ECONOMIC

PROCESSES

AND POLICIES

ECONOMIC

PROCESSES

AND POLICIES

BY

William J. Baumol

Associate Professor of Economics
Princeton University

AND

Lester V. Chandler

Gordon S. Rentschler Professor of Economics
Princeton University

HARPER & BROTHERS   PUBLISHERS   NEW YORK

Library of Congress catalog card number: 54–5850

CONTENTS

PART VI. INTERNATIONAL TRADE AND FINANCE

PART VII. DISTRIBUTION OF INCOME

GRAPHIC APPENDIX

PREFACE

This book grew out of our need for satisfactory reading materials in a beginning economics course which we were both teaching. It seems to us desirable that such a course have at least the following characteristics: (1) It should deal primarily with matters that have important policy implications. These ought to be not mere issues of the day that will be forgotten tomorrow, but problems of basic and continuing importance. (2) It should be essentially analytical. It should seek not to provide the student with ready-made answers, but to help him analyze processes and problems. At the same time, it ought not require the student to spend most of his time and effort learning and reciting standard theoretical results whose applicability is quite unclear to him. (3) It should include institutional, historical, and statistical materials only to the extent that they illustrate and elucidate economic analysis and policy problems.

In line with these desiderata, this volume is essentially a book on economic theory and principles which are introduced and developed in relation to policy problems. Our aim throughout has been to equip the student with analytical tools and to indicate how they may be applied to policy problems which will continue to be of interest to him even after he leaves college, but we have avoided specific policy recommendations and political judgments. These the student must arrive at for himself, though we hope we have helped him avoid at least some fallacies and facile oversimplifications.

For the beginner who will go on to further work in the field we believe it highly advantageous to emphasize application as we have sought to do here. This can enable him to evaluate and assess the significance of the more detailed teachings to which he will later be exposed. For the majority of the students in the introductory course who will have no further work with the economics department, it seems to us even more essential that the significance and applicability of the things they are taught be made perfectly clear. Otherwise, the material is likely to seem pointless and to be forgotten quickly.

Because of its orientation, this book is somewhat differentiated from others in the field, both in content and in organization. For example, our discussion of free enterprise and planning led us to draw on such areas as welfare economics and input-output analysis. On the other hand, while several aspects of value and distribution theory are developed and employed in the body of the text in connection with our analysis, we thought it expedient to confine the more formal and systematic development of some of the principal topics in these fields to a long appendix. The analysis in the body of the book does not depend at all on the appendix, but the latter should be useful to those who wish to place greater emphasis on the formal aspects of value and distribution theory.

Several chapters begin with quotations, some of them from the words of prominent politicians. The main purpose of this is to show the reader that we are not dealing with straw men and with arguments that never left the ivory tower.

By way of acknowledgment, we wish above all to express our gratitude to Jacob Viner, whose generous help has undoubtedly made this a better book. We have also received highly useful comments on various parts of the manuscript or other types of assistance from Arthur Arkin, Edgar O. Edwards, Edward Karpoff, Richard A. Lester, Oskar Morgenstern, Gardner Patterson, and George Stolnitz. We also thank our student assistants—Robert T. Golembiewski and Tom Davis—for their patient research, and Miss Martha Roberts for her careful typing of the manuscript. It is hardly necessary to add the conventional note that they are not to be blamed for those things which remain to the reader's displeasure.

Finally, though it be not meet, we thank each other for making it relatively easy to complete this book as a truly cooperative enterprise. The purely alphabetical ordering of our names on the title page constitutes no attempt at the impossible task of ranking contributions.

Princeton

W. J. B.
L. V. C.

ECONOMIC

PROCESSES

AND POLICIES

CHAPTER 1

The Nature of Economic Problems and Processes

---

1. A World of Alternatives and Choices

We all like to dream of a world in which no one has to work, and in which nature lavishes on us all the goods and services we could possibly desire. Whether we would actually be happier in such a world we shall never know, for it is not the kind of world in which we live, of which we have any record, or which we have any reason to expect in the future. The harsh and inescapable fact is that man has to work for a living. Nature does supply him with various natural resources with which he can work—soil, water, air, sunlight, minerals, and wild animals and plants. But man must use at least part of his limited time and energy to convert these resources into things capable of satisfying his desires—into food, clothing, living quarters, heat, house furnishings, medicine, music, books, places of worship, and a host of other things capable of supporting life and making it more enjoyable.

Yet despite our work and sacrifice of leisure, we are still unable to produce enough to satisfy all the wants of all the people all the time. Millions of people in this world have too little food, clothing, housing, and medical care to keep them healthy and strong. Other millions have little more than is necessary to cover these minimum needs. Even those whose standard of living is comfortably above "the minimum level of health and decency" have many unsatisfied desires; they want more leisure, more and better foods, better and more stylish clothes, bigger and better houses, more and better television sets, more books, music, and plays, and many other things. Our ability to create new wants seems always to outrun our ability to satisfy them. What family, be its

1

yearly income $3000 or $30,000, feels that it has as much as it "really needs"?

In short, we live in a world of scarcity; there cannot be enough of everything to satisfy all the wants of everybody. Because of this fact we cannot escape the problem of alternatives and choices. We have to balance our innumerable wants—including our desire for leisure—against each other, determine the extent to which each will be satisfied or denied, and choose among the various alternative methods of satisfying them. And we must realize that we can have more of one thing only at the price of having less of others. In other words, the fact of scarcity forces man to "economize" or "practice economy." These terms have been defined in various ways, but through all the definitions runs the central idea of prudent management, of securing maximum benefits from limited resources, and of "making the most" of our scarce means.

2. The Central Interest of Economics

The preceding paragraphs indicate the central interest of economics. It is to describe and analyze the processes by which people make a living. Economics is a study of the processes of using scarce productive resources—such as natural resources, labor, and capital equipment—to produce goods and services capable of satisfying human wants. It is a study of the processes of determining what particular types of goods and services are to be produced, how much of each is to be produced, and how the resulting output is to be divided among the various members of society.

Because all these processes are group processes, economics is a "social" science. With such disciplines as history, political science, sociology, social anthropology, psychology, and philosophy, economics shares the task of studying the behavior of men in groups. As in the other social studies, the ultimate interest of economics is in individual human beings; but since men live, work, and consume as members of groups it is necessary to study the social processes and social institutions that are employed in making a living.

3. Some Basic Problems of All Economic Systems

In order to indicate somewhat more specifically the types of subject matter to be treated more fully in later sections of this book, we shall now look briefly at some basic economic problems that must be faced by any society. It is to be emphasized that because of scarcity these problems inevitably exist in every type of society—in rich as well as in poor societies, and in communist, fascist, socialist, and anarchist, as well as in capitalist types of economic systems. One type of economic system may cope with these problems better than others, but the problems themselves cannot be escaped merely by changing the arrangements for dealing with them.

These basic economic problems may be grouped under four main headings: (1) the rate of output as a whole, (2) the composition and pricing of output, (3) the allocation of productive factors among their alternative uses, and (4) the distribution of income. We shall separate these problems for analytical purposes, but we must emphasize that in fact they are closely interrelated, that they coexist and must be dealt with simultaneously, and that an economic system can function smoothly only to the extent that the solutions of the various problems are consistent with each other.

A. THE RATE OF OUTPUT AS A WHOLE

It is evident that the ability of an economic system to satisfy people's wants depends to a great extent on its overall rate of output of goods and services. This is the real income of a society. One basic economic problem, therefore, is to secure as much production as possible without an overbalancing sacrifice of leisure and other values. Included here is the problem suggested by the popular slogan, "Maintain full employment!" An economic system obviously falls far short of ideal performance when, as in the decade of the 1930's, millions of people who are willing and able to work and who prefer income to their enforced leisure are left unemployed and in need. But the problem is much broader than this, encompassing many other factors relating to the overall rate of output.

For example, what should a society mean by "full employment"? How many in the population should work? How long should they work? How intensively should they work? Few want literally "maximum employment" and "maximum production." At some point, usually short of complete physical and nervous exhaustion, most people prefer more leisure and a slower pace of work to more goods and services. They may also prefer to sacrifice some real income rather than subject themselves to the stricter discipline that a higher rate of production would require.

Also included here as affecting the rate of output as a whole are many other things relating to the overall "efficiency" of an economy—

the amounts of output that can be achieved with each unit of input of natural resources, labor, and capital. Among these are the promotion of technological change, the allocation of every specific type of natural resource, labor, and capital to the particular use for which it is best suited, the establishment of productive units of the most efficient size, and so on. But the achievement of these ends must be weighed against such possible disadvantages as the obsolescence of old skills and the unhappiness caused when some workers have to move away from cherished relatives, friends, and familiar surroundings.

We shall later have much to say about the many factors that affect the overall rate of output of an economy.

B. THE COMPOSITION AND PRICING OF OUTPUT

Since no economy can produce all the goods and services that might be useful to people, it is necessary to pick and choose among the various possible types of output. That a certain quantity of some particular good is useful is not sufficient to justify its production; the more relevant test is whether it has greater utility than the other things that could be produced with the same amount of productive resources. Thus every economy faces the problem of determining somehow the composition of its output—of arriving at the particular types of goods and services it will produce and the amounts of each. The welfare of the community can be seriously affected, for with any given overall rate of output the production of more of one thing necessarily means a smaller production of something else.

In arriving at the composition of its output a society must somehow determine what proportion of its output shall be in the form of consumer goods and services to satisfy current wants and what proportion shall be in the form of capital goods to facilitate future production. Within each broad category many more details must be determined. For example, society must somehow settle on the particular types and styles of consumer goods it will make and the amounts of each, as well as the types it will not make at all. The well-being of people may depend as much on the achievement of a "well-balanced" composition of output as it does on the overall rate of output. We may all want some spinach, but who wants nothing but spinach? Society must also determine the particular types of capital equipment that it will produce, and the amounts of each.

In an economy based on specialized production and trade among the specializers, it is also necessary to arrive at relative prices for the various types of output. We shall see later that in the American type of economic system, as in many others, the relative prices of the various types of output play important roles as major determinants of actual consumption patterns, of the composition of output, and of the distribution of income.

c. The Allocation of Productive Factors Among Their Alternative Uses

Interrelated with the problem of determining the composition of output is that of allocating the limited supply of productive resources among an almost unlimited number of alternative uses. This is not simply a problem of determining some aggregate amount of productive resources to be used in producing each particular type of output. Details as to the specific types and quantities of productive factors to be allocated to each particular use must be settled. Society must somehow determine what particular types and amounts of land will be used for various agricultural, manufacturing, mining, and other purposes. Similarly the uses of the many types of labor and capital goods must in some way be decided.

Resource allocation is a basic problem of economics, for in the last analysis it is the scarcity of productive resources that is the source of all scarcity problems. We would have no problems of scarcity if we had so many productive factors that they could produce more than enough to satisfy all the wants of everybody. But since the supply of productive factors is always scarce—because work competes with leisure, if for no other reason—we always face the problem of "making the most" of the available supply.

d. The Distribution of Income (or Output)

Unable to produce enough to satisfy all the wants of everybody, every society faces the thorny problem of dividing or distributing its limited output (income) among its members. This raises many difficult questions. What share of the output pie shall go to each member? Shall each receive an equal share regardless of his "needs" or "contributions to output"? Shall each receive a share determined by his "needs," and if so, who shall weigh the alleged "needs" of the various members? Shall each receive a share based on the size of his "contribution to output," and if so, how is the contribution of each to a cooperative productive process to be measured? Should other criteria be used?

In view of the sharp conflicts of interests, the wide differences of opinion as to the most appropriate principles to be applied, and the conceptual and practical difficulties of measuring relative "needs" and relative "contributions to output," it is no wonder that the distribution of income is always a controversial subject.

E. INTERRELATIONS OF THE BASIC ECONOMIC PROBLEMS

In summary, we have found that the basic economic problems that must be faced by every society are those of determining the overall rate of output, the composition and pricing of output, the allocation of a scarce supply of productive factors among their alternative uses, and the distribution or sharing of output or income. Though we discussed these problems separately for purposes of analysis and exposition, they are interrelated in many ways. They coexist, they must be solved simultaneously, and actions taken to deal with one problem are almost certain to have impacts on others. The sum of real income shares must be in line with the total amount of real output to be shared. A pattern of income shares that would be acceptable when goods and services are abundant may prove to be quite unacceptable at low output levels, when the same degree of inequality will result in some people starving to death. Decisions relating to the composition of output cannot be carried out unless productive factors are appropriately allocated. It is impossible to produce both hats and books if all our resources are put into producing hats. The determination of the composition of output must take into consideration the size of total output; to have 60 percent of output in the form of food may be wise in an impoverished economy but undesirable in a wealthy, highly productive community. The distribution of income may affect the overall rate of output. When income shares are determined largely by "need" rather than "contributions to production," incentives to hard work may clearly be affected.

These are only a few examples of the almost innumerable interrelationships among economic problems and processes. This interrelatedness is one of the reasons why economics is such a challenging study.

4. Economic Control Systems

Economic problems of the types discussed above do not solve themselves. Human beings must solve them, or at least find working compromises. In other words, every society must have some "system" or set of arrangements for controlling its economic processes. And where, as in modern societies, economic processes are social or group processes, there must be some sort of social control of these processes. Only anarchy and chaos would result if every person were completely free of all social restraint and direction and could without penalty do just as he pleased without considering the effects of his actions on others. Complete freedom for every individual is possible only if each lives, works, and consumes in complete isolation.

A. THE FUNCTIONS OF ECONOMIC CONTROL SYSTEMS

As often employed, the term "control" has purely negative connotations, implying putting restraints on people and preventing them from doing certain things. Economic controls must, of course, serve this negative function of restricting, or at least discouraging, types of behavior that are judged to be undesirable. A few familiar examples are the prevention of theft, of price "gouging," of the sale of contaminated foods, and of "unfair" methods of competition.

But an economic control system must also serve the affirmative function of setting goals, of providing positive direction, and of promoting types of behavior that are considered to be desirable. It must somehow determine what particular goods and services are to be produced and how much of each, and the shares of total output and of each type of output that shall go to each member of society. It must also allocate the scarce supply of productive factors among their many possible uses, organize these factors into functioning productive units, and continuously direct them toward the selected goals. Moreover, to be considered acceptable in the United States and many other countries, a control system must be capable of achieving a continually rising level of productivity and a continuing adjustment of productive processes to the shifting demands of the people.

Because of the fact of scarcity, every economic control system must operate in the midst of conflicting interests and ideas which sometimes lead to sharp controversy. The system must therefore be powerful enough to arrive at some sort of working compromise and to enforce its decisions even though these decisions are unpalatable to some members of the group. To this end it needs powerful sanctions in the form of rewards, or penalties, or both.

B. ALTERNATIVE SYSTEMS OF ECONOMIC CONTROL

When we said that there must be *social* control of economic processes as soon as these come to involve groups of people we did not mean either that this control must be exercised through government, or that it must be centralized. We meant only that each person must be subject to some degree of restraint and direction by other members of the group.

At least some of this control may, of course, be exercised through government. But it may also be exercised in many other ways—by custom, the pressure of group opinion, labor unions, employers, competition in the market place, and so on. In fact, an almost unlimited variety of social control systems is possible. It is partly because of this great number of alternatives that a society finds it so difficult to choose a particular type of control system. It would perhaps be difficult enough for some societies to make a broad choice among capitalist, socialist, fascist, communist, and syndicalist systems. But the number of alternatives is far greater than this classification would imply, for there can be many variations in the control systems included within each broad category.

To illustrate this point, let us look briefly at just a few of the choices that must be made in devising an economic control system. We shall limit ourselves to three types of choices—the allocation of control functions among the various types of social institutions, the location of control power, and the types of sanctions to be employed.

C. THE INSTITUTIONS EXERCISING CONTROL

Control may be exercised through many different types of social institutions: governmental units at international, national, state, and local levels; family units; churches; corporations and other business firms; guilds; trade associations and cartels; labor unions; consumer and producer cooperatives; and so on. Control functions can be allocated among such social institutions in almost every conceivable way. At one extreme, as in Soviet Russia, the central government may exercise virtually all control. At the other extreme, the government may exercise only a minimum of control, leaving that function largely to private competition in the market place. As many buyers and sellers can testify, competition in the market can be a powerful method of restraining and directing individual actions. Between these two extremes an unlimited number of gradations and combinations is possible. One of the great problems of social policy involves not only deciding what control institutions to develop and utilize, but also defining their respective jurisdictions and functions.

D. ALLOCATING POWER AMONG THE MEMBERS OF SOCIETY

A closely related problem is that of allocating control power among the members of society. How is this power to make and enforce decisions to be distributed? Shall it be shared equally by all persons regardless of age, income, wealth, and other characteristics? If power is to be shared unequally, what is to be the basis for giving more to some and less to others? Shall it be age, wisdom, size of income or wealth, hereditary status, physical power, sheer aggressiveness, or some other basis? How great should be the differences in the shares of power? Should each person exercise his power in his role as a consumer, as a worker, as an owner of wealth, as a voter, or in some other role? These are but a few of the questions that must be faced in allocating control power. They are likely to be highly controversial, for power is much sought after, both as an end in itself and as a means to other ends.

E. TYPES OF SANCTIONS

Every control system must, of course, develop and utilize sanctions strong enough to enforce its decisions. These generally include both rewards for approved types of conduct and penalties for undesired types of behavior. Rewards and penalties may take various forms. For example, one can be rewarded by social approbation, elevation to positions of prestige and power, larger wealth, higher income, and so on. With so many alternatives, every society must somehow determine what combinations of rewards and penalties it will employ to enforce its decisions and it must adjust the types and sizes of rewards and penalties to merits and offenses. We all abhor inappropriate and excessive penalties. Inappropriate and excessive rewards can be just as offensive. At the same time, however, society must employ sanctions powerful enough to make its controls effective.

In summary, every society faces the difficult problem of developing and operating some sort of system for controlling its economic processes, and the problem is made more difficult by the very large number of alternatives from which a choice must be made. In later chapters we shall have much more to say about the structure, functions, and policies of economic control systems.

5. Economics and Economic Policies

Though we have discussed several types of economic processes and problems, we find that all of them present at least one common aspect: in every case there is a necessity of weighing alternatives and of choosing among them.

A. THE NATURE OF POLICYMAKING

This process of choosing among alternative lines of action is usually called *policymaking*. It is the choosing of a *policy*—a course or line of action. Wherever alternatives exist, there must be a policy. Thus there are *economic policies* with respect to many types of economic phenomena—in choosing the wants to be satisfied or left unsatisfied, in choosing the means of satisfying these wants, in choosing an economic control system, and so on. Moreover, every person and institution has power to make economic policy to the extent that he or it possesses alternatives. Thus within their realms of discretionary powers governments, business firms, labor unions, consumers, and many others make economic policies.

B. RATIONAL POLICYMAKING

We do not mean to infer that economic policies are always arrived at through completely rational processes. Custom, inertia, ignorance, and mental laziness are certainly not without their influence. But to the extent that policymaking is rational, it involves the following steps: (1) Identification of the available alternatives. If people do not know about all the alternatives that are available to them, they may fail to select the course of action that they would consider "best." (2) Understanding of the significant effects of each of the alternative lines of action. If people fail to understand the effects of the various possible policies, and even misunderstand them, they are hardly in a position to make rational choices. (3) The making of value judgments as to the effects of the alternative policies. Are they "good"? Are they "bad"? How "good" or how "bad" are they? Presumably any person or group will select the policy that, on balance, is expected to yield the most net "good" results or the least net "bad" results. But what is to be considered "good" or "bad" is a matter of social values and depends on the ethics, morality, and culture of the group.

C. THE ROLE OF THE ECONOMIST

This brings us to an important question. What are the appropriate roles of economics and of economists in the determination of economic policies? Can economics tell us what economic policies should be? Can the economist, as an "expert," tell us which courses of action we should reject and which we should adopt? The answer is clearly "no," for the economist cannot claim any special qualifications as a judge of what social values ought to be—what people ought to consider "good" and what they ought to consider "bad." As a person he may or may not have intelligent ideas on these subjects, but he can claim no special expertness simply because he is a student of economic problems and processes.

Nevertheless, students of economics can serve a highly useful purpose in the policymaking process by increasing and disseminating information concerning alternative courses of action. They can make people aware of the alternatives available to them, pointing out the various ends that might be sought and the various possible ways of achieving them. They can also increase the knowledge about the probable effects of each of the alternative courses of action so that policymakers can base their decisions on a better understanding of what is being chosen and what is being rejected. Thus the primary purpose of economics is to increase understanding of economic alternatives and processes, not to prescribe specific economic policies.

Even with these restrictions the task of economics is both valuable and difficult. It is valuable because ignorance, misunderstanding, and even misrepresentation of economic alternatives and processes are widespread. One of the major tasks of economics is to expose prejudiced and fallacious reasoning and try to replace it with objective and logical analysis. It is difficult because economic processes, involving the interactions of millions of people, are complex, and because any course of economic action has so many different types of effects on society. For these reasons economics cannot—at least not in its present stage of development—provide a complete and accurate prediction of all the effects that will flow from any given course of action. It can, however, expand the area of understanding and narrow the area of ignorance, which is about all that can be claimed for any study.

6. Conclusions

In this introductory chapter we have tried to indicate the types of basic economic problems, processes, and policy decisions that we shall consider in the remainder of the book. Up to this point we have intentionally dealt with these matters in somewhat general terms in order to emphasize their basic nature. As we go on, however, our discussion will become more specific and detailed. We shall study many of the forms in which economic problems manifest themselves, describe and analyze more fully the various economic processes and institutions, and consider a number of specific policy issues.

In the first group of chapters we shall concentrate mainly on real national income or output, indicating the meanings of these terms and analyzing the many factors that determine a nation's ability to turn out real goods and services with which to meet its people's needs.

We shall then go on, in later chapters, to describe and analyze the various processes and policy decisions involved in determining the composition of a nation's output, the relative prices of the many types of output, the allocation of productive factors among their alternative uses, and the distribution or sharing of national income or output.

SUGGESTED READINGS

Robbins, Lionel, *The Nature and Significance of Economic Science,* Macmillan, London, 2nd ed., 1940.

QUESTIONS

1. a. Why must every type of society cope with the problems of the rate of output as a whole, the composition of output, the allocation of productive factors, and the distribution of income?
   b. Why does this not mean that any economic principle is equally applicable to every economy now and in the past?
   c. Can you think of some economic questions which apply to our economy but not to that of Russia?
   d. To our economy today but not to the economy of the colonial period?
2. Give some plausible examples of:
   a. The effect of a change in the level of output on the composition of output.
   b. The effect of a change in the level of output on the pattern of income distribution which most people consider acceptable.
   c. The effect of a change in the system of distributing income on the overall rate of output.
   d. The effect of a reallocation of resources on the composition of output.
3. Give some examples of economic and social control exercised through agencies other than the government, and describe the sanctions employed in each case.
4. Suppose you are a congressman considering a bill to raise the tariff on wool.
   a. What sort of relevant information could you expect from an economist working for you?
   b. What sort of question would you not want to ask him?
5. "The only reason we do not have all the good things of life we want is that our economy is run by businessmen and politicians rather than engineers." Discuss.

PART I

Productivity, Income, and Wealth

CHAPTER 2

Wealth and Income

Real wealth and real income, especially the latter, are the focal points of economics. Although their studies range over broad areas and include many subjects, the central interest of economists centers ultimately on the ability of the economy to satisfy human wants. This is where the concepts of real income and real wealth come in, for it is, roughly speaking, our ability to satisfy wants that income and wealth are designed to measure. They are meant to indicate the economic achievement of a community or an individual. An understanding of these concepts is therefore crucial for a comprehension of our economic goals and some of our central economic problems.

1. Wealth and Income

A. THE CONCEPTS DISTINGUISHED

To begin with, we must distinguish clearly between the concepts of wealth and income. Though related, they are obviously not the same thing. For example, a wealthy man may retire, live off his capital, and have little or no income. A spendthrift with a high income may accumulate no wealth, as the sad experience of many retired athletes and actors has shown. The same is true of nations and other communities. Thus, despite their connection, wealth may be low and income high, or vice versa.

The nature of this relationship can be made clear only after a brief digression.

B. STOCKS AND FLOWS

A standard example employed in economics involves water and a reservoir. The amount of water in the reservoir is a *stock*. The rate at which the water enters or leaves is a *flow*. It is as simple as that.

Note that the level of water in the reservoir may be high even though little or none is coming in, or the level in the reservoir may continue low even though much water is coming in, if it flows out rapidly enough. Thus the flow may be great and the stock low, or vice versa. We all know enough about the mechanics of filling and emptying bathtubs to make unnecessary any further laboring of the relationship.

The characteristic that distinguishes the concepts of stock and flow is the question of time. To measure a flow we must specify some interval of time. Water flows over Niagara Falls at a rate of so many gallons per second. No such time interval is relevant to the measurement of the magnitude of a stock. There are simply ten million gallons in our reservoir at present, and it makes no sense to say that there is so much per week or per second.[1]

There are many economic examples of stocks and flows, and a large number of these occur in this volume. We list a few examples, leaving a clear definition of the terms for later. (1) The quantity of real capital in a country—its factories, machines, and equipment—is a stock. The nation's real investment—its creation of new machines, etc.—is the corresponding flow; investment must therefore be described as being so much *per year*. (2) Consumption is a flow, as is saving. (3) The number of dollar bills in a man's wallet is a stock. The rates at which he receives and spends dollars are related flows. (4) By now the reader will have realized that wealth is the stock of possessions of an individual or community, and that income is the rate of inflow of wealth to that individual or community. More specifically, any income that is not consumed increases wealth. Real national income minus consumption is the rate of increase of real national wealth per unit of time.

C. REAL WEALTH

Real wealth consists of two principal parts. (1) Natural resources. These include the stock of useful goods which were not created through the efforts of man, but were supplied solely by nature—such things as soil, mineral deposits, waterfalls and other water supplies, and so on.

---

[1] To the reader who is acquainted with the rudiments of calculus the distinction is even simpler. A flow is the rate of change or derivative with respect to time of the relevant stock.

And (2) capital goods. These capital goods at any point of time include the existing stock of all goods that have been created by man and that are still in existence. Real capital includes the following types of things: existing buildings of all types; man-made improvements in the form of roadways, canals, irrigation and drainage systems, and terracing; farm equipment; transportation and communication equipment; factory, mine, and store equipment; and inventories of finished, semi-finished, and raw materials.

It is important to note that capital goods, being the stock of accumulated man-made goods existing at a point of time, are a result of two necessary processes: (1) They must have been produced in the past, or they would not be in existence. And (2) they must not have been consumed or "used up" in the past, or they would not be in existence. In short, the stock of capital goods at any point of time represents the amount of goods accumulated or "saved" out of man's past production. We shall later have much to say about this process of capital accumulation.

d. REAL INCOME

We saw above that real wealth is the *stock of useful goods existing at a point of time*. In contrast, *real income is the flow of output or production of useful goods and services over a period of time less the capital goods used up in their production.*[2] It is the net flow of useful goods and services out of the production process per period of time, and the flow of output is usually measured at an annual rate. At first it may seem strange to think of "income" as being synonymous with "output" or "production." Being somewhat egocentric, most of us like to use the term "income" as "the flow of things to me," the emphasis being on their receipt rather than on their production. But the goods and services which people receive must constitute their respective shares of the current net output of goods and services. And the sum of the shares of real income flowing to all the claimants during a period is equal to total real net output or production for that period. In the following pages we shall use interchangeably the terms real income, real output, and production of goods and services.

e. THE EMPHASIS ON INCOME

We noted earlier that economics focuses more of its attention on real income than on real wealth. This is not because real wealth is

[2] For an explanation of the last phrase, see below, pp. 19–20.

unimportant. Largely it is because most of our stock of real wealth is of such a nature that it cannot satisfy human wants directly, but can serve this end only to the extent that it enhances real income by increasing the nation's productivity. This is true, for example, of land, factory buildings, mining machinery, farm implements, railroads, and many other things.

We are also more interested in income because it is here that things "are happening." Like the inflow tap in the bathtub, it is the more active changing element, by its very nature. Sudden sharp changes in our economic circumstances are usually associated with income changes. For example, depression and unemployment necessarily reduce a nation's real income, but unless the slump is protracted it may not have great effects on the stock of real wealth. In most of this book we shall therefore concentrate primary attention on real income, and deal with real wealth as one, but only one, of the important factors determining the ability of an economic system to produce real income.

2. "Real" Versus Money Income

A. THE BASIC SIGNIFICANCE OF REAL INCOME

We shall also emphasize the basic importance of real wealth and real income rather than of money wealth and money income. This emphasis is necessary to counteract the popular tendency to think too much in terms of money. We are so accustomed to measuring and stating economic magnitudes in terms of dollars or other monetary units that we are inclined to jump to the conclusion that the economic welfare of a community depends solely on the size of its money wealth and money income. Some people even go so far as to assume that economic welfare can always be assured and improved simply by creating sufficiently large amounts of money!

The solution of economic problems would be simple indeed if we could abolish all scarcity by this process, for money creation is easy. However, a little reflection shows the fallacy of this argument. In the final analysis we cannot satisfy our wants with money itself; money cannot allay our hunger, or clothe us, or shelter us from the elements, or meet our other needs. Only real goods and services can satisfy our wants, and money is significant only to the extent that it affects the supply of real goods and services and their distribution among the members of the community. This point should be kept in mind even while we are studying money and monetary policy.

B. MONEY INCOME AND PRICES

Money income, that is to say the money value of output or the sum of the money earnings accruing to the members of the economy, is in itself of little significance, for fluctuations in prices can make it largely meaningless. With high prices a relatively high money income may obviously represent less purchasing power than does a smaller money income at much lower prices. The significance of changes in money income can be assessed only if we know how prices behaved.

3. National Income: Problems of Definition

A. THE BASIC CONCEPT

What we are really getting at when we speak of real national income is the aggregate quantity of goods and services that is made available to the public during a given period, and the additional plant and equipment which accrues to the nation. In effect, it is the net amount produced during that period. However, formidable difficulties arise as soon as we try to be more specific about the definition and measurement of real national income.

B. PROBLEMS OF INCLUSIONS AND DEDUCTIONS

What is to be included in real output? We are clear that the production of a marketable consumer good represents an addition to national income. So also does a newly produced piece of machinery which adds to a nation's wealth by enabling it to produce more in the future. But how do we classify an item that turns out to be unmarketable because fashions have changed since its production was first planned? What do we do about the intangible product in the form of "good will" which results from advertising activities during the period? How do we classify housewives' services? What do we do about the services yielded by owner-occupied houses? Do we include the pleasures derived from amateur sports? There can be no clear-cut answer as to what to include and what to exclude from real income, but we can come to reasonable though somewhat arbitrary decisions.

C. CAPITAL REPLACEMENT

At least as vexing is a problem that arises out of the using up of equipment in the production process. The nation is no wealthier for having a new machine if its production involved the using up of an old one equally good. Thus what we are interested in is what is called net income, i.e., income after allowance has been made for equipment used up in the production process. It is the amount produced minus the amount used up in production.

Unfortunately, it is very difficult to estimate the depreciation or quantity of capital used up during a period. For example, during a year's production there is some wear and tear on a machine, but it is not used up entirely. There is no clear-cut way we can decide what proportion of that machine has been used up in the process. Businessmen try to estimate the rates of depreciation and obsolescence of their capital equipment, but all their methods are necessarily somewhat arbitrary conventions. Or suppose the machine is used up entirely and is replaced by a machine of new and superior design. We cannot say to exactly what extent this represents replacement pure and simple, and to what extent an addition to our national wealth.

4. National Income: Problems of Measurement

A. THE PROBLEM OF AGGREGATION

The most disturbing problem encountered in trying to measure real national income is aggregation—adding together the millions of different things included in national output. This is the sort of operation the concept of real income demands, for it is meant to measure the totality of all the various things that have been produced during a period. Yet we all know that we cannot really add apples and bananas, to say nothing of the millions of other types of physical products. There is no physical unit of measurement—whether of weight, volume, or length—that indicates in any meaningful sense the economic significance of different types of products. Who would claim any economic significance for a sum secured by adding together pounds of concrete, strawberries, penicillin, Cadillacs, and bananas?

To clarify the nature of the problem let us imagine we are in a world in which only two items are produced—say our old friends, apples and bananas. Suppose that banana output has gone up 10,000 tons and apple output has declined 30,000 bushels. Has national income increased, decreased, or stayed the same? As things stand, we cannot decide, for we do not have any sort of table of equivalents to tell us whether in some sense one bushel of apples is worth 5, or 10, or 20 pounds of bananas. But once we have such a figure our problem is solved, for we can then say how much of a rise in banana output would be required to make up for the 30,000-bushel decrease in apple production.

B. PRICES AS A BASIS FOR COMPARISON

The usual way of trying to get out of this dilemma is to use the market's evaluation of the commodities in terms of their prices, a dollar's worth of apples being assumed to be equivalent to a dollar's worth of bananas. Thus if the market prices are $2 a bushel for apples and $100 a ton for bananas, a ton of bananas will be considered equal to 50 bushels of apples. Having established such a table of equivalents, we could proceed to measure national income and changes in national income.

C. CHANGES IN RELATIVE PRICES

Though this seems quite simple and straightforward, our troubles are not over. We still face the problem of deciding what prices to use —wholesale prices or retail prices? And even after we have more or less arbitrarily selected the type of prices to be used, we face the fact that relative prices change through time. For example, in year X the average prices may be $2 a bushel for apples and $100 a ton for bananas, indicating that a ton of bananas is equivalent to 50 bushels of apples. But in year Y the average prices may be $3 a bushel for apples and $75 a ton for bananas, indicating that a ton of bananas is equivalent to only 25 bushels of apples. Which figure should we use? In computing changes in national income between years X and Y, shall we assume that a ton of bananas is equal to 25 or to 50 bushels of apples? Since there is no absolutely "true" or "correct" answer to this question, we have to be content with somewhat arbitrary decisions. Even when we have made these decisions another important measurement problem remains.

5. Correcting for Changes in Price Levels

In the preceding section we found that the millions of different things included in national output can be aggregated only if we employ a common unit of measurement, and that price is the only meaningful common unit we have. Thus everything is measured in dollars or other monetary units. But when we attempt to measure changes of real national income through time, we encounter the troublesome fact that the dollar itself is a far from constant unit of measurement. Sometimes prices rise and the dollar will buy less. At other times prices fall and the dollar will buy more. Thus if we are to get an indicator of changes in real national income through time we must find some way of eliminating the effects of changes in prices or in the purchasing power of the dollar. This presents many difficulties.

A. VALUING OUTPUT AT "BASE YEAR" PRICES

One method of attempting to eliminate the effects of changes in prices would be to value output for every year at the average prices prevailing in some one selected period. This might be done as follows. (1) Select some year as the "base year." There is no a priori reason for selecting one year over another. Suppose we select the year 1939. (2) Find out the average prices of every type of output during the base year. (3) To find the value of output during any year, multiply the physical volume of every type of output during that year by the average price of that type of output during the base year, 1939. For example, for 1954 you would multiply the number of tons of steel produced in 1954 by the 1939 price of steel, the number of bushels of apples produced in 1954 by the 1939 price of apples, and so on. (4) Add together all the products just computed to get the value of total national output as measured in 1939 prices. Since this process presumably eliminates the effects of price changes, any changes in national income revealed by the statistics should indicate, in some sense, a change in real income.

Though at first glance this method seems simple, it actually presents many conceptual and practical difficulties and involves a number of discretionary decisions. We shall consider only a few of these. The first is the great difficulty of securing accurate price data for the millions of products during the base year and other years. Errors in estimating actual prices may sometimes be large. In the second place, this method arbitrarily assigns to each type of product a weight determined by its price in the base period. If the 1939 prices were $100 a ton for bananas and $2 a bushel for apples, a ton of bananas would be considered equal to 50 bushels of apples during every year. If we had selected as a base some other year in which the price of bananas was lower relative to the price of apples, bananas would have been weighted less heavily relative to apples. The same principle applies to every other component of output. Thus the behavior of output as measured in constant prices may be influenced somewhat by the selection of a base period.

A third serious difficulty arises from changes in the types of output.

Changes in products are an outstanding characteristic of the American economy. The sizes, styles, and other characteristics of familiar products change markedly through time, new products are developed and offered for sale, and old products are discontinued. Consider, for example, the case of a Chevrolet whose price may have been $700 in 1939 and $2000 in 1954. Should a 1954 Chevrolet be considered the same "product" as the 1939 model and included in output at the 1939 price of $700? Almost everyone will agree that the 1954 Chevrolet is in many respects "more car" than its 1939 predecessor. But how much more? Since we have no way of answering this question accurately, we cannot with certainty say just how much of the increase from $700 to $2000 is an increase in "real" output and how much a pure price increase. This is by no means an isolated case.

Similar problems arise with respect to things that were not produced in the base period. Television receivers, many wonder drugs, room air conditioning, and various other things that made up a considerable part of output in 1954 were not produced for general sale in 1939. What would their prices have been in 1939 if they had been produced at that time? We have no way of knowing for sure.

In summary, this method of measuring real output, as well as all other methods, necessarily involves many difficulties and permits many discretionary decisions.

This particular method of estimating the value of output at constant prices is not the one actually employed by government statistical agencies and others. However, the time you spent studying it has not been wasted, for it brings out several useful points. (1) It indicates what economists and statisticians are getting at when they try to value output at constant prices. (2) It suggests the types of difficulties and decisions involved in constructing index numbers of prices. Every problem that we faced here must be confronted in constructing price indexes. (3) It suggests why we use price indexes which are based on a sample of prices and so avoid the collection of huge amounts of data on all prices. Otherwise the cost of constructing the index would be prohibitive and it would require millions of computations.

B. USING PRICE INDEXES TO CORRECT FOR CHANGES IN PRICE LEVELS

The method actually used to arrive at values of output at constant prices, which we employ as an indicator of the behavior of real income, is to use price indexes to correct for price changes. This involves two steps. (1) Estimate the value of output for each year at the prices prevailing during that year by using a sample of outputs and their prices as indicators. (See Column 1 of Table 1.) Changes in this value

TABLE 1.   Values of National Output at Current and 1939 Prices for Selected Years[3]

Year	Col. 1 Values of Output in Billions of Dollars at Current Prices	Col. 2 Indexes of Prices of Output 1939 = 100	Col. 3 Indexes of Purchasing Power of the Dollar Over Output 1939 = 100	Col. 4 Values of Output in Billions of Dollars at 1939 Prices	Col. 5 Indexes of Output at 1939 Prices 1939 = 100
1929	$104	121	83	$ 86	95
1933	56	91	110	62	68
1939	91	100	100	91	100
1946	211	153	65	138	152
1948	259	181	55	144	158
1951	329	197	51	167	185
1952	348	202	49	172	188

of output figure reflect changes in both physical output and the prices of output. (2) Adjust this figure by using an index of the average level of prices for output (based on a sample of prices) in order to eliminate the effects of price changes and leave only the effects of changes in real output.

The price index used for this purpose, like any price index, indicates the average height of prices at various times *as a percentage of their average height in some period taken as a base period.* In Column 2 of Table 1 we have chosen 1939 as the base period. The index number for that year is 100 for the obvious reason that prices in that year were 100 percent of themselves. The index of 91 for 1933 indicates that in that year the prices of output were 91 percent of their level in 1939. The index of 202 for 1952 indicates that prices then were 202 percent of their level in 1939. And so on. Another way of stating the same thing is to say that at 1952 prices it would on the average require $202 to buy as much real output as $100 would buy at 1939 prices.

Once you have computed the price indexes for the various years, it is easy to convert the values of output at current prices into values of output at 1939 prices. You simply divide the value of output at current prices by the price index for that year and multiply by 100. The reason

[3] Source: *National Income Supplements to the Survey of Current Business,* July, 1951, 1952, and 1953.

you *divide* by the price index can be made clear by an example. Suppose in years X and Y outputs are exactly the same but prices are four times as high in the latter. The money value of output in year Y will then be four times as high as in year X. For our index of real output to show the fact that there has been no change in production, we must *divide* the value of output during Y by 4, the relative price rise. You multiply by 100 because the price index you used as a divisor is stated in hundreds rather than units. In our example the price index for year Y would be 400, using X as the base year. The figures in Column 4 of Table 1 were derived in this way.

The figures showing the values of output at 1939 prices which we have just obtained are themselves a sort of index of the behavior of real output. It is therefore simple to convert them into formal index numbers showing real output in the various years *as percentages of the 1939 level*. All we have to do is divide the figure for each year by the value of output in 1939 and multiply by 100. Column 5 of Table 1 shows an index of real output.

While we are on the subject, it will be useful to note the relationship between price levels and the purchasing power of the dollar. The general nature of the relationship is clear; the higher are prices the less will a dollar buy, and the lower are prices the more will a dollar buy. To be more precise, the purchasing power of the dollar varies reciprocally with the level of prices. For example, when prices double, the dollar loses half of its purchasing power. When prices fall by half, the purchasing power of the dollar doubles. The general formula for this relationship is as follows:

$$\text{Index of purchasing power of the dollar} = \frac{100}{\text{price index}} \times 100.$$

The figures in Column 3 of Table 1 reflect this relationship.

6. Problems of Index Number Construction

Though index numbers are convenient and are widely used to correct for price changes, we must not beguile ourselves into believing that they yield completely "true" or "accurate" results and involve no discretionary decisions. The fact is that they involve almost all the difficulties we have already encountered, and more besides. This is brought out by looking at one method of constructing index numbers.

A. Constructing a Price Index

As noted earlier, an index number of prices is based on only a sample of prices rather than on all prices. Even the most inclusive index includes few more than a thousand items. The steps involved in constructing such an index are as follows: (1) Select the goods and services to be included in the "market basket," indicating not only the types but also the specific amounts of each. These amounts are kept constant for all periods. (2) For each period, ascertain the prices of all these things and the total value of the contents of the market basket at the prices prevailing in that period. (3) Select some period as the base period, and let the total value of the market basket in that period equal 100, or 100 percent of itself. (4) State the total value of these same things in each period as a percentage of their total value in the base period. Table 2 illustrates in a highly simplified way a method of constructing such an index.

TABLE 2. An Example of a Price Index Number Construction

Type of Commodity	Amount of Commodities	Price in Base Year	Total Value in Base Year at Base Year Prices	Price in Year 1	Total Value in Year 1 at Year 1 Prices
Steel	2 tons	$ 50.00	$100	$ 75.00	$ 150
Cotton	100 lbs.	0.10	10	0.20	20
Autos	1 unit	800.00	800	900.00	900
Total value			$910		$1070

Computation of the price index:

$$\text{Index for base year} = \frac{\$910}{\$910} \times 100 = 100$$

$$\text{Index for year 1} \quad = \frac{\$1070}{\$\ 910} \times 100 = 118$$

It will be noted that this index measures an "average" behavior of the prices included. Moreover, this is a "weighted" average; each price does not have an equal effect on the average. Rather, the effect of each on the average depends on the relative amounts of the various types of goods and services included and on the relative prices of each. For example, cotton would have had a greater influence on the average if the market basket had included more cotton relative to steel and autos or if the base year price of cotton had been higher relative to the prices of steel and autos. The failure of the average to rise more than 18 percent despite the 100 percent increase in cotton prices and the 50 percent rise in steel prices was due to the heavy weight given to autos, whose prices rose only 12½ percent.

B. INDEX NUMBER PROBLEMS

What, then, are the problems of index number construction? The basic index number problem is almost always that *an index number is used as a device for aggregating and comparing the incommensurable,* for adding apples and bananas. A price index encounters this problem when it tries to decide what happens to the price level as a result of a $200 rise in the price of Chevrolets and a drop of 10 cents a pound in the price of steak. Has the price level then risen or fallen? Because it must compare incomparable items, no such index number can yield absolute and unchallengeable answers.

There are other problems involved in the computation of index numbers. In the first place there may be errors in data. Second, the specifications of some commodities may change so much as to make largely meaningless any comparison of their outputs or prices at different times. Third, the average behavior of the items included in the sample may differ significantly from the average behavior of the items they are meant to represent. In other words, we cannot be sure that the sample is really representative. For this there may be several reasons. The average of prices in a sample may move from year to year more than the average of all prices because a disproportionate number of highly volatile prices are included in the sample or are weighted too heavily. Or the reverse may be true. Even if the sample was in some sense satisfactory at the beginning, it may cease to be so as new products appear, old ones are discontinued, and the proportions among the various types of output are altered.

In short, the construction, use, and interpretation of price or other indexes involve many difficulties and choices. This is true not only of indexes of real output or price indexes used to derive estimates of real national income, but also of almost all other types of index numbers. For example, it is true of the so-called "consumer price index" which is so widely used to indicate the behavior of the cost of living and as a basis for escalator clauses in wage contracts designed to adjust wages to compensate workers for changes in the purchasing power of the dollars they earn. It is true of the indexes of average prices received by farmers and average prices paid by farmers, which are used to com-

pute indexes of parity prices in terms of which the government supports the prices of farm products. It is true of the various indexes of
wholesale prices. Because so many choices are open to them, even the
most objective and well-intentioned constructors of indexes may come
out with differing results. And the way is left open for the unscrupulous
to manipulate the indexes to favor themselves.

7. National Income: Conclusion

It turns out, then, that the concept of national income is not clear-
cut. To get figures for it we must make a variety of discretionary decisions which leave room for different people to come up with different
answers. Though the term is widely used, the apparent simplicity of the
idea serves only to obscure its intrinsic difficulties. We shall find, as we
go along, that this is also true of many other economic concepts we
shall employ.

Within limits there is much virtue in a skeptical attitude toward
these terms. Indeed, the inculcation of skepticism is perhaps the first
stage in education. But we must beware of going to the other extreme
of denying ourselves the use of such convenient, if imperfectly defined,
concepts. It is one thing to employ them with our eyes open, knowing
what questions we are begging in the process. It is quite another to
reject them entirely and to have nothing better to take their place.

Certainly these indexes or indicators of output tell us roughly what
we want to know. For example, they agree fairly well as to the dating
of depressions and recoveries and the impressiveness of the increase in
our ability to satisfy human wants over the course of the last century.
Moreover, much of our analysis would become even more difficult and
complex if we were to shun the income concept. The great importance
of this concept will become clearer as we proceed.

SUGGESTED READINGS

Kuznets, Simon, *Economic Change,* Norton, New York, 1953, Chapters
6–8.
Mitchell, Wesley C., *The Making and Using of Index Numbers,* Bulletin
No. 656, U.S. Department of Labor, Bureau of Labor Statistics, Washington, 1938.

QUESTIONS

1. Suppose you were offered the alternative of being wealthy or having a
high income.

   a. On what basis would you make your choice?

   b. Are there any circumstances under which you would be indifferent as between these alternatives?

2. "Living off one's capital" means converting a stock of capital (wealth) into a flow (consumption).

   a. For what sort of stock of capital can this conversion be effected without any substantial passage of time?

   b. How can the owner of a factory or a machine live off his capital if he can't sell it?

3. "It is not possible for the real incomes of all the members of the community to add up to more or less than the net output of that community during a given period."

   a. Discuss.

   b. Is this true for the world as a whole?

   c. For Venezuela?

4. Why can the level of national income usually change more rapidly than the nation's stock of wealth?

5. If a foreign nation can pay off its war debt to us either in wine and fine linens or in gold which will be hoarded by our government, which will more directly increase our real income?

    What are some implications of the preference for payment in gold displayed by many nations?

6. How would you deal with the following items if you were trying to measure our national income:

   a. Dresses just off the production line but made unsalable by a change in fashion.

   b. Preserves made by self-employed housewives to earn some pocket money.

   c. Preserves made by housewives for their own use.

   d. The services obtained by a house owner from his own house.

   Which of these would you include in national income?

    If (d) is excluded, show how national income can be increased when two house owners decide to rent each other's houses.

7. Suppose you were a businessman owning a $10,000 machine whose physical life expectancy is twenty years, but which will probably become obsolete long before then.

   a. How might you decide what proportion of the machine is used up in this year's production?

   b. How does your decision affect your net income?

8. Suppose you were an unscrupulous statistician trying to make a rise in price level look as large as possible.

   a. Show two ways in which you might go about juggling your figures to get this result without actually using any false data.

b. Illustrate by using the values in Table 2 to construct a *two* commodity price index.

9. a. Distinguish clearly between the effect of a change in relative prices and of a change in price level on an index of output in which nothing has been done to correct for these.

   b. Construct a numerical example showing these effects.

   c. Construct an index number of real output for your numerical example and show explicitly how each of these effects is dealt with.

CHAPTER 3

Determinants of Productivity

---

1. Introduction

We have now discussed the meaning and measurement of real income and have emphasized that, roughly speaking, it is the size of real income that measures the ability of an economic system to satisfy people's wants. We now turn to the important task of studying the various factors that determine the amount of real income a nation's economy can produce. At this point we shall concentrate on explaining the amount of real income that a nation's economy can turn out when it is operating at what is considered at that time to be "full employment" and "full production." We shall reserve "underemployment" and "underproduction" for later consideration.

Our discussion should help us understand many economic facts and processes. Among these are the sharp upward trend of real incomes in the United States, the great differences among real incomes in the various parts of the world today, the possible methods of raising real income levels, and some of the problems encountered in attempts to raise real incomes.

In the course of our discussion we shall use three different measures of real income. (1) Total national income. Unless otherwise specified, this will be stated at an annual rate and measured in dollars of constant purchasing power. This measure does not, of course, indicate the size of the population by whom the total output must be shared. (2) Average per capita income. This is simply the total national output divided by the size of the population. Though this measure indicates the average amount of real output for each person it tells us nothing about

31

the deviations of individual incomes from the average. Incomes are so unequally distributed in most countries that considerably more than half of the people have incomes below the average. (3) Average output per man-hour worked. This is a useful index of productivity, for it indicates the average amount of goods and services produced for each hour of work.

We cannot emphasize too strongly that we claim no high degree of accuracy for the figures we shall use. They are subject to all the qualifications that were noted earlier, and more besides. The most that can

TABLE 3.   Indexes of Real Output in the United States, 1869–1951[1]
(Annual average for the years 1869–1878 = 100)

Period	Col. 1 Index of Total Output per Year	Col. 2 Index of Population	Col. 3 Index of Real Output per Capita
1869–1878	100	100	100
1879–1888	189	126	150
1889–1898	259	156	166
1899–1908	400	187	214
1909–1918	549	225	244
1919–1928	755	260	290
1929–1938	793	290	273
1940	1047	303	346
1948	1508	336	448
1950	1618	348	464
1951	1753	354	495

be claimed for them is that they are the best available and that they do indicate general orders of magnitude.

As a first step, we shall look briefly at some statistics indicating the trend of real income in the United States and the differences among real income levels in the various parts of the world. These will suggest the importance of understanding the determinants of productivity and will cast light on a number of policy issues.

2. The Trend of Real Income in the United States

One of the most striking characteristics of the American economy has been the rapid increase of its productivity. This rise of output, not only in aggregate amount but also in amount per capita and per man-

[1] These indexes were computed from estimates of gross national product. The basic data for 1869–1938 are from Simon Kuznets, *National Product Since 1869*, National Bureau of Economic Research, New York, 1946. Those for later years are from *Survey of Current Business*, July, 1952, p. 28.

hour worked, seems to have begun very early in our history, though reliable statistics for the early period are scarce. Table 3 presents indexes of real output for the period 1869–1951. The level of output for each year, or the annual average for each decade, is stated as a percentage of the average annual level during the 1869–1878 decade. The rise of real income was rapid during this period. Column 1 shows that in 1951 total national output was more than 17 times as large as it had been during each year of the 1869–1878 decade and more

TABLE 4. Actual Hours Worked per Week and Output per Man-Hour, 1850–1940[2]

Year	Col. 1 In Agriculture	Col. 2 In Non- agriculture	Col. 3 Weighted Average	Col. 4 Index of Output per Man-Hour 1870 = 100
1850	72.0	68.0	70.6	80
1860	72.0	64.0	68.7	93
1870	71.0	61.0	66.3	100
1880	71.0	60.0	65.4	103
1890	70.0	58.0	63.2	138
1900	69.0	56.0	60.9	166
1910	68.0	53.0	57.5	186
1920	63.0	48.0	51.9	200
1930	59.0	44.0	47.2	245
1940	52.3	41.7	43.0	344
1950	. . .	. . .	. . .	432

than 4 times as large as in 1900. A considerable part of this increase was due to the increased number of workers, for in 1951 the population was about 3½ times as large as in 1869–1878. Nevertheless, real output rose so much faster than population that in 1951 the average output per capita was more than 4 times as high as in the 1869–1878 decade, and more than twice as high as it had been at the turn of the century. In the middle decade of the twentieth century there is no reason to believe that this rise of productivity is at an end or even that it is slowing down.

This dramatic rise of per capita real income was achieved despite a marked reduction in the length of the work week. As shown in Table 4,

[2] The data for 1850–1940 are taken from tables in J. Frederic Dewhurst and associates, *America's Needs and Resources,* Twentieth Century Fund, New York, 1947. The statistics on the length of the work week are from p. 695 and those relating to output per man-hour are from p. 23. The estimate for man-hour productivity in 1950 is based on data for selected industries as given in *Productivity Trends in Selected Industries,* Bulletin 1046, Bureau of Labor Statistics, 1952.

the average length of the work week declined 25 percent in agriculture and nearly 40 percent in nonagricultural industries between 1850 and 1950, with the larger part of the decrease occurring after 1900. This trend toward a shorter work week is still continuing. The increase of real output per capita has been due primarily to the rise of output per man-hour worked. It is estimated that in 1950 real output per man-hour was more than 5 times as high as in 1850, more than 4 times as high as in 1870, and more than twice as high as in 1900. (See Column 4 of Table 4.) And productivity continues to rise.

In short, ours has been a rapidly expanding economy. Output has risen much faster than population, and average per capita incomes have shown a sharp upward trend despite a continuing reduction in the length of the work week. We have used our increasing productivity per man-hour to achieve more goods and more leisure too. The American belief in the possibility of continued economic progress grows naturally out of our past experience. This rapid change in productivity has been accompanied by almost revolutionary changes in our productive processes and social institutions. Later pages will describe some of the most important of these changes and their relationships to the rise of productivity.

TABLE 5.   Average per Capita Incomes in 70 Countries in 1949[3]
(In U.S. dollars of 1949 purchasing power)

Country	Average per Capita Income in Dollars	Average per Capita Income as Percentage of That in the U.S.
United States	$1453	100
Canada	870	60
New Zealand	856	59
Switzerland	849	58
Sweden	780	54
Great Britain	773	53
Denmark	689	47
Australia	679	46
Norway	587	41
Belgium	582	40
Luxembourg	553	38
Netherlands	502	35
France	482	33
Iceland	476	32

[3] Source: United Nations Statistical Office, *National and per Capita Incomes in Seventy Countries,* 1949, New York, October, 1950. The Statistical Office emphasizes the highly approximate nature of these estimates.

TABLE 5. Average per Capita Incomes in 70 Countries in 1949 (*Continued*)

Country	Average per Capita Income in Dollars	Average per Capita Income as Percentage of That in the U.S.
Israel	389	27
Czechoslovakia	371	26
Finland	348	24
Argentina	346	23
Ireland	342	23
Uruguay	331	22
Venezuela	322	21
Germany (Western)	320	21
U.S.S.R.	308	21
Poland	300	20
Cuba	296	20
Hungary	269	19
South Africa	264	19
Portugal	250	17
Italy	235	16
Austria	216	15
Chile	188	13
Panama	183	12
Yugoslavia	146	10
Colombia	132	9
Greece	128	9
Costa Rica, Turkey, Lebanon	125	8
Mexico	121	8
Brazil	112	8
Southern Rhodesia, Egypt, Japan, Syria, Peru	100	7
El Salvador	92	6
Nicaragua	89	6
Iran, Iraq	85	6
Paraguay	84	6
Honduras	83	6
Guatemala	77	5
Dominican Republic	75	5
Ceylon	67	5
India	57	4
Bolivia	55	4
Pakistan	51	3
Afghanistan	50	3
Philippines	44	3
Ecuador, Saudi Arabia, Yemen, Haiti	40	3
Ethiopia, Liberia	38	3
Burma, Thailand	36	2
Korea (Southern)	35	2
China	27	2
Indonesia	25	2

3. International Differences in Average per Capita Incomes

Even more striking than the rise of per capita real incomes in the United States during the past century are the great international differences in per capita real incomes at the present time. At the top are the United States and a few other countries with relatively high per capita real incomes. At the bottom are many countries containing a major part of the world's population with per capita incomes that are only a small fraction of those in the United States. This fact is illustrated in Fig. 1, and in Table 5, which presents estimates of per capita output, stated in U.S. dollars of 1949 purchasing power, for 70 countries during 1949. Though these estimates cover only one year and are admittedly highly approximate, they do indicate general patterns. Other estimates for recent periods present roughly the same picture.

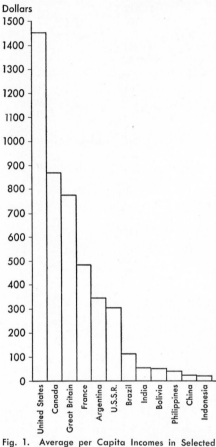

According to these admittedly rough estimates, the 70 countries had in 1949 a total population of 2,079,000,000 and a total output worth $513,101,000,000, so that average per capita output for all countries was $247. There

Fig. 1. Average per Capita Incomes in Selected Countries, 1949. (In dollars of 1949 purchasing power.)

were, however, wide deviations from this world average. At the top was the United States with an average per capita output of $1453, which was nearly 6 times the world average. Twenty-seven other countries also had per capita incomes above the world average, though most of them were considerably below the United States. The other 42 countries, with far more than half of the world's population, had per capita incomes below the world average. In 36 of them average per capita incomes were 10 percent or less of the United States average, and in 17 of them average per capita incomes were 5 percent or less of those in the United States.

Table 6 shows in another way this highly unequal distribution of the world's output. The United States with only 7 percent of the world's population accounted for 42 percent of the world's output, and the 8 countries with the highest per capita incomes had only 11

TABLE 6. Distribution of 70 Countries by Size of per Capita Income in 1949[4]

Size of per Capita Income	Col. 1 Number of Countries	Col. 2 Size of Population (In millions)	Col. 3 Size of National Income (In millions of dollars)	Col. 4 Percent of Total World Population	Col. 5 Percent of Total World Income
Over $900 (U.S.)	1	149.2	$216,831	7	42
$600–899	7	89.6	69,977	4	14
$400–599	7	66.5	33,258	4	6
$200–399	15	393.5	118,073	19	23
$100–199	15	253.0	28,832	12	6
$ 50– 99	13	477.2	27,768	23	5
Less than $50	12	650.9	18,362	31	4
Total	70	2079.9	$513,101	100	100

percent of the world's population but accounted for 56 percent of the world's output. At the lower extreme, the 12 countries with average per capita incomes of less than $50 a year had 31 percent of the world's population and produced only 4 percent of the world's output. The 25 countries with per capita incomes of less than $100 had 54 percent of the world's population and only 9 percent of its output. More than a billion people live in countries with per capita incomes below $100 a year. These are, of course, averages. In most countries incomes are quite unequally distributed so that much more than half of the people have incomes below the average for the country.

These figures, inaccurate and probably biased as they are, do emphasize the fact that scarcity is not a thing of the past. A large majority of the world's people suffer scarcity of even the most essential things. They do not have enough food to keep them healthy and vigor-

[4] Source: *Ibid.*, p. 29.

ous. Partly because of malnutrition and inadequate medical care they have high rates of infant mortality, low life expectancy, and numerous diseases. Many have inadequate clothing; much of their housing is unsanitary and of very low quality; and many of them are illiterate. Taken as a whole, the world is still poor.

These statistics also cast light on many aspects of the current world situation. For example, they help explain why the United States, with only 7 percent of the world's population, is the greatest economic, political, and military power in the world today. They help to explain why we hear so much about the plight of the "underdeveloped areas" of Asia, Latin America, Africa, the Middle East, and elsewhere. They help explain why so many of these countries are engaged in ambitious development programs and are requesting foreign assistance for them. And they suggest some of the reasons why the United States is considered to be the principal source of international aid.

Low average incomes are, of course, a reflection of low productivity, and the task of raising average real incomes is primarily that of raising productivity. This leads us to a series of important questions. What determines productivity? What accounts for the fact that average output per capita, per worker, and per man-hour worked is so much higher in the United States than in the rest of the world? Why has productivity increased so much in the United States during the last century? Can we extend this trend into the future? What actions might other countries take to raise their productivity? The following pages will try to provide some basis for answering questions of these types.

4. Determinants of Productivity

Many people have tried to discover a single "ultimate cause" which could by itself explain the productivity of a society. Geo-determinists find it in the natural-resources situation, stressing geographic, geologic, and climatic factors. Proponents of racialism find it in racial differences. Some others find it in patterns of culture and social values. Still others find it in economic control systems and stress the superiority of some specific type of system, such as capitalism. And so on.

We shall make no attempt to discover any single "ultimate cause," partly because we doubt its existence. Our objective is the less ambitious one of surveying the many factors existing in a nation at any given time which collectively determine the productivity of the nation's economy. These can be grouped into six broad categories: (1) the quantity and quality of natural resources, (2) the quantity and quality of labor, (3) the supply of capital, (4) the state of technology—the types and amounts of knowledge employed in economic processes, (5) the types and degrees of specialization and exchange, and (6) the system of economic control. We shall emphasize that the actual productivity of a nation's economy at any time is determined not by any one of these factors alone, but by all of them collectively and by their interactions on each other. And we shall find that these interactions are both numerous and complex.

Since these factors determine the productivity of an economy, it should be evident that differences in productivity are to be explained by differences in these factors. It should also be evident that successful attempts to raise the level of a nation's productivity must operate through one or more of these factors.

Though we shall have something to say about total national output, our primary interest will be in real output per capita and per man-hour worked.

5. Natural Resources

Since production is a process of applying human effort, knowledge, and capital to natural resources in order to produce useful output, it is clear that a nation's productivity is greatly influenced by both the quality and quantity of its natural resources. And output per capita and per man-hour of work depends greatly on both the quality and quantity of the natural resources available to each worker. In these respects nations vary greatly.

A. AGRICULTURAL RESOURCES

This is clear in the case of agriculture. In some countries each farmer is assisted by large amounts of high-quality land so that he can get a large output for each hour of work and for each unit of capital he employs. Soil conditions, topography, rainfall, temperature, and humidity are favorable to the growing of one or more crops that can be used domestically or exported in exchange for foreign products. In other countries each farmer is hindered by having only a small amount of land, or low-quality land, or both. He is plagued by poor soil, or steep hillsides, or swamps, or inadequate rainfall, or too much rainfall, or excessive heat, or excessive cold, or some combination of these conditions.

We have no satisfactory way of comparing statistically the qualities of the agricultural resources of different countries. For this reason a comparison of the average sizes of farm holdings is of only limited significance. Nevertheless, it is interesting to note that while the average size of each farm holding in the United States is over 150 acres, it is only 40 acres in Denmark, 20 acres in England, and 5 acres or less in China, India, Ceylon, Java, Siam, the Philippines, and many other areas. Where the amount of land per worker is so small, agricultural output per man-hour of work must be small. The total output on each acre may be increased by applying more and more capital and labor to it, but after some point the amount of output per man-hour and per unit of capital will fall.

B. MINERAL RESOURCES

The mineral resources of countries also differ widely. Some nations are richly endowed with large amounts of high-quality minerals that are located in accessible areas and are relatively easy to extract, refine, and process. They may have good supplies of coal and petroleum which are so useful as sources of heat, power, and chemicals; iron, copper, zinc, lead, bauxite, magnesium, and many other metallic ores; limestone; potash, sulfur, and other chemicals, and so on. Other nations are less fortunate; they have much smaller supplies of minerals relative to their population, or their minerals are more costly to extract, refine, and transport. For this there may be many reasons. For example, the minerals may be located in mountains or other inaccessible areas. They may occur in such a diffused state that they are hard to extract and refine. They may be located far underground, or beneath rock or other substances that are hard to penetrate. Veins of coal may be so narrow that it is hard to work them. These and many other conditions determine the amount of pure, usable minerals that can be secured for each hour of work and each unit of capital employed.

In these days when the productivity of economic systems depends so much on power, metals, and chemicals, a shortage of mineral resources can be a great handicap.

C. OTHER NATURAL RESOURCES

Some nations have large amounts of potential water power which can be developed at relatively low cost. Others have little or none. Some can have cheap transportation because of their navigable streams, lakes, and oceans, their natural ports, and their favorable terrain. Others lack these advantages and face serious obstacles to transportation—mountains, marshes, jungles, and deserts. Some have climates favorable to manufacturing activity. Others do not.

Many other examples could be mentioned, but those already cited should establish the point that natural resources are an important determinant of a nation's productivity. At the same time, it should be clear that the amount of real output a nation can achieve with the natural resources it does have also depends greatly on the other factors that we shall consider.

6. Labor

Another major determinant of a nation's output per capita and per man-hour of work is the quantity and quality of labor, both physical and mental, actually utilized in productive processes. And average output per capita depends not only on output per man-hour worked but also on the proportion of the population that works and on the number of hours each person works per year. Nations differ widely in all these respects. Let us look at just a few of these differences.

A. Nutrition and Health

In countries like the United States, most people have enough food and medical care to keep them healthy and vigorous most of the time. This is not true in many other parts of the world. People there have too little food in general and are especially deficient in meat, milk, eggs, and other foods that build up resistance to disease. Partly because of their poor diets but also because of unsanitary conditions, inadequate disease prevention, and lack of medicines and medical care, large parts of the population suffer almost chronically from many debilitating diseases. Tuberculosis, malaria, typhoid, yaws, and other diseases are common. Malnutrition and disease are, of course, objectionable in themselves, but they also lower productivity, both by reducing the proportion of the people who are capable of working and by lowering the efficiency of those who do. A man who is undernourished and ill is unlikely to have the strength, stamina, and mental alertness necessary for high productivity.

B. Literacy

Differences in literacy are still another important source of differences in productivity. Thanks to both public and private education, almost every adult in the United States, Canada, western Europe, and some other areas can at least read and write. We take for granted a labor force that can, as a minimum, read written instructions, learn by reading after they have left school, and do at least simple computations. But in many parts of the world less than half the adult male population can read and write, and illiteracy among women is even higher.

Illiteracy and low educational standards lower productivity in many ways. They obviously reduce a nation's supply of educated scientists, doctors, business leaders, technicians, and others who can contribute so much to productivity. But they also lower productivity by decreasing the ability of workers to follow instructions and learn new ways of doing things and by strengthening traditionalism and decreasing people's willingness to try new methods and new products. We shall have more to say about this when we discuss technology.

C. SOCIAL VALUES AND CUSTOMS

In the United States economic activity is held in high regard. We respect the man who is industrious and thrifty, pride ourselves on the fact that a lowly born person can "get ahead," and accord the highest prestige to those who become leaders in the economy. Such social attitudes are conducive to high productivity. They encourage large numbers of the most capable people to strive for economic leadership and they provide incentives to industriousness, thrift, and economic innovation.

Social values and customs in many other areas are less favorable in these respects. For example, business activity is held in lower regard than literary, government, military, and religious careers. Strict caste systems reduce economic incentives by making it clear that a person cannot rise out of the class into which he was born. Land tenure systems and methods of wage payment provide little economic incentive to extra effort and initiative. Close family ties lower the geographic mobility of labor. These and many other social conditions tend to hold down productivity in various parts of the world.

D. METHODS OF IMPROVING THE LABOR SUPPLY

Many nations might achieve significant increases in productivity by improving the diets of their workers, by preventing and curing disease, by raising literacy and educational standards, and by creating more favorable attitudes toward economic activity. But such programs are highly expensive and cannot be completed in any short period by a country starting from a condition of low productivity.

⋇Cost is not the only obstacle to the success of such programs aimed at raising per capita real incomes. Many countries also face the possibility that measures taken to increase food supplies and improve health would lead to such a great upsurge of population that real income per capita would rise little if at all. They now have very high birth rates and their populations are held down only by very high death rates, especially in the early age groups. Improvements in diet and health would almost certainly lower death rates, and this would increase the rate of population growth unless birth rates fell sufficiently.⋇

7. The Supply of Capital Goods

A. CAPITAL AS A DETERMINANT OF PRODUCTIVITY

The amount of capital goods available to assist each worker in his productive activities varies greatly from country to country. The United States has very large amounts per worker. This will be evident to anyone who looks at the huge amounts of land improvements, buildings, engines, machinery, and other equipment and inventories employed in all of our lines of production. Most other countries, and especially the "underdeveloped" areas, have much less capital per worker. It is not only that many of them lack the large numbers of buildings and the large amounts of power machinery and equipment that can contribute so much to productivity in manufacturing. They also lack dams, irrigation systems, drainage systems, farm equipment, and fertilizers to raise farm output. They lack improved roads, railways, canals, and the other transportation equipment necessary for fast and cheap transportation. They lack equipment to raise productivity in forestry and mining. These are but a few examples of the acute shortages of capital goods that help depress productivity to very low levels in much of the world.

It is clear, therefore, that a nation may raise its level of real output by increasing the supply of capital goods at its disposal. But this process involves many problems, a few of which we shall now consider.

B. INCREASING CAPITAL SUPPLIES THROUGH DOMESTIC SAVING AND INVESTMENT

⋇ A nation can increase the supply of capital goods at its disposal in two ways: (1) by saving and investment at home, and (2) by importing savings (borrowing) from other countries. The general nature of the process of capital accumulation through domestic saving and investment was indicated earlier. The people of a nation can build up their stock of capital goods by saving part of their real income; that is, they can use part of their output not for current consumption but to increase their supply of capital. Or, to state the analysis in more basic terms, they can use some part of their productive resources to produce capital goods rather than goods and services for current consumption. For example, a farmer may use only part of his labor to produce consumer goods and spend part of his time improving his land, constructing buildings, or making tools. Or some members of the community may specialize in producing capital goods while living on consumption goods produced by the others.

We emphasize that in the final analysis the process of accumulating real capital is one of using some part of a nation's productive resources to produce capital goods rather than goods for current consumption. Thus capital accumulation could occur even in a purely barter economy. But as specialization and exchange develop, the process of capital accumulation becomes increasingly one of saving out of money incomes and of using these money savings to buy capital goods produced by specializing persons and firms. People "save" part of their money incomes; this is the part they do not spend for current consumption. These money savings can be used for "investment"—that is, to buy new capital goods from specialized producers. The process of saving—of not spending for consumer goods—tends to repel productive factors from the job of turning out consumer goods. Spending for investment tends to draw productive factors into the production of capital goods.

The process of capital accumulation in a money economy involves three necessary steps. (1) Saving out of money incomes. The actual rate of saving varies with both the ability and the willingness to save, which in turn depend on the real purchasing power of money incomes and on people's attitudes toward consumption and saving. (2) The transfer of money savings from the savers to those who will spend them for investment. For this to occur, the savers must part with their savings on terms that are acceptable to the potential spenders for investment. (3) Investment—the actual spending of money to finance the construction of new capital goods. This step requires that someone be willing to take the initiative and bear the risks involved in constructing and using the new capital goods. Nations vary greatly with respect to all three parts of this process. In some, social attitudes and conditions are quite favorable to the saving-investment process. In others they are much less favorable.

Conditions in the United States are favorable to a high rate of saving. Per capita incomes are so high that people can save large amounts without serious hardship. This is especially true of the higher-income groups. Moreover, thrift is considered to be a social virtue. In contrast, per capita incomes are so low in the underdeveloped areas that most of the people could save very little without subjecting themselves to severe hardships. The rich do, of course, have incomes high enough to permit large savings, but many of them prefer luxurious living or use their savings in ways that add little to productivity.

There are also great differences in the willingness of people to transfer their money savings to those who will spend them for investment. Most Americans are willing to part with their money savings at relatively low rates of dividends or interest in exchange for shares of ownership or for debt obligations issued by business concerns or the government. This process is aided by a highly developed system of financial institutions. In contrast, savers in many underdeveloped countries refuse to make their savings available for capital construction, or will do so only on prohibitive terms. They prefer to hold their money idle, to build luxurious mansions, or to accumulate stores of gold, silver, and precious gems. For this there are many reasons, such as the prestige of holding precious metals, gems, and mansions, and the fear of political instability, inflation, excessive taxation of factories and other capital goods, and revolution and confiscation.

Though capital accumulation cannot occur if people do not save and offer their savings for use, neither can it occur if no one is willing to assume the responsibility of spending for new capital goods and of using them for productive purposes. The performance of this positive function requires knowledge as to how additional capital may be used profitably, imagination, initiative, and a willingness to bear risks.

In general, Americans have shown a great capacity and willingness to assume such responsibilities. Venturesome, imaginative, and optimistic as to the profitability of employing larger amounts of capital goods, private enterprisers have spent huge amounts to increase capital supplies in almost all lines of industry. Moreover, our governmental units have shown great enterprise in constructing and operating capital goods in the form of roads, highways, streets, canals, ports, water systems, sewage systems, and many others.

Such enterprise is lacking in many of the underdeveloped countries, for many reasons. For example, social values are such that many of the best potential leaders in economic activity prefer other careers. They lack the knowledge and imagination required for the efficient use of more capital. Their governments fail to protect property rights adequately and do not actively promote capital construction.

✻In short, many of the underdeveloped countries face serious obstacles when they pursue programs to increase their capital supplies through domestic saving and investment. Low per capita incomes hold down the ability of their people to save. Even those whose incomes are high enough to permit a high rate of saving may elect to consume rather than save. People may refuse to make their savings available on acceptable terms. And such countries may not have an adequate supply of enterprisers who possess the knowledge, imagination, and courage to construct and manage large amounts of new capital.✻

c. Imports of Savings from Other Nations

A nation may also increase the amount of capital goods at its disposal by importing savings from other countries. For example, Brazil may get dollars from the United States by selling to us shares of ownership in Brazilian businesses or by borrowing from us. She could use the dollars acquired in this way to import more goods and services than she exports. In some cases she may use the dollars to import capital goods, such as rails, locomotives, construction equipment, or fertilizers. In others she may use the dollars to import consumption goods so that some of her own workers and other productive factors can be released from the job of producing consumer goods and diverted to the construction of capital goods. In either case, capital accumulation is encouraged.

In some cases imports of savings are accompanied by imports of management and technical skill. For example, General Motors might establish a factory in Brazil, providing the capital and also the key management and technical personnel. In other cases Americans may simply lend to the Brazilian government or to business firms or buy shares of ownership in Brazilian businesses without supplying management or technical assistance.

International movements of savings from areas where capital is relatively plentiful to areas where capital is scarcer can be advantageous to both the importing and exporting countries. A nation importing savings must, of course, use some of its output to pay interest and dividends to foreign savers, but the additional capital goods may increase its productivity so much that it has more real income left for its own people after the payment of interest and dividends. At the same time, the nation exporting savings may benefit because the interest or dividends it receives can be used to import an amount of goods and services greater than the amount that would be added to domestic output if these savings were invested at home.

Nevertheless, there are many serious obstacles to international movements of savings. Savers in countries where capital is relatively plentiful are often ignorant of investment opportunities elsewhere in the world or fear for the safety of any savings that they might export. They fear that their rights will not be adequately protected in foreign courts, that foreign moneys may depreciate, that they will not be permitted to bring their money back home when they want it, that they will be subject to unfair taxation or confiscation, that their savings will be wasted by incompetent or corrupt foreign managers, and so on. These fears are sometimes justified. The assurance that governments in the capital-importing countries would protect and encourage foreign investments in the underdeveloped areas could do much to promote an international flow of savings. But in many of these areas the governments are notoriously unstable or hostile to foreign investments, and the people fear that foreign investments would lead to foreign domination, both economically and politically.

Even if these countries could get large amounts of foreign savings on favorable terms many of them would still lack the technology and trained managers and workers necessary to utilize capital most effectively.

8. The State of Technology

Knowledge is generally considered to be a worthy end in itself; it is also a powerful means to other ends. Technology, the types and amounts of knowledge utilized in economic processes, is one of the most powerful determinants not only of productivity but also of the entire structure of economic and social relationships. No one can understand the great economic and social changes that have occurred in the United States and the rest of the western world without considering the scientific and technological revolutions that began more than two centuries ago and are still continuing at a rapid rate. Moreover, no one can explain the vast differences in economic and social conditions in the various parts of the world today without reference to the differing degrees to which these areas have felt the impact of scientific and technological changes. The current emphasis on technical assistance to underdeveloped areas is based on a recognition of these facts.

Since the scientific and technological revolutions are such basic forces, it will be useful to consider briefly their nature and history.*

A. THE SCIENTIFIC REVOLUTION

Attitudes and methods of thought during the Middle Ages were quite unfavorable to scientific discoveries. Men's minds were chained to the past. They looked not forward but backward, insisting that ultimate truth was to be found only in the ancient writings. They lacked zeal for expanding the area of knowledge and were biased against new discoveries. Rapid scientific advances were impossible so long as these attitudes prevailed.

Gradually, however, men were able to free themselves from traditionalism and to develop new attitudes and new modes of thought. They came to believe that the area of knowledge can be expanded, that such an expansion is both meritorious and useful, and that the validity of any proposition is to be judged by its capability of being verified through observation and experiment rather than by its agreement with some weighty authority.

This growth of the scientific method, which only in the seventeenth century began to have a substantial effect on the attitudes and thinking of the general public, made possible a growing torrent of scientific discoveries. These discoveries have not been limited to any one science; they have occurred in almost all fields—astronomy, geology, mathematics, physics, chemistry, biology, and psychology, among others. They include the discovery of new products as well as of new ways of making or using old products.

*Though scientific discoveries are a necessary basis for great technological changes, they can increase productivity only to the extent that they are actually used in economic processes. Technological change therefore involves at least two necessary steps: (1) discovery of new knowledge or of new applications of existing knowledge, and (2) the actual use of the knowledge in economic processes. Someone must act as innovator; he must have the imagination, initiative, and courage to use the new discovery as a basis for developing and using new methods of production or for turning out new products, or both. Moreover, many discoveries and innovations can yield maximum results only if large numbers of appropriately educated workers are available to exploit them. Thus, scientists, inventors, enterpriser-innovators, and educators all play essential roles in technological change. Some countries are liberally supplied with all of these; others suffer a serious shortage of one or more. ✳

B. SOME EXAMPLES OF TECHNOLOGICAL CHANGE

The pervasiveness of the technological revolution in the western world can be suggested by a few examples selected from the millions that might be cited. Perhaps the most familiar examples are in the field of power production and utilization. Most economic processes require power—power to plow, cultivate, and harvest; to transport goods and people; to hoist; to separate, combine, compress, and shape materials; and to perform a host of other functions. The only sources of power before the eighteenth century were human beings, animals, water, and wind. Man had yet to discover how to convert fuel into mechanical power. A vast new field was opened in 1705 when New-comen built the first steam engine.

The usefulness of steam engines and turbines has since been en-hanced by thousands of discoveries increasing their reliability, dura-bility, and efficiency. Electric power became available for widespread use only after Faraday showed how to convert electric current into mechanical motion and after numerous improvements of dynamos and electric motors. The invention and improvement of the internal-combustion engine, which dates only from the latter part of the nine-teenth century, opened up still further uses of power. These have been supplemented by many other discoveries: geologic discoveries of fuels, such as coal, petroleum, and uranium; chemical discoveries permitting the manufacture of cheaper and more efficient fuels; great changes in metallurgy; and so on. As a result of this surge of discoveries, man's economic activities in the western world are now aided by huge amounts of mechanical power derived from fuels and water power. In fact, the role of labor is decreasingly that of providing physical power and increasingly that of directing the operation of tools and machinery driven by engines and motors. Yet there are still areas of the world in which men and beasts must provide most of the power.

Also familiar are numerous discoveries relating to tools and ma-chinery. A century ago, and even fifty years ago, man had not yet learned how to make a large part of the tools and machinery that we employ so productively today. But the technological revolution extends far beyond these familiar examples. Chemists have shown us how to eliminate impurities from iron ores that were previously worthless; how to make aluminum out of bauxite clay; how to make magnesium out of sea water; how to derive the sulfas and thousands of other products from coal tar; how to make penicillin, aureomycin, and other life-saving substances out of molds; how to make cloth out of limestone, water, air, and coke; and so on.

Research by chemists and biologists in the field of plant physiology have shown us how to adapt plants to the various types of soils, to use fertilizers to remedy soil deficiencies, and to prevent or cure many plant diseases. Geneticists have taught us how to improve and produce more efficiently both plants and animals through selective breeding and hybridization. For example, cows are no longer "general purpose" animals, but are specialized and more efficient converters of vegetable matter into milk or beef. There are now hundreds of types of wheat that vary as to strength of stalk, resistance to rust, resistance to drought, length of growing period, requirements as to soil, and so on.

We cannot list here the host of other significant technological changes in this country during the last century or even during the past fifty years; such a list would fill several volumes. But even our limited number of examples should suggest the pervasiveness of the scientific and technological revolutions, their great contributions to productivity, and their far-reaching effects on our entire economic and social structure. The latter point will be developed in the next chapter.

c. Technological Change as a Method of Increasing Productivity

Advances in technology are a necessary condition for improving productivity in many areas of the world. But the achievement of these advances presents many problems. One is, of course, the cost. It is expensive, especially for a low-income country, to import scientists and highly trained technicians, to send students abroad to become highly trained, and to provide educational facilities at home. But the cost of acquiring technical know-how is not the only obstacle. There is also the problem of overcoming opposition to change and of creating enthusiasm for doing things new ways and of producing and using new products.

9. Specialization and Exchange

Productivity also depends on the extent of specialization and exchange. Each person could, of course, attempt to be completely self-sufficient. He could be a jack-of-all-trades, making all his own tools and consumer goods and services. But the penalty would be chronic poverty. Output can be greatly increased through specialization accompanied by an exchange of output among the specializers. And within limits, productivity rises along with increases in the degree of specialization.

A. SPECIALIZATION

Greater specialization enhances output in many ways.

1. Geographic specialization permits the natural resources of each area to be used for the specific purposes for which they are best suited or least unsuited. The various areas of the world are far from uniform. They differ as to soil, topography, rainfall, temperature, mineral deposits, availability of water power, and so on. Total output can be maximized only by devoting the natural resources of each region to those particular uses in which they are most productive or least unproductive. Canada is better off when other countries grow its tea and oranges. This is possible only under regional specialization and trade.

2. Specialization permits each person to concentrate on those particular functions for which his native abilities are best suited or least unsuited. People display great natural variations in strength, in coordination and dexterity, in quickness of comprehension, in capacity for imaginative thinking, in temperament, and so on. A group can maximize its output only through the most effective utilization of the almost unlimited variations in its members' abilities. This, too, is possible only under specialization.

3. Personal specialization enhances productivity by facilitating the acquisition of knowledge and skill. This would be true even if all people had exactly the same innate abilities. By specializing on only one or a few tasks, each person can acquire greater skill, can learn and apply greater amounts of knowledge relevant to that task, and can even increase the total amount of knowledge available. Our rapid accumulation of knowledge is itself largely attributable to specialization.

4. Personal specialization enhances productivity by reducing the time lost in passing from one job to another. If a person attempts to do many jobs in many places, he is likely to waste time, not only in actually going from one place to another, but also in adjusting himself to the requirements of different jobs.

5. Specialization increases productivity by permitting the use of larger amounts of capital goods of more highly specialized types. A man who attempted to produce all the goods he consumed could not

possibly have adequate supplies of even the simple farm tools, carpenter tools, spindles, looms, and blacksmith tools, to say nothing of tractors, combines, power saws and sanders, power looms, drop hammers, grinding machines, and lathes. A machine may make no addition to productivity if it stands idle most of the time, yet it may increase output manyfold if used more steadily.

The greater the degree of specialization, the greater is the amount of capital equipment that can be used advantageously. For example, if each publishing house tried to print its own books it might be able to use profitably only small and relatively inefficient printing machinery. But if publishers let out their printing to specialized printing companies the work can be done with the most efficient machinery that man knows how to make.

A higher degree of specialization permits the use of more highly specialized machinery—machinery more closely adapted to the specific job. A general-purpose power lathe may be capable of turning out table legs, camshafts, wagon axles, and many other things. But despite its versatility, the lathe is not the most efficient tool for each specific job; it will be too powerful or not powerful enough for maximum efficiency, or more precise than is necessary or not precise enough, and so on. A machine constructed for only one type of job can be closely adapted to that specific function. Power can be saved, the machine need have no more size and quality than the performance of the particular function requires, labor and time need not be wasted in adjusting the machine to different types of jobs, and the machine can be more nearly automatic. A machine that does nothing except make a certain type and size of screw may require virtually no labor for its operation.

In summary, specialization enhances productivity in many ways. It enables each specific type of natural resource and human ability to be devoted to the use in which it is relatively most efficient or least inefficient, it facilitates the acquisition and use of knowledge and skill, it decreases the time wasted in going from one job to another, and it permits the use of larger amounts of capital goods of more specialized types.

The increase of productivity resulting from the more effective use of variations in natural resources and innate human abilities is large, but it should be emphasized that specialization would increase productivity even if the natural resources of all regions were uniform and even if all human beings had exactly the same combination of natural capacities and limitations. This is because specialization makes it possible to take advantage of "the economies of large-scale production"—for each function or group of functions to be performed in a productive unit large enough to employ the most advantageous specialization of labor, the most favorable amounts of capital, and the most favorable adaptation of capital goods to their specific functions.✳

B. EXCHANGE

Specialization must be accompanied by exchange. People and regions will specialize only if they can trade their specialized output for the things they want. The extent of specialization is limited by the costs and other obstacles to the exchange process. If the process of exchange is very expensive or is obstructed by other factors, specialization will not proceed very far. But if exchanges can be effected easily and cheaply, specialization can reach a high level of development.

The costs and other obstacles to exchange are associated with—or removed or minimized by—the following elements of the exchange process: (1) transportation, (2) merchandising—the gathering of information relating to demand and supply conditions and the transfer of ownership of goods and services, (3) the making of payments, and (4) the policies related to trade.

Costs of transportation can be a serious limitation on the extent of specialization. When goods can be transported only in small boats, or on the backs of men and animals over unimproved roads, the cost is so great that trade is likely to be limited to small areas and to goods having a high value in relation to their weight and bulk. But as roads are improved, vehicles developed, railroads constructed, and ships enlarged, the cost of transportation is lowered and trade can be expanded to cover larger areas and more types of goods. Specialization could not have proceeded so far in the United States without the great cheapening and speeding up of our transportation facilities. Many underdeveloped countries still suffer from slow and costly transportation.

✳Exchange also involves changing the ownership of goods and services and the collection of information as to what things are wanted, how much of them is wanted, where they are wanted most, when they are wanted, and how much will be paid for them. This fitting together of supply and demand we shall call the merchandising function. The extent of specialization depends greatly on the cheapness and smoothness with which this function is performed.✳

The degree of specialization also depends on the efficiency of the monetary system. It is possible, of course, to carry on some trade by means of barter, but this method is so wasteful of time and effort that to rely on it exclusively would limit the expansion of specialization. The use of money can greatly facilitate trade and expand specialization. But we shall see later that imperfections in money and monetary policies have often inhibited the orderly flow of trade and have seriously interrupted productive processes.

The extent of trade and specialization is greatly influenced by the policies of governments and other social institutions. Trade has often been discouraged by the failure of governments to protect traders from personal danger, theft, and robbery, by failure to enforce trade contracts, by the exclusion of outside traders and outside products from home markets, by heavy and discriminatory taxation of importation and sales, and by many other restrictions on both domestic and foreign trade. Governments can facilitate trade by removing such obstructions and establishing favorable conditions.

✳In summary, the productivity of an economic system is greatly influenced by the types and degrees of specialization employed. Greater specialization can increase productivity in many ways. But the development of specialization can be limited by the costs of trade and other obstacles to trade. The greater the efficiency of transportation, merchandising, and the monetary system, and the more favorable are governmental policies toward trade, the easier will it be to increase the degree of specialization and to raise productivity. This applies to specialization and trade among nations as well as to domestic trade and specialization.✳

10. Economic Control Systems

As we saw earlier, every economy must have some system for controlling its economic processes—some method of determining what ends are to be sought, of organizing the available productive resources into a coordinated system for the production and distribution of output, and of resolving conflicts among its people. The productivity of a nation depends greatly on the manner in which its economic control system performs these functions. In these respects nations differ widely.

1. There are wide differences in the attitudes of the leaders—not only in government but in business and other social institutions as well —toward changes that might increase productivity. Some leaders strive to prevent change and to maintain the *status quo* in order to protect their own economic and social positions, to protect certain entrenched

economic groups, or to preserve a social structure that might be disrupted by a more productive economic system. Others welcome and actively promote changes capable of increasing productivity.

2. The capabilities and motivations of the leaders differ greatly. In some countries, leadership is exercised by men who lack native ability, training, and an urge to promote productivity. In others the leaders are highly capable, well trained, and strongly motivated to promote output.

3. Control systems also differ greatly as to the types of conduct they reward or penalize and the effectiveness with which their sanctions promote desirable types of conduct and suppress those considered undesirable. Some systems actually discourage economic activity; they hold it in low regard, grant the highest social positions to those who shun it as much as possible, and prevent people from acquiring and keeping large economic rewards for extra ability and extra effort. Such deterrents to economic activity may result from confiscatory taxation, failure to protect property rights, limitations on trade and the size of business firms, and so on. In other nations economic activity is highly rewarded with general social approbation, prestige, and wealth and income.

These are but a few examples of the differences in control systems that affect productivity. Many nations could promote their productivity by developing more favorable attitudes toward changes capable of enhancing output, more highly qualified leaders with a greater interest in economic problems, more appropriate institutions through which to organize and control economic processes, and a system of rewards and penalties that would promote more effectively the types of conduct that would raise the productivity of the economy as a whole.

11. Conclusions

The ability of economic systems to produce real income has varied enormously over both time and space. One of the most striking characteristics of the American economy has been the marked upward trend of its output, not only in total amount but also in amount per capita and per man-hour worked. Even more striking are the great differences in productivity in the various areas of the world today. A large part of the world's population lives in countries where output per capita and per man-hour is only a small fraction of that in the United States. To raise productivity in underdeveloped countries is widely considered to be one of the most urgent of the world's economic problems.

These facts emphasize the importance of understanding the factors that determine the productivity of an economic system. Only if we understand basic causes and processes are we in a sound position to point out effective preventives and cures. We found that the many specific determinants of productivity can be included in six broad categories: (1) the quantity and quality of natural resources, (2) the quantity and quality of labor, (3) the supply of capital, (4) the state of technology, (5) the types and degrees of specialization and exchange, and (6) the economic control system. The productivity of an economy does not depend on any one of these factors alone; it is a resultant of all of them and of their interactions on each other. In all these respects nations vary widely.

A nation wishing to raise its level of productivity has open to it many possible lines of action. It may seek to improve the efficiency of its workers through better diets, the prevention and cure of disease, and better education. It may study its natural resources more thoroughly to discover any that may have been unused or used only inefficiently. It may try to increase its supply of capital goods by promoting domestic saving and investment and by importing capital from abroad. It may promote technology by research and education at home, by educating some of its people abroad, and by importing technologists. It may increase specialization and trade in order to utilize more effectively the resources at its disposal. And it may seek to change its control system so as to produce more favorable attitudes toward economic activity, more effective leaders, more efficient institutions, and a system of rewards and penalties more conducive to the enhancement of output. Each of these objectives may be approached through many specific types of programs. Thus in promoting productivity, as in other economic problems, the people of a nation face many alternatives and must choose among them.

We shall not attempt to lay down specifications for the "best" or even a "good" program for enhancing productivity. A few comments may be in order, however. (1) There is probably no one program that is most appropriate for all times and all countries. What will work best depends on many conditions, such as the natural-resources situation, the history of the people, their social attitudes and institutions, the nature of the causes of their low productivity, the types and amounts of foreign aid available, and so on. (2) In most cases, the most efficient program will have several facets. For example, it may require simultaneous action to improve technology, to increase capital, and to improve the diet, health, education, and attitudes of leaders and workers. (3) A large increase in productivity may in some cases be achievable only through almost revolutionary alterations in the economic and social structure. For example, it may require a shift from a relatively simple and predominantly agrarian society to one much more complex, urbanized, and industrialized. However, industrialization is no panacea—some poor countries are totally unsuited to it by their location or their natural-resources situation. To them a program for this purpose can prove a costly disappointment. How in other more appropriate circumstances industrialization can promote productivity will become clearer as we trace some of the principal trends in American economic history.

SUGGESTED READINGS

Kuznets, Simon, *Economic Change,* Norton, New York, 1953, chapters 6–10.

Rostow, Walter W., *The Process of Economic Growth,* Norton, New York, 1952.

Viner, Jacob, *International Trade and Economic Development,* Free Press, Bloomington, 1953, chapter 6.

QUESTIONS

1. Try to describe the daily existence of the recipient of an income:
   a. Of $2000 per year.
   b. Of $1000 per year.
   c. Of $50 per year.
   Draw up budgets for these income levels.
2. Explain why we must question the accuracy and comparability of the income figures:
   a. For India or China with the United States.
   b. For Great Britain with the United States.
   c. For the United States in 1880 with the U.S. today.
3. Contrast the significance of the following concepts:
   a. National income (output).
   b. Output per capita.
   c. Output per man-hour.
4. "Incomes are so unequally distributed in most countries that considerably more than half of the people have incomes below the average." Explain.

5. Some people talk as though any "underdeveloped area" can solve its economic problems by switching from agricultural production to manufacturing and by investing heavily in machinery and other expensive capital equipment.
   a. When would such a policy fail unless supplemented by other programs? What other programs?
   b. Can you imagine a country in which such an industrialization program would be no help at all in raising standards of living?
   c. Is there any validity at all to the suggestion?
   d. What might lead people to advocate such a naïve approach?
6. In Egypt there is about as much land per person as in the United States. Comment on the significance of this fact, if any.
7. In many areas social values and customs discourage productivity. For example, business activity and other industrial pursuits are often held in lower regard than literary, military, religious, or scholarly careers.
   a. Would you say that such a people ought certainly to change their outlook on life, and that they must be silly to sacrifice productivity this way?
   b. What can economics say on this point?

CHAPTER 4

Trends in the American Economy

At several points we have referred to the upward trend of real incomes in the United States and to the accompanying changes in our entire economic and social structure. The rapidity, pervasiveness, and persistence of these changes are suggested by the title of a recent book issued by Fortune magazine—*U.S.A.: Permanent Revolution.* We have no reason to believe that this revolution is approaching its end.

This chapter will survey some of the most important aspects of these continuing changes. More specifically, it will describe some of the major changes in the structure and functioning of our economic system and suggest the relevance of these changes to economic policy. Because of its brevity it will obviously have to omit many relevant factors that would be included in a more comprehensive economic history. But this very brevity will enable us to highlight some major trends that might be obscured by a more detailed account.

To provide a background for our narrative, let us look briefly at some of the principal characteristics of the American economy around 1800. Most of these facts will be familiar to the reader but some of their implications may not.

1. The American Economy in 1800

At the beginning of the nineteenth century the American economy was still relatively primitive. It was predominantly rural, most families were largely self-sufficient, specialization was not yet highly developed, trade was quite limited, capital was very scarce, and technology was still backward.

There were only 5,300,000 people in the country, most of them living along the Atlantic seaboard. The population was predominantly
rural. No city had a population as large as 100,000 and only six had
populations exceeding 10,000. Thus there was no city as large as Wa-
terbury, Connecticut, or Corpus Christi, Texas, or Lowell, Massachu-
setts, is today. Only 6 percent of the people lived in places of 2500 or
more; 94 percent lived on farms or in small villages. Though there
were large plantations in the South, most of the farms were quite small.
Farming methods showed few improvements over those that had been
used in western Europe for centuries; farmers still relied largely on
hand tools, crude wooden plows, and plants and animals which by
modern standards would seem very poor indeed.

Most manufacturing was still carried on in homes or little shops with
the aid of only small amounts of simple tools and equipment. Each
family manufactured many of the things it used, not only processing
its own foods, but also doing much of its own spinning, weaving, knit-
ting, sewing, furniture making, and construction of its tools and equipment. Most of the manufacturing for the market was done in homes or
small handicraft shops. Factories had begun to develop, but by modern
standards they were quite small and poorly equipped. Each had only
a few employees, relied almost solely on human and water power, and
used only a few rather simple tools and machinery.

Under these conditions only a small proportion of output entered
into trade. There was some trade, of course. There was trade with
Europe, trade with the West Indies, trade up and down the Atlantic
coast, and internal trade via rivers and roads. Nevertheless, only a
small proportion of the goods produced entered into trade, and most
of the trade covered only a small area. The high cost of transportation
was a major limitation on both the amount of trade and the size of
trade areas. Ocean transportation was expensive, slow, and risky.

Inland transportation was even more expensive in most cases. Where
navigable streams were available, transportation downstream was
sometimes relatively easy, but transport upstream was far more expensive because of the absence of mechanical power. Overland transport was very costly. Most of the roads were poor, and in many areas
they were muddy a large part of each year. This was true even in many
cities—the muddiness of Washington streets was still notorious decades later. Vehicles were crude, and human beings, oxen, and horses
were the sole means of propulsion. In 1800 animals could pull a wagon
over the very bad roads only a few miles per day. Freight charges of

30 cents per ton-mile and more were common in those days. Today the cost of haulage has decreased to something nearer one cent per ton-mile despite the considerable fall in the purchasing power of money.

With the amount of trade still rather small, there was no need for elaborate institutions to perform exchange functions. Most merchants operated on a scale very small by modern standards. There were few banks and other financial institutions. Money was used, of course, and it performed important functions in the market sections of the economy, but it was far less important than it is today. Ours was not yet a predominantly money and credit economy.

Such were the outstanding characteristics of the primitive American economy of a century and a half ago. The great transformation that has occurred since that time, and is still continuing, will be evident to anyone who looks at our contemporary society.

2. Changes Since 1800

Since 1800 there have obviously been tremendous changes in America's productive capacity.

First to come to mind are doubtless the many inventions and discoveries and the revolution they caused in our mode of production. No one can understand our rapid rate of capital accumulation, the continuing growth of specialization and exchange, the rising trend of real output per man-hour, the continuously changing composition of output, or the sweeping changes in our social institutions without considering the continuing surge of scientific discoveries and their application in every line of economic activity.

Equally important has been the tremendous improvement in our system of transportation and communication. We need hardly mention the development of the great network of railroads, roads, and airlines and of telegraphic, telephonic, and radio communication systems. This has been an integral part of the continuing process of expanding the areas of trade, increasing the proportion of output entering into trade, increasing specialization, and making the country into a truly "national economy" rather than a collection of largely isolated local markets.

Our labor force has increased perhaps 30 times—and in quality as well as quantity, for today's worker is far healthier and better educated than his counterpart at the end of the eighteenth century.

We have accumulated huge quantities of capital. During the nineteenth century much of this was acquired by importing foreign savings, mostly from western Europe. However, our net imports of savings ceased at about the end of the century. During the twentieth century we have been a large net exporter of savings. Taking our history as a whole, by far the largest part of our capital accumulation has occurred through saving and investment by the American people themselves.

Perhaps less obvious is the contribution made by our expanding territory. Geographic and geologic exploration revealed that a large part of our most productive farm land and rich mineral deposits lies west of the Appalachians, almost all acquired since 1800. A few examples are the great areas of rich farm land between the Appalachians and the Rockies; the iron ore deposits of Wisconsin; the great gas and petroleum deposits in Louisiana, Oklahoma, Texas, California, and other western areas; the lead and zinc deposits in Missouri, Oklahoma, and Arkansas; and the large deposits of gold, silver, and copper in the Rocky Mountain area.

This is not to say that our natural-resources situation leaves nothing to be desired. Obvious shortcomings are the acute shortages of rain and water supplies in a large part of the West; the thinness of New England soils; the scarcity of nickel, tin, manganese, and various other metals; eroded soils in many areas, and so on. Yet it is still true that the supply of high-quality natural resources available to assist each worker is far more abundant here than in most parts of the world.

The availability of large amounts of good land at low cost has also influenced our economic development in other ways. For example, it enabled a large proportion of our farmers to own their own land rather than accept the status of tenant or farm employee. It helped force wage rates up in both rural and urban areas. And it assisted in creating a feeling of freedom and opportunity; people dissatisfied with their current status had the alternative of migrating to the frontier where they could make a living and perhaps reap gains as land values rose.

We see that our nation's productive capacity has expanded since 1800 in just about every one of the ways mentioned in the preceding chapter. We have increased our resources, increased and improved our labor force, increased our capital supply, improved our technology, and increased economic specialization and exchange.

The various developments that we have considered are often referred to collectively as the industrial revolution. This revolution has been accompanied by a sweeping transformation of both the structure and functioning of our society. Our task now is to look at some of the most striking aspects of these social changes and to see how they may be relevant to current policy issues. Perhaps the best approach is to ask this question: "If an American who was thoroughly familiar with conditions in the early nineteenth century should return today, what are the most striking changes that he would find?"

3. Urbanization and the Agricultural Revolution

Our visitor would find that our society has been transformed from one predominantly agricultural to one predominantly nonagricultural. In 1800 farmers made up about 90 percent of the total population. In 1950 they constituted only 16 percent of the total. This has been accompanied, of course, by a great increase in the proportion of the population living in cities. In 1950 rural dwellers, even including those who do not farm, made up only 36 percent of the total population; 64 percent were urban dwellers. More than a third of our people now live in places of 50,000 or more.

This trend toward urbanization would have been impossible in the absence of a great rise of productivity in agriculture. With the crude technology and tools available in 1800, output per worker in agriculture was so low that most of the available labor had to be used to produce the necessary food and fibers. Urbanization and industrialization could take place only to the extent that a smaller proportion of the total labor supply came to be required for farming. This has occurred in three principal ways. (1) Farmers have discontinued many of their old functions, such as manufacturing, and have specialized in agriculture. (2) Automobiles and other motor vehicles have substituted urban-made transportation and power for horses and their feed. (3) Agricultural output per man-hour has risen tremendously. In 1800 a farmer could produce little more than enough to feed his own family. Today a farmer can produce enough to feed many families.

A. TECHNOLOGICAL ADVANCES IN AGRICULTURE

This increase of productivity in agriculture has been achieved largely through technological advances, increased capital supplies, and increased specialization. We have already noted that in 1800 farmers were aided by a few crude tools. To plow and cultivate the soil they used inefficient wooden plows, hoes, and hand rakes. For harvesting they used knives, sickles, and scythes. They threshed with flails or by tramping out the grain. Many types of new and improved machinery were invented and put into use during the nineteenth century—steel walking plows, wheeled plows, wheeled cultivators, harrows, reapers, binders, threshers, and so on. By the end of the century farmers were employing large amounts of horse-powered equipment and their productivity was far higher than it had been at the beginning of the century.

The increase of agricultural output per man-hour has been even more rapid during the last fifty years as mechanical power has come to be used in farming. Steam engines had been employed for threshing and a few other farm purposes after 1860 but were not suitable for traction work in the fields. Only after 1915, when internal-combustion engines began to be adapted to traction purposes, did it become feasible to use tractors on a wide scale. Farmers now employ millions of tractors to pull and operate larger and more efficient plows, harrows, seeders, harvester-threshers, cornpickers, haybalers, and many other types of machinery. Their hauling, both on the farm and between farm and market, is speeded up and cheapened by millions of tractors, trucks, and autos. Rural electrification has recently contributed much to farm output as well as relieving the dreariness of farm life. Many other discoveries have contributed to productivity. Among these have been better plant and animal nutrition, fertilizers, the prevention and cure of plant and animal diseases, insecticides and fungicides, selective breeding, hybridization, and so on.

This continued rise of farm output per worker during recent decades has been reflected in a continued shrinkage of the proportion of the population engaged in farming. In the forty years between 1910 and 1950 this proportion fell from 36 to 16 percent. There is no reason to believe that this trend will not continue. Output per farmer continues to rise, both because of new discoveries and because of the more widespread use of the knowledge already at hand.

B. CHANGES IN RURAL LIVING

Along with these great increases in farm productivity has come a complete transformation in farm life. Even as late as 1900 a "typical" farmer lived a primitive and isolated life. With horse-drawn vehicles and dirt roads, the nearest city was several hours away. His children went to a one-room country school. His home was equipped with kerosene lamps, a wood-burning stove, no telephone, and no refrigerating facilities. His reading materials were often limited to a weekly newspaper and a farmer's magazine. Now all this has been changed. Hard-surfaced roads and an automobile enable him to reach the city in a few minutes. His home is equipped with a gas or electric stove, refrigerator, many other electrical appliances, and an indoor toilet. His children go to a consolidated school, and many continue to college. He is kept up to date on the latest news by daily newspapers, telephone, radio, and television. Whether or not he approved of the change, our visitor would certainly agree that farm life isn't what it used to be.

c. CHANGES IN FARM ECONOMICS

Our visitor would also find many other changes on the farm. He would find that farms are now much larger than they used to be and require far more capital equipment. A farmer can no longer get along with "a few acres, a plow, and a mule." He would find farmers complaining about overproduction and low prices for their products. And he would find that farm families have lost a large amount of their earlier self-sufficiency. They no longer produce any large part of the things that they consume. Like urban dwellers, they now sell their specialized products in the market for money and use the money to buy products of other specialized producers. Their economic welfare therefore depends on market processes. Even among farmers, family self-sufficiency is largely a thing of the past.

d. EFFECTS OF URBANIZATION

The trend toward urbanization has many economic and social implications, of which we can mention only a few. As greater numbers of people come to live closer together, the actions of each one have greater effects on the others so that each must be subjected to more social control. For example, a farmer may safely be permitted to dispose of his garbage as he sees fit, to erect fire hazards, and to burn any type of fuel he wishes, but urban dwellers must restrict each other. Urban dwellers also demand many types of community services that are not required on farms: streets, sidewalks, street lighting, parks, sewage systems, fire prevention, slum clearance, and sanitation control. We shall find later that the trend toward urbanization has been an important factor in raising government expenditures.

4. The Size of Business Firms

Our hypothetical visitor from the past would be startled by the huge size of many of our business firms, some employing several hundred thousand workers and billions of dollars' worth of assets. He would be unable to understand our offhand references to G.M., the A.T. & T.,

Du Pont, Metropolitan Life, U.S. Steel, and other great corporations.

The rise of large business firms has been an inevitable accompaniment of the changes we have already described. There was little reason
to develop very large firms when trade areas were small, technology
backward, and capital supplies quite limited. A relatively small firm
could produce about as efficiently as a much larger one. But all this
changed as trade areas expanded, technology advanced, capital supplies increased, and new methods of specialization became more productive. Under the new conditions a firm can approach maximum
efficiency in many industries only by employing very large numbers of
workers and great aggregations of capital.

The great growth in the size of business firms has many implications, of which we shall mention only a few.

1. It has created a large class of wage and salary workers, most
of whom will never own a business enterprise. When business firms
were small with only a few employees and a little capital, a large proportion of workers did own their own businesses and more expected to
do so before they died. Now, with such large firms and great capital
requirements, few can succeed in becoming the sole owner of a business. Most will be wage and salary workers all their lives. In this role
they may earn higher incomes than they could have made in earlier
years as enterprisers, but they tend to become "class-conscious"—to
differentiate between themselves and the employer groups.

2. It has changed drastically the relationships between "owners"
and their businesses. In the earlier period, people usually owned their
individual businesses alone or in partnership with only a few others,
lived near their businesses and worked in them, and kept in close touch
with their operations. This relationship has changed greatly with the
growth of large corporations, some of which have thousands, or even
hundreds of thousands, of shareholders or "owners." Each absentee
part-owner of a corporation is likely to know little about its operations
and to exercise very little control over it. This splitting up of ownership and control functions leads to a number of problems which we
shall consider later.

3. The growth of large firms has concentrated tremendous economic power in the hands of corporate management. The management of a large corporation often has great power over thousands of
workers, over many suppliers of raw materials and services, and over
the prices of products. Directly and indirectly it can affect the welfare

of millions. The power of "big business" is a source of many policy controversies.

5. Consuming, Living, and Working

Our visitor would be amazed at the sweeping changes in family consumption patterns and in the conditions of everyday life. They have occurred not only because real incomes per family have risen to several times their level at the beginning of the nineteenth century, but also because families now spend a major part of their income for things that were unknown earlier. To be impressed with the magnitude of the change it is not necessary to go back to 1800. Even in the past half century our mode of living and working and our consumption patterns have been transformed by the appearance of a host of new commodities.

It is hardly necessary to remind the reader that automobiles, airplanes, movies, radio, electric refrigeration, plastics, nylon, and even rayon were all things of the future as the "gay nineties" drew to an end. Some of the readers of this volume would not now be alive were it not for the wonder drugs—the sulfas, penicillin, etc.—that have so recently appeared. The authors can remember the indescribable terror felt by a family when a member of it came down with an illness, such as pneumonia or an ear infection; today such illnesses are routine matters usually cleared up in a few days.

In his vivid book, *The Big Change,* Frederick Lewis Allen recalls some of the things that might attract our attention were we suddenly set down in the world of 1900:

A six-mile drive would take an hour, for there was that sandy stretch by the cemetery where the horses moved at a straining walk, and there were a couple of long hills (now taken by all automobiles in high).

. . . . Most of the city houses of the really prosperous were now electrified; but the man who was building a new house was only just beginning to install electric lights without adding gas, too, lest the current fail suddenly. And the houses of the great majority were still lighted by gas (in the cities and towns) or oil lamps (in the country). Millions of Americans of the older generation still remember what it was like to go upstairs of an evening and then be consumed with worry as to whether they had really turned off completely the downstairs gas jets. A regular chore for the rural housewife was filling the lamps; and a frequent source of family pride was the possession of a Welsbach burner that would furnish adequate light for a whole family to read by as they gathered about the living-room table. . . .

For a good many years there had been refrigerator cars on the railroads, but the great national long-distance traffic in fresh fruits and vegetables was still in its infancy; and accordingly the prevailing American diet would have shocked deeply a visitor from 1950. In most parts of the United States people were virtually without fresh fruit and green vegetables from late autumn to late spring. During this time they consumed quantities of starches, in the form of pies, doughnuts, potatoes, and hot bread, which few would venture to absorb today.

. . . Even in the gracious houses of well-to-do people beyond the reach of city water lines and sewer lines, there was likely to be no bathroom at all. They washed with pitcher and basin in their bedrooms, each of them pouring his dirty water from the basin into a slop jar, to be emptied later in the day; and after breakfast they visited the privy behind the house.[1]

The new products which have appeared since this time have obviously affected work as well as consumption patterns. The buggy maker is no more, and many people are now engaged in producing the new items we have mentioned as well as many others not listed. Partly because of the increasing size and complexity of business firms, there has been a marked decrease in the proportion of manual laborers and a corresponding increase in the number of "white-collar" workers—managers, bookkeepers, clerks, purchasing agents, salesmen, etc. Change has destroyed some jobs and created many others.

6. Economic Interdependence

Another important and inevitable consequence of the industrial revolution has been the decline of self-sufficiency and the rise of economic interdependence. Families no longer produce any large part of the things that they consume. Each is almost completely dependent on market processes—on the market demand for its specialized goods and services and on the market supply of goods and services produced by others. This interdependence is not limited to local areas; it is as wide as the market and extends far beyond our national boundaries.

A. INTERDEPENDENCE IN EARNING AND CONSUMING

Consider, as an example, the case of Charles Smith, an auto worker. If he is typical, he does not produce any of his own food, clothing, medicines, or other necessities. He depends on his employer for a job and money wages, he depends on the purchasing power of his money

[1] Frederick Lewis Allen, *The Big Change*, Harper, New York, 1952, pp. 18–20.

wages, and he depends on many suppliers to provide him with consumer goods and services.

But his employer is no less dependent on others. He cannot supply jobs to Smith and his other workers and make a money income for himself without depending on financial institutions to supply him with money, on the machinery and construction industries to supply equipment, on transportation facilities to carry raw materials and parts to him and to carry his finished product away, on many other producers to supply him his raw materials and other components, and on buyers to purchase his product at adequate prices.

In turn, each of the employer's suppliers cannot perform the required functions for him without depending on many others. They too depend on others for materials, labor, finance, equipment, transportation, communication, and a market. If we traced all the interdependences of those who enable Smith to earn a money income we would have to cover a large part of the world's economic system.

The trip is no shorter when we try to trace the interdependence of those who supply Smith with the goods and services he desires. We again find ourselves involved with many types of marketing institutions, monetary and financial organizations, transportation and storage systems, factories, farms, mines, labor, and management. And these are located all over the world. Smith can enjoy the living standards made possible by modern techniques of production only if all the parts are properly coordinated. If all the parts are not properly coordinated, he may even lose his job and have to depend on charity. His employer may face the same fate.

At the same time, other people are dependent on Smith. They rely on him to help produce a useful product, and they depend on his demand for their products.

B. THE EFFECT ON ECONOMIC SECURITY

This great growth of economic interdependence and reliance on market processes has many important implications. It brings new sources of economic insecurity. A self-sufficient family is by no means free from economic insecurity; it faces hazards such as illness or death of the breadwinner, drought, floods, fire, insect invasions, and many others. But a family dependent on the market can be adversely affected by thousands of events that are largely beyond its control. These include everything that can dislocate market processes, lower employment or other sources of money income, decrease the purchasing power of money wealth and income, or interrupt supplies.

C. INTERDEPENDENCE AND THE CONTROL SYSTEM

Greater economic interdependence necessitates a greater degree of social control over economic activities. As soon as each individual affects others and is affected by them, it is only to be expected that he will insist that their activities be prevented from hurting him and that he will have to submit, however reluctantly, to some social control over his own activities. This is a price that must be paid for living in groups and participating in cooperative group processes. But it should again be noted that this greater degree of social control need not always be greater control by government.

The spread of trade and economic interdependence over wider and wider areas has tended increasingly to shift control power to institutions with broader geographic jurisdiction. When trade and economic interdependence are largely limited to small local areas, control may be exercised satisfactorily through local institutions such as towns, counties, manors, or guilds. But as economic interdependence spreads, there is created a strong pressure to lodge control authority in institutions with jurisdictions as wide as the area of interdependence. This has been an important reason for the progressive shift of control power from local governments to states, to national governments, and even to international institutions. The trend toward wider jurisdictions is also evident in other types of control institutions—in business firms, labor unions, trade associations, and cartels.

D. REASONS FOR WIDER CONTROL JURISDICTIONS

A few examples will indicate why this is true. Detroit cannot eliminate unemployment in its automobile industry that results from a decrease in the national or international demand for motor vehicles or from a stoppage of coal mining in other areas. Iowa alone cannot solve the problem of low corn prices arising out of nation-wide or world-wide developments. The condition of highways in New Jersey is of interest not only to residents of that state but also to the millions of others who drive in the state or buy and sell products transported in it. New York alone may not be able to eliminate the exploitation of child labor in the garment industry; its attempts to do so may merely lead to the industry's migration to other areas.

In short, the progressive broadening of the areas of trade and economic interdependence has been a powerful force in shifting economic control power from governmental units with only local jurisdictions to those covering broader areas. Similarly, the scope of labor unions has broadened so that many now cover the entire country. The same is true of many trade associations and other employer organizations.

The growth of international trade and economic interdependence has even modified somewhat the principle of national sovereignty. What we may like to consider as "purely domestic" monetary, fiscal, or tariff policies may lead to serious unemployment in other parts of the world. Import or export restrictions by Britain, Bolivia, Australia, South Africa, or any other country may injure many of our industries and people. As soon as international economic interdependence becomes important, strong incentives are created to delegate some control power to an international authority, or at least for nations to enter into treaties and agreements limiting the freedom of each to take action that may harm others. Long-range bombers and fighters, atomic bombs, and guided missiles may be the most dramatic forces tending toward a modification of the principle of national sovereignty, but no one familiar with the growth of international economic interdependence will argue that these new weapons of war are the original or only important forces tending in this direction.

7. "The Permanence of Economic Laws"

Our discussion sheds some light on a much, and perhaps needlessly, debated question: How permanent are economic "laws"? Do they apply only to a particular type of economy and for a limited period or can they encompass all conceivable economies?

Some principles do apply to all economic situations. All people must somehow decide on how to allocate their scarce resources among their alternative uses. To do this rationally they must balance gains against losses for any change they consider. We have listed other economic problems which must be faced by all societies.

But such observations, because of their generality, can give us only a limited amount of information and guidance for the world in which we live. To be of more help, our economic principles must take into account the peculiar institutions and characteristics of the society to which they are meant to apply.

An example should help bring out our point. Today we can accept it as a rather firm principle that the prices of many commodities will rise or fall in New Orleans, San Francisco, and New York whenever they rise or fall in Chicago, Pittsburgh, and Denver. If meat prices go up substantially in Boston without rising elsewhere, shipments will quickly be rerouted to Boston. The increase in supplies will tend to lower Boston meat prices and raise prices in the other cities from which supplies have been diverted. In this way the prices will be brought back into line.

When General Motors bonds, or wheat, or steel rises substantially in price in one city, we can be quite sure it will also rise elsewhere in the United States. This is of much significance to buyers and sellers, most of whom need not follow prices in many cities at once. They know that it will ordinarily pay them to continue buying and selling in the place which was most convenient and profitable last year and the year before.

In colonial times the picture was different. Because of difficulties of communication and transportation, prices could and sometimes did rise in one city while they were falling in another. Sellers in the low-price area often did not find out about such a price spread for a long time. Even when they did there was often little they could do about it. Costs of transportation were so high that it might not have paid to reroute the goods to higher-price areas which (by today's standards) were very close.

Here then is an example of a useful economic principle which loses much of its validity in the primitive American economy of a century and a half ago. Even had it been valid then, it might have been much less useful than it is today.

8. Conclusions

An outstanding characteristic of the American economy has been pervasive and continuous change—change in techniques of production, change in the types of output produced, change in the size and types of producing units, and change in all other parts of our social and economic structure. We have no reason to expect that our economy will be more static in the future. Scientists and innovators are still at work, and the flow of discoveries and inventions continues.

These changes have affected our lives in many ways. They have increased urbanization, they have affected our consumption patterns and our mode of living, and, perhaps most important from the point of view of economic policy, they have increased our dependence on one another.

SUGGESTED READINGS

Allen, Frederick Lewis, *The Big Change,* Harper, New York, 1952.
Johnson, E. A. J., and Krooss, Herman E., *The Origins and Development of the American Economy,* Prentice-Hall, New York, 1953.

QUESTIONS

1. Since the beginning of the nineteenth century what have been the principal developments:
   a. In metallurgy?
   b. In chemical products?
   c. In applied biology?
2. Discuss the quantities and qualities of the natural resources of several countries. Can you tie this in with recent events?
3. Name some types of employment which have largely disappeared since 1800.
4. Discuss some factors that have encouraged saving and the accumulation of capital in the United States.
5. a. List some of America's larger business firms.
   b. How many of these manufacture products that were not produced in 1800?
   c. What were the nearest substitutes for these products then?
   d. For each of the firms you have listed, discuss why a firm producing the same products or their eighteenth-century counterparts would have been smaller.
6. a. How do you reconcile the increase in urbanization with the view that American agriculture is suffering from chronic overproduction?
   b. How does such overproduction affect the migration from farm to city in times of industrial depression?
   c. In times of industrial prosperity?
   d. What is the relevance of government farm price support?
7. a. From the newspapers list some problems arising out of the growing interdependence of the economy that have led to federal economic intervention.
   b. Discuss the policy alternatives with respect to these problems.
   c. How could some similar problems have been handled in 1800?

PART II

Economic Organization and Control

CHAPTER 5

Business Firms

1. Introduction

At various points in our discussion we noted that every nation must have some sort of control system to organize and direct its economic processes. In the next chapter we shall discuss the American type of free-enterprise system. There we shall find that by far the largest part of our economic activity is carried on in more than 11 million privately owned and privately operated business firms located in all branches of the economy.

Though the economic activities of the government are large, these private business firms account for the major part of our production and trade and employ a correspondingly large proportion of our natural resources, labor, and capital. They are the basic productive organizations in the private sectors of the economy. No one can understand the operation of a free-enterprise type of economic system without understanding the purposes and functions of these basic economic units. The primary purpose of this chapter is to contribute to such an understanding.

We shall start out by discussing the various functions performed in every business firm, regardless of its size or legal form. But we shall also deal with the great differences among firms. Their sizes vary all the way from little one-man shops with no employees and only small amounts of natural resources and capital to huge corporations with hundreds of thousands of employees and billions of dollars' worth of assets. Their legal forms include individual proprietorships, partnerships, corporations, and cooperatives. We shall analyze the relationships among the size, legal form, and functioning of firms. Such questions as these will be in the forefront: Why does the size of business firms differ so widely in different industries? Why are there so many different legal forms? Why has the corporation developed and spread so widely? Why is the corporate form dominant in some lines and not in others? What are some of the social implications of the large corporation?

2. The Common Characteristics and Functions of All Business Firms

Let us begin by looking at some basic characteristics and functions that are common to all business firms, regardless of their size and legal form. The term "business firm" means, of course, a legal entity that owns and operates a business enterprise. This legal entity has the power to own property, to enter into contracts, to sue and be sued in the courts, and so on. From the point of view of its owners, the primary purpose of a firm is to "make money"—that is, to make a net money income. From the social point of view the function of the firm is to employ productive resources in producing and trading useful goods and services.

On closer examination we find that a business firm commands certain amounts of labor, natural resources, and capital, all organized into a productive process under common management or control. The person or group of persons with the ultimate responsibility for organizing and controlling a business firm is called an *enterpriser* or *entrepreneur*. And this function is called *enterprise* or *entrepreneurship*. In some firms the functions of entrepreneurship are concentrated in one person; in others they are split in various ways among several or even very large numbers of people. The functions of entrepreneurship are threefold: (1) organization and control, (2) risk-bearing, and (3) the supplying of assets to the firm in exchange for ownership claims.

A. Organization and Control

The enterpriser in a business firm is faced with many decisions in the field of organization and control, some of them very difficult because of the large number of alternatives available. Among the decisions which the enterpriser must make and carry out are these: (1) Whether and when to establish or discontinue a firm. (2) What types of products to turn out—not just the general classes of product but the exact specifications of each. (3) The geographic location of the firm's plant or plants. (4) The size of the firm and of each plant—whether small, medium-sized, or large. (5) The combination of productive factors to be used in producing each type and amount of output. Such decisions are sometimes difficult, for it is often possible to produce a given output with various combinations of the different types of labor, capital, natural resources, and raw materials. (6) The types of technology and degrees of specialization to be employed. (7) The rate of output of each type of product. (8) The area of the market he will try to serve. ✳

The efficiency of the entire economy depends greatly on the effectiveness of enterprisers, acting within a framework of government controls and market competition, in solving problems of these types. The term "efficiency" presents difficulties of definition, but we shall use it here in the general sense of getting the greatest value of output from the value of inputs of productive factors and materials. Though all the types of decisions listed above are important determinants of economic efficiency, we shall single out the size of firms for special comment.

If the economy is to operate at maximum efficiency, each business firm must be of "optimum size"—just large enough to permit it to achieve the highest possible efficiency. We all recognize that a firm can be too small and that it can achieve "economies of scale" by increasing its size up to some point. Up to this point it can reap greater economies as it uses more capital of more specialized types, hires more laborers and increases their degree of specialization, commands better and more varied management skills, buys and handles supplies in larger lots, and uses more efficient marketing methods.

But a firm can also be too large for maximum efficiency; beyond some point the "diseconomies of scale" are likely to predominate. Further increases in size will not bring further economies, or any further economies will be more than offset by diseconomies. The latter are most likely to appear in management, as further increases in size increase business bureaucracy, red tape, difficulties of communication and discipline, and problems of maintaining incentive and initiative. In this age of high respect for giant business enterprises it is well to remember that a firm can be too large as well as too small for maximum efficiency.

There is, of course, no one optimum size for firms in all industries, at all times, and in all places. In fact, there may not be just one optimum size for all firms producing a given type of product. Some firms may achieve or approach their most efficient size only if they are very large. Some others may at least approach their most efficient size while they are still somewhat smaller. The optimum size of a firm depends on many things, such as the nature of its product, the state of technology, the size of the market, the qualities of its management, and the availability and cost of capital. We have already noted that the industrial revolution has, in general, increased the optimum size of firms. As markets widened, capital supplies increased, technology advanced, and greater specialization became advantageous, firms had to become larger to approach their greatest possible efficiency. It is no accident that the rise of large-scale firms has paralleled these basic developments.

Even today, however, there are great differences in the optimum size of firms in different industries. There are still some lines in which the optimum size is relatively small. For example, a shoe repair firm may be able to achieve maximum efficiency with no more than a score of employees and a few thousand dollars' worth of equipment. Despite the enlarging effects of the agricultural revolution, a corn farm can gain little or nothing in efficiency by expanding beyond a few hundred acres of land and somewhat less than $100,000 worth of capital equipment.

On the other hand, there are now many industries in which a firm must be extremely large to attain, or even approach, maximum efficiency. This is clearly true in iron and steel, automobiles, railroads, telephone and telegraph, radio and television transmitting, long-distance pipe lines, life insurance, and many other industries. In these and other similar industries very large firms are likely to predominate.

Competition tends to force the firms in each industry to be of approximately optimum size and to penalize those that are either too small or too large. The efficacy of competition in achieving this result should not be overestimated. Many firms remain of less than optimum size because of such things as the inertia of their enterprisers, imperfections in the money market that prevent them from acquiring the money necessary for expansion, and so on.

On the other hand, some firms are almost certainly too large to achieve maximum efficiency. Imperfections in competition may permit them to survive despite their higher costs. They may be willing to sacrifice some net earnings in order to command a larger share of the market. And in some cases greater size gives them monopolistic buying or selling power which permits them to exploit their suppliers or customers more than enough to offset the diseconomies that come with excessive size. These and other types of imperfections in competition are important in many cases and should not be forgotten.

Nevertheless, it is also important to remember that as the power of competition increases, it brings pressure for the establishment of optimum-sized firms in each industry. In the first place, each firm has an incentive to pioneer in moving toward optimum size in order to reap higher profits by achieving the lowest possible costs per unit of output. And in the second place, laggard firms are put under pressure as they compete. They must be able to meet the terms set by their more efficient rivals or else go broke, and to meet these terms they will have to move toward a size that will enable them to achieve maximum efficiency.

We cannot understand the actual structure of our various industries —the numbers and sizes of the firms in them—without remembering both the competitive pressures that tend to force firms toward a size that will be optimal for a particular industry and also the imperfections of competition that interfere with the process.

B. RISK-BEARING

The second function of entrepreneurship that is present in every firm is risk-bearing. The entrepreneur assumes the position of residual claimant of both the income and assets of the business unit; he claims only what is left over after the claims of others have been met. He may gain or lose by accepting this position, but in any case he must bear risk because production is a time-consuming process and involves many uncertainties.

A firm makes long-term commitments in buying or renting natural resources and durable capital goods. It buys raw materials, semi-finished goods, or finished inventory to process and sell in the future. It enters into labor contracts for short or long periods. It may borrow money, promising to repay fixed dollar amounts in the future. But in making such commitments, a firm faces many uncertainties as to the future—uncertainty as to the future demand for its products, uncertainty as to the future costs of raw materials and productive factors, and uncertainty as to how much output it can get from inputs of materials and productive factors. These uncertainties are the sources of risk which must be borne by someone.

The entrepreneur, as residual claimant, is the primary risk-bearer. If things turn out well, he may reap very large profits and capital gains.

If they turn out badly, he may reap only losses. In some cases, the losses may be so great as to ruin the entrepreneur and cause even the creditors to suffer losses.

In the individual proprietorship the function of primary risk-bearer is concentrated in a single owner. In partnerships and corporations this function may be split among many owners, either equally or unequally.

C. BUSINESS FINANCE

Every business firm needs assets with which to carry on its operations. These assets take many forms, such as land, buildings, capital equipment, inventories, and some money with which to meet payrolls and other current expenses. Business finance refers to the process by which firms acquire the assets they use. Business firms as legal entities acquire assets by creating and issuing two types of claims against themselves: debt claims and ownership claims. In some cases these claims are issued directly to those who supply the firm with real goods, such as durable capital goods or inventories. In more cases, however, a firm issues these claims in exchange for money, which it then uses to buy the assets it desires.

Debt claims against itself are created by a business firm and issued to those who lend to the firm and thereby become its creditors. Such claims usually require the firm to repay a specified number of dollars on a specified date and to pay interest at a specified rate. Some of these debts are long-term, being repayable only after the lapse of many years; others are short-term or even payable on demand. But despite differences in their maturities and other provisions, almost all debt claims issued by business firms have these characteristics in common: (1) Their amounts are stated as fixed numbers of dollars, and (2) they represent claims against both the assets and income of a firm that take precedence over ownership claims. The owners have only a residual claim against the part of a firm's assets and income that is not owed to its creditors.

As already noted, a firm also acquires assets by issuing ownership claims against itself, these being residual claims against any of the firm's assets and income that are not owed to creditors. A firm issues these ownership claims by two principal processes: (1) It issues them to owners who actually pay in money or other assets to the firm. For example, it may issue ownership claims to an owner who pays $100 to it. (2) It "plows in" or retains net earnings which would otherwise have gone to its owners. For example, a firm may use $5000 of its net earnings during some period to increase its assets rather than to pay income to its owners, in which case the owners have a $5000 increase in their claims against the firm. Ownership claims usually carry with them the right to control the firm. However, we shall find later that in complex business firms the rights and obligations of ownership are split up in various ways.

Up to this point we have concentrated on the characteristics and functions that are common to all types of business firms, regardless of their size or legal form. We now turn to some important differences. Our classification will be based on legal form, but our primary interest will be the relationship between the legal form of a firm and its size and performance.

3. The Individual Proprietorship

The oldest and simplest type of firm is the individual proprietorship, by which we mean one natural person in his business capacity. In this case the law makes no distinction between the natural person and the firm; the firm's income is considered to be income to the owner, and both the business and nonbusiness assets of the person may be taken to satisfy either his business or his nonbusiness debts.

Two characteristics of this simple form of business enterprise should be noted. (1) In this case there is only one owner, and in him are concentrated all the functions of entrepreneurship—control, the supplying of assets in exchange for ownership claims, and risk-bearing. (2) In this case the owner is subject to unlimited liability for the debts of the firm. To satisfy their claims, creditors may take not only the assets that the owner has put into the firm but all his other assets as well.

The individual proprietorship possesses certain advantages, especially for small-scale business. The first is the ease of starting or discontinuing business. The proprietor can establish or discontinue an enterprise quickly and without the necessity of consulting others or of going to the trouble and expense of securing a charter from the government. The second is the centralization of responsibility in the single owner. This not only permits quick decisions and flexibility, but also provides a maximum incentive to initiative and efficiency, for the owner-manager reaps all the profits and bears all the losses. In some cases the individual proprietor enjoys a third advantage in the form of lower taxes. This, however, depends on the nature of tax policies, for there are some cases in which taxes on this type of firm are higher than those on corporations.

Individual proprietorships are still by far the most numerous type of business firm in this country, and they account for a major part of production in many lines where relatively small firms can approach maximum efficiency. There are more than 11 million of them, mostly in such lines as farming, fishing, retailing, and services.

However, the individual proprietorship has proved incapable of amassing the very large amounts of assets that a firm needs to be successful in many lines of industry today. There is no one person in the United States who has or can borrow enough money to buy as many assets as are now commanded by our largest business firms, and there are very few people who have or can borrow enough to buy the amount of assets possessed by firms that are now considered only medium-sized. Moreover, the unlimited liability of the owner makes many people unwilling to invest all their money in a sole proprietorship and risk losing everything. Other legal types of firms without these limitations had to be developed to amass the very large amounts of assets now required for efficient operation in many lines.

4. The General Partnership

Another common and very old type of firm is the partnership. This form sometimes becomes complex, but we shall consider only the simplest and most common type, the general partnership. A general partnership consists simply of two or more persons acting as a unit in conducting a business. The law does not distinguish between the firm and the partners; the income of the firm is considered to be income to the partners, and all of the partners' assets may be taken to satisfy the firm's obligations. The general partnership differs from the individual proprietorship in one major respect: in it the functions of ownership—the supplying of assets to the firm, ultimate responsibility for control of the firm, and risk-bearing—are not all concentrated in one person but are split as many ways as there are partners. These functions may be split either equally or unequally.

The general partnership has several advantages over the individual proprietorship. It can command more assets, for it can secure the contributions of two or more partners and can borrow additional amounts on the security of the partners' contributions. Where there are several partners, the firm may amass a considerable amount of assets. The partnership can also secure greater specialization in management without resort to nonowners. One partner may be an expert in buying, another in technology, another in finance, another in selling, and so on. If the firm has plants in several places, each may be managed by a partner.

Despite these advantages, the general partnership has shortcomings that limit the extent of its use. The first of these is the unlimited liability of the partners for the debts of the firm. This unlimited liability is joint and several; a creditor may seek payment from all the partners together or from any one of them, and he may claim all the assets of any partner. A partner who has paid more than his share of the firm's debts may seek restitution from the others, but this sometimes affords him little relief. Because of this unlimited liability many people refuse to enter into partnerships.

The danger inherent in unlimited liability is enhanced by a second potential shortcoming of the partnership, the ability of each partner to bind the others in anything pertaining to the firm's business. One incompetent, dishonest, or careless partner can bankrupt all the owners. In addition to their usual warnings against wine, women, and gambling, many fathers have warned their sons against becoming involved in partnership arrangements.

A third disadvantage of the partnership is the nontransferability of ownership. When one partner dies or withdraws for other reasons, the partnership is dissolved. No heir of the deceased may demand the right to become a partner, and no partner may sell his share to anyone not acceptable to the others. Though this rule is necessary to protect the remaining partners, it often makes a partnership interest an illiquid asset, leads to bad feelings among the partners or their heirs, and may prevent the heirs of a deceased partner from receiving the full value of the partnership interest. In some cases it may force the sale of the firm's assets at a price far below the value of the enterprise as a going concern.

Owing to the types of shortcomings described above—the unlimited liability of partners, the ability of each partner to bind the others, the nontransferability of shares of ownership, and the necessity of dissolving the firm upon the withdrawal of a partner—the general partnership has proved incapable of amassing the very large quantity of assets required for efficient operation in many lines. For this purpose it has been necessary to develop a type of firm that will combine limited liability for its owners, quick and easy transferability of the shares of ownership, continuity of the firm over long periods, and specialized management.

5. The Corporation

Many societies have developed institutions similar to the business corporation, in that these institutions have possessed continuity as legal entities over prolonged periods despite the death or withdrawal of the individual human beings associated with them at various times. Examples of such institutions with a continuing legal identity, despite the death or withdrawal of their individual human members, include political units, churches, colleges, charitable foundations, fraternal societies, and many other social institutions. Such a concept is highly useful for any organization that wishes to function over a long period or uses highly durable assets.

The first business corporations resembling the modern type were the British East India Company and the Dutch East India Company, which were established in the first years of the seventeenth century after the commercial revolution had made larger-scale trading units advantageous. Only after 1750, with the beginning of the industrial revolution, did the corporation begin to spread into such lines as manufacturing and mining. In the United States the corporate form of business was largely limited to railroads, canal companies, turnpike companies, banks, and textile companies until the Civil War. But after 1865 the corporation spread rapidly, and today is the dominant type of firm in many lines. It is certainly no accident that the rise of the corporation has paralleled the rise of large-scale business firms during the economic revolution.

We shall concentrate on the business corporation as it exists in the United States, but other countries have similar types of firms. Examples include the joint-stock company in England, the *société anonyme* in France, and the *Aktiengesellschaft* in Germany.

A. THE NATURE OF THE BUSINESS CORPORATION

In his famous decision in the Dartmouth College case, Chief Justice Marshall defined the corporation in the following terms:

A corporation is an artificial being, invisible, intangible, and existing only in contemplation of law. Being the mere creature of law, it possesses only those properties which the charter of its creation confers upon it, either expressly, or as incidental to its very existence. These are such as are supposed best calculated to effect the object for which it was created. Among the most important are immortality, and, if the expression may be allowed, individuality; properties, by which a perpetual succession of many persons are considered as the same, and may act as a single individual. They enable a corporation to manage its own affairs, and to hold property, without the perplexing intricacies, the hazardous and endless necessity, of perpetual conveyances for the purpose of transmitting it from hand to hand. It is chiefly for the purpose of clothing bodies of men, in succession, with these qualities and capacities, that corporations were invented, and are in use. By these means, a perpetual succession of individuals are capable of acting for the promotion of the particular object, like one immortal being.[1]

This definition brings out the most important characteristics of the corporation.

1. It is legally an artificial being or person, with a legal existence in-dependent of its owners. We have seen that in the case of the individual proprietorship and partnership the law does not distinguish between the firm and its owners; the firm's income, assets, debts, and contracts are considered to be those of the owners. But the corporation as a legal artificial person distinct from its owners has its own income, assets, liabilities, and contracts.

This legal fiction has greatly influenced both public thinking and public policy. For example, we often hear people refer to the General Motors Corporation in such a way as to suggest that it is a real person with a real personality. And corporate property and income are sometimes taxed without much consideration of the effects on the real people who are the owners of the corporations concerned.

2. The corporation has the attribute of immortality; unlike an individual proprietorship or partnership, it persists as an entity even if some of its owners die or withdraw for other reasons. This continuity is especially valuable for business units which wish to operate over a long period of time, which profit from accumulated "good will," and which use large amounts of specialized fixed capital.

3. The corporation as an artificial person created by law has only the powers conferred upon it by law. It cannot claim "human" rights, "natural" rights, or the rights of citizenship unless these are conferred by law. The powers of a corporation are set forth in its charter, which is granted by a state government or, less frequently, by the federal government. The charter authorizes the establishment of a corporation, defines its powers and obligations relative to the government, and fixes the rights and obligations of the corporation, its owners, its creditors, and its managers relative to each other.

In the earlier period, governments tended to grant charters only

[1] Dartmouth College v. Woodward *United States Reports*, vol. 17, 4th ed., p. 634.

sparingly and to restrict corporate powers. For many decades, however, the growing public approval of the corporate form and competition among the states for the business of issuing charters have led to great generosity, both in the number of charters granted and in the amount of power granted to corporations. In most states the right to incorporate is now issued to anyone who will pay a small fee, meet the minimum requirements of a general incorporation law, and file the proposed charter with a designated state official. It is not at all uncommon now for a charter to contain a long list of specific corporate powers followed by a blanket grant of power "to do anything else not prohibited by law."

4. An attribute of almost all modern corporations is the limited liability of owners for the corporation's debts. The corporation's creditors can take all of the corporation's income and assets to satisfy their claims, but they cannot sue the owners for any deficiency if the owners have paid in full for their shares of ownership. Thus, the owners' losses are limited to the amount they contributed to the corporation's assets. It is evident that the privilege of limited liability has greatly increased the willingness of savers to become part-owners of corporate firms.

5. Another characteristic of the corporation is the free transferability of shares of ownership in it. The total ownership of a corporation is split into units which are commonly called *shares*. A large corporation may issue millions of these shares of ownership which may be freely bought and sold either in direct deals between sellers and buyers or through the channels of the widespread securities markets. The feeling that they can transfer their ownership shares to others whenever they wish makes many people more willing to assume the position of shareholder or part-owner. But anyone who believes that he can always sell his shares without loss may be disappointed.

These attributes of the modern corporation—limited liability of its owners, immortality, and free transferability of shares of ownership—enable it to command huge amounts of assets. A single corporation can sell shares of ownership to thousands or even hundreds of thousands of people and can borrow from at least as many. This will become clearer as we consider methods of corporation finance.

B. CORPORATION FINANCE

A corporation, like any other type of business firm, acquires assets by creating and issuing two broad types of claims against itself: debt claims and ownership claims.

The debt instruments issued by a corporation in order to acquire money or other assets have one common attribute: they represent a promise of the corporation to repay a fixed sum of money at or before a stipulated future date and to pay a fixed amount of interest each year until the debt is retired. These lenders' or creditors' claims against the corporation's assets and income take precedence over the claims of the owners. Beyond this the debt instruments issued by corporations show a great variety. Some run for long periods; these are usually called *bonds*. Others run for only short periods; most of these are evidenced by some sort of promissory note. Some, such as mortgage bonds, have specific income or assets pledged for their satisfaction and represent claims that are prior to those of other creditors. Other debt instruments are simply general claims against all the assets and income of a corporation and are subject to the prior claims of other creditors.

By issuing such a wide variety of debt instruments, a corporation can secure money from many types of savers and can fit the amount and duration of its borrowings to its needs. For example, a corporation may borrow $100 million for twenty years, this debt being represented by 100,000 bonds, each of a $1000 denomination. These bonds may be sold through financial channels to thousands of individual and institutional buyers throughout the United States and some foreign countries. Or a $50-million short-term debt may be evidenced by 50,000 promissory notes with denominations of $1000, and these may be sold widely through the money markets to individuals, banks, insurance companies, and other buyers.

The ownership claims against a corporation, often called the *stock*, are divided into units or *shares*. Some corporations divide their ownership into only a small number of shares; others sell millions of them. Collectively, the shareholders or stockholders, whether they number a million or only three, are the owners of the corporation. As such they are the residual claimants of the corporation's assets and income and possess, at least nominally, ultimate control. They have the legal power to elect the board of directors and to vote directly on certain major policies. In short, the stockholders as a group share the functions of entrepreneurship; they assume the functions of contributing assets to the firm in exchange for ownership claims, they assume ultimate responsibility for control, and as residual claimants they are the risk-bearers. How these functions are split up we shall indicate later.

A corporation acquires assets by issuing ownership claims in two principal ways: (1) by selling shares, and (2) by retaining net profits.

The first method is relatively simple; the corporation issues shares to stockholders who pay in money or other assets. But many corporations add greatly to their assets by retaining net earnings rather than paying them out to the shareholders. For example, a corporation may use $50 million of its net earnings to increase its assets, in which case the owners do not get this amount in dividends but do have claims against more assets in the corporation. Some corporations have built up a large part of their assets in this way.

We have found that collectively the shareholders of a corporation have all the rights and responsibilities of entrepreneurship—the contributing of assets to the firm, ultimate responsibility for control, and risk-bearing. These functions may be divided either equally or unequally among the shares. Let us look first at the rather simple case in which all these functions are divided equally among the shares. Suppose that a corporation has issued only one type of stock, usually called common stock, that there are 1 million shares outstanding, and that each share carries with it the same rights and obligations. In this case, each share represents one one-millionth part of the ownership of the corporation. Each carries one one-millionth of the voting power, one one-millionth share of the total ownership claims against the income and assets of the corporation, and one one-millionth of the risk-bearing. And, in a legal sense at least, the proportion of the ownership function performed by each shareholder depends on the proportion of the total shares he owns.

In practice, however, many complex business corporations divide the various ownership functions quite unequally among their various shares of stocks. They issue not one but many types of shares, each carrying different priorities and amounts of claim against income and assets, different degrees of risk, and different voting rights. For example, one type of share may give its holder the right to receive $5 a year in dividends before other types of shares receive any, or upon dissolution of the corporation to receive $100 of assets before any return to other types of shares. In this way the holders of the other shares come to bear a larger proportion of the risk. In return, the shares with only a deferred claim may be given all the voting power, or at least an amount of voting power far out of proportion to their contribution of assets.

Control and risk-bearing are divided among the various types of shares in almost every conceivable way in modern corporations. It is common to refer to shares with a prior claim on earnings or assets as *preferred stock*, and to shares with a deferred claim as *common stock*. But such nomenclature is not very informative. Some corporations have issued several types of shares within each classification, each type of share carrying different voting rights and different claims on earnings and assets. The actual legal rights and obligations of any particular type of share can be ascertained only by studying the entire financial structure of the issuing corporation.

The corporate practice of issuing different types of shares which split up quite unequally the entrepreneurial functions of control, risk-bearing, and contributions to corporate assets raises a number of serious problems, a few of which will be noted later. But it does enable a corporation to amass greater assets by selling shares to more people, for it permits the attributes of shares to be adjusted to the tastes of different types of investors. For example, those who are willing to bear heavy risks and want control can buy the types of shares that carry control but whose claims on income and assets are junior to the claims of others. Those who demand somewhat more safety can buy types of shares with prior claims but less power of control. And those who demand the highest degree of safety can buy bonds or other debt obligations whose claims are prior to those of all stockholders.

C. THE HOLDING COMPANY

One type of corporation, the *holding company*, deserves special mention. This is a corporation that holds the securities of one or more other corporations in order to control them. A corporation that only holds the securities of other corporations is called a *pure holding company;* one that owns one or more plants directly as well as the securities of one or more other corporations is called a *mixed holding company*. The corporations controlled by a holding company are called its *subsidiaries*. A holding company may own 100 percent of the stock of its subsidiaries, in which case the controlled corporations are called *wholly owned subsidiaries*, or it may own a smaller percentage of the subsidiaries' stocks. Ownership of shares carrying 51 percent of the voting power assures control; but when the remaining shares are widely scattered, anyone holding as much as 10 or 15 percent of the voting power may have effective control under normal circumstances. The principle of "divide and conquer" applies as well in finance as on the battlefield.

Even a relatively simple holding-company structure may include several holding companies, each controlling the corporations beneath it. Such a simple pyramided structure is represented in the accompanying diagram. By possessing shares carrying effective voting control, Holding Company 4 can elect a majority of the board of directors of Holding Company 3, which in turn elects a majority of the board members of Holding Companies 1 and 2, which elect a majority of the directors of Operating Companies A, B, C, and D. In this way a number of separately incorporated firms can be brought under centralized control. By using a pyramided holding-company structure, an individual or group of individuals can exercise control over a large industrial domain with only a very small investment of their own funds.

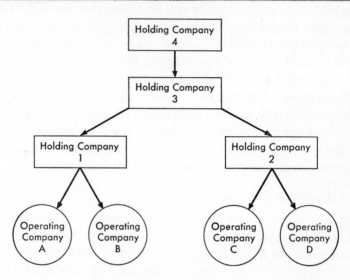

Suppose, for example, that each of the corporations in our diagram has outstanding only one type of security, common stock, and that each corporation owns exactly 51 percent of the stock of the corporation or corporations immediately below it. Thus, Holding Company 1 owns 51 percent of the shares of Operating Companies A and B, the other 49 percent being held by an outside minority group. Holding Company 2 owns 51 percent of the shares of Operating Companies C and D, the other 49 percent being held by an outside minority group, and so on, with each holding company having 51 percent of the stock of the company below it. It is clear that any person, say John Jones, who holds 51 percent of the shares of Holding Company 4 can control the entire holding-company structure. But 51 percent of the stock of Holding Company 4 is equal to less than 7 percent of the total stock of Operating Companies A, B, C and D (51% of 51% of 51%

of 51%). By investing $100,000 in Holding Company 4 John Jones
could indirectly control the four operating companies with total outstanding stocks of about $1,500,000.

It should be emphasized, however, that this example is much simpler
than many actual cases. The number of corporations involved is frequently much larger, the pattern of ownership and control is much
more involved, and the investment required to assure control is much
smaller. On the other hand, many holding companies do not try to
establish control with such small investments relative to the total assets
of the operating companies.

TABLE 7. Some of the Largest Corporations in the United States, 1951

	Assets (Millions of dollars)	Number of Shareholders	Number of Employees
Industrials			
Standard Oil Co. (N.J.)	$ 4,707	254,000	120,000
General Motors Corp.	3,672	478,924	469,197
United States Steel Corp.	3,141	268,226	301,328
Standard Oil Co. (Indiana)	1,801	116,800	49,740
Socony Vacuum Oil Co.	1,792	158,000	64,000
E.I. duPont de Nemours & Co.	1,599	138,168	86,874
Texas Company	1,549	113,642	39,747
Bethlehem Steel Corp.	1,542	98,207	152,578
Gulf Oil Corp.	1,512	38,021 (Feb. 1952)	46,873
Ford Motor Co.	1,469 (1950)	. . .	130,000
General Electric Co.	1,460	252,993	210,200
Standard Oil Co. of Calif.	1,366	104,857	32,339
Westinghouse Electric Co.	1,004	102,912	108,654
Union Carbide & Carbon Co.	978	102,460	65,000
Cities Service Co.	973	203,402	21,802
Public utilities			
American Telephone & Telegraph Co.	$ 6,960	1,092,400	551,400
Consolidated Edison of New York, Inc.	1,601	132,800 (common) 26,800 (preferred)	28,800
Commonwealth and Southern Corp.	636	115,400	11,000
American Power & Light Co.	66	11,600	. . .

TABLE 7. Some of the Largest Corporations in the United States, 1951 (*Continued*)

	Assets (Millions of dollars)	Number of Shareholders	Number of Employees
Railroads			
Pennsylvania Railroad Co.	$ 2,451	179,900	137,600
Southern Pacific Transport Cos.	1,898	51,400	64,100
New York Central Railroad Co.	1,866	47,600	109,000
The Atchison, Topeka & Santa Fe Railway Co.	1,408	39,600 (common) 20,100 (preferred)	65,600
Union Pacific Railroad Co.	1,272	59,200	55,100
Baltimore & Ohio Railway Co.	1,261	14,100 (common) 5,100 (preferred)	58,000
Great Northern Railway Co.	897	32,300 (Feb. 1952)	30,000
Banks			
Bank of America	$ 7,531	200,000	17,000
National City Bank	5,910	59,900	7,334 (domestic) 4,989 (overseas)
Chase National Bank	5,607	82,300	7,500 (domestic) 1,200 (overseas)
Guaranty Trust Co.	3,137	22,700	4,100
Continental Illinois National Bank & Trust Co.	2,703	14,100	3,200
Bankers Trust Co. (N.Y.)	2,172	19,800	3,800
Other financials			
Metropolitan Life Insurance Co.	$10,901	. . .	45,000
Prudential Insurance Co.	9,537	. . .	44,500
Equitable Life Assurance Society of the U.S.	6,095	. . .	8,000 (1950)
New York Life Insurance Co.	5,093	. . .	. . .
Northwestern Mutual Life Insurance Co.	2,748	. . .	1,400
Mutual Life Insurance Co. of New York	2,196	. . .	. . .

The holding company is very important in our economy. Of the 200 largest corporations in the United States, roughly 90 percent control one or more other corporations through stock ownership. And many smaller corporations also act as either pure or mixed holding companies. The holding company has proved to be a powerful device for bringing numerous corporations and their great aggregations of assets under one common control. Sometimes this creates or increases monopoly power; sometimes it does not.

D. THE NUMBER AND SIZE OF CORPORATIONS IN THE UNITED STATES

There are now about 500,000 active business corporations in the United States. Not all of these are large. In fact, most corporations are relatively small, having only a few owners, a very small number of employees, and a small amount of assets. Their purpose is not to bring together large amounts of resources, but to take advantage of certain other advantages of the corporate form, such as limited liability and the free transferability of shares. But some of our corporations are huge. A few of the largest are listed in Table 7.

The size of some of these corporations almost surpasses comprehension. For example, the $10.9 billion of assets under the control of the Metropolitan Life Insurance Co. is equal to nearly $70 for every man, woman, and child in the United States. Only about 5 American cities have populations as large as the number of shareholders in the American Telephone and Telegraph Co.—more than a million. And only about 13 American cities have populations as large as the number of employees in either the American Telephone and Telegraph Co. (551,000) or General Motors Corp. (469,000).

The establishment of such huge business units would not have become advantageous in the absence of the revolutionary economic developments mentioned earlier—the technological revolution, the cheapening and quickening of transportation and communication, the growth of population and other factors increasing the size of markets, and the growth of capital. But neither could such huge business units have developed in the absence of some institution, such as the corporation, which would combine the attributes of limited liability, immortality, free transferability of shares, and delegation of management functions.

E. THE LARGE CORPORATION AND THE NATURE OF OWNERSHIP

As indicated earlier, the development of the large corporation with thousands or even hundreds of thousands of owners has brought revolutionary changes in the relationships of "owners" to their business firms. To illustrate this point, let us compare a huge corporation with an individual proprietorship. We found that in an individual proprietorship all the functions of ownership are concentrated in one person. In the one owner are centered all the functions of contributing assets to the firm in exchange for ownership claims, of assuming ultimate responsibility for control of the firm, and of bearing risk. Moreover, the single owner usually has an intimate and long-continuing relationship to his firm, participates actively in its management, is well acquainted with its operations and problems, and is personally acquainted with some, if not all, of its employees.

All this is likely to be changed in a huge corporation. Most shareholders are likely to feel little continuing responsibility for the corporation, whose plants may be located hundreds of miles away. In fact, some look upon their shares only as a medium for speculation, to be bought and sold for capital gains purposes. Moreover, they often know little or nothing of the corporation's operations and problems and are personally acquainted with none of its employees or their working conditions. In short, many shareholders are merely temporary, absentee part-owners.

Several factors contribute to divorcing the function of control or management from those of contributing assets and bearing risks. One is comparable to what in the political sphere is often called the apathy of the electorate. A person with shares in several corporations and perhaps with only a small interest in each is likely to know little about the business of any one of them and to be passive in his attitude toward them, especially if he expects to hold the shares only temporarily. He is unlikely to attend stockholders' meetings and may not even take the trouble to sign over his proxy (the authorization to another to vote in his place) to someone who will use it. Even if he does sign his proxy, he is likely to sign it over to the proxy committee of the board of directors, which usually votes as the existing management wishes. This passivity of stockholders often permits the hired management to maintain its power and to determine practically all of the corporation's policies.

Stockholders frequently find themselves powerless to assert themselves even when they do take an interest in corporate affairs. Since shares carrying 51 percent of the votes can control policy, a minority having as much as 49 percent of the votes may be powerless to prevent actions injurious to it. Sometimes, however, a minority may defeat the majority. A small, close-knit group holding only 4 or 5 percent of the votes may outmaneuver large numbers of unorganized shareholders who nominally possess the great majority of voting power. When a corporation has issued some nonvoting stock or stock with only a small vote per share, those who contributed a large part of the corporation's assets often have to stand aside and let those with only a small financial interest control it. Similar results may be achieved by using a holding-company structure. We cannot here mention all the ingenious methods by which ownership and control are effectively separated.

This separation of ownership and control may be either advantageous or disadvantageous socially. On the one hand, it can result in much more efficient management than could be had from a large group of inexpert and poorly informed owners. The management may also be more socially enlightened than the owners. On the other hand, it may enable an unimaginative, bureaucratic management group that lacks the incentives of ownership to perpetuate itself in office and to benefit at the expense of the owners and perhaps also of the public. The management may follow unprogressive policies, believing itself less likely to be dismissed for inefficient passivity than for bold and progressive actions that probably would increase earnings but do carry some risk of failure. It may vote itself unreasonably large salaries or bonuses that bear little or no relationship to managerial efficiency. It may load the corporation payrolls with its relatives and friends. It may cause the corporation to purchase materials or services at exorbitant prices from the management members or from other firms in which they are interested.

Though legally the corporation is a single entity, the interests of the various groups associated with it—the management and the different classes of shareholders and creditors—often conflict. Two of the most difficult problems of the modern corporation are to secure maximum efficiency and honesty from management and to prevent the various classes of security holders from exploiting each other. In any case, it is clear that the shareholders of a large, widely held corporation have a relationship to their firm that is far different from that of a single owner to his individual proprietorship.

6. Other Forms of Business Firms

We shall note only briefly a few of the other types of firms that carry on business. One of these is the cooperative. Consumers may band together and establish a business firm which will produce or buy certain products purchased by them. This is a consumers' cooperative. The consumer members supply ownership funds, assume ultimate responsi-

bility for management, bear the risks, and share any resulting profits.
2. Producers' cooperatives, on the other hand, are formed and directed by a group of producers. The principal producers' cooperatives in the United States have been formed by farmers to process or sell their products.

Another great class of economic enterprises are those established and operated by governmental units. In most cases the governmental unit itself—federal, state, or local—owns an enterprise directly and carries on entrepreneurial functions. In other cases these units operate

TABLE 8. Percentage Distribution of Legal Forms of Business Enterprises Outside Agriculture, Forestry, and Fisheries, 1947[2]

Industry	Total, All Types of Firms	Individual Proprietor- ships	Partner- ships	Corpora- tions	Others
All industry	100.0	69.5	18.0	10.7	1.8
Mining	100.0	52.8	21.4	23.5	2.3
Contract construction	100.0	78.2	15.5	6.2	0.1
Manufacturing	100.0	45.3	23.6	29.4	1.8
Transportation, com- munication, and other public utilities	100.0	76.8	7.5	12.3	3.3
Wholesale trade	100.0	44.6	25.5	27.9	2.0
Retail trade	100.0	72.5	20.5	6.1	0.9
Finance	100.0	54.3	14.3	22.2	9.2
Service industries	100.0	81.4	13.6	4.4	0.6

through public corporations somewhat similar to the business corporations we have studied. Examples are the Reconstruction Finance Corporation, the Export-Import Bank, and the Commodity Credit Corporation.

The following sections will deal only with privately owned business firms.

7. The Variety of Business Firms

Let us now look at a few facts concerning the size and relative importance of the various types of business firms in American industry.

A. CORPORATE AND NONCORPORATE FIRMS

In 1947, the latest year for which we have detailed data, there were about 11,400,000 business firms in the United States. Well over 90

[2] Source: *Survey of Current Business,* June, 1951, p. 10.

percent of these were of noncorporate types. But though the number of corporations was considerably less than 10 percent of the total, their average size was so great that they accounted for 61 percent of the total value of output in the private sectors of the economy.

The relative importance of the various types of firms differs greatly from industry to industry. In agriculture, which includes about half of the total number of firms, the corporation is still relatively unimpor-

TABLE 9. Sizes of American Corporations, 1947[3]
(Based on Federal Income Tax Returns)

Size Class Based on Total Assets (In thousands of dollars)	Total Number of Corpora- tions	Percent of Total Number of Corpora- tions	Percent of Total Corporate Assets	Percent of Total Corporate Receipts
Under $50	218,623	44.1	0.9	3.3
$50–100	89,002	18.1	1.3	3.9
$100–250	90,709	18.1	2.9	8.3
$250–500	39,571	8.0	2.8	7.6
$500–1000	23,258	4.7	3.3	8.0
$1000–5000	26,447	5.3	11.6	17.1
$5000–10,000	4,576	0.9	6.5	7.0
$10,000–50,000	3,565	0.7	14.5	14.3
$50,000 and over	1,070	0.2	56.2	30.5
Total	496,821	100.0	100.0	100.0

Addenda:
   Total corporate assets in 1947 = $494,615 million.
   Total corporate receipts in 1947 = $361,521 million.

tant, both in numbers and in proportion of output. It is only slightly more important in forestry and fisheries. But in other industries the corporation tends to dominate. Table 8 shows the distribution of firms in these other industries by legal types. Though corporations made up less than 11 percent of all firms in these industries, their average size was so great that they accounted for a major part of total output.

B. THE SIZE DISTRIBUTION OF CORPORATIONS

We must not, however, leave the impression that all corporations are large. In fact, Table 9 shows that 44 percent of all active corpora-

[3] Source: *Statistical Abstract of the United States*, 1951, p. 439. The data come from federal income tax returns and exclude inactive corporations and corporations failing to give full balance-sheet data.

tions in 1947 had assets of less than $50,000 and 62 percent had assets of no more than $100,000. Only 0.2 of 1 percent had assets of $50 million or more, and only 1.8 percent had assets of $5 million or more.

But this is only in terms of numbers; we get a very different picture when we measure importance in terms of total corporate assets or total corporate receipts. For example, the 62 percent of all corporations that were in the smallest asset groups accounted for only 2.2 percent of total corporate assets and 7.2 percent of total corporate receipts. At the same time, the largest 0.2 of 1 percent of all corporations accounted for more than 56 percent of total corporate assets and more than 30 percent of total corporate receipts. In 1947 these 1070 huge corporations commanded total assets of more than $278 billion and had total receipts exceeding $110 billion.

C. THE NUMBER AND SIZE OF FIRMS IN PARTICULAR INDUSTRIES

If we had the space here to extend our analysis to individual industries we would find still greater variety in both number and size of firms. We would find some industries with very large numbers of firms producing the same or similar products for sale in a common market. For example, in the production of wheat, corn, cotton, eggs, hogs, and many other agricultural products there are hundreds of thousands of competing farmers, no one of whom produces as much as 1 percent of the total output of the industry. At the other extreme are industries in which no more than a handful of firms produce all or most of the output for the national market. A few examples are aluminum production, nickel production, auto manufacturing, sulfur extraction and refining, the manufacture of tin cans, and iron and steel production. Entry into such industries is often difficult because of the large amount of capital required, the difficulty of overcoming established consumer habits of buying familiar brands, and other reasons.

The structure of an industry has a great influence on its behavior. One of our important tasks later in this book will be to investigate the effects of industrial structure on the functioning of industries.

SUGGESTED READINGS

Berle, Adolph A., Jr., and Means, Gardiner C., *The Modern Corporation and Private Property,* Macmillan, New York, 1950.
Lilienthal, David E., *Big Business: A New Era,* Harper, New York, 1953.

QUESTIONS

1. a. Give some examples of commodities that can be produced with various combinations of the different types of labor, capital, natural resources, and raw materials.
   b. How does a businessman make up his mind which combination of productive factors to use in making such items?
   c. Are there any commodities in whose production there is no option regarding the combination of productive factors—that is, in which the proportion of labor to machines to raw materials, etc., cannot be varied?
2. a. Aside from the examples given in the text, can you think of any industries in which it is most efficient to operate fairly small firms?
   b. Why are there no net economies of large scale in the production of these items?
3. One economist has suggested that entrepreneurs have as a whole lost money on their risk-bearing.
   a. What motives, then, has any businessman to undertake risks?
   b. Why isn't there a marked and steady decrease in the number of firms because of widespread bankruptcy?
4. Try to evaluate the role each of the three functions of entrepreneurship has played in the development of the corporation.
5. Suppose corporation A is held by holding company B, which is held by C, which is held by D, which is in turn held by holding company B.
   a. If anyone who holds effective control of 10 percent of any one of these firms controls it, how much must be invested in company D to control A whose outstanding voting stock is worth $1 million?
   b. In practice, what factors would tend to make your answer too small?
   c. Too large?
   d. What are some of the other devices that have been invented to enable a small money investment to control a large corporation?
6. Why doesn't every businessman incorporate to avoid the risks inherent in unlimited liability?
7. Some writers have suggested that the separation of ownership from management in large corporations has caused these firms to avoid predatory business practices and activities which the public is likely to consider antisocial.
   a. Why might this be so?
   b. Give examples of business decisions which may be affected in this way.
   c. Show how an increase in "socially undesirable" acts might also sometimes result.

    d. How do you think separation of management from ownership might affect the frequency of bankruptcy?

    e. The frequency of spectacular profits?

8. a. Why do you think the consumer or producer cooperative form of firm is not very widespread in the United States?

    b. Why, for example, are consumers willing to buy from a private corporation when a consumer cooperative would return to them all the profits earned from their purchases?

CHAPTER 6

This chapter is pure theory.

The Free-Enterprise System

ie. Theory of Laissez-Faire Capitalism.

1. Introduction

In the first chapter we found that every society—primitive or highly developed, rich or poor—must have some sort of system for controlling its economic processes.[1] Because of scarcity, each society inevitably faces the basic economic problems of determining the overall rate of output, of determining the composition of output, of allocating the scarce supply of productive factors among their alternative uses, and of distributing or sharing output among the various members of the community. These problems do not automatically solve themselves. They must be solved by human beings through some sort of control system that will determine what ends shall be sought, organize the available productive factors into productive units for the achievement of the selected ends, and resolve conflicts among the members of the community. To accomplish its purposes a control system must employ powerful sanctions, which usually include both rewards and penalties.

We also found that there are many types of economic control systems. Those existing today range all the way from that of Soviet Russia, where economic processes are largely controlled through a dictatorial government, to that of the United States, where a major part of control is exercised through competition in relatively free markets. Other types of systems have been used in the past and still others will probably be developed. We shall have more to say on this subject later.

This chapter will discuss the free-enterprise type of control system

[1] See especially pp. 6–9.

found in the United States. We shall consciously oversimplify and shall concentrate on its main principles and processes in order to make its basic logic clear. Its complexities and complications will be postponed for later treatment. However, we must emphasize that the actual control systems included in the free-enterprise category are by no means uniform in every respect. Our own control system has changed almost continuously in response to such things as changes in technology, changes in people's attitudes and aspirations, and changes in the relative powers of the various economic and social groups. Moreover, there have been wide international differences among the actual control systems that belong in this general class. Anyone who persists in believing that the free-enterprise type of control system is static will not be able to understand economic history.

2. The American Type of Control System: General Characteristics

A. NOMENCLATURE

The American type of economic control system has been given many names, each an incomplete description but emphasizing some particular aspect of the system. The "capitalist system" suggests that a large amount of capital is employed and also that the system is controlled by the owners of capital. We shall see that the latter implication —that the owners of capital control the system—is a misleading oversimplification. The "system of economic individualism" suggests that the goal of economic activity is to promote the welfare of individual human beings rather than that of some abstract entity such as the state, that individuals rather than the state are the best judges of their own welfare, and that chief reliance is placed on individual initiative rather than state direction and control. The "price system" centers attention on the powerful role of prices in guiding output and the allocation of resources. The "free-enterprise system" emphasizes the high degree of freedom of individuals and groups to establish and operate their own business enterprises. Because it is short we shall use this name.

It will be useful to consider another name—the "laissez-faire competitive system"—because it suggests both the negative and positive aspects of the system. The term "laissez faire" indicates the negative aspect—that the government exercises only a minimum amount of control over economic activities. The word "competitive" indicates the positive aspect—that the major part of control is exercised through competition among private buyers and sellers in the market. Both the negative and positive aspects of the system are worthy of further analysis.

B. LAISSEZ FAIRE AND THE ROLE OF GOVERNMENT

The term "laissez faire" originated in protests against the wide-spread restrictions and controls over economic activity by a mercantilist French government in the eighteenth century. These protests had their counterparts in England and some other countries. Galled by many tight government restrictions and directives, merchants and other businessmen demanded that the government let them alone— laissez faire. But neither these men nor the many businessmen and economists who have shared their general philosophy meant literally that they wanted the government to leave economic affairs completely alone. They were not anarchists. Rather, theirs was the "theory of the limited state"; they wanted only a limited amount of control by government and a wide scope for free enterprise.

Adam Smith, the great eighteenth-century exponent of free enterprise, defined the appropriate scope of government in the following terms:

According to the system of natural liberty, the sovereign has only three duties to attend to; three duties of great importance, indeed, but plain and intelligible to common understandings: first, the duty of protecting the society from the violence and invasion of other independent societies; secondly, the duty of protecting, as far as possible, every member of the society from the injustice or oppression of every other member of it, or the duty of establishing an exact administration of justice; and, thirdly, the duty of erecting and maintaining certain public works and certain public institutions, which it can never be for the interest of any individual, or small number of individuals, to erect and maintain; because the profit could never repay the expense to any individual or small number of individuals, though it may frequently do much more than repay it to a great society.[2]

Most advocates of a free-enterprise system have indeed found some of the government functions outlined by Smith to be "plain and intelligible to common understandings." In fact, they have insisted that a free-enterprise system can function and develop satisfactorily only within an orderly framework maintained by the government as it provides protection against depredations from abroad, protects persons and property at home, enacts and enforces laws of contract,

[2] *Wealth of Nations,* book IV, chapter IX.

provides a monetary system to facilitate trade, and raises the money necessary to cover its expenditures. But two of the governmental functions described by Smith—protection from injustice and oppression and the erection and maintenance of certain public works and public institutions—have proved to be not so "plain and intelligible." These can be construed either narrowly or broadly.

N.B.

✳ Here we wish to emphasize just two points. (1) Laissez faire has never meant the complete absence of government control over economic activities. It has meant only that the amount of control by government should be limited and that a major part of control should be exercised through private competition in the market. (2) Ours has always been a "mixed" control system in the sense that control power over economic processes has been divided between governmental units and market competition. Despite much verbiage to the contrary, the real issue here has never been complete control by the government versus complete control by competition. Rather it has been the more difficult problem of defining the relative scope of government and competitive controls in a "mixed" control system.✳

Let us look now at the logic of a competitive control system.

C. COMPETITION - see p.127.

By competition we mean, of course, rivalry among buyers and sellers. It includes rivalry of seller against seller, of buyer against buyer, and of buyer against seller. Moreover, we usually assume that the primary motive of each buyer and seller is to promote his own advantage.

Some critics of free-enterprise systems have alleged that these are not systems at all but only anarchies—that they have no logic, and that they afford no means of welding productive factors into a co-ordinated economic process to satisfy human wants. It is easy to show that this crude argument is fallacious. Whether or not competition is a better control system than any other, the fact is that it does work; systems relying largely on competitive control have achieved high and rising levels of productivity and they have somehow determined the composition of output, the relative prices of the various types of output, the allocation of resources, and the distribution of income among the members of the community.

In brief outline, this is the logic of the competitive systems: (1) The goals of production—the particular types and amounts of goods and services to be produced—are set by the free choices of consumers. This is often called consumers' sovereignty. Consumers have at their disposal certain amounts of money income which they are free to spend as they see fit for the various types of output that might be produced by business firms. They communicate their choices to the market and bring pressure on business firms to adjust output to these choices by the way they spend their money incomes. In effect, they cast "dollar ballots" for the different types of output.

(2). Production and trade are carried on by many business firms, each intent on making as much net money income as it can. But these firms can make maximum profits only if they use the available productive factors to turn out the particular types and amounts of goods and services that consumers demand. If they produce things for which consumers cast no dollar ballots they will obviously be unable to sell them. If "too much" of some article is produced relative to consumers' demands, its price will fall so low as to penalize its producers. If "too little" of some article is produced relative to consumers' demands, its price will be so high as to encourage an increase in its production. Thus business firms can realize their desire to avoid losses and maximize profits only by adjusting output to consumers' choices as expressed in their market demands.

These ideas are beautifully expressed in Adam Smith's *Wealth of Nations,* the work which was to serve as a chief source of inspiration to those who favored a free-enterprise system.

In almost every other race of animals each individual, when it is grown up to maturity, is entirely independent, and in its natural state has occasion for the assistance of no other living creature. But man has almost constant occasion for the help of his brethren, and it is in vain for him to expect it from their benevolence only. He will be more likely to prevail if he can interest their self-love in his favour, and shew them that it is for their own advantage to do for him what he requires of them. Whoever offers to another a bargain of any kind, proposes to do this. Give me that which I want, and you shall have this which you want, is the meaning of every such offer; and it is in this manner that we obtain from one another the far greater part of those good offices which we stand in need of. It is not from the benevolence of the butcher, the brewer, or the baker, that we expect our dinner, but from their regard to their own interest. We address ourselves, not to their humanity but to their self-love, and never talk to them of our own necessities but of their advantages. Nobody but a beggar chuses to depend chiefly upon the benevolence of his fellow-citizens.[3]

As every individual, therefore, endeavours as much as he can both to

[3] *Ibid.,* book I, chapter II.

employ his capital in the support of domestic industry, and so to direct that industry that its produce may be of the greatest value; every individual necessarily labours to render the annual revenue of the society as great as he can. He generally, indeed, neither intends to promote the public interest, nor knows how much he is promoting it. By preferring the support of domestic to that of foreign industry, he intends only his own security; and by directing that industry in such a manner as its produce may be of the greatest value, he intends only his own gain, and he is in this, as in many other cases, led by an invisible hand to promote an end which was no part of his intention. Nor is it always the worse for the society that it was no part of it. By pursuing his own interest he frequently promotes that of the society more effectually than when he really intends to promote it. I have never known much good done by those who affected to trade for the public good. It is an affectation, indeed, not very common among merchants, and very few words need be employed in disuading them from it.[4]

To show that the argument is not mystical in spite of the reference to "the invisible hand" we shall describe competitive processes in more detail. As a first step we shall identify the various participants.

3. Participants in the Competitive Process

Ignoring the government for the moment, we can divide the participants in the competitive process into three broad classes: (1) households, which receive and dispose of money incomes; (2) business firms, which produce and trade goods and services; and (3) the owners of productive factors, who either use their own factors or sell their services to business firms or in some cases directly to households. It is immediately evident that each individual is likely to be a member of two or more of these groups. Thus a worker may be both a seller of his labor services and the head of a household. Or a man may be both the head of a business firm and the head of a household. Our functional classification is useful, however, for it enables us to analyze the various motivations and functions of each person or institution in the competitive process.

A. HOUSEHOLDS

By households we mean families and certain other small groups that pool their money incomes and as a unit determine how these will be disposed of. We shall concentrate on this income receipt and disposal function of households. We deal with the household rather than a person as the basic consuming unit to avoid becoming ensnarled in

[4] *Ibid.*, book IV, chapter II.

the difficult question, "Who determines a family's spending pattern?" It is true, of course, that some production occurs within the household; dishwashing, cooking, housecleaning, and other similar examples come quickly to mind. But this part of production does not enter into the competitive market process and we shall ignore it.

Each household receives some amount of money income. Most of it is usually received as compensation for the services of productive factors owned by the household—wages and salaries for labor, interest on savings, rent on real estate, and profits for the services of being a business owner. Each family has a wide degree of freedom in disposing of its money income, and it is to be presumed that each will spend the money in the way that appears to be most advantageous to it. Some of this income may be saved; this part we shall consider later. The part spent for consumption will be spread among the many available types of goods and services in accordance with the family's tastes. In making such choices, each family in effect casts dollar ballots for the various types of output.

But the amount of any good or service that a household will buy depends not only on its income and tastes but also on the price of that particular good or service relative to the prices of other things. For example, the cheaper beef is, relative to other things, the more of it is the family likely to purchase. A statement giving the different amounts of beef which the family will buy at each different beef price is called that family's *demand schedule* for beef.

Owing to differences in tastes as well as to differences in incomes, different households are likely to have quite different demand schedules for each of the various types of goods and services. One household may be willing to buy a large amount of article A at a high price, whereas another will buy none of it at that price.

By adding together the many individual household demand schedules for each product we can get the *total market demand schedule* for that product. Thus, the total market demand for article A at a price of $10 is the sum of the amounts that all households would buy at that price. And the total market demand at a price of $5 is the sum of the amounts that all households would buy at that price. The same is true at all other levels of prices.[5]

Thus we find that with any given total amount of money income

---

[5] For a formal treatment of this point see the Graphic Appendix, pp. 603–610. By formal we mean the purely analytical aspect of the argument without attention to its practical implications.

for households, any given distribution of this money income among the households, and any given set of tastes of the households, there will be in the market at any time a complex of demand relationships. For any particular good or service this will take the form of a market demand schedule which usually has this characteristic: the larger the amount of the article offered for sale, the lower will be the price at which all of it will be purchased; and the smaller the amount of the article offered for sale, the higher will be the price at which all of it can find purchasers.

These total market demand schedules for each of the various possible types of output, reflecting consumers' choices, are the guides to production. Or, as it is sometimes said, they are the means by which consumers exercise sovereignty over the market. If producers wish to make maximum profits they must adjust their activities to consumers' choices as indicated by the series of market demand schedules for the various possible types of output. This brings us to the role of business firms in the competitive process.

B. BUSINESS FIRMS

Production and trade are carried on by millions of business firms. The primary purpose of each firm is to make net money income in the form of profits. Enterprisers create new firms, discontinue old firms, expand and contract the size of their firms, vary rates of output in their plants, and shift their production from one type of output to another as opportunities for greater profits or smaller losses appear.

These millions of firms compete with each other in two principal ways. (1) They compete for the buyers' dollars. We are all familiar with the fact that the producers of the same type of output, such as radios, compete for the consumers' dollars. But in a broader sense every producer competes with every other producer for consumers' dollars. Thus the sellers of radios, autos, cigarettes, movie admissions, and all other goods and services compete for the buyers' dollar votes. (2) They compete for production factors. All firms enter the market and compete for labor, for the use of natural resources, for the rental of buildings and other durable equipment, and for the use of money savings. Each firm will vary its purchases of each type of productive factor according to their respective prices. That is, each firm has a demand schedule for the services of each type of productive factor.

It is important to note that a firm's demand for each type of productive factor is a *derived demand*—a demand derived from the market demand for the firm's output. The firm buys the services of productive factors only because they are capable of producing goods or services that can be sold in the market for money. And both the amount of any productive factor that a firm will buy and the price it will be willing to pay for the factor depend on how much successive units of the factor can be expected to add to the value of the firm's output.

C. THE OWNERS OF PRODUCTIVE FACTORS

The owners of the various types of productive factors make up the third group of participants in the competitive process. These include workers of all kinds who are the sellers of their own services, owners of natural resources who offer them for use, owners of buildings and other durable capital goods who offer them for rent, and owners of money savings who offer them for loan or shares of ownership. Subject to some qualification, these owners wish to get as much money income as they can and will therefore sell the use of their productive factors to the firms that offer the highest price. Whenever it is profitable to do so, they will shift their factors not only from firm to firm within a given industry but also among firms in different industries.

D. SUMMARY

In short, there are three broad classes of participants in the competitive process. Households provide the ultimate guides to production through their demand schedules in the market. Business firms, intent on making as much profit as they can, organize and direct production and hire productive factors. And the owners of productive factors sell them to the firms that will bid the most for them. We can now proceed to see how competition among all these participants controls economic processes.

4. Competitive Equilibrium: General Characteristics

A. ADJUSTMENT TO CONSTANT DEMAND SCHEDULES

Let us look first at the process by which competition adjusts output, prices, and the allocation of resources to a set of household demand schedules that remain constant during the adjustment period. We assume that consumers' choices, as reflected in their market demand schedules, remain fixed, but that the demand for each product is such that the more of it that is offered, the lower will be its price, and the less of it that is offered, the higher will be its price.

We may expect that the price of any commodity will rise if the demand for it exceeds the supply, and that it will fall if more is offered for sale than consumers are willing to buy. Only if demand and supply are equal will there be no tendency for the price to change. Only then can we have competitive equilibrium.

Business firms, intent on avoiding losses and making as much profit as possible, adjust their supply to consumer demand schedules. They will avoid producing any items whose prices are so low as to cause losses or to yield profits below those in other lines. The increased scarcity then tends to raise the prices of these items. At the same time, they will increase their output of items whose prices are so high as to yield larger profits than could be secured elsewhere. This tends to lower the prices of these items. Thus the process of adjustment will continue, with producers decreasing their output of items that yield only losses or lower profits than can be made in other lines, and increasing their output of any items on which profits are higher than in other lines. The adjustment process will end only when the relative prices of the various types of output, the rates of output, and the allocation of factors are such that no one finds it profitable to make any further adjustment. This is what we mean by competitive equilibrium.

Three important characteristics of competitive equilibrium should be noted. (1) Prices are such as to clear the market. That is, all the supply that is offered at these prices finds buyers and (at these prices) there is no unsatisfied demand. (2) Prices are such that firms in the aggregate have no net incentive to make further changes in either the types or the rates of their output. (3) The allocation and prices of productive factors are such that the owners of these factors have no incentive to make any further net shifts from one industry to another. If all these conditions are not met, competitive equilibrium has not been established.

B. ADJUSTMENT TO CHANGES IN CONSUMERS' DEMANDS

In the preceding section we outlined the process of adjusting prices, the composition of output, and the allocation of resources to a set of constant consumer demand schedules. Let us now consider the process of adjusting to changes in consumers' preferences. Suppose that consumers decrease their demands for radios and increase their demands for television sets. In the radio industry the first effect will be to lower the prices of radios, or at least to decrease the number that can be sold at the old prices. Under these new conditions, radio production will be less profitable than before and at least some of the producers will probably suffer losses. Some may even go bankrupt. In any case, the rate of radio output will decline and smaller amounts of productive factors will be used in radio production. This reduction of output will continue until the amount of output remaining can be sold at prices high enough to yield profits as high as those in other lines.

The rise of consumers' demands for television sets will raise their prices, or at least increase the number of sets that can be sold at the old prices. This greater profitability will increase the output of television sets and cause more productive factors to be employed for this purpose. Some new firms may set up business in the television industry. This expansion will continue until television output has been increased so much and prices have receded to such an extent that profits in the industry will be no higher than those elsewhere.

We see that resources will have been reallocated from radio to television production in accord with changed consumers' desires. This is but one example of the general process of adjusting output and the allocation of resources to consumers' preferences as indicated by their market demand schedules.

c. COMPETITIVE SANCTIONS

We noted earlier that a control system can succeed only if it employs powerful sanctions. The competitive system meets this test. It uses both rewards and penalties to induce business firms to adjust to consumers' demands. Those that adjust the types and rates of their output to consumers' demands promptly, especially those that correctly anticipate changes in consumers' demands, may reap large profits. But those that persist in producing things that consumers do not want or that contribute to the overproduction of a particular type of product are penalized by losses. If they get too far out of line with consumers' demands they will be eliminated from the market by bankruptcy.

The same is true of labor and other productive factors. Those that are shifted promptly to the production of the things that consumers want most may be rewarded by steady employment and high incomes. But those who persist in offering their services for the production of things that consumers do not want at all or will buy only at very low prices are likely to be penalized by low incomes or unemployment.

D. COMPETITIVE PROMOTION OF EFFICIENCY

Competition brings powerful pressures on business firms to improve their efficiency—that is, to get as large a value of output as they can from the value of inputs they use up in the process of production. For this purpose it uses both rewards and penalties. A firm can reap large profits by pioneering in reducing its costs below those of its competitors. Thus every firm has a strong incentive to develop and employ technological innovations, to achieve optimum size, to use the most economical combination of productive resources, and to do anything else that will reduce its costs relative to its selling prices. The hope of reward for pioneering is supplanted by an even more powerful sanction—the fear of penalty for being a laggard. The firms that fail to lower costs as much as their competitors may suffer losses and even bankruptcy as their more efficient competitors lower the selling prices of their products, or bid up the prices of productive factors, or both.

The principal results of this competitive race to raise efficiency and lower costs may be to lower prices to consumers, or to increase the incomes paid to productive factors, or both. But any firm that lags behind in this race may be eliminated by losses or even by bankruptcy. It is therefore easy to understand why competition has been such a powerful force for continuous technological change and rising efficiency. This includes not only the development and use of cheaper methods of production but also the development of new products that will meet the approval of consumers.

5. Competition and the Solution of the Basic Economic Problems

Though it has already been implied in our discussion, we should note specifically that the competitive process provides a simultaneous solution of the basic economic problems mentioned earlier—the determination of the overall rate of output, the composition and pricing of output, the allocation of resources, and the distribution of income.

A. THE OVERALL RATE OF OUTPUT

We shall later discuss in more detail the actual behavior of total output under a free-enterprise system. At this point it is sufficient to note that the overall rate of output of business firms is determined by the competitive interactions of buyers' demands, the responses of business firms, and the supplies of productive factors. Buyers' payments provide the rewards for production, and to these demands of buyers business firms adjust both the overall rate of output and the total amount of productive factors employed.

B. THE COMPOSITION AND PRICING OF OUTPUT

As we have already seen, the types of goods and services to be produced, the amounts of each, and the relative prices of the various types are determined by buyers' demands and the supplies offered by business firms as they try to make as much profit as possible.

C. THE ALLOCATION OF PRODUCTIVE FACTORS

This same competitive process also allocates the scarce supply of productive factors among their many alternative uses. As we have already seen, each of the millions of business firms has a derived demand for the various types of natural resources, labor, and capital— a demand based on the amount that the productive factor can add to the value of the firm's output. At the same time, the owners of the productive factors stand ready to supply them to the firms that will offer the most for them. These demand and supply conditions determine a market price for the use of each type of productive factor—a wage or salary rate for each type of labor, a rental rate for each type of natural resource, and an interest rate on capital.

These prices of the productive factors serve as an allocative or rationing device. Each firm will presumably hire additional units of productive factors so long as these additional units will add to the value of its output an amount greater than the price that must be paid for the factor. For example, if the price of a particular type of labor is $10 a day, each firm will hire as many man-days of that labor as will add more than $10 to the value of its output. But we may assume that no firm will hire at $10 any man-days of this labor that will add less than this amount to the value of its output. Thus the price of the factor, which is determined by competition, rations the available supply. It allocates the factors to those who can make them add the most to the value of output and denies these factors to those who cannot derive so much value from their use.

D. THE DISTRIBUTION OF INCOME

The competitive process which we have just described also determines the distribution of income among the owners of the various types of productive factors. As we saw above, it determines the wage or salary rates for the various types of labor, rental rates for the various types of natural resources, interest rates on capital, and profits of enterprisers. The income of any family depends on the prices of the productive factors it offers for use and on the amounts of these factors it has. This subject will be discussed in more detail in a later chapter.

6. Conclusions

We have seen that economic control in the United States and other similar economies rests primarily in two entities, the government and market competition. The essence of the free-enterprise system is the fact that by far the larger part of the control function devolves on the market. We may again note three things which the market tends to accomplish. (1) It makes for the efficient operation of the firm. (2) It promotes responsiveness of output composition to consumers' desires. (3) It organizes the productive system and arranges for the factors of production to be where they are needed when they are needed.

The market is thus, at least in its ideal form, an amazingly efficient means of giving effect to the desires of the members of an economy, insofar as this is permitted by the scarcity of resources. Is it not surprising that, practically without central supervision and without any centrally formulated and administered overall plan, consumers find their desires catered to—provided they have the money to pay—and that the great complex of processes competing for raw materials and productive factors is so organized that the goods the consumer wants are there when he asks for them?

The type of analysis presented in this chapter should be a useful antidote to the beliefs of some that there are no economic controls except controls by government and that free enterprise is no system at all but only chaotic anarchy with no logic and no method of making and enforcing decisions. But the numerous omissions of this chapter should be emphasized. In order to bring out sharply the basic logic and broad outlines of the free-enterprise system, we have deliberately omitted many complexities and complications. For example, we have said nothing about monopoly, about the effect of market structures on the behavior of industries, about limitations on the mobility of productive factors, and so on. We have also been careful to avoid pronouncements concerning the relative scope of competitive and government controls. In which areas are competitive controls likely to yield results that are generally acceptable, and in which areas are people likely to demand that they be supplemented or superseded by government intervention? Many problems of these types will be considered later.

SUGGESTED READINGS

Graham, Frank D., *Social Goals and Economic Institutions,* Princeton University Press, Princeton, 2nd ed., 1949.
Wright, David McCord, *Capitalism,* McGraw-Hill, New York, 1951.

QUESTIONS

1. Can you think of some limitations to the notion of consumers' sovereignty, i.e., the view that the economy is set up to serve the consumer efficiently?
   a. Does the economy always serve the most meritorious consumer? Explain.
   b. Does it ever sacrifice the interests of the consumer to other groups? If so, give examples.
   c. Does it ever operate wastefully and inefficiently? If so, give examples.
   d. How do you reconcile the arguments of this chapter with your answers to the preceding parts of this question?
2. How is the view that the desires of households control the productive process affected by advertising whose aim is to mold the desires of households?
3. The cost of producing the various commodities clearly helps determine how profitable it will be to make them, and hence affects the quantities which firms manufacture. How do you reconcile this with the view that the composition of output is determined by consumers' desires?

   Suppose, for example, that most people prefer a house of type A to one of type B, but that it takes much more labor and other resources to build the former.
   a. If more type-B houses are built, is this a violation of consumers' sovereignty?
   b. How might the scarcity of resources make a preponderance of type-B houses preferable in the judgment of the consumers themselves?
4. Explain what takes the place of a central planner in coordinating activities in a free-enterprise economy.
   a. Why do not all firms and individuals always end up working at cross-purposes?
   b. What keeps the makers of raw materials, machine tools, watch parts, watches, and watch buyers acting in relative harmony?
5. Explain the influence of the owner of a factor of production on the composition and size of output and the allocation of resources.

    a. Does this violate consumers' sovereignty?

    b. What is the relevance of the fact that workers sometimes want better working conditions—e.g., a cleaner, lighter, quieter, safer factory—rather than an increase in pay?

    c. What is the relevance of a landlord's decision to keep his land for hunting rather than renting it out to a farmer?

    d. What is the relevance of a housewife's decision to take a defense job?

6. a. Do you consider it advantageous to have prices at a level where the market is cleared, i.e., where supply is exactly equal to demand?

    b. Wouldn't consumers be happier if prices were lower?

    c. What may be some of the effects of price ceilings designed to keep prices from rising in times of inflation?

    d. Of government price supports, e.g., those designed to keep farm prices from falling?

7. a. What is a derived demand?

    b. Discuss the determination of the demand schedule for some commodity whose demand is derived.

    c. Discuss the motivation behind this sort of demand and contrast it with the motivation behind consumers' demands.

8. When the demand (schedule) for some commodity rises, the supply of that item is likely to be increased under a free-enterprise system.

    a. Does this prove that no other system could serve consumers' demands more effectively?

    b. How can we judge whether one economy serves consumers' demands more effectively than another?

CHAPTER 7

Economic Functions of Government

1. Introduction

We have all heard the complaint that government intervention in economic affairs has gone too far. Yet most of those voicing this opinion believe that anarchists, who advocate the abolition of all government, are a rather harebrained lot. This brings up some basic questions: Why precisely do we reject the anarchist viewpoint? In other words, why government at all? Why not rely completely on competitive market controls? One might reply that the government ought to intervene when competition does not yield the results that people want and when the government can produce results that are considered more acceptable. But this is quite unsatisfactory, for it leaves the crucial questions unanswered. Why in some particular cases do people consider competition less capable than the government of yielding desirable results? Why in some other cases do they find the results of competition acceptable enough to oppose government intervention?

The purpose of this chapter is to throw light on problems of these types. It will make no attempt to indicate precisely where the lines should be drawn between government and competitive controls, but it will suggest some of the relevant considerations.

2. Cases of Universal Benefit from Government Intervention

Let us start with some cases in which everybody, or almost everybody, agrees that he is better off as a result of being coerced, along with others, by the government into behaving differently from the way he would have behaved in the absence of such coercion. Each is happier for being prevented from doing what he would otherwise have done, or for being forced to do something he otherwise would not have done.

At first this may appear to be an impossible case. Why, it may be argued, would not each person voluntarily modify his activities so as to make government intervention unnecessary? How could anybody feel better off as a result of being coerced by the government? Yet the fact is that we frequently find people approving of government interventions that prevent them from behaving as they otherwise would. Many a man who would otherwise drive like the wind approves of speed limits applicable to himself as well as to others. Many people who would voluntarily contribute nothing to the government approve of laws that compel them as well as others to pay large amounts of taxes.

The nature of the problem can be clarified by an example that has no obvious relation to economics. Suppose that as a result of bitter controversies every inhabitant of a western town has become a pistol-toter. Unlike a movie hero, every person fears that he may be killed, is violently opposed to pistol-toting, and believes that he and everyone else would be better off if no one carried a gun. Yet in the absence of coercion no one will quit. Each will reason that if he disarms himself the others will still carry guns and he will not only fail to realize his desire for a peaceful life but will actually be in a worse position. The only way each individual can realize his desires is through government intervention that will force everyone to modify his behavior.

In this case the individuals were interdependent, could not realize their individual desires through competition, but could realize them through government intervention. There are many similar cases in economics. In the cases considered in this section we shall emphasize the relevance of interdependence—the fact that what each person does or does not do affects others, and that each is affected by the action or inaction of others. But we shall also have to consider the motivations of individuals and business firms.

A. INDIVIDUAL AND SOCIAL CALCULATIONS OF BENEFITS AND COSTS

In our discussion of competition we indicated that each buyer and seller in the market is likely to base his decisions on a calculation of his own benefits and his own costs. Each will undertake a project only if he calculates that the value of its benefits to him is at least as great as its costs to him. He cannot be depended upon to allow his decision to be influenced by any benefits to others for which he is not compensated or by costs to others which he does not have to bear. But in some cases his action will affect others, either by benefiting them or by imposing costs on them. For example, if a man builds a very attractive house he may raise the "tone" of an entire neighborhood, delight those who see it, and raise real estate values in the area. These benefits which accrue to others may not enter into the calculations on which the builder's decisions are based. On the other hand, an ugly firetrap of a house may decrease the happiness of all the neighbors, increase fire hazards in the entire area, and lower real estate values. The builder may not let these costs to others influence his decision.

In short, where there is interdependence there may be differences between the total *value* of benefits to the entire community and the *value* of the benefits to the individual or firm undertaking a project, and between the total *costs* to the entire community and the *costs* to the individual or firm. When this occurs there is a danger that one of two things will happen. (1) Individuals and business firms will refuse to undertake some projects whose social benefits exceed their social costs. Each will refuse because his own benefits are not great enough to justify his own costs and he has no feasible way of getting compensation from others for the benefits that the project would confer on them. (2) Individuals and business firms may behave in a way that is injurious to everyone because each will not allow his decisions to be influenced by the costs that he may impose on others. Let us consider some examples.

B. CERTAIN PUBLIC WORKS AND PUBLIC INSTITUTIONS

It will be remembered that one of the functions which Adam Smith considered to be appropriate for government was that of "erecting and maintaining certain public works and public institutions which it can never be for the interest of any individual or small number of individuals to erect and maintain; because the profit could never repay the expense to any individual or small number of individuals, though it may frequently do much more than repay it to a great society."

The construction and operation of lighthouses is an oft-cited example. Everyone might agree that the costs of lighthouses are far outweighed by the benefits they confer by reducing shipwrecks, saving the lives of seafarers, cheapening transportation, and lowering the costs of products to millions of people. Yet it might well turn out that no person or business firm would voluntarily build and operate lighthouses. No one of the hundreds of shipping companies would construct and operate them because its own costs would exceed its own benefits. No specialized business firm would find it profitable to perform these services because it would have no feasible way of charging for them. It might not be able to count on voluntary contributions from the millions of beneficiaries, for each would be likely to reason as follows: "Whether or not I contribute will not determine whether or not I get the benefits afforded by lighthouses. My contribution would be such a small part of the total that it would not appreciably affect the outcome. If others will pay in enough to operate lighthouses with my contribution they would also pay in enough even though I pay nothing. If others do not pay in enough, my small contribution will not get them built. I shall therefore pay nothing voluntarily." Lighthouses may be built and operated only if the government takes the initiative and coerces people into paying for them. And everybody may consider himself better off for having been coerced.

The same principles apply in many other cases. Military preparation is a classic illustration. Not enough people may be willing to join the army voluntarily, no matter how ardently they want their country to be strong. Each would point out that any one soldier is but a drop in the bucket, that if his country could win a war with him in the army it could also win without him, and that if it would lose without him it would also lose with him. If we relied solely on volunteers we might not realize our desires for national security. This is another case in which people may be able to realize their desires only through government intervention. The application of this argument to other types of citizen contributions to military preparation should be obvious.

Flood control is another example. All the people might agree that a flood-control program in a great river valley would much more than repay its cost by saving lives, protecting land and other property spread over hundreds of miles, and lowering the cost of consumer goods. Yet private enterprise would not undertake the project because it would have no way of getting revenues from the millions of people who would be benefited. The beneficiaries may refuse to contribute voluntarily, yet feel better off when the government forces them to do so in order to make possible a flood-control program.

The applicability of this argument to the provision of sidewalks, streets, roads, police and fire protection, weather forecasting, public parks and playgrounds, and other similar services should be evident. Private enterprise might be willing to construct and operate toll roads, but it is not feasible to charge fees for the use of all roads, especially not those on which traffic is quite light. It would also be possible to charge fees to those who visit public parks and playgrounds. But parks and playgrounds often benefit many who do not actually visit them. They increase real estate values in the area, diminish air pollution in the vicinity, improve the health of all in the area, and make driving less difficult and hazardous by keeping children off the streets. Private enterprise would have no way of charging for these benefits.

Both education and public health are services that can be—and indeed have been—provided by private enterprise on a fee basis. Under this arrangement the recipient of instruction or medical service pays for it himself, and if he cannot or does not want to pay for it he must go without it.

On these problems Americans appear to be divided. Free public education is generally accepted as an untouchable feature of the American way of life, whereas publicly supported medical treatment is viewed with considerable horror. Yet the grounds for accepting or rejecting state interference in these matters seem to have some similarities.

One argument against government intervention in education and health services is that state support is paternalistic, the community telling the citizen that it knows better than he how he ought to spend his money. It is maintained that a citizen's health and schooling are his own business, and that if he prefers to spend his money on automobiles or fine clothes the government has no right to take it away from him in taxes and respend it for him as it thinks best.

A second argument against public health and education holds that public sponsorship would seriously impair the efficiency with which these services are performed. It is a common argument nowadays that under socialized medicine the doctor would become a bureaucrat swamped with paper work, with no motivation for efficiency and no interest in his patient. Similar arguments about teachers' salaries were once employed, as witness the remarks of Adam Smith:

In [some] . . . universities the teacher is prohibited from receiving any honorary or fee from his pupils, and his salary constitutes the whole of the revenue which he derives from his office. His interest is, in this case, set as directly in opposition to his duty as it is possible to set it. It is the interest of every man to live as much at his ease as he can; and if his emoluments are to be precisely the same, whether he does, or does not perform some very laborious duty, it is certainly his interest, at least as interest is vulgarly understood, either to neglect it altogether, or, if he is subject to some authority which will not suffer him to do this, to perform it in as careless and slovenly a manner as that authority will permit. If he is naturally active and a lover of labour, it is his interest to employ that activity in any way, from which he can derive some advantage, rather than in the performance of his duty, from which he can derive none.

If the authority to which he is subject resides in the body corporate, the college, or university, of which he himself is a member, and in which the greater part of the other members are, like himself, persons who either are, or ought to be teachers; they are likely to make a common cause, to be all very indulgent to one another, and every man to consent that his neighbour may neglect his duty, provided he himself is allowed to neglect his own. In the university of Oxford, the greater part of the public professors have, for these many years, given up altogether even the pretence of teaching.[1]

On the other side, those favoring public health and education often urge that private enterprise in these fields must discriminate against the poor in matters which are vital to them. An unhealthy or poorly educated man cannot be said to have the equality of opportunity that is considered fundamental in our political creed. People using this argument claim that our object is not to guarantee prosperity to everyone, but rather to give each person an opportunity to achieve it, and good health and adequate education are cited as prerequisites to this opportunity.

However, there is another ground on which public assistance in education and medical care might be defended. The health and education of its citizens are an asset to a country as a whole. Sickly and uneducated people cannot be highly productive, and a country lacking in these respects may expect a low standard of living and slow progress in science and technology. If anyone doubts that the nation as a whole is benefited by an educated, healthy populace, he need only consider its importance for the country's military power. If it is true that everyone benefits from the health and education of the individual, it may well pay the country to invest an amount greater than the individuals themselves would voluntarily spend for these purposes. If general health and universal education are appropriate goals for the community, government intervention may be the only way to achieve them.

It must be made clear that the authors are not seeking to take sides on the controversial question of a national health scheme, or even to give a complete list of all the important arguments pro and con. They

[1] *Wealth of Nations,* book V, chapter I, article II.

wish merely to indicate how this analysis of the role of government applies, and incidentally to indicate some of the relevant issues. Even a complete listing could never by itself yield a definite policy recommendation. For example, the expected loss in the efficiency of doctors, if any, must be weighed against the expected social gains in better health, if any, and one's dislike of the extension of the powers of government must be weighed against the value of the increased equality of opportunity.

In this section we have considered several examples in which government intervention is necessary to provide certain goods or services that people want but cannot get from private enterprise. And the basic reason why private enterprise will not provide these things is that it has no way of charging the many beneficiaries for the benefits they receive. Let us turn now to some cases in which everybody, or almost everybody, may feel better off because of government intervention that prevents individuals and business firms from doing what they would otherwise do.

c. Government Control of Private Practices

We found earlier that in the absence of government intervention each person or business firm is likely to base its decisions on a weighing of its own benefits and its own costs. Any costs that its decisions impose on others and which it does not bear itself may not influence its behavior. There is therefore a danger that each will take actions which are justified in terms of its own costs but would not be if the total costs to the entire community were included.

A classic example is air pollution. It may be that in a certain town the cheapest way to get heat and power is by burning soft coal in furnaces that cover the entire area with soot and smoke. Though everyone despises the smog and wishes for its elimination, it may be that no individual citizen has any incentive to change his fuel or to install expensive devices to eliminate smoke. Each may reason that such action will only increase his own expenses and will make no significant contribution to improving the situation because most of the pollution comes from others. All may welcome government intervention that forces everyone to cease generating smog. The same principles may apply to water pollution.

There are similar examples in the field of natural-resources conservation. Each of the hundreds of lumber companies operating in the hills and mountains may find it profitable, if they consider only their own costs, to denude the watersheds and not reforest them. But such practices may impose heavy costs on others by creating floods and serious soil erosion over a great area, perhaps in river valleys hundreds of miles downstream. Every individual lumber company may admit that the total effects are bad and yet have no incentive to alter its practices because this would increase its own costs and make only a negligible contribution to the prevention of floods and erosion. All may welcome government intervention that forces everyone to conserve natural resources. And even if some of the lumber companies object, the great majority of people may approve.

Another case is child labor. It may be that the cheapest way of producing a certain product is by using large amounts of child labor. But this may injure the children's health and deprive them of educational opportunities. All the employers may be ashamed of the practice and desire its elimination. Yet no one of them may be able to cease employing children so long as his competitors continue to do so; he will only raise his own costs, perhaps be eliminated by his lower-cost competitors, and see the use of child labor continue in the firms that take over his business. All may be happy when the government forbids the use of child labor.

The same may be true of dishonest and misleading advertising. Advertising for a group of products may have become so blatantly untruthful that every seller wishes for its reform. Yet these misleading tactics may be so successful in promoting sales that no one seller can afford to reform if his competitors do not. All sellers may be happy when the government intervenes to ban misrepresentation.

D. UNEMPLOYMENT AND INFLATION

There are many reasons why our analysis of the role of government is applicable to the problems of unemployment and inflation. Most of these we shall not discuss here, partly because the necessary background materials are presented at a later point. It should be clear, however, that increased expenditures and demands for output are desirable in times of unemployment in order to make it profitable for businessmen to provide more jobs. Yet at just such a time anyone who by himself undertakes to increase his expenditure is likely to act to his own disadvantage. In such uncertain times it is prudent for him to put aside every penny he can spare against the rainy day which has become so imminent. With jobs hard to find and business firms shaky, he can ill afford to spend his money foolishly. Moreover, there is a premium on not spending; if prices are falling, every dollar he puts away will buy more tomorrow than it would today if he should rush out and spend it in a futile gesture to promote the national interest.

Similarly, it would help combat inflation if people were to reduce their expenditures, so that decreased demands for goods might exert a downward pressure on prices. Yet at such times it will pay each individual who can afford it to do his spending quickly before rising prices destroy much of the purchasing power of his money.

If, then, it is universally desired to eliminate unemployment or inflation, it may well be that government intervention will be called for to give effect to the will of the citizens, and to organize and perhaps coerce them all into doing what they consider appropriate but are unable to undertake by themselves individually.

3. Some Other Examples of Government Intervention

There are other cases where government intervention cannot possibly benefit everyone, yet where many people feel that the government ought to intervene because so many people stand to benefit so substantially. In practice almost all government regulations are of this variety. The armed robber objects to being deprived of his weapon, and some taxpayers may not want to pay for lighthouses, preferring to live in lighthouseless worlds. We shall mention two cases in which government intervention *must* harm someone, and yet in which intervention often has popular approval.

A. MONOPOLY

As we saw earlier, a laissez-faire policy of a government is ordinarily supported by the argument that competition will control the economy and yield results that are generally acceptable. Yet there is a danger that in some markets competition will be suppressed and monopoly power enhanced because there are so few sellers or buyers, or because of collusion, or both. Monopoly power may become so great that people demand government intervention.

When this occurs, the government may intervene in any one of three ways. (1) It may intervene to prevent monopoly and to preserve or reestablish a degree of competition that will yield acceptable results. This is a type of government intervention whose purpose is to make reliance on competitive controls feasible. (2) It may permit and even enforce private monopoly but regulate its prices, quantity and quality of service, investment, and so on. This is done in the so-called public utility field—in railroads and several other common carriers, electric and gas utilities, and telephones, among others. (3) The government itself may own and operate industries in which the maintenance of a satisfactory degree of competition is not considered feasible and monopoly is deemed advantageous.

We shall find later that one of the big issues in our public policy is that of deciding what types and degrees of competition are necessary to yield acceptable results and of determining what to do when monopoly power is, or threatens to become, excessive.

b. The Distribution of Income

As we saw earlier, market competition determines a distribution of income. But the distribution of income arrived at in the market is highly unequal, as is also the distribution of wealth. These great inequalities may so offend the ethical standards, as well as the economic interests, of a majority of the people that they will demand government intervention to alter the distribution of wealth and income. Income and wealth redistribution is at least one of the objectives of many types of government intervention. These include highly progressive taxes on incomes and inheritances, subsidized public housing, free education, free medical services, aid to widows and orphans, old-age pensions, minimum wage laws, etc.

Our purpose here is neither to defend nor to attack government intervention that alters the distribution of income and wealth arrived at by market processes. It is only to point out one example in which a majority of the people have found the results of market processes unacceptable and have demanded government intervention to alter them, though in the one case it is disadvantageous to the monopolist and in the other it presumably harms the individual whose share of the national income is reduced.

c. Summary

In the preceding pages we have presented some of the cases in which the American people—who generally favor a wide scope for consumers' sovereignty, free enterprise, and market competition—have considered government intervention to be desirable. Other cases could have been mentioned. In many of these cases government intervention and coercion are considered necessary to enable all individuals, or at least a majority of them, to realize desires that could not be realized through competitive processes.

4. Why Should Government Not Intervene?

We began this chapter by asking why it would ever be in an individual's interest to have the government intervene and thus have himself as well as others coerced or restrained. In answering this question things seem to have gotten out of hand, and we appear to have opened the door to government intervention throughout the economy, for we have shown that interdependence can make government intervention advantageous and we have seen how interdependent we are in our every economic act. This is certainly not our intention. Even if there are ways in which government intervention can benefit the members of the economy, it does not follow that just *any* government act is desirable. Clearly, a misanthropic and tyrannical state can work, and has done so, to the disadvantage of those whom it governs. Nor is good will on the part of a government enough. Misguided policies undertaken by an ignorant or inefficient ruling body may be objectionable, however desirable its aims. Moreover, the cost and inefficiency of a huge bureaucracy may more than outweigh any benefits from it. Finally, some types of government intervention may have harmful net results even though they enjoy the support, or at least acquiescence, of a large majority of the citizens.

A. NONECONOMIC CONSIDERATIONS

We have been primarily concerned, insofar as a distinction can be made, with economic considerations. It may well be that on purely economic grounds we would be inclined to favor a certain type of government intervention, yet we might consider it unacceptable for other reasons. For example, if we strongly dislike any extension of government authority, considering it reprehensible because it is likely to curtail our liberties, no strictly economic benefit may justify a new regulation.

However, there are also important economic reasons why we might want even the most efficient and best willed of governments to limit the scope of its economic activity.

B. COMPETITION

There are broad areas in which people believe that market competition can give effect to their desires more efficiently than can government controls. This is because of the attributes of consumers' sovereignty and the strength of competitive pressures in increasing efficiency and adjusting output to consumers' choices as expressed in their market demands. Even if the government tried to achieve the same results it might be less efficient in many areas.

C. HARMFUL GOVERNMENT ACTIONS WITH POPULAR APPROVAL

Some government actions may work to the disadvantage of all, or almost all, concerned even though they are approved and even demanded by a great majority of the electorate. The voters do not consider *all* the costs and benefits of the actions they approve. In part, this is due to ignorance of the results of the policies. Misrepresentation, lack of understanding, and misunderstanding of the economic results of government policies are all too common. Knowledge is not always necessary for wise decisions, but it is often helpful.

The tariff can be used as an example that has considerable practical significance. Employers and employees in each line of industry may desire tariff protection against foreign competition in the belief that they can thereby raise the prices of their products and get higher money incomes. When the government has granted tariff protection to everybody, each individual, as we shall see later, may have lost more as a consumer than he gained as a producer. Yet each may approve of the tariff program because of the actual or imagined increase of his money income, being less influenced by—and perhaps less conscious of—the probably greater increase in his cost of living. This is but one example of a broad class of cases in which voters may approve of a government program because they are more conscious of its benefits than of its costs.

Certain public works projects are another example. The people in some locality may want the federal or state government to undertake in that locality a public works project which will cost $10 million. They are not willing to pay more than $1 million to get its benefits, but they figure that if it is financed by the federal or state government their share of the expense will be far less than a million. Many other localities may have similar projects about which they feel the same way. Through the logrolling technique of "you vote for my project and I'll vote for yours," all the projects may be adopted despite the fact that all who weighed the total costs against the total benefits would agree that the programs were not worth while. Yet each voter, impressed by the benefits of his local project and less conscious of the total cost of all the projects that had to be adopted in order for him to get his, may register his approval.

It would be easy to list many other cases in which government intervention may have dubious value or actually be harmful even though they have the approval, or at least the acquiescence, of a majority of the voters. It certainly cannot be taken for granted that people are in every case wiser when they vote than when they make decisions in the market place, or that competition at the polls and in the halls of government is always a more effective means of achieving people's economic goals than competition in the market. Nor is the reverse true.

5. Conclusions

We have found that the American economy is, and always has been, a "mixed" system, in that economic control functions are divided between the government and the competitor in the market. Most Americans have insisted upon maintaining a wide scope for free enterprise and competitive controls. At the same time, they have not hesitated to permit and even to demand government intervention when they believed that it would yield desirable results. Very few have seriously suggested that competitive controls be completely superseded by government controls, and the extremists who heatedly demand that "government get out and stay out of economic affairs" probably do not mean literally what they say and do not enjoy wide support.

This commitment to a pragmatic approach and a mixed control system raises a host of policy questions, such as these: What should be the relative scope of government and competitive controls? In what cases and to what extent should we rely on competition in the market? In what cases should market competition be limited, supplemented, or superseded by government intervention? If it is decided that the government should intervene in a particular case, what precisely should it do?

In this chapter we have presented some cases in which government intervention may be necessary to enable people to satisfy desires that they could not satisfy through their individual efforts or through competitive market processes. We have also noted other cases in which government intervention may be more harmful than beneficial. But we have not presented any magic or simple formula for determining when, where, and how the government ought or ought not to intervene. In fact, we doubt that it is possible to develop any simple yet useful formula for this purpose. One can say, of course, that the government ought to intervene when it can produce more desirable results than market competition. But this broad principle yields no specific policy prescription in a particular case.

To arrive at a rational policy decision in any particular case, two steps are necessary. (1) One must arrive at an understanding of the probable results in the absence of government intervention and under each of the various possible types of government intervention. These should include both economic and noneconomic results. (2) One must evaluate these results and make a choice in light of the ethical and political preconceptions of the people. Both of these steps present great difficulties. It is often difficult to predict all the significant short-run and long-run economic and noneconomic results that would flow from each of the alternative policies.

At least as difficult is the problem of attaching weights or values to each of the various predicted results. This is true partly because so many of the results of government intervention do not have a "market value" which can be used as a measuring stick. For example, what value should we place on the annoyance and discomfort felt by those who are restricted or coerced by the government? How should we value better education for the masses? How should we value a 50 percent decrease in infant mortality? What is the value of the discomforts of people who pay taxes to clear slums and the value of better living conditions to those who no longer have to live in slums? How should we value the greater degree of national security afforded by 100 additional jet fighters?

There is no simple rule that can answer questions of these types. In the final analysis, policy decisions must rest on some sort of social judgment that is usually a compromise among the conflicting views of people with different predictions of the effects of the alternative policies, conflicting interests, and differing sets of social values.

In the following pages we shall encounter many cases in which people have to decide whether or not the government should intervene and precisely what it should do if intervention of some sort is considered desirable. Though many of these decisions will depend to a large extent on considerations that are not strictly economic, economic analysis can still be valuable and sometimes indispensable for rational decision-making.

SUGGESTED READINGS

Baumol, William J., *Welfare Economics and the Theory of the State,* Harvard University Press, Cambridge, 1952.
Bowen, Howard R., *Toward Social Economy,* Rinehart, New York, 1948.

Graham, Frank D., *Social Goals and Economic Institutions,* Princeton University Press, Princeton, 2nd ed., 1949.

QUESTIONS

1. a. Describe the likely consequences of a completely government-free (anarchist) world.
   b. Are there any conceivable circumstances under which it would operate smoothly and satisfactorily?
   c. What would you consider the minimal functions of government that are necessary to make an economy function satisfactorily in the judgment of its members?
   d. How does your list compare with Adam Smith's?
   e. How does it compare with the current situation?
2. In light of the examples discussed in the earlier sections of this chapter:
   a. Just how do you resolve the paradox that a preference for government intervention means that people prefer to be coerced into doing what they would not otherwise have done?
   b. Why would you not have done voluntarily what the government now forces you to do if you prefer the results now obtained?
   c. What is the significance of the fact that government intervention involves coercion of others, not of yourself alone?
3. What prevents the problems listed from being solved by voluntary agreement?
   a. Why can't lighthouse building always be financed by passing the hat?
   b. Why can't "pistol-packing" always be stopped by an unpoliced peace pact?
   c. Why will not smoke elimination always be accomplished in this way?
4. What motivation would people have to "welsh" and "chisel" on agreements of the sort referred to in the preceding question?
   a. How do you reconcile this motive for "welshing" with the assertion that the voluntary agreement in these cases can benefit everyone?
   b. Does the "chiseler" only gain so long as the voluntary agreement is adhered to by others?
   c. Are the others "suckers" to continue to adhere to the agreement when others are "welshing"?
   d. When others are not "welshing"?
5. In arranging for smoke elimination, lighthouse building, etc.:
   a. Show that the government's role as an instrument of coercion is only part of its job.
   b. List the difficulties that private enterprise might encounter in organizing, negotiating, and administering, as well as policing the agreements necessary to accomplish these ends without state intervention.

6. a. What other noneconomic grounds might there be for objecting to an act of government intervention in addition to the possibility of government inefficiency and the restriction of liberty?

   b. Can you think of any noneconomic ground which might increase the desirability of an act of government intervention?

   c. Are there some measures involving state intervention whose economic consequences you approve of but which you would reject on noneconomic grounds?

   d. Can you think of some measures whose economic consequences you disapprove of but which you would advocate on noneconomic grounds?

7. Do you know of some "paternalistic" arguments for government intervention, that is, cases where the government can reasonably be expected to protect people from themselves either because:

   a. These people are in no position to judge what is good for them, or because they cannot resist harming themselves, though aware they are doing so?

   b. Where do you think the government has intervened on "paternalistic" grounds without adequate justification?

8. a. What, precisely, has the public overlooked when it helps harm itself by approving of a series of relatively useless public works?

   b. In this case, are the citizens of Crayfish Corners being irrational in pressing for the construction of the giant marble Crayfish Corners post-office building and war memorial?

   c. Do they have any reason to believe that other wasteful projects elsewhere will be abandoned, if they refrain from pressing their request for federal funds?

   d. Can you think of any remedies?

PART III

Income, Unemployment, and Inflation

CHAPTER 8

Economic Instability

---

1. Introduction

In an earlier chapter we considered the long-term upward trend of real incomes in the United States and some of the basic developments that have made it possible. It would indeed be pleasant to report that the actual rate of output has always hovered close to the long-term upward trend, that all who wanted jobs have always been able to find them, that our national wealth has grown at a fairly steady rate, and that the purchasing power of the dollar has remained relatively steady. Unfortunately, as the reader no doubt knows, such a report would not be true.

Despite its other great achievements, the free-enterprise system has suffered from serious economic instability. On far too many occasions, millions of able and willing workers have been without employment; factories, mines, and other productive facilities have lain idle or been underutilized; and the actual rate of output has been far below the levels that the economy was capable of achieving. Moreover, the purchasing power of the dollar has fluctuated widely. In some periods, usually periods of depression and unemployment, prices have fallen and the purchasing power of the dollar has risen. In other periods prices have risen and the dollar has lost a considerable part of its value.

This type of economic instability has generated so much suffering and discontent that some countries have either abandoned free-enterprise systems or modified them drastically. One of the major economic problems of the United States—perhaps the most pressing problem—

is preventing economic instability and maintaining continuous high-level employment, high-level production, and a relatively stable purchasing power of the dollar. It is probably no exaggeration to say that the future of the free-enterprise system in this country, as well as the economic welfare of our people, depends on our ability to solve this problem.

This chapter will describe the principal characteristics and social implications of business depression on the one hand and of inflation on the other. To make our treatment more concrete and realistic we shall deal largely with the period since 1929, a period that has included one of our worst depressions and one of our greatest inflations. At this point we shall have little to say about the causes of depression and inflation; this analysis will come later. Here it is enough to note that depressions reflect the fact that the demand for output is so low that business will not employ all the available factors of production. And inflation reflects the fact that expenditures for output are so large relative to the real output of the economy that prices are forced up.

To illustrate the nature and seriousness of business depressions, we shall study in some detail the great depression that plagued the United States during the entire decade of the 1930's. Though we shall concentrate on this particular depression in our country, several points should be kept in mind. (1) This depression was not confined to the United States. In fact, it was almost world-wide. The suffering, discontent, and frustrations it generated led to serious social and political upheavals in many countries, undermined faith in liberal institutions, helped elevate authoritarian government, and were an important factor in producing World War II. (2) Though this was our most serious depression to date, it was by no means the only one. We also had serious depressions during periods beginning in 1920, 1907, 1893, and 1873, to mention only the major ones since the Civil War. And in various other periods we have had considerably less than full employment. (3) Depressions are not uniform; they differ in depth and duration, and in many other respects.

2. The Depression and the Decline of Real Income

Let us look now at the great depression which began in late 1929. The latter part of the 1920's was a period of relative prosperity. Output was at a high level, only about 3 percent of the labor force was unemployed, and the prices of output had been practically stable for several years. From the point of view of our productive potential, we should have been able throughout the 1930's not only to maintain but even to surpass by large amounts the rate of output achieved in 1929. We had rich natural resources, a huge and rising supply of capital goods, an expanding labor force, and an advancing technology. But what happened? Real output declined abruptly, as indicated in Fig. 2 and Table 10.

TABLE 10.   National Output, 1929–1941[1]
(Indexes, 1929 = 100)

Year	Index of National Output at Current Prices	Index of the Price Level of Output	Index of Real Output
1929	100	100	100
1930	88	96	91
1931	73	87	84
1932	56	78	72
1933	54	75	72
1934	63	79	79
1935	70	81	86
1936	79	81	97
1937	87	85	102
1938	82	83	98
1939	88	83	106
1940	98	84	115

Table 10 shows the behavior of national output and prices. The value of output at current prices, reflecting the declines of both physical output and prices, fell 46 percent between 1929 and 1933. Part of this decline was accounted for by the 25 percent decrease in the average prices of output. But even after allowing for the price decline, real output fell 28 percent. As indicated in Table 11, output in the various sectors of the economy behaved quite differently. At one extreme, agricultural output declined but little. At the other, the output of durable manufactured goods fell more than half.

After reaching its low point in 1933, real output began to recover somewhat, but not until the late 30's did it again reach and surpass its

[1] These statistics refer to gross national product. They were computed from U.S. Department of Commerce data presented in *Survey of Current Business*, July, 1952, pp. 14, 15, and 28.

Many of the data in this chapter are taken from Department of Commerce publications. The sources of data in some tables are not indicated because they were gathered in so many different places.

Billions of Dollars (Ratio Scale)

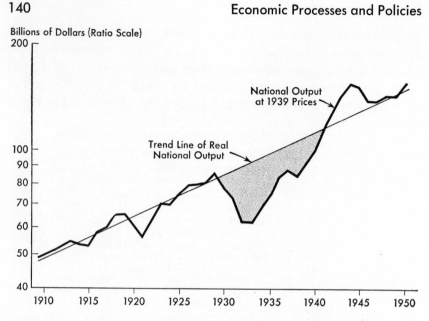

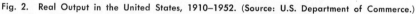

Fig. 2. Real Output in the United States, 1910–1952. (Source: U.S. Department of Commerce.)

1929 levels. And even then it was far below capacity levels, for both the size of the labor force and technology had continued to grow.

We can attempt to measure in two different ways the nation's loss of real income due to underemployment and underproduction. (1) We can use the amount of employment as a rough index of the amount of

TABLE 11.   Decreases in Selected Types of Real
Output, 1929–1933

Types of Output	Percentage Decline
Total	28
Agricultural	4
Nondurable manufactured goods	15
Minerals	29
Durable manufactured goods	59

unutilized productive power. Table 12 shows that by 1933 the number of unemployed was about 13 million, or almost 25 percent of the total labor force. Some others were only working part-time. From that time until 1941 there was no year in which the average number of unemployed fell below 7.7 million, or 14 percent of the labor force.

(2) We can also attempt to estimate the loss of real income by com-

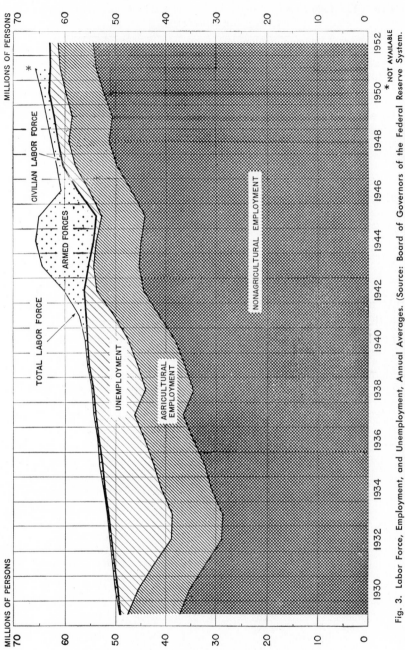

Fig. 3. Labor Force, Employment, and Unemployment, Annual Averages. (Source: Board of Governors of the Federal Reserve System. Based on Bureau of Labor Statistics Estimates, 1929–1939; and Bureau of the Census Estimates, 1940–1952.)

* NOT AVAILABLE

MILLIONS OF PERSONS

TABLE 12. Labor Force, Employment, and Unemployment, 1929–1941[2]
(In millions)

Year	Total Civilian Labor Force	Total Employment	Total Unemployment	Unemployment as Percent of Total Labor Force
1929	49.2	47.6	1.6	3.2
1930	49.8	45.5	4.3	8.7
1931	50.4	42.4	8.0	15.9
1932	51.0	38.9	12.1	23.6
1933	51.6	38.8	12.8	24.9
1934	52.2	40.9	11.3	21.7
1935	52.9	42.3	10.6	20.1
1936	53.4	44.4	9.0	16.9
1937	54.0	46.3	7.7	14.3
1938	54.6	44.2	10.4	19.0
1939	55.2	45.8	9.5	17.2
1940	55.6	47.5	8.1	14.6
1941	55.9	50.4	5.6	9.9

paring actual output with "potential" output, the latter meaning the levels that could have been achieved with only a normal advance over the levels actually attained in 1929. Table 13 presents such an estimate. Column 1 shows the actual rates of output during the decade, stated in dollars of 1951 purchasing power. Column 2, stated in the

TABLE 13. Actual and "Potential" Output, 1930–1939
(In billions of dollars of 1951 purchasing power)

Year	Col. 1 Actual Output	Col. 2 "Potential" Output	Col. 3 Loss of "Potential Output" (Col. 2 minus Col. 1)
1930	$ 152	$ 173	$ 21
1931	141	178	37
1932	119	183	64
1933	118	188	70
1934	131	194	63
1935	143	200	57
1936	164	206	42
1937	171	212	41
1938	164	218	54
1939	180	224	44
Total for decade	$1483	$1976	$493

[2] Source: *President's Economic Report,* July, 1952, p. 150.

same dollars, shows the rates of output that could have been attained with a 3 percent annual increase over the level actually achieved in 1929. This rate of increase had been attained in the past. These estimates indicate that underproduction during the decade cost the country more than $490 billion of lost income, measured in dollars of 1951 purchasing power. Real output during the decade could easily have been a third higher than it was.

3. The Impact of the Decline of Real Income

Let us look now at the impact of this decline of real income on the various economic groups. A decline of real income of more than 25 percent, such as occurred between 1929 and 1933, would have been serious enough if it had been spread proportionally over the entire population. Few of us can suffer a 25 percent cut in real income without pain, and for low-income families such a cut can be calamitous. But the reduction was not shared proportionally. Some people actually gained; others suffered much more than the average reduction.

A. THE GAINERS

The cost of living declined 25 percent between 1929 and 1933, so that all those whose money incomes rose, remained the same, or decreased less than this amount had higher real incomes. There were many people in this group—workers who were able to keep full-time jobs and escape serious pay cuts; those who were able to collect their pensions, annuities, interest, and fixed rents; and some others. But to the extent that some people actually enjoyed higher real incomes or suffered a reduction that was less than the average, others had to undergo real income reductions that were greater than the average. Some would have had no income at all if they had not received private or public relief. Who were these people who suffered most?

B. THE UNEMPLOYED

Outstanding among the sufferers were the unemployed. We have already seen that in 1933 one out of every four members of the labor force was jobless, and in no year from then until 1941 did unemployment claim less than one out of every seven potential workers. Many of these people were jobless for several years.

Who were the jobless? We can dismiss the blanket statement, made by some, that the unemployed were just a bunch of bums who didn't want to work anyway. It is probably true that in each plant there was some tendency to dismiss the least efficient first. But this was by no means the invariable rule. Considerations such as favoritism, age, seniority, and race and religious prejudice were also important. Young people were especially hard hit. Those leaving school and college and seeking to join the labor force for the first time were told everywhere, "No help wanted." Many of those who already had jobs were discharged because of their lack of seniority or because they had no de-

TABLE 14.   Percentage Decreases in Employment in Selected
Industries, 1929–1933[3]

Industry	Percentage Decrease
All industry (average)	23.2
Food and kindred products	9.8
Textile-mill products	14.3
Finance, insurance, and real estate	14.4
Apparel and finished products	18.1
Agriculture, forestry, and fisheries	18.4
Water transportation	19.2
Services	23.2
Wholesale and retail trade	23.6
Communications and public utilities	24.0
Mining	30.2
Total manufacturing	30.9
Furniture and finished lumber products	36.2
Iron and steel products	38.5
Railroads	41.2
Nonferrous metals and products	44.0
Automobiles and equipment	44.4
Stone, clay, and glass products	46.6
Machinery, except electrical	48.7
Electrical machinery	51.6
Contract construction	52.6

pendents. At the bottom of the depression millions of youths, including some from our best colleges, loafed disconsolately or roamed the country looking for something to do. Workers in the oldest age group also suffered, especially when they sought reemployment after losing their jobs. Employers wanted younger and more vigorous men. Negroes and some other minority groups were hard hit. Not without justification did they complain that they were "the first fired and the last hired."

A man's chance of holding his job also varied greatly from industry

[3] Derived from data on the number of full-time equivalent employees, U.S. Department of Commerce, *National Income,* 1951, p. 180.

to industry. As indicated in Table 14, there were several industries in which the total number of jobs decreased no more than 10 or 15 percent between 1929 and 1933. At the other extreme, however, were numerous industries in which the number of jobs fell more than 40 percent. In some cities specializing heavily in the durable-goods industries, a large proportion of all workers were unemployed and local resources were insufficient to meet even the minimum needs for unemployment relief.

It is almost impossible to translate these unemployment statistics into an adequate account of the human suffering, feelings of insecurity, and personal defeat that accompanied prolonged unemployment. How would you feel if you lost your job and remained unemployed for a long time despite your most persistent efforts to find work? If you used up all your savings and piled up debts? If you had to watch your children go to school shabbily dressed and perhaps even hungry? If you were forced to accept private charity and public relief with all their social stigma? If you were taunted as a failure—a man unable to get and keep a job or take decent care of his family? The social costs of unemployment cannot all be stated in dollars and cents or even in terms of bread and butter. They also include long dreary hours of loafing with nothing interesting to do, dull defeatism, loss of self-respect, broken homes, postponed marriages, frustration, and loss of faith in established mores and institutions.

C. FARMERS

Farmers, who had not shared the prosperity of the 1920's, were hit very hard by the depression. Their loss of real income was not due to any decline in the amount of work they did or to any decrease in their production; in fact, farm output stayed close to 1929 levels except in drought years. They were ruined by the drastic decline of farm prices resulting from the decreased incomes and spending power of consumers not only in the United States but in other countries as well. Between 1929 and 1933 the prices received by farmers fell more than 50 percent, but the prices that entered into farmers' costs fell considerably less. It was largely because of this great fall of farm-product prices that the net money incomes of farmers fell 60 percent between 1929 and 1933. For millions of farmers, many of them already in the lowest-income groups, this further fall of income was nothing short of ruinous.

The plight of farmers was worsened by their large outstanding mortgages and other debts, most of which had been contracted when the prices of both farm land and farm products were much higher. With the decline of farm-product prices it took more than twice as much wheat, cotton, or other farm products to cover each dollar of interest or principal payment on debt. Hundreds of thousands of farmers were unable to meet their obligations and foreclosures were widespread. The decline in the price of farm land was so great that when a farmer's property was sold to satisfy his debts he usually found that his entire equity—in many cases representing his life savings—had been wiped out and he was still in debt. In view of these facts it is not hard to understand why farmers were discontented and sometimes resorted to riots as well as to political action.

D. OTHER OWNERS OF BUSINESSES

With the great decrease in the money demand for output, it was inevitable that, as residual claimants, the owners of business firms would suffer serious reductions in both their money and their real incomes. That this occurred is indicated by Table 15. In 1929 all corporations

TABLE 15.   Percentage Reductions in the Net Money
Incomes of Business Firms, 1929–1933[4]

Types of Firms	Percentage Reductions
Corporate profits—total	119
Unincorporated enterprises—total	63
Farmers	60
Business and professional	65

had total net profits of more than $10 billion; in 1933 they had net losses of nearly $2 billion. In the same period the net money incomes of unincorporated businesses fell more than 60 percent. Owners as well as employees felt the impact of the depression.

Business failure rates were abnormally high and the number of new businesses established was abnormally low. Many owners lost everything they had. More than one enterpriser probably shared the feelings of the little New York shopkeeper who disgustedly locked up his store and hung on the front door a sign reading: "Opened by mistake."

Included among the enterprisers who suffered drastic decreases in both money and real incomes were many professional people such

[4] Source: *Ibid.*, 1951, p. 150.

as doctors, dentists, lawyers, engineers, accountants, and architects. They could not prosper while their potential clients had low incomes.

E. CREDITORS

The incomes of creditors behaved in widely different ways. Some creditors, as we have already seen, actually gained as they continued to collect relatively fixed dollar amounts of interest while the cost of living fell. But many were not so fortunate, for their impoverished debtors were unable to make the promised payments. Hundreds of thousands of farmers, homeowners, business firms, and governmental units defaulted on their obligations.

4. Effects of the Depression on National Wealth and Its Distribution

A. TOTAL NATIONAL WEALTH

National wealth increased very little if at all during the depression decade, for the depreciation of capital continued and the rate of new capital construction was very low. National wealth at the outbreak of World War II was far smaller than it would have been if investment had continued at the rate actually achieved in the 1920's. However, there were very large shifts in the distribution of wealth during the depression.

B. SHIFTS OF WEALTH FROM DEBTORS TO CREDITORS

Falling prices and the rising purchasing power of the dollar shifted large amounts of wealth from debtors to creditors. Every type of debtor—business firms, farmers, homeowners, and others—found that they had to repay dollars that had greater purchasing power than the dollars they had borrowed earlier.

This can be illustrated by a simple example. Suppose that in the 1920's Jones borrowed $5000 and used $5000 of his own money to buy a house which, at current prices, was worth $10,000. By 1933 the price of the house had fallen to $5000. If Jones had to sell the house to pay his debt on it, the entire proceeds would be required to retire the debt. Thus the decline of prices wiped out Jones' ownership claim and increased the purchasing power of the creditor's claim. Though the example is hypothetical and the figures arbitrary, the principles involved should be clear.

It was in this way that owner-debtors lost so much of their wealth.

Millions of farmers and homeowners lost their properties and in many cases everything else they had. Corporate stocks depreciated markedly and many became practically worthless. And thousands of individual proprietors and partners sorrowfully realized the disadvantages of unlimited liability. But one type of business boomed—the business of the bankruptcy courts.

Generally speaking, creditors fared better than debtors. But many creditors were not so fortunate; because of the great decline in debtors' incomes and in the values of the properties on which loans were made, many debts proved to be uncollectable. Billions of dollars' worth of debts fell into default, and many creditors lost seriously in real terms as well as in money terms. Thousands of banks, savings and loan associations, and other financial institutions failed, imposing large losses on their creditors as well as their owners.

Though we have emphasized the loss of real income due to unemployment and underproduction, we should not underestimate the suffering of millions who lost all, or at least a large part, of their accumulated wealth. Many people lost the savings of a lifetime, their only protection against poverty during old age, illness, and other contingencies.

5. Other Social Effects of the Depression

Up to this point we have concentrated largely on the great losses of real income and wealth during the depression. But the social effects were far broader. People could not experience such serious suffering and frustrations without protests and without beginning to question the existing social order.

Their protests took many forms. In fewer instances than might have been expected under the circumstances, people resorted to bitter direct action. In violent but largely ineffective protest against low prices for their products, groups of farmers intercepted supplies of milk and other farm products bound for the market and dumped them along the roadside. They tried to halt foreclosures of farm mortgages by such devices as locking sheriffs in their offices, intimidating bidders at foreclosure sales, and threatening bodily harm to creditors and their agents. Thefts increased markedly. A large number of unemployed veterans marched on Washington to demand prepayment of their bonuses, only to be scattered by the army. Groups of unemployed stormed factory gates demanding jobs to keep their families from starving. Others rioted because of inadequate relief benefits. In many cases the demonstrators were dispersed with tear gas, clubs, and even guns. Such riots and near-riots were not on a wholesale scale, but they were numerous.

People also turned to political action. The number of socialists and communists increased, though Marxism made much less headway here than in many other countries. For the most part the violent protesters turned to American brands of radicalism—to Huey Long's "share-the-wealth" and "every man a king" movement, to Dr. Townsend's old-age benefit program, to technocracy, and to many radical movements with a strong fascist tinge. In the end, however, the two-party political system triumphed, and in 1932 the Republicans were roundly defeated by the Democrats, who soon undertook a more aggressive if not always well-designed program to deal with underproduction and its evils.

The great depression left many legacies that still exert an important influence on public thinking and public policies. Among these are the following.

1. A deep fear of depressions. No one can understand public policies since World War II without reference to the gnawing fear of another period of serious underproduction, mass unemployment, and falling prices. This has persisted through more than a decade of inflation.

2. A demand for greater government intervention to prevent unemployment and provide economic security to millions of people. So great is this demand that it is now impossible for any political party to attain and hold office if it does not promise to use the great power of government to prevent unemployment and deflation and to ameliorate their evils if they do occur. One manifestation is the Employment Act of 1946, under which the federal government expressly stated its responsibility to use all its powers to maximize production, employment, and purchasing power. Others include the price-support program for farm products, unemployment insurance, old-age insurance, more generous unemployment relief programs, benefits to widows and orphans, and fiscal policies to cope with depression. Some of these programs might have been adopted even without the depression, but there can be little doubt that the depression experience paved the way for them.

3. A shift of functions from state and local governments to the federal government. Because the depression was a nation-wide and even a world-wide rather than a local phenomenon, state and local governments could not prevent or remedy it. Many state and local govern-

ments proved incapable of financing adequate relief payments. This created a general belief that only a national government can deal with the nation-wide problem of preventing and remedying depressions.

4. A breakdown of the system of international specialization and trade. Free international trade has always had many enemies, but the depression precipitated a great increase of trade barriers. With millions of unemployed, many countries—including our own—adopted programs for excluding foreign goods from their markets, forcing people to buy home products, and "keeping our own money for our own people." It may take many years to restore international trade to its predepression position.

These are but a few of the legacies of the great depression. They should, however, indicate the pervasive social effects of this historic catastrophe.

6. Inflation: World War II and Its Aftermath

Before analyzing the effects of inflation it will be useful to sketch briefly the history of the inflationary period during and following World War II.

When war broke out in September, 1939, our economy had not yet recovered fully from the depression. Production was still far below capacity levels, 17 percent of the total labor force was still unemployed, and other productive facilities were still underutilized. In 1940 we began lend-lease aid to our future allies and embarked upon an expanding armament program. Government expenditures began to rise, as did also private consumption and investment expenditures. Until late 1941 the economy responded to this rising level of demand largely by increasing real output and employment and only to a lesser extent by raising prices.

However, beginning late in 1941 the continuing rise of both government and private expenditures, in the face of greater difficulties of achieving further increases in the rate of real output, led to a more rapid rise of prices. To prevent or at least retard further price increases the government placed legal ceilings on both wages and prices, so that prices rose only slowly until after the end of the war. This did not prevent the creation of inflationary pressures; it merely suppressed them.

Soon after the end of the war both price and wage ceilings were removed so that prices were again free to rise. Government expenditures were reduced markedly from their wartime levels, but this decrease was much more than offset by the rise of private consumption and investment spendings. From 1945 until 1952, with a lull only in 1949, both expenditures and prices continued upward. With the outbreak in Korea in June, 1950, the government again began to increase its expenditures, and this was accompanied by a further rise of private spending.

Table 16 summarizes some of the principal developments during

TABLE 16. Some Developments in the American Economy, 1939–1951
(Indexes, 1939 = 100)

Year	Value of Output in Current Dollars	Real Output	Price Level of Output	Consumer Prices	Wholesale Prices
1939	100	100	100	100	100
1945	236	168	140	129	137
1948	284	157	187	173	208
1951	360	183	197	187	230
1952	379	188	202	191	223

the period. These data show that between 1939 and 1952 total expenditures for output rose 279 percent, real output 88 percent, the price level of output 102 percent, consumer prices 91 percent, and wholesale prices 123 percent.

Taken as a whole, the period from 1939 through 1952 was indeed one of rising real output and price inflation. However, it is very important to note that a major part of the increase of real output had been achieved by 1945, whereas the largest part of the price rise occurred after that time. Later we shall make several comments about this phenomenon.

7. Inflation: Some Problems of Definition

A. POPULAR USAGES

Following popular custom, we have used the term "inflation" without defining it precisely. Just what does it mean? To some it means "high" prices. But high prices in relation to what? High prices in the United States relative to those in China? High prices in 1954 relative to those in 1609? This connotation of "high" prices is not very meaningful and is not what most people mean by inflation.

The more usual connotation of inflation is rising prices—the fact that prices are actually rising or would do so if they were legally free to move. And the implied reason for the upward pressure on prices is that buyers are spending, or trying to spend, at such a high rate relative to the volume of goods and services available for purchase. This is the general sense in which we use the term inflation. We shall distinguish two types: suppressed inflation and open inflation.

B. SUPPRESSED INFLATION

Suppressed inflation refers to the situation in which buyers' demands are so high as to exert a strong upward pressure on prices but the government is attempting, by imposing price ceilings, to prevent prices from rising. Such a situation prevailed in the United States and many other countries during World War II and it continued long after the war in several countries that were unwilling to remove their price ceilings. Even if the government succeeds in preventing black markets and in holding prices down to the legal levels, suppressed inflation gives rise to many problems.

One important characteristic of suppressed inflation is the prevalence of obvious shortages of goods and services. At the legal ceiling prices, which are lower than those that would be established by free competition, buyers want to purchase more than is available.[5] If prices were allowed to rise freely, shortages could be eliminated by pricing some consumers out of the market. But with prices kept down by government fiat there is no such restraint on consumers' demands, and since the very concept of inflationary pressure implies that the supply of goods is not large enough to meet demands, overt shortages must be expected.

If prices are not allowed to adjust in such a way as to perform the rationing function and if the government does not ration the available supplies, the distribution of goods is likely to be inequitable. The goods are likely to go to those who "know the right people," who queue up earliest and longest, who violate the law by slipping sellers something extra under the table, or who are in a position to do other favors for sellers.[6] Thus, suppressed inflation may lead not only to a haphazard distribution of output but also to the waste of large amounts of time. It is especially disadvantageous to a family all of whose adult members are working. They do not have time for queuing up and are likely to be busy at just the times when retailers receive their supplies,

---

[5] For a formal discussion of this point see the Graphic Appendix, pp. 624–625.

[6] The wife of a formerly sober English butcher finally had to divorce him because his customers kept him overly supplied with alcoholic beverages.

many of which will be exhausted by evening when the members of the family have finished their work. This may discourage housewives, and perhaps others, from joining the labor force at the very time when it is desirable to increase the labor supply in every possible way.

These problems may be reduced somewhat by government rationing, but rationing itself presents problems. It is a cumbersome, expensive, and unpleasant business. Moreover, it is extremely difficult to devise a system that will adjust the rations of the different types of goods to the particular needs and tastes of different families.

Price ceilings to suppress inflationary pressures are also likely to prevent prices from acting as an efficient guide to the composition of output and the allocation of resources. Some prices are likely to be set so low relative to other prices that production of those products will be far less than is generally agreed to be desirable. On the other hand, some prices may be set so high relative to others that production of these particular things will be overstimulated. If prices are not permitted to adjust in such a way as to guide the production and rationing of supplies, the government may have to impose a comprehensive system of direct controls over a large part of the economy.

Suppressed inflation over a prolonged period can also diminish incentives to work and lead to a high rate of absenteeism. Suppose that the people of some country have very high money incomes and that because of the combination of price ceilings and a shortage of consumer goods a considerable part of their incomes cannot be spent for consumption. They will be forced to save at a high rate. As time goes on they may accumulate very large stocks of money savings. When this occurs, many may reason as follows: "I already have enough money to buy all the goods and services that can be made available to me for a long time. Why should I work merely to accumulate more money that I shall not be able to use in the foreseeable future and that may lose most of its purchasing power when price ceilings and other direct controls are removed?" This sort of thing appears to have been a serious drag on production in a number of European countries during the period of suppressed inflation after World War II.

We are not arguing that it is never wise for a government to suppress inflationary pressures through the use of price ceilings and other direct controls. Suppressed inflation may be less disadvantageous than a runaway open inflation. There may even be cases in which suppressed inflation is less disadvantageous than the restrictive measures that would be required to prevent the generation of inflationary pressures. Our only purpose here is to point out that suppressed inflation raises serious problems.

c. OPEN INFLATION

The term *open inflation* connotes a situation in which inflationary pressures are not suppressed and the general level of prices is actually rising. However, if we make the term synonymous with any general increase in prices we must be especially careful not to imply that all inflation is "bad." Such a broad use of the term covers many types of situations. It includes the rise of prices that occurs when a country is recovering from a deep depression as well as price increases after full employment and full production have been reached. It includes slow "creeping inflation" as well as rapid "runaway inflation." We shall see that these different types of open inflation may have quite different results.

In the following sections we shall concentrate on open inflation, using the term to mean simply a general rise of prices.

8. Inflation and the Rate of Output

It is clear that rising prices are likely to be accompanied by a rise in real output so long as there are large amounts of unemployed labor and other productive facilities. Consider, for example, the depressed conditions of the 1930's. Employment and production were at such low levels because the effective demand for output was deficient and prices were so low relative to costs. An increase in the demand for output was a prerequisite to economic recovery.

This very rise of demand was almost certain to raise some prices before full employment and full production could be achieved. At first, the increase of demand may be reflected largely in increased employment and production. However, as the quantity of unemployed labor and unused productive facilities shrinks, one industry after another may encounter increasing difficulties and increasing costs of achieving further increases of output. As a result, further increases of demand will be reflected to a greater extent in price increases and to a lesser extent in expansion of real output. Thus some price increases above depression levels may be necessary for an economy to achieve, or even approach, full employment and full production.

Some believe that a slow and continuous rise of prices is necessary and inevitable if an economy is to achieve and maintain maximum production. They assert that if demand is high enough to elicit anything like full production, labor unions and monopolists will take advantage of the situation to drive up wages and prices. To avoid such price increases demand would have to be kept so low as to cause a considerable amount of unemployment. We do not know whether this is true. The opposing view is that production is best promoted by maintaining a relatively stable price level after full employment has been reached.

It is clear, however, that inflation, especially prolonged and rapid inflation, can actually decrease output and lower the efficiency of an economy. The rising cost of living may lead to numerous labor disputes, costly strikes, and damaged morale. Subsidized by inflation, even the most inefficient firms may be able to succeed, whereas they would otherwise be forced to relinquish their labor and other productive factors to their more efficient competitors. Large numbers of people may find it more profitable to speculate and hoard goods rather than contribute to orderly production and distribution.

In rapid ("galloping") inflations, such as occurred in Germany, Hungary, China, and several other countries, the whole economic process became deranged. Farmers refused to sell their products for money. Hungry people trudged through the country carrying clothing or other articles which they hoped to barter for food. Speculators bought and hoarded large amounts of raw materials and inventories rather than making them available for consumption or production. With little regard for efficiency, speculators bought plants and merged them in order to reap capital gains as prices rose. These experiences indicate clearly that rising prices do not always elicit higher production.

To simplify the discussion, the following sections will deal with "pure price inflation"—situations in which prices rise without any accompanying changes in the rate of real national output.

9. Inflation and the Distribution of Real Income

Inflation obviously cannot lower everybody's real income if it does not lower total national output. But it does redistribute income, giving to some and taking from others.

A. THE GAINERS

The gainers include all those whose money incomes rise faster than the cost of living. Suppose that the cost of living doubles. Everyone whose money income is more than doubled actually gains in real purchasing power. Of course many of these people will complain bitterly about their injury from inflation, pointing out how much better off they would be if prices had remained stable while their money incomes rose. They fail to recognize and admit that the increase in their money incomes was generated by the same inflationary processes that raised prices.

Stockholders and other owners of business are likely to be in the group that gains from inflation. As expenditures for output rise and costs lag behind, profits are likely to rise faster than prices. However, this tendency may be lessened by excess profits taxes or other heavier taxes on business income and by the increased power of labor unions.

Also in this group are likely to be doctors, lawyers, other professional people in independent practice, and workers who are in a strong bargaining position.

B. THE LOSERS

The losers include all those whose money incomes rise less than the cost of living. Suppose the cost of living doubles. Those whose money incomes remain constant lose half of their real incomes just as surely as they would if someone stole half of their money incomes while prices remained constant. And all those whose money incomes rise less than 100 percent suffer some decrease in real income.

Among those whose real incomes are likely to be decreased by inflation are many types of workers—ministers; employees of hospitals, churches, and charitable institutions; schoolteachers and college professors; government employees, especially at state and local levels; and others whose wages and salaries rise only slowly and after a delay. Interest receipts, being relatively fixed in terms of dollars, lose in purchasing power. The same is true of rentals, many of which are fixed for long periods, and of pensions and annuities.

The aged and others living on fixed pensions and annuities may be hit very hard. Consider, for example, the plight of a person who before World War II retired on a fixed pension which was even then barely adequate to cover his needs. Or the person who laboriously saved high-purchasing-power dollars before World War II to assure himself an income of $150 a month, only to see its purchasing power cut in half by the increased cost of living.

During some of the great inflations, such as that in Germany after World War I when prices rose to several billion times their prewar levels, the so-called fixed-income groups lost practically all their real incomes.

10. Inflation and the Distribution of Real Wealth

It is clear that inflation cannot lower everybody's real wealth if it does not lower the nation's total stock of natural resources and capital goods. However, it does redistribute wealth, giving to some and taking from others.

A. EFFECTS ON CREDITORS AND DEBTORS

Rising prices transfer real wealth from creditors to debtors, for debts are stated in fixed numbers of dollars. This is the reverse side of the proposition we encountered earlier in the chapter when we were discussing the effects of deflation on debtors and creditors. Again it can be clarified by an example. Suppose that in 1939 Smith bought a $10,000 house, using $2000 of his own money and borrowing $8000 from Brown. Suppose further that by 1954 the price level has doubled and the price of the house has risen to $20,000. Inflation has halved the purchasing power of Brown's $8000 debt claim, so it will buy only as much as $4000 would have bought in 1939. But Smith's ownership claim has increased from $2000 to $12,000, and the $12,000 will buy as much as $6000 would have bought in 1939. In effect, inflation has transferred from Brown the creditor to Smith the debtor an amount equal to $4000 of 1939 purchasing power.

The same principle applies in other cases. Inflation takes purchasing power from creditors and transfers it to debtors of all types—to owners of business firms, farms, homes, and other borrowers. It is not difficult to understand why lenders may oppose inflation while debtors look upon it more favorably.

B. THE LOSERS

In our example, creditor Brown lost because his claim was fixed in terms of dollars. This is just one example of the general principle that inflation lowers the purchasing power of all types of assets whose money values decline, stay the same, or rise less than the price level. Clearly in this group are such things as money itself, savings accounts, mortgages, government and corporate bonds, all other debt claims, life insurance policies, and the accumulated values of annuities and pension rights. A doubling of price levels can cut their purchasing power in half, and extreme inflations can rob them of practically all their purchasing power. Many a person who put his savings into these "conservative" types of assets can testify that they do not "conserve" purchasing power in time of inflation. Inflation has robbed many a church, college, hospital, and welfare institution of much of the purchasing power of an endowment that was accumulated over decades and even centuries.

c. THE GAINERS

All assets whose money values rise more than average prices increase in purchasing power. This includes many types of ownership claims—shares of stock in corporations and ownership equities in unincorporated businesses, buildings, and land. It should be recognized, however, that the money values of some types of ownership claims will not rise as much as the general price level.

11. Other Social Effects of Inflation

Rapid and prolonged inflation often has many other social effects. For example, the decreased purchasing power of private schools and colleges may decrease the quality of their instruction, force them to seek government aid, or drive them out of existence. Churches, private hospitals, children's homes, and other charitable institutions may become unable to perform their functions. Lagging salaries of government employees may deteriorate the quality of government personnel and services. The frequent renegotiation of wage contracts accompanying rising living costs may generate increasing animosity between employers and employees and increase the working time lost in labor disputes. Businessmen may cease to be respected by the public and instead be branded as speculators, gamblers, and profiteers. The aged and others who have been robbed by inflation are likely to demand government intervention to restore their status. Victimized by inflation and disillusioned with the existing economic and political system, conservative middle groups may throw their support to revolutionary movements.

These are but a few of the widespread social consequences of rapid and prolonged inflations.

12. Full Employment and Unemployment

We have already used the terms "full employment" and "unemployment" many times and shall have to repeat them many more times before we are through. The connotations of these terms are fairly clear, but we must admit that they are difficult to define precisely and that policy decisions may be influenced by the choice of definition. Let us look at a few of the problems involved.

A. DEFINITION AND MEASUREMENT OF UNEMPLOYMENT

The number of unemployed is obviously equal to the total labor force minus the number employed. The total labor force includes all who are more than 14 years old and who are both able and willing to work. We have already run into trouble. Who is able to work? How ill, handicapped, or irresponsible must a person be in order to be classified as unemployable and excluded from the labor force? Who is willing to work? People may be willing to work on some terms but not on others. Because of such conceptual difficulties, as well as the problem of gathering accurate statistics, estimates of the total labor force are only approximate.

We run into similar problems when we try to define the employed. Shall we include in the employed category those who have only part-time jobs, are on vacation, or are idle because of industrial disputes? In the official statistics all these people are classified as employed.

Estimates of the size of the labor force, the number employed, and the number unemployed are useful indicators, but we should recognize that they are highly approximate and are affected by many arbitrary decisions.

B. TYPES OF UNEMPLOYMENT

For policy purposes it is useful to classify unemployment into at least three categories: unemployment due to a deficiency of total demand, seasonal unemployment, and frictional unemployment.

Some unemployment at a given time may be due to the fact that at the prevailing prices and wages the demand for output is so low that there simply aren't enough jobs to go around. Even if workers knew about all the existing jobs and were willing to move quickly to take them, some would be left jobless.

Climatic conditions and social customs lead to some seasonal unemployment. For obvious reasons some farm hands, construction workers, and lifeguards are likely to be out of jobs during part of each year. Garment workers are often jobless until the next season's rush begins.

There is also what is known as *frictional* unemployment. People are always changing jobs, moving from firm to firm, from area to area, from industry to industry. In the process they are often unemployed. Moving itself may take time. Moreover, time may be needed to find a new job, to decide which job to take if plenty are available, or to learn a new skill. Frictional unemployment is an inevitable accompaniment of shifts in demand and of technological change.

Though subject to a number of objections, this classification of the types of unemployment is useful for policy purposes. Unemployment due to a deficiency of total demand may perhaps be eliminated through expansionary policies aimed at raising the demand for output. But such measures may be incapable of eliminating seasonal and frictional unemployment, or may be able to do so only by increasing demand so much as to create many more jobs than there are workers and to produce rapid inflation.

c. Full Employment

We often hear people say that they favor government policies to maintain continuous full employment. But precisely what do they mean by full employment? Do they mean literally that every member of the labor force has a job, that not one person in the entire nation is jobless? In this sense we have never had full employment and probably never shall. There is always some seasonal and frictional unemployment. If pressed, most advocates of full employment as a national goal would say they are not using the term literally but mean only that unemployment should be kept at a minimum, with seasonal and frictional unemployment alone remaining.

This still leaves serious questions for the policymakers. Should they aim at preventing unemployment from rising above 7 percent of the total labor force, or 5 percent, or 3 percent, or 1 percent? The results of policy may be greatly affected by this choice of goals. For example, we might be able to reduce unemployment to 1 or 2 percent of the labor force only by raising demand so much as to produce rapidly rising prices. But we might be able to reduce unemployment to 5 percent while maintaining relatively stable prices. If so, which choice should we make?

We shall use the term full employment in the general sense of minimum unemployment. We shall not attempt to answer the difficult policy question of what this minimum should be.

13. Conclusions

This chapter has described some of the principal characteristics and social implications of economic instability—of widespread unemployment, underproduction, and deflation on the one hand and inflation on the other. In the period since 1929 we have experienced our most serious depression and perhaps our most serious inflation. Both have had millions of victims. Largely as a result of these experiences it is now a professed national objective to decrease economic instability and to maintain maximum employment, maximum production, and, some would add, relatively stable price levels. This brings up important questions. Are these goals reconcilable? What are the causes of economic instability? What can we do to control the behavior of employment, production, and price levels? Such questions as these will be discussed in the following chapters.

SUGGESTED READINGS

Bresciani-Turroni, C., *The Economics of Inflation,* Allen and Unwin, London, 1937.

Chandler, Lester V., *Inflation in the United States, 1940–1948,* Harper, New York, 1951.

Wallace, Donald H., Despres, Emile, Friedman, Milton, Hart, Albert G., and Samuelson, Paul A., "The Problem of Economic Instability," *American Economic Review,* September, 1950, pp. 505–538.

Wecter, Dixon, *The Age of the Great Depression,* Macmillan, New York, 1948.

QUESTIONS

1. a. What are some possible explanations of the fact that during the depression the output of farm products decreased much less than the production of durable consumer goods?
   b. How would you expect consumers to respond to price and income changes in their purchases of each of these two types of commodity?
   c. Would you expect farm prices to fluctuate more or less than those of consumer durables? Why?
2. The loss in American income which resulted from the great depression has been estimated at $450 billion in terms of 1951 dollars.
   a. How much is this per person?
   b. How much per family with three children?
3. "The great depression was an important factor in producing World War II." Explain. Is this far-fetched?
4. "Depressions are not uniform. They differ in depth, duration, etc."
   a. How is this relevant to the concept of the business cycle?
   b. Do you believe there is any point in searching for *the* cause of depressions?

5. Reduced prices benefit the creditor at the debtor's expense, and rising prices do the reverse.
   a. Show how this discourages spending in depression and encourages it during inflation.
   b. Are these effects on the incentive to spend desirable?
   c. How is the effect on the creditor and debtor relevant to the position of farm groups on the free-silver controversy at the turn of the century?
6. a. How can severe open inflation reduce production?
   b. How can severe suppressed inflation reduce production?
   c. It has been said that Germany's experience after the First World War indicates that open "galloping" inflation can at first encourage investment, whereas suppressing such an inflation stops investment at once. Why might this be so?
7. a. What do we mean by inflationary pressure?
   b. What are the immediate sources of that pressure?
   c. How might you measure it?
8. If all prices, incomes, and wealth holdings increased proportionately during an inflation:
   a. Could the inflation help stimulate production?
   b. Could it cause a reduction in output?
9. a. Why do we distinguish between the stockholder's gain in income and his gain in wealth during an inflation?
   b. How would each of these types of gain manifest itself?
10. "Unemployment is the price of progress." Explain.
    a. Which of the three types of unemployment mentioned in the text is involved?
    b. Why would an increase in demand not eliminate this cost of un-employment?
    c. How could an increase in demand help reduce seasonal and frictional unemployment?
    d. How may the statement about unemployment and progress affect our attitude toward full employment as a goal?

CHAPTER 9

National Income Accounting

1. Introduction

In the preceding chapter we found that national income has fluctuated widely. We turn now to the task of explaining what determines the level of national income at any given time, and its fluctuations over periods of time. In the process we shall also cast light on the behavior of employment and prices. As a first step we shall present some of the essentials of national income accounting. This will be an extension and elaboration of the general treatment of the subject in Chapter 2.

Strictly speaking, national income accounting does not attempt to explain *why* national income is what it is during any given period. Its purpose is merely to show what national income actually was during a stated period and what its components were. Nevertheless, income accounting is an essential basis for income analysis. We can explain the behavior of national income only if we know what it is, what its components are, and some of the most important quantitative relationships among the components.

The growth of national income accounting, statistics, and analysis constitutes one of the most important developments in economics during recent decades. Before the 1930's neither the United States nor most other countries had developed comprehensive estimates of national income. However, interest in the field was stimulated greatly by the depression, the war, and the wartime and postwar inflation. A number of American economists and research institutions—notably Professor Simon Kuznets and the National Bureau of Economic Research—did valuable pioneering work. The U.S. Department of Commerce has built on their work and developed comprehensive and detailed estimates for the United States which it publishes periodically. A full description of the different measures of national income together with detailed statistics for the years 1929–1950 was published by the Department in 1951 under the title, *National Income.* Data for the last completed calendar year are included in each July issue of the Department's *Survey of Current Business.* Quarterly estimates appear currently in the *Survey of Current Business,* the *Federal Reserve Bulletin,* and many popular publications.

These concepts and statistics are now widely discussed and used for many purposes. Businessmen use them to analyze total output and its composition, the behavior of consumers' buying power and probable consumers' demands for broad categories of goods, the behavior of private saving, and so on. Military planners use them to estimate the total output of the economy, the amounts of output required for essential civilian purposes, and the amounts that can be made available for military uses. Government financial officials use them to forecast tax receipts and to analyze the effects of taxes and expenditures on the economy. Economists use them for an even greater variety of purposes. These are but a few of the analytical purposes for which national income accounting is now employed by business, government, journalists, and economists.

2. Measures of National Income or Output

A. DIFFERENT CONCEPTS AND MEASURES

We shall consider three different concepts and measures of national income or output: *gross national product, net national product,* and *national income.* Each of these has a specialized meaning. It is not possible to say that any one of them is "right" and the others "wrong." Each measures a different thing. One measure may be more useful for one purpose, and another more useful for another purpose.

We shall also consider *disposable private income*—the part of the total remaining at the disposal of the private sectors after their tax payments.

B. THE VALUE OF OUTPUT OR INCOME AT CURRENT PRICES

In every case we shall deal with the money value of output or income at current prices. Changes in money income therefore reflect changes in both the real output of goods and services and their price levels. To get an index of real output we would have to adjust these money values by using an appropriate index of prices. Some of the difficulties of doing this were indicated in Chapter 2.

C. THE VALUE OF OUTPUT EQUALS THE SUM OF THE CLAIMS AGAINST OUTPUT

In Chapter 2 we pointed out that income or output can be measured in either of two ways with the same result: (1) as the value of output, and (2) as the sum of all the claims against output—that is, the sum of all the income shares. Each method should give the same result, for the whole is equal to the sum of its parts. We shall see that this is true for each of our measures of national income. In effect, we shall be using double-entry accounting. On one side we enter the value of output. On the other we enter all the claims against the value of output, and these must account for the entire value of output.

TABLE 17.   A Simplified Income Statement for a Business Firm
Covering the Calendar Year 1953

Output		Claims Against the Value of Output (Costs and Profit)	
Value of output	$1000	Wages and salaries	$ 500
		Interest	100
		Rent	200
		Taxes	100
		Total costs	$ 900
		Profits (value of output minus costs)	100
Total	$1000	Total	$1000

This is illustrated by the highly simplified income statement for a business firm in Table 17. During 1953 the value of the firm's output was $1000. Costs of producing and selling constitute the first claim against the value of the output. But the firm's costs are income to the recipients. Wages and salaries are income to workers, interest is income to lenders, rent is income to those who lease property to the firm, and taxes are income to the government. Anything left over from the value of output after deducting costs constitutes profits for the owners. Total claims, including the claims of the owners, must exactly equal the total value of output.

People sometimes wonder why this is true. They ask, "What happens if a firm is badly managed or going bankrupt? How will the two sides of its accounts balance then?" The answer is simple. The two sides must balance because the profit item is purely residual; it is arrived at by deducting total costs from the value of output in order to find out what profit, if any, is left over for the owners. These profits can be negative (losses). If one avoids simple arithmetic errors he should get a sum equal to the total value of output if he adds to total costs a profit figure arrived at in this way.

We shall now look at the various measures of national output, starting with gross national product which is popularly referred to as GNP.

3. Gross National Product: Definition

Gross national product or *expenditure* is the market value of the output of goods and services produced by a nation's economy during a stated period of time *before deduction of allowances for capital consumption* during the period. We say that this is a measure of "gross" income because it includes the output of capital goods to replace capital worn out during the period as well as to make net additions to the nation's stock of capital. The term "capital consumption" is synonymous with "capital depreciation" used in its broad sense to include obsolescence as well as physical wear and tear. GNP is usually stated at an annual rate.

It is important to note that GNP may be viewed and measured in at least two principal ways: (1) as expenditures—i.e., the market value of output or expenditures for output during a stated period; and (2) as receipts—i.e., the sum of the gross income shares accruing to the members of the community during the period. These two are obviously the same since every dollar spent must be received by someone, and every dollar received must have been spent by someone.

4. GNP as the Market Value of Output or Expenditures for Output

As just noted, GNP is the market value of output or expenditures for output during a stated period. This flow of spending is a key factor in the operation of the economy, for it constitutes the money reward for producing. It is this effective money demand that greatly influences producers' decisions relative to the level of output, employment, and prices.

From this point of view, GNP is composed of three broad types of expenditures for output: (1) personal consumption, (2) gross private investment, and (3) government purchases of goods and services.

A. PERSONAL CONSUMPTION

This category includes all personal or household expenditures for current output to be used for consumption purposes. It includes consumers' spendings for new durable goods, such as autos and refrigerators; for nondurable goods, such as food and clothing; and for services, such as medical care and amusements.

B. GROSS PRIVATE INVESTMENT

This category includes all private expenditures for output to maintain or increase the nation's supply of capital. It is composed of two broad categories—gross private domestic investment and net foreign investment (American investment in foreign countries).

Gross private domestic investment includes all expenditures of individuals and business firms for current output with which to maintain and increase the domestic stock of capital. It includes expenditures for replacement as well as for net additions to the total stock. It is made up of three parts: (1) new construction, both residential and nonresidential; (2) producers' durable equipment, such as machinery, fixtures, railroad rolling stock, etc.; and (3) net changes in the size of business inventories.

The net changes in the size of business inventories may require some explanation. Inventories consist of goods held by businessmen and not (yet) sold by them. They are essential for many business operations. A grocer could not operate without goods on his shelves for customers to choose from. Similarly, a manufacturer must keep inventories of raw materials, etc. Otherwise he would have to arrange to buy them every time he set out to make another item. Let us now consider three cases.

1. There is no net change in the size of business inventories during the stated period. In this case total production is just equal to total sales to final buyers. That is, the flow of production into inventories is exactly offset by the flow of goods out of inventories and into the hands of final buyers.

2. There is a net increase in the size of business inventories during the stated period. In this case total production exceeds sales to final buyers, and this part of output is used to increase the stock of wealth held by producers.

3. There is a net decrease in the size of business inventories during

the stated period. Sales to final buyers exceed total production, thereby drawing down the stocks held by producers.

Changes in the size of business inventories may have an important influence on the behavior of national output and employment, especially during short periods. If firms make net additions to their inventories, either by purchasing from other firms or by producing in their own plants, they tend to support output and employment, thereby tending to cushion a recession or accentuate an expansion. But if they allow net reductions in their inventories they may accentuate a recession or damp an expansion, for they are buying from other firms or producing in their own plants less than they are selling to final buyers.

The other component of private investment is net foreign investment—American investment abroad during the period. This represents the net amount of our output during the period that is exported to increase our claims against foreigners.

In the future we can use the interest and principal receipts on these claims to buy real goods and services from foreigners. Thus our net foreign investment is like investment at home in that it may enable us · to have more goods and services in the future. Its nature and effects can best be clarified by a simple example. Suppose that during some year we make no gifts to foreigners but export to them $2 billion more of goods and services than we buy from them. This $2 billion worth of our output has been used to increase our claims against foreigners, and these claims can be in the form of gold or of debt and ownership claims. In this case, foreigners have contributed a net amount of $2 billion to the total demand for our output by buying more from us than we bought from them. And this was financed by their shipping gold to us or borrowing from us. Thus our net foreign investment— American investment abroad—constitutes part of the demand for our output. We shall emphasize later that this is one way in which saving can be injected back into the market as investment demand for our output. In effect, we lend dollars to foreigners and they use the dollars to buy from us.[1]

---

[1] Our net foreign investment can also be negative. That is, we may during a period decrease our claims against foreigners by using some of our income to import more from foreigners than they buy from us. This obviously represents a net drain of spending from our economy into foreign economies, with results that are the reverse of those when our net foreign investment is positive.

We also make net gifts to foreigners during some periods. Net gifts by our government are included in government purchases of goods and services. Private gifts to foreigners are included in personal consumption expenditures. In both cases it is assumed that in effect we buy the goods and services and give them to the foreign

c. GOVERNMENT PURCHASES OF GOODS AND SERVICES

These expenditures by federal, state, and local governments can be broken down into two principal classes. (1) Direct expenditures for the services of productive factors, primarily for labor. Included here are the services of both the military and civilian personnel used by the government. These services are valued for GNP purposes at their cost to the government. These expenditures obviously constitute income to the productive factors hired directly by the government.

TABLE 18. Gross National Product as Expenditures for Output During Selected Years[2]
(In billions of dollars)

Year	GNP	Personal Consumption	Gross Private Investment	Government Purchases of Goods and Services
1929	$103.8	$ 78.8	$16.6	$ 8.5
1933	55.8	46.3	1.5	8.0
1939	91.3	67.5	10.8	13.1
1944	213.7	111.6	5.6	96.5
1946	211.1	146.9	33.3	30.9
1948	259.0	177.9	44.6	36.6
1950	286.8	194.6	50.2	42.0
1951	329.8	208.1	58.8	62.9
1952	348.0	218.1	52.3	77.5

(2) Government expenditures for the output of business firms. Modern governments buy very large amounts of many types of output from business firms located all over the country. Business firms provide employment and produce in response to government demands just as they would if the demands emanated from private sources.

d. SUMMARY

We find, then, that GNP for any period is the sum of expenditures for output in the form of personal consumption, gross private investment, and government purchases of goods and services. It therefore

recipients. These gifts obviously do not increase our claims against foreigners. In more precise terms, our net foreign investment during any period is equal to our exports plus net earnings of our factors of production located abroad minus our imports and our net gifts to foreigners.

[2] The data in this table and in all others in this chapter unless otherwise specified are from the U.S. Department of Commerce. See *National Income*, 1951, and the *Survey of Current Business* for July of each year.

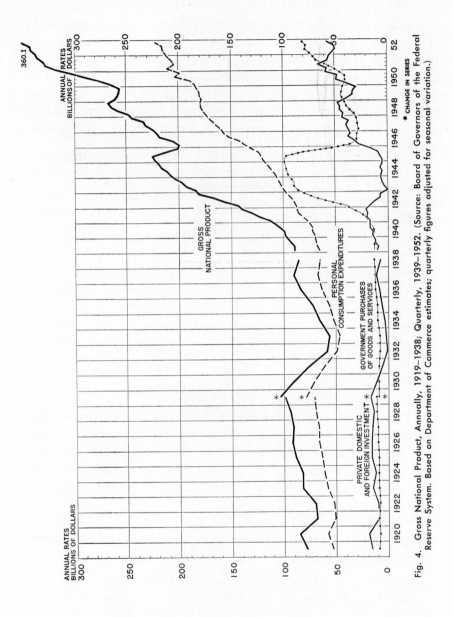

Fig. 4. Gross National Product, Annually, 1919–1938; Quarterly, 1939–1952. (Source: Board of Governors of the Federal Reserve System. Based on Department of Commerce estimates; quarterly figures adjusted for seasonal variation.)

fluctuates with the sum of these three types of expenditures. This is shown in Table 18. The reader may profitably study this table, noting the size and fluctuations of GNP and the relative sizes and degrees of variability of its components.

5. GNP as the Sum of Gross Income Shares

As already indicated, GNP can also be viewed as the sum of the shares of gross national income accruing to the members of the community. Every dollar spent for output must accrue to someone as income, and the total amount of money income accruing to the community as a whole cannot exceed the amount spent for output during the period. In short, the sum of gross income shares during any period must be exactly equal to total spending for output during the period, and it fluctuates with the rate of expenditures for output.

TABLE 19.   GNP as the Sum of Gross National Income Shares[3]
(In billions of dollars)

Year	Total GNP	Indirect Business Taxes	Capital Con- sumption Allow- ances of Business	Com- pensa- tion of Em- ployees	Rental Income of Persons	Net Inter- est In- come	Profits of Unincor- porated Business	Cor- porate Profits
1929	$103.8	$ 7.0	$ 8.8	$ 50.8	$ 5.8	$6.5	$13.9	$10.3
1933	55.8	7.1	7.2	29.3	2.0	5.0	5.2	−2.0
1939	91.3	9.4	8.1	47.8	3.5	4.2	11.3	5.8
1944	213.7	14.1	11.9	121.2	6.5	3.1	29.0	24.0
1946	211.1	17.3	12.2	117.1	6.6	2.9	35.4	18.3
1948	259.0	20.4	17.6	140.2	7.5	4.3	39.8	31.7
1950	286.8	23.7	21.6	153.4	8.5	5.7	37.0	36.0
1951	329.8	25.7	24.2	178.9	9.0	6.4	41.6	42.4
1952	348.0	28.1	27.0	193.2	10.0	7.0	41.1	40.2

This is shown in Table 19. For each stated period, the sum of the various shares of gross national income indicated by the column heads is determined by and is equal to total expenditures for output during the period.

Some of these expenditures become government income in the form of indirect business taxes, by which we mean all business taxes except those on corporate net income. They include taxes on production and

[3] For some years the components do not add to exactly the totals shown. This is due partly to rounding, partly to statistical discrepancies in the original data, and partly to the elimination of minor items under the headings of "government subsidies minus current surplus of government enterprises" and "business transfer payments."

sales by business, taxes on business property, business license fees, and so on. All the remainder of GNP accrues to private business and individuals as gross money incomes before any taxes except indirect business taxes. The other types of taxes will be considered later.

Some expenditures for output accrue to business firms as receipts in the form of capital consumption allowances. This share is *not* net income, but it is a share of spendings for output that is left at the disposal of business firms to cover the estimated depreciation and obsolescence of their buildings and equipment. Another part accrues as compensation of employees in the form of wages, salaries, commissions, and so on. Still another part accrues as rental incomes of persons, and another in the form of interest income. All the remainder accrues as business profits—as incomes to the owners of both unincorporated and incorporated business firms.

The relationships brought out in this section will be emphasized in our later analysis. Spending for output, and only spending for output, creates money income for the nation as a whole. Hence an increase in the rate of expenditures for output creates correspondingly higher money incomes for the nation as a whole. And a decline of these expenditures reduces correspondingly the nation's money income.

We shall later have more to say about GNP. First, however, we shall look at two other concepts of output or income—net national product and national income.

6. Net National Product

Net national product during any stated period is simply GNP minus capital consumption during the period. We saw that gross private investment includes the amount of output required to replace capital used up in the process of production during the period as well as the amount used to make a net addition to the stock of capital. By deducting capital consumption during a period from gross private investment we get *net private investment*—the net increase in the nation's stock of privately owned capital goods.

Thus, from the point of view of the value of output, net national product is equal to the sum of personal consumption, government purchases of goods and services, and *net* private investment. From the point of view of income shares, net national product is equal to GNP minus capital consumption allowances. That is, it is the sum of indirect business taxes, compensation of employees, rental incomes of persons, net interest income, and business profits.

7. National Income

We shall here use national income in its technical rather than its general sense. In this sense it is the total earnings of labor and property that arise from the current production of goods and services by the nation's economy. Or, to state the same thing in other words, it measures the total costs of the factors of production used in turning out these goods and services. It is equal to the sum of the compensation of labor, rental incomes of persons, interest income, and business profits before any taxes except indirect business taxes.

We should also note that national income in this sense is equal to GNP minus capital consumption allowances and indirect business taxes. All the expenditures for output that are not claimed as capital consumption allowances and indirect business taxes become money income to the factors of production.

8. Disposable Private Income

A. Definition and Determination

In our earlier discussion of gross national product we dealt with the shares of expenditures for output that accrue to the various types of income receivers before any taxes except indirect business taxes. However, we shall want to analyze the *disposable incomes* of business and households—that is, the amount of money income remaining at their disposal after they have paid their taxes and have received certain transfer payments from the government. Private disposable income is important for our analysis because it is the amount of money income left at the disposal of the private sectors to be used for consumption and saving. We shall find that private disposable income in any period is equal GNP minus government tax collections but plus government transfer payments to the private sectors.

It is clear that government tax collections tend to decrease private disposable incomes. All types of taxes—indirect business taxes, taxes on corporate profits, and personal taxes—are subtractions from private money incomes. However, *government transfer payments* add to private money incomes. These are government payments for which the government currently receives no goods or services in return. They include such things as unemployment relief payments, benefits to the aged, veterans' pensions, interest payments, and subsidies to business. Thus we find that private disposable incomes during any period are

equal to GNP minus taxes and plus government transfer payments.
This is shown in Table 20. Column 2 shows the amount of GNP
taken by the government as taxes. Column 3 indicates the amounts returned to the private sectors as transfer payments. Column 4 shows
what might be called the government's net tax receipts—that is, its
total tax collections minus the amounts returned as transfer payments.
Column 5 indicates that private disposable incomes for any stated
period are indeed equal to GNP minus taxes and plus government
transfer payments.

TABLE 20.   GNP and Private Disposable Incomes[4]
(In billions of dollars)

Year	Col. 1 GNP	Col. 2 Government Tax Receipts	Col. 3 Government Transfer Payments	Col. 4 Government Tax Receipts minus Trans- fer Payments	Col. 5 Total Dispos- able Private Income (GNP minus Col. 4)
1929	$103.8	$11.3	$ 1.7	$ 9.6	$ 94.1
1933	55.8	9.3	2.6	6.7	47.8
1939	91.3	15.4	4.7	11.2	78.7
1944	213.7	51.8	6.6	45.2	164.5
1946	211.1	51.7	16.2	35.5	173.7
1948	259.0	59.8	15.0	44.8	216.8
1950	286.8	69.8	19.3	50.5	236.3
1951	329.8	86.8	16.8	70.0	259.8
1952	348.0	92.0	16.9	75.1	271.5

The private disposable income with which we are dealing here may
be called disposable gross income, for it includes the capital consumption allowances of business. To get disposable private incomes corresponding to net national product we need only deduct capital consumption allowances.

B. A DIGRESSION—INSTRUMENTS OF GOVERNMENT POLICY

It will be useful to digress for a moment to note that we have discovered three ways that the government can influence the behavior of
national income. (1) Government purchases of goods and services are
both a component of the effective demand for output and a contribution to private money incomes. (2) Government transfer payments

[4] The careful reader will note that for some years the components do not add to
exactly the totals shown. This is partly because of rounding, but largely because of
discrepancies in the original data. The same will be true of some of the tables that
follow.

are not directly a demand for output but they do contribute to private money incomes. (3) Taxes subtract from private money incomes.

The government may therefore exert an expansionary influence by increasing its purchases of goods and services, by increasing its transfer payments, or by decreasing its tax collections. It may exert a contracting influence by decreasing its purchases of goods and services, by decreasing its transfer payments, or by increasing its tax collections.

c. COMPONENTS OF PRIVATE DISPOSABLE INCOME

Let us now see how total disposable private income is divided between business firms and persons or households. It is clear that households do not receive all of the private disposable income; some remains at the disposal of business. Business retains control of capital con-

TABLE 21.   Private Disposable Income and Its Components
(In billions of dollars)

Year	Col. 1 Capital Consumption Allowances	Col. 2 Undistributed Corporate Profits	Col. 3 Total Disposable Business Income	Col. 4 Disposable Personal Income (Equals Col. 5 minus Col. 3)	Col. 5 Total Private Disposable Income
1929	$ 8.8	$ 2.8	$11.6	$ 82.5	$ 94.1
1933	7.2	−4.6	2.6	45.2	47.8
1939	8.1	0.4	8.5	70.2	78.7
1944	11.9	5.6	17.5	147.0	164.5
1946	12.2	2.6	14.8	158.9	173.7
1948	17.6	10.8	28.4	188.4	216.8
1950	21.6	7.8	29.4	206.9	236.3
1951	24.6	9.6	34.2	225.0	259.8
1952	27.0	9.5	36.5	235.0	271.5

sumption (depreciation) allowances, as shown in Column 1 of Table 21. Corporations also retain certain amounts of undistributed profits in some years. In years of very high profits these undistributed profits are likely to be large. In bad years corporations sometimes distribute dividends greater than their current profits; at such times undistributed profits are negative. The total of capital consumption allowances and undistributed corporate profits is shown in Column 3 under the heading of total disposable business income. This is the part of total private disposable income that does not flow to households or persons.

We may therefore arrive at the disposable income of households or persons in either of two ways. (1) We may arrive at it by subtracting

from total private disposable income the amounts left at the disposal
of business in the form of capital consumption allowances and undistributed corporate profits. (2) We may add up its components, as
is done in Table 22. Total personal income is the sum of the compensation for labor, profits of unincorporated business, personal rental incomes, personal interest incomes, dividends from corporations, and

TABLE 22.   Personal Income and Disposable Personal
Income, 1952
(In billions of dollars)

Compensation of labor (less social insurance deductions)	$184.6
Proprietors' and rental income	51.2
Dividends	9.1
Personal interest income	11.9
Transfer payments	12.9
Equals: Personal income	$269.7
Less: Personal taxes	34.6
Equals: Disposable personal income	$235.1

transfer payments received from government and business. Total personal income minus personal taxes leaves disposable personal income.
This is the amount left at the disposal of households for personal consumption and personal saving.

9. The Disposition of Private Disposable Incomes

A. CONSUMPTION AND SAVING

What do the private sectors do with the incomes remaining at their
disposal after their tax payments? Some part they spend for consumption. (See Column 2 of Table 23.) The remainder is private saving
(see Column 3). We shall emphasize that private saving during any
period is equal to total private disposable income during that period
minus consumption, and that the act of saving is the purely negative
one of failing to spend some part of disposable income for consumption.

Total gross private saving during any period is the sum of *gross
business saving* and *personal saving*. Gross business saving is the same
as the disposable gross income of business—capital consumption allowances and undistributed corporate profits. This part of private income is clearly not spent for consumption. Personal saving is simply

the part of disposable personal income that is not spent for consumption.

In the preceding paragraph we dealt with *gross* private saving, which included capital consumption allowances. If we wish to arrive at the disposable private income and *net* private saving that correspond to net national product we deduct capital consumption allowances from disposable private income as shown in Column 1, and from business gross savings as shown in Column 4. Thus net private saving during any period is the sum of undistributed corporate profits and personal saving.

B. CONSUMPTION, SAVING, AND THE LEVEL OF DISPOSABLE INCOMES

The recipients of disposable income are, of course, free to determine how much of their disposable income they will spend for consumption and how much they will save. How are these decisions influenced by

TABLE 23. Disposal of Private Disposable Income
(In billions of dollars)

Year	Col. 1 Private Disposable Income	Col. 2 Personal Consumption	Col. 3 Total Private Gross Saving (Col. 1 minus Col. 2)	Col. 4 Gross Business Saving (Capital Consumption Allowances plus Undistributed Corporate Profits)	Col. 5 Personal Saving (Col. 6 minus Col. 2)	Col. 6 Disposable Personal Income (Col. 1 minus Col. 3)
1929	$ 94.1	$ 78.8	$15.3	$11.6	$ 3.7	$ 82.5
1933	47.8	46.3	1.4	2.6	−1.2	45.2
1939	78.7	67.5	11.2	8.5	2.7	70.2
1944	164.5	111.6	52.9	17.5	35.4	147.0
1946	173.7	146.9	26.8	14.8	12.0	158.9
1948	216.8	177.9	38.9	28.4	10.5	188.4
1950	236.3	194.6	40.5	29.4	11.3	205.8
1951	259.8	208.1	51.7	34.2	16.9	225.0
1952	271.5	218.1	53.6	36.5	16.9	235.0

the size of the disposable incomes? How do consumption and saving respond when disposable incomes fall? When disposable incomes rise?

A comparison of the annual data in Table 23 cannot yield definitive conclusions that will hold in all circumstances but it is quite suggestive. It suggests that a fall of private disposable income is likely to be accompanied by declines in both consumption and saving, and that a rise of disposable income is likely to be accompanied by increases in both consumption and saving.

Business saving tends to be quite responsive to changes in income levels. (Compare Columns 1 and 4 in Table 23.) For example, when incomes fell between 1929 and 1933, business saving declined markedly, largely because corporations did not have profits to retain. But with the general rise of incomes thereafter, the rate of business saving rose. Generally speaking, personal consumption and personal saving both respond to changes in disposable personal incomes. For example, the decline of disposable personal incomes between 1929 and 1933 was accompanied by decreases in both personal consumption and personal saving. But as disposable personal incomes rose they were accompanied upward by both consumption and personal saving.

Our later analysis will make considerable use of this common-sense observation that a rise of disposable private income is likely to be accompanied by increases of both consumption and saving, and that a decline of this income is likely to be reflected in decreases of both consumption and saving.

c. SAVING AND THE CIRCULAR FLOW OF INCOME

Income creation and distribution are a circular flow process—a flow of spendings into the market for output, into the income shares of recipients, back into the market for output, into income shares again, and so on. Income can continue to flow at an even rate only if this circular flow remains unbroken. This raises important questions concerning the effect of saving on the circular flow process. Consumption spending clearly tends to create money income and to maintain the circular flow. But saving is the part of disposable private incomes that is not returned as spending for consumption. Taken by itself, saving tends to reduce the flow of spendings for output.

How can the part of income representing saving by the private sectors as a whole be returned to the market as spending for output? What are the offsets to saving? Since saving represents a failure of consumers to buy, we must look to the other purchasers of GNP— investors and the government—to make up the difference. Saving can be offset or returned to the market as spending for output in only two ways. (1) Private investment. For example, business may use its own savings, borrow savings, or issue shares of ownership in exchange for savings and buy new capital goods. Thus all private investment is an offset to saving. (2) Government deficit spending. The government can borrow savings and use them to cover a deficit—that is, an excess of its expenditures over its income in the form of tax receipts.[5] Thus a deficit involves the government's injecting more purchasing power into the circular flow than it withdraws from that flow by taxes. As an offset to saving or as a way of channeling savings back into the market as expenditures for output, government deficits are quite similar to private investment.

In summary, the only two offsets to saving are private investment and government deficits. These are the only ways that private savings can be channeled back into the market as expenditures for output.

10. Conclusions

The primary purpose of this chapter has been to present the principal concepts and measures of national income, the components of national income, and some of the quantitative relationships among the components. These may be summarized as follows:

A. MEASURES OF NATIONAL OUTPUT OR INCOME

1. Gross National Product

GNP as the value of output or as expenditures for output	GNP as the sum of gross income shares
a. Personal consumption	Indirect business taxes
b. Gross private investment	Capital consumption allowances
c. Government purchases of goods and services	Compensation of employees
	Rental incomes of persons
	Interest incomes of persons
	Profits of unincorporated business
	Corporate profits
Total =	Total

N.B. [5] A government surplus—an excess of government income over its expenditures—may be regarded as a negative deficit. This has the same effect as private saving because it involves the government's withdrawing purchasing power from the circular flow without returning a corresponding amount in the form of expenditure. To maintain the flow, private investment must then offset this surplus as well as private saving.

2. Net National Product = GNP minus capital consumption allowances.

NNP as the value of output	NNP as the sum of net income shares
Personal consumption	Indirect business taxes
Net private investment	Compensation of employees
Government purchases of goods and services	Rental incomes of persons
	Interest incomes of persons
	Profits of unincorporated business
	Corporate profits
Total _____ =	Total _____

3. National Income in the Technical Sense

National income as the value of output	National income as the sum of income shares
GNP minus capital consumption allowances and indirect business taxes	Compensation of employees
	Rental incomes of persons
	Interest incomes of persons
	Profits of unincorporated business
	Corporate profits
Total _____ =	Total _____

4. Total Disposable Private Income
   a. Total disposable gross private income = GNP minus all taxes but plus government transfer payments.
   b. Total disposable net private income = disposable gross private income minus capital consumption allowances.

5. Disposable Personal Income = total disposable gross private income minus capital consumption allowances and undistributed corporate profits. It may also be arrived at in the following way:

   Compensation of labor (less social security deductions)
   Rental incomes of persons
   Interest incomes of persons
   Profits of unincorporated business
   Dividends from corporations
   Transfer payments from government and business

   Total: Personal income _____
   Less: Personal taxes
   Equals: Disposable personal income _____

6. Private Saving

    a. Total private gross saving = total disposable gross private income minus consumption. Gross saving is the sum of capital consumption allowances, undistributed corporate profits, and personal saving.

    b. Total private net saving = gross saving minus capital consumption allowances. It is the sum of undistributed corporate profits and personal saving.

B. SOME IMPLICATIONS OF NATIONAL INCOME ACCOUNTING

Though our principal purpose has been to show the nature and composition of national income, we have also discovered several things that will be highly useful in our analysis of the determination of national income. For example, we found that national income for any period is equal to expenditures for output in the form of consumption, private investment, and government purchases of goods and services. The major task of our analysis, therefore, will be to explain the behavior of these components and their relationships to each other. This will lead us into a discussion of saving and its relationship to investment and the level of national income.

Our discussion has also implied some interrelationships among government, business, and household expenditures and receipts. Changes in any one of these will affect the receipts and expenditures of the other two. For example, changes in the rate of government purchases of goods and services represent changes in the government's effective demand for the output of the private sectors and in the government's contributions to private money incomes. By increasing or decreasing its transfer payments, it tends to increase or decrease disposable private incomes. And by increasing or decreasing its tax collections the government tends to decrease or increase disposable private incomes. In these ways the government's operations affect not only private money incomes but also the rates of private consumption, investment, and saving.

Business expenditures for investment also affect both the government and households. For instance, an increase in the rate of investment spendings creates more money income for those engaged in the capital goods industries. This increase of income will affect consumption, saving, and tax payments.

Household decisions as to the distribution of their incomes between consumption and saving affect both business and government. For example, if people decide to save more and consume less at each level of income they may lower the incomes of those in the consumer goods industries, lower national income, affect business investment decisions, and decrease government tax receipts.

These complex interrelationships among the various types of expenditures, incomes, and saving are largely responsible for the fact that national income analysis cannot be simple.

SUGGESTED READINGS

Ruggles, Richard, *An Introduction to National Income and Income Analysis,* McGraw-Hill, New York, 1949.

U.S. Department of Commerce, *National Income,* Washington, 1951.

QUESTIONS

1. The accountant's magic makes many things equal that you might not expect to be so.
   a. Explain how, by including I.O.U.'s, he can always make a person's or a nation's expenditures equal its receipts.
   b. Show that the secret of making any sort of double-entry sheet or balance sheet balance lies in taking the same total and dividing it up in two different ways.
   c. Show how confusion can result when conventional terms are applied to the accountant's categories so that expenditures become always equal to receipts even for the profligate, and the costs of the firm always equal its revenues, though it is losing money or earning large profits.
2. a. Describe the operation of an imaginary firm which uses absolutely no inventories.
   b. Do you know of any industry in which very little inventory is employed?
   c. If so, why is this?
   d. Does this help the efficiency of operation of that industry?
   e. How can a firm go about reducing its use of inventory?
3. "In 1929 GNP was below $104 billion; in 1953 it was above $350 billion. The people of the country were thus about 3½ times as well off in 1953 as they were a scant 24 years earlier." Comment.
4. An American who builds a factory in Ecuador is clearly investing there in a sense that corresponds to real investment in domestic operations.
   a. Is an American's acquisition of a French I.O.U. or of stock in a

South African gold mine analogous to an act of domestic investment from his point of view?

b. Is it from the nation's point of view?

5. In the chapter we have spoken alternatively of "the value of output" and "expenditures for output."

  a. Need these always be equal?

  b. What definitional convention must we be using in order to treat them as equal?

6. Can you think of some policy problems for which you would be most interested in the figures of:

  a. Gross national product?

  b. Real national income?

  c. Disposable national income?

7. a. Distinguish between government transfer payments and other types of government expenditure.

  b. Why do you think the economist is interested in this distinction?

8. The income-reducing influence of saving can be offset only by private investment or government deficit spending.

  a. The accountant, by means of his usual tricks, always makes savings exactly equal the sum of private investment plus the government deficit. How is he able to perform this feat?

  b. Does this accounting convention imply that saving can really never affect expenditure because it will always be counterbalanced by governmental or private investment demands?

CHAPTER 10

Determination of National Income: Basic Relationships

---

1. Nature of the Analysis

We shall now proceed to study the factors that determine the level of national income at any time. This is essential as a basis for our later discussion of economic stabilization policies. Before we can hope to understand what might be done to prevent or remedy depression and inflation we must discover how they come about. As a first step let us make a few remarks about the nature of our analysis.

A. THE INTERRELATEDNESS OF THE PARTS

National income determination has one aspect that makes exposition very difficult. It has many parts, all are interrelated, and none can be understood in isolation. They are like the parts of a clock; the function of no one of its wheels can really be explained without a thorough understanding of the operation of the rest of the mechanism. Such a situation is said to involve *mutual interdependence*. Ideally, each part of our exposition should come last after all other parts of the mechanism have been explained. Such an arrangement being obviously impossible, we have been forced to resort to a less satisfactory mode of organization.

Especially in the earlier part of our exposition we shall discuss things whose bearing on the rest is somewhat obscure. However, all will work out well in the end when the loose strands have been gathered together.

B. OVERSIMPLIFICATION OF REALITY

The apparent simplicity and neatness of the final outcome will not be entirely accidental. To some extent it will be the result of deliberate oversimplification and abstraction to which we are forced to resort in order to prevent things from getting out of hand.

In a sense this simplifying process is quite legitimate. Without it scientific research would be reduced to pure description. In our analytic work we seek primarily to set up a model—i.e., to describe an imaginary world—that is sufficiently complex and sufficiently similar to reality to permit us to make some legitimate inferences about the behavior of our environment, but which is at the same time simple enough for us to understand or manipulate with the analytic tools at our disposal. This is analogous to what the natural scientist does in setting up an experiment under artificial laboratory conditions which are arranged for analytic convenience.

We do pay a price for this simplification and abstraction. We must constantly be on the lookout lest we be misled into facile conclusions and mistaken policy measures in cases where the things we have omitted turn out to be crucial or where the conditions assumed in the model are significantly different from those of the real world.

2. Purpose of the Analysis

Our primary purpose here is to explain the determination of the level of net national income or product in real terms at any given time. Every part of this statement is worth emphasis. In the first place, we shall concentrate on net national income or product. We may think of this as being net national product as defined in the preceding chapter.

In the second place, we shall be interested in real income rather than money income. Values must of course be measured in money, but we shall assume that we have used an appropriate price index to correct for price changes. All our quantities—national income, saving, investment, consumption, and even the money supply—are assumed to be measured in dollars of constant purchasing power. This fact must constantly be borne in mind for we shall not often repeat it.

In the third place, we are interested in the determination of the level of income at a given time. In general, we shall not concern ourselves with the movement of income over periods of time. We shall certainly not be interested here in the long-run changes in national productive capacity resulting from such things as technological change, growth of the labor force, and larger capital supplies. These were discussed earlier. At this stage we shall deal with periods so short that we can assume that not only productive capacity but also economic customs and expectations remain practically unchanged.

Another feature of our analysis should be noted. At the beginning we shall concentrate largely on the production and use of income by the private sectors of the economy. Thus our analysis will deal mostly with private output, private consumption, private saving, and private investment. We exclude the government's activities at this point not because they are unimportant; later we shall emphasize their importance. We exclude them for two reasons: (1) to simplify our exposition in its earlier stages, and (2) to highlight the determinants of the behavior of income production and use by the private sectors. After we have analyzed this, we can superimpose the government's activities and discuss some of the things the government might do to offset fluctuations arising in the private sectors. However, this does not imply that government activities may not generate or accentuate fluctuations. To make our analysis formally correct we shall include government purchases of goods and services under investment, but in the earlier stages we shall have little to say about them.

An analysis of the level of real national income or output will throw light on the behavior of employment and prices. Clearly, in any given state of technology the volume of employment, measured in manhours, varies roughly with the level of real output. More output requires more labor, and less output less labor. As a very rough approximation we may assume that in the short run the amount of employment varies proportionally with the rate of real output.

An analysis of income and of the demand for it will also shed light on the process of inflation. As we saw earlier, price increases occur when the effective money demand for output rises faster than the quantity of goods and services made available for purchase. This is most likely to happen when effective demand continues to rise while output is approaching or has reached capacity levels.

3. Outline of the Analysis

Having disposed of the preliminaries, we now outline our analysis of national income determination.

A. THE GOODS MARKET AND THE MONEY MARKET

Essentially, ours will be a supply and demand analysis. We shall argue that in a free-enterprise system the level of real output depends on demand and supply. In fact, we shall deal with demand and supply in two different but closely interrelated types of markets: the goods market and the money market.

By the goods market we mean the market for the output of all goods and services, i.e., the market for all the items that constitute the net national product. The state of demand and supply for all these goods and services is of great significance for a nation's welfare. For example, overproduction can be viewed as an excess of supply over demand on the goods market, and inflationary pressure may be regarded as the reverse situation.

The money market is somewhat more difficult to define, as we shall see later, but the term will be used here to indicate the interactions and effects of the supply of money and the demand for money.

B. Equating the Goods Supply and Demand: The Role of Income

Real national income may be considered as the supply of goods and services. We may expect that if the quantity of goods and services demanded falls short of the supply, there will be a downward pressure on national income, for businessmen will not long be willing or able to produce more goods than they can market, and so they will tend to reduce production (national income). In this way the supply of goods will drop toward the demand. Similarly, if the quantity of goods and services demanded exceeds the quantity supplied we may expect an upward pressure on national income, which tends to move the supply of goods toward the quantity demanded. This suggests that national income tends to move toward a level at which goods supply and demand are equal.

When we have gone into the analysis in greater detail we shall conclude that national income at any given time will tend toward the level at which *both* of the following conditions are met simultaneously:

  1. The demand for goods = the supply of goods, and
  2. The demand for money = the supply of money.

C. The Demand for Goods and Services

Whether the quantity of goods and services demanded falls short of, exceeds, or is equal to the quantity of national income supplied is crucial for our analysis. It is convenient to classify the demand for goods and services into three categories—the public's demand for consumer goods, businessmen's demand for goods to be used in their business operations (investment goods), and the government's demand for goods and services. Again for the moment ignoring the government, we shall come to the following conclusions: (1) The demand for consumption goods is dependent on the level of national income, for the higher the level of income the greater will be the purchasing power in the hands of the public. (2) Investment demand of businessmen will be determined by profit prospects and by the interest rate, for the interest rate can be an important cost of investing. This is particularly easy to see when the investment is financed by borrowing. For example, if a businessman is considering borrowing to invest in a new factory, the higher the interest rate the more expensive will this investment be to him. (3) The interest rate is affected by the supply of and demand for money (the money market), though it is also affected by the goods market. This is the way the money market enters the analysis.

These are the basic relationships we shall employ in our analysis of the determination of national income. Let us now examine these in greater detail. We begin with a discussion of supply and demand in the goods market.

4. The Supply of and Demand for Goods

A. GOODS SUPPLY

We shall use the term "supply" in its schedule sense to indicate the amounts of real output or income that business would produce per unit of time at the various levels of demand. Within any given level of capacity and with a given state of technology, business will produce larger amounts of output or income at higher levels of demand and smaller amounts at lower levels of demand.

It will be convenient to divide the supply of income or output into two parts—consumption and saving. Saving is thus defined in accord with ordinary usage as the difference between the amount of income received and the amount of that income used by consumers for their own purposes. It consists of the goods which are produced but not consumed. For later use, this may be written as:

National income (output) = consumption plus saving.

B. THE DEMAND FOR GOODS

The total demand for output may also be divided into two classes— consumption demand and investment demand. Thus:

Demand for output = consumption demand + investment demand. Investment demand is the demand for output to be used in making net additions to the stock of producer goods, or to be used by the government.

It is convenient to divide things up in this way because these two types of demand tend to be conditioned by different influences. The demand for producer goods is determined primarily by considerations of profitability, whereas the demand for consumer goods depends on the purchasers' tastes and desires and on the purchasing power which happens to be in their hands.

It is not always possible to distinguish an investment (or capital) good from a consumer good simply by looking at it. A blast furnace is usually an example of the former, and an ice cream soda of the latter. Coal on the other hand can be either, as can a piece of cloth or some flour. Even such things as shoes, which are clearly not raw materials, can and do serve as investment goods, for they are bought by businessmen for inventory purposes. An item held in inventory is just as much a producer good as a drill press is, for the lack of either may equally well cause a business operation to come to a standstill.

In common parlance the word "investment" is also used to mean a quite different thing—the purchase of a stock or bond. In this volume we shall never mean this use when we speak of an investment. The confusion that can arise from the ambiguous use of this term is well illustrated in the effect of a rise in the rate of interest. Since interest is the return for bondholding, a rise in its rate can encourage the demand for bonds, i.e., encourage the demand for "investment" in the sense in which we are *not* using the term. On the other hand, since investment in our sense—the purchase of producer goods—is often financed by borrowing, a rise in the rate of interest makes the operation more expensive and hence may be expected to discourage it.

Note finally that we have lumped government expenditures for output under investment because this classification will simplify our exposition somewhat. This is not, however, perfectly in accord with general usage. Nor is it meant to imply that all government expenditures consist of the purchase of producer goods or even that they are all useful.

We shall now analyze consumption, saving, and investment, the components of the supply of and demand for goods.

5. Consumption and Saving

The level of consumption demand obviously depends on many things, among the most important of which is the level of national income. Given the level of income, the rate of consumption depends somewhat on the distribution of income, social attitudes toward consumption and saving, and expectations as to future prices and incomes, among many other things.

We shall confine our analysis to a period so short that these factors may be considered constant. Then the following proposition, whose validity seems to be attested by experience, is plausible: The higher the level of the public's incomes, the higher will be both consumption and saving; the lower the level of incomes, the lower will be both consumption and saving. That is, each increase of income will go partly into higher consumption and partly into higher saving. And each decrease of income will be reflected partly in lower consumption and partly in lower saving.

This common-sense idea does not commit us to very much. Yet it is all the information about saving and consumption that we shall use in our analysis.

It is sometimes suggested that the richer we are, the greater the *proportion* of our incomes we will save. But this is *not* relevant to what we have said, though the two ideas are often confused. We require only that the total amount saved and the total amount spent for consumption both rise when income rises, even if one of them rises only by one dollar when income rises by a million.

This proposition is summarized in the first of the assumptions to which we shall refer throughout our analysis:

Assumption 1. Any increase in national income will go partly into saving, partly into consumption.

Note that we attempt no numerical estimate for this relationship. We cannot say, even given the circumstances, how much a specified increase in real net national income will increase saving. For it to be possible for us to determine this (and it never may be), statistical techniques must become much more powerful than they are today. All our assumptions will be of this general nature, indicating direction rather than magnitude of changes, stating that something will go up or down but never saying much about the amounts involved. As may be imagined, this makes specific prediction with the aid of our analysis quite impossible. Nevertheless, and perhaps surprisingly, it will be found that with such little information we can construct a fairly powerful apparatus for the examination of important policy questions.

6. Investment Demand

As already noted, investment demand is used here to include both government purchases of goods and services and private investment. The relevance of government demand for output should be apparent, so we shall not discuss it further at this point.

Private investment demand is the demand for output to be used in making net additions to the stock of privately owned producer goods. It includes all private demands for new construction, new durable producer goods, and net changes in business inventories. We shall assume that the buyers of this output are guided by the profit motive.[1]

When a businessman faces a decision regarding any investment project, his question is essentially this: "Will this addition to my stock of capital goods increase my net profits, after I have paid interest on the money used to finance it? Will the annual addition to my net profits, measured as a percentage of the cost of the investment project, be at least as great as the interest cost on the money required to pay for the project?" Presumably he will undertake the project if its profits are expected to exceed its interest costs, but will not undertake it if interest costs exceed the expected profits.

We may conclude, then, that private investment demand depends on two classes of factors: (1) the expected profitability of investment at the time of investment, and (2) interest rates. Both are measured in percentage per year. Expected profits are annual profits as a percentage of the original cost of the investment goods. Interest rates are annual interest costs as a percentage of the principal amount of money required to pay for the investment goods.

A. EXPECTED PROFITS AND INVESTMENT

It is expected profits rather than the profits actually realized that are relevant in investment decisions. Investment yields its total returns only over a future period of time, and the amount of profits that will actually be realized cannot usually be forecast with accuracy. This is even true of investment in inventory. The businessman cannot forecast

---

[1] We also subsume net foreign investment under private investment and assume that it too is determined by the profit motive. However, we shall not discuss it further until we begin our study of international economic relationships.

accurately the prices at which he will be able to sell the goods, how long it will take him to sell them, or what their selling and storage costs will be. It is even more true of new construction and durable producer goods which will yield their full returns only over a very long period.

Much of the fluctuations of private investment demand emanates from changes in the expected profitability of investment. At some times expectations improve greatly and businessmen see many more investment opportunities that they expect to yield high rates of profit. This will raise private investment demand if it is not choked off by a sufficient rise of interest rates. At other times, expectations deteriorate and businessmen see fewer opportunities that they expect to yield high rates of profit. This will lower private investment demand if it is not offset by a sufficient decline of interest rates.

Later we shall have more to say about changes in private investment demand that are initiated by changes in the expected profitability of investment. At this point we are interested in explaining private investment demand during a period so short that the state of expectations regarding the profitability of investment may be considered to remain constant. However, it is important to emphasize that changes in profit expectations, though ignored for the moment, are a most important influence on the level of investment, and that their omission can never be wholly legitimate.

B. THE RATE OF INTEREST AND INVESTMENT

Even if he uses his own money to finance it, an investment costs the businessman interest. By tying up his funds in a producer good he gives up the interest earnings he could have obtained by lending out his money. The higher the interest rate, the more he gives up by buying a producer good. More obvious is the interest cost of an investment financed by borrowing. An increase in the rate of interest must increase investment costs. It is therefore plausible that the higher the rate of interest, the less will be the willingness of the public to invest.

There will always be projects which a businessman considers on the border of profitability, and any decrease in the cost of obtaining funds should therefore induce someone to change his mind and try to borrow funds for some borderline investment. A rise in the interest rate might for the same reason be expected to reduce investment. At least this is plausible for long-term investments like office buildings and hydroelectric plants in which money will be tied up for considerable periods. In such investments interest costs are a very high proportion of their total costs. For example, suppose $1 million is invested in an office building which is sold after ten years, the proceeds being used to pay off the loan with which the construction was financed. Even neglecting compounding, a rise in interest rates of 0.5 of 1 percent can raise interest costs over the ten years by $50,000, or 5 percent of the original investment. This surely will carry some weight with a man who is hesitating in deciding on an investment.

If we remember that we are assuming the expected profitability of investment to remain constant, we may sum this up by another assumption which will be useful in our analysis:

Assumption 2. Investment demand will tend to be reduced by a rise in the interest rate, and stimulated by a fall in the interest rate.

In a few moments we shall consider the money market and the factors that determine the height of the interest rate. First, however, we must delve further into the role of the goods market in determining the level of income.

7. Equating Supply and Demand on the Goods Market

A. SAVINGS, INVESTMENT, AND GOODS SUPPLY AND DEMAND

Earlier we adopted the classifications which we summarized as:
1. Supply of goods   = consumption + saving.
2. Demand for goods = consumption (demand) + investment demand.

For practical purposes we can take consumption to be equal to consumption demand. During wartime shortages consumers may find that they cannot buy as much as they want to; dealers' stocks of cars, nylon stockings, or sugar may run out before the demand for them (at controlled prices) is satisfied. A consumer may also be forced to buy furniture he does not want in order to get an apartment. But consumers usually find that they can buy as much as they care to at current prices and they are almost never forced to buy more than they want of an item.

We can draw the following conclusions:
1. The demand for and supply of goods will be equal when, and only when, the rate of saving is equal to the rate of investment demand.
2. If saving exceeds investment demand, the supply of goods will exceed the demand.
3. When investment demand exceeds saving, the demand for goods will exceed the supply.

This can perhaps be better visualized in the following way: Saving constitutes a decision on the part of the people not to employ a portion of production for their personal use. If some of these same people in their role as investors do not offer to buy all that residue, there will be some goods for which there is no demand. If investors seek to buy more than the residue (savings), demand will exceed supply. Only if investors seek to buy neither more nor less than the residue will the goods market be exactly in adjustment.

B. INCOME AND GOODS SUPPLY AND DEMAND

The reader will recall that one of the goals of our analysis is to show that income will be driven toward a level at which the supply of and the demand for goods are equal. He may well ask why this should be so. What will influence income not to go higher or lower than this?

We shall deal only with the case in which at the current level of income the supply of goods exceeds the demand (saving is greater than investment demand), leaving the reader to show that the argument holds in the reverse situation. Since with supply greater than demand sellers will find that there is not an adequate demand for all their goods, they may be expected, ultimately, to reduce production. So long as they remain optimistic and stick to the old output levels, they will find themselves stuck with goods they cannot sell at going prices (undesired additions to their inventory), and sooner or later they will be forced to cut back on production.

Assumption 1 tells us that this reduction in income will reduce saving. Thus saving will tend to fall toward investment demand, and goods demand and supply will move toward equality.

We shall see later that in these circumstances the rate of interest will also help by causing investment to increase. However, further discussion of this point must wait until we have analyzed the determination of the interest rate.

Until then we shall have explained only part of:

Assumption 3. National income and the rate of interest will both tend to be at levels at which the supply of and demand for goods are equal, i.e., at which saving equals investment demand.

8. The Money Market

We noted earlier that national income at any time will tend to be at the level at which the demand for goods is equal to the supply of goods and the demand for money is equal to the supply of money. We shall now analyze the supply of and demand for money and their relationship to demand in the goods market. We shall be especially concerned with their influence on the rate of interest, and with their effects, through the rate of interest, on investment demand and national income.

A. THE SUPPLY OF MONEY

We shall have much to say later about the money supply, the processes by which it can be increased and decreased, and the methods the government may use to regulate it. Here it is enough to note that the money supply is made up of the outstanding supply of coins, paper money, and checking deposits, and that it is controlled largely by the government and the banks.[2]

It should be remembered, however, that here we are measuring the money supply, as well as all our other quantities, in dollars of constant purchasing power. Thus a rise of prices will reduce the money supply as measured in dollars of constant purchasing power, and a fall of prices will have the reverse effect.

B. THE DEMAND FOR MONEY

By the demand for money we mean simply the amounts of money that the members of the community, including both persons and business firms, demand to hold at any given time.

The demand for money obviously depends on a great many things. For example, the rich in many underdeveloped countries elect to hold a large part of their assets in the form of gold or silver money, whereas Americans are much more willing to part with money and hold stocks, bonds, and other earning assets.

The demand also depends to a considerable extent on business practices relative to the frequency of payments. In general, the less frequently payments are made, the more money will people demand to hold relative to their expenditures. For example, if it were suddenly to become standard practice to pay wages twice a year rather than every week, the demand for money would be increased considerably. An expenditure of $100 a week corresponds to an expenditure of $2600 in six months. If a man starts out with $100 at the beginning

---

[2] The student may not be accustomed to thinking of checking deposits as money. But they clearly serve the same purposes as dollar bills do. As a matter of fact, by far the greater proportion of payments in this country are made by check.

of each week and spends it gradually until it is all gone at the end of the week, his average holding of money is $50. But if he acquires the full $2600 at the beginning of a six-month period and spends it gradually until it is all gone at the end of the period, his average holding of money has increased to $1300 even though his weekly income and expenditures remain unchanged. Thus the less frequent are income receipts, the greater tends to be the demand for money even though income is constant.

The demand for money also depends to a considerable extent on people's expectations. If they expect that business conditions are going to be poor and defaults on debts common, moneylenders may prefer to hold money themselves rather than lend it out. But if they are more optimistic about the future, they may be willing to reduce their own money holdings by bond buying and other forms of lending.

It will be well to remember that the demand for money may be increased or decreased markedly by changes in customs and expectations (among other things), thereby affecting the behavior of national income. Here, however, we are dealing with a period so short that we may consider customs and expectations to be constant. We may therefore state that the demand for money depends on the level of national income and the height of interest rates.

c. Income and the Demand for Money

With any given set of customs and expectations, the demand for money tends to rise as national income rises and to fall as national income falls. As business firms undertake higher rates of production, have larger payrolls, buy more materials, and have higher gross incomes, they are likely to find it convenient to hold larger money balances. The same is true of households; with higher incomes and higher expenditures they are likely to hold more money.

We can summarize this general idea in another assumption that will be useful for our analysis:

Assumption 4. The demand for money will increase with the income of the community.

d. Interest Rates and Money Demand

The demand for money also depends on the height of interest rates. Interest rates may be considered as the cost of holding money. This is quite clear in the case of a person who is holding money that he has borrowed; he may use his money to repay the debt, thereby escaping interest costs. It is equally true of someone holding his own money, for he is thereby giving up an opportunity to lend out the money and earn interest.

It is therefore quite plausible that some individuals and business firms will demand less money to hold at higher interest rates than at lower interest rates. At higher interest rates some borrowers will borrow less money to hold, and some owners of money will decide to part with some of it in exchange for earning assets. At lower interest rates the reverse will occur; some borrowers will elect to hold more money and some owners of money will elect to hold more of it because the interest reward for holding earning assets is lower.

It is true that many people neither know nor care much about changes in interest rates. It does not pay people whose money holdings are small to undergo the trouble of lending out their funds, especially since any interest earnings may be wiped out by the cost of negotiating to lend the money. However, for large money holders and lenders, the wealthy, big speculators, and large firms, these calculations are well worth their while.

We may therefore conclude that:

Assumption 5. The public's demand for money varies inversely with the rate of interest.

Putting together Assumptions 4 and 5 we find that the demand for money tends to vary directly with the level of the community's income and inversely with the rate of interest. We have emphasized its dependence not on just one factor but on two. It follows, therefore, that any given demand for money may result from various combinations of national income and interest rate levels. For example, the demand for money may be equal to the existing supply of money with national income at a high level and interest rates at a high level or with national income at a low level and interest rates at a low level. This point will be clarified in the next section.

E. ADJUSTMENT OF THE DEMAND FOR MONEY TO A FIXED SUPPLY OF MONEY

We stated earlier that for national income to be at an equilibrium level the demand for money must be equal to the supply of money. Let us now see how this adjustment comes about, on the premise that the government and the banks have fixed the total supply of money at a given level.

Suppose now that the demand for money is less than the available supply. This amounts to saying that the levels of national income and interest rates are such that some members of the community are actually holding more money than they want under the circumstances. Those who are holding the excess money try to get rid of it by increasing their expenditures for goods, by repaying some loans, or by lending more. But the public as a whole cannot get rid of its cash in this way. What one now spends or lends, another must receive.

Since the quantity of money supplied will not accommodate itself, the quantity of money demanded must be adjusted to the quantity of money available. This is just what the changes in national income and interest rates resulting from the public's attempts to get rid of its excess money will accomplish.

1. As people try to get rid of their excess money by spending more for goods, this obviously tends to raise the level of national income, which in itself makes people want to hold more money (Assumption 4).

2. Some people will try to get rid of their excess money by repaying loans or by offering more loans to others. Business and other borrowers may use some of their excess money to repay loans, in effect reducing their demand for loans and tending to lower interest rates. Those who try to get rid of money by offering more for loans also tend to lower interest rates. The tendency toward lower interest rates has a double effect. In the first place, lower interest rates stimulate investment demand and raise the level of national income, and hence the demand for money (Assumption 4). In the second place, the very fall of interest rates tends to increase the demand for money (Assumption 5).

This adjustment will continue so long as the demand for money is less than the available supply of money. It will come to an end only when the levels of national income and interest rates have been adjusted in such a way that the public's demand for money is as great as the available money supply.

Adjustment in the reverse situation in which the demand for money exceeds the available supply takes place in exactly the same way. To replenish their money supplies the public will try to: (1) Increase borrowing and decrease lending, which will raise the interest rate and so reduce the excess demand for money. (2) Reduce their expenditures. This will reduce national income and thereby cut down the excess demand for money. In addition, (3) the rise in interest rate will also deter investment and so reduce income. This will further reduce the excess demand for money.

We may sum up our findings in:

Assumption 6. The rate of interest and the level of national income will tend to be at the level at which the demand for money is equal to the supply of money.

9. Interest and Goods Market Equilibrium

In Assumption 3 we asserted without explanation that the rate of interest will tend to a level where the supply of and the demand for goods are equal. It is now easy to show why this is so.

Again we consider only the case in which goods supply is greater than demand. As we saw, this will force producers to cut their outputs, and so reduce national income.

But the fall in income will in turn reduce the demand for money (Assumption 4). This will tend to lower interest rates as the public seeks to lend its excess money. Thus the excess goods supply will make for lower interest rates. This verifies our assertion, for it shows that unless goods supply and demand are equal, the interest rate will be forced to change. Only when they are equal is no further movement in the interest rate necessary.

We can carry this result further. The lower interest rates will stimulate investment (Assumption 2), and the reduction in income will reduce saving. Together they will make saving and investment move closer together—that is, they will serve to equate goods demand and supply.

10. Summary of the Analysis

After a somewhat long and difficult journey we have now reached a point where we can stop and look back to see where we have been and what we have accomplished.

It will be remembered that our primary objective is to explain the determination of the level of real national income at any time, though we also want to shed light on the level of employment and prices. It is important to keep in mind that we are here trying to explain the level of income at a given time rather than its movements through time. This permits us to assume as constant several things that change through time—such things as total productive capacity, technology, customs, and expectations.

To accomplish our objective we decided to use a supply and demand analysis. We stated that the level of national income is determined by the supply of goods, the demand for goods, the supply of money, and the demand for money.

We quickly found, however, that two of our aggregates—the supply of goods and the demand for goods—could be broken down into smaller classes. We discovered the following relations:
1. Supply of goods   = consumption + saving.
2. Demand for goods = consumption (demand) + investment demand.
Consumption and saving we found to be influenced by the level of national income, while investment demand is influenced by the rate of interest. Thus we can say that the level of national income is determined by the following six classes of factors:
    1. Consumption demand.
    2. Saving.
    3. Investment demand.
    4. Supply of money.
    5. Demand for money.
    6. Rate of interest.
We then proceeded to analyze these factors and their interrelationships. Let us review some of our principal findings.

A. CONSUMPTION AND SAVING

The proportion in which a nation will divide any given amount of income between consumption and saving obviously depends on many things, such as the distribution of income, attitudes toward consumption and saving, expectations as to future prices and incomes, and so on. But by confining our attention to such a short period that these things may be considered constant, we were able to make Assumption 1: Any increase in national income will go partly into saving, partly into consumption.

B. INVESTMENT DEMAND

Investment demand is made up of two parts: government demand for output and private investment. We assume the level of government demand to be given and constant.

Private investment depends on the expected profitability of investment and interest rates. Expectations as to the profitability of investment fluctuate over time and bring about changes in investment demand. But by dealing with a period so short that we could assume expectations to be constant, we were able to make Assumption 2: Investment demand will tend to be reduced by a rise in the interest rate, and stimulated by a fall in the interest rate.

To explain the behavior of interest rates we turn to the supply of and demand for money.

c. The Supply of Money and Demand for Money

The supply of money is simply the total stock of coins, paper money, and checking deposits. We assume it to be fixed by the government and the banks.

The demand for money also depends on many things, such as social customs, the frequency of income receipts and expenditures, expectations as to future incomes and prices, and so on. But by again employing our device of dealing with a period so short that we could consider these things constant, we were able to make two more assumptions: Assumption 4: The demand for money will increase with the income of the community. Assumption 5: The public's demand for money varies inversely with the rate of interest.

d. The System as a Whole

We have now considered all six of the factors that determine the level of national income—consumption demand, saving, investment demand, supply of money, demand for money, and the interest rate. The level of national income is not determined by any one of these factors alone; it is determined by all of them together and by their interactions on each other. The interdependence and interactions of these factors are to be emphasized.

Let us now return to our earlier statement concerning the equilibrium level of national income. We said that national income will be determined at the level at which *both* of the following conditions are met simultaneously: (1) the demand for goods = the supply of goods, and (2) the demand for money = the supply of money. Let us now see why no other level of national income would be maintained.

We found that we could restate the first condition as follows:

Consumption + investment demand = consumption + saving.

By subtracting consumption from both sides, we get the equation:

Investment demand = saving.

That is, the only level from which national income will not tend to change is that at which investment demand is just equal to the supply of goods represented by saving. If income were higher than this, the supply of saving would exceed investment demand. Some part of output would remain unsold and producers would reduce their output. If income were lower than this, the supply of saving would be less than investment demand, and the excess demand would induce producers to increase their output. These changes in income will also affect the demand for money, and through it the interest rate. These results were summarized in Assumption 3: National income and the rate of interest will both tend to be at levels at which the supply of and demand for goods are equal, i.e., at which saving equals investment demand.

At the same time, the second condition must be met. National income can be at an equilibrium level only if the demand for money is equal to the supply of money. Suppose, for example, that the demand for money is less than the available supply. In their attempts to get rid of their excess money holdings, the members of the community will lower interest rates, stimulate investment demand, and raise the level of national income.

Suppose, on the other hand, that the demand for money is greater than the available supply. In their efforts to build their money balances up to the desired level by borrowing, decreasing loans, and reducing expenditures for goods, the members of the community will increase interest rates, reduce investment demand, and lower the level of national income. Thus we come back to our conclusion that national income can be at an equilibrium level only when the demand for money is equal to the supply of money, and when investment demand is equal to saving. As stated in Assumption 6: The rate of interest and the level of national income will tend to be at the level at which the demand for money is equal to the supply of money.

11. Comment: A Vicious Circle?

It may appear that parts of our analysis involve circular reasoning, and in a sense they do. For example, we stated that the level of national income depends on consumption, saving, investment demand, the supply of money, and the demand for money. But we found that consumption, saving, and the demand for money depend in part on the level of national income. Moreover, most of these factors are at least partially dependent on each other.

Now this is undoubtedly arguing in a circle, but it is not a vicious circle. A moment's thought will indicate that it is inherent in the nature of the problem. In fact, it is precisely what we meant when we said earlier that the system involves mutual interdependence. The clock analogy is again appropriate. The movement of every part of the clock is dependent on that of every other part. Similarly (using a famous illustration from economic literature) the position of each of a bunch of balls piled in a bowl will depend on that of every other ball, and the removal or movement of any one of them will cause them all to shift.

This sort of mutual interdependence of the various parts of a system is, therefore, in reality a common phenomenon. The mathematician knows how to deal with it analytically. That is what the solution of a system of simultaneous equations amounts to. For example, the two equations:

$$y = 6 - 2x$$

and

$$x = 5 - y$$

may, if one wishes, respectively be taken to indicate a dependence of y on x and a dependence of x on y. Yet together they yield the perfectly determinate result $x = 1$ and $y = 4$, obtained by a simple computation which the reader may remember.

In the next chapter we shall seek to analyze further this situation of mutual interdependence, using what may appear to be nonmathematical methods. But actually the essence of the trick will always be the same—the solution of a system of simultaneous equations.

SUGGESTED READINGS

Gordon, Robert A., *Business Fluctuations,* Harper, New York, 1952.

Hansen, Alvin, *Business Cycles and National Income,* Norton, New York, 1951.

Weintraub, Sidney, *Income and Employment Analysis,* Pitman, New York, 1951.

QUESTIONS

1. a. How does one go about measuring the money supply in dollars of constant purchasing power?
   b. What happens to the supply of money measured in this way if the number of dollar bills remains unchanged but all prices double?
   c. What is the significance of this way of measuring the quantity of money for Assumptions 4 and 5?
2. a. Can you think of cases in which an individual will increase his consumption by more than a rise in his income?

    b. Can you think of cases where an individual will increase his saving by more than a rise in his income?

    c. Why would you consider these cases less likely for the community as a whole?

    d. Give a numerical example in which saving increases as income increases but the proportion saved decreases.

3. Many businessmen have stated in interviews that the rate of interest does not influence their investment decisions.

    a. Show why this is plausible in the case of short-term investments.

    b. Show why the results of these interviews need not be conclusive.

    c. Do you know your own conscious and unconscious motivations in making any decisions?

    d. Show that the statistics might be even less illuminating, and explain why they would often show that the level of investment went up when the rate of interest went up. (Hint: What is likely to happen in prosperity? In depression?)

    e. Why is this statistical observation irrelevant for Assumption 2?

4. With goods demand greater than supply, show:

    a. That national income will tend to rise.

    b. That the rate of interest will tend to rise.

    c. That the rise in income will increase saving.

    d. That the rise in interest rate will decrease investment.

    e. That all this will move goods supply and demand toward equality.

    f. That this is the argument behind Assumption 3.

5. a. Construct a numerical example showing that the practice of paying bills at the end of the month rather than as purchases are made can decrease the demand for money.

    b. Show how more careful planning ahead of purchases can reduce the demand for money.

    c. Can you think of reasons why firm A, which does ten times as much business as B, might need less than ten times as much money on hand?

6. a. Show how the supply of loans may be influenced by changes in interest rates.

    b. Show that bond buying is a form of lending.

    c. Show that calling in loans or selling bonds is equivalent to demanding money.

    d. Show therefore that bond buyers' and potential bond buyers' demands for money are affected by the rate of interest.

    e. A rise in the rate of interest can cause a serious loss to people who bought bonds before the interest rise occurred because the price of their bonds must consequently fall. Can you explain this?

   f. Why, then, might the fact that interest rates are abnormally low reduce the demand for bonds?

   g. How do all these points relate to Assumption 5?

7. Show that when the demand for money is greater than the available supply:

   a. The rate of interest will rise.

   b. The level of income will fall.

   c. The demand for money will fall.

   d. Show that all this implies Assumption 6.

   e. Why are there fewer parts to this question than to Question 4?

8. a. Can you give an example of a "vicious circle" argument?

   b. How does it differ from the circularity of our analysis?

CHAPTER 11

Determination of the National Income Level

The purpose of this chapter is to tie together all the elements that have just been discussed. We shall show how all these elements together serve to determine the level of national income, and incidentally the values of our other variables—consumption, investment, saving, and the rate of interest. The full significance of our results will only become apparent in the next chapter.

Though it may at first seem difficult and pedantic, we shall translate the discussion into graphic terms. This is necessitated by the mutual interdependence of the variables in our model. The reader who has not previously worked with this technique will find it explained in the appendix to this chapter.

1. Graphic Description of the Goods Market

We begin with a graphic review of our analysis of the goods market. We shall consider first the investment-interest relationship, because its representation is a bit simpler than that for the relationship of saving and consumption to income. This entire discussion will be in terms of the six assumptions of the preceding chapter.

A. THE DEMAND FOR INVESTMENT

Assumption 2 summarizes the investment-interest relationship. This assumption can be translated into the graph shown in Fig. 5, in which the line LL' indicates how the *demand for investment* varies with the rate of interest. Thus if the rate of interest falls, say from Oi to Oi', the quantity of investment demanded will rise from *OI* to *OI'*, and vice versa. This graph says exactly what Assumption 2 does—that a fall in interest rate will stimulate investment and a rise will deter it. Except for the negative slope—the fact that it slants downward toward the right—the details of the shape of the curve are of no particular significance. Having no quantitative information, we do not know whether it falls sharply or is flat, whether it is smooth or bumpy, high or low. Its downward slope is all that concerns us. The same sort of warning must be applied to all our graphs.[1]

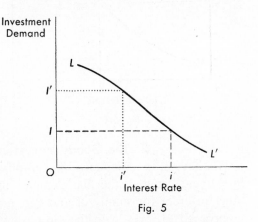

Fig. 5

B. CONSUMPTION AND SAVING

We may interpret Assumption 1, our basic result on saving and consumption, in the same way. Line *MM'* in Fig. 6A shows the influence of the level of income upon consumption demand. In accord with Assumption 1 it shows consumption demand rising as national income does.

Similarly, line *NN'* in Fig. 6B shows saving rising with the level of income. Here, however, a complication arises. We cannot simply draw this second diagram in an arbitrary manner after consumption has been graphed. By definition, saving is the residue from income after consumption. Since Fig. 6A shows the level of consumption corresponding to every level of national income, we can derive Fig. 6B from it by a mechanical procedure. How to do this is shown in the footnote for anyone interested in the details.[2]

---

[1] We ordinarily begin to draw the curves representing our relationships well away from the axes. For example, point *L* on the investment curve does not lie on the vertical axis because, for lack of experience, we have no good idea what would happen to investment if the interest rate were zero. For the same reason we cannot make realistic guesses at what would happen to saving and consumption levels at zero national income, so only limited segments of these curves are shown.

[2] In Fig. 6A consider any level of national income *OY*, and let *OC* be the desired consumption at this level of income. With a ruler measure off the length of *OY* and *OC*. Subtract the length of *OC* from that of *OY;* let us call the remainder *L*.

Now measure off *OY* along the horizontal axis of Fig. 6B. Having done this, draw the vertical dotted line *YA* of length *L* directly above *Y*. *A* is the point on the savings curve corresponding to income *OY*. By drawing in a series of points like this

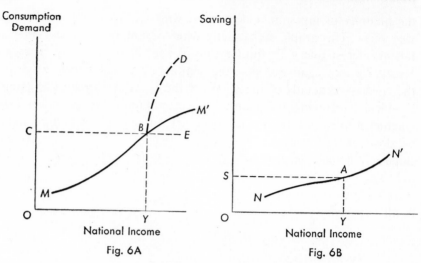

Fig. 6A

Fig. 6B

2. The Goods Market in Adjustment

We have now completed the graphic translation of savings and investment demand, the two elements that must be equated to each other in order for supply of and demand for goods to be equal. Let us proceed to investigate the circumstances which can yield supply-demand and equality on the goods market.

Since savings and investment are influenced by the rate of interest and the level of income, our object will be to find the combinations of income and interest rate that are compatible with equality of supply and demand on the goods market, that is, with equality of saving and investment.

A. Points of Goods Market Adjustment

Fig. 7 really consists of three diagrams. Figs. 7A and 7B are reproductions of Figs. 5 and 6B. Fig. 7A shows the relation between

for various levels of income and joining them, we can construct the entire savings curve NN′ from the consumption curve.

The reasoning behind the construction is simple enough. The length OY represents income, and the length OC is consumption. Saving being the difference between income and consumption, its level at income OY must be given by length L, the difference between the two other lengths.

We also note that Assumption 1 precludes either line MM′ or NN′ rising at an angle greater than or equal to 45 degrees with the horizontal. This is because such a rise would involve a movement upward, say by distance ED (Fig. 6A), greater than the corresponding horizontal part of the movement (BE); i.e., it must involve an increase in either consumption or saving greater than the rise in the level of income that brings it about. Suppose, for example, that consumption increases in this way. Then, in violation of Assumption 1, there must actually be a reduction in saving despite the increase in income.

the level of investment and the rate of interest (line *LL'*). Fig. 7B shows the connection between the level of income and saving (line *NN'*).

Now consider any particular level of income *OY*. This will result in a level of saving *OS*, according to Fig. 7B. But if the goods market is to be in adjustment, investment demand must be at that same level; it must be at level *OI = OS*, which is found by drawing a horizontal

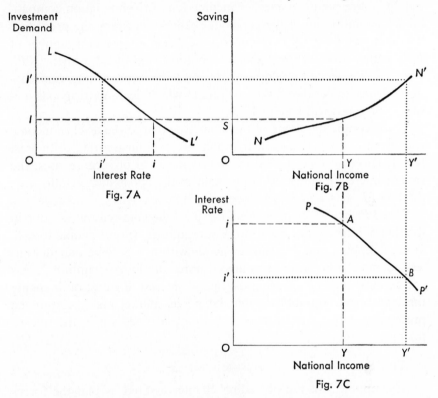

Fig. 7A

Fig. 7B

Fig. 7C

line *IS* across from *OS* in Fig. 7B to *OI* in Fig. 7A. Investment demand will be at the level *OI* required for equilibrium only if the rate of interest happens to be *Oi*. Thus, if national income happens to be at *OY*, supply of and demand for goods will be equal if and only if the rate of interest happens to be at *Oi*.

We record this information in Fig. 7C, where we intend to show all combinations of interest rate and income levels compatible with equilibrium of the goods market. Thus we have just shown that point *A* in this figure, which corresponds to income *OY* and rate of interest *Oi*, is such a point of adjustment. This point is determined simply by measuring off the distances OY and Oi in Figs. 7A and 7B and drawing the same lengths on the axes of Fig. 7C.

B. THE LINE OF ADJUSTMENT

Now take any other level of income, say OY', and repeat the procedure. With that level of income, the demand for and supply of goods will be equal only if the interest rate is Oi'. Thus point B in Fig. 7C corresponds to another income-interest combination compatible with equilibrium of the goods market. By repeating the procedure beginning with several different income levels we obtain a number of such points. Connecting them we obtain a line of adjustment, PP'. This may be defined as the locus of all points representing combinations of income level and interest rate at which demand for goods and supply of goods will be equal.

To determine the shape of this line, note that as the level of income rises from OY to OY', the corresponding equilibrium rate of interest falls from Oi to Oi'. It follows that as the level of income rises, the rate of interest making for adjustment in the goods market falls; i.e., the line PP' has a negative slope.

Line PP' has a negative slope for the following reasons. A rise in the rate of interest, according to Assumption 1, will get people to save more. Supply of and demand for goods will then become unequal unless people can be induced to invest more. But by Assumption 2, this can be done only by lowering the rate of interest, the cost of financing the investment. Equilibrium on the goods market can therefore be preserved, after a rise in income, only by a reduction in the rate of interest.

C. THE SIGNIFICANCE OF ASSUMPTION 3

Assumption 3 of the preceding chapter assured us that the forces of supply and demand on the goods market will help determine national income and the rate of interest. Income and interest will be induced to move toward levels at which the supply of and demand for goods are equal. This means, graphically, that the interest-income combination actually encountered in practice will be represented by a point which tends to lie on the line of adjustment, PP' in Fig. 7C.

3. The Money Market

We now translate our analysis of the working of the money market into graphic terms. Let point A in Fig. 8 represent a combination of interest rate and national income at which the demand for cash just happens to coincide with the supply. The national income is given by distance OY, and the rate of interest by distance Oi.

A. AN INCOME RISE WITH NO CHANGE IN INTEREST RATE

Suppose now that the level of income were to rise from its initial level OY to the higher level represented by OY'. If this occurred with no change in the interest rate (the new interest rate-income combina-

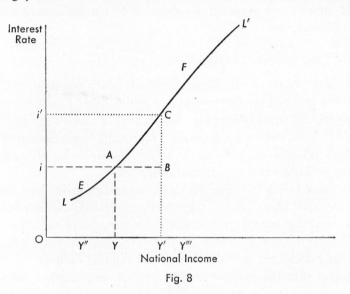

Fig. 8

tion then being represented by point B), we would expect a rise in the demand for money to result. Since we assume the supply to be given, this must cause the demand for money to exceed the supply. In consequence, a horizontal movement to the right from a point of adjustment like A to a point like B must involve an excess demand for money.

B. EQUILIBRIUM REGAINED BY RAISING INTEREST RATE TOO

However, at the higher level of income the demand for cash can be cut down again by a rise in the rate of interest. By raising it sufficiently, say to Oi', the quantity of money demanded can once again be cut down to equal the quantity supplied.

At any level of income OY' there will therefore be a point, say C, which represents a combination of interest rate and income at which the money market is in adjustment. With OY' greater than OY, the point of adjustment C, corresponding to the former, must lie above the point of adjustment A, corresponding to the latter. For if the demand for cash is to remain unchanged (and equal to the supply), the influence of the increased income, which makes for an increased demand, must be offset by an increased cost of holding cash, i.e., by a higher rate of interest.

In the same way, corresponding to incomes OY'' and OY''', there will respectively be points E and F representing combinations of the rate of interest and the level of income at which the money market is in equilibrium.

C. The Line of Adjustment

All these points of adjustment, one for every possible level of income, will presumably form some sort of line like LL', the locus of all points yielding equality between the quantity of money demanded and supplied. Any point not on the line represents some combination of income level and interest rate at which the quantity of money demanded will not equal the quantity supplied.

The line LL' slopes up to the right. It has a positive slope because, as we have just seen, a rise in the income level, which tends to increase the demand for money, will destroy the adjustment between supply and demand if it is not accompanied by a rise in the interest rate which sufficiently decreases the attractiveness of holding money.

Observe that the positive slope of the money market adjustment line contrasts with the negative slope of the line of adjustment for the goods market. This will prove to be very convenient when, later in the chapter, we put the pieces of our analysis together and examine the working of the whole system.

D. The Significance of Assumption 6

By Assumption 6 supply of and demand for cash do in fact tend to be equal, so we may expect that the interest rate and national income will tend to be given by some (as yet unknown) point on line LL'.

4. Finding the Income Level

We have now substantially completed the examination of the elements of our analysis of the determination of national income, and therefore are ready to get down to serious business. Now, and in the next chapter, we go on to see the working of the whole system. Having looked over the construction of every wheel in our watch, we can put it together and see how it ticks.

We have seen what is required for equality between supply and demand in the money and goods markets. In both these markets the quantity supplied can be brought into equality with the quantity demanded by appropriate combinations of the interest rate and the level of income. As we shall see in a moment, there are only one rate of interest and one level of national income that will do the trick in both markets at once. Any other interest-income combination will involve disequilibrium in either the goods or the money market, or both.

Assumptions 3 and 6 tell us that we may expect the forces of supply and demand to drive the actual interest rate and national income level toward this one equilibrating interest-income combination. When we have located this combination we shall know the level of income that market forces tend to establish and we shall have completed our formal analysis of the determination of national income.

A. THE RELEVANT GRAPHS

Since we shall employ the conditions of adjustment between supply and demand in both the goods and the money market, we turn to the graphs which summarize them. These are Fig. 8 for the money market, and Fig. 7C for the goods market. Both these graphs show the required relationships between the level of national income and the rate of interest, and it will be convenient to bring them together by superimposing one on the other. In effect we trace one of the two diagrams on transparent paper, and paste it over the other. The result will look like Fig. 9. Here MM' is the line of money market equilibrium and GG' the line of goods market equilibrium.

B. THE POINT OF EQUILIBRIUM

We see that there will be many points, like A, which represent an income-interest combination at which the money market will be in equilibrium but the goods market will not. Similarly, there are many points like B where the reverse will hold. There are also a good many points like C at which neither market will be in adjustment. Usually there will be just one point, E, that represents an interest-income combination at which supply and demand will be equal in both markets.

Since both markets tend to move toward adjustment (Assumptions 3 and 6), the rate of interest will tend toward the equilibrium rate, Oi,

and income toward the equilibrium level, *OY*. We have thus completed our graphic analysis of the determination of the level of national income. In the process we have incidentally examined the
determination of the interest rate, and with almost no additional effort
we can similarly examine the levels of investment, saving, and consumption.

To do this we turn first to Fig. 5 and observe that with *Oi* the equilibrium interest rate, the investment demand will be at level *OI*.

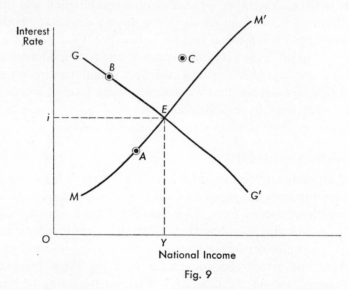

Fig. 9

Similarly from Figs. 6A and 6B we see that with income at *OY* consumption will tend to be at *OC* and saving at *OS*. Thus, except for a
discussion of the level of employment, we have in a purely mechanical
way completed the task we set ourselves.

c. Recapitulation of the Analysis

A summary survey of the route we have traversed may be in order
at this point. We have in effect argued that national income tends to be
adjusted to the demand for it, that is, to consumption demand plus
investment demand. These two demands we suggested are respectively
determined primarily by the level of income and the rate of interest.
The rate of interest and national income tend to such levels as make
for equality between income and the sum of consumption demand
plus investment demand, i.e., the levels that make for supply-demand
equality on the goods market.

We have also indicated that the rate of interest, which helps determine the level of investment demand, is in turn influenced by the quantity of money, adjusting itself so as to make the demand for money equal to the supply at whatever level income happens to be.

This is the path we have followed in our graphic analysis. We have found that for each of the variables in our system—rate of interest, income, investment, savings, and consumption—there is a level that is in conformity with all these relationships.

D. INCOME AND THE LEVEL OF EMPLOYMENT

At this point it is convenient to tie the discussion in briefly with the question of employment level and inflation. We stated earlier that since we are for the present concerned merely with the situation at a moment

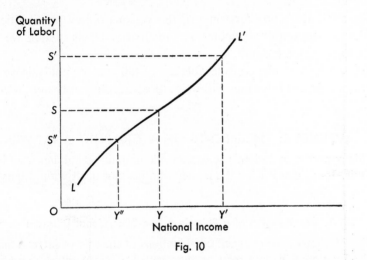

Fig. 10

of time, we may take equipment, production methods, industrial know-how, etc., to be given and unchanged. We also assume wages to be constant, postponing for later a discussion of the effects of changes in wage levels.

In this case there is a fairly simple relationship between the level of income and the demand for labor (the level of employment). The greater the volume of production, i.e., the higher the level of income, the greater will be the demand for labor, since, with equipment given, production can be increased only by an increase in the labor effort devoted to it.

This result can readily be shown on a graph, though here a diagram is by no means indispensable. Thus, in Fig. 10, the demand for labor is shown by line *LL'*, which increases as the level of income rises.

With national income determined at level *OY*, the demand for labor, according to the graph, will be *OS*. If the supply of labor happens to be at level *OS'*—i.e., if it is greater than the equilibrium level *OS*—there will be unemployment whose magnitude is given by *SS'*. Only by somehow increasing the level of income from *OY* to *OY'* can unemployment be eliminated. If the labor force happens to be in short supply, e.g., if it is *OS''*, the quantity of labor demanded will exceed the quantity supplied by *S''S*. This is likely to have inflationary consequences.

In the next chapter we shall see how the economy gets itself into these difficulties. We shall try to find some of the influences that push national income toward levels making for unemployment or inflationary pressures.

We shall also consider some of the various policy possibilities for stabilizing the national income at satisfactory levels, which we shall study later in some detail.

We shall also make considerable use of the graphic analysis we have developed here. Only then will its purpose become fully apparent.

APPENDIX: ELEMENTS OF A GRAPHIC ANALYSIS

This appendix is designed to explain the graphic techniques used in our analysis. It is intended for the reader who has not dealt with graphs elsewhere.

1. The Meaning of a Point in a Two-Dimensional Diagram

Fig. 11 shows how different combinations of the rate of interest and the level of national income may be represented. Thus point *A* represents a situation where the rate of interest is 5 percent and national income $100 billion; point *B* a situation where the rate of interest is 3 percent and national income $150 billion; at point *C* the interest rate is 3 percent and income $50 billion.

2. The Meaning of a Line in a Two-Dimensional Graph

A movement from *A* to *B* in Fig. 11 represents a fall in interest rate and a rise in income, a movement from *A* to *C* represents a fall in both, and a movement from *A* to *D* represents a rise in both. In Fig. 12 a movement along line *LL'* from any starting point to any other, say from point *E* to point *F* or from point *G* to point *H,* involves the interest rate and income moving in opposite directions (one rising and one falling). Any such movement along line *MM'* must involve income and interest both rising or both falling. Before proceeding, the student should convince himself that this is the case, taking various points on the line and seeing what they represent.

In sum, in these graphs the values of the variables are measured along the

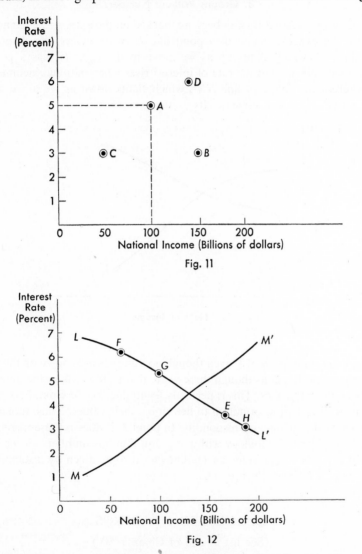

Fig. 11

Fig. 12

axes, a point on the graph represents a specific combination of the values of these variables, and a line represents a relationship between the movements in these variables. It is important to note that this need *not* represent a cause-and-effect relationship. In this way line *MM'* involves a relationship which may be stated as a rising rate of interest when the level of income rises (however this may come about), whereas LL′ involves a falling rate of interest as income rises. We say that *MM′* has a *positive slope* and that *LL′* has a *negative slope*.

3. Graphs Without Numbers

Note in Fig. 13 that no numbers are marked on the axes, so we cannot determine the exact meaning of a point like *J*. Nevertheless, the shape of a line like *PP′*, which slants up as we move to the right (it has a positive slope), still tells us that the rate of interest rises when national income goes up, whereas the shape of line *NN′*, which slants down as we move to the right (it is a negative slope), tells us the reverse.

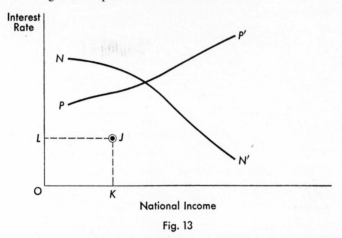

Fig. 13

In a diagram like Fig. 13, even though no numbers are shown on the axes, it is convenient to act as though there were, that is, to speak of the unknown numbers along the axes. This is perfectly legitimate, because numbers would be shown if we had information to determine their values. Thus, though we don't know the income corresponding to point *J*, it does represent some income level. Hence in analogy with the graph that has numbers on the axes, we will say that *J* represents an (unknown) income given by distance *OK*, and a rate of interest given by *OL*.

SUGGESTED READINGS

(See list at end of Chapter 10.)

QUESTIONS

1. a. Show what will happen to line *LL′* in Fig. 5 if businessmen's profit expectations become more optimistic.

   b. What will happen to the quantity of investment demanded at interest rate *Oi?*

   c. What will happen to the level of income necessary to make saving equal investment demand, with interest rate *Oi* (Fig. 7A)?

   d. What will happen to the goods market line of adjustment (Fig. 7C)?

   e. What will happen to the level of income (Fig. 9)?

   f. Can you explain what has happened in each of these cases in common-sense terms?

2. Explain in common-sense terms:

   a. The negative slope of *LL'* in Fig. 5.

   b. The negative slope of *PP'* in Fig. 7C.

   c. The upward slope of *LL'* in Fig. 8.

3. a. Show what it would mean if line *NN'* in Fig. 6B were to have a negative slope.

   b. Show how this violates Assumption 1.

   c. Show why, if this were correct, an excess of supply over demand on the goods market would lead to a decrease in saving.

   d. Show that in this event Assumption 3 might not be valid.

   e. Attempt a common-sense interpretation of all this.

4. In terms of Fig. 9, what would we know about the level of national income:

   a. If Assumption 3 were untrue?

   b. If Assumption 6 were invalid?

   c. If both these assumptions were invalid?

5. a. Show that when technology changes there may be no simple relationship between the level of employment and the level of national income.

   b. Point out the relevance of labor-saving inventions.

   c. Do any practical inventions ever increase the amount of labor needed to produce a given output?

   d. How can inventions of the type referred to in (c) help raise standards of living in view of the fact that they reduce the product per man-hour in the industry in which they are used?

CHAPTER 12

Changes in National Income Levels

In this chapter we shall analyze some of the causes of the inflationary and deflationary problems that have plagued our economy. We shall first center attention on the private sectors to see how their behavior can lead to these difficulties. Then we shall see what might be done about them.

It is important to note how both the purpose and the analysis of this chapter differ from those of the two chapters immediately preceding. In the two earlier chapters our purpose was to show how a unique level of national income is determined, assuming many things to be constant. Both those chapters and the present one assume technology and the total productive capacity of the economy to be given. But the earlier chapters also assumed several other things to be constant, among them (1) the supply of money; (2) the various expectations, social customs, and business practices that affect the public's demand for money at each given level of national income and interest rate; (3) social attitudes, expectations, and other factors affecting the public's choice between consumption and saving at each given level of income; and (4) expectations as to the profitability of new investment. We emphasized that our analysis of the determination of a unique level of national income at some given time rested on the assumption that these things were given and remained constant.

Now, however, we are interested in *changes* in the level of national income. We shall find that the national income level can be changed by a *shift* in any one or more of the things we previously assumed to be constant. The income level can be changed by a shift in the money supply, a shift in the quantity of money demanded by the public at each level of national income and interest rate, a shift in consumption and saving at each level of national income, or a shift in the expected profitability of new investment. To show that this is true we shall shift these variables one by one. But it will quickly become apparent that a shift of one variable has repercussions on the others.

1. Shifts in the Supply of Money

We shall begin by examining the effect of a shift in the money supply. The ways it can occur will be discussed later in detail.[1] We shall assume without explanation that something causes the banks to change the supply of money, and we shall then go directly into an examination of the effects.

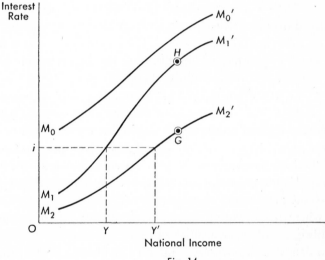

Fig. 14

Let us start with the money supply at such a level that the line representing equilibrium of supply of and demand for money is given by $M_1 M_1'$ in Fig. 14. Suppose now that the monetary authorities take actions which result in an increase in the money supply. We shall see that this results in a shift in the money market equilibrium line from $M_1 M_1'$ to $M_2 M_2'$ which represents the new set of interest-income

[1] See chapters 14 and 15.

combinations at which the quantity of money demanded is equal to the increased quantity of money supplied.

A. THE PROCESS OF ADJUSTMENT

If the market is initially in equilibrium, people will suddenly find that they have more money than they want, so long as income and interest rates remain unchanged. Equilibrium can then be restored only if the demand for money can be increased enough to match the rise in its supply.

B. THE NEW LINE OF EQUILIBRIUM

Assumptions 4 and 5 of our model tell us how such an increase in the demand for money can be produced. The demand for money can be stimulated by a fall in interest rates or by a rise in the level of national income.

At every level of income there will be some rate of interest below the old equilibrium interest rate at which the public will be willing to hold the new quantity of money. Thus point G, directly below a point H which lies on the old equilibrium line, may represent a rate of interest sufficiently low to induce the public to hold the increased quantity of money when income is the same as at H. Corresponding to every point on M_1M_1' there will be another point below it representing an income-interest combination at which the public will be willing to hold the increased quantity of cash. These new points will form the (not necessarily straight) line M_2M_2', which is the locus of all points representing combinations of income and interest at which the demand is equal to the new supply of money.

Thus when the supply of money increases, the line of money market equilibrium shifts downward—it takes a lower interest rate to get people to demand the increased quantity of money at any given level of income.

In sum, a rise in the money supply will work to decrease the equilibrium interest rate corresponding to every level of income. Or, to look at it the other way, it will increase the equilibrium income level at every interest rate. This is just what the shift in the money market equilibrium line means. For example, with interest at Oi, the increase in the money supply just considered will increase equilibrium income from OY to OY'.

In precisely the same way a decrease in the supply of money from our original amount must raise the line of money market equilibrium from M_1M_1' to some higher and positively sloping line M_0M_0', because only at a higher rate of interest will the demand for money be reduced to the new and lower supply at any particular level of income. The decrease in money supply will therefore increase the equilibrium interest rate corresponding to every level of income. In other words, it will decrease the equilibrium level of income corresponding to every rate of interest. The reader can verify that this is the meaning of the shift in the money market line of adjustment from M_1M_1' to M_0M_0'.

C. THE EFFECT ON INCOME AND EMPLOYMENT

As this may suggest, an increase in the supply of money will serve to increase income and lower the interest rate, and a decrease in the supply of money will do the reverse. In Fig. 15, which is in essence a

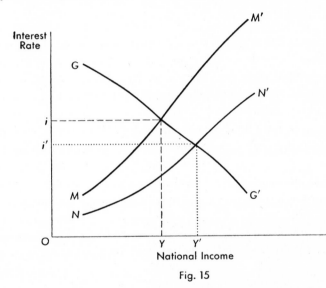

Fig. 15

reproduction of Fig. 9, let the line of goods market equilibrium be given by GG', and the line of money market equilibrium before the increase in the money supply be given by MM'. Let MM' be shifted to NN' as a result of an increase in the cash supply. We see at once that the interest rate will fall from Oi to Oi', and the level of national income will rise from OY to OY'.

This result is really quite plausible. The increased money supply has simply decreased the price of money loans and induced increased expenditures, thereby raising national income.

We can readily see what the change in the quantity of money has done to the rest of our system. The fall in interest rates may be expected to increase the level of investment, having reduced the cost of financing any investment project. This is confirmed by Fig. 5, according to which a reduction of interest rate from Oi to Oi' will result in a rise in investment from OI to OI'. (Note that in equilibrium, since supply equals demand, we need not distinguish between the level of investment and the quantity of investment demanded.)

In the same way we see that the rise in income will result in an increase in consumption and saving. The rise in national income will then have resulted from a combined rise in consumption and investment, the latter resulting from the eased lending terms which accompany the augmented money supply, and the former from the increased income which results from increased expenditure.

D. CONCLUSION

Grave effects can result from a change in the quantity of money. A rise in money supplies at the wrong time and of sufficient magnitude can produce inflationary pressure, as we have always heard. Similarly, an inappropriate reduction in the quantity of money can lead to depression and unemployment.

There have been many times in our history when the money supply has behaved in this perverse manner. We do not know to what extent any particular boom and bust can be ascribed to the behavior of the banking and monetary system. But in many cases things almost certainly would not have been so bad had money supplies behaved otherwise.

We shall find, however, that appropriate shifts in the money supply can also be a useful device for income stabilization.

2. Shifts in the Demand for Money

Spontaneous changes in the demand for money can lead to the same troubles.

When we first spoke of the demand for money, we listed many things besides the level of income and the rate of interest which can affect the public's demand for money. Changes in hoarding habits and changes in the frequency with which payments are made can influence it substantially.[2] But these are things which may change only slowly.

[2] For an explanation of the influence of the frequency of payments see above, pp. 195–196.

We would therefore not look to them as a source of the shorter-run changes in national income with which we are now concerned.

The demand for money is also affected by expectations. For example, a sudden deterioration in prospects may precipitate a rush by security holders to get rid of stocks and bonds. Stocks and bonds are offered for sale in exchange for money, and any increase in the attempted sales of these securities is tantamount to an increased demand for money. These same circumstances may impel other lenders (beside bondholders) to call in old loans and refuse new ones for fear that falling prices will make borrowers unable to repay. Potential lenders will therefore demand for themselves the money which they might otherwise have loaned to others. Deteriorating expectations usually increase the demand for money.

For the same reason, an upward change in anticipated prices will reduce the demand for money. Changes in anticipations can thus have severe effects on the demand for money.

A spontaneous rise in the quantity of money demanded will have exactly the same effects as a decrease in the quantity of cash supplied. Either of these can make the demand for money exceed the supply. If the two are to be equalized by market forces, demand must be cut down to size by a suitable rise in interest rates and/or fall in national income. The end result of an increase in the demand for money must then be a fall in national income and a rise in interest rates. That, as we have seen, is also the result of a decline in the quantity of money supplied.

Common-sense reasons can be adduced for this result. People who want more money can obtain it in any one of four ways—by buying (spending) less, by selling more, by borrowing more, or by lending less. An increased demand for money will exert a downward pressure on national income by increasing supplies of goods and reducing the demand for them. The attempt to borrow more money will force interest rates up, as will also reduced lending. In these ways an increased demand for money will work to increase interest and reduce national income.

Similarly, a spontaneous decline in the demand for money has the same effects as a rise in the supply of money, for both will increase the money supply relative to the demand. Both will therefore make for a higher national income and lower interest rates.

Thus a change in the public's expectations can cause income to rise or to fall. It can cause these results through its effects on the demand for money or its effects on consumption and investment, which we shall observe later in the chapter. A sudden change in psychological climate can therefore lead to inflationary pressure or to recession. Perhaps more often such a change in anticipations will arise not from inexplicable caprice but as the result of changes in economic circumstance that have already occurred. If, for example, a decline in business conditions leads to a deterioration in potential lenders' price expectations, it may induce them to increase their demand for money. In this way the original decline can be further aggravated. Movements in prices and incomes can be accelerated or retarded by their effects on expectations.

In the next chapter we shall see the role that expectation changes can play in just such a process when we examine how wage declines can affect income and employment.

3. Shifts in the Saving-Consumption-Income Relationship

National income can also be changed by shifts in the public's saving and consumption desires.

The quantity of goods the public stands ready to buy at any time depends not only on the purchasing power at its disposal, but also on how badly it wants those goods and how badly people want to retain their purchasing power for the future. These desires may change slowly as the result of changing attitudes toward thriftiness and worldly possessions. More relevant for us are the changes in consumption and saving desires that can and do occur more quickly and more frequently.

A. SOME CAUSES OF SHORT-TERM SHIFTS

The public's division of its income between consumption and saving can be affected by the quantity and the condition of goods in consumers' hands. For example, right after World War II American households were relatively low on durable consumer goods. Many families owned old refrigerators, old cars which were on their last legs, and many other items which were obsolete or even totally unusable. During the war they were irreplaceable, but as supplies became available a burst of consumer spending resulted. Innovations can also affect saving and consumption. The introduction of new products can increase consumer spending at the expense of saving. The appearance of television may very well have had this effect.

Expectations, as usual, have their effects here too. Fear of a depres-

sion and unemployment can get people to save more for that anticipated rainy day, and expected price declines can induce people to put
off purchases. If we think the price of a washing machine will be much
lower next year, we may save our money until then rather than buying
one now. The demand for durable consumer goods is particularly
sensitive to changes in expectations. It is usually possible to make the
old car or stove last a little longer, and in favorable circumstances they

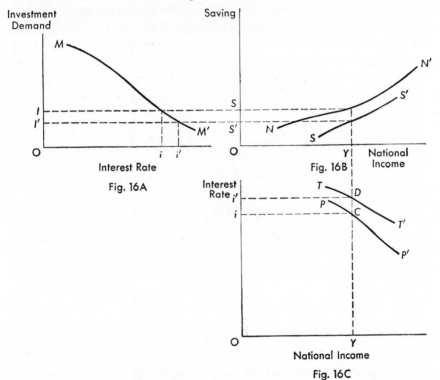

Fig. 16A

Fig. 16B

Fig. 16C

can certainly be replaced ahead of schedule. For the same reasons
optimistic income expectations or expectations of higher prices can
induce people to spend more and save less.

Experience indicates that for these reasons the relationship between
saving and income (and hence that between consumption and income) has shifted frequently and significantly. Let us see how this
affects national income.

B. THE EFFECT ON GOODS MARKET EQUILIBRIUM

In Fig. 16, which is substantially a reproduction of Fig. 7, we
examine the effect of a shift in the saving curve.

Suppose, for example, that at the end of a war, because people rush out to buy all sorts of goods they had been hungering for, the saving curve shifts downward from *NN'* to *SS'*. For any level of income, *OY*, in Fig. 16B, the equilibrium interest rate will rise from *Oi* to *Oi'* in Fig. 16A. For now with decreased saving at the old income level, it will take a higher interest rate to keep investment demand down to the level of saving. With saving down from *OS* to *OS'* investment must fall by the same amount, from *OI* to *OI'*, and this can be accomplished by the rise in interest rate just mentioned. Thus, in Fig. 16C, where we record this information, the equilibrium interest rate corresponding to income *OY* will rise from *Oi* to *Oi'*. This is represented by a change

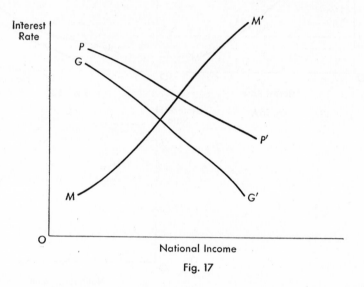

Fig. 17

in equilibrium points from *C* to *D*. If we repeat this process for several income levels, we see that the increase in consumer spending desires shifts the curve of goods market adjustment upward from *PP'* to *TT'*.

In sum, a downward shift in the saving curve, i.e., an upward shift in the consumption curve, will serve to increase the equilibrium rate of interest corresponding to every level of income. Or, looking at it the other way, it will serve to increase the equilibrium income level at every rate of interest.

C. THE EFFECT ON INCOME AND INTEREST

In Fig. 17, which is again based on Fig. 9, we let the line of money market equilibrium stay unchanged at *MM'*, and let the line of goods market equilibrium shift upward and to the right from GG' to PP', as the result of a decrease in consumer saving desires. We see at once that the effect is a rise in income and interest rate.

This is to be expected, since the increase in expenditure should increase income directly. This in turn will lead to an increased demand for money, and so to an increased interest rate.

D. THE EFFECT ON CONSUMPTION, SAVING, AND INVESTMENT

We can see the effect on the other variables in our system. The increased interest rate will serve to reduce investment, and the increased income will further increase consumption. The increased income will also serve partly to offset the original reduction in saving. Nevertheless, saving will still be below its old level. We know this because saving will tend to be equal to the reduced investment demand.

It follows that the increased income that occurs in this case will be based entirely on an increase in consumption, and will actually take place despite a reduction in investment demand.

At least some of the instability of our economy can be ascribed to shifts in the consumption-saving-income relationship. An increase in consumption desires (a decrease in saving desires) can help get us out of a depression or into an inflationary situation. A decline in the public's willingness to spend for consumption can be deflationary and can even precipitate depressions.

4. Shifts in the Investment-Interest Rate Relationship

A. PROFIT EXPECTATIONS AND INVESTMENT DEMAND

When we first discussed investment we indicated how important is the influence of profit expectations on investment demand. This cannot be emphasized too strongly. A businessman's guess about the future is the most essential element on which he bases his investment decisions. Investment really means buying things in the present in order to be able to sell the same or other things in the future. The businessman buys a machine or a factory now in order to be able to sell its product next week, next month, or perhaps ten years from now. The clothing store invests in suits for inventory in order to be able to sell them in the future. Rising prices mean that the investor can "buy cheap" now and "sell dear" later. For this reason a "bullish psychology" (the anticipation of rising prices) and optimism about market conditions generally are favorable for investment.

B. DETERMINANTS OF PROFIT EXPECTATIONS

We cannot list here all the many factors that determine the expected profitability of private investment, but we can mention a few.

1. The stock of unexploited technological innovations. If practically all plants are already equipped with the most efficient machinery, fixtures, and other capital goods that man knows how to make, businessmen may see few opportunities to make high profits from new investment. But if much of the existing plant, machinery, and production methods is obsolete, businessmen may see many opportunities to make high profits by investing in modernized equipment.

2. The relation between the existing stock of capital and the existing level of demand for output. If plant capacities are already large enough to satisfy the existing demand for output, and to do so efficiently, businessmen may see few opportunities for profitable net additions to capacity. But they may see many opportunities for profitable investment if plant capacities are already inadequate relative to the current level of demand for output.

3. The expected rate of increase of demand for output in the future. This is highly important. If plant capacities are already adequate to satisfy the current level of demand, and if demand is not expected to rise in the future, businessmen may see no opportunities for profitable net additions to their stock of capital goods. Even though demand is high they may do no more than replace capital as it wears out. But if demands for output are expected to rise rapidly, businessmen may expect large amounts of net investment to be highly profitable.

Many factors are relevant to expectations as to the future demand for output—the expected rate of population growth, expected rate of increase of productivity, expected distribution of income, expected expenditure patterns of the public, expected government policies, expected course of the business cycle, and so on.

Businessmen can get some objective evidence to guide their expectations about the future. For example, electric utilities or the telephone company may project past trends and use information regarding local populations to forecast demands for their services. But in the end, expectations must be based to a large extent on guesswork—on guesses regarding the probabilities of depression and inflation, the nature of government policies, consumers' tastes, and so on. These guesses can be greatly influenced by the general state of mass psychology.

c. INCOME AND SHIFTS IN INVESTMENT DEMAND

A change in profit expectations can profoundly affect national income through its influence on investment demand. To see how this works, suppose that as the result of an increase in business optimism the investment demand line in Fig. 18A shifts upward from *LL'* to

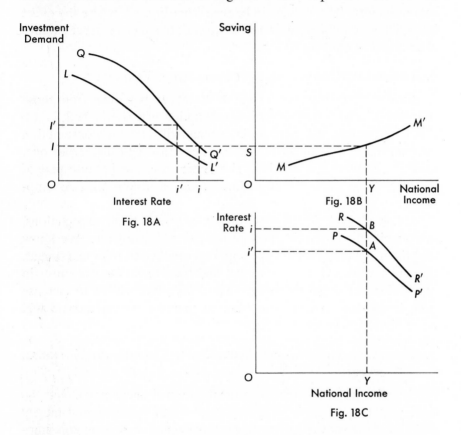

Fig. 18A

Fig. 18B

Fig. 18C

QQ'. With income at *OY* the equilibrium rate of interest rises from *Oi'* to *Oi;* for unless it is discouraged in this way, money investment demand will rise to *OI'* and so it will exceed saving (*OS = OI*). The corresponding equilibrium point in Fig. 18C thus rises from *A* to *B*. Proceeding in this way for other levels of income, we can see that the equilibrium line will be shifted upward from *PP'* to *RR'*.

Fig. 18C then shows that a rise in investment demand (an upward shift in the investment curve) will result in a higher equilibrium rate of interest corresponding to every income level. Or, to look at it the other way, it will result in a higher equilibrium income corresponding to each interest rate.

The effect of an upward shift in the investment curve on the goods market adjustment curve is just like that of a downward shift in the savings curve. Both of these will serve to increase both income and the rate of interest. This can again be seen from Fig. 17, where the effect of the increase in investment will be to shift the goods market equilibrium line upward from GG' to PP'.

D. THE EFFECT ON INVESTMENT AND OTHER VARIABLES

However, the effects on the rest of the system will differ from those of a decrease in saving desires. Consumption will rise in both cases, this time because the increase in income will increase consumption demand indirectly. But in this case, in contrast with the earlier one, saving and investment will both rise. Saving will rise because part of the increase in income will go into saving in accord with Assumption 1.

Investment will rise because of the increased profit expectations, and despite the offsetting effect of the rise in interest rate. We know that the net effect of these opposing forces will be to raise investment, because savings will have gone up, and investment demand must, in equilibrium, be equal to savings. Thus, the effect will be to increase both investment and consumption, so that the rise in income will come partly from each of these.

E. SUMMARY: THE PRIVATE SECTOR AND CHANGES IN NATIONAL INCOME

The behavior of the nongovernment part of the economy affects the level of national income in a variety of ways. By increasing money supplies, decreasing the demand for money, and increasing consumption and investment demands, we can work ourselves out of a depression or into an inflation. The reverse changes are deflationary and can lead to depression. It will be noted how crucial is the role of expectations in influencing each of these items. The variables of our system can also be profoundly affected by objective changes, such as new inventions and the availability of consumer goods, which may increase consumption demand and the profitability of investment. Here, then, we have found some of the important sources of the instability of our national income and the resulting unemployment and inflation.

5. Some Policy Possibilities

This analysis also suggests ways in which the government can use its influence to help stabilize income at a satisfactory level. It can do this by appropriately influencing the quantity of money, the level of consumption and saving, and investment demand. Let us consider each of these possibilities in turn.

A. THE GOVERNMENT AND THE MONEY SUPPLY

This possibility needs little elaboration at this point. In times of inflationary pressure our analysis indicates that it will be appropriate for the government to do what it can to reduce the supply of money or at least to arrest its expansion. During a depression an increase in the money supply appears desirable. Precisely how the government can go about this will be discussed in several later chapters.

B. GOVERNMENT AND SAVING: CREDIT AND TAX POLICY

The government can influence saving levels—i.e., shift the saving curve—in two principal ways: by making it easier or harder for consumers to borrow, and by increasing or reducing taxes.

1. By making it easier to buy on credit the government may succeed in inducing the public as a whole to spend a greater proportion of its income for consumption. This it can do through control over the terms of installment purchasing—reducing the required down payments or increasing the length of time over which payment is permitted to extend. The effect of this may be to get some people to dissave—to spend more than their current income. For the community as a whole, then, the amount spent out of every level of income can be increased, i.e., the amount saved decreased. By tightening up on consumer credit, this process can be reversed.

2. For our present purposes, taxes may be considered a way of getting money out of the hands of consumers. An increase in taxes may be expected to result in a reduction of the proportion of every level of income (before taxes) spent on consumption. Taxes must then be included in the saving of the public, albeit they are involuntary savings. Some of the money collected would, of course, have been saved anyhow, but a considerable part of it will often come out of consumption.

It may be objected that an increase in taxation is likely to result in an increase in government spending which can even surpass the reduction in private spending, since some of the tax money would not have been spent had it remained in private hands. However, in these days of deficit financing there is a somewhat elastic relation between government receipts and expenditures. An increase in taxes may be kept by the Treasury to help reduce a deficit or build up a surplus for the future. Especially in wartime, important decisions on government expenditure are made largely on considerations other than the quantity of tax money collected.

To get back to our main point, a reduction in taxes may be expected to result in an increase in the amount consumed (a decrease in the amount saved) at every level of national income. An increase in taxes will have the reverse effect.

Inflationary pressure can, we saw, be reduced by a decrease in consumption demand, and a depressed economy can be aided by a rise in consumption. It therefore may be desirable to have high taxes and tight consumer credit controls in boom times and low taxes and liberal consumer credit terms when income is low.

c. Government and Investment Demand

To increase investment demand, the government need only demand goods and services itself. It can do this by constructing highways, bridges, TVA projects, post offices, or war monuments. It can invest in military equipment or bigger and better government offices. It can finance the painting of murals on public buildings or the draining of marshland or the replanting of forests. In fact, it can increase invest-ment demand by purchasing more goods and services of any kind.

The net effect of these expenditures is to raise the investment de-mand curve (shift it upward) throughout its length by the amount of government investment.

But this will be the result only if private investment is not deterred by the flood of government purchases. If, for example, government investment in a TVA leads private firms to feel that government has entered into competition with them, private investment may be re-duced and total investment may therefore rise by substantially less than the amount of the government's purchases.

It appears that an increase in government expenditure may be an appropriate policy for reducing unemployment, and that the reverse may be called for in times of inflation.

We shall not at this point elaborate further on any of these policy possibilities. This is as far as our abstract model will carry us. It yields a list of suggestions, but throws little light on the many political, administrative, and other concomitant practical problems that are relevant to intelligent policy decisions. Detailed discussion of these problems will occupy several of the chapters that follow.

6. The Multiplier Process

Essentially our remedial measures call for reduced expenditures in inflation, and increased spending in depression. It will be useful to look somewhat more carefully at the influence of a change in the level of spending. Let us follow through an increase in expenditure and see just how it works itself out in an increase in national income. Although our discussion is presented in terms of an increase in government public works expenditure, we want to emphasize that it is equally applicable to an autonomous rise in private investment, or to a spontaneous increase in consumption. Anything that induces the government, consumers, or business to spend more at each level of national income can start the process we are about to describe.

A. THE EXPENDITURE CHAIN

Suppose that the government increases its expenditure on public works by $1 million. This money will be received by the laborers who helped level the roads, the contractors in charge of the operation, the sellers of the raw materials, etc.

These people, on finding themselves in possession of larger cash balances by the amount of those receipts, will in turn increase their consumption expenditures. We may expect that they will save some but not all of the money. Suppose that of the original million some $700,000 is respent, the other $300,000 being saved. This $700,000 will go to other members of the economy, say grocers, farmers, tailors, etc. These recipients in turn will save some of this money and spend the rest. They may save $200,000 and spend $500,000 for consumption. The process will continue in this way, part of the original money being transferred from hand to hand to buy more consumer goods, but in ever-diminishing amounts.

B. THE INCOME RISE CAN EXCEED THE GOVERNMENT EXPENDITURE

We see, then, that the initial addition to investment sets in motion a chain of consumption expenditures. *The total increase in national income that results must therefore be greater than the original in-*

crease in investment. This is another way of saying, as we did earlier, that the rise in income that results from a spontaneous change in investment will be composed partly of a rise in investment, partly of an increase in consumption expenditure. To put it in a stronger way, a net increase of a dollar in investment may be expected to increase national income by more than that dollar.

c. THE MULTIPLIER

The ratio of the resulting increase in income to the initial increase in expenditure which brings it about is called the *multiplier*. Thus, if a dollar of government expenditure results in a two-dollar rise in income, the multiplier will be 2, whereas if the dollar expended causes income to rise by three dollars, the multiplier will be 3.

We may observe that the smaller the amount saved out of every given increase in the nation's income receipts, the greater will be the multiplier. This is because more of the money received from the government or the spender for investment will be respent for consumption, and so added again to income, and more of this respent money will in turn be respent by its recipients, etc. If the proportion saved out of an increase in income is rather small, the initial expenditure will give rise to a chain of rather large consumption demands which will serve to raise national income considerably. On the other hand, a considerable amount saved out of every income receipt will mean that the initial expenditure will give rise to considerably smaller reexpenditures which will add up to a relatively small addition to national income. That is why the greater the public's saving out of every income receipt, the smaller will be the multiplier.

The assertion that every dollar of government expenditure may be expected to bring in more than a dollar's worth of added income— that the multiplier is greater than unity—seems a powerful argument for greater government expenditure as a means of combating unemployment. There are many practical considerations to be examined before jumping to any conclusion about the relative desirability of the different means of increasing income. But even the poker-faced conclusion that the multiplier is greater than unity requires some provisos.

d. THE EFFECT OF COMPETITION WITH PRIVATE INDUSTRY

It must be remembered that a dollar of public works investment will not necessarily result in a one-dollar increase in net investment demand at every interest rate, because businessmen, feeling that government is poaching on their territory, may think it advisable to reduce their own investment. For this reason the net increase in investment at any interest rate may be less than the government's investment expenditure. On the other hand, it must be realized that if businessmen expect the government's policies to be successful, they may be led to expect better business conditions, and so may invest even more than they would have otherwise.

E. THE EFFECT ON THE INTEREST RATE

Moreover, we have seen that government expenditure may produce some rise in the interest rate. If there is no simultaneous counteracting move by the government in the money market, the rise in the cost of borrowing may result in some reduction in private investment expenditure.

Hence there is some question whether a dollar spent by the government will add something close to a dollar to total investment. It is conceivable, therefore, that in practice the multiplier will turn out to be somewhat smaller than unity, though the meager statistical evidence we have on this point seems to indicate that this will usually not be the case; it suggests that in practice the multiplier will ordinarily be somewhat greater than unity.

7. Conclusion

Before leaving this discussion it is well to remind the reader again that things have been left out of our sketch of the economy. We have tried to indicate step by step the process of abstraction employed in order to present a picture sufficiently simple to be comprehensible and analyzable. We hope, however, that none of the omissions have seriously biased our results or misled the reader in any important way. It can only be said that, at least in outline, the model is the one accepted by most economists as the most useful one to date.

A. AGGREGATION AND MACROECONOMICS

We have oversimplified throughout, in particular in our persistent use of aggregate categories like investment, consumption, and national income. In doing so we have left out important things that might occur in the individual sectors of the economy from which these aggregates are composed. For example, a situation involving a high overall level of employment and general prosperity may conceal serious unemployment in the New England textile industry, or a piling up of unsold tele-

238 Economic Processes and Policies

vision sets because purchasers are holding back in anticipation of improved models. Moreover, it is not inconceivable that a crisis might be set off by trouble in a key industry, and an inflation sustained for a considerable period because some industry constitutes an important bottleneck and prevents a general expansion of production.

This aggregative approach is usually labeled macroeconomics. It is contrasted with microeconomics, in which the individual economic elements are examined in detail—with a microscope, so to speak. We shall have occasion to employ a microeconomic approach in some of our later discussions.[3] Macroeconomic analysis is appropriate for examining the problems with which we are at present concerned—the broad problems of unemployment, depression, prosperity, and inflation. Yet we must recognize that in dealing with such broad aggregates we may be leaving important elements out of our analysis.

B. "KEYNESIAN ECONOMICS"

The general type of analysis employed in these chapters is associated with the work of the late Lord Keynes. Though in many respects it is based on the work of earlier writers, and though our emphasis and premises differ in several ways from Keynes's, the general form taken by the discussion owes much to him.

As the reader probably knows, the term "Keynesian" has been the center of great controversy. Objections have been raised to the policy recommendations made by some of Keynes's more extreme followers, many of which might not have met his approval. Equally controversial has been the prediction, taken up by this same group of followers, that capitalism is destined to provide ever-diminishing economic opportunities unless assisted by government.

Discussion of Keynes's analytic structure, with which we are primarily concerned, has been more dispassionate. Ideally such an analytic structure should be quite neutral and above political passions and purposes, for it is no more than a device for recording observed phenomena and examining their consequences. However, in its choice of emphasis and in the things it leaves out in the process of simplification, bias may be introduced even here.

C. THE FUNCTION OF THE MODEL

Our model has indicated how employment and the level of income are determined by the public's willingness to spend for consumption

[3] See especially chapters 20–24.

and investment and by the availability and cost of funds on the money market. It has also suggested various policy measures which can help to produce economic stability without unemployment or inflation. These are the purposes for which it was developed.

It is customary and convenient to class these income-influencing policy measures under the two heads "fiscal" and "monetary." Fiscal policy refers to government finance, its expenditures and revenues. Tax manipulation and government expenditure decisions therefore fall under this head. Monetary policy obviously includes maneuvering of the money supply as well as credit conditions. Though the distinction between the two types of policy is somewhat artificial and can sometimes even be misleading, because of the expository advantages we shall discuss the practical details of this policy area under these two headings. But first we shall devote a chapter to an analysis of the effects of wage rates on income, employment, and prices.

SUGGESTED READINGS
(See list at end of Chapter 10.)

QUESTIONS

1. a. Explain how printing money can sometimes help increase real national income.
   b. Explain why this is not the same as the assertion, made by some monetary cranks, that all a nation needs at any time to be rich and well off is to have lots and lots of money.
   c. How does this suggest that there are times when we should like foreigners to send us lots and lots of money and other times when it might be to our advantage for them not to do so?
2. Expectations of falling prices can lead people to increase their demands for money because it means that the purchasing power of money is going to increase so that it pays to hold the less valuable money until it becomes more valuable in the future.
   a. Explain, giving concrete examples of how this might plausibly apply to a businessman-investor.
   b. To a housewife.
   c. Show how a decision to sell goods or not to buy goods may be construed as an increased demand for money.
   d. Show that we took care of the proposition in this question in discussing the effects of changed expectations on investment and consumption.

3. An increase in the nation's wealth requires saving, for wealth is added to only by the part of production that is not consumed.
   a. How do you reconcile this statement with the possibility that saving will reduce real national income?
   b. Explain when and how an increase in willingness to save will increase productivity and wealth as discussed in Chapter 3.
   c. Explain when and how it will reduce production and income.
4. The demand for investment may be influenced more by the expected rate of increase of national income than by its level.
   a. Show by examples how the rise of national income can be great when national income is small, and vice versa.
   b. Why might producers want new machines when business is poor but they expect sales to rise?
   c. Why might they not want new machines if production is high but not rising?
   d. How does this explain the original statement in this question?
5. a. Explain why saving will rise if there is an upward shift in the investment curve, whereas the reverse occurs when there is a downward shift in the saving curve.
   b. Since in both cases national income rises, is not the fall in saving a violation of Assumption 2?
6. Show some ways in which, through their effects on expectations, government programs might affect the demand for:
   a. Investment.
   b. Consumption.
   c. Money.
   d. What are the policy implications?
7. Compare and contrast the multiplier effects of an investment expenditure when there is substantial unemployment and when there is full employment, showing:
   a. The process whereby jobs are increased in the one case and not in the other.
   b. The process whereby real national income is increased in the one case and not in the other.
   c. How money national income is increased in both cases.
8. Discuss circumstances, practical and theoretical, under which the multiplier might be less than unity.

CHAPTER 13

Wages, Unemployment, and Inflation

The first of these measures [to expedite recovery] was an agreement of leading employers to maintain the standards of wages. . . . In consequence the buying power of the country has been much larger than would otherwise have been the case. (Herbert Hoover, December 2, 1930.)

. . . General unemployment is in reality to be explained almost in the same way as particular unemployment. . . . In all employments *taken together* . . . indefinite numbers can be employed if they do not ask for too high a remuneration. General unemployment appears when asking too much is a general phenomenon. (Edwin Cannan, *Economic Scares,* 1933, pp. 37–38.)

1. Introduction

A. THE NATURE OF THE PROBLEM

The relationship between the behavior of money wage rates and the behavior of national income, employment, and price levels is an important, difficult, and highly controversial problem. With the total wage bill making up more than half of all costs of production and more than half of national income, it is clear that the behavior of money wage rates is capable of exerting important influences on the economy. However, neither the nature nor the direction of these influences is clear in every case. Just what are the effects of a refusal to lower money wage rates during a period of depression and widespread unemployment? What are the effects of general wage cuts in such a period? What

241

wage policy would be most conducive to the restoration of full employment? What types of wage policy should be followed in times of
actual or threatened inflation?

These questions were important long before labor unions became a
powerful force in our economy. They are even more important now
that over a quarter of all our workers are unionized and the wage rates
negotiated by labor unions exert a significant influence on the wages
of many nonunion workers. We shall refer frequently to the wage policies of unions, but it should be remembered that wage behavior would
still be of interest even if unions were much weaker or even non-
existent.

B. CONFLICTING VIEWS

Popular arguments on this subject are of little help. Consider, for
example, two rather common views as to the proper wage policy for a
period of depression and unemployment. Mr. A declares vehemently,
"Wage rates ought to be raised whenever a depression occurs or even
threatens. Insufficient purchasing power in the hands of the public is
the only reason for depression. By raising wage rates we can raise the
public's purchasing power, increase demands for the products of industry, induce an increase of output, and create job opportunities for
everybody." One might expect Mr. A, following his own logic, to favor
wage cuts in time of inflation in order to reduce the public's spending
power. But if he is like many others he will argue that money wages
should also be raised during inflation to protect labor's real purchasing
power. Thus he concludes that money wage rates should be raised
during both depression and inflation.

With equal vehemence Mr. B advocates wage reductions during depression. "The only reason people are unemployed is that wages are
too high; labor just costs too much. Everybody knows you can sell your
product if you lower your prices enough. All the workers have to do to
get jobs is lower the prices of their labor." We might expect Mr. B,
following his own line of reasoning consistently, to favor wage increases during periods of overfull employment and inflation in order to
reduce the effective demand for labor and end the apparent labor
shortage. But many people with Mr. B's general views assert that wage
rates should be held constant, or even reduced, during inflation in
order to hold down inflationary pressures. In other words, wages
should be reduced in depression and either kept constant or reduced
during inflation.

We begin to suspect that there is something wrong somewhere. Unfortunately we shall find it much easier to criticize such popular views than to forecast the effects of each type of wage policy and point toward appropriate policy decisions. Nevertheless, we can at least identify some of the crucial questions and evaluate the usability of wage policy as a means of income stabilization.

c. WAGES AS COST AND INCOME

Though the argument between Messrs. A and B was largely inconclusive, it did bring out one point: Wages have not one but two important aspects, and it is highly dangerous to concentrate on one to the neglect of the other. To the employer, wages are a cost; to the worker they are money income. Thus a 10 percent increase in hourly wage rates is both an increase in the cost of labor to employers and an increase in money income and spending power for each hour the worker is at his job. If we concentrated on the cost aspect alone, we might infer that increased wage rates would tend to decrease the amount of labor purchased. If we concentrated on the income aspect alone, we might infer that increased wage rates would raise labor's demand for output and induce employers to hire more men.

Similarly, a wage cut is both a decrease in the cost of labor to employers and a decrease in workers' money income per hour of work.

Thus it becomes clear that any valid analysis must consider both the cost and income aspects of wage rates. We shall find that the behavior of wage rates also exerts other important influences on the economy.

2. Prices and Sales: An Analogy

A. THE ANALOGY

Some have suggested that the problem of disposing of an oversupply of labor is exactly like that of disposing of an excess supply of any other commodity. In both cases, it is argued, a price reduction is the way out. Suppose, for example, that a South Carolina mill has an excess inventory of cotton gray goods. It can sell the goods by lowering their prices sufficiently. From this it is argued that an excess supply of all goods and of all labor can find buyers if their prices are reduced enough.

B. CRITICISMS OF THE ANALOGY

In arguments of this sort we must beware of "the fallacy of composition"—the fallacy of assuming that what is true for one person or small group must also be true for much larger groups or even for the economy as a whole. We are all properly skeptical of this argument: "Saddleback Sam earned enough by prospecting for gold to keep up a mansion with 18 servants. This shows that if everybody spent his life at gold prospecting, we could all have 18 servants." For somewhat less obvious reasons the argument that because one seller can increase his sales by lowering his prices all sellers can do likewise may also lead us into the fallacy of composition.

To indicate why this argument can be fallacious, let us consider several cases in which sellers lower the prices of their products. In each case we should remember that a price also has at least two aspects; it is a cost to the buyer and income to the seller.

1. The South Carolina mill lowers the price of its cotton gray goods 10 percent, while all other cotton goods producers and the producers of all other products keep their prices constant. In this case the South Carolina mill will probably have a very large increase in sales. Not only will its lower price induce some people to buy more cotton goods, but it will take a lot of business away from the other cotton sellers. Moreover, its price reduction will have very little effect on the total money income of the public as a whole.

2. The South Carolina mill, and all the other cotton mills, lower their prices of gray goods 10 percent, but the producers of all other products keep their prices constant. The South Carolina mill and all its competitors will probably be able to sell somewhat more cotton goods because they are now cheaper relative to other types of products. But it is clear that the increase in the South Carolina mill's sales will not be as great as it would have been if its competitors had not lowered their prices. The effect on the total money incomes of the public will not be very large because the cotton manufacturing industry is such a small segment of the economy.

3. The South Carolina mill, all other producers of cotton goods, and the producers of all other types of products lower their prices by a uniform 10 percent. In this case it is not at all clear that the South Carolina mill, or the cotton producers as a whole, or even industry as a whole, will enjoy any increase in sales. Cotton is now no cheaper than before, relative to other types of goods. Moreover, the fall in the prices of all types of output may lower the public's total money income, for we saw earlier that total money income is equal to the money value of output. Thus we cannot be sure that a general price cut on all

types of goods will increase the total quantity of goods demanded. It is even conceivable that the quantity of goods demanded will be reduced.

c. Application of the Analogy to Wage Rates and the Quantity of Labor Demanded

Similar reasoning can be applied to the relationship between wage rates and the quantity of labor that can be sold. Let us consider several cases of wage cuts, remembering both the cost and income aspects of wages.

1. All the workers in a single plant offer their labor at a 10 percent lower price while wage rates remain unchanged in all other plants in the industry and also in other industries. Having lower labor costs, this employer is likely to hire more labor. The increase in employment may be quite large if the firm allows its cost decrease to be reflected in lower prices for its product and if its competitors do not lower their prices. At least some of the increased employment at this plant may be at the expense of decreased employment elsewhere. The decrease of wage rates in just one plant will not have much effect on the public's total money income.

2. The workers in all plants in an industry, such as cotton manufacturing, offer their labor at a 10 percent lower price, but wage rates in all other industries remain constant. With lower labor costs, all the textile firms can now afford to lower the prices of their product. If they do, a greater quantity of it can probably be sold because each unit will be cheaper relative to other types of products. These greater sales will probably be reflected in a somewhat higher level of employment in the industry. But the percentage increase in employment will almost certainly be smaller than in the case where one plant alone lowered its wage rates and took business away from its competitors. Wage reduction in a single industry may still have little effect on the public's total money income, especially if the industry comprises only a small segment of the economy.

3. Workers in all industries take a uniform wage cut of 10 percent. We cannot be at all sure that the cotton industry or industry as a whole will employ more labor. In the first place, the uniform wage cut throughout industry may lead to something like uniform price reductions so that the relative prices of products will remain unaltered. But even if some industries lower their prices more than others, attract sales from other industries, and increase their employment, this may be offset by

decreased sales and employment in the remaining industries. In the second place, the general wage reduction throughout all industries lowers the workers' money income for each hour of work and will lower the total amount of wage income received by all workers if the amount of employment does not rise enough to offset the lower wage per hour. Thus a general decrease of wage rates may even conceivably lower the quantity of output demanded.

The net outcome of our analysis up to this point is quite unclear. A universal wage reduction will lower employers' costs, which we would expect to increase their demand for labor. But the same wage cut decreases workers' money incomes for each hour of work, which tends to lower their spending for output. This may reduce the employers' demand for labor. Which influence will dominate we do not know. Further analysis is called for.

3. Wage Cuts, Prices, and the Purchasing Power of Incomes and the Money Supply

A. WAGE CUTS AND THE PRICE LEVEL

A fall in wages makes for price reductions in a number of ways. First, the fall in wages reduces costs, and this may in many cases induce businessmen to lower commodity prices.

Second, the fall in wages tends to reduce the price of labor-saving machinery and of all sorts of capital equipment in two ways. (1) The labor cost of producing that equipment will fall. (2) If the manufacturers of equipment do not cut its price, the demand for labor-saving machinery will decrease. A machine that displaces three workers will not be bought any more if wages fall to a point where the three men can be hired at less cost than the purchase and maintenance of the machine involve. When wages fall, competition will therefore force equipment manufacturers to lower the prices of their products too.

Finally, the diminished money income per worker, together with the reduced money income of machine producers, may cut money demands for finished goods, and so help drive their prices down. In these ways a general wage cut will tend to drive all prices down.

B. THE EFFECT ON REAL INCOMES AND COSTS

The fall in wages will change incomes and costs. But the effect of these changes on employment may be negligible. Though costs and incomes tend to fall in money terms, *real* costs and *real* incomes may even be higher when all is said and done. With prices lower, each dollar will be worth more than before. Costs now involve the expenditure of a smaller number of more valuable dollars, and for the same reason the change in money income may not enable consumers to buy substantially more or less goods and services than before.

c. The Effect on the Purchasing Power of Money

There is, however, one item that is certain to be affected substantially by a price-wage fall. The purchasing power of money is increased. A 50 percent fall in prices doubles the purchasing power of every dollar in existence.

The effect of this change on employment can be deduced directly from the analysis in the preceding chapters. There we decided to measure the quantity of money, not in terms of the number of actual dollars but in terms of its purchasing power.[1] *Given the number of dollars,* the increase in the purchasing power of each dollar, which accompanies a wage-price fall is equivalent to an increase in the quantity of money.

We saw in the preceding chapter that a rise in the supply of money (in purchasing-power terms) can produce a higher level of national income, a lower interest rate, and increases in both consumption and investment.[2]

This suggests that a wage cut will have helpful effects in depression, for by increasing the quantity of money in terms of total purchasing power it will help raise income, consumption, and investment. More surprisingly, it suggests that rising wages and prices can reduce the excess of the demand for goods over the supply of goods during inflation by serving, in effect, to reduce the supply of money. Thus the price rise might help eliminate an important source of further inflation if the actual number of dollars is not allowed to rise.

Though this argument is valid as far as it goes, there is still much more to the story.

4. Wage Cuts and Expectations

A price-wage fall is also very likely to affect people's anticipations of the future. A sharp decline in price levels is likely to make businessmen stop and think. Even when it sets into motion no conscious thinking about future prospects, a severe drop in prices can hardly fail to affect the climate of optimism or pessimism.

[1] See p. 195.
[2] See above, pp. 221–224.

We saw in the last chapter how a change in expectations can have profound effects on the demand for money, consumption, and investment, and how these in turn can affect national income and employment. Let us see how this works out in our present problem.

A. REVISED EXPECTATIONS AND INVESTMENT

For the same reason that rising prices are favorable for investment, a revised guess that leads people to believe that prices will have more of an upward trend *or less of a downward trend* than they had originally expected will motivate them to revise investment plans upward.

Even if prices are expected to fall, some investment will usually take place. At least some resources will be invested in maintenance and replacement to prevent plant and equipment from deteriorating completely. Should a revised view of the future, even though still gloomy, be less pessimistic than the original view, at least slightly more investment than the small amount initially planned will be induced. If the price-wage fall then leads businessmen to hope for less of a deterioration or more of an improvement in business conditions than they had counted on formerly, investment will be stimulated. If the wage-price fall leads them to fear even greater declines or smaller improvements in the future than they had previously counted on, investment will be discouraged to the detriment of employment.

B. THE EFFECT ON OTHER PURCHASES AND SALES

In general our wage-induced price fall will affect purchases and sales as follows. Suppose the fall in price leads people to expect still greater price declines in the future. This will cause consumers to hold off on purchases, expecting the future to bring even more of a buyers' market. The same sort of anticipation will clearly make sellers try to get rid of stocks of goods in a hurry before prices become even more unfavorable. But this effect of the price-wage fall will aggravate unemployment problems. For by increasing supplies and decreasing demands it must increase the excess supplies of goods. It will become more difficult for sellers to find purchasers for their wares, and the demand for labor will decline.

If, on the other hand, the price-wage fall has little effect on people's anticipations of the future, if the downward pressure on prices is considered only temporary, employment will be stimulated. Present prices will have gone down as compared with anticipated future prices, and this will serve as an inducement to buyers to purchase some things now which they had originally planned to buy in the future. Similarly, this may motivate sellers to offer less for sale currently in order to have more to sell later when prices are expected to be relatively more favorable than had originally been anticipated.

These consequences of the wage-price fall represent increases in demands and decreases in supply, both of which should help stimulate employment.

c. Expectations and the Demand for Money

We know that expectations may also affect the demand for money. If the price-wage fall leads lenders to become pessimistic about the ability of potential borrowers to repay loans, they will prefer to hold on to their money. The supply of loans will be decreased, and interest rates may be turned upward. This will tend to affect employment adversely. The reverse will tend to occur if lenders regard the price fall as a sign of improvement in future business conditions.

d. Comment

The effect of the wage-price fall on employment seems to depend very much on whether it affects price anticipations adversely or favorably, whether it is taken as an omen of further cuts yet to come or as a prelude to an upturn.

In practice it will sometimes have the one effect and sometimes the other. If the public has been expecting a depression, a price decline can convince people that it has arrived. By acting on this conviction— by holding out on purchases and dumping goods on the market—they can, as we have seen, make their prediction come true. If on the other hand the public is convinced that the economy tends to "normalcy" so that the price decline brought about by a wage fall is viewed as a temporary aberration, it can produce favorable results.

Our experience suggests that at different times in our history the attitude of the public has varied between these extremes. But we can never be sure. Indeed, we may have hardly an inkling about its attitude at any particular time. These questions are more delicate than any of those usually posed by the public opinion polls. A person may not even know how he himself will react to a drop in prices.

5. Wage Cuts and Employment: Summary

We have been dealing with a highly oversimplified and incomplete model of reality, and many relevant elements have not been considered. Nevertheless, we can draw several conclusions. It appears that general wage cuts may have some stimulating influence on employment by inducing price reductions which increase the purchasing power of the community's money supply if it remains fairly constant. Yet this effect may be offset or more than offset if the wage cuts lead to pessimistic anticipations about the future.

While wage cuts may conceivably help alleviate widespread unemployment, it is by no means certain that they will do so. In some circumstances a wage rise may be needed to increase the demand for labor, and it is by no means easy in practice to distinguish one circumstance from the other. The same sort of doubts apply to the efficacy of wage cutting as a means of combating inflation. At best, therefore. wage manipulation is a doubtful instrument for stabilizing employment and income. Other methods appear to be considerably more reliable.

6. Wage Versus Money Manipulation

We have seen that there is some similarity between the effects on employment and income of wage cutting and money "printing," i.e., the creation of money by the banks and the monetary authorities, for both may be used to increase or decrease the purchasing power of the money supply.[3] Yet there are important differences between these two methods.

A. EXPEDIENCY

It may be easier and politically more advisable to arrange for money to be created than to induce general wage reductions for the purpose of increasing the real money supply and raising employment. It is hard to imagine just how a government would go about implementing a decision to lower wages, whereas increasing the quantity of money by encouraging bank loans can be done rather easily. One can also visualize the political consequences of a decision to force wages down—a veritable politician's nightmare of indignant labor.

B. THE EFFECT ON EXPECTATIONS

There is another important difference between the two methods of augmenting the total purchasing power of the community's money. An increase in the money supply, unlike a general wage fall, will usually be associated with rising prices. This suggests that the influence of a fall in wages on expectations would be in the opposite direction from

[3] For the methods and explanation of procedures see chapters 14 and 15.

that of an increase in the quantity of money. Where the expectations effect of the one may work against an increase in employment, the other may work for it.

We cannot generalize regarding which will be the better, for, as we have seen, the effect of a wage fall on expectations may sometimes be favorable, sometimes unfavorable. We only remark that the general climate of pessimism during a depression might indicate that the rising prices which may accompany money creation will be welcomed. Similarly, a drop in prices, which results when the money supply is reduced, may be salutary during a period of inflationary pressure.

c. The Effect on Income Distribution

There is still another consideration that appears to favor monetary as against wage rate manipulation. We saw earlier that in a depression, when prices fall, there will be a redistribution of purchasing power in favor of fixed-income recipients, and in favor of creditors and savers generally, as against debtors.[4] The rise in prices accompanying an injection of money will tend to offset this redistribution, whereas a wage-induced price fall will only aggravate this redistribution.

Aside from the objection that may be raised in terms of distributive justice, the change in distribution produced by a wage cut can be considered undesirable because it may encourage the wrong people, as far as getting out of a depression is concerned. It rewards the saver—the nonspender—for his savings are increased in value. It penalizes the borrower—the spender for investment purposes—by increasing the burden of his debt. Expected wage falls thus give comfort and encouragement to precisely those whose activities tend to work against the elimination of depression and unemployment.

Exactly the same considerations favor monetary manipulation in inflationary periods. At such times a reduction in the quantity of money serves to reduce prices, thereby encouraging the saver and discouraging the investor-borrower. A wage increase, which tends to raise prices, clearly works in the other direction.

7. Wage Levels and Full Employment

A. Rising Prices Without Full Employment: Bottlenecks

Though it appears from the discussion in this chapter that wage manipulation is not a reliable instrument for eliminating short-run fluctuations in income and employment, the behavior of the wage level may

---

[4] See above, pp. 147–148.

at times have important and serious impacts on the effectiveness of other instruments of employment policy.

As we have said earlier, full employment or something very close to it is usually considered to be the border line between inflationary pressure and its absence. Yet wages may begin to rise while unemployment still exists. Bottlenecks may appear at key points in the economy. For example, skilled mechanics or engineers may come to be in short supply and prevent the expansion of production in response to unsatisfied demand even though a considerable body of unemployed remains.

B. RISING EMPLOYMENT AND UNION WAGE DEMANDS

Moreover, a rising level of employment may be enough to prompt labor unions to press for higher wages while there is still a considerable amount of unemployment. In such cases an increase in the demand for labor may lead to higher wages rather than to an increase in employment.

It may be quite rational for workers to press for higher wages while there is still unemployment. It may be good monopoly practice to do so. As implied earlier, increasing wages in one industry will usually decrease employment; but even so, it may increase the total amount paid out to workers. Though fewer men are hired, each is hired at a higher wage. Whether it does or does not pay union members to raise their price depends at least partly on the nature of the demand situation. Only if the demand for labor is very responsive to a wage change,[5] so that a small increase in wages causes a relatively large decrease in employment, will higher wages decrease the total wage receipts of union members.

It may then pay a union to keep part of its membership unemployed or to keep its members employed only part time, for the total amount paid to union members may thereby be increased. Though it is usually not done, such a policy might even be made profitable to the unemployed members by giving them sufficiently large unemployment benefits from a fund collected by assessments on the wages of employed members. There is a greater amount to divide among the same number of men, so all the union members will benefit.

C. INFLATION WITH OR WITHOUT FULL EMPLOYMENT

Thus, an increase in the demand for workers may result in a demand for higher wages rather than a substantial increase in employment. In

[5] This is called the case of *elastic demand*. For a more detailed analysis of this and other points in this section, see the Graphic Appendix, especially pp. 671–674.

such unhappy circumstances the various monetary and fiscal policies that have been mentioned in earlier chapters as possible remedies for unemployment will in the long run be able to reduce unemployment to only a minor extent, if at all. Even though a significant amount of unemployment remains, further increases in the demand for labor may only produce inflationary pressures.

That inflationary wage pressure is a real danger, at least when employment is high, is indicated by the postwar experience of some European countries where runaway wage rises were prevented only by the more or less complete submission of the trade union leadership to government requests for moderation. In many cases this apparently caused the union members to lose confidence in their own leaders. All the feasible alternatives proposed up to this time would involve permanent wage and price control by the government. In the United States this possibility is not viewed with equanimity in the light of our bias against unlimited government intervention. Much thinking remains to be done before a way will be found to establish a satisfactory long-run relationship between the unions and the rest of the economy in a situation of nearly "full employment."

It must be emphasized that this is not peculiarly a unionization problem. Shortages of special skills may hold back production and lead to rising prices even if there is still considerable unemployment and workers are not unionized. Some economists have argued that the net effect of unions has been to hold back wages during inflationary times.[6]

The problem of achieving full employment with stable prices therefore need not feature the unions as the villains. The experience of European trade unions just cited shows clearly that labor organizations can sometimes play an important assisting role in policy designed to cope with these difficulties.

8. Summary

In this chapter we have been concerned primarily with the effect of wage levels on employment and inflation. We have argued that in a small sector of the economy, such as a firm or an industry, a fall in wages is likely to stimulate employment by reducing costs. The extension of this argument to industry as a whole is not legitimate, for though a fall in all wage rates reduces money costs, it can also reduce

[6] See below, pp. 594–597, for more details. See also the Graphic Appendix, pp. 673–674.

consumers' spending power, and hence demand. More careful argument showed that in some cases a cut in all wages might be expected to increase employment, but that in other cases it is likely to have the opposite effect.

For similar reasons, the effect of a wage rise or a wage cut on inflationary pressure is not always certain, though in this case anticipations may perhaps be expected to be such as to make wage rises inflationary more often than not. We concluded, therefore, that wage manipulation was, at best, a poor method of combating general unemployment and inflation. Manipulation of the money supply, which in theory has much in common with wage adjustment as an instrument for that purpose, seems to possess overwhelming advantages in practice.

While manipulation of the wage level offers little hope as a means of achieving income stability at a satisfactory level, it can pose a serious threat to the achievement of this goal by other means. The tendency for upward pressures on wages and prices to accompany full employment and even to commence before that aim is achieved is of the utmost concern to long-run economic policy. As yet no very satisfactory solutions to the problem have been proposed.

SUGGESTED READINGS

Wright, David McCord (ed.), *The Impact of the Union,* Harcourt, Brace, New York, 1951.

QUESTIONS

1. In the first section of this chapter show:
   a. Where Mr. A's argument neglects the cost aspect of a wage change.
   b. Where it neglects the income aspect.
   c. Where B's argument neglects the cost aspect.
   d. Where it neglects the income aspect.
2. Define the fallacy of composition. Explain the fallacy in each of the following examples:
   a. If a small necktie manufacturer produces many ties, his income will rise. Therefore all necktie producers can gain by doubling their production.
   b. If any one factory installs smoke elimination devices, it will not clear the air in a smoky city. Therefore smoke elimination devices cannot clear up the city air.

   c. A rise in an individual's expenditure may get him into worse trouble during a depression. Therefore increased expenditure by the community is very bad during such a period.

   d. One employed worker will become poorer if he accepts lower wages. Therefore lower wages for all employed workers will reduce living standards.

   e. Give more examples, using the discussion in Chapter 7 for clues.

3. a. Show how the fact that lower wages in one factory can increase employment there depends on the fact that lower prices of that factory's products can increase its sales.

   b. Show similar connections for an industry.

   c. For the economy as a whole.

   d. Show how technological change can make it pay workers to accept lower wages in one industry even though there are plenty of jobs available elsewhere.

4. a. Show how a proportionate fall in all incomes, prices, and money supplies will neither harm nor benefit anyone if there are no private debtors or creditors.

   b. If there are debtors and creditors in this situation, who will gain and who will lose?

   c. Show therefore that though some lose and some benefit, there may be no net gain in the community's purchasing power as a result of a general wage-price-money-supply fall.

   d. Show that a proportionate fall in prices and incomes will affect neither real incomes nor costs, but will benefit money holders.

   e. Review the effect of this increase on the purchasing power of the money supply on national income and the rate of interest.

5. a. Explain why investment and other demands will tend to be higher and supplies to be lower when prices are expected to rise than when they are expected to fall.

   b. Explain how investment and other demands can be stimulated and sales discouraged by a change in anticipated price trends from sharply to gradually falling prices.

   c. What sort of effects on anticipated price trends will stimulate and what sort will deter employment?

6. Show that every effect of a change in expectations on national income, which was discussed in the preceding chapter, plays a part in the discussion in Section 4 of this chapter.

7. a. What methods might you use in trying to find out about businessmen's expectations for next year?

   b. In your opinion, which of the following is most likely to be representative of a businessman's views of the future:

      "The price of my product will probably be $5.27."

"I'll be very surprised if the price goes much below $4.50 or goes much higher than $6."

"It's a 50–50 chance that it will be $5.27 and a 2 to 1 chance that it will not be above that figure."

Or do you think they simply have a hazy notion, say, that the price is likely to rise a little?

   c. Do you think economists are in a position to answer this question?

8. a. What sorts of redistribution of income might increase the demand for goods?

   b. Show that the price rise which accompanies an inflation may redistribute incomes in a way that increases demands.

   c. Show therefore that inflation may "feed on itself."

   d. Show the analogous result for deflations.

   e. How can a reduction of the money supply (the number of dollars) in inflation and its increase in depression help offset these effects?

9. a. Why is it suggested here that a rise in wages is very likely to add to inflationary pressures even though a fall in wages may or may not help get rid of depression?

   b. Show how higher prices can lead to demands for higher wages.

   c. Show how higher wages can in turn cause prices to rise.

   d. Why is this process called a "wage-price spiral"?

   e. Show how a rise in wages might conceivably eliminate any further inflationary pressure.

   f. In such a case discuss the advisability of a price ceiling, wage control, and rationing program.

   g. If a situation in which wage rises had this effect were to occur, would it be easy for government policymakers to find out about it?

10. a. When might it be to a union leader's selfish interest to increase the employment of the union membership to a maximum?

   b. When would it pay *all* union members to have some unemployed in their ranks?

   c. When might it be to the selfish interests of a controlling group in a union to have fewer members employed, even though this cuts down the total wage receipts of the union membership?

11. Show exactly how union policies might prevent any increase in demand that results from the government's fiscal and monetary policies from decreasing unemployment.

PART IV

Monetary and Fiscal Policies

CHAPTER 14

The Money Supply and Monetary Institutions

---

1. Introduction

We have seen that the size of the money supply is one of the major determinants of national income, employment, and price levels. Increases in the money supply tend to increase the supply of loans and to lower interest rates, thereby working to raise investment demand and national income. Under some circumstances, increases in the money supply produce or accentuate inflationary pressures; under other circumstances they can be a useful means of combating depression and unemployment. Decreases in the money supply, on the other hand, tend to decrease the supply of loans and to raise interest rates, thereby working to lower investment demand and national income. At times this may create or accentuate depression and unemployment; at other times it may be a useful method of combating inflation. To regulate the money supply in such a way as to promote economic growth and stability, rather than militate against them, is still one of our important economic problems.

The purpose of this chapter, and of the two that follow, will be to analyze further the interrelationships between money and the behavior of the economy, the processes of increasing and decreasing the money supply, methods that may be used by the government and the Federal Reserve to regulate the money supply, and some of the major policy problems in this field. Our emphasis throughout will be on the functioning of money in the economy. We shall discuss the forms of money and monetary institutions only to the extent necessary to clarify the be-

259

havior of money. As in our other analysis, we shall have to simplify
somewhat and concentrate on the major institutions and processes.

2. The Composition of Our Money Supply

As a first step toward measuring the money supply, we must define
what we mean by "money." Here we are forced to use a functional
definition: Money includes all those "things" that are in practice generally accepted as a means of payment—that are generally accepted
in payment of debts and in payment for goods and services.

Applying this definition to the means of payment used in the United
States, we find that our money supply includes coins, paper money,
and checking or demand deposits at banks. The relative proportions

TABLE 24.   Types of Money in the United States on Selected Dates[1]
(In billions of dollars)

Year (June 30)	Amounts of Money in the Form of				Percent of Total Money Supply		
	Total	Coin	Paper Money	Checking Deposits	Coins	Paper Money	Checking Deposits
1914	$ 13.3	$0.6	$ 2.6	$10.1	4.5	19.5	76.0
1920	24.8	0.6	4.6	19.6	2.4	18.6	79.0
1925	25.9	0.4	4.1	21.4	1.6	15.8	82.6
1929	27.0	0.5	4.0	22.5	1.9	14.8	83.3
1933	19.5	0.4	5.0	14.1	2.1	25.6	72.3
1939	34.4	0.6	6.4	27.4	1.7	18.6	79.7
1952	124.8	1.7	27.3	95.8	1.4	21.9	76.7
1953[a]	127.4	1.7	28.2	97.5	1.3	22.1	76.6

[a] End of May.

of these types of money have changed greatly during our history. At
first a considerable part of our money was in the form of coins; paper
money and bank deposits were relatively less important. Gradually,
however, paper money and checking deposits rose in amount relative
to coins, and checking deposits rose relative to both coins and paper
money. As a result of this evolution, checking deposits have for many
decades been far larger than coins and paper money together, and the
volume of paper money has been much greater than that of coins.

Table 24 bears out this statement, for it shows that during most of

[1] Computed from data in *Federal Reserve Bulletins* and other Federal Reserve
publications. The term "checking deposits" corresponds to the Federal Reserve term
"demand deposits adjusted." Coin and paper money include all outside the Treasury
and the Federal Reserve. It thus overstates the amounts held by the public by the
amount held in commercial banks. Except where otherwise indicated, all the statistics
in this chapter are from the *Federal Reserve Bulletin*.

the time since 1914 more than 75 percent of our total money supply has been in the form of checking deposits, about 20 percent in the form of paper money, and only about 2 percent in the form of coins. Metallic coins are indeed "small change" in the monetary system.

It has been estimated that more than 90 percent of all payments in the economy are made by transferring checking deposits from payers to payees. This is usually done by checks, when the owner of a deposit orders a bank to transfer dollars from his account to the account of the payee. Table 24 also shows that the size of the money supply has fluctuated widely, and that changes in the volume of checking deposits have accounted for a major part of these fluctuations.

3. The Issuers of Our Money

Let us now see what institutions create and issue our money. As indicated in Table 25, our money is created and issued by three types of institutions: the United States Treasury, the Federal Reserve banks, and more than 14,000 privately owned and privately operated commercial banks. The Treasury creates and issues all of our coins and a small part of our paper money. In mid-1953 these Treasury issues accounted for only 3.5 percent of our total money supply. Most of our paper money is issued by the Federal Reserve banks in the form of Federal Reserve notes.

TABLE 25.   Types of Money and Their Issuers, June 30, 1952

Type of Money	Issuer	Amounts in Billions	Percent of Total Money Supply
Coins	Treasury	$ 1.7	1.4
Paper money	Treasury	2.7	2.2
	Federal Reserve	24.6	19.7
Checking deposits	More than 14,000 commercial banks	95.8	76.7
Total		$124.8	100.0

All our checking deposits, which make up more than three-quarters of our total money supply, are issued by the privately owned commercial banks.

4. The Public's Choice of Money

It is important to note that the distribution of the money supply among the categories of coins, paper money, and checking deposits reflects the choices of individuals and business firms. The size of the total money supply is determined by the issuers of money—the Treasury, Federal Reserve, and commercial banks. But the public is free to determine the form in which it will hold its money. It may exchange its coins or paper money for checking deposits, or it may surrender checking deposits for coin or paper money, and the issuers of money, particularly the banks, stand ready to make these exchanges on a dollar-for-dollar basis. Since the commercial banks cannot create and issue paper money or coins they must get them from the Federal Reserve.

Under ordinary circumstances, relative convenience is the basis of people's choices as to the forms in which they will hold their money. Coins and paper money are the most convenient types of money for meeting some payrolls and payments in retail trade. But for several reasons individuals and business firms find it convenient to hold the larger part of their money in the form of bank deposits, and to make most of their payments with checks on these deposits. (1) Deposits are not so liable to loss or theft as other forms of money. (2) They can be transported very cheaply, no matter how large the payment or how great the distance between payer and payee. (3) Checks can be written for the exact amount of the payment, thereby obviating the necessity of making change and of counting bills and coins. (4) When endorsed by the payee, checks serve as a convenient receipt for payment.

For reasons of this sort the public ordinarily holds the largest part of its money in the form of deposits. Commercial banks can therefore operate on the expectation that deposits will be left in the banking system when they are transferred from one owner or another and that there will not be large net withdrawals of coin and paper money. But there have been occasions when the public has feared that the banks would be unable to redeem deposits in coin and paper money. At these times there have been widespread runs on banks, leading to banking crises and panics. The banks either could not get enough coin and paper money to meet the demands, or could do so only by paying out most of their reserves and reducing their loans so much as to create widespread economic distress.

5. Money as Debt

All of our money is debt. An understanding of this fact is basic to an understanding of our monetary system. Of course, not all debt is money. Most debts, such as real estate mortgages, corporation bonds,

government bonds, and personal obligations, are not generally acceptable as payments, and are therefore not money. Our money includes only the particular types of debt that have come to be generally
acceptable as a means of payment. The holders of these debts consider
them to be assets, for they are valuable claims against the issuers.

A. CHECKING DEPOSITS AS DEBT

Checking deposits are only debt liabilities of the commercial banks
—debts payable on demand to the owner of the deposit claim, or to
anyone to whom the owner of the deposit claim orders payment. The
term "deposits" has misled many people into two fallacious beliefs:
(1) that deposits are "backed" 100 percent by coin and paper money
in the banks' vaults, and (2) that most, if not all, deposit debts were
created and issued in exchange for the "deposit" of coin and paper
money. Both of these beliefs are quite wrong. Rare indeed is the bank
that holds coin and paper money equal to more than 2 or 3 percent
of its deposit debts. Deposits are merely debt claims against the general assets of the banks, and most of these assets are in the form of
bank claims against others. Moreover, most of the deposits were not
created and issued by the banks in exchange for coin and currency;
most of them were created and issued to those who borrow from the
banks or sell securities to them. For example, if you borrow $100 from
a bank, giving it your I.O.U., the money that you get will usually be
in the form of a newly created checking deposit.

B. OTHER TYPES OF MONEY AS DEBT

Paper money is also debt. However beautiful and finely engraved
they may be, the "bills" that we use in payment are only promissory
notes representing debts of their issuers. Federal Reserve notes are
only debt liabilities of the Federal Reserve banks, representing general
claims against the assets of the Federal Reserve banks. Similarly, the
paper money issued by the Treasury is but debt of the United States
government.

The same is true of coins. They are debts of the United States government, even though the evidence of the debt is stamped on metal
rather than paper. The market value of the metals in these coins is
considerably below the face value of the coins, and there is no good
reason why even cheaper metals could not be used. Iron or steel coins
would serve just as well, leaving aside questions of corrosion, aesthet-
ics, and ease of counterfeiting.

c. Conclusions

In short, our entire money supply is made up of debts—debts of particular kinds that have come to be generally acceptable in payment. The process of increasing the money supply is therefore one of increasing the quantity of these particular types of debts. And the process of destroying money is one of decreasing the outstanding quantity of these particular types of debts.

Understanding of this point is important for two reasons. (1) It brings out one common character of all types of moneys—they differ only in the agency whose debt they represent, and the confidence of the public in these agencies constitutes the money supply's only ultimate "backing." (2) It shows why banks are able to create money. So long as a bank is willing and legally able to add to its promises to pay (debts) it can add to the money supply by issuing these promises to business and private borrowers in return for their I.O.U.'s.

6. The Processes of Creating and Destroying Money

A. Creating and Destroying Money by Buying and Selling Assets

In later sections we shall examine in detail the processes of creating and destroying money. However, a brief outline of these processes may be useful at this point.

The money-issuing agencies—the Treasury, the Federal Reserve, and the commercial banks—create and issue money to pay for *assets* that they acquire, and they withdraw and destroy money as they sell assets. Roughly, a bank asset may be defined as any valuable item purchased and held by a bank or other institution, which is useful to it in the conduct of its business. Included is a wide variety of items ranging from bank buildings to bonds which earn interest for the institution holding them.

To pay for assets that they purchase and hold, these institutions create and issue debt money in the form of coins, paper money, or deposits. This can be clarified by an example. Suppose that at some time the public sells to the monetary institutions $10 billion worth of gold, bonds, or any other sort of assets. The monetary institutions pay for them by creating and issuing to the public additional coin, paper money, or checking deposits. Thus in paying for the assets they bought, the monetary institutions have created and issued additional money to the public.

On the other hand, these institutions withdraw and destroy money by making net sales of assets to the public. As the public makes net purchases of assets from the monetary institutions, it pays in coins, paper money, or checking deposits, and this debt money is retired. Suppose, for example, that the public buys from the monetary institutions $5 billion worth of gold, bonds, or any other sort of assets. To pay for these assets the public must relinquish an equal amount of its coin, paper money, or checking deposits. Thus the net sale of assets by the monetary institutions has reduced the public's money supply.

B. TYPES OF ASSETS BOUGHT, HELD, AND SOLD BY THE MONETARY INSTITUTIONS

The principal types of assets purchased, held, and sold by the monetary institutions are gold and debt claims against others.

Debt claims against others are by far the larger part of the total. These include debt claims against federal, state, and local governments, corporations, other businesses, individuals, and so on. Specifically, they include bonds, mortgages, and many other forms of I.O.U.'s. In fact, there is almost no type of debt claim that is not bought or sold by one or more of these monetary institutions. When they buy debt claims against others, these institutions create and issue in payment coins, paper money, or deposits. And when they make net sales of these debt claims against others, they withdraw coins, paper money, or deposits.

Of the greatest importance to an understanding of our monetary system and its relationship to general credit conditions is this fact, that the monetary institutions create and issue money largely by purchasing debt claims against others, and that they withdraw and destroy money largely by decreasing their holdings of debt claims against others. When these institutions are willing and able to buy and hold very large amounts of debt obligations at low interest rates, the supply of loans is likely to be large and interest rates low. But when they will hold only smaller amounts of debt obligations and at higher interest rates, the total supply of loans is likely to be smaller and interest rates higher.

Gold is the other principal asset purchased, held, and sold by these monetary institutions. When they buy gold, they create and issue debt money to pay for it. And when they sell gold, they retire the money received in payment for it. The role of gold in the monetary system will be discussed more fully later.

7. Functions of the Monetary Institutions

With this general background, we can now examine the specific monetary functions of the Treasury, the Federal Reserve, and the commercial banks. These will be treated separately, but it will quickly become apparent that they are interrelated in many ways. For our present purposes, the following interrelationships are most important: (1) The commercial banks hold deposits at the Federal Reserve banks. As we shall see, these are the reserves of the commercial banks. Banks also pay each other by transferring these deposit claims against the Federal Reserve from payer to payee banks. (2) The commercial banks may borrow from the Federal Reserve or sell U.S. government securities to it. When they do this, the Federal Reserve gives them deposit claims against itself. When the commercial banks repay loans to the Federal Reserve or purchase government securities from it, they must surrender in payment an equal amount of their deposit claims against the Federal Reserve. (3) The commercial banks may get coin and paper money from the Federal Reserve by surrendering an equal amount of their deposit claims against it, and they may ship coin and paper money to the Federal Reserve in exchange for deposit credits there. (4) The Treasury borrows from both the Federal Reserve and the commercial banks. Some of the other interrelationships among these institutions will be brought out in the following pages.

8. The Monetary Functions of the Treasury

Though the United States Treasury has a wide range of duties, we shall concentrate here on its monetary functions. Two of these will be discussed at this point: its function (1) as issuer of "Treasury currency," (2) as purchaser, holder, and seller of gold.

A. TREASURY CURRENCY

As we have already seen, the Treasury itself issues all the coins that we use, and a small part of our paper money. In practice, this component of our money supply has been only a very small part of the total, and has fluctuated slowly and within narrow limits. We therefore need not discuss it further.

B. GOLD

Of much greater importance is the Treasury's function of buying, holding, and selling gold. Since January, 1934, the United States has been on a *gold-bullion standard,* with the official price of gold at $35 an ounce. Under this standard the Treasury must buy at $35 an ounce all the gold that is offered to it, whether the gold comes from imports, domestic production, or the melting of gold scrap. It must also sell at $35 an ounce all the gold that is demanded from it for "legal purposes." In general, these "legal purposes" include only demands for gold for export or for "legitimate" industrial, artistic, or professional uses. Gold will not be supplied for other purposes, such as hoarding. As a result, all of our monetary gold is under Treasury ownership. Most of it is locked up in Fort Knox, though some is in vaults elsewhere. Except as already noted, neither the public, nor the commercial banks, nor the Federal Reserve may hold gold for their own account.

C. GOLD FLOWS AND THE MONEY SUPPLY

Even though our monetary gold is all locked up in Fort Knox or other Treasury vaults, changes in the size of our monetary gold stock can have an important influence on monetary conditions, for the Treasury must pay money for the gold it buys, and must collect money for the gold it sells. To show that this is true, let us suppose that you indirectly sell $100 million of gold to the Treasury. You may get the gold by importing it, mining it, or melting scrap. The following transactions are not the only ones which may occur, but the results will be the same even if the procedure is different: (1) You sell the gold to your commercial bank, which pays you by adding $100 million to your deposit account. Thus, the public's total money supply has been directly increased by $100 million. (2) Since the commercial bank may not legally hold gold, it will sell the gold to the Federal Reserve, which will pay by adding $100 million to the commercial bank's deposit at the Federal Reserve banks. Since these deposits at the Federal Reserve are legal reserves for the commercial banks, the latter's legal reserves are increased by $100 million. (3) The Federal Reserve will sell the gold to the Treasury, which will pay by creating and issuing $100 million of "gold certificates" to the Federal Reserve. These gold certificates may be held only by the Federal Reserve banks and constitute the legal reserves of those banks.

This example illustrates a general principle: When gold flows into the monetary system it must be paid for, and the net gold inflow tends directly to increase by an equivalent amount (1) the public's money supply, (2) commercial bank reserves in the form of deposits at the Federal Reserve, and (3) Federal Reserve bank reserves in the form of gold certificates. Moreover, as we shall see later, this increase of bank reserves tends to increase the power of commercial banks to lend and create more money. It is for these reasons that large gold inflows can have highly expansionary effects.

Conversely, gold outflows from the monetary system tend directly to reduce the money supply, commercial bank reserves, and Federal Reserve bank reserves. Suppose, for example, that you indirectly buy for export $50 million of gold from the Treasury. The process may be as follows: (1) You buy the gold from a commercial bank, paying for it by relinquishing $50 million of your deposit claims. Thus, the public's total money supply is reduced by this amount. (2) The commercial bank buys the gold for you from the Federal Reserve, paying for it by relinquishing $50 million of its deposits at the Federal Reserve. Thus, commercial bank reserves are correspondingly reduced. (3) The Federal Reserve relinquishes $50 million of gold certificates to the Treasury in payment for the gold, thereby losing some of its own legal reserves.

This example illustrates the general principle that net reductions of our monetary gold stock tend directly to decrease by equivalent amounts the public's money supply, commercial bank reserves, and Federal Reserve bank reserves. And because of their loss of reserves, the banks may have to decrease their loans and reduce the money supply still further. Hence, gold outflows may tend both directly and indirectly to reduce the money supply and tighten credit conditions.

Thus, the Treasury affects the monetary situation both as issuer of coins and certain types of paper money, and as purchaser and seller of gold. However, its influence as a buyer and seller of gold is largely passive, for the effect on the money supply depends on how much gold is sold to or bought from the public, and about this the Treasury has no direct say. Under the law it must passively buy or sell whatever quantities the public offers or demands for legal purposes. In this way the supply of money can be subjected to influences not directly controllable by the government. The effects of this autonomous influence of gold on the money supply, as well as the Treasury's other powers to influence monetary conditions, will be considered later.

9. The Federal Reserve System: The U.S. Central Bank

Almost every economically advanced country has its "central bank" whose major function is to regulate, if not to exercise precise control over, its monetary system. Thus, there are the Bank of England, the

Bank of France, the Bank of Canada, the Central Bank of Bolivia, the National Bank of Cuba, and so on. The Federal Reserve System is the central bank of the United States. And like other central banks, its primary function is monetary management—the regulation of not only its own activities in creating and destroying money, but also those of the private commercial banks.

A. STRUCTURE AND CONTROL

At first glance, the structure of the Federal Reserve appears far more complex than that of other central banks. No other country has more than one central bank. But in the United States, with its fear of excessive centralization, this solution was considered unacceptable when the Federal Reserve System was established in 1914. The country was therefore divided into twelve districts, each with its own Federal Reserve bank. Each of these banks has its own corporate charter, its own board of directors, and its own executive officers. The twelve Federal Reserve banks are located in the following cities:

Boston	Chicago
New York	St. Louis
Philadelphia	Minneapolis
Cleveland	Kansas City
Richmond	Dallas
Atlanta	San Francisco

These regional banks are not autonomous, however. From the very beginning the location of control over the System has been a controversial subject. Some wanted a very high degree of centralized control; others demanded a large degree of regional autonomy. The advocates of centralized control have been largely victorious. Control over the entire Federal Reserve System is now largely centralized, so that we can, without much violence to the facts, consider the System as one central bank with one monetary policy and one balance sheet.

The System has two central control agencies. The Board of Governors of the Federal Reserve System is composed of seven members appointed by the President with the advice and consent of the Senate. To give them a high degree of independence from the executive department, the members of the Board are appointed for fourteen-year terms. The other central control agency is the Federal Open-Market Committee. It is composed of twelve members, including the seven members of the Board of Governors, and five of the presidents of the Federal Reserve banks. The Open-Market Committee controls Federal Reserve purchases and sales of U.S. government securities. The Board of Governors controls most of the other Federal Reserve policies.

B. FUNCTIONS

The Federal Reserve performs many types of functions. It acts as fiscal agent for the Treasury, supervises and examines banks, clears and collects checks for the banks, and does many other financial "chores." Here, however, we shall concentrate on the primary function of the Federal Reserve—the function of general monetary management. This is the job of controlling the size of the money supply and the availability and cost of credit. In performing this task, the Federal Reserve not only controls its own creation and destruction of money, but also regulates the money-creating and -destroying activities of the commercial banks.

10. Monetary Management by the Federal Reserve

The ability of the Federal Reserve to control the amount of money created by the commercial banks is derived from two powers: (1) control over the reserve requirements of commercial banks, and (2) control over the dollar volume of commercial bank reserves.

A. COMMERCIAL BANK RESERVE REQUIREMENTS

American commercial banks are required by law to hold legal reserves equal to at least a stated percentage of their deposits. These are called *legal reserve requirements*. For the commercial banks that are members of the Federal Reserve—and these banks hold most of the deposits at commercial banks—both the form of the legal reserves and the minimum ratio of these reserves to deposits are stipulated. All their legal reserves must be in the form of deposits at the Federal Reserve banks.

Within limits set by law, the Board of Governors is empowered to set and to vary the percentages of reserves that member commercial banks must hold against their deposits. Though these requirements are complex and vary with the class of bank, we can summarize the situation by saying that the Board may fix average reserve requirements against checking deposits at member commercial banks at not less than 10 percent or more than 20 percent. Fixing a minimum ratio of reserves that must be held against deposits is a device for limiting the amount of deposits that may be created. For example, to decree that banks must hold reserves equal to at least 10 percent of their checking deposit liabilities is the same as saying that their checking deposits may not exceed 10 times the volume of legal reserves available to them. Or to decree that the banks must hold legal reserves equal to at least 20 percent of their checking deposit liabilities is to say that their checking deposit liabilities may not exceed 5 times the volume of their legal reserves.

The amount of checking deposit liabilities that commercial banks may have outstanding at any time is indicated by a simple formula. Let us use the following symbols:

D for the maximum amount of checking deposit liabilities that may be outstanding.

A for the dollar volume of legal reserves available to banks.

R for the minimum legal ratio of reserves to deposits, stated as a fraction (e.g., $\frac{1}{5}$).

Then we must have

$$D \cdot R = A.$$

This states, for example, that if $R = \frac{1}{5}$, reserves, A, must be (at least) $\frac{1}{5}$ of deposits, D. It is convenient to rewrite this formula as:

$$D = A/R.$$

This tells us that if $R = \frac{1}{10}$ (i.e., 10 percent), each dollar of reserves will support up to $10 of deposits; but with reserve requirements at 20 percent (i.e., $R = \frac{1}{5}$) each dollar of reserves will support no more than $5 of deposits.

The Board of Governors uses its power to determine R as a means of regulating the volume of deposits that commercial banks may create and have outstanding. By raising R the Board can force the banks to decrease the amount of deposits supported by each dollar of their reserves. And by lowering R the Board can create excess reserves for the banks, and enable them to increase the amounts of their deposits relative to the dollar volume of reserves.

The Federal Reserve also regulates the money-creating and -destroying activities of the commercial banks through its power to create and destroy commercial bank reserves—the A in our formula. Given the reserve ratio, R, the lending ability of the commercial banks can obviously be restricted by reducing their reserves, and vice versa. The Federal Reserve can create bank reserves by lending to banks and by purchasing government securities. And it can decrease bank reserves by decreasing the amount of its loans to banks and by selling government securities.

B. FEDERAL RESERVE LOANS TO BANKS

Let us look first at Federal Reserve loans to banks. Suppose that
the Federal Reserve increases the volume of its loans to banks. These
loans consist of additions to the deposit accounts of the banks borrowing from the Federal Reserve. This creates bank reserves that did
not exist before. On the other hand, when the Federal Reserve decreases the volume of its loans to banks, it collects from the repaying
banks by deducting from their deposits at the Federal Reserve, thereby
destroying bank reserves.

The Federal Reserve employs two instruments to regulate the volume and cost of its loans to banks: (1) its discount rate—the interest
rate it charges on its loans, and (2) moral suasion or direct action. To
encourage banks to borrow from it, the Federal Reserve may lower its
discount rate, thereby lowering the cost of getting bank reserves and
signifying its own willingness to lend more freely. It may also use various types of moral suasion, such as public speeches and letters to
banks, to induce banks to borrow from it, and to lend more freely
and at lower rates of interest. If, on the other hand, it wishes to
tighten credit and raise interest rates in general, it may raise its discount rates and employ moral suasion in an attempt to discourage
bank borrowing from it and to reduce the supply of bank credit.

C. FEDERAL RESERVE OPEN-MARKET OPERATIONS

The founders of the Federal Reserve System expected that it would
extend its credit primarily by lending to banks, and the System did this
in its early years. However, in recent decades, as the size of the federal
debt expanded greatly, the Federal Reserve has lent much less to
banks, and has extended its credit largely through the purchase of
U.S. government securities in the open market. These so-called "open-
market operations" are now the principal method used by the Federal
Reserve to regulate the volume of bank reserves and general credit
conditions. By purchasing government securities, the Federal Reserve
creates bank reserves, and by selling governments it destroys bank reserves. These operations are so important as to merit further consideration.

Let us consider two types of Federal Reserve purchases of government securities: (1) from commercial banks, and (2) from nonbank
holders. When the Federal Reserve purchases securities from commercial banks, the effect is to reduce commercial bank holdings of

government securities and to increase their holdings of legal reserves, for the Federal Reserve pays the banks by adding to their deposit accounts at the Reserve banks. Thus, the Federal Reserve manufactures deposits with itself to pay for the securities it buys.

When the Federal Reserve buys securities from nonbank holders, it directly increases both the public's money supply and commercial bank reserves. For example, suppose that you sell $10 million of government securities to the Federal Reserve and receive a check drawn on a Reserve bank. You will deposit the check with a commercial bank, which will add $10 million to your deposit, and your bank will forward the check to the Federal Reserve to get a $10-million addition to its reserve account. In short, all purchases of government securities by the Federal Reserve tend to create commercial bank reserves, but purchases from nonbank holders also add directly to the public's money supply.

Federal Reserve sales of securities have just the reverse effects; they decrease bank reserves. When the Federal Reserve sells securities to a commercial bank, it collects by reducing the bank's deposit account with it. In this way it destroys bank reserves. When the Federal Reserve sells securities to nonbank buyers, it directly reduces both bank reserves and the public's money supply. For example, suppose you buy $1 million of governments from the Federal Reserve and pay for them with a check on your commercial bank. On receiving the check, the Federal Reserve will deduct its amount from your bank's reserve account and send the check to your bank, which will deduct its amount from your deposit account. By this process of selling governments to a nonbank purchaser, the Federal Reserve has directly reduced both commercial bank reserves and the public's money supply.

It should be evident that through these open-market operations in U.S. government securities, of which more than $200 billions are held outside the Treasury, the Federal Reserve can greatly influence the money supply and the availability and cost of credit. This influence is exerted both through the effects on commercial bank reserves, and through the direct effects of Federal Reserve purchases and sales on the prices and interest yields on government bonds.

To understand the Federal Reserve's influence on interest rate (the cost of credit) we must digress momentarily. We must see that the market price of a bond is directly related to the market rate of interest, the higher the market rate of interest the lower being the price of the bond. This is because a bond is a contract by the firm or government which issues it to return a fixed amount of money (its face value) to its holder after a specified amount of time, and in the meantime to pay him a fixed dollar amount of interest per year.

If, when a bond is first sold, the rate of interest is 3 percent, and its face value is $100, it involves the firm in a contract to pay the bond-holder $3 a year, say for ten years, and to repay $100 at the end of the period. Suppose that a few days after the initial sale of the bond, the market rate of interest suddenly rises to 6 percent. One hundred dollars will now pay a purchaser of a new bond $6 per year for ten years, and the return of the $100 at the end of that period. Clearly no one will any longer be willing to pay $100 for the first bond, and its price must fall. In sum, a fall in interest rates is the same thing as a rise in bond prices. Saying that bond prices have fallen is just another way of saying that the rate of interest has risen.

We can now see how the open-market purchases of the Federal Reserve System affect the economy. Suppose that the Federal Reserve stands ready to buy an unlimited volume of government securities at low interest rates. These purchases will tend directly to hold up the prices of government securities and *so hold down their interest yields,* and every purchase will add to the volume of commercial bank reserves. The public's money supply will be directly increased to the extent of the Federal Reserve's purchases from nonbank sellers. On the other hand, the Federal Reserve can raise interest rates and decrease the supply of credit by selling government securities, so as to lower their prices and raise their interest yields. Every sale will lower commercial bank reserves, and sales to nonbank buyers will also directly reduce the public's money supply.

D. FEDERAL RESERVE NOTES

Besides controlling the quantity of money issued by the commercial banks, the Federal Reserve influences the money supply by issuing paper money of its own. These bills are called Federal Reserve notes. The supply of these notes has tended to fluctuate rather widely in the past. They account for the larger share of the changes in the stock of paper money.

11. Reserve Requirements of the Federal Reserve Banks

We have found that the Federal Reserve has the power to manufacture paper money in the form of Federal Reserve notes and also deposits with itself, the latter serving as legal reserves for commercial banks. These notes and deposits are created and issued by the Federal Reserve to pay for assets acquired by it, these assets being primarily gold certificates, promissory notes of borrowing banks, and U.S. government securities. We are thus led to this question: What are the limits to the amount of Federal Reserve notes and of deposits at the Reserve banks that may be created? The formal limit is to be found in the law requiring the Federal Reserve banks to hold gold certificates equal to at least 25 percent of their outstanding Federal Reserve notes and deposit liabilities. In other words, the sum of outstanding Federal Reserve notes and deposits may not exceed 4 times the gold certificate reserves of the Federal Reserve.

In practice, however, this requirement has not often restricted Federal Reserve actions, for as a matter of policy the System has usually held the volume of its outstanding notes and deposits far below the level that would have been permitted by its gold certificate holdings and its reserve requirements. Moreover, the Board of Governors may, if it wishes, suspend these reserve requirements. For these reasons we may assume that the System's actions in creating or destroying Federal Reserve notes and deposits are determined by its policy decisions rather than by its reserve requirements.

12. Summary

Before discussing commercial banking, which will be the subject of the next chapter, it will be useful to summarize some of our most important findings up to this point.

1. Listed in order of size, the components of our money supply are checking deposits, paper money, and coins. These are created and issued by more than 14,000 privately owned and privately operated commercial banks, the Federal Reserve, and the Treasury.

2. All this money is debt money; it includes the particular types of debt that, largely as a result of convenience and custom, have achieved the status of general acceptability as a means of payment. Money can therefore be created or destroyed easily by increasing and decreasing the outstanding volume of these types of debt.

3. The monetary institutions—the Treasury, the Federal Reserve, and the commercial banks—create and issue money to pay for assets acquired by them, and they withdraw and retire money by making net sales of assets.

4. The principal assets purchased and sold by these institutions are gold and debt claims against others. The latter include debt obliga-

tions of all types of government and private borrowers and are by far the larger part of the total.

5. The primary function of the Federal Reserve, as the central bank of this country, is general monetary management. This includes regulating not only its own money-creating and -destroying activities, but also those of the private commercial banks.

6. The Federal Reserve can regulate the money-creating and -destroying activities of commercial banks in two principal ways: (a) by fixing their legal reserve requirements, and (b) by regulating the volume and cost of their legal reserves.

7. The Federal Reserve can bring pressure on the commercial banks to curtail the money supply, restrict the availability of credit, and raise interest rates by taking one or more of the following actions: (a) raising the reserve requirements of the member commercial banks; (b) discouraging bank borrowing at the Federal Reserve by raising discount rates (the interest rate on commercial bank borrowing from the Federal Reserve) and using moral suasion in a restrictive manner; (c) selling U.S. government securities in the open market.

8. The Federal Reserve can encourage the commercial banks to expand the money supply, increase the availability of credit, and lower interest rates by taking one or more of these actions: (a) lowering the reserve requirements of the member commercial banks; (b) encouraging bank borrowing by lowering discount rates and using moral suasion in an expansionary way; (c) buying U.S. government securities in the open market.

SUGGESTED READINGS

Board of Governors of the Federal Reserve System, *The Federal Reserve System—Its Purposes and Functions,* Washington, 2nd ed., 1947.

Chandler, Lester V., *The Economics of Money and Banking,* Harper, New York, rev. ed., 1953.

QUESTIONS

1. a. How would you define money?
   b. Show that checking deposits perform all the ordinary monetary functions.
   c. What are the advantages of holding money in the form of checking deposits?
   d. Why is it not advantageous to hold all money in the form of checking deposits?

2. a. Why are some debt claims against the government and the banks usable as money, whereas debt claims against the Lower Slobovia Gold Prospecting Company are not?
   b. Can you think of any private debt claims that might conceivably perform some monetary functions? Explain.
   c. How can you collect on a debt claim against a bank?
   d. Against the government?
3. a. What is meant by money "creation"?
   b. Who can create it?
   c. When does the creation of a bank deposit involve a net addition to the stock of money?
   d. Who obtains such bank deposits?
4. a. List some of the types of claims against others that might be bought by banks.
   b. What is bought by the bank when it lends money to a man to help him finance his automobile purchase?
   c. Why should a bank want to buy debt claims?
   d. Explain the process whereby the purchase of such a claim by banks adds to the coins, paper money, or deposits held by the public.
5. Suppose gold is sold by Jones to a commercial bank, which sells it to the Federal Reserve, which sells it to the Treasury.
   a. Show why the addition to the commercial bank's deposits with the Federal Reserve may have more influence on the public's money supply than the equal increase in Jones' deposits in the commercial bank.
   b. Show why the influence of the former *need* not be greater than that of the latter.
   c. Why is the effect of the gold inflow on the Federal Reserve's holding of Treasury gold certificates likely to have little or no effect on the public's money supply?
6. It has been proposed that the law be changed to require banks to hold 100 percent reserves against deposits.
   a. How would this affect the likelihood and seriousness of runs on banks?
   b. How would this affect the ability of the Federal Reserve to influence the nation's money supply?
   c. Is this likely to help eliminate inflation and deflation?
7. a. Why might a bank borrow from the Federal Reserve even though it makes no immediate profits by doing so?
   b. Suppose a commercial bank finds that the public's cash withdrawals have reduced its reserves below the legal requirements; what can it do?
   c. Will a bank ever allow its reserves to fall to the legal requirement?

    d. How will the discount rate affect how close to its minimum reserves the bank is willing to go?

    e. How does this suggest that a change in the discount rate can affect the public's money supply?

8. Show how the Federal Reserve's purchase of bonds in the open market affects:

    a. The supply of money in the hands of the public directly.

    b. The reserves of the commercial banks.

    c. The supply of money in the hands of the public indirectly.

    d. The price of government bonds.

    e. The rate of interest on government bonds.

9. If the rate of interest on one type of government bond rises from 4 percent to 6 percent,

    a. What will tend to happen to comparable General Motors bonds which have been yielding 5 percent?

    b. What will happen to comparable bonds of the Super-Bonanza-We-Hope-We-Find-Oil-Gushers Company, which had been promising 8 percent?

    c. Show how Federal Reserve open-market operations can affect interest rates on private loans.

    d. How is this relevant to the influence of the Federal Reserve on private investment, income, and employment?

10. a. If the price of a bond falls, how does this automatically affect its interest yield?

    b. If the rate of interest on newly issued bonds falls, show how this affects the price of old bonds.

    c. The yield on old bonds.

11. a. Reconcile the statements that some 75 percent of our currency consists of checking deposits, and that some 90 percent of payments are made by the transfer of checking deposits.

    b. What does this imply about the average frequency with which such a dollar changes hands as compared with a dollar in coin or paper money?

CHAPTER 15

Commercial Banks

1. The Nature of Commercial Banks

The distinguishing characteristic of a commercial bank is its power to create checking deposits which serve as money. Many other types of financial institutions can lend and can purchase securities, but they cannot create checking deposits or any other type of money. They can only lend money that they get from others. It is because commercial banks are our only privately owned institutions with the power to create and destroy money that we single them out for study.

We shall consider only the commercial banking functions that are directly related to the creation and destruction of money. In passing, however, it is worth noting that many of these banks are in effect financial department stores, also acting as savings banks, managers of trust funds, financial advisers, dealers in foreign exchange, sellers of insurance, and so on.

There are more than 14,000 commercial banks in the United States. About 5000 are national banks operating under charters granted by the federal government. More than 9000 are state banks operating under charters granted by the 48 states. Since we are here interested in the overall economic effects of commercial bank activities, most of our discussion will relate to the commercial banking system as a whole. We shall have little to say about the activities and problems of individual banks.

2. Commercial Bank Creation and Destruction of Money

As indicated in the preceding chapter, commercial banks create and issue money to pay for assets they purchase, and they withdraw and destroy money by making net sales of assets. When banks buy assets, they usually pay for them by creating new checking deposits, giving these deposits to the sellers of assets. And when banks sell assets, they collect payment for them, usually by reducing their deposit liabilities to the purchasers of assets. These principles apply regardless of the nature of the assets purchased or sold by the banks.

A. TYPES OF BANK ASSETS

But what types of assets do the banks purchase, hold, and sell? Table 26 indicates that loans and securities constitute by far the largest

TABLE 26. Assets of All Insured Commercial Banks in the United States, June 30, 1952[1]

Type of Asset	Amount (in billions)	Percent of Total Assets
Coin and paper money in vault	$ 2.4	1.5
Deposits at the Federal Reserve	19.3	12.3
Debt claims against others (loans and securities)	132.8	84.7
Other assets	2.3	1.5
Total	$156.8	100.0

Addendum: Types of Loans and Securities Held

Type	Amount (in billions)	Percent of Total Loans and Securities
Securities of:		
U.S. government	$ 60.2	45.1
Other governments, mostly state and local	9.7	7.3
Corporations and other	4.0	3.0
Loans:		
Commercial and industrial	25.2	18.9
Loans to farmers (except on real estate)	3.6	2.7
Loans to buy or carry securities	3.0	2.3
Real estate loans	14.9	11.2
Other loans to individuals	11.2	8.4
Other loans	1.5	1.1
Total loans and securities	$133.3	100.0

part of the total. In mid-1952, loans and securities made up nearly 85 percent of total bank assets. All of these are debt claims against others, most of them evidenced by some sort of promissory note. The adden-

[1] Source: Federal Deposit Insurance Corporation Report. Claims of commercial banks against each other have been eliminated in this table.

dum to Table 26 shows the wide variety of debt obligations held by commercial banks. These include debts of the federal government, other governmental units, corporations, other businesses, farmers, and consumers. Many are *short-term;* they are repayable not more than a year later. Others, such as government bonds, mortgages, and corporation bonds, are *long-term;* they are repayable only after many years. In short, commercial banks deal in almost all types of debt obligations.

This point deserves emphasis because many people, noting that these are called "commercial" banks, assume that they make only "commercial" loans, i.e., loans to businessmen, and only short-term loans at that. Whether or not this may have been true at some time in the past, it is not true today. For example, in mid-1952 more than 52 percent of all the debt obligations held by banks were government debts. Some of these had been purchased directly from the government units, others from other holders. Another 11 percent were loans on real estate and more than 8 percent were consumer loans.

B. BANK PURCHASES OF ASSETS

Banks acquire debt obligations in two principal ways. (1) In many cases banks buy the debt obligations from the borrowers who create them. For example, you may borrow money directly from a bank to help buy a factory, a house, or an automobile, giving in return your own newly created promise to repay in the future. (2) In other cases the banks buy obligations not from the debtor himself but from an intermediate holder. For example, you might get money from a bank by selling to it some of your holdings of U.S. government securities, corporation bonds, real estate mortgages, or any other kind of debt obligation.

In each case, however, the banks create and issue money in the form of checking deposits to pay for the debt obligations they buy. Suppose, for example, that the banks increase their holdings of loans and securities by $2 million. This would show up on the banks' financial statements as follows:

		INCREASE IN BANK DEBT	
ASSETS ACQUIRED		TO OTHERS	
Increase of loans and		*Increase* of checking	
securities	$2 million	deposits	$2 million

This example shows how the banks create and issue checking deposits to pay for assets in the form of debt claims against others. And

since the volume of other types of money is not reduced, this constitutes a net addition to the total money supply.

C. BANK SALES OF ASSETS

Conversely, banks reduce both the volume of checking deposits and
the total money supply by decreasing their holdings of debt claims
against others—that is, by making net sales of these debt obligations.
Those who buy these debt obligations from the banks pay for them by
surrendering checking deposits.

This is true whether the banks reduce the volume of their outstanding loans to customers or make net sales of debt obligations to others.
For example, suppose that you buy $1 million of debt obligations from
the banks—either your own debt obligations or those of someone else
—and that you pay for them by surrendering $1 million of your check-
ing deposits. The effect on the banks' financial statement will be as
follows:

		DECREASE IN BANK DEBT TO OTHERS	
ASSETS LOST			
Decrease of loans and		*Decrease* of checking	
securities	$1 million	deposits	$1 million

By this process of reducing its assets in the form of loans and securities,
the banking system has destroyed $1 million of checking deposits. And
since this reduction of checking deposits is not offset by any increase
in other types of money, there is a net reduction in the total money
supply.

We now summarize our principal findings up to this point. (1)
Banks create and issue checking deposits to pay for assets they acquire, and they withdraw and destroy checking deposits as they make
net sales of assets. (2) Loans and securities constitute by far the largest
part of bank assets, and fluctuations of bank holdings of loans and
securities account for a major part of the fluctuations in both the volume of checking deposits and the total money supply.

D. OTHER BANK ASSETS

While emphasizing that the banks create and destroy checking deposits primarily by expanding and contracting their holdings of loans
and securities, we must not forget that checking deposits may also be
created or destroyed as banks increase or decrease their other assets.
The most important of these other bank assets, as indicated in Table

26, are deposit claims against the Federal Reserve banks, which count as legal reserves for commercial banks.[2] Transactions that increase or decrease bank assets in this form may also directly increase or decrease the volume of checking deposits. These transactions will be discussed in the following section in which we deal with commercial bank reserves.

3. Reserve Limitations on the Creation of Money by the Banks

The creation of checking deposits through the purchase of loans and securities is likely to be profitable to the banks, for they earn interest on the debts that they buy and hold, and they usually do not pay interest on the checking deposit debts that they create and issue to pay for the earning assets. This raises some interesting questions: Why don't the banks expand the supply of checking deposits indefinitely? Why don't they buy up all the debt obligations in existence, and even go so far as to induce individuals, governmental units, and business to create many more debt obligations by borrowing huge amounts from the banks? What factors limit the amount of money that can be created by banks?

A. RESERVES AS THE LIMIT TO DEPOSIT CREATION

We found the basic answer to these questions in our discussion of the legal reserve requirements of banks.[3] As we saw then, the maximum volume of checking deposits that may be outstanding at any time is indicated by the formula,

$$D = A \cdot \frac{1}{R},$$

where D is the maximum volume of checking deposits,
      A is the dollar volume of legal reserves, and
      R is the minimum ratio of reserves to deposits, expressed as a fraction such as $\frac{1}{10}$ or $\frac{1}{5}$.

Thus the upper limit on the volume of checking deposits is imposed by (1) the height of R, which is fixed by administrative action of the Board of Governors of the Federal Reserve within the limits fixed by law, and (2) the volume of legal reserves (A) available to the commercial banks. If R is $1/10$, the banks may create and have outstanding a volume of checking deposits equal to 10 times the amount of

---

[2] Because its volume fluctuates only narrowly, we shall omit here the item "coin and paper money in vault."
[3] See pp. 270–271 above.

reserves available to them; but if $R = 1/5$, the banks may have outstanding checking deposits equal to only 5 times the volume of their reserves.

This fact, that the volume of checking deposits is a multiple of bank reserves, is very important in understanding commercial banking operations. It means that for every change of $1 in the volume of its legal reserves, the banking system may change the volume of its checking deposits by several dollars. Suppose, for example, that while its reserve requirements are 20 percent, the banking system gets a $1 increase in its supply of legal reserves. If these reserves remain within the banking system, the banks can expand their deposits by $5, and can do so by increasing their holdings of loans and securities. On the other hand, suppose that at a time when they have no excess reserves, the banks lose $1 of reserves. In order to meet their legal reserve requirements, the banks may have to decrease their deposits by $5, and do so by decreasing their loans and security holdings. It is because of this "leverage effect" that changes in the volume of bank reserves can influence so greatly the supply of money and the availability and cost of credit.

B. PRINCIPAL FACTORS THAT CHANGE THE SUPPLY OF BANK RE-
    SERVES

We have already studied two of the principal factors that determine the supply of legal reserves for commercial banks—the size of the monetary gold stock, and the volume of Federal Reserve holdings of loans and securities that are acquired by the Federal Reserve through its open-market purchases or its loans to commercial banks.[4] Increases and decreases of these items tend to bring corresponding increases and decreases in bank reserves.

We now note a third major determinant of the volume of bank reserves—net inflows of coin and paper money to the banking system, and net outflows from the banking system. Net inflows tend to increase bank reserves, and net outflows to decrease them. Suppose that the public elects to decrease by $1 billion its holdings of coin and paper money. It will surrender this amount of coin and paper money to the banks, which will give the public deposits in payment. The banks will send the coin and paper money to the Federal Reserve, which will add their amount to commercial bank reserve balances. The net inflow of

[4] See pp. 267–268; 272–274 above.

coin and paper money to the banks has thus increased bank reserves, and may lead to a multiple expansion of deposits.

Net outflows of coin and paper money from the banking system have just the reverse effect; they decrease bank reserves. Suppose, for example, that the public as a whole withdraws $1 billion of coin and paper money from the banks, paying for it by surrendering $1 billion of deposit claims. The banks will get the cash from the Federal Reserve, and pay for it by surrendering an equal amount of their reserve balances. Thus, net outflows of coin and paper money from the banks tend to decrease bank reserves and necessitate a multiple contraction of bank deposits.

We may summarize the principal factors tending to increase and decrease the volume of bank reserves:

Factors Tending to Increase Commercial Bank Reserves	Factors Tending to Decrease Commercial Bank Reserves
1. Increases in the monetary gold stock.	1. Decreases in the monetary gold stock.
2. Increases in Federal Reserve loans and security holdings.	2. Decreases in Federal Reserve security holdings.
3. Net inflows of coin and paper money into the banking system.	3. Net outflows of coin and paper money from the banking system.

c. The Influence of the Federal Reserve

One fact about these determinants of bank reserves deserves special notice. The Federal Reserve can directly control its own loans and security holdings. It has no direct control over either the size of the monetary gold stock or inflows and outflows of coin and paper money. If inflows or outflows of gold, coin, or paper money tend to produce undesired effects on bank reserves, the Federal Reserve can only try to vary the volume of its loans and security holdings in such a way as to produce the desired net effects on the banks' reserve positions.

4. Actual Versus Maximum Volume of Checking Deposits

Up to this point we have considered only the maximum volume of deposit liabilities that the banks may create and have outstanding at any time, and we found that this depends on the height of their legal reserve requirements and the dollar volume of their reserves. But do the banks actually expand to the maximum permitted by their reserves? What are their incentives to expand to the maximum? Why might they fail to expand to the maximum, electing instead to hold excess reserves?

A. MOTIVES FOR EXPANDING DEPOSITS

The banks' principal incentive to expand to the maximum is their desire for profits. They receive no interest on their deposits at the Federal Reserve banks, and excess reserves represent unutilized power to make loans or buy securities which would yield interest income. They are therefore likely to expand their loans and security holdings to the maximum if they do not consider the risks too high.

B. FEAR OF RUNS AS A DETERRENT

However, there are occasions, especially in times of actual or threatened depression, when banks may prefer to hold excess reserves rather than assume the risks of expanding their earning assets to the maximum. These risks are of two general types: fear of bank runs and fear of deterioration of asset values.

The bank may fear runs—that the public may try to withdraw large amounts of coin and paper money. On various occasions, especially during prolonged depressions, large numbers of banks have failed, and the fear of failures has occasioned large cash withdrawals. In such periods some banks have preferred to hold excess reserves with which to meet some of the threatened drains. The insurance of deposits up to $10,000 for each account, which is now provided by the Federal Deposit Insurance Corporation for most banks, will no doubt lessen but may not eliminate such fears in the future.

C. FEAR OF LOSS IN THE VALUE OF ASSETS

Banks may also be deterred from expanding loans to the legal maximum by the fear that they may suffer losses on their loans and security holdings. This risk may be subdivided into two types. One is that debtors may fail to meet their obligations to pay interest and repay principal. Banks are likely to fear this greatly during a serious depression. As they watch businesses fail in large numbers and the financial positions of others deteriorate, banks may decide that it is wiser to hold idle reserves rather than assume the risk of losing both interest and principal.

The other risk is that interest rates will rise in the future and lower the prices of bonds and other outstanding debt obligations. We have already seen why a rise of interest rates must have this effect.[5] But a fall in the value of the securities which constitute a large proportion of their assets can be a serious financial blow to the banks. They may therefore prefer to hold excess reserves rather than make long-term loans at very low interest rates.

These low interest rates discourage bank lending not only because they offer low earnings to the bank. When interest rates are low the chances are that they will rise eventually (certainly they can't fall much since no one will ordinarily lend money at a zero rate of interest). Low interest rates therefore tend to increase the risk that securities will fall in value since this is what an interest rise means. Low rates will therefore discourage security purchasing (lending) by the banks.

D. BANK POLICIES AND ECONOMIC INSTABILITY

Partly because of these considerations, bank policies may tend to accentuate economic instability. Sharing the general optimism of the business community, banks tend to expand up to the maximum in boom periods, thereby supplying large amounts of credit and retarding, if not preventing, the rise of interest rates. This encourages a high rate of spending for investment purposes. The high rate of investment, together with a high induced rate of consumption spendings, may promote inflation. In this way the banks may tend to "boom the boom." But in periods of recession and depression, when they fear that borrowers may default and they anticipate that interest rates have hit bottom and will soon turn up, the banks may refuse to expand to the maximum and may elect to hold excess reserves. This tends to reduce the supply of credit and to raise interest rates, or at least to reduce the extent to which credit can be made more available and interest rates lowered.

Thus the banks may tend to defeat Federal Reserve efforts to combat depression. No matter how much the Federal Reserve lowers its discount rates, the banks may be reluctant to borrow and lend. And no matter how much the Federal Reserve floods the banks with excess reserves by purchasing securities in the open market and by lowering the banks' reserve requirements, the banks may elect to hold a large part of their reserves idle. This is not to say that such an easy-money policy by the Federal Reserve will be completely ineffective. An easy-money policy usually has some effect in making interest rates lower

[5] See pp. 273–274 above.

and loans more available than they would be in the absence of such a policy. The only point here is that the banks' fear of risks is one of the factors decreasing the effectiveness of an easy-money policy during depression.

_N.B._   ### 5. An Individual Bank in the Banking System

In the preceding sections we emphasized that the banking system as a whole, operating under a system of fractional reserve requirements, can expand its deposits by a multiple of any increase in the volume of its legal reserves, and that it must decrease its deposits by a multiple of any decrease in its supply of reserves if it is not holding excess reserves at the time. For example, if reserve requirements against deposits average 20 percent, each $1 change in the volume of reserves may induce a $5 change in the total deposits of the banking system. It was proper for us to concentrate our attention on the operation of the banking system as a whole because we are here interested in the total money supply, the total supply of credit, and the general behavior of interest rates. However, to avoid misunderstanding we must also emphasize that what is true of the banking system as a whole need not be true, and usually is not true, of any individual bank within the system.

A. DEPOSIT EXPANSION BY AN INDIVIDUAL BANK

For example, an individual bank whose reserves are increased by $1 usually cannot expand its deposits by $5 if its reserve requirements are 20 percent. This is because by lending, the individual bank is likely to lose reserves to other banks in the system. Jones, who borrows from Bank A or sells securities to it, is likely to write checks on his deposit account at A and use them to make payments to Brown, who will deposit them in his own bank, B. Bank A will therefore have to transfer some of its reserves to Brown's bank, B, to pay the checks. Bank A, therefore, will not dare to lend five times as much as it receives in new reserves for fear that it will be unable to pay the checks drawn on these loans. The expansion of the loans and deposits of the individual bank following an initial increase of its reserves is for this reason less than the multiple expansion possible for the banking system as a whole.

B. HOW THE BANKING SYSTEM EXPANDS DEPOSITS MORE

How, then, can the banking system as a whole work $1 of reserves into $5 in deposits if no one bank will make this move? This can be answered by an example which is summarized in Table 27. Let us make the following assumptions: (1) Bank 1 receives a $10-million addition to its reserves in a way that also adds directly to its deposits but is not a transfer of either deposits or reserves from any other bank. This increase at Bank 1 may be due to a net inflow of coin and paper money, or a net import of gold, or Federal Reserve purchases of securities from nonbank sellers. (2) Reserve requirements are 20 per-

TABLE 27. Deposit Expansion on New Reserves by a Banking System[6]

	Additional Deposits Received	Additional Reserves Retained Against Deposits Received (20%)	Additional Loans Made (80%) (The deposits created by these loans are all checked out to the next bank)
1st bank	$10,000,000	$ 2,000,000	$ 8,000,000
2nd bank	8,000,000	1,600,000	6,400,000
3rd bank	6,400,000	1,280,000	5,120,000
4th bank	5,120,000	1,024,000	4,096,000
5th bank	4,096,000	819,200	3,276,800
6th bank	3,276,800	655,360	2,621,440
7th bank	2,621,440	524,288	2,097,152
8th bank	2,097,152	419,430	1,677,722
9th bank	1,677,722	335,544	1,342,178
10th bank	1,342,178	268,436	1,073,742
Total, first ten banks	$44,631,292	$ 8,926,258	$35,705,034
Other banks in turn	5,368,708	1,073,742	4,294,966
Grand Total	$50,000,000	$10,000,000	$40,000,000

cent for all banks. (3) All the deposits created by each bank as it expands its loans are paid out in checks which are deposited in the next bank, and as a result an equal amount of reserves is paid to the transferee bank.

Let us now trace the expansion process. Receiving a $10-million addition to both its deposits and its reserves, Bank 1 has an increased reserve requirement of $2 million and an $8-million addition to its excess reserves. It therefore increases its loans by $8 million, thereby creating deposits which its customers pay out to others who transfer the money to Bank 2. Bank 1 must transfer $8 million of its reserves to Bank 2 in payment. Bank 2 thus gets an $8-million increase in both

[6] This table is based on Board of Governors of the Federal Reserve System, *The Federal Reserve System—Its Purposes and Functions,* 2nd ed., 1947, p. 18.

its deposits and its reserves. Its legal reserve requirements rise $1.6 million (20 percent of $8 million) and its excess reserves by $6.4 million. It therefore increases its loans by $6.4 million, thereby creating deposits which its customers transfer to Bank 3. Bank 2 must transfer $6.4 million of its reserves to Bank 3 in payment. Bank 3, having an increase of $6.4 million in both its deposits and reserves, increases its loans by the amount of its excess reserves, and the new deposits are transferred to Bank 4. And so the process continues. Fairly elementary algebra assures us that when it is finished, the deposits of the banking system as a whole will have been increased by $50 million, of which $10 million represents the initial increase of deposits and $40 million the manufacture of deposits through bank loan expansion.[7]

This example brings out some important points. (1) An individual bank usually cannot expand its deposits by a multiple of any initial increase in its reserves, because in the process of expansion it is likely to lose deposits and reserves to other banks. Each individual banker in our example could quite truthfully say, "But all I did was to expand my loans by an amount equal to my excess reserves!" Yet the banking system as a whole expanded deposits by a multiple of the increase of reserves. (2) An injection of new reserves into any bank or group of banks is likely to lead to a wave of expansion through the system. For example, gold imports into New York banks increase their reserves, this induces them to lend more, some of their reserves are thus transferred to banks in other cities, these banks expand, and so on. Similar results follow when individual banks expand their reserves by borrowing at the Federal Reserve or selling government securities to it.

c. Decreasing Deposits

Similarly, an individual bank that suffers an initial loss of reserves usually need not reduce its deposits by a multiple, though the banking system as a whole must. This is because the individual bank may re-

[7] To see this, suppose Bank 1 receives A dollars in new deposits and reserves. Its reserve requirements go up only by the ⅕ needed to back the A in new deposits, and it can lend out the remaining ⅘ A. Bank 2 receives this ⅘ A and must increase its reserves by ⅕ of this amount. It lends out the remaining ⅘ of its receipt $= ⅘ \cdot ⅘ A$. This is received by Bank 3, which in turn can lend out ⅘ of this amount $= ⅘ \cdot ⅘ \cdot ⅘ A$, and so on. Thus the total deposits created by all the banks, including the original A dollars, will be

$$A + (⅘) A + (⅘ \cdot ⅘) A + (⅘ \cdot ⅘ \cdot ⅘) A + (⅘ \cdot ⅘ \cdot ⅘ \cdot ⅘) A + \text{etc.}$$

This is a simple geometric series. The standard formula to be found in second-year high-school algebras tells us that it all adds up to $5A$. In Table 27 A is $10 million, so that $5A$, the total expansion of the money supply, must be $50 million.

store its reserve position by drawing reserves away from other banks.

This point can best be explained by reversing the process described in our earlier example. Suppose that Bank 1 suffers a $10-million reduction in both deposits and reserves owing to net withdrawals of coin and currency, gold exports, or Federal Reserve sales of securities to its customers. With a $10-million reduction in its actual reserves and only a $2-million reduction in its required reserves, it will now be in a deficient reserve position. It will therefore reduce its loans or sell securities, and at least some of the money used to repay loans and to pay for the securities will be drawn from other banks. These banks now have a deficiency of reserves, so they reduce loans and sell securities, thereby drawing reserves from other banks. Thus the contraction process continues until total deposits in the banking system have been reduced $50 million.

This example illustrates the general principle that a loss of reserves by one bank or group of banks can lead to a wave of contractions through the system. The total contraction is felt not by one bank alone but by all banks.

6. Conclusions

We have described in this chapter the great powers of commercial banks to create and destroy money, increase and decrease the availability of credit for both government and private purposes, and raise and lower interest rates. The behavior of the entire economy depends to a great extent on the way these powers are used. It is largely for this reason that these privately owned and privately operated institutions are subjected to so much more government regulation than most other types of private business.

SUGGESTED READINGS

Sayers, R. S., *The American Banking System,* Oxford, London, 1948.
(See also list at end of Chapter 14.)

QUESTIONS

1. In a bank's financial statement (called a *balance sheet*), assets and liabilities to others (debts and other claims against the bank) always are equal to each other in total.
   a. Show how the accountant can perform this trick.

    b. Will the balance sheet still balance if the bank is in financial trouble? Why?

    c. Can you guess how the bank's profits are balanced out?

2. Suppose the required ratio of reserves to deposits is 20 percent, and that banks always create deposits up to the full legal limits. Show the effects of the following on (1) the public's money supply; (2) commercial bank reserves; and (3) the financial position of the Federal Reserve:

    a. Mr. A's sale of $1 million worth of gold through the banking system to the Treasury.

    b. Mr. B's deposit of one million paper dollars.

    c. Mr. C's sale of $1 million worth of government bonds to the Federal Reserve in an open-market operation.

    d. A loan of $1 million by the Federal Reserve to the First National Bank of Hambone Hollow.

3. a. Explain why the Federal Reserve has no direct control over inflows or outflows of coin or paper money to the public.

    b. Can the public force the Federal Reserve to print more Federal Reserve notes?

    c. How do you think this would affect the supply of paper money in an inflationary period?

    d. How would it affect the supply of bank reserves? Bank deposits?

4. a. Why is a rise in the interest rate another way of saying that the price of bonds has fallen?

    b. Why may the fact that the rate of interest will not fall to zero make it unprofitable to buy bonds when the interest rate is low?

    c. Why may this stop interest rates from falling any more when they reach a fairly low level but one that is still quite a bit higher than zero—i.e., how may it set a floor under interest rates?

5. Suppose the Federal Reserve is trying to increase the money supply.

    a. How can it go about this?

    b. Why might its efforts be frustrated by the behavior of the individual commercial banks?

    c. Why might its efforts be frustrated by the behavior of businessmen and others who are potential borrowers?

    d. Is the Federal Reserve equally in danger of being frustrated in an attempt to reduce the money supply?

6. Repeat the argument of Table 27 on the assumption that the required ratio of bank reserves to deposits is 1/10.

CHAPTER 16

Objectives of Monetary Policy

1. Introduction

We have now completed our general survey of the American monetary system. We have described the money supply, the institutions that issue it, and the processes by which it is increased and reduced. We have also noted the monetary management functions of the Federal Reserve and the various instruments it may use to regulate the supply of money, the availability of credit, and the level of interest rates. This brings us to the problem of the objectives of monetary policy. What should the monetary authorities try to accomplish through the use of their control powers? What should be their goals? If two or more objectives conflict with each other, which should be sought and which rejected?

The problem of selecting appropriate objectives is highly important because the instruments of monetary management can be powerful forces for either evil or good. For example, a perverse policy of increasing the money supply and lowering interest rates in the midst of inflation and of decreasing the money supply and raising interest rates during depression can accentuate fluctuations of national income, employment, and prices. On the other hand, the reverse type of policy may make important contributions to general economic stability.

It would be a serious mistake to assume that the primary and dominating objective of monetary policy has been to achieve and maintain full production, full employment, and stable prices. Our monetary policies have been greatly influenced by other objectives which at times conflict with the achievement of this goal. One of the major

293

purposes of this chapter is to describe some of these objectives and to see how they have influenced the monetary policies that have actually been followed. We shall have to omit several objectives that have influenced policy and concentrate on a few that have been most influential in recent years.

Though admittedly not its only goal, the Federal Reserve has at least professed that one of its important objectives is the achievement and maintenance of economic stability at full employment levels. To simplify matters, let us first look at some of the problems that would be presented by this objective even if it were the sole or dominating goal of monetary policy.

2. Economic Stability at Full Employment

A. THE NATURE OF STABILIZING MONETARY POLICIES

It is easy to outline the types of monetary policies that can be used to regulate the level of national money income. To raise the level of national money income, or to prevent it from declining, the Federal Reserve should attempt to increase the money supply and to lower interest rates. For this purpose, it can take one or more of the following actions: (1) Lower the reserve requirements of commercial banks, thereby creating excess reserves. (2) Lower its discount rate on loans to banks, thereby making it cheaper for the banks to borrow and to add to their reserves. (3) Use moral suasion in an attempt to induce banks to lend more freely. (4) Purchase government securities in the open market so that the money paid for these securities will add to the reserves of commercial banks.

To lower the level of national money income or to prevent it from rising, the Federal Reserve should attempt to decrease the money supply, or at least to halt or retard its increase, and to raise interest rates. To this end it can simply reverse one or more of the four expansionary actions just listed.

Thus, the general nature of a stabilizing type of monetary policy is quite simple. But the actual formulation and administration of such a policy present serious problems. Let us look at a few of these.

B. FULL EMPLOYMENT VERSUS PRICE STABILITY

As we saw earlier, the very concept of "full employment" is somewhat vague. Does "practically full employment" mean that unemployment affects only 7 percent, or 5 percent, or 3 percent of the labor force? The monetary authority should not be vague about this; it should have some specific goal.

Moreover, there may be occasions when stability of prices and the attainment and maintenance of full employment, however defined, conflict with each other. In such cases, which should be sacrificed? How much of a cost in terms of unemployment should we be willing to pay to get price stability? How much of a price increase should we be willing to take to provide employment for another million workers? These are very difficult choices to make.

C. PROBLEMS OF TIMING AND DEGREE

Economic forecasting is notoriously unreliable. Standing at any point of time, it is very difficult for anyone to peer into the future and predict whether national income, employment, and prices will rise, fall, or remain the same. Faced with this fact, should the monetary authorities try to anticipate changes and prevent them, or should they wait until changes have begun and then try to deal with them? Either course is dangerous. If they base their action on forecasts they may often be wrong. For example, if on the basis of forecasts they act to prevent a recession that has not yet begun they may create or accentuate inflationary pressures. On the other hand, if they wait until a recession or inflation has already gained momentum their actions may be much less effective.

A closely related problem is determining the degree to which money should be expanded or restricted. If the policy should be restrictive, just how restrictive should it be? If it is to be expansionary, how expansionary should it be? Too much can be just as dangerous as too little. For instance, measures to halt inflation can be carried so far as to produce depression. And measures to remedy a slight downturn in business can be carried so far as to induce inflation. There is no easy formula for solving problems of this sort.

D. PROBLEMS OF EFFECTIVENESS

There may be occasions when even the most highly expansionary type of monetary policy will not be very effective in halting a depression and restoring full employment. This is especially likely when expectations as to the profitability of investment and the safety of loans have deteriorated seriously. The obstacles to the effectiveness of an expansionary monetary policy may be classified into three groups. (1) Even though they are flooded with excess reserves, commercial banks may estimate risks at such a high level that they will not lend large amounts at low interest rates. Thus the banks may be reluctant to supply more money. (2) Even if the banks are persuaded to make loans more easily available and at lower interest rates, business may be unwilling to borrow the money. This is because the expected profitability of investment has fallen to such low levels that even low interest rates cannot make investment attractive. Thus the public may be reluctant to accept more money. (3) Even if its money supply is increased, the public may prefer to hold its money idle rather than use it for investment, consumption, and lending. Fear of further declines in prices and incomes may prevent increased expenditures for goods. And fear of defaults and future increases in interest rates may prevent or limit the increase in the supply of loans and any consequent decline of interest rates. Thus even if more money is forced on the public, people may be reluctant to use it.

At such times monetary policy alone may be incapable of restoring full employment. It may have to be supplemented by an expansionary type of fiscal policy. This does not mean, however, that an expansionary monetary policy is useless during depressions. It rarely fails completely. Such a policy is likely to make interest rates somewhat lower and the supply of loans somewhat greater than they would be if the monetary policy were more restrictive. This is almost certain to have some buoyant effect on the levels of investment and national income. Combined with appropriate fiscal policies it can prove quite useful in helping improve economic conditions.

E. THE CASE OF INFLATION

These problems need not arise in case of inflation, at least not to the same extent. In depression the job is to *persuade* the banks to create more money and the public to accept and use it. In inflation persuasion plays a less important role in a stabilizing monetary policy. Though the banks may *want* to increase the money supply, the Federal Reserve may *force* them not to do so by raising reserve requirements or by depleting their reserves through open-market operations. The public may therefore find no more money to borrow and use, though it still *wants* more.

F. CONCLUSION

The formulation and administration of monetary policy would present many problems even if the achievement and maintenance of full employment were its sole or dominating objective. But actual Federal Reserve policies have been much influenced by other objectives, some of which have at times conflicted with the achievement of this goal. Let us look at a few of these.

3. The Maintenance of a Gold Standard

A. MONETARY POLICY REQUIREMENTS OF A GOLD STANDARD

One objective of our monetary policy for many years has been to maintain some sort of gold standard with a fixed dollar price for gold, or, what is the same thing, a fixed gold value for the dollar. Since early 1934 the official price of gold has been $35 an ounce; the gold value of the dollar has been kept at $\frac{1}{35}$ of an ounce of gold. In order to prevent the price of gold from falling below this level the monetary authorities must, as in any price-support program, passively buy at the fixed price all the gold that is offered to them. And in order to prevent the price of gold from rising they must passively sell at the fixed price all the gold that is demanded from them for legal purposes. As we found earlier, net gold purchases tend to be expansionary, and net gold sales contractionary.

B. POSSIBLE CONFLICT WITH INCOME STABILIZATION

This objective of maintaining a gold standard, with its requirement that the monetary authorities passively buy and sell gold at the behest of other sellers and buyers, has on occasion conflicted with the objective of combating deflation or inflation. For example, under the depression conditions of 1931 large gold withdrawals for export and domestic hoarding were an unwelcome deflationary influence, for they decreased bank reserves. In the inflationary conditions following World War II, large gold inflows increased bank reserves and added still further to inflationary pressures. It is true, of course, that the Federal Reserve could have offset to at least some extent these undesired influences of gold flows by appropriate changes in the volume of its own security holdings, but its task was made considerably more difficult by the changes in our monetary gold stock over which it had no direct control.

This is not necessarily to argue that the country is unwise to maintain a gold standard. For example, a gold standard may be useful for international purposes. Our only point here is that the objective of maintaining a gold standard has at times conflicted with the objective of fighting inflation and deflation.

4. Facilitation of Treasury Finance

Another influential objective of monetary policy, which at times conflicts seriously with the objective of fighting inflation, is that of enabling the Treasury, acting for the federal government, to borrow large amounts of money at low interest rates.

A. LONG HISTORY OF THIS OBJECTIVE

Subordination of monetary policy to the fiscal needs of government is by no means a recent development. Almost from the beginning of modern nation-states, governments have resorted to increases in the money supply to cover part of their expenditure needs during periods of emergency, and especially during wars.

But recent policies have differed from earlier ones in at least two respects: (1) In the extent to which this objective has shaped monetary policy in peacetime. In earlier periods, the subordination of monetary policy to government fiscal needs was largely limited to war periods. Recently, however, the objective of facilitating Treasury finance and holding down interest rates on the national debt has greatly influenced monetary policy in time of peace, even when the Treasury was not making net additions to the national debt but was only managing the debt already outstanding. (2) In the techniques of money creation. In the earlier period, the new money created to cover government expenditures was largely in the form of paper money issued by the Treasury itself. The continental paper money during the Revolutionary War, paper money during the War of 1812, and the greenbacks of the Civil War are examples of direct Treasury issues. This technique is too obvious and crude for the twentieth century.

B. CURRENT MONETARY TECHNIQUES FOR FACILITATING GOVERN-
    MENT FINANCE

The Treasury itself no longer manufactures the newly created money it wishes to spend; it calls upon the Federal Reserve and commercial banks to do the job for it. In effect, the banking system buys government securities from the Treasury and in return gives newly created money, mostly in the form of new checking deposits. Though the Federal Reserve may itself buy some securities directly from the

Treasury, its primary function in the process is to assure that the commercial banks will be both able and willing to buy the necessary amount of securities at low interest rates. To this end it assures the banks of an adequate supply of low-cost reserves, doing so primarily by standing ready to lend to them at low discount rates or to purchase government securities from banks and other holders at high prices and low yields.

Such an *easy-money policy*—the assurance of a large supply of credit to the Treasury at low interest rates—also tends to assure large supplies of low-cost credit to private borrowers. Having access to large amounts of low-cost reserves, the banks are likely to grant loans liberally to private borrowers as well as to the government. This may be in accord with the needs of the Treasury, for it provides money to the public with which to buy government securities as well as other things, though it raises the costs of the government's purchases at the same time.

c. Conflict with Income Stabilization

The objective of facilitating Treasury finance does not always conflict with the objective of promoting economic stability. In some periods, especially during actual or threatened deflation and unemployment, both objectives call for an easy-money policy. In fact, the provision of easy money for both the government and private borrowers, coupled with government deficit spending financed largely by borrowing from banks, may be a highly useful program for promoting recovery. But in the face of actual or threatened inflation the two objectives may call for quite different policies. At such times an easy-money policy to facilitate Treasury finance and hold down interest rates on the national debt may actively promote inflation.

In the following pages we shall examine American monetary policy since 1940 in some detail in order to show how it was subordinated to the fiscal needs of the Treasury during a large part of the time. In the course of this description we shall encounter many of the principles we have just been discussing, and some previews of the analysis of fiscal policy in the following chapters.

It will be convenient to divide this longer period into two subperiods: (1) The period from mid-1940 to mid-1946, which included the armament and war periods, and (2) the postwar period since mid-1946.

5. Monetary Policy from Mid-1940 to Mid-1946

A. GOVERNMENT WAR EXPENDITURES

One of the most striking economic developments during this period was the great rise of government expenditures for armament and war purposes. Before the initiation of the preparedness program in mid-1940, federal expenditures were running at an annual rate of about $9 billion. But under the impact of the expanding military program they rose rapidly. At the time of Pearl Harbor they had reached an annual rate of nearly $30 billion. After our entrance into the war they rose still more rapidly, reaching a peak annual rate of nearly $100 billion. At the peak of the war effort, federal expenditures alone, in

TABLE 28.   Cash Outgo, Income, and Deficits of the
Federal Government, 1940–1946
(In billions of dollars)

Fiscal Year Ending June 30	Cash Outgo	Cash Income	Cash Deficit
1941	$ 14.1	$ 9.4	$ 4.7
1942	34.6	15.3	19.3
1943	79.0	25.2	53.7
1944	94.1	48.0	46.1
1945	96.0	51.1	44.9
1946	65.7	47.8	17.9
Total	$383.4	$196.7	$186.7

terms of current dollars, exceeded the rate of total private and government spending for output in 1939, and were equal to more than 40 percent of the total value of national output. During the six years following June, 1940, the federal government spent $383 billion (Table 28); this was more than twice its total spendings during the preceding 150 years, 100 times its total spendings during the Civil War, and 10 times its total spendings during World War I.

B. DEFICIT FINANCING AND ITS INFLATIONARY EFFECTS

This great rise of government expenditures was accompanied by inadequate taxation. Many new taxes were levied and the rates of existing taxes were increased, but total tax collections for the six-year period were only $197 billion, leaving a total deficit of $187 billion. During some years the deficit was more than $50 billion.

This huge deficit-spending program was highly expansionary. Rising government expenditures tended to expand total spendings for output in two principal ways: (1) They represented a very large increase in the government's own demands for output, and (2) all these expenditures entered into private money incomes. But taxation extracted from private money incomes far less than rising government expenditures contributed to them, so that private incomes after taxes were greatly increased. In the early stages, while government expenditures and deficits were still relatively small and there was still widespread unemployment, the rise of spending produced but little infla-

TABLE 29.   Federal Net Borrowings and Their Sources, 1940–1946[1]
(In billions of dollars)

Fiscal Year Ending June 30	Net Cash Borrowing	By Nonbank Holders	By Federal Reserve and Commercial Banks—Total	By Commercial Banks	By Federal Reserve Banks
			Net Increase in the Amount of Federal Debt Held		
1941	$ 5.4	$ 2.1	$ 3.3	$ 3.6	$ −0.3
1942	19.7	12.9	6.8	6.3	0.5
1943	60.3	28.5	30.8	26.2	4.6
1944	56.8	32.9	23.9	16.2	7.7
1945	49.5	27.2	22.7	15.8	6.9
1946	7.4	5.4	2.2	0.2	2.0
Total increase for the period	$199.0	$109.0	$89.6	$68.3	$21.3

tionary pressure; the principal response was increased real output and employment. Later, however, as actual output approached capacity levels and expenditures continued to rise, serious inflationary pressures appeared.

The Treasury had to borrow money to cover its huge deficits. In fact, during this six-year period it added $199 billion to its outstanding debt, $187 billion to cover its deficits and $12 billion to increase its money balance. But from what sources was the Treasury to borrow? Economists advised the Treasury that borrowing from nonbank investors would be least inflationary. To the extent that it was successful, such borrowing might inhibit inflation in two principal ways. (1) It could encourage people to save rather than spend for consumption,

[1] These figures include only Treasury borrowings from outside sources. They do not include increases in the debt held by Treasury trust funds.

and (2) it could decrease the need for borrowing from banks, thereby lessening the expansion of the money supply. The Treasury did induce nonbank investors to add $109 billion to their holdings of government debt (Table 29). However, this was far from enough, so it had to borrow $89.6 billion from the commercial and Federal Reserve banks. The commercial banks increased their holdings of governments by $68.3 billion and the Federal Reserve by $21.3 billion. These net purchases of government securities by the Federal Reserve and the commercial banks were largely responsible for the increase of the public's money supply from $38.7 billion in mid-1940 to $106 billion in mid-1946—a rise of $67.3 billion, or 174 percent.

C. MONETARY POLICY SUBORDINATED TO BORROWING NEEDS

In this process the Federal Reserve played an essential role. It subordinated all other considerations to the dominant objective of insuring that the Treasury would be able to borrow all the money it wanted without any increase in interest rates. For several years before the war interest rates, and especially those on short-term obligations, had been very low. There were two principal reasons for this: (1) the large supply of credit based on the great volume of excess reserves in the hands of the commercial banks, largely because of huge gold inflows, and (2) the low demand for credit for investment purposes. It was at this very low level that interest rates were frozen throughout the war.

The principal method employed by the Federal Reserve to assure the sale of Treasury issues and to prevent interest rates from rising was basically simple; it was the technique which is used in all price-support programs, only this time bonds were the item whose price was supported. The Federal Reserve stood ready to buy at the agreed-upon prices and yields all the government securities that were offered to it. No matter how many securities the Treasury might issue, the Federal Reserve stood ready to buy all that other purchasers were not willing to purchase and hold at the low level of interest rates. It is easy to see why the Treasury was able to sell as many securities as it wished, and without any rise of interest rates (i.e., no fall in security prices), so long as the Federal Reserve followed this monetary policy.

D. LOSS OF MONETARY CONTROLS OVER INFLATION

By following this policy the Federal Reserve surrendered its control over the money supply and lost its power to decrease the availability and to increase the cost of credit to private borrowers. Anyone who wished to do so could get new money by selling low-yield government securities to the passive Federal Reserve. Commercial banks could increase their reserves at will by selling to the Federal Reserve some of their holdings of low-yield government securities. And whenever anyone else sold his bonds to the Federal Reserve both bank reserves and the public's money supply were directly increased. The failure of private spendings to rise more than they did during the war period was certainly not due to any scarcity of money or to any increase in its cost.

E. USE OF DIRECT CONTROLS (SUPPRESSED INFLATION)

Committed to huge deficits and an easy-money policy, the government relied largely on a comprehensive system of *direct controls,* including price and wage ceilings and many regulations directing or limiting the use of labor and materials, to deal with inflationary pressures. These direct controls did not prevent the creation of inflationary pressures, but they did limit the extent to which these pressures were converted into open price inflation during the war period. They also limited private expenditures during the war and forced both individuals and business firms to save abnormally large amounts of their swollen money incomes after taxes.

F. SEEDS OF FURTHER INFLATION

In the following section we shall see that the period from 1945 until the time this was written in 1953 was predominantly inflationary, with an abatement of inflationary pressures during only a few years. Several developments during the war period played an important role in creating these inflationary pressures. (1) The great accumulation of savings by both individuals and business firms during the war. This was due largely to the huge government deficits which added so much to private money incomes after taxes. (2) The convenient form of these savings from the point of view of expenditure (liquidity). A large proportion of these savings were held in the form of money itself, and most of the rest were in the form of government securities or savings accounts that could be easily converted into money. This meant that anyone who saw something he wanted to buy could run right out and offer money for it. If his savings had been sunk in a house or a factory instead, he would first have had to wait until he could sell it or earn enough profits to make his purchase. The liquidity of savings thus permitted easier and quicker spending. (3) The accumulated backlog of demand. Unable to buy many of the things that they wanted during the war, both consumers and business firms were in a mood to go on a buying spree. And they did just that when direct controls over prices, wages, and materials were first weakened and then abandoned soon after the end of the war.

6. Monetary Policy Since World War II

A. CONTINUATION OF EASY MONEY

As already stated, the period since 1945 has been predominantly inflationary. By 1953 the cost of living had risen 48 percent and wholesale prices 60 percent above the levels prevailing on V-J Day. One might expect that under these conditions the Federal Reserve would have abandoned its wartime easy-money policy, and would have actively restricted the supply of credit and raised interest rates in order to fight inflation. But this was done only after a long delay, and even then to only a very limited extent. Until July, 1947, nearly two years after V-J Day, the Federal Reserve continued its wartime easy-money policy with no significant change. It still stood ready to buy all government securities offered to it at the wartime pattern of interest yields. After mid-1947 it did permit interest rates to rise slightly, but until early 1951 the increases were confined to short-term obligations. In general, the monetary policy of the period was one of easy money despite the onrush of inflation.

There appear to have been two principal reasons for continuing to pursue an easy-money policy in the face of inflation. One we have already noted—the desire to promote "full employment and full production" and the fear that a more restrictive monetary policy might jeopardize the attainment of this objective. But of at least equal weight was the dual objective of facilitating Treasury financing and holding down interest charges on the national debt.

B. CESSATION OF GOVERNMENT DEFICITS

During most of this period the Treasury was not making net additions to its debt; in fact, during much of the time it had tax surpluses which could be used to retire debt. For several years it did "better" than balance the budget. But much of the debt was in short-term securities which fell due frequently. The government therefore had to go into the market frequently to renew its borrowings, that is, to borrow money with which to pay off maturing obligations. Hence it demanded that the Federal Reserve maintain stable prices and yields on governments in order to facilitate these refinancing operations. It also demanded that the Federal Reserve prevent interest rates from rising in order to hold down interest charges on the national debt. Time after time, the Secretary of the Treasury pointed out that every 0.5 of 1 percent rise in the average interest rate on the national debt would increase annual government interest payments on the debt by $1.25 billion.

c. PARTIAL REEMERGENCE OF FEDERAL RESERVE INDEPENDENCE

For a time the Federal Reserve submitted to Treasury demands with no more than feeble resistance. But gradually, as inflation continued, it grew more restive and was able to secure Treasury acquiescence to slightly more restrictive policies. A real showdown on this issue came only after the outbreak of hostilities in Korea in June, 1950. This outbreak touched off a new surge of inflation. Both consumers and business firms increased their spendings markedly, financing them partly out of idle money balances and partly out of increased borrowings from the banks. The Treasury insisted on an easy-money policy to prevent any rise of interest rates. The Federal Reserve, on the other hand, insisted that it should restrict the supply of credit in order to fight inflation, even if this would force the Treasury to pay higher interest rates.

The controversy culminated in a Federal Reserve-Treasury "accord" in March, 1951. Under this accord it was agreed that the Federal Reserve would no longer "peg" the prices and yields on government securities; that is, it would no longer buy them so freely as to prevent any decline in their prices or any increase in their yields. Instead, it would have some freedom to allow their prices to fall and their yields to rise in order to discourage their sales to itself.

From the time of the accord in March, 1951, until 1953 the Federal Reserve used its greater independence to permit some tightening of credit and some rise of interest rates. How much this more restrictive monetary policy contributed to stopping price inflation in 1951 and maintaining relatively stable prices from that time until 1953 is still a disputed subject.

The March, 1951, accord did not mean that Federal Reserve policy would no longer be influenced by the objective of facilitating Treasury finance. It meant only the end, or at least a temporary suspension, of the inflexible pegging of security prices. The Federal Reserve still stands ready to assure the success of Treasury financing and assumes responsibility for preventing "disorderly movements" in the prices and yields on government securities. Just what constitutes a "disorderly movement" remains to be defined. Does it include only "excessively rapid" and "erratic" movements? Or does it also imply limitations on the extent to which prices on government securities will be allowed to fall and yields to rise, even if the movement is gradual and "orderly"? Answers to these and other similar questions remain for the future.

D. SOME POLICY PROBLEMS

The objective of facilitating Treasury finance and holding down interest rates on the national debt has been for several years, and will probably continue to be, an important determinant of monetary policy. It has inhibited the use of restrictive monetary policies to combat inflation, and may do so in the future. An important policy problem, therefore, is determining the extent to which this set of objectives should be allowed to influence monetary policy. In attempting to solve this problem, the following questions, among others, should be considered:

1. Just how important is the objective of holding down interest charges on the national debt as compared with the other objectives that may have to be sacrificed in order to achieve it? With annual interest charges on the national debt already above $6 billion, we cannot dismiss the height of interest rates paid by the Treasury as of no significance whatever. But neither can we take lightly the creation or accentuation of economic instability that may result from maintaining an easy-money policy in the face of inflation.

2. How can the Treasury itself alter its debt management policies in such a way as to assist, rather than inhibit, the effectiveness of monetary policy in achieving socially desirable objectives? Debt management refers to the methods used to finance the debt—whether by sale of bonds or short-term securities, whether by sale to the public or to the banks, whether at low or high interest rates, etc. These decisions clearly can have powerful effects on the economy. It should not be assumed without investigation that the presence of a large national debt must necessarily be a "drag" on monetary policy. The Treasury might even manage this debt in such a way as to increase the effectiveness of a restrictive monetary policy. For example, it might decrease

the availability and increase the cost of credit for private purposes by offering highly attractive government obligations to the owners of savings. However, the possibility of using debt management in such a way as to increase the effectiveness of a restrictive monetary policy remains largely unexplored.

7. Conclusions

We cannot examine here the many other interesting aspects of monetary policy. However, there have emerged from this discussion several conclusions that are important for public policy. (1) The behavior of the monetary system inevitably exerts a powerful influence on the behavior of the entire economy through its influence on the supply of money and the availability and cost of credit. It may either promote or inhibit the achievement of socially desirable economic objectives. (2) The monetary authority cannot escape responsibility for the behavior of money and credit. Passivity, as well as positive action, inevitably affects the behavior of the economy. (3) The monetary authority therefore faces the difficult problem of weighing the various economic objectives against each other, and of formulating specific policies that will promote the attainment of the objectives that are selected. And here, as in most other areas of economic policy, it must recognize that objectives may conflict—that it will have to sacrifice some economic objectives in order to achieve others.

SUGGESTED READINGS

Chandler, Lester V., *Inflation in the United States, 1940–1948,* Harper, New York, 1951.

Goldenweiser, Emanuel A., *American Monetary Policy,* McGraw-Hill, New York, 1951.

U.S. Senate, 81st Congress, 2d Session, *Report of the Subcommittee on Monetary, Credit, and Fiscal Policies,* Senate Document 129, Government Printing Office, Washington, 1950.

QUESTIONS

1. a. Discuss the relevance of the government's ability to predict, to the maintenance of a successful monetary policy to stabilize income.
   b. Give some reasons why the prospects for accurate economic prediction are dim.

2. Suppose businessmen do not want more money because profitable investment opportunities are not to be found.
   a. How may the monetary authorities nevertheless be able to increase
      the money supply in the hands of the public?
   b. Show that this can sometimes be done, though no one wants the
      money for expenditure purposes.
   c. Why, then, may this procedure be ineffective as an antidepression
      measure?
3. Under the inflationary conditions following World War II large gold
   inflows were an unwelcome expansionary influence.
   a. Show how this increased the money supply, and follow through the
      effects on the public's deposits with commercial banks and on com-
      mercial bank reserves.
   b. Show diagrammatically how this increase in money supply affected
      the money market line of adjustment and so gave the level of na-
      tional income an inflationary direction.
4. The financing of wars has long induced government to resort to increases
   in the money supply. An old technique, used when money consisted
   exclusively of gold coins, involved the government's short weighting
   them or adulterating them with base metals. More recently the printing
   of paper money and borrowing from the Federal Reserve (or other
   central banks) have been resorted to.
   a. Show how each of the three methods serves to increase the nation's
      money supply.
   b. Why could a given number of dollars obtained in any one of these
      ways add more to the money supply in the modern world than it
      would have formerly?
   c. How do you think public reaction to these three measures might dif-
      fer? Which do you therefore suspect might be most inflationary?
   d. Analyze your last answer graphically in terms of the effects on the
      public's expectations.
5. Where are each of the following pairs of objectives of monetary policy
   in conflict and when in harmony:
   a. Income stabilization and maintenance of the price of gold.
   b. Income stabilization and facilitation of federal finance.
   c. Maintenance of the price of gold and facilitation of federal finance.
   d. From the material of this chapter give historical illustrations of con-
      flict in each of these pairs of objectives.
6. Why might economists argue that federal borrowing from the public is
   less inflationary than borrowing from commercial banks or the Federal
   Reserve?
7. Give several reasons why inflation may directly facilitate government
   financing operations, considering:

    a. Tax collections.

    b. The purchasing power of interest payments.

    c. The ease of borrowing.

    d. Is there some duplication in these reasons?

    e. How might inflation make government financing more difficult?

8. a. Some advocates of a cheap-money policy have defended it on the ground that its abandonment could cause severe losses to those who lent money to the government, and would hence be a breach of faith. Can you explain this?

    b. Another argument of cheap-money advocates was that postwar profit expectations were such as to assure a continued demand for loans even with a considerable rise in interest rates. Therefore, they said, any likely rise in interest rates would neither stop the expansion in the money supply nor decrease investment expenditure. Can you explain this point?

    c. What does this imply about the shape of the demand for investment curve?

CHAPTER 17

Government Expenditures and Taxes

---

1. Introduction

A government's fiscal problems relate to its expenditures, its revenues, and its debts. Its *fiscal policy* refers to its aims, its strategy, and its tactics in dealing with these important financial problems.

As we have already noted, the fiscal policies of our governmental units—federal, state, and local—have always exerted some influence on the behavior of the entire economy, and the extent of this influence has increased greatly as government expenditures, tax collections, and debts have risen not only in absolute amounts but also as percentages of national income. We shall now explore more fully some of the most important effects of these policies, paying special attention to their effects on the behavior of national income, employment, and price levels, but noting also several others, such as the effects on the distribution of real income and on the production and consumption of specific types of goods and services.

Owing to the fact that they have quite different economic effects and need not be equal to each other in any given period, government expenditures and revenues will be analyzed separately. Of course there are many who argue that the budget should be in exact balance all the time. We shall examine the merits of this proposal later. But whatever may be its merits, the principle of an annually balanced budget does not always rule fiscal policy. In some periods the government has deficits, its expenditures exceeding its revenues. In others it has surpluses, its revenues exceeding its expenditures. And these deficits or surpluses are sometimes very large.

2. Types of Government Expenditures

Because they have somewhat different economic effects, it will be useful to divide government expenditures into two broad classes: (1) purchases of goods and services, and (2) transfer payments—the expenditures for which the government currently receives no goods or services in return. Table 30 indicates that in 1952 purchases of goods

TABLE 30. Government Expenditures, 1952[1]
(In billions of dollars)

Type of Expenditure	Federal	State and Rural	Total
Purchases of goods and services—Total	$54.2	$23.4	$77.6
Direct purchases of labor services	18.7	12.2	30.9
Other purchases of goods and services, mostly from business firms	35.5	11.2	46.7
Transfer payments—Total	$14.4	$ 2.4	$16.8
Old-age insurance benefits	2.2	. . .	2.2
Other old-age and pension benefits	0.5	0.5	1.0
Life insurance benefits	0.8	. . .	0.8
Unemployment insurance benefits	1.0	. . .	1.0
Direct relief and other social security benefits	0.8	2.3	3.1
Veterans' benefits	3.6	. . .	3.6
Interest on government debt	4.6	0.3	4.9
Net subsidies to agriculture, business, etc.	1.0	−0.7	0.3
Total	$68.6	$25.8	$94.4

and services accounted for 82 percent of total government expenditures, the other 18 percent being transfer payments.

A. PURCHASES OF GOODS AND SERVICES

As pointed out in our discussion of national income, government purchases of goods and services may be looked at in two different ways.

1. Government purchases are the value of output taken for government purposes, and therefore not available for private use, this output being valued at its cost to the government. Part of this output is in the form of the labor services of workers employed directly by the government. The rest consists of output purchased from private industry. This includes a wide variety of things, such as new construction, motor vehicles, fuel, munitions, office supplies, foodstuffs, and so on. The important point here is that expenditures of this type do represent

[1] Adapted from materials in *Survey of Current Business*, July, 1953, pp. 15 and 25.

amounts of productive resources used by government, and therefore not available for private purchase.

Stated in other words, these purchases are the government's effective demand for national output. The behavior of national output, employment, and price levels is responsive to government demands no less than to private demands. A rise in the rate of government purchases therefore tends directly to be expansionary, and a decline to be contractionary.

2. Government purchases are a government contribution to private money incomes. Money spent by government for goods and services constitutes income for someone. Payments for labor services are income for government employees, and payments for the output of private industry become income to the owners of business firms, workers, and others who participate in producing the goods and services sold to the government. Thus, an increase in the rate of government purchases tends directly to raise private money incomes, and a decline in the rate of government purchases tends directly to lower private money incomes.

We find, therefore, that changes in the rate of government expenditures for goods and services, considered by themselves, directly affect the total demand for output in at least *two* ways—not only by changing the government's own demands for output, but also by changing private money incomes and spending power. This is of course equally true of any purchase of goods and services by a private individual or firm. It, too, will take goods or services off the market and increase the purchasing power in the hands of those from whom the items are bought.

B. GOVERNMENT TRANSFER PAYMENTS

We saw that transfer payments are expenditures for which the government currently receives no goods or services in return. Table 30 indicates that these are in such forms as benefits paid out under old-age insurance programs, other old-age and pension benefits, benefits under the national life insurance program for veterans, benefits to the unemployed, veterans' benefits, interest on government debt, subsidies to agriculture and business, and so on. Transfer payments represent neither a value of output used for government purposes nor a direct government demand for output. They do, however, contribute to private money incomes. Thus, an increase in transfer payments, considered by itself, tends to increase private money incomes and spending power, and a decrease has the opposite effect.

3. The Trend of Government Expenditures

The sharp upward trend of government expenditures is, of course, widely known. Column 3 of Table 31 indicates that between 1890 and

TABLE 31.   Trend of Government Expenditures, 1890–1951[2]

Year	Col. 1 Federal Expenditures (In billions)	Col. 2 State and Local Expenditures (In billions)	Col. 3 Total Government Expenditures (In billions)	Col. 4 Government Expenditure Per Capita	Col. 5 Government Expenditures as Percentage of National Output
1890	$ 0.3	$ 0.6	$ 0.9	$ 14	9.6
1902	0.5	1.0	1.5	19	8.7
1913	0.7	1.8	2.5	26	8.7
1929	2.5	7.7	10.2	84	9.8
1939	8.0	9.3	17.3	132	18.9
1951	55.4	24.1	79.5	516	24.1
1952	68.6	25.8	94.4	601	27.1

1952 the annual rate of government expenditures rose from less than $1 billion to more than $94 billion. This is indeed a tremendous rise; some view it as almost calamitous.

A. MISLEADING ASPECTS OF THE STATISTICS

While interpreting these figures, we should bear in mind several other economic developments during the period. (1) The upward trend of price levels. In 1952 price levels were about three times as high as in 1890; each dollar represented only about a third as much purchasing power as in 1890. In real terms, therefore, expenditures rose some 35 times, not 105 times as indicated by the money figures.

2. The increase of population. As the number of people rose from 63 million in 1890 to 157 million in 1952, it was only to be expected that government expenditures would also rise. Nevertheless, expenditures rose so much faster than population that government spending per capita increased from $14 in 1890 to $601 in 1952. If we take into account the decline in the value of the dollar, this may be viewed as an increase from the earlier $14 to $200 per head in 1952 when measured in 1890 dollars. This is still a great increase, but of the order of 14 to 1 rather than the 105 to 1 indicated by the figures when unadjusted for changes in population or the purchasing power of the dollar.

[2] Most of these figures are highly approximate and should be considered only as indicators of general magnitudes. They were gathered from several sources.

3. The sharp upward trend in the value of national output or income. Reflecting increases in both price levels and the rate of real output, national money income rose more than 35-fold between 1890 and 1952. Until about 1929 its rate of increase just about kept pace with the rise of government expenditures, so that government expenditures as a percentage of national income rose only slightly, if at all. But since 1929 government expenditures have risen even as a percentage of national income; in 1952 they were equal to more than a quarter of the total value of national output.

B. REASONS FOR THE RISE OF GOVERNMENT EXPENDITURES

Why have government expenditures risen so much? One popular explanation—the desire of scheming politicians to expand their power and impose more government services on an unwilling citizenry—is both too simple and actually misleading. Though it may contain some element of truth, there is little evidence that the majoritiy of voters have disapproved of the expansion. An adequate explanation must be far more complex and take into account a great variety of social and economic developments. Two of these have already been noted—the increase of price levels and the rising population to be supplied with government services. But there are also many others, such as wars and international tensions, industrialization and urbanization, the increased use of motor vehicles, the desire of the public for more and better government services, and so on.

C. MILITARY AND QUASI-MILITARY EXPENDITURES

Defense, wars, and the aftermath of wars have accounted for a major part of the increase in government expenditures. During the twentieth century we have engaged in two world wars and a "cold war" against communism. During each of these periods expenditures for national security purposes have risen to very high levels. But the fiscal effects of wars do not end with the termination of hostilities. Instead, wars leave a heritage of higher price levels, increased debt and service charges on the debt, and obligations to pay large benefits to veterans.

The large part of federal expenditures directly related to wars and national security is indicated in an approximate way in Table 32. In the fiscal year 1952, expenditures related to war and national security constituted about 85 percent of all federal spending. It is impossible to forecast the future course of these expenditures. Though spendings directly related to the cold war against communism were higher in 1953 than in 1952, they may decline in the future if international tensions ease, but will probably not go back to the levels prevailing before World War II. Two other types of war-related expenditures will be even more difficult to reduce. Interest on the national debt, most of which was incurred during the two world wars, will probably continue for a long time at or above $6 billion a year, which is more than twice

TABLE 32.   Federal Budget Expenditures During Fiscal Year 1952[3]

Type of Expenditure	Amount (In billions)	Percent of Total
National defense	$39.1	59.2
International aid	4.8	7.3
Atomic energy	1.6	2.4
Veterans' benefits	4.9	7.4
Interest on national debt	5.9	8.9
Total expenditures related to war and defense	$56.3	85.2
All other	9.8	14.8
Total	$66.1	100.0

as high as total federal expenditures in 1929. And if past history is any guide, benefits to veterans are more likely to rise than to decline; in 1952 these, too, were about twice as great as total federal expenditures in 1929.

D. URBANIZATION, ROAD CONSTRUCTION, AND OTHER CAUSES

Though the rise of government expenditures related to war and international tensions has accounted for a major part of the total increase, other expenditures have also risen. For this there have been many reasons, of which the following are but a few examples.

1. Increased urbanization. As a larger proportion of our people have come to live in cities the government has provided them with services considered essential for urban dwellers but not for farmers. Among these are sidewalks, sewage systems, street lighting, public parks and playgrounds, police and fire protection, garbage collection and disposal, slum clearance, and so on.

2. The demand for more and better highways. As the number of autos, trucks, and buses expanded rapidly, voters have demanded not only more miles of paved highways, but also more expensive types of highways to support heavier loads and permit higher speeds. In 1953 the annual rate of highway expenditures was already above $3 billion and was expected to rise still higher.

3. More public education for more people. For many decades the

[3] Source: U.S. Treasury *Bulletins*.

trend has been toward a higher percentage of school attendance by those of school age, more school days per year, a larger proportion of students in public rather than private schools, more years of schooling for each student, more varied curriculums, better school facilities, and higher pay for teachers.

4. The quest for economic security. For a complex of reasons, the government has assumed increasing obligations to provide a degree of economic security against many contingencies. This has led to large expenditures to combat unemployment, provide unemployment insurance and relief, support farm prices and incomes, provide old-age insurance and relief, provide medical and hospital care for the needy, construct and operate low-cost housing, and so on.

5. Increased government promotion and operation of economic enterprises. These include hydroelectric projects, flood control, irrigation, rural electrification, soil conservation, airport construction and operation, numerous types of lending, and many others.

E. SUMMARY

This brief discussion has not attempted either to approve or to condemn the rising trend of government expenditures. It has, however, suggested several facts that are useful in evaluating government policies in this area. (1) Taken by itself, the upward trend in government expenditures measured in absolute amounts of current dollars has but limited meaning. It should be interpreted in light of the downward trend in the purchasing power of the dollar, the upward trend in population, and the upward trend in both total and per capita incomes. (2) To analyze government expenditures rationally, one must consider the purposes for which the money is spent. This leads to the broad question of the proper scope of government economic activity and the relative efficiency of government and private enterprise in performing the various types of economic functions. (3) Government expenditures are now such a large part of total national income that they are inevitably a major influence on the behavior of the economy.

4. Financing Government Expenditures

A. MONEY COSTS AND REAL COSTS OF GOVERNMENT EXPENDITURES

The costs of government must be paid for somehow. But this is not true in the obvious sense that may first come to mind. A government with the power to create money need not collect money from its citi-

zens to pay for the goods and services it buys and uses. Wisely or unwisely, it can always print new money for the purpose, or it can have
the Federal Reserve and commercial banks manufacture the new
money for it.

Though the government does not have to collect money from the
public to obtain the goods and services it requires, the costs of these
things must in a very real sense be paid for by its citizens. Every pencil,
every ton of steel, and every hour of labor used by the government must
be produced by the people and is not available for private purchase.
Every good and service the government uses it receives from its citizens.

B. TAXES, BORROWING, AND REAL RESOURCES

The function of taxing and borrowing in helping finance government expenditures can now be better understood. In essence, they are
means of depriving the public of purchasing power with which the
public would otherwise demand and pay for the goods and resources
that the government wants for itself. Of course the public does not directly compete with the government for many items. There is normally
no private demand for battleships and heavy artillery. But the public
is likely to want goods in which the raw materials or productive resources needed by the state are used. Steel used in tanks cannot be used
in refrigerators or in automobiles. When taxes cut down private purchasing power and hence the demand for pleasure cars and washing
machines, the metals that would otherwise have gone into these items
become available for government use.

C. MONEY CREATION AND THE TRANSFER OF RESOURCES

Suppose now that the government decides to finance its expenditures
by money creation, either directly or through the banking system. To
understand how the state acquires the real resources and products it
desires, we must distinguish between the case where there is widespread
unemployment and the case where employment is at a high level.

Unemployment means essentially that a large quantity of unused
resources is available. In such a case government acquisition of goods
and services does not, in a sense, compete with the public's. There are
plenty of resources available to meet all demands. Even if the state's
increased demand for steel initially limits the amounts available to the
public at large, the steel industry can make up the deficiency by hiring
more people and expanding its facilities. As soon as the steel-making
equipment can be built or idle steel-making facilities put into opera-

tion, the reduction in the supply of steel for private use due to increased government requirements can cease.

If, on the other hand, there is a high level of employment, an increase in the use of steel by the state must mean a persistent reduction in private use. In this case the reduction of private purchasing power by taxing or borrowing becomes particularly desirable. Money creation by the state can just as effectively deprive the public of this purchasing power, but the process is likely to have other serious consequences. For the way this is done is by a process of inflation, which reduces the purchasing power of the money in the hands of the public.

When in times of full employment the government increases its demands and does nothing to decrease the amount of money in private hands, there is an increase in the money demand for commodities, but their supply cannot increase. Prices therefore rise, and the public finds that it cannot buy as much as it wants to, not because it has paid taxes or made loans to the government, but because the value of its money assets and money incomes has fallen. The creation of money does not necessarily make the financing of government expenditures less painful. In some circumstances it can have serious and highly undesirable effects. And certainly it is never a magic formula for avoiding the real cost of the government's operations—the goods, the services, and the leisure of which it deprives the citizens. This point will be important later when we examine how, when, and by whom wars and other large government expenditures are paid for. We shall see that though they have been financed to a considerable extent by borrowing, there is an important sense in which we and not, as often alleged, "our grandchildren" pay for our wars.

We turn now to an examination of the various methods of financing public expenditures, starting with taxation.

5. Taxation

A. The Influence of Taxes on National Income

We shall find that the government levies taxes on many bases—incomes, property, the production or sale of goods and services, the transfer of estates at death, and so on. But regardless of their bases, all taxes are paid out of private incomes. Considered by themselves therefore, tax collections tend to lower private disposable money incomes— that is, private money incomes after taxes. Thus, with any given level of national income, an increase of tax collections serves to decrease private disposable incomes, thereby decreasing the abilities of the private sectors to consume and save. A decrease of tax collections has the opposite effect; it tends to increase private disposable incomes and the ability of the private sectors to consume and save.

B. TRENDS AND SOURCES

Though the government sometimes has large deficits or surpluses, the long-term trend of its tax collections has been roughly the same as the trend of its expenditures. In 1953 more than 25 percent of national money income was taken by taxes. When taxes are at such a high level, tax policy cannot avoid being a major influence on economic behavior.

The principal sources of government revenue in recent years are shown in Table 33. These include taxes levied on personal incomes,

TABLE 33.   Government Revenues, 1952[4]
(In billions of dollars)

Type of Tax	Federal	State and Local	Total Revenues	Percent of Total Revenues
Personal income taxes	$30.2	$ 0.9	$31.2	34.0
Taxes on corporate profits	19.8	0.8	20.6	22.1
Taxes on production and sales	9.6	5.2	14.8	16.1
Contributions for social insurance	7.5	1.2	8.7	9.5
Property taxes	. . .	8.6	8.6	9.5
Death and gift taxes	0.9	0.2	1.1	1.2
Other	0.8	6.2	7.0	7.6
Total	$68.8	$23.2	$92.0	100.0

corporate profits, the production and sale of goods and services, property, estates and gifts, and contributions for social insurance. The federal government relies largely on taxes levied on personal incomes, corporate profits, the production and sale of goods, and contributions for social insurance. State and local governments, on the other hand, depend mainly on property taxes, sales taxes, and contributions for social insurance. A further breakdown would show that local governments rely to a major degree on property taxes, particularly real estate taxes.

[4] Adapted from *Survey of Current Business*, July, 1953, p. 14. The figure for state and local revenues does not include $2.6 billion received from the federal government as grants-in-aid.

C. PROPORTIONAL, PROGRESSIVE, AND REGRESSIVE TAXES

Taxes can be classified into three general types: proportional, progressive, and regressive. A *proportional* tax is one which, as its name suggests, collects from each taxpayer an amount that varies exactly in proportion to his income. If A receives twice as much income as B, A pays twice as much in taxes. Proportional taxation does not redistribute income; after both have paid their taxes A still retains twice as much income as does B.

If a tax is designed to redistribute income in favor of the lower-income groups, it must tax the wealthy at higher rates than it does the lower-income groups. Such a tax is called *progressive,* because the rate grows progressively higher as the size of income rises. The term progressive is not to be taken as a verdict on the desirability of the tax. Indeed we shall note later that this type of tax has peculiar drawbacks.

There are also taxes which work the other way round and serve to increase the inequality of income. That is to say, they tax the poor at higher rates than the wealthy. Taxes of this variety are called *regressive*.

6. Types of Taxes

We turn now to a more detailed examination of our various taxes.

A. PERSONAL INCOME TAXES

The personal income tax is the largest single source of revenue for the federal government, constituting some 40 percent of its tax collections and nearly a tenth of our national income. It is considerably less important to states, and is used hardly at all by local governments. This is one of the few types of taxes clearly designed to be progressive.

Progression is achieved in two ways. (1) By exempting from the tax a certain amount of income, say $600, for the taxpayer and each of his dependents. In this way some people with low incomes are completely exempted from the tax; the higher the income, the higher is the proportion of total income subject to the tax. Thus, there would be some progression in the effective income tax rate—that is, in the percentage of one's total income taken by the tax—even if a flat tax rate were applied to all taxable income. (2) Graduated rates on taxable income. Taxable income is divided into "brackets," and successively higher brackets are taxed at progressively higher rates. For example, under the federal income tax law in effect during 1953, the first $2000 of taxable income was subject to a tax rate of 22.2 percent, the next $2000 to a rate of 24 percent, the next $2000 to a rate of 29 percent, and so on. A top rate of 92 percent applied to taxable income in excess of $200,000.

State income taxes are similar in structure, though their rates are much lower. In only a few states do the rates rise above 7 percent, and in several they do not reach this level. Some states have no income tax.

Perhaps this is the appropriate place to clear up a rather widespread misconception. This is the view that progressive income tax rates make it unprofitable to get into a higher bracket in the sense that a man may, by earning an additional dollar, be forced to pay two dollars more in taxes because this puts him into the next tax bracket. Our taxes are generally computed in a way that avoids this difficulty. This is done by charging the lowest rate on the first X dollars earned, a higher rate *only* on the next Y dollars earned, and so on. Thus if by earning an extra dollar a man goes into the 50 percent tax bracket, his tax will be 50 cents more than it would have been had he not earned that dollar. An additional dollar earned will always add something to one's income after taxes.

B. CORPORATE INCOME TAXES.

At first glance at least, there seems to be no special reason for taxing the income of corporations. Why not confine our taxes to the *recipients* of corporate income? Is not the corporation tax discriminatory and does it not involve double taxation of individuals whose assets are largely composed of corporate shares? Why not tax the equally wealthy landholder or owner of a partnership just as much? Isn't this tax merely a political expedient? To some extent these questions must no doubt be answered affirmatively. Yet there is one reason why a corporation tax or something like it must be levied in order to plug an important loophole in our income tax structure.

To see this, let us see what would happen if there were no such taxes. Consider two individuals, A and B. A receives $5000 in dividends from his shares in a corporation; the firm in which B is a shareholder, though able to pay $5000 in dividends to B, decides to keep the money and plow it back into the business, thereby increasing the value of B's claim against the firm by $5000. Suppose A, after paying $1000 in taxes, decides to put the remaining $4000 into B's company. Note that both of them have received the same income, and have invested as much of it as they can in the same firm. Yet A, having received his money from elsewhere, will have paid $1000 in taxes and will end up with only $4000 in the firm, whereas B will have $5000 more in the firm and will have paid nothing in taxes on this sum. This device could be a very effective way for a large income earner to postpone taxes indefinitely, if he could arrange to have his income paid into a "personal corporation" which he owned himself and which kept or invested the money for him. Such corporations designed solely to avoid taxes have in fact been created, though the tax laws now limit their use.

It turns out that some sort of corporation tax is necessary if the personal income tax is to be an equitable and effective instrument of taxation. Nevertheless, much of our present corporate taxation appears to be based on little more than the legal fiction that the corporation is a legal entity, separate and distinct from its owners. The fairness of corporate taxes, as levied at present, has therefore been questioned, primarily because it subjects the stockholders to double taxation, and because it tends to be regressive since it makes no distinction between richer and poorer stockholders, taxing their corporate revenues alike.

By a flat levy of 53 percent after a small exemption (1953), corporation taxes have in recent years produced about a quarter of all federal tax revenue, and are thus the federal government's second largest source of taxes. State taxes in this field are similar in structure but much lower in rates.

During the war and cold war period the need for taxes has continued at unprecedented heights, so that it has proved very difficult politically to do much about corporate taxes. The fear of losing this important source of revenue (as well as the fear of seeming to weaken the progressiveness of the tax structure) has prevented any serious attempts at revision.

c. Taxes on the Production and Sale of Goods and Services

Sales (excise) taxes are measured by the amount of goods and services produced or sold. Some are *specific* taxes, being so much per physical unit; others are *ad valorem,* being stated as a percentage of value. Some, such as state taxes on retail sales, are *general,* applying to all goods and services not specifically exempted. Others are *selective,* applying to only selected commodities or services. The states, and to a lesser extent local governments, employ both general and selective taxes; the federal government has used only selective taxes. These include taxes on liquor, playing cards, tobacco, and so-called "luxury items" generally. Moreover, many sales taxes are charged not when the item in question is bought by the consumer, but rather when it is purchased by some middleman or processor. An important example is the customs duty (tariff), which is essentially a tax on a commodity sold by a foreigner to a domestic middleman. A tax on flour is also a sales tax even though it affects the price of bread only indirectly. Including all their varieties, sales taxes have accounted for about one-sixth of total federal revenue and more than half the revenue of our state governments.

Sales taxes are significant from the point of view of income redistribution because they tend to be regressive. To cite an extreme case, a tax on cigarettes is likely to collect as much from a poor smoker as from a rich smoker. Thus they take a much greater percentage of the income of the poor man and tend to increase inequality of real income. In general they will be somewhat less regressive (though still regressive), because the poor will buy less of most commodities than do the rich. Taxes on luxury goods like furs and jewelry may even be progressive up to a point, in that the very poor will not pay them at all. But at some point even these taxes are likely to become regressive. For example, a family with a $500,000 income is likely not to spend fifty times as much on furs as a family making $10,000 a year. In any case the bulk of sales tax revenues does not come from these extreme luxury items. For example, in 1951 taxes on tobacco and alcoholic beverages accounted for about a third of all excise taxes collected. We may therefore be quite sure that, on the whole, excise taxes are regressive.

Excise taxes on particular items also can influence consumers' purchase decisions. By increasing the prices of the items taxed they deter consumers from buying these goods. They thus distort the consumers' expenditure patterns. Sometimes people consider this a good thing. For this reason Prohibitionists generally approve of high taxes on alcoholic beverages if they are unable to have liquor outlawed entirely. But generally this property of excise taxes—their tendency to dictate his purchases to the consumer—is regarded with disfavor.[5]

Why are such taxes levied at all? There are several reasons. (1) Need for revenue. In times when any source of revenue is precious to the politician, he will be reluctant to give up so lucrative a tax. (2) Political expediency. Sales taxes can be levied on the producer or the

[5] For a more detailed analysis of the possible advantages of leaving prices unaffected by taxation, see below, pp. 402–404.

middleman and "hidden" from the consumer, who may not notice that they increase the prices he pays for his goods. Public grumbling may be less than that aroused by an income tax.

(3) Incentive effects. Precisely because they are regressive, sales taxes are likely to minimize the effects on incentives, about which we shall say more presently. For example, a progressive tax tends to discourage overtime work because a greater percentage of additional wages will be taken in taxes. A regressive tax, on the contrary, increases the reward for *additional* effort, for it means that a higher income bracket is taxed at a lower rate. However, when their collection involves much paper work and other nuisances, sales taxes, too, have a substantial disincentive effect which offsets their inherent advantage in this respect.

(4) Counterinflationary effects. By falling on the poor, who save little and spend a high proportion of their incomes, sales taxes and regressive taxes in general may be more effective than a progressive tax in combating inflationary pressure. A tax on a rich man may be paid out of money he would not have spent anyway. A tax on a poor man, who cannot afford to save, is more likely to reduce consumption expenditure and inflationary pressure. Of course, in times of depression and unemployment this aspect of the sales tax makes it less attractive than an income tax.

We see, then, that there is something to be said for sales taxes, at least in some circumstances. Whether we wish to keep them in spite of their regressive nature and their distortion of consumers' expenditure patterns is something each must judge for himself.

D. CONTRIBUTIONS FOR SOCIAL INSURANCE

Most of these contributions are to finance old-age and employment insurance programs, though some are to finance pensions for government employees. They are based on payrolls and paid partly by employers and partly by employees.

E. PROPERTY TAXES

Because of the constitutional provision that its direct taxes other than income taxes must be allocated among the states in proportion to population, the federal government does not use property taxes. However, this tax is the chief source of revenue for local governments, providing them with nearly 90 percent of their tax income. It is of lesser and steadily declining importance to states, several states having abandoned it altogether. At one time most state and local governments attempted to tax both personal property and real estate in the same way, but as a result of the complex administrative problems of appraisal and enforcement in the case of personal property like jewelry, furs, etc., the property tax has become largely a tax on real estate.

F. DEATH AND GIFT TAXES

The federal inheritance tax applies to the part of an estate in excess of $60,000, although many states permit a considerably smaller exemption. On amounts over the exempt minimum, tax rates run from 3 percent on the first $5000 to 77 percent on amounts above $10 million. Some allowance is provided for state taxes already paid on the estate.

Inheritance taxation must be integrated with a system of gift taxes if it is to be effective. Otherwise its intent could easily be avoided because heirs could receive most or all of their legacy in the form of gifts during the lifetime of the prospective testator.

Almost all states also levy death taxes, some taxing total estates at graduated rates and others levying graduated taxes on the shares of an estate received by inheritors. Though the annual yield of death and gift taxes is relatively small, this type of tax has an important long-run influence on the distribution of wealth.

G. OTHER TAXES

Though the taxes already discussed yield most of the government's income, many other sources of revenue are also used. For example, state and local governments tax the privilege of doing business and collect license fees for motor vehicles, operators of motor vehicles, marriages, dogs, bicycles, and so on. There are other minor sources of revenue that cannot be mentioned here.

7. Who Pays the Taxes?

Who pays the many types of taxes collected by the federal government, the 48 states, and the thousands of local taxing units? How is the tax burden divided among the various income classes? Unfortunately, we know only little about the final distribution of the real tax burden. It would not be too difficult to find out the amounts of taxes actually paid into the government by the various classes of individuals, corporations, and other business firms. But for several reasons this information would tell us little about the final distribution of the tax burden among the various groups of human beings.

A. THE PAYERS OF CORPORATE TAXES

Being only a legal fiction, neither a corporation nor any other form of business firm can itself "feel" a tax burden. This can be felt only by human beings whose real incomes tend to be lowered by a tax. The final bearers of a tax may be the owners of the business firms or others. It may be paid primarily by poorer or richer stockholders or by holders of common or preferred stocks. Knowing what taxes are paid by corporations, therefore, is not enough to discover how tax burdens are distributed among the populace.

B. THE INFLUENCE OF CONSUMPTION PATTERNS

Even the distribution of the tax burden among families in a given income class depends somewhat on consumption habits. A family that spends a large part of its income for such highly taxed things as cigarettes, cigars, alcoholic beverages, and gasoline may bear far more of the tax burden than a family that has the same income but spends more of it for things that are taxed less heavily. It is therefore impossible to generalize on the way tax burdens are distributed among income classes.

C. THE SHIFTING AND INCIDENCE OF TAXES

The very levying of a tax on a business firm, person, commodity, or process may set in motion a chain of reactions that will shift the burden of the tax to others. The fact is that the individual from whom the government collects the tax may not be the person who ends up being made poorer by it. Suppose, for example, that the federal government levies a tax of 7 cents on every package of 20 cigarettes, the tax to be paid by the manufacturer. Since this is a cost of producing and selling, the manufacturer may shift at least some of it forward to buyers by increasing the price of cigarettes, provided this does not make him lose too many sales. The manufacturer may also shift some of the burden backward to his suppliers by forcing them to take lower prices for the tobacco and other supplies they sell to him. But some of the burden may remain on the manufacturer. Thus, depending on supply and demand conditions, the burden of a tax paid initially by a business firm may be borne by the buyers of its product, by its suppliers, or by its owners, or be divided in various ways among all of them.[6]

[6] For a formal discussion of this problem, see the Graphic Appendix, pp. 625–627.

Some other taxes may be shifted by similar processes. For example, property taxes on buildings may decrease the net profits from buildings, discourage construction, and pass forward the tax burden by raising rental rates; at least part of the burden may be passed backward to suppliers by lowering the prices of construction materials and services. A tax on employers' payrolls may tend to fall on workers in the form of lower wage rates, and so on. The processes of shifting taxes and arriving at their final incidence are so complex and depend on such a wide variety of demand and supply conditions that it is difficult to generalize about them.[7]

D. CONCLUSION

Because of these and other difficulties, it is safe to make only a few generalizations about the distribution of the real burden of taxes in this country. Primarily because of the personal income tax, with its exemptions and graduated rates, the tax system as a whole is almost certainly progressive for incomes above the average level; that is, the higher the incomes above this level, the higher is the percentage taken by taxes. It is more dangerous to generalize about tax burdens on those whose incomes are below the average. Owing to the heavy taxes on residential property, autos, gasoline, and other consumer goods, it is doubtful that taxes are more than proportional to incomes in this lower range.And in the lowest part of the range they may be regressive, taking a larger percentage of lower than of higher incomes.

8. Some Tax Principles

Let us now examine some principles that have been advocated as guides for distributing the tax burden among the populace.

A. EQUITY IN THE DISTRIBUTION OF THE TAX BURDEN

Everybody favors an "equitable" distribution of the tax burden; no one champions "inequity." But just what is equity in this case? Two of the most popular principles are taxation in proportion to benefits received from government services,and taxation in proportion to ability to pay. On closer examination both principles present many difficulties, and only by unlikely coincidence would they suggest exactly the same distribution of tax burdens.

[7] At this point the perceptive reader may wonder why the levying of a tax may cause a firm to raise its price above the level it would have charged in the absence of the tax. If this pays, why didn't the firm raise its price before the tax was imposed? It turns out that if a firm was charging the most profitable price it could before the tax was levied, it will usually find it profitable to raise its price after the tax is instituted. This problem is treated in the Graphic Appendix, pp. 641–642.

B. THE BENEFIT PRINCIPLE

The central idea of taxation according to the benefit principle is simple; every family should pay for the benefits it receives from government activities, just as it pays for the services it buys in private markets. Many believe that such a distribution of taxes is not only equitable but also tends to promote economy in government by preventing people from demanding government services for which they themselves are unwilling to pay.

This principle assumes that it is possible to determine the amount of benefits received by each person or family from government services. There are, of course, some specific government activities that can be shown to benefit particular persons. For example, a sewage system benefits the residents in the area, a public playground benefits those who play there, a hard-surfaced road benefits the farmers who use it, an old-age insurance program benefits those covered by it, and fire protection benefits property owners in the area.

But even in these cases there are also likely to be more general benefits. For example, sewage systems may reduce the danger of disease and epidemics over a very wide area; playgrounds may lessen juvenile delinquency, raise the health and vigor of the citizenry, and improve the attractiveness of the city; a hard-surfaced road may benefit not only local farmers, but also travelers through the area and urban dwellers who get cheaper food; and fire protection may provide safety for those who own no property. Even in these cases, therefore, it would usually be very difficult to estimate with any accuracy the value of benefits received by each person or family.

It is even more difficult to estimate the benefits received by each person or family from many other government activities whose effects are much more widely diffused. How, for example, would you determine the benefits received by each of the millions of families from national defense? From the services of legislative bodies, the courts, the police? From the development of atomic energy? From public education?

This is not to argue that the benefit principle is useless as a guide to taxation. When it can be shown that identifiable persons or families receive measurable benefits from specific government expenditures, it may be appropriate to tax them by amounts not exceeding the value of the benefits they receive, even though there are also benefits that cannot be allocated. But the benefits of many, if not most, government expenditures are so widely diffused that it is practically impossible to assign them.

c. Ability to Pay

Most of those who favor taxation in proportion to ability to pay reject the benefit principle not only because of its administrative difficulties but also because they believe that it would be inequitable even if perfectly administered. They hold that people should bear tax burdens in proportion to their ability to pay, regardless of the amount of services they receive from the government. This is likely to involve a redistribution of real income, as some pay taxes in excess of the benefits they receive and others receive benefits in excess of their tax payments.

Just what is meant by ability to pay? How are we to measure it, and how are we to translate it into a specific tax system? For example, how much weight should be given to a taxpayer's income? To his wealth? To the number of his dependents? To his age? Even if we agree that ability to pay should be measured by income, perhaps with adjustments for the number of dependents, at what rate should total tax payments rise with income? Do we mean merely that the higher the income, the higher the total amount of taxes? Even a regressive tax could meet this test—for example, a tax of 5 percent, or $500, on a $10,000 income and a tax of 1 percent, or $10,000, on a $1 million income. Or do we mean that the tax should be proportional, taking the same percentage of all incomes? Or do we mean that the tax should be progressive, taking a higher percentage of higher incomes? If so, at what rate should the tax progress, and how high should it go?

Since value judgments are involved, economics cannot provide answers to these questions. In the end both the extent to which this principle will guide the tax policy and the definition of ability to pay embodied in the tax laws must depend on such things as social attitudes toward the distribution of wealth and income, social evaluation of the wants of the rich as against those of the poor, the distribution of political power among the various income and wealth classes, and other considerations.

d. Other Considerations in Tax Policy

We can mention here only briefly some of the considerations, other than the principles of benefit and ability to pay, that have strongly influenced American tax policies.

1. Sheer political expediency. Faced with the unpopular job of collecting more taxes, legislators have often been guided by the "least-squawking theory of taxation," plucking dollars in the ways calculated to produce the least effective protests from voters.

2. Incentive effects. Taxation does not necessarily reduce incentives to work, save, invest in capital goods, and operate business efficiently. In fact, by lowering disposable incomes some taxes may actually stimulate people to work harder, save more, and otherwise strive to raise their incomes in order to replace the amounts taken by the government. Yet there is a real danger that high tax rates, taking a large proportion of each additional dollar of net income, may tend to reduce incentives and damage productivity. People may simply feel that it is not worth their time, effort, and risk to start new businesses or expand old ones. As we have seen, overtime work may be discouraged, and so on. Fear of this result has been a major factor in preventing the use of some types of taxes and in limiting the rates of others. This concern about the effect on incentives is frequently a pressure toward less progressivity and even toward regressivity in the tax system.

3. Effects on consumption patterns. This consideration has influenced tax structures in several ways. It helps explain the high taxes on alcoholic beverages and tobacco—types of consumption that many believe should be penalized; it is also partially responsible for high taxes on many so-called "luxuries" and for generally lower taxes on food, medicines, and other things considered "necessities."

4. Effects on the location of industry and of taxpayers. The federal government has taxed many types of imports in order to penalize their purchase from foreigners and to promote the growth of these industries at home. This consideration has also influenced state and local tax policies. To prevent business from migrating to other jurisdictions or to attract business from them, these governmental units have in many cases sought to avoid higher business taxes, to tax business at rates below those in other areas, and even to grant tax exemptions and subsidies to business. To a lesser degree they have also competed to retain residents, avoiding higher personal taxes—such as income and death taxes—and striving to offer the advantage of lower taxes than in other areas.

5. Effects on the structure of industries. The desire to encourage small business firms and to discourage "bigness" has also influenced tax policy. Examples are the preferential treatment of small corpora-

tions under the federal corporate income tax and the graduated tax on chain stores employed by some states.

6. Income redistribution. Some people have viewed the tax system as an appropriate means of ironing out what they regard as unjust differences in income levels. In part the progressiveness of our income taxes arises from this motive. We shall have more to say about it later.

9. Summary

In conclusion, we find that the American tax structure is shaped by many considerations, most of them controversial and many in at least potential conflict with each other. These include conflicting concepts of equity in the distribution of the tax burden, conflicting notions as to how benefits and ability to pay should be measured, conflicting estimates of the effects of various taxes on socially useful incentives, and conflicting attitudes toward the effects of taxes on consumption patterns, the location of industry, the location of taxpayers, the structure of industries, and so on. It is no wonder, therefore, that our tax system reflects an uneasy and shifting compromise.

SUGGESTED READINGS

Groves, Harold M. (ed.), *Viewpoints on Public Finance,* Henry Holt, New York, 1947.

Somers, Harold M., *Public Finance and National Income,* Blakiston, Philadelphia, 1949.

QUESTIONS

1. a. How do the economic effects of transfer payments differ from those of government purchases of goods and services?
   b. Which do you think would have more powerful expansionary effects? Why?
2. a. In the text why is the magnitude of government expenditures compared with *money* national income?
   b. Do you think government expenditures ought to be a constant rising or falling proportion of national income?
   c. How about expenditure on potatoes?
   d. Expenditure on entertainment?
3. If the government is forced to curtail its expenditures, where do you think cuts are:

   a. Most feasible politically?
   b. Most desirable?
   Go through the list of uses of government funds in giving your answer.
4. Suppose the government were in 1956 to collect enough taxes to pay off $20 billion of the debt incurred during World War II.
   a. Would taxpayers as a whole in 1956 be paying the money costs of the war expenditure?
   b. Would they be paying the real costs of that expenditure?
   c. Would all taxpayers together suffer real income losses in 1956?
   d. Would some taxpayers be suffering real income losses? Who?
5. "The personal income tax is the one type of tax clearly designed to be progressive."
   a. Why does not the tax exemption on small corporate incomes have this effect?
   b. How about property taxes?
   c. Gift and estate taxes?
6. Suppose a man has been earning $2000 of taxable income and that his income suddenly goes up to $2020.
   a. Compute his federal income tax both before and after his income rise.
   b. Did it pay him to accept the additional $20 even though it put him into a higher bracket?
7. Show the fallacy in businessman X's assertion that it is profitable for him to embark on an advertising campaign only because of the height of his income taxes:
   a. If the advertising campaign is successful.
   b. If it is unsuccessful.
   c. Show how his anticipations of future tax rates may eliminate the fallacy.
   d. Show why taxes may induce him to make tax-exempt gifts.
8. a. Describe the operation of a "personal corporation" set up to avoid income taxes.
   b. Why is this lucrative only for rich men?
   c. How might you go about plugging up the tax loophole which could appear in the absence of corporate taxes and yet avoid double taxation and unprogressive tax rates?
9. Discuss the pros and cons of excise taxes on:
   a. Cigarettes.
   b. Entertainment.
   c. Mink coats.
   d. All commodities.
10. Who bears the burden of a corporation tax:
   a. If it is all covered by a rise in the price of the firm's products?

   b. If it is not covered by a rise in the price of its products and all profits are paid out in dividends?
   c. If profits are not paid out in dividends?
   d. If it is not covered by a price rise and the corporation is sold after the tax has been in effect for some time?
11. a. Can you think of some cases where a rise in taxes will increase production?
    b. Decrease production?
12. Show why most of the functions of government discussed in Chapter 7 cannot be financed by taxing on the "benefit principle."

CHAPTER 18

Government Borrowing and the Public Debt

If the Nation is living within its income, its credit is good. . . . But if, like a spendthrift, it . . . continues to pile up deficits, then it is on the road to bankruptcy. (Franklin D. Roosevelt, October 19, 1932.)

Are your children and mine going to be free men or are they being sold into the bondage of debt? . . . Now, there are some people who say, "Let's just run a little deficit." They want to go just a little bankrupt. (Thomas E. Dewey, January 23, 1940.)

1. Introduction

A. RECENT DEFICITS AND SURPLUSES

We have already noted that government expenditures and tax revenues are not always equal to each other. In some periods the government has a deficit as its expenditures exceed its revenues. In others its revenues exceed its expenditures, giving it a surplus. These statements are borne out by the data in Table 34. In fact, government deficits or surpluses have sometimes been large and persistent. For example, the total government deficit during the 30's was nearly $16 billion, reflecting a federal deficit of $18 billion and a state and local surplus of $2 billion. But this deficit was quite small as compared with that of World War II, which was nearly $170 billion. This reflected a federal deficit of more than $181 billion and a state and local surplus of more than $11 billion. During the five years immediately following the war the government had a total tax surplus of nearly $32 billion, most of it at the federal level.

TABLE 34. Deficits (−) and Surpluses (+) of American Government Units[1]
(In billions of dollars)

Calendar Year	Total	Federal	State and Local
1929	$+ 1.1	$+ 1.2	$−0.1
1933	− 1.3	− 1.3	0.0
1939	− 1.9	− 2.2	+0.3
1944	−51.4	−54.0	+2.6
1947	+13.7	+12.8	+0.9
1949	− 2.8	− 1.9	−0.9
1950	+ 8.0	+ 8.9	−0.9
1951	+ 7.3	+ 8.3	−1.0
1952	− 2.4	− 2.3	−0.1
Addenda:			
Total for the ten years, 1930–1939	$−15.9	$− 17.9	$+ 2.0
Total for the six war years, 1940–1945	−169.7	−181.4	+11.7
Total for the postwar years, 1946–1950, inclusive	+ 31.7	+ 31.0	+ 0.7

B. DEFICITS AND GOVERNMENT BORROWING

It would not be quite accurate to say that when the government has a deficit it always borrows to get money to cover it, and that it always uses any tax surplus it may have to retire debt. For this there are two principal reasons. (1) As we have already seen, a central government with money-creating power may meet some part of its deficit simply by printing new money. However, our Treasury has used this power very little during the twentieth century. (2) The government may make net increases or net decreases in its own money holdings. It may add to them by borrowing or by using part of a tax surplus for the purpose. Or it may decrease its money holdings to cover part of its deficit or retire some of its debt.

These qualifications should be kept in mind. Yet without serious inaccuracy we may assume that net borrowing by the government during any period will be equal to the government deficit, and that any tax surplus will be used to retire debt.

The major aim of this chapter is to describe the various types of borrowing and public debt and their influence on the operation of the economy. Let us start with government borrowing, assuming that the borrowing is done to cover the government's current deficit.

[1] These are Department of Commerce data which appear in the *Survey of Current Business.*

The immediate purpose of any government borrowing is, of course, to provide the government with money which it can spend to command real resources for its use. But the effect of borrowing depends greatly on the source of the money.

2. Foreign Versus Domestic Borrowing

The first important point is that the effects of government borrowing from foreigners are quite different from those when it borrows from its own citizens.

A. BORROWING FROM FOREIGNERS

A government can add to the total real resources available for use by itself and its citizens by borrowing from foreigners. Suppose that during some year our federal government covers its deficit by borrowing from the British an amount in pounds equivalent to $1 billion. The government is buying goods and services worth $1 billion more than its tax revenues. But the pounds borrowed from the British can be used to make net imports of $1 billion worth of foreign goods and services. In effect, we borrow from foreigners $1 billion worth of real goods and services, so that this part of government expenditures does not have to be met out of our current domestic production.

Foreign borrowing, of course, leaves a heritage of government debt to foreigners. Some part of the nation's future income must be used to pay interest to foreigners and to repay the principal of the debt if it is not renewed. This can be a drain on the nation's real income, for some part of its output will have to be exported to get the money with which to meet the interest and principal payments to foreigners.

Since our government has not borrowed significant amounts from foreigners for many decades, we can confine our discussion to domestic borrowing.

B. DOMESTIC BORROWING

The effects of government borrowing from its own citizens are quite different. In the first place, such borrowing does not add to the total quantity of resources available for use by the government and its citizens. It is merely a method of enabling the government to command more domestic resources. All the goods and services bought by the government with borrowed money as well as those purchased with taxes must be provided by its citizens.

In the second place, such borrowing does not leave a heritage of debt to foreigners. It leaves a heritage of government debt to its own people; some of them will own more assets in the form of debt claims against their government. Collectively, the people as taxpayers owe the debt to the people as creditors of the government.

In the following sections we shall deal exclusively with domestic borrowing. In order to emphasize the importance of the different types of borrowing we shall proceed as follows. We shall assume that the government deficit is of a given size and that the government has the option of borrowing from the public, the commercial banks, or the Federal Reserve. Thus we may assume a given expansionary effect flowing from the excess of government expenditures over its tax collections, and then see how the extent of the expansionary effect is influenced by the type of borrowing used to cover the deficit.

3. Types of Domestic Borrowing

A. A COMMON ASPECT OF ALL TYPES OF BORROWING

All types of domestic government borrowing have one aspect in common: they require that the government issue valuable claims. If the government had collected enough taxes to cover all its expenditures, the public would have only its canceled tax bills to evidence its contributions to the government. But to the extent that the government covers its expenditures by borrowing, it must issue valuable debt claims to the public. The form of the claims received by the public depends on the type of borrowing employed.

B. BORROWING FROM THE PUBLIC

By borrowing from the public we mean government borrowing from anyone within the country except the Federal Reserve and commercial banks—that is, from anyone who does not have the power to create money. Under this type of borrowing the government gets money that was already in existence and the public receives government securities in return.

Borrowing from the public is likely to be less effective than taxation as a means of decreasing private expenditures. Taxation is a way of coercing people into contributing to government. The people would probably have spent a large proportion of the dollars they are forced to pay in taxes. Moreover, they feel poorer for having paid taxes; they receive no valuable claims in return and are therefore less inclined to spend. But a government program of borrowing from the public is ordinarily not so coercive; it usually relies on efforts to persuade people to give up their dollars. A larger proportion of the money lent to the government is therefore likely to be spare dollars that would not have been spent anyway. Sometimes people just withdraw money from their savings accounts to buy government bonds. Moreover, people do not feel poorer for having lent to the government; they receive government securities in exchange for their money. For these reasons, borrowing from the public is likely to be less effective than taxation in reducing the rate of private spending.

Nevertheless, government borrowing from the public may tend to lower private spending. In the first place, the government may, through patriotic appeals and the offer of attractive securities, induce people to save more and spend less for consumption. In the second place, the government demand for loans may tend to raise interest rates and lower private investment spending. If the total money supply is not increased, government borrowing can decrease the supply of loans for private use. But this is less likely to happen if an easy-money policy does permit the money supply to increase.

It should be remembered that government borrowing from nonbank lenders increases the public's holding of securities and does not directly increase the money supply.

c. Borrowing from Commercial Banks

Government borrowing from commercial banks tends to increase the public's money supply. It works as follows: The banks buy securities from the Treasury, creating new deposits for it. The Treasury then transfers this deposit money to the public to pay for goods and services purchased by the government. This type of borrowing therefore tends to increase the amount of money in the hands of the public. There will be a net increase in the money supply if the banks have excess reserves or can get additional reserves so that they do not have to reduce their loans to private borrowers in order to lend to the government. But this effect is offset to the extent that larger bank loans to government do lead to smaller bank loans to private borrowers.

It should be clear that government borrowing from commercial banks is likely to be less effective than borrowing from the public as a means of decreasing private spending. In fact, it may actually increase private spending, for it tends to increase the public's money supply, and so can even reduce interest rates.

D. Borrowing from the Federal Reserve

Government borrowing from the Federal Reserve tends directly to increase both the public's money supply *and the dollar volume of commercial bank reserves.* It happens this way. The Treasury sells securities to the Federal Reserve and receives in return new deposits at the Federal Reserve banks. It then writes checks on these deposits and uses them to pay for goods and services purchased by the government. The public deposits these checks at the commercial banks, which increases the public's checking deposits. The banks then send these checks to the Federal Reserve, which adds their amount to commercial bank reserves. Thus the process of borrowing from the Federal Reserve directly increases both the public's money supply and the volume of commercial bank reserves and lending power.

There is no reason to believe that government borrowing from the Federal Reserve would tend to reduce private spending. Rather, it tends to increase private expenditures. It directly increases the public's money supply and the banks' lending power and tends to increase the availability of credit for private use and to lower interest rates. For practical purposes the effect is much the same as if the Treasury or the Federal Reserve had printed paper dollars to meet government needs.

E. Summary of Borrowing Methods

There is no type of government borrowing from domestic sources that is as effective as taxation in decreasing private spending. But the different types of borrowing have widely different effects. Borrowing from the public tends to reduce private spending to some extent. Borrowing from commercial banks is less effective for this purpose and may actually increase private spending. Borrowing from the Federal Reserve almost certainly tends to increase private spending.

These points are very important for fiscal policy. If the government wishes its expenditures to be as expansionary as possible it may reduce the part financed by taxes and increase the part financed by borrowing. And it may prefer borrowing from the Federal Reserve and commercial banks to borrowing from the public. On the other hand, if it wishes to offset as much as possible the expansionary effects of its spending it may rely more heavily on taxes and less heavily on borrowing. And it may seek to borrow more from the public and less from the Federal Reserve and commercial banks.

4. Debt Retirement

A. THE USE OF TAX SURPLUS TO RETIRE DEBT

The only way by which a government can make a net reduction in its debt is to have a tax surplus. The very collection of taxes tends to reduce private disposable incomes and private spending. But the net effect of collecting a tax surplus *and* using it to retire debt depends to a considerable extent on the type of debt that is paid off. To make this point let us assume that the contractive effects of collecting the tax surplus are given, and then go on to compare the effects of two types of debt retirement: (1) government retirement of debt held by the public, and (2) government retirement of debt held by the Federal Reserve. Let us assume that the amount of tax money available for debt reduction is $10 billion.

B. RETIREMENT OF DEBT HELD BY THE PUBLIC

The use of a tax surplus to retire debt held by the public has no direct effect on the total money supply. The taxpayers send $10 billion to the Treasury; the Treasury returns it to the public in repaying debt. The public is, of course, $10 billion poorer because after the tax collection it has to surrender $10 billion worth of government securities to get its money back. But its money supply is not reduced.

There is no reason to believe that this process of retiring debt held by the public will reduce the supply of credit for private use or raise interest rates. In fact, the reverse may occur. The former holders of government bonds now have more money to lend. This can stimulate private investment and may even offset the contractive effects of the collection of the tax surplus.

C. RETIREMENT OF DEBT HELD BY THE FEDERAL RESERVE

The use of a tax surplus to retire debt held by the Federal Reserve reduces directly both the public's money supply and the dollar volume of commercial bank reserves. Here is how it works. Taxpayers send $10 billion of checks to the Treasury, which deposits them at the Federal Reserve. The Treasury uses these deposits to buy back its securities from the Federal Reserve. Meanwhile the latter deducts $10 billion from the reserves of the banks on which the checks are drawn, and sends the checks to the banks. The banks deduct the amounts of the checks from the taxpayers' deposit accounts.

The use of a tax surplus to retire debt held by the Federal Reserve can therefore have highly restrictive monetary effects, for it directly reduces both the public's money supply and the reserves and lending power of the commercial banks.

D. SUMMARY

Our findings in this section are highly important for fiscal policy. For example, if the government wants to use a tax surplus in the way that will be most restrictive on private spending, it should retire debt held by the Federal Reserve. If, on the other hand, it wishes its tax surplus to have the least restrictive effect it should use the surplus to retire debt held by the public.

This result ties in with our previous finding that borrowing from the Federal Reserve is more inflationary than borrowing from the public. For paying off debt reverses the borrowing process; it is, so to speak, "disborrowing." Since borrowing from the Federal Reserve is most inflationary, undoing this process—i.e., retiring debt held by the Federal Reserve—must be most deflationary.

Let us look now at some other aspects of the public debt. Much of what we say will relate to the very existence of a public debt that was built up in the past and is currently neither increasing nor decreasing. However, we shall also make further comments about the processes of increasing or decreasing the size of the debt.

5. The Public Debt

A. THE FIGURES

The debts of American government units have grown enormously during the past half century (Table 35). In 1912, shortly before World War I, the total public debt was only $5.7 billion, of which $1.2 billion was owed by the federal government and $4.5 billion by state and local governments. But by 1951 the total had risen to more than $282 billion, with the federal debt above $255 billion and state and local debts above $27 billion. Commentators tirelessly point out that this represents a debt of about $1800 for every man, woman, and child in the country. As in the case of expenditures and taxes, these figures should be interpreted in light of the decrease in the purchasing power of the dollar, the growth of population, and the rise of both total national income and per capita incomes. But even with these adjustments the increase in the debt has been very large.

The increase of the public debt indicates, of course, the net amount of deficit spending by the government during the period; the government issued its debt obligations to get the money needed to cover the excess of its expenditures over its revenues. Practically all this debt is held by Americans; very little is in foreign hands.

TABLE 35. Debts of American Government Units on Selected Dates[2]
(In billions of dollars)

End of Fiscal Year	Total	Federal	State	Local
1902	$ 3.4	$ 1.2	$0.3	$ 1.9
1912	5.7	1.2	0.4	4.1
1919 (August)	. . .	26.6	. . .	. . .
1922	33.2	23.0	1.2	9.1
1930 (December 31)	. . .	16.0	. . .	. . .
1940	. . .	48.5	. . .	. . .
1946	285.3	269.2	2.4	13.6
1951	282.3	255.2	6.4	20.7

Most of the state and local debt was issued to finance durable public works, such as highways and school buildings, though some was created to finance operating deficits during the great depression, to pay bonuses to veterans after World War II, and for other purposes. Most of the federal debt was created during three periods—World War I, the great depression, and World War II.

B. THE BURDEN OF THE DEBT

As already noted, this huge debt would clearly represent a real "drain" on American wealth and income if it were owed to foreigners. In figuring the net worth of all Americans, including our government, we would have to deduct the amount of foreign claims against our wealth, and part of our income would have to be used to pay interest, and, if the loans are not renewed, to repay principal, to our foreign creditors. But since very little of our government debt is held abroad we need not consider this further.

The great growth of our domestically held public debt has raised this highly controversial question: "Does the growth of public debt tend to impoverish the nation?" Reasoning by analogy, many people unhesitantly answer "Yes." They argue that a government is just like a person, and everybody knows that a person is worse off if he goes into debt. His net worth is reduced because he is in debt, and part of

[2] Source: The Tax Foundation, *Facts and Figures on Government Finance, 1952–1953,* New York, p. 189.

his income must be used to pay interest to his creditors. Even applied to private debts this is poor reasoning, and it is even worse when applied to the public debt.

C. PUBLIC BORROWING DIFFERS FROM PRIVATE BORROWING

The issue here is not the effect of borrowing on the government as a "person"; it is its effect on the wealth and income of the nation as a whole. As a minimum, therefore, we must consider the effects not only on the government, but also on the lenders to the government. On doing this, we find that government borrowing has a two-sided effect; the government owes more debt, but lenders own more assets in the form of claims against the government. The government is poorer but the public is richer, so there need be no change in the net worth of the nation as a whole. The same is true of national income. Though the government may have to collect more taxes to pay interest on the debt, this income is paid out to the government's creditors. Thus, the mere issue of more public debt obligations does not *necessarily* increase or decrease the wealth and income of the nation as a whole.

This indicates the fallacy of the argument that by borrowing to cover a large part of government expenditures during World War II we shifted much of the cost of the war to our grandchildren. We did no such thing. When some of our grandchildren pay interest and principal on the war-created debt to our grandchildren, they will only be redistributing income. Total national income then would not necessarily be reduced.

In a very real sense we paid for the war ourselves during the time it was fought, even though much of the government's expenditure was financed by borrowing. The analysis in the preceding chapter showed us where to look for the real cost of government spending. The real cost of the war was the use of our resources in the production of military rather than civilian goods, and the resulting shortages. The cost of the war also consisted in the loss of time, leisure, and personal comforts, especially by those who were in the armed forces, to say nothing of the lives lost in the fighting. This real material cost of the war was paid by us at the time and will not be "paid by our grandchildren."

D. PRODUCTIVE BORROWING

Even if the analogy between public and private debt were valid, it would not follow that an increase in government—or private—debt is always undesirable. To judge this we must consider the uses to which the borrowed money is put. Of course we all know of people who got into financial difficulties by borrowing money to spend for riotous living or for unsuccessful business ventures. But we also know of people who increased their wealth and earning power by going into debt. We need only cite the case of the impoverished law or medical student who must go into debt to complete his training. Borrowing is an integral part of a transaction in which people acquire assets that can prove to be worth more than the debt and that yield an income in excess of the interest payments on the debt. In fact, a considerable part of private investment is financed in this way. All corporate bonds represent indebtedness by the firms that issue them, yet no one suggests that this is unsound business practice. Thus it is foolish to try to evaluate private borrowing without considering the use to which the money is put.

The same is true of government borrowing. In some cases the government uses the borrowed money to increase its own assets. It may borrow money to pay for additions to the national wealth in the form of highways, school buildings, hydroelectric facilities, and so on. Government borrowing and deficit spending may also tend to increase the real income and wealth of the country even though the government's assets are not increased. For example, such spending of borrowed money in a depression period may directly and indirectly increase the demand for output, thereby eliciting increased employment, increased real output, and a higher rate of private investment. Incidentally, all this may increase the government's tax yields, so that the debt may be at least partly "self-liquidating."

On the other hand, deficit spending under other conditions may not raise real output at all, and may produce only price inflation. This subject will be discussed more fully in the following chapter. However, it should already be clear that an increase of the public debt does not inevitably reduce the wealth and income of the nation in either real or money terms. The net effect depends on the uses to which the borrowed money is put, the state of employment at the time, and other factors.

E. DISADVANTAGES OF THE DEBT

Does this mean that we must accept the conclusions of some optimists that the size of the public debt is of no economic significance at all because "we owe it to ourselves"? The answer is emphatically "no."

We have already seen that the process of increasing the debt is one of deficit spending, which may have either favorable or unfavorable effects on the economy, depending on the circumstances. But the answer is still "no," even if we consider only the existence of a large public debt of constant size.

The mere presence of such a large debt may disadvantageously influence economic behavior in several ways, some of which may assume serious proportions as the magnitude of the debt grows in relation to our national income. (1) Holders of these debts consider them to be assets, and feeling themselves wealthy they may increase their rate of consumption expenditure. This may be desirable if there is a tendency toward deflation, but undesirable if it will induce or accentuate inflation. (2) Because of its large outstanding debt, the government may press for a continuous easy-money policy, even in the midst of inflation, to hold down its interest payments and facilitate its refinancing operations. It may be prepared to flood the market with money to provide a source of funds with which the public can buy government securities but which may be used for other purposes. The inflationary consequences are obvious and have already been discussed in detail. (3) If the debt is held largely by the wealthy, interest payments to them may aggravate inequalities in the distribution of income. (4) The collection of additional taxes to cover interest payments on the debt may have many effects other than those on the distribution of income. For example, the addition of these taxes to those levied for other purposes may impair useful economic incentives. (5) The existence of an already large debt may make the government less willing to contract additional debt, even for worthy purposes. Or the necessity of taxing to cover interest payments may make the government less willing to levy taxes for other purposes, whether worthy or unworthy.

In the following discussion of fiscal policies, we shall deal with some other effects of increasing and decreasing the public debt.

SUGGESTED READINGS

Abbott, Charles C., *The Federal Debt,* Twentieth Century Fund, New York, 1953.

Poole, Kenyon E. (ed.), *Fiscal Policies and the American Economy,* Prentice-Hall, New York, 1951.

QUESTIONS

1. Why might a government prefer to build up a surplus rather than borrowing or collecting taxes for only as much as it pays out?
2. Explain why if a war debt were held by foreigners, future generations might indeed pay for the war.
3. Examine the effects on the money supply when reserve requirements are 20 percent if the Treasury obtains $1 million:
   a. By borrowing from the public.
   b. By borrowing from the commercial banks when they have no excess reserves.
   c. By borrowing from the commercial banks when they have large excess reserves.
   d. By borrowing from the Federal Reserve.
   e. By printing one million paper dollar bills.
   f. Compare your last two answers and comment.
   g. Show what happens in each case when the government retires its debt; include the effect on national income.
4. a. If government bonds are held primarily by the very rich, would you guess that government retirement of debt held by the public would be expansionary or contractionary?
   b. What does your answer imply about the saving propensities of rich and poor?
   c. Does this suggest that in a depression we want more equality or more inequality?
5. Why is the effect on national income of retiring debt by taxing somewhat easier to analyze, in the abstract, than the effect of the government spending that originally produced the debt?
   Hint: What two types of expenditure have we considered, and what is the difference in their economic effects?
6. Cite cases in which it is good financial policy for firms or individuals to live on borrowed funds.
7. Weigh the disadvantages of a large debt of constant size in depression as against inflation, considering:
   a. Interest payments.
   b. The effect of the Treasury's needs on Federal Reserve policy.
   c. The effect on incentives.
   d. The effect on governmental willingness to spend.
8. a. Show that when large amounts of bonds are held by the public, falling prices during a depression can increase the public's purchasing power.

b. That rising prices can decrease its purchasing power.

c. Show thus how a large debt might help mitigate inflations or depressions.

d. Compare this result with the analysis in Chapter 13 of the effects of a price-wage fall on the purchasing power of the stock of money.

CHAPTER 19

Fiscal Policy

. . . You do not have to be an expert to know that when anything happens that violently contracts sales and incomes and the prices of securities and commodities, . . . a Government . . . is under a very solemn duty . . . to take immediate steps to avoid a deficit. (Franklin D. Roosevelt, October 19, 1932.)

. . . There was a deficit of over three billion dollars. . . . And the result was natural. Business recovery slowed up. (Thomas E. Dewey, February 10, 1940.)

1. Introduction

We shall now explore more deeply a topic already encountered several times—the overall effects of government expenditure, tax, and debt policies on the behavior of national money income, real output, employment, and price levels. We shall pay special attention to the types of fiscal policies that tend to initiate or aggravate economic instability, those that may be used to promote economic stability, and some of the practical problems of formulating and administering income-stabilizing types of fiscal policy.

A. SUMMARY OF EARLIER RESULTS

To provide a background for our discussion, it will be useful to recall some of our earlier findings. The government exerts an expansive influence on the economy by taking one or more of the following actions: (1) Increasing its rate of purchase of goods and services. This increases both the government's own demand for output and its contribution to private money incomes. (2) Increasing its transfer

348

payments. Though this does not increase the government's own demand for output, it does increase government contributions to private money incomes. (3) Lowering its tax collection. This tends to increase private disposable incomes. All these actions tend to enhance the ability of the private sectors to consume and save, and a rise of government purchases also adds directly to the demand for output. The government exerts a contractive influence by taking the reverse types of action—by lowering its rate of purchase of goods and services, by decreasing its transfer payments, and by increasing its tax collections.

At any time the government may take some actions that make for expansion and others that make for contraction. For example, it may increase both its expenditures and its tax collections. Whether the net effect will be neutral, expansive, or contractive depends on the relative powers of these counteracting forces. This will be examined in the following sections.

B. ALTERNATIVE POLICIES

In recent years we have heard much about deficit spending as a means of eliminating unemployment and about tax surpluses to fight inflation. It is maintained that the government ought to spend more than it receives in revenues in times of depression, and collect more in taxes than it spends in times of inflationary pressure. We have already seen that there is much to be said for this advice. We shall find that there are many different policy measures of this type that might be used to stabilize national income at a high level of employment. In addition it turns out that deficits in depressions and surpluses during inflation are not even the only possible fiscal methods for stabilization, though for various reasons we may wish to reject other alternatives as practical policy measures. Let us examine the alternatives in greater detail.

2. Balanced Budget Expenditures as a Stabilizing Device

Those who are suspicious of government surpluses and deficits may derive some meager consolation from the observation that, at least in theory, the government can combat inflation and depression by fiscal measures and yet never depart from an annually balanced budget.

A. EXPANSIONARY EFFECTS OF BALANCED BUDGET EXPENDITURES

The assertion that the government can exert an upward pressure on national income via a balanced budget expenditure may strike the reader as paradoxical. With one hand the government spends more and so pushes income upward, and with the other it taxes away an equal amount and so pushes the economy in the reverse direction. Yet it happens that when the government spends this money on goods and services rather than on transfer payments the two forces usually do not cancel out. The net effect may be expected to make for expansion in most cases.

To see this let us suppose that the government increases by $20 billion both its annual rate of expenditures for goods and services, and its tax collections. Private disposable incomes may remain unchanged, at least initially; the $20 billion contributed to them by the increased rate of government expenditures is offset by the $20-billion increase in tax collections. It therefore seems unlikely that there will be a substantial decline of private spending to offset the $20-billion expansionary rise of the government's own demand for output. Looked at another way, the result is that the public will come to market with no substantial change in its purchasing power, only to find that unless the nation's output has meanwhile increased, the supplies available for their purchase will have gone down because the government has taken these items for its own use. We can usually expect an increase in national money income, an increased demand for labor, and under some conditions an upward pressure on prices.[1] Thus we find that a rise of government expenditures for goods and services may have an expansive influence, even though it is accompanied by an equal rise of tax collections so that the budget is continuously in balance. To prevent the rise of its expenditures from having a net expansive effect, the government would have to increase its taxes by a somewhat greater amount.

Perhaps it is well to examine this feat of magic a bit further to see where the secret lies. We observed, when first discussing government purchases of goods and services, that their expansionary effects are exactly the same as those of any similar purchase by a private firm or individual. In other words, if a business firm had decided to spend this money the net effect on the economy would have been exactly the same as if the money had been taken from that firm in taxes and spent by the government. Both acts would have given the purchasing

[1] We can see that this balanced budget argument is inapplicable to governmental transfer payments, for these involve only a redistribution of income and no demand for goods and services by the government. Even then, appropriately planned transfer payments might make for expansion if they take money out of the hands of people who do not want to spend it and give it to those who will use it to demand goods and services.

power back into the hands of the public and would have taken goods and services off the market.

But the fact is that individuals and firms usually do not spend all their money income. They save some of it and do not use that money to make purchases. On the other hand, under a balanced budget arrangement the government spends every penny it takes in. This is the secret of the expansionary effect of a balanced budget expenditure. The government takes money, only part of which would have been spent had it been left in private hands, *and spends it all*.

B. A BALANCED BUDGET ANTI-INFLATION POLICY

The same reasoning applies to a reduction of government expenditures. Suppose that, starting from a situation of a balanced budget, full employment, and stable prices, the government decreases by $10 billion the annual rates of both its expenditures and its tax collections. Private disposable incomes may not be changed; the $10-billion decrease of the government's expenditure contributions to them is offset by the $10-billion decrease in tax collections. Nevertheless, there remains the contractionary influence of the $10-billion decrease in the government's own demand for output. Thus, reduced government spending for output may have a net contractive effect even though it is accompanied by an equal decrease of taxes and a continuously balanced budget. To avoid exerting a net contractive effect the government would have had to lower its taxes more than it reduced its expenditure and run a deficit.

The reasoning here ignores some complicating factors. Yet the outcome is clear. At least in theory it is possible to combat inflation or depression by fiscal means while maintaining an annually balanced budget.

3. Expenditures Financed by Borrowing

In the preceding chapter we discussed the sources from which the government can borrow: the public, the commercial banks, and the Federal Reserve. We also compared the effects of these alternatives on the economy. Let us recall these results and apply them to our analysis of income stabilization policy.

A. BORROWING FROM THE PUBLIC

The government may combat depression by increasing its expenditures of funds borrowed from the public rather than out of taxes. In periods of inflationary pressure it can contract both its expenditures and its borrowings. Clearly this method can use the approach mentioned earlier—deficit spending in depression and acquisition of surpluses during periods when inflation threatens.

This technique may be expected to be more powerful in producing economic expansion (and contraction) than the balanced budget methods just discussed. The reason is quite simple. By taxing for revenue the government obtains its funds relatively indiscriminately by coercive means. Much of the income collected may come from people who would have spent part of it themselves had they been permitted to retain it. Borrowing, on the other hand, is a request that people volunteer their spare funds. It may therefore be surmised that much of the money obtained in this way will come out of "spare cash" —out of money that would not otherwise have been spent. As a result we may guess that a greater proportion of the money acquired by the government will come out of the public's idle cash holdings when the money is borrowed than when it is obtained by taxation. If so, a balanced budget expenditure will have its expansionary effects offset to a greater extent by reduced private expenditure than will a government expenditure financed by borrowing.

For the same reason, it may be expected that a reduction in expenditures which were financed by borrowing will be more potent as a counterinflationary device than a decrease in expenditures matched by an equal tax reduction.

B. BORROWING FROM THE BANKING SYSTEM

As we have seen, the government can finance its expenditures by borrowing from commercial banks or the Federal Reserve System. It is easy to see that government borrowing from commercial banks will be more effective in producing expansion than either of the two methods already discussed, if the banks are not thereby forced to reduce their loans to the public. The process takes no money out of the hands of the public, so there is no offset to the expansionary effect of the expenditure, as there would be if the expenditure were financed out of higher taxes or by borrowing from the public.

Borrowing from the Federal Reserve (which for our present purposes is equivalent to the printing of money by the Treasury) is still more expansionary. By adding to the reserves of the commercial banks such borrowing may even add more to the money in the hands of the public than the people receives from the government's expenditures.[2]

[2] See above, p. 339.

This will occur when the money spent by the government is deposited by its recipients in the commercial banks, which can then use it as part of their reserves.

For the same reasons the government may very effectively reduce inflationary pressure by diminishing expenditures that were financed by commercial banks, and still more by decreasing expenditures that were financed by borrowing from Federal Reserve banks or the direct printing of money by the Treasury.

C. STABILIZING BY MANIPULATING GOVERNMENT RECEIPTS

The foregoing discussion also suggests that the government can carry on an income stabilization policy without doing anything at all about the magnitude of its expenditures. To combat inflationary pressure it can increase the proportion of its expenditures financed by borrowing from the public or, even better, the proportion financed by taxation, and reduce the proportion of its expenditures financed by the creation of money by the commercial banks, the Federal Reserve banks, or the Treasury.

This is the reason the government has been so anxious to finance its military expenditures by selling bonds to the public. Such sales are generally not really indispensable for getting bullets to the front lines, as some overenthusiastic government security advertisers have suggested. Military equipment can almost always be obtained through a process of money creation. It is only because these large expenditures usually occur at a time of full employment that the government considers it imperative to reduce the purchasing power in the hands of the public. Otherwise, as we have seen, the competition of the government and the public for the nation's fully employed resources can lead to serious inflationary consequences. If allowed to go too far, this might result in a runaway inflation and a breakdown of production, so that the soldier really would not get bullets because the public did not buy enough bonds.

In times of inflation the government may even want to increase its taxes and reduce its borrowing so much that it ends up with a surplus. The Treasury may keep this surplus or use it to pay off its debt (the reverse of borrowing), as we saw in the preceding chapter.[3] This will be most effective in combating inflation when it is used to retire securities held by the Federal Reserve, for the same reason that selling these securities to the Federal Reserve is the most inflationary way of borrow-

[3] See pp. 340–341.

ing. Retiring debt held by the public, on the other hand, may be less helpful in fighting inflation, since it transfers back to some members of the public the tax money collected from other people, and so leaves the public's money supply unaffected.

Analogously, the government can fight depression with a fiscal program that involves no increase in its expenditures. A reduction in taxes and perhaps a shift away from borrowing from the public and toward an increase in the proportion of expenditures financed by money creation can exert a powerful expansionary effect on income.

4. Choosing Among the Alternatives

It is impossible to say in advance which of the alternative routes to economic stabilization will be most appropriate. Different policies may be called for in different historical circumstances, as we shall presently see. Moreover, because the disadvantages of some of these methods increase with the extent to which they are employed, it may be desirable to use them in combination in combating an inflation or a depression. Let us look at a few of the advantages and disadvantages of each of the methods we have examined.

A. The Balanced Budget Method

Because of a traditional respect for the financial prudence of a balanced budget and for other reasons about which we shall have more to say later, this alternative may appear very attractive indeed. But it has very serious drawbacks. In times of inflationary pressure it simply may not be possible to use this technique. This may be true for two reasons: (1) The public and the government may be unwilling to see some types of government expenditures decreased. This may apply to public education, law enforcement, and, perhaps most significant, military expenditure whose reduction in time of war or international tension might be tantamount to national suicide. (2) Even if the government is willing to reduce its expenditures this may not have much effect on the economy if government spending was not pretty high to begin with. If government spending is an insignificant portion of national income, even its total elimination cannot contribute much toward reducing severe inflationary pressures. In varying degree these difficulties clearly apply to any program for combating inflation by reduced expenditures, not just to a cut in expenditures that are fully covered by taxes.

In times of depression an effective expansionary balanced budget policy is theoretically always possible. But even if it is feasible, it may have a concomitant effect that may be most unpalatable to many of us. It is likely to involve an extreme expansion of government activity and influence over our economy. Because it is the least powerful of the fiscal weapons for combating unemployment, expansion via a balanced budget requires a greater increase in government expenditure and activity to achieve any given increase in national income than does any of the other methods. A dollar of balanced budget expenditure will very likely add much less to national income than a dollar borrowed from the Federal Reserve. It is probable that the expansion of tax-financed government expenditure required to have gotten us out of the depression of the 30's would have been stupendous. With such an expansion of government expenditure and taxation there are serious doubts as to whether the free-enterprise system could have survived at all. The effects of the enormous tax collections alone might have destroyed business incentives.

B. Expenditures Financed by Borrowing from the Banks

Having examined in the preceding chapter some of the dangers inherent in a large government debt, it should be clear to us that unlimited borrowing may also produce mixed blessings. The amount of borrowing required to raise national income by any given amount would of course be minimized by having the Treasury print the money directly or getting the Federal Reserve to create it. Moreover, these methods, being the most powerful expansionary devices, would require the smallest extension of government expenditure and activity to bring us out of a depression. But they also involve an increase in the outstanding money supply which might prove very embarrassing and difficult to control if the depression turned into inflation.

C. Borrowing from the Public

Borrowing from the public requires greater expansion of government activity to halt a depression than does borrowing from the other possible sources. In any event the public is usually not prepared to lend indefinitely large amounts to the government. This is forcefully indicated by the bond-selling drives the government had to undertake in wartime when all the factors were favorable. The public had the funds to lend, civilian goods were low so that opportunities for spending the money were limited, and there was the strong emotional patriotic appeal to back up the drives. Yet they were not always as successful as the government had hoped.

D. MANIPULATION OF RECEIPTS

Not until recently did an antidepression policy involving only a decrease in taxes and no increase in government spending offer any possibility of being effective. The reason is that until recently government taxation rarely constituted a very large proportion of national income. As a result, even the total elimination of tax collections would not have had a very significant effect in a serious depression. Now, however, with about a quarter of national income going into taxes, things are quite different. But though this procedure is in the realm of feasibility, it too has the drawback of being debt-creating and therefore can leave us with serious debt problems if used too extensively to fight unemployment and deflation.

In a sense it has always been possible to fight inflation by increasing taxes and leaving government expenditures constant. In principle there is no limit on the magnitude of the tax surplus that can be collected. But here again we run into the problem of incentives after a point. Too high a percentage of national income going into taxes may, as we have seen, pose a serious threat to the free-enterprise system.

E. CONCLUSION

We have surveyed five fiscal methods that the government can use in striving for economic stability. These include an increase or decrease in expenditure financed by (1) taxes, (2) borrowing from the public, (3) borrowing from commercial banks, (4) borrowing from the Federal Reserve banks (or money printing), and (5) leaving expenditure unchanged but shifting the method of financing, particularly increasing or decreasing the reliance on borrowing as compared to taxes.

We saw that none of these methods is without its drawbacks, particularly when it is used extensively. There is no path of roses to economic stability. Yet inflation and depression are too serious to leave unchallenged even though the methods of fighting them are not without cost. We saw also how the fiscal methods we want to use may vary with time and circumstances, and that the government is very unlikely to find it desirable or even feasible to use only one method to the exclusion of the others.

Fiscal measures are likely to prove most effective when coordinated with monetary policies. Monetary and fiscal policies at loggerheads can defeat each other. It may not even be possible to treat decisions in these two areas as independent. We have several times seen how the government's debt has influenced monetary policy and for a long period made it difficult to depart from an easy-money policy. Conversely, the government cannot always make its borrowing plans and decisions effective without appropriate conditions in the money market. We have also seen how seriously borrowing and debt retirement can affect money supplies. The separation of monetary and fiscal policies thus becomes more a convenient expository device than a matter of practical operation.

The preceding paragraphs imply that there is much to be said for giving government officials considerable discretion in tailoring fiscal policy to fit the circumstances. However, there are many suggestions, some of them rather popular, that propose more precise formulas for fiscal decisions. Let us now consider some of these.

5. Automatic Flexibility in Budgets

It has been proposed that legislation be enacted which would leave little to administrative wisdom and foresight and would predetermine the response of government receipts and expenditures to changes in the national income. This idea is referred to as "built-in" or "automatic" flexibility. It would require no change in tax laws or other legislation affecting fiscal policy in times of inflation and depression.

A. THE PROPOSAL

Briefly, this formula would work as follows. The government would enact tax laws that would yield just enough revenue to balance the budget at a level of national income consistent with "practically full employment and stable prices." This level of national income might, for example, be defined as that at which no more than 5 percent of the labor force would be unemployed. At lower levels of national income, the budget would automatically show a deficit, owing both to automatically lower tax yields and to automatically higher government expenditures. And the lower the level of national income, the greater would be the deficit. This would tend to be stabilizing, at least in the sense of reducing the extent of the decline in national income.

On the other hand, any increase of national income above the level of "practically full employment with stable prices" would automatically produce a tax surplus, both by automatically increasing tax yields and by automatically lowering government expenditures. And the higher the level of national income, the greater would be the tax surplus. This would tend to be stabilizing, at least in the sense of reducing the extent of the rise of national income.

B. BUILT-IN FLEXIBILITY IN OUR ECONOMY

Our present laws provide a certain amount of just this sort of "built-in flexibility." It appears that under the tax structure in effect during 1953 every $1 increase or decrease in the level of national money income would automatically increase or decrease total tax collections by at least 30 cents, this without any change in the structure of tax rates or in the legal definition of things subject to tax. To see how this happens we must look at the effect of changes in national income on the main sources of the government's tax revenue: taxes on personal incomes, corporate profits, contributions to social insurance, and the production or sale of goods and services.

For the very high sensitivity of personal income tax yields to changes in national income there are two principal reasons.

1. The automatic change in the amount of taxable personal income. A large part of every change in national money income is reflected in personal incomes. Moreover, because a relatively constant total amount of personal income is exempt from the tax, the percentage change in *taxable* personal income is greater than the percentage change in total personal income. Suppose, for example, that total personal incomes and total exemptions are at such levels that only half of total personal incomes is taxable. If total exemptions remain constant, a 10 percent rise of total personal incomes will mean a 20 percent rise in taxable income.

2. The graduated rate schedule. For each person, any increase in the amount of his taxable income is taxed at the highest bracket rate to which he was previously subject, or at an even higher bracket rate. And with each decrease in his taxable income he escapes an amount of tax determined by the highest bracket rates to which he was previously subject. For example, suppose that most of a man's income is taxed at 25 percent but that a small part of his income is in the 30 percent bracket. Even though on his income as a whole he pays less than 30 percent in taxes, on any addition to his income at least this percentage will go to the government.

The yields of taxes on corporate net income are also highly unstable, primarily because the volume of corporate profits is so highly responsive to changes in national money income. Contributions for social insurance, being based on payrolls, fluctuate with both the amount of employment and wage rates. Though to a smaller extent, taxes on the production and sale of goods and services are also sensitive to changes in the level of national income. The yields of specific taxes—those based on the number of physical units—fluctuate with real output or sales, and the yields of ad valorem taxes of this type fluctuate with both real output or sales and price levels.

Thus, even now total tax yields go up and down with the level of national income, just as is required by a system involving built-in flexibility.

Certain types of government expenditures also tend to be automatically responsive to national income, rising as national income declines, and falling as national income rises. Two of the most sensitive of these are unemployment insurance and relief benefits and government benefits to agriculture. A decline of national income tends to increase both of these. The accompanying rise of unemployment makes more people eligible for benefits, and the accompanying decline in the demand for agricultural products tends to lower their prices and enlarge government payments to farmers. Conversely, both of these types of expenditures tend to decline as national income rises, owing to the accompanying shrinkage in the number of unemployed and the rise of private demands for farm products.

We see that our economy already has these elements of an automatically stabilizing fiscal mechanism. Taxes do tend to rise and some expenditures to fall automatically in inflation, and vice versa. Yet experience shows that it may not be nearly enough. The advocates of this sort of device therefore propose a considerable increase in the economy's built-in flexibility.

c. EVALUATION

This formula for fiscal policy has several attractive features. (1) It does not discard the goal of balancing the budget when this can be done without contributing to inflation or deflation. (2) It would almost certainly contribute more to general economic stability than would a haphazard fiscal policy of the sort that has sometimes been employed in the past. (3) These stabilizing influences operate quickly in response to changes in national income. They do not have to wait for changes in the laws governing taxes and expenditures which may be made only after long delays, and they may also avoid other types of red tape.

Most people who favor the use of fiscal policy to promote economic stability are happy about this type of automatic flexibility and consider it a useful part of a stabilization program. Nevertheless, this particular formula is subject to at least two types of criticism.

1. A fiscal policy that would balance the budget at a level of national income consistent with practically full employment and stable prices may militate against the actual achievement of just that level of income. For example, suppose the private sector of the economy is behaving in a way that makes for inflation, so that a steady price level at a high level of employment will soon turn into rapidly rising prices. Private consumption and investment demands may be so high that the government could prevent inflation only by having a large tax surplus at the level of national income corresponding to full employment. On the other hand, private propensities to spend for output may be so low that a level of national income consistent with practically full employment and stable prices can be achieved only with government deficits at that level of national income. Sometimes the one and sometimes the other will in fact be the case, depending on circumstances to which the automatic formula permits no adaptation.

2. At times the automatic flexibility of tax yields and government expenditures which is dictated by the rules may not be great enough and at other times it may be too great to assure an acceptable degree of economic stability. Though the built-in flexibility serves to reduce the extent to which national income will fall or rise, it may still permit fluctuations that will be considered intolerably wide. The fixed arrangements may not be powerful enough to reverse cataclysmic initial changes in national income and restore a level of income that is considered satisfactory. Or they may be so powerful that they quickly turn a mild inflation into a depression, or vice versa. An automatic rule thus becomes a strait jacket which prevents the administration from tailoring fiscal policy to the nature and severity of the particular inflation or depression it is trying to combat.

For reasons of this type, many believe that this formula requires modification, and that in at least some cases it will prove necessary to supplement and reinforce automatic flexibility by positive government action that will change effective tax rates or expenditure programs, or both.

6. An Annually Balanced Budget

However much it may be violated in practice, the principle that is probably most widely advocated is that of an annually balanced budget

—that during every 12-month period, and almost regardless of economic circumstances, the government should collect enough taxes to cover all its expenditures. Though we shall have to criticize this principle, its attractive features should not be neglected.

A. ADVANTAGES

(1) Because it is simple and easy to understand, the balanced budget principle is a guide to fiscal policy that can command powerful support from the voters. It is a criterion against which they can measure the performance of their elected representatives. This is not so easy for some of the more complex principles. (2) It may promote economy in government, both by discouraging the undertaking of projects that are not worth their cost, and by promoting efficiency in carrying out projects of a worth-while nature. A legislature may be more careful in balancing benefits against costs if it must face the distasteful task of levying enough taxes to cover all its appropriations. (3) It may prevent fiscal policy from having an almost continuous inflationary bias. Some government officials seem to believe that the best formula for political success is "Vote for every appropriation and against every tax increase." Adherence to the principle of an annually balanced budget helps curb this potentially inflationary practice.

These objectives are important, and they are promoted, however imperfectly, by the principle of an annually balanced budget. If this principle is abandoned, some other way of promoting these objectives should be found.

B. DRAWBACKS

Though it is theoretically possible to carry on an income-stabilizing fiscal program while never departing from an annually balanced budget, we have seen that this is not really feasible in practice. In inflation it may not work because it may not be possible to reduce government expenditure (and taxes) sufficiently, and in depression an intolerable expansion of government activities (and taxes) might be required for it to be effective. This is generally the last thing the advocates of a balanced budget would like to see, for they usually view it as a device for preventing large government expenditures—a method of preventing "too much government."

But haphazardly employed balanced budget expenditures can initiate inflation or deflation. We have seen that an increase in the government demand for goods and services, even though matched by tax increases, can make for economic expansion, and vice versa. Thus if

they are ill-timed, changes in balanced budget expenditures can precipitate a fairly stable economic situation into inflation or depression.

c. The Balanced Budget May Aggravate the Cycle

Balanced budget expenditures are likely to have more serious and
systematic destabilizing effects. Close adherence to a balanced budget
policy works to offset the built-in fiscal flexibility which we have already seen to be present in our economy, and so tends systematically to
aggravate inflation and unemployment.

To see this let us again start from a situation of a balanced budget,
practically full employment, and stable prices. Suppose now that
private investment and consumption expenditures decline sharply,
thereby lowering national money income, and perhaps also real output,
employment, and prices. The decline of national income will automatically lower the yields of the existing tax system and produce a
deficit. To reestablish a budget balance, the government would have
to decrease its expenditures, raise its taxes, or take some combination
of these actions. But each of these actions would tend to accentuate
the contraction. Any decrease in the rate of government purchases of
goods and services would lower both the government's own demand
for output and private money incomes. Private disposable incomes and
spending power would also be lowered by any decrease in the government's transfer payments and by any increase of its tax collections.
This is hardly the way to arrest a downward spiral.

The same reasoning applies in an expansion. Suppose that, again
starting from a situation of a balanced budget, practically full employment, and stable prices, there occurs a large increase in private
investment and consumption expenditures, thereby raising national
money income and inducing inflation. The rise of national money income will automatically raise the yield of the existing tax system and
tend to produce a tax surplus. To bring its budget back into balance,
the government would have to increase its expenditures or lower its
taxes, or both. But each of these actions would tend to accentuate the
inflation. Any increase of government spending for output would raise
both the government's own demand for output and its contributions to
private money incomes. And private disposable incomes would also be
raised by any increase of government transfer payments or any decrease of taxes.

We must conclude, therefore, that despite its attractive features, the
principle of an annually balanced budget is a highly imperfect guide to
fiscal policy.

7. An Annual Surplus for Debt Reduction

Another principle of fiscal policy that has numerous advocates would require the government to achieve an annual tax surplus to be used for debt retirement. For example, some have proposed that the federal government have a $10-billion tax surplus every year in order to retire practically all of its debt over a 25-year period. This can be considered a variant of the balanced budget principle, with a constant amount of debt retirement included in the government expenditures to be covered by taxes. As such it is subject to all the criticisms we have made of the balanced budget principle. But it also presents some special problems which we can approach by looking at two of the principal arguments for a complete repayment of the debt, or at least a marked reduction of it. (1) If the government does not retire the debt, its securities will become worthless and it will be unable to borrow. (2) The debt should be retired because its very existence has an unfavorable effect on the economy.

A. Creditworthiness of the Government

The first argument is clearly fallacious. All the government needs to do in order to retain its creditworthiness is to maintain public confidence that it will be both willing and able to meet its annual interest obligations. The securities will be purchased and held for the annual income they yield, even though the debt is never retired or even reduced in size. This is clearest in the case of perpetual bonds which some governments have issued; in these the governments make no promise to repay principal, but they do pay an annual income. Holders of these bonds can "get their money back" only by selling them to other buyers. The same result can be achieved by a succession of shorter-term obligations, maturing issues being retired with money obtained by selling new securities. And new securities, either perpetual or shorter-term, can find a market so long as people are confident that the government can meet its interest payments.

B. The Burden of the Debt

The second argument—that the debt should be retired because its very existence has an unfavorable effect on the economy—cannot be dismissed so briefly. But its validity seems to turn on two questions—whether the presence of the debt does on the whole have an unfavorable effect on the economy, and whether any net unfavorable effects it may have are worse than the unfavorable effects of collecting the tax surplus to retire the debt.

We have already considered the first question; we found that the answer is unclear and depends somewhat on circumstances.[4] But even if we concluded that the debt does have unfavorable net effects, it would not necessarily follow that these outweigh the unfavorable effects of collecting every year the extra taxes required for debt retirement. The very act of collecting a tax surplus tends, of course, to lower private disposable incomes. This may be desirable in periods of inflationary pressure, though even then the formula does not necessarily indicate the amount of tax surplus that would be appropriate for stabilization purposes. And on other occasions it may initiate or aggravate a deficiency of demand for output, leading to unemployment and underproduction. Under such conditions attempts to retire public debt may tend to lower both the real income and the real wealth of the nation.

8. A Balanced Budget over the Span of a Business Cycle

Another fiscal policy formula that has gained many adherents in recent years is balancing the budget over the course of an entire business cycle. The advocates of this principle envisage the use of deficit spending to combat depression and the use of tax surpluses to fight inflation, but they believe that any deficits incurred in the depression phase of the cycle should be balanced by tax surpluses in the prosperity phase.

At first glance this formula appears quite attractive. It does not wholly discard the balanced budget principle but seeks to secure a budget balance over a period of greater economic significance—the period of time required for overall business activity to run through its cycle, rather than the time required for the earth to make its cycle around the sun. It does not envisage any net increase in the public debt over the cycle as a whole. And it would almost certainly be more consistent with the objective of promoting high employment and economic stability than would an annually balanced budget.

A. VAGUENESS OF THE CRITERION

Unfortunately, however, even this ointment contains at least a couple of flies. The first is the vagueness of the term, "the business cycle." To begin with, it is not always easy to decide when a cycle "begins" and "ends." For example, there were definite signs of business trouble before the stock market crash in the fall of 1929. When can we say

[4] See pp. 342–345 above.

the great depression began? Moreover, statisticians believe they have found many types of business cycles—short-term cycles averaging about 30 months, medium-term cycles averaging about 7 years, and cycles of even greater length. Over which type of cycle should the budget be balanced? In addition, the cycles in each category are by no means of uniform length. These facts, together with the highly unsatisfactory state of economic forecasting, would make it difficult for a government to plan its finances in such a way as to achieve a balanced budget over "the" business cycle.

B. Imbalance Between Depression and Inflation

Even if these problems could be solved satisfactorily, it is by no means certain that a balanced budget during a cycle as a whole would promote an acceptable level of employment and an acceptable degree of price stability, to say nothing of making the maximum contribution to stability that fiscal policy can make. In different cyles the relative lengths and intensities of the depression and prosperity phases vary greatly. In some the depression phase is relatively short and shallow, while the prosperity phase is much longer and characterized by strong inflationary pressures. Merely to balance the budget over such a cycle may permit serious inflation. A large tax surplus for the cycle as a whole may be more appropriate. On the other hand, some cycles have a protracted and serious depression phase, and only a relatively brief and weak "prosperity" phase in which a considerable amount of unemployment persists and there is little or nó inflationary pressure. A balanced budget over such a cycle might leave large amounts of unemployment and underproduction, even during the weak prosperity phase. In these cases a net deficit over the cycle might be more appropriate.

9. Fiscal Policy and the Private Sectors of the Economy

Having examined some of the government's fiscal policy alternatives, let us see how these policies are likely to react on the rest of the economy. We consider only expansionary policies, leaving the reader to draw the analogy for counterinflationary techniques.

The principal types of actions that the government may take to increase the total demand for output or to arrest or retard its contraction generally involve an increase in the rate of government purchases of goods and services, an increase in transfer payments, or a decrease in taxes. Only the first of these adds directly to the government's own demand for output, but all tend to increase private money incomes after taxes, which is likely to affect the rates of private spending for consumption and investment purposes.

A. EFFECTS ON PRIVATE CONSUMPTION

In response to the initial increase in its disposable income, the public is likely to increase its rate of consumption. This contributes a further increase of income to those producing consumer goods, and they in turn are likely to raise their rates of consumption. And so on. Through this process, which we earlier called the multiplier process, the level of national income may be raised by some multiple of the initial increase in government expenditures or decrease in its tax collections.[5] The size of the multiplier depends, of course, on the responsiveness or sensitivity of consumption to changes in private disposable incomes. If consumption is highly sensitive to disposable income, a large part of each additional dollar of income being used to increase consumption, the multiplier may be quite large. But the induced rise in income will be smaller to the extent that increases in disposable income are used to increase the rate of private saving rather than consumption.

The actual responsiveness of consumption may depend on many things, only two of which will be mentioned here. (1) Who gets the increased disposable income? It is often assumed that the consumption expenditures of the rich are less responsive to changes in disposable income than are those of the poor, so that a larger multiplier effect can be achieved by increasing the disposable incomes of the lower-income groups. However, it is not certain that this is true. (2) What are the effects on expectations as to future disposable incomes and prices of consumer goods? If people believe that the recovery program will not succeed, that any improvement in their incomes will be no more than temporary, and that the prices of consumer goods will not be raised, they may save rather than spend for consumption a large part of each increase in their disposable incomes. But if the government actually succeeds in creating expectations of higher future incomes and higher consumer goods prices, a larger part of each increase in income may be used to increase consumption spending. For this reason a spectacular program which people believe will be resolutely pursued until full recovery is achieved may have larger multiplier effects than a smaller and irresolute program which people believe may be abandoned before full recovery.

In any case, government actions of these types may be expected to

[5] See pp. 235–237 above.

increase private consumption to some extent, and under favorable conditions the rise of consumption may be considerably larger than the initial increase of government expenditures or the initial decrease in taxes.

B. EFFECTS ON PRIVATE INVESTMENT

These types of expansionary action by the government are also likely to affect the rate of private investment, both by influencing expectations as to the profitability of new investment, and by influencing the availability and cost of credit for private investment purposes. To the extent that private investment is increased, it will directly increase national income and will have its own multiplier effects by inducing increases in consumption. But if it is decreased, it will militate against the government's expansionary program.

It is often assumed that the government's expansionary fiscal actions will tend to increase the expected profitability of new investment. Any rise of the government's own demand for output and any induced rise of private consumption demand can make business more optimistic as to the profits to be made on new capital. But the extent of this improvement depends on many things, among them the extent of unused productive capacity, the extent of the increase in the demand for output, and the expected duration of the increase in demand.

Investment may rise only little if there is a large amount of unused equipment and other types of idle capital, if the rise of demand is so small as still to leave large amounts of idle productive capacity, and if the improvement of demand is expected to be only temporary. But investment may increase greatly if there is little unused capacity or if the increase in demand is great enough to eradicate it, and if the rise of demand is expected to be enduring.

C. COMPETITION WITH PRIVATE INVESTMENT

Certain types of fiscal actions may tend to lower businessmen's expectations as to the profitability of new investment. For example, large government expenditures for the construction of hydroelectric projects or housing may discourage private investment in these fields, and perhaps induce a general fear of competition by the government and even "socialization." Or large deficit spending may lead business to fear extremely high tax rates in the future. But if these adverse effects are avoided, the expansionary types of fiscal policy may be expected to improve expectations as to the profitability of new investment.

D. EFFECTS ON BORROWING

These types of fiscal policy may also affect the availability and cost of credit for private investment purposes. If the money supply is kept constant and the government borrows large amounts of money to cover its deficits, credit for private purposes may be made less available and more costly. This result can be avoided, however. In the first place, to the extent that expansionary fiscal policies lead to expectations of higher incomes in the future, the expected risks of lending to business may be reduced. This may be reflected in a greater availability of credit, and perhaps in lower interest rates.

In the second place, an easy-money policy, under which the banks are kept supplied with a sufficient volume of excess reserves, can prevent any lessening in the availability and any rise in the cost of money for private use. In fact, we have already seen that deficit spending can be used as a means of increasing the public's money supply if the government borrows newly created money from commercial banks and spends it. Deficit spending can be used to increase both the public's money supply and the volume of commercial bank reserves if the government borrows newly created money from the Federal Reserve and spends it. This shows again how fiscal and monetary policies must be integrated for maximum effectiveness.

In summary, expansionary types of fiscal policy may increase the total demand for output in several ways: (1) by increasing the government's own demand for output; (2) by inducing an increase in private consumption; and (3) by inducing an increase in private investment, which adds directly to the demand for output and also tends to induce increases in private consumption. It would be most convenient to be able to forecast accurately the responsiveness of private consumption and investment to each of these fiscal actions. Unfortunately, we cannot do this, for so much depends on such volatile things as consumers' expectations as to the future behavior of their incomes and the prices of consumer goods, business attitudes toward the government's policies, and business expectations as to the future behavior of demand and prices.

E. "BOONDOGGLING"

Many believe that to advocate expansionary fiscal policies to combat unemployment is synonymous with advocating higher government expenditures for goods and services, and defending the idea that it doesn't matter who spends the money, what it is spent for, or how inefficiently resources are utilized, so long as the demand for output is increased and the unemployed get jobs of some sort. The late Lord Keynes may have strengthened this belief by his famous, and partly facetious, remark that real national income would be increased through the induced rise of private consumption and investment, "if the treasury were to fill old bottles with banknotes, bury them at suitable depths in disused coal-mines which are then filled up to the surface with town rubbish, and leave it to private enterprise on well-tried principles of *laissez-faire* to dig the notes up again."[6] Useless projects have even been said to have the advantage of minimizing governmental competition with private industry.

This type of reasoning is correct as far as it goes. In fact, such "boondoggling" might be wise public policy if it were the only alternative to doing nothing at all to break an unemployment deadlock. But it is not the only alternative. The other alternatives are to use unemployed resources to produce useful goods and services for the government or for private consumption or investment purposes. Here, as in full employment situations, resources should be used to produce the most desirable goods and services. In some cases this may call for the production of more useful goods and services for government; in others it will indicate that the government should increase its transfer payments or decrease its taxes, or both, in order to enable the private sectors to buy more consumption and investment goods of their own choosing. In short, even an inefficient use of resources may be superior to their unemployment, but an efficient use of resources is superior to both. And a stabilizing type of fiscal policy need not be inconsistent with the attainment of efficiency.

We cannot list here all the problems of defining "the most efficient use of resources"[7] and of selecting the combination of expansionary fiscal actions to be used in any given unemployment situation. It should be evident, however, that the choice should depend on many things, such as estimates of the relative usefulness of the various possible types of public works on the one hand and of goods and services for private

---

[6] J. M. Keynes, *The General Theory of Employment Interest and Money,* Harcourt, Brace, New York, 1936, p. 129. But note that Keynes adds, "It would, indeed, be more sensible to build houses and the like; but if there are political and practical difficulties in the way of this, the above would be better than nothing."

[7] But see below, chapters 20 and 21.

purchase on the other, the types and amounts and locations of the unemployed resources, their efficiencies in their alternative lines of production, and so on.

10. Some Problems of Formulating and Administering Fiscal Policies

Several of the problems of formulating and administering fiscal policies to promote high employment and economic stability have already been discussed. A few others should be mentioned.

A. ECONOMIC FORECASTING AND SLOWNESS OF FISCAL ACTION

Of all the stabilizing types of fiscal actions that have been mentioned, only the "automatic" changes in tax collections and expenditures come into play without specific action by the government. The others require positive government action, in most cases involving legislative bodies. But except during emergencies such action is notoriously slow. Months may be required to change tax or expenditure laws, and expanding or contracting an expenditure program after the necessary legislative action has been taken is often a slow process. This, together with the highly unsatisfactory state of economic forecasting, has constituted a serious limitation on the timely flexibility of fiscal policy. The problem has been aggravated by the difficulty of coordinating the fiscal policies of the federal government, the 48 states, and the tens of thousands of local taxing and spending units.

There have been many proposals to improve the flexibility of fiscal policy, among them the following: (1) Preplan public works so that efficient action can be taken quickly. (2) Change legislative procedure to secure more rapid action. (3) Have the legislative bodies enact in advance three alternative tax laws—one for periods of inflation, one for periods of stability, and one for periods of deflation—so that the appropriate one can be put into effect by a simple resolution. (4) Do the same for expenditure programs. (5) Have legislative bodies delegate to the executive some discretionary power over expenditures or taxes, or both. (6) Secure coordination of state and local fiscal policies through an appropriate system of federal grants-in-aid.

Though proposals of these types are worthy of consideration, some of them have important implications for the division of power among the various layers of government and between the legislative and executive branches which must be judged largely on noneconomic grounds.

B. SOME POLITICAL PROBLEMS

It is always well to remember that fiscal policies are formulated and administered by men who have their own "political" interests. An expansionary fiscal policy, giving them a chance to spend more or tax less, is often consistent with their own interests as politicians. But they may be much more reluctant to take restrictive actions that will necessitate higher taxes or fewer government benefits for their constituents.

11. Conclusions

Again we have encountered a series of economic problems for which we have found no easy solutions. Because it must use resources, spend, tax, and manage its debt, the government must have fiscal policies of some sort, and these inevitably influence in many ways the behavior of the entire economy. It is easy to say that these powers should be used to avoid "unfavorable" effects and to promote "favorable" economic behavior. To prescribe exactly the types of fiscal policy that would yield these results is far more difficult. There is no simple formula that can serve as an unerring and adequate guide.

SUGGESTED READINGS

Poole, Kenyon E. (ed.), *Fiscal Policies and the American Economy,* Prentice-Hall, New York, 1951.

Wallace, Donald H., Despres, Emile, Friedman, Milton, Hart, Albert G., and Samuelson, Paul A., "The Problem of Economic Instability," *American Economic Review,* September, 1950, pp. 505–538.

QUESTIONS

1. a. "Because it adds nothing to private disposable incomes, a dollar's worth of 'balanced budget' government expenditure adds only one dollar's worth of production to national income." Explain.
   b. Why would we then say that the value of the multiplier for this type of expenditure is unity?
   c. Suggest some cases where this rule would not hold and the multiplier would be either greater or less than unity. (Hints: What if the tax is on saving? On consumption? If land is the commodity bought by the government? If the public's expectations are affected?)

2. a. List *all* the things you can think of that the government can do to combat a depression.
   b. An inflation.
   c. Evaluate each of these monetary and fiscal programs from the point of view of its interference with the operation of the free-enterprise system.
3. a. Try to formulate a combined program that might have been appropriate for the great depression of the 30's.
   b. What sort of additional information about the period would you want to have to set up a really satisfactory program?
   c. How much of this sort of information is available to the government?
4. Discuss the effects on national income if government expenditures are kept small and unchanging from year to year and the budget is always balanced.
5. a. Show how each of the methods of financing government expenditures is likely to have effects that are considered undesirable as the size of the expenditures grows.
   b. Show why an effective fiscal approach to income stabilization has become more feasible in recent times.
   c. Which stabilization policies might formerly have run into trouble in combating inflation, and which in fighting depression?
6. a. Formulate the details of a program of "built-in flexibility" to stabilize national income.
   b. Evaluate and criticize your program.
7. Can you think of any sort of program which might be more effective in stabilizing income and yet have some or all of the advantages of a balanced budget?
8. a. Why would anyone want to buy the British securities which pay interest but will never be redeemed by the government?
   b. How can anyone who buys them "get his money back"?
   c. Does the existence of this sort of debt, which a government never intends to retire, mean that the government is insolvent?
9. In a depression, if you were a potential private investor and heard that the government was about to engage in expansionary fiscal policy:
   a. What would you want to find out about it?
   b. How might this information influence your investment decisions?

PART V

Composition of Output, Free Enterprise, and Planning

CHAPTER 20

Composition of Output and the Allocation of Resources

---

1. Introduction

Most of the preceding chapters have dealt primarily with aggregate output and aggregate employment—with the total production of all types of goods and services and with the total quantities of productive factors employed in the economy. When they were concerned with the composition of output and the allocation of resources they usually dealt with very broad categories of goods and services, such as the aggregate amounts taken for personal consumption, for government use, and for private investment purposes.

In this part of the book we shall consider another but closely related set of problems—the problems of determining the composition of output and the allocation of scarce productive resources among their alternative uses. We shall analyze some of the problems and processes of determining the specific types and amounts of goods and services to be produced, and the specific types and amounts of productive resources to be allocated to the creation of each particular type of output.

We have already touched upon these topics at two points. In the first chapter we noted that all societies—rich or poor, capitalist or socialist—must make choices of these types. They all suffer from scarcity; they simply do not have enough productive power to satisfy all the wants of everybody, and so must weigh alternatives and choose among them. They must weigh each possible type of good or service—including leisure—against others, and realize that to have more of one they must have less of others. As a part of this process, they must somehow de-

375

termine not only the aggregate amounts but also the specific types of scarce productive resources to be allocated to each particular type of output. In Chapters 6 and 7 we noted in a preliminary way the functions of the market and of government in solving these and other problems in a free-enterprise type of economy. The purpose of the present section is to elaborate and extend our earlier treatment.

We shall proceed as follows. This chapter will indicate some of the problems of determining the composition of output and the allocation of resources in any kind of economic system. It applies to collectivist as well as to free-enterprise economies. The next three chapters discuss the solution of these problems in a free-enterprise economy. Finally, we shall see how these problems may be solved in a centrally planned economy.

2. Some Allocation Problems

In our earlier brief treatment of resource allocation many of the complexities of the problem were necessarily ignored. Because some of these are of fundamental importance we shall consider them now. However, to avoid repetition and elaboration of the obvious we shall attempt neither to deal with all aspects of the problem nor to present them in a systematic framework. Our treatment will be illustrative rather than exhaustive. In light of what has gone before and what is yet to come, the parts should fall readily into place. This simple listing of problems should indicate the great variety and difficulty of resource allocation problems.

A. ALLOCATION BETWEEN PRESENT AND FUTURE AND BETWEEN
    FUTURE AND FUTURE

The problem of allocating scarce resources obviously includes weighing all types of goods for present consumption against each other —raincoats versus butter versus leisure, and so on. Perhaps less obviously, it also includes weighing goods for present use against goods for the future, and weighing the various possible types of future goods against each other. A nation, like an individual, can within limits have more for present use by having less in the future, or more for future use by consuming less in the present.

The allocation of our resources between present and future can be illustrated by the way we deal with scarce natural resources. The scarcity of these gifts of nature, which is an important source of the problem of output composition, can often be alleviated temporarily. By sending more men and machines into the pits we can get up more coal for present use. But this does nothing to augment the supply of fuel under the earth's surface. More coal today means less for tomorrow. This is one of the many ways in which we allocate between present and future.

A decision to mine more intensively, to do nothing about soil conservation, to fail to replace or maintain a machine—these are all ways to reduce the productivity of society in the future by using more labor and materials for current consumption.

On the other hand, a decision not to use up some raw material, to work toward conserving natural resources, to accumulate inventory, to construct a building, or to produce a machine is a decision to allocate resources to production for some future use. For example, the construction of a hat-making factory is a decision to make possible the manufacture of more hats in the future. *Any* investment is a decision to allocate more to future production.

As in allocating resources among current uses, we must weigh what we will have to give up when we consider producing more of some item. We must decide whether to produce more dairy cattle for the future or more beef for today, whether more steel for use today or more aluminum capacity for tomorrow. It has been charged that the Soviet Union allocates too much of its resources to increasing future productive capacity as part of its program to build up military strength, and that as a result the Russian people are grossly deprived of goods for present consumption. On the other hand, it is sometimes said that our capitalist system allocates too little to the future, and that both the ruthlessness with which some of our natural resources have been depleted and the neglect of conservation are symptomatic of this. Whether or not these allegations are true, they do indicate the importance, in the allocation problem, of arriving at some sort of "appropriate balance" between goods for present as against future use.

B. MUTUAL INTERDEPENDENCE OF THE DECISIONS

It has already been implied that decisions in this field are mutually interdependent; we cannot decide on any one particular type of output or any one use of resources without weighing it against all others. Each type of output must be determined in relation to others, and others in relation to it. One aspect of this mutual interdependence is worthy of special mention—the aspect of complementarity. Complementary goods are those that are used together in such a way that each loses at least part of its usefulness if it is accompanied by only inadequate quantities of the other. Examples of complementary finished goods are ham and eggs, coats and pants, autos and gasoline, and furnaces and fuel. It is clear that decisions relating to complementary finished goods are mutually interdependent.

Many intermediate goods are also complementary. An auto cannot be manufactured without tires, wheels, gears, spark plugs, ball bearings, and a host of other things. A shortage of ball bearings will stop auto production, but a superabundance of ball bearings would be a wasteful use of resources. Satisfactory decisions as to coal output cannot be made without reference to the expected output of steel and other things that directly or indirectly use coal or make coal production possible. Decisions as to steel output are in turn dependent on decisions relating to coal and everything else that directly or indirectly uses steel or makes steel output possible. Neither the allocation of resources to steel nor their allocation to coal production can be "decided first." And so on throughout industry.

This mutual interdependence greatly complicates the problem of arriving at an optimum composition of output and allocation of resources, especially when it is attempted by conscious and systematic planning, as we shall presently see. For it means that actions and decisions must somehow be coordinated. Otherwise we may end up with factories overstocked with some raw materials and equipment which they cannot use for lack of still others, and with automobiles standing idle for lack of fuel, tires, or highways.

C. TECHNOLOGICAL ALTERNATIVES IN PRODUCING A PARTICULAR GOOD

A decision to produce a certain quantity of some particular type of output also involves a decision to allocate productive resources to that purpose. But there are often many technological alternatives for turning out any given type and amount of output. For example, a farmer may produce 100 bushels of wheat with much labor, little machinery, much land, and no fertilizer. Or he may produce the same amount with less labor, more machinery, less land, and more fertilizer. A given rate of wheat output can be achieved with many different combinations of the various types of productive factors. The same is true in most other industries. Butadiene for synthetic rubber can be derived from either petroleum or alcohol, and alcohol can be produced from molasses, corn, wheat, rye, old newspapers, and many other substances. A store can provide a given amount of selling space by using more land and less capital, or less land and more capital to increase the height of the building.

One aspect of the allocation problem thus involves choosing for each purpose the particular combination of productive factors that is considered most desirable.

D. TECHNOLOGICAL ALTERNATIVES IN SATISFYING A PARTICULAR CONSUMER WANT

Each consumer, with his limited resources, must balance his various types of wants against each other and determine the extent to which each will be satisfied or left unsatisfied. But like producers, each consumer often has several technological alternatives for satisfying each type of want, especially if the "want" is defined somewhat broadly. For example, a man's want for "some good meat" may be satisfied by steak, roast, or mutton chops. A woman's desire for "a good-looking dress" may be satisfied by one made of wool, silk, nylon, or cotton. A family's desire for warmth in its house may be satisfied by either coal or fuel oil, or by more insulation and less fuel.

E. TECHNOLOGICAL MEANS AS GOALS

We are not always satisfied to choose the most efficient or cheapest means of producing a given item. Since a great proportion of our lives is spent working, we are often willing to accept lower pay in a job that offers more interesting work or better working conditions. Similarly, from society's point of view it may sometimes be preferable to produce less or at greater expense if the owners of the factors of production are thereby benefited. Thus rich land is often used for its owner's pleasure rather than to grow crops, and trade union demands sometimes deal primarily with working conditions rather than wage rates.

3. The Choice of Goals

A. ETHICS AND THE COMPOSITION OF OUTPUT

Owing to the inescapable fact of scarcity, there are certain to be conflicts of interest and opinion concerning the choice of output goals —the quantities of the different goods and services to be produced. A decision to produce more beef cattle and less milk benefits beefeaters at the expense of those who want milk. Every such decision is likely to benefit some at the expense of others. How are these conflicting interests and opinions to be weighed? What weight or value is to be attached to each? Ultimately this is a matter for ethics and value judgments, matters in which the economist can claim no special competence.

B. METHODS OF SELECTING OUTPUT GOALS

There are, of course, many ways of weighing alternatives against each other, of selecting output goals, and of allocating resources to each of the selected types of output. It may be done by a dictator, who decides what part of output to use for each type of military manpower and supplies, what part for each type of plant expansion, and what part for each type of consumption. With all his power the dictator faces a very difficult problem. If he is a benevolent dictator, wanting to do as much as he can to promote his people's welfare as he sees it, he faces all the difficult decisions we have described. But no matter how ruthless and callous he may be and no matter how much he may wish to concentrate resources on increasing the nation's military prowess he cannot completely ignore consumers' desires. To have efficient workers and soldiers, as well as to prevent revolt, he must allocate some resources to consumer goods. And he still faces the problem of deciding what part of output shall be used to increase each type of productive capacity and what part for each type of armament.

In the United States and some other countries it is generally accepted that the composition of output ought to be decided largely, but with exceptions, by the desires of individuals. Individuals should be sovereign. It is contended that the choice of output goals should be made by individuals in their role as consumers, these choices being expressed in the market through consumers' demands for the various types of goods and services that could be produced. And in their role as producers individuals should influence the allocation of resources through their choices of occupations, hours of work, working conditions, and so on.

However, we encounter difficulties as we try to define more precisely the meaning of individual choices. We have already noted the difficulty of reconciling the conflicting choices of different individuals. In addition, serious problems arise out of the nature of each individual consumer's wants.

1. The vagueness of consumer wants. The desires of each consumer are often rather ill-defined; choice is likely to be hesitant or capricious. If we are asked whether we would be happier with a pound less of peas

and two more pounds of apples we may not be sure of the answer.

2. Malleability of consumers' demands. Consumers' demands are not only vague but also subject to outside influence. The main purpose of advertising and other selling efforts is, of course, to shape or alter consumers' demands. Incidentally, this raises the question of the amount of resources that should be devoted to advertising.

3. Interdependence of consumers' demands. We are all creatures of fashion. We wish to imitate others, especially the "right people." Our demands are conditioned by the consumption patterns of social leaders, movie stars, the Joneses, and even the "vulgar horde" whose purchase of a commodity makes it wholly undesirable to us. Thus our desires are fixed only in relation to the desires of others, which in turn are dependent on ours.

All in all, it is clear that even the desires of a single consumer are not sharply defined.

c. A Consumer's Demand as a Schedule

In dealing with the desires of an individual consumer we run into another and very important complication. The amount of any product that a consumer will demand is not just one fixed quantity regardless of its price. The amount he will actually demand depends partly on price. In general, he will demand more at a lower price and less at higher prices. Thus a consumer's demand for any product can be represented only by a schedule showing the amounts that would be purchased at various prices. Having to deal with schedules rather than fixed quantities inevitably adds to the conceptual difficulty of comparing and reconciling the desires of the various consumers.

d. The Desires of the Body of Consumers

When we turn to the problem of determining the preferences of consumers as a group, which must be done in allocating the resources of society, we run into the extremely difficult job of weighing the conflicting choices of different consumers. Suppose A prefers that resources be shifted so as to produce fewer peas and more potatoes, while B prefers the reverse. Which preference should prevail? What weight should be given to A's desires? What weight to B's?

Majority rule provides no satisfactory answer. The majority of the people may have only a very mild desire to have some of society's resources devoted to the production of souvenir kewpie dolls. If these same resources can alternatively be devoted to the production of anesthetics, which a small minority of the public wants very badly, giving the majority what it wishes may not be a solution to which we would all subscribe.

There is no simple way out of this difficulty. Aggregating and weighing the desires of different consumers is like the apple-banana problem we encountered earlier. We must compare the incommensurable. There can be no perfectly correct answer to such a problem, yet an answer there must be if resource allocation is somehow to obey consumers' dictates. We shall see in the next chapter how the market deals with this.

E. CHANGES IN DEMAND

To avoid future misunderstandings we must distinguish clearly between mere changes in a quantity demanded and the shift of a demand schedule or curve.

Up to this point we have dealt only with a given demand schedule. We indicated that the quantity demanded will tend to increase as prices fall and to decline as prices rise. This indicates no change in attitudes or tastes. It simply implies that with a given set of tastes people will be willing to buy more shoes at a price of $5 than at a price of $10. This is a mere change in the quantity demanded in response to a price change. If the price goes back to its old level, the demanded quantity may be expected to follow suit.

By a shift of the demand schedule or curve we mean a change in the amount that will be demanded at each price. For example, at $5 and also at each other price, consumers may demand more than they did before at that price. Here the quantity demanded has not changed *because* the price changes. Indeed, the amount demanded will change despite an unchanging price.

The difference can best be brought out by a simple graph. In Fig. 19 we measure the price of shoes along the vertical axis, and the quantity demanded along the horizontal axis. Let *DD'* be the demand curve (or schedule). At price *OP*, *OQ* pairs of shoes will be demanded. Now if the price falls from *OP* to *OP'*, the number of shoes demanded will rise from *OQ* to *OQ'*. This is what we mean by a change in the *quantity* demanded. It can also be described as a change in demand involving a movement along the demand curve.

Suppose that with an increase in the popularity of shoes, the entire demand curve shifts from *DD* to *EE'*. More shoes will now be demanded at each price. For example, at price *OP* the quantity demanded will rise from OQ to OQ'', and there will be a similar increase in the quantity demanded at every other price. We refer to this as a shift in the demand curve (or schedule).

This rightward shift of the demand curve is an increase of the demand schedule or curve. It indicates that more can be sold at each price, or that any given quantity can be sold at a higher price than before. This sort of shift may reflect the fact that people have had an increase in their incomes, or that the product has become more popular, or that some other item for which this good can be substituted has become more expensive. A leftward shift of the demand curve, as from EE' to DD', is a decrease of the demand schedule or curve. It indicates

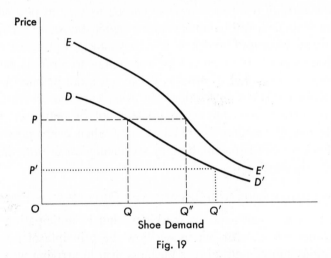

Fig. 19

that less can be sold at each price, or that a given quantity can find buyers only at a lower price than before. Such a shift may reflect such things as a decrease in buyers' incomes, or a decline in their taste for the product, or a decline in the price of a competing product.

These distinctions should be kept clearly in mind when we talk about supply and demand adjustments.

4. Optimal Decisions

A. THE PRINCIPLE OF NO WASTED OPPORTUNITIES

In trying to get the most out of anything—whether it be society trying to get the most out of its resources, or consumers or firms trying to get the most for their money—there is a simple rule that proves quite useful even though it seems trivial at first. It is the self-evident proposition that so long as any opportunity, however minor, of getting more out of your (money or real) resources goes begging, you have not done as well as possible. We shall call it the principle of no wasted opportunities, because a person has made the most of his limited resources only when he has wasted no available opportunity to get more of something by sacrificing less of something else. He has used up every available opportunity to shift his resources in a way that will give him more gain than loss. This is also called "the marginal principle" for reasons which will presently become apparent.

We shall use this so-called "marginal analysis" throughout this section of the book in describing how a consumer can attain the optimum allocation of his money income among its various possible uses, how a business firm can balance revenues against costs to arrive at an optimum rate of output, and how a society can move toward an optimum allocation of its resources by continuing to shift its resources from one use to another as long as it can get more of one thing and lose a less valuable batch of others. In every case the principle of no wasted opportunities is applicable. The point of optimum or most favorable use of resources is reached only when every possible opportunity to get more of something by sacrificing less of something else has been exhausted.

B. No Wasted Opportunities and the Output of a Firm

To get some insight into its workings, and in anticipation of our needs in the next chapter, let us see how the principle of no wasted opportunities can be helpful to a business firm in arriving at a rate of output that will maximize its profits.[1] This problem, like the other cases we have considered, involves arriving at an optimum, this optimum being defined as maximum total profits.

To illustrate the process, let us assume that our business firm is producing autos whose price is fixed by law or some other agency at $2000 per car. We are not interested here in how the price was fixed at $2000; all that concerns us is that the price is $2000, that it cannot be altered by our one business firm, and that it is not affected by the firm's decisions relating to its rate of output. All the firm can do is adjust its rate of output, by which we shall mean the number of autos produced each hour.

Though the price he can charge is beyond his control, the owner of the firm can adjust his rate of output to the level that will give him the

---

[1] For a formal analysis, see the Graphic Appendix, pp. 632–640.

largest possible total profits, that is, his total revenues minus his total costs. To accomplish this, he must waste no opportunity of producing any unit that adds more to his revenues than it adds to his costs. Neither can he waste any opportunity to avoid producing any unit that will add more to his costs than it will add to his revenues. In more technical terms, he produces every car whose *marginal revenue* is greater than its *marginal cost,* and he produces no car whose marginal cost is greater than its marginal revenue.

Two of these terms—marginal revenue and marginal cost—require definition. By the firm's total revenue we mean the total amount of money collected from all its customers. It differs from profits in that it makes no allowance for cost. A firm may thus prefer low revenues and very low costs to higher revenues and very high costs. *Marginal revenue is the addition to total revenue* (per hour) *resulting from producing one more unit of* (auto) *output* (per hour). In this case, when the price of each auto remains at $2000 regardless of the rate of output, marginal revenue is obviously the price of the car—$2000 (see Column 1 of Table 36). Marginal cost is the cost of producing an ad-

TABLE 36. Marginal Revenues, Marginal Costs, and Profits from Auto Production

Rate of Auto Output per Hour	Col. 1 Marginal Revenue	Col. 2 Marginal Cost	Col. 3 Marginal Profit (Col. 1 minus Col. 2)	Col. 4 Total Hourly Profit[a]
1	$2000	$1000	$1000	$1000
2	2000	1200	800	1800
3	2000	1600	400	2200
4	2000	1700	300	2500
5	2000	1750	250	2750
6	2000	1820	180	2930
7	2000	1900	100	3030
8	2000	2000	0	3030
9	2000	2500	−500	2530
10	2000	3000	−1000	1530

[a] This table assumes that the firm will have no cost at all if its rate of output is zero.

ditional auto per hour. That is, it is *the addition to total cost* (per hour) *resulting from increasing* (auto) *output by one unit* (per hour). (Total cost is the sum of all the costs on all the cars produced each hour.) In Column 2 we have assumed that marginal cost rises as the rate of output rises. That is, the cost of the second car per hour is greater than the cost of the first per hour, the cost of the third per hour is greater than the cost of the second per hour, and so on.

Assuming the conditions indicated in the table, we see that the firm's most profitable rate of output will be at least 7 cars per hour. If it were less than this, the firm would be wasting opportunities to produce cars whose price is greater than their marginal cost. (See Columns 1, 2, and 3.) For example, adding a seventh car per hour will add $2000 to revenues at a marginal cost of only $1900, thereby yielding a net gain of $100 and raising total profits from $2930 to $3030 per hour. On the other hand, the firm would be foolish to produce a ninth car per hour, for this additional car would add only $2000 to revenues at a marginal cost of $2500. On this car the firm would have a net loss of $500 and lower its total profits per hour from $3030 to $2530. This illustrates the general principle that the production of any unit whose marginal cost exceeds its marginal revenue will lower total profits.

We cannot say whether the firm's rate of output should be 7 or 8 autos per hour. The firm will be indifferent to the eighth unit because its marginal cost is exactly equal to its price, so that it involves no net gain and no net loss and leaves total profits unchanged at $3030. All we can say is that the firm can maximize its total profits only if its rate of output is at least 7 and not more than 8 cars per hour.

Thus the principle of no wasted opportunities leads to an important conclusion. When the price of a commodity is fixed and beyond the control of a firm, it pays the firm to produce up to the point at which its marginal cost is (approximately) equal to the price of the commodity.

This tendency toward equality between marginal cost and price when price cannot be influenced by the individual businessman will be referred to in the next chapter. Together with the analogy between the resource allocation problem of the consumer and the economy as a whole, it will help to throw light on the relationships between consumers' desires and the composition of output and the allocation of resources determined by the market.

SUGGESTED READINGS

Lerner, Abba P., *The Economics of Control*, Macmillan, New York, 1946.

QUESTIONS

1. a. Show why every investment decision is a decision to allocate resources for the future.

    b. Explain why this is true in particular of the building of machinery and investment in inventory.

    c. Explain the difficulties in judging whether the Soviet Union has allocated too much and the U.S. economy too little to the future, even if we knew all the facts.

    d. What can the economist say on this point?

2. a. Show how the production of trucks depends on the production of glass.

    b. Show how the production of glass can depend on the production of trucks.

    c. Give some other examples of outputs which are mutually interdependent.

    d. How might you go about deciding on the outputs of such items if you were the commissar of central planning?

3. a. How does a worker set about "purchasing" leisure?

    b. Better working conditions?

    c. How does the landowner "purchase" his land away from agricultural uses?

    d. How are desires of these sorts catered to under a profit system?

    e. Explain how this fits in with the notion of individual sovereignty.

4. a. What do we mean by "the aggregation of the desires of different consumers"?

    b. Explain the analogy with the index number problem treated in Chapter 2.

    c. Give examples in which majority rule offers a solution that you consider unsatisfactory.

    d. Have you any idea how you might deal with the problem?

5. ". . . Floors under prices [can] bring about adequate production. . . . We all know it to be a fundamental principle of economy that prices are largely fixed by the law of supply and demand, and the chief factor in any price fixing is the quantity of commodities offered on the market. The best way to hold down prices of any commodities, and especially of agricultural commodities, is to produce in ample quantities, and the ample supply will in itself automatically bring about fair and reasonable prices." (Senator John H. Bankhead, *Congressional Record,* 1943, p. 2961.)

    a. Disentangle the confusion between movements along a supply curve and shifts in a supply curve. (A supply curve gives the quantities of a commodity which its producers will offer for sale at each price of the item.)

    b. Criticize the statement otherwise.

6. "The businessman described in the last section of the chapter is a sucker for going on and producing up to a point where marginal cost equals

marginal revenue. He should have stopped while the going was still good, at an output where marginal cost is less than price, where the firm is still making a good profit on the last car produced." Explain the fallacy in terms of the principle of no wasted opportunities.

7. a. Why do we say that the firm will produce to a point where marginal cost is *approximately* equal to marginal revenue?
   b. What would have been the firm's profit-maximizing output if in Table 36 the marginal cost of the eighth unit had been $1999?
   c. $2001?
   d. $2450?
   e. Explain then why it is a peculiarity of our example that it does not matter to the firm whether it produces 7 or 8 autos per hour.
   f. Discuss the realism of the analysis.

CHAPTER 21

Competition and the Allocation of Resources

The irrational and planless character of society must be replaced by a planned economy. . . ." (Erich Fromm, *Escape from Freedom,* 1941, p. 272.)

1. Introduction

In the preceding chapter we dealt with some of the basic problems of determining the composition of output and the allocation of resources. We noted the source of these problems and the types of alternatives and decisions that must be faced by every economy, whatever its type of control system may be. Now we shall see how a free-enterprise system deals with these matters by means of the market price mechanism, without any centralized overall plan and without government direction and control of detailed decisions relating to the specific types of goods to be produced, the amounts of each, the specific types of productive resources to be allocated to each use, and the amount of each.

These processes have already been outlined in Chapter 6, which described the logic and functioning of the American free-enterprise system. We found that in this type of system output goals are set by the choices of households and consumers as they try to get the most from their money incomes. Consumers' choices are communicated to the market through their demand schedules for the various possible types of output. Production and the use of resources are carried on by business firms whose owners' motives are to maximize their profits. But they can maximize their profits only by adjusting both the composition of output and the allocation of resources to consumers' choices as com-

389

municated to the market by consumers' demands. If they get too far out of line with consumers' choices they may be driven into bankruptcy.

We shall now elaborate on these processes and point out some of their implications.

2. The Price System

A. PRICES AS GUIDES

This type of control system is often called the *price system* or price mechanism because prices play such an important role in guiding consumption, production, and the allocation of resources. Prices are not, of course, the ultimate guides. The height of any price is itself determined by basic demand and supply conditions. But to any individual participant in the market—whether he be a consumer, an enterpriser, or the owner of a productive factor—price is an important guide and determinant of his behavior. The price he must pay for an item affects a consumer's decision as to whether and how much he will buy. The price he can get for a product affects an enterpriser's decision as to whether and how much he will produce. The price a firm must pay for any productive factor affects the amount of the factor it will hire. And the price the owner of a productive factor can get for its services affects his supply decisions.

An individual buyer or seller may consider the market price of some commodity to be beyond his individual control; all he can do under the circumstances is to decide whether to demand or supply the product at the prevailing price and how much to demand or supply. But all these decisions of demanders and suppliers *taken together* will determine whether the price stays the same, rises, or falls.

Thus we reach an interesting conclusion. Even though each demander and supplier may consider the market price beyond his control, so that he can only decide how much to demand or supply at that price, the decisions of all demanders and suppliers taken together determine the price. Price will tend to be forced toward the level at which demanders are willing to buy just the amount that suppliers are willing to offer at that price.[1]

B. THE INFLUENCES OF PRICE

To see how this happens it is important to note three different influences of price. (1) Price is a deterrent to purchase or consumption.

[1] For a formal discussion of this point see the Graphic Appendix, pp. 623–624.

Since the price of a good represents the value of other things that must be sacrificed to get one unit of it, we should expect that a price rise will reduce the consumption of a commodity, whereas a price decline will stimulate its use. (2) Price is an inducement to produce and sell. Ordinarily a price increase on a commodity will induce a larger output, and a price reduction will decrease its output. (3) Price is a determinant of real income. Price affects the real income of an individual in both his producer and consumer roles. A rise in the price of his product or service will raise his income, other things being unchanged. Price increases on the things he consumes will lower his real income, and a fall of these prices will raise his real income.

c. CLEARING THE MARKET

These various functions of price help explain how price adjustments equate the quantities of a good which are supplied and demanded. Suppose that at some time the price of a good is so low that the amount demanded exceeds the amount supplied. The price rise which usually follows will bring into equality the quantities demanded and supplied in two ways. (1) It will heighten the deterring effect on consumption and will ordinarily reduce the amount demanded. (2) It will usually stimulate production. The price rise will also raise the real incomes of producers and decrease the real incomes of buyers. Suppose now that at some time the price of the good is so high that the amount supplied exceeds the amount demanded. The price decline which may be expected in such circumstances can equate the amounts demanded and supplied both by stimulating consumption and by reducing production. In the process buyers' real incomes will be increased and producers' real incomes reduced.

Concentration on one function of price to the neglect of the others has often created serious problems when the government has intervened to fix prices. An outstanding example is its intervention to raise farm prices in order to raise the real incomes of farmers. Suppose that at some time the quantity of wheat supplied is so great relative to the quantity demanded that its price is only $1 a bushel. Declaring that $1 wheat yields an unbearably low income for farmers, the government may decide to raise the price to $2 by standing ready to buy all the wheat that private buyers are unwilling to take at that price. If the government does not place restrictions on output, this price increase will reduce wheat consumption and stimulate wheat production, so the quantity supplied may greatly exceed the amount demanded by the public at the $2 price. The government has to buy this large excess. It then faces the problem of what to do with the wheat. Since attempts to sell all of it in the domestic market may only lower the price again, the government may hold it, dispose of it for fuel, destroy it, or dump it in foreign markets and erect tariffs to prevent its reimport. At least some of these uses of the wheat clearly are a waste of resources. Although the foreigners may receive the wheat as a gift, it may represent a misallocation of resources even from their point of view because they might have preferred something else that could have been produced with the resources used to produce the wheat.

Even if the government does try to restrict production as part of its price-support scheme it runs into other equally serious resource allocation problems which will be discussed later.

Similar complications may arise from government efforts to hold a price considerably below the level that would be established by private demand and supply. In order to protect the real incomes of tenants, the government sometimes holds rental rates on apartments and houses considerably below the levels that would be established by the market. It does this by freezing rental rates at their levels as of some base date, and refusing to allow them to increase as demand rises during an inflation. The relatively low rental rates stimulate the quantity of housing space demanded. As housing space becomes cheap relative to other things, people try to buy more of it. At the same time, the low rental rates may discourage landlords from constructing new houses or apartments for rental, some of the existing space may be withdrawn from the rental market and sold to owner-occupiers, and some of it may be allowed to deteriorate and become unusable.

This freezing of rental rates at a low level may give rise to a large apparent shortage of rental housing, both by stimulating the quantity demanded and by reducing the quantity supplied. Those who are lucky enough to get rented space enjoy cheaper rents; others may have to go without housing, double up with friends or relatives, or buy their own homes. This does not necessarily represent the most efficient use of limited resources.

We should make it quite clear that we are not making any judgment on these and other similar government policies. We refer to them only to emphasize this point: price exerts at least three influences—as a deterrent to consumption, as an inducement to produce and sell, and as a determinant of real income. Any decision that does not take all these aspects of price into account is likely to lead to embarrassing complications.

3. Human Calculations and Choices

In analyzing the processes by which competition determines the composition of output and the allocation of resources we shall deal with the calculations and choices of individual human beings as they try to make the most of the limited resources at their disposal. We shall have individual consumers, enterprisers, and owners of productive resources weighing alternatives and arriving at an optimum use of their resources by wasting no available opportunity to get more of something by sacrificing less of something else.

At points the reader may get the impression that these "economic" people think only in terms of economic calculus, are always wholly rational, know everything, never make a mistake, are always alert, and are extremely willing to adjust their behavior at the slightest provocation. He may object that these commercialized intellectual robots bear little resemblance to the real human beings who consume, run businesses, and offer their labor for hire. These real people often lack information that is relevant to their decisions, sometimes appear irrational, are to a considerable extent creatures of habit, and do not always think in terms of money values.

We admit, and wish to emphasize, that our analytic model contains numerous oversimplifications and that the reader's suspicions of this are not wholly without foundation. But at this point we are not trying to explain all aspects of human behavior. We are only trying to explain typical behavior in the market. Moreover, we recognize that human behavior both in and out of the market is motivated by values other than the money values registered in the market.

A man may work in his old home town for $40 a week even though he knows that he could sell his services for $80 a week in a distant city. Is he being irrational and violating our principle of no wasted opportunities? Not necessarily. He may so love his family, friends, and surroundings that he would be willing to sacrifice $60 a week in pay to live among them. If he has made his decision with full knowledge of his alternatives, who can say he was wrong? And who can say that society as a whole would be better off if every person were forced by the government to leave low-pay jobs and take available higher-pay jobs whether they wanted to or not?

There are many other similar cases. A consumer may strongly suspect that he could get better bargains by spending more time and energy shopping around. But since his time and energy, as well as his money income, are limited, it may be perfectly rational for him to decide that spending more time and energy in shopping is not worth while.

We conclude that no rational man will allow his behavior to be determined completely by the money values registered in the market place. He may arrive at his decisions through a more or less conscious weighing of alternatives, but in determining the relative weights of the alternatives he will include not only market values but also others.

We shall not contend that all human choices are rational, that everyone knows what is best for him, or that everyone actually behaves in the way that will maximize his own happiness. Ignorance of alternatives and of the consequences of our actions, lack of sufficient will power to do what we believe will make us happiest in the long run, and later remorse are all too common. At the same time, we will do well to remember that our own judgment as to what is best for the other fellow has its limitations. We may think he is choosing and acting so unwisely that someone else ought to manage his affairs. He may think the same of us.

We shall take the choices registered in the market at their face value and shall not try to say whether they are right or wrong.

4. Adjustment to a Constant Set of Consumers' Choices

We start out by describing the process and results of a competitive adjustment of the composition of output and the allocation of resources to a constant set of consumers' demand schedules in the market. For most goods, the consumers' demand schedule is such that more will be taken at lower prices than at higher prices.

A. BUSINESS FIRMS IN THE ADJUSTMENT PROCESS

Business firms perform the function of adjusting output and the allocation of resources to consumers' demands. The primary objective of each firm is, of course, to make profits, as much profit as possible under the circumstances. This means the greatest possible excess of the value of its output over its costs. It achieves this by wasting no opportunity to get more by sacrificing less. This adjustment process has many facets. Each firm will shift its production from one product to another whenever this promises to be more profitable. Having chosen its type or types of product, it will adjust its rate of output to the level that promises to yield maximum profits. To do this, it must waste no opportunity to avoid producing any unit that will add more to its costs than to its revenues.

The firm has strong incentives to achieve the lowest possible costs—to use up a minimum value of resources—in producing its output. To achieve minimum costs, the firm must adjust in several ways. (1) It must adjust the size of its plants appropriately. (2) It must develop and apply the most efficient technology that it can. (3) If there are several alternative combinations of productive factors that will yield the same rate of output, it must choose the one that costs least.

As the late Joseph Schumpeter emphasized, every entrepreneur has powerful incentives to act as innovator in applying or making as well as in discovering and developing new products, new techniques of production, new markets, and new sources of raw materials. Pioneering business innovators may reap rich rewards. Businessmen who lag too far behind may be eliminated from the market.

Thus we may think of business firms adjusting both the composition of output and the allocation of resources by shifting from one product to another, adjusting their plant capacities, adjusting their rates of output, competing for resources, and striving for minimum costs.

B. THE CHARACTERISTICS OF AN EQUILIBRIUM

The adjustment process will tend toward an equilibrium situation—a situation in which everyone has wasted no opportunity to better his position and in which no further adjustment will tend to occur unless basic demand and supply conditions change. In a dynamic economy like ours it is unlikely that such a static equilibrium will actually be attained. But there may nevertheless be a strong tendency toward an equilibrium which itself shifts as new events occur.

What would be the characteristics of such an equilibrium with a constant set of consumers' demand schedules? The composition and relative prices of output would be such that the following conditions would obtain: (1) In each market the amount demanded would be just equal to the amount supplied at the prices established by competition. (2) Consumers would have wasted no opportunities to increase their money incomes to buy more of one thing and less of others at these prices. (3) Business firms would have wasted no available opportunities to increase their profits by shifting from one product to another, by adjusting their rates of output, and by lowering their costs. (4) The owners of productive factors would have wasted no opportunities to make net gains by shifting their factors from one industry to another or by increasing or decreasing the supply of their services. In calculating these gains, the owners of productive resources balance the attractiveness or unattractiveness of working conditions against the pecuniary earnings to be obtained in the various possible occupations. This is the way in which the individual can influence the market to take account of his interests as a producer as well as his desires for gloves and model airplanes.

Thus individuals' choices have set the goals and business firms have adjusted both the composition of output and the allocation of resources to the achievement of those goals.

5. Adjustment to Changes in Consumers' Choices

The nature of the competitive process of adjusting the composition of output and the allocation of resources to consumers' demands can be seen even more clearly by assuming a change in consumers' demands. Let us assume that consumers' demand schedules for buggies decrease and that their demand schedules for autos increase. That is, the demand curve for buggies shifts to the left; fewer buggies can be sold at each price. At the same time, the demand curve for autos shifts to the right; more cars are demanded at each price.[2]

A. THE PROCESS OF ADJUSTING SUPPLY

When the change is cataclysmic, as might have been the case had a perfected automobile suddenly hit the market and caused a complete cessation of demand for buggies, the process is fairly clear. Buggy makers, finding that no one will buy their product, must get out, salvaging what they can from the wreckage. Machinery and equipment are probably best converted to some other use or sold for their scrap value, and production must cease immediately if good money is not to be thrown after bad. Labor and raw materials at once cease to be allocated to this industry and are thrown back on the market to be bid for and used by other industries whose products continue in demand.

Things rarely happen this way in practice. Even in the case of the automobile, demand changed slowly. It took time before people became used to the idea of a self-propelled vehicle, before satisfactory roads were constructed, and before the cost of autos could be lowered enough to make them generally accessible. Changes in demand usually are gradual rather than cataclysmic. When the demand for an item

[2] See pp. 382–383 above.

falls it rarely goes out of use altogether, but continues to be employed by the more conservative consumers or to have more limited uses. The appearance of detergents has lowered but not eliminated the demand for soap flakes.

In such a case, the adjustment may take several forms. As in the preceding examples, producers will tend to decrease their output simply because fewer customers will buy their product. In addition, the price of the less desired product will tend to fall because the quantity supplied now exceeds the quantity demanded. This will make for reduced output. The firms that remain in the industry may be expected to contract their production. Others may find it necessary to leave the industry entirely, particularly those that were already on the borderline of profitability. But even these may find it profitable to shut down only gradually. Being fully equipped and in operation at the time the change occurs, they may prefer to continue in business until some of their equipment wears out.

This is an important illustration of the principle that from the point of view of profits bygones must be considered bygones. It may be true that current price is too low to repay the money the firm has sunk in equipment. Nevertheless, the businessman gains nothing by wasting tears over the money he spent in the past which is now beyond recovery. He will be better off continuing to produce and recouping only $50,000 by using machines that cost him twice that amount, rather than recouping nothing at all. Eventually, however, such a firm will leave the industry. Though it may pay the enterpriser to use up his equipment, it will be unprofitable to replace it. Even if he wants to stay he will be forced out either because the money market refuses to supply funds with which to renew his equipment or because bankruptcy, the ultimate sanction on business behavior, takes the matter out of his hands entirely. The reallocation of resources in accord with changes in consumers' desires is speeded by businessmen who quickly heed the call of greater profits elsewhere, but even when businessmen are irrational it will surely take place.

B. ADJUSTMENT AND THE FACTORS OF PRODUCTION

This reduced allocation of resources to the industry that has suffered a decrease in the demand schedule for its product may also be assisted by the owners of the factors of production. With prices for their product lower, businessmen will generally be neither willing nor able to pay as much as before for their factors of production. In this industry there will be a downward pressure on wages and on prices of raw materials, machinery, etc. Workers will tend to go elsewhere so long as jobs are available. Manufacturers of specialized equipment designed just for this industry will tend to cut down their outputs since in equipment production as elsewhere a fall in price makes for reduced outputs. All this will occur because the demand for the factors of production is a "derived demand," one that is based not on the consumption pleasure of the person buying the factors but on his ability to make money by using his purchases in his business. His demand (schedule) for these items will fall when the demand for his commodity is reduced, and so the prices of the factors of production and their supply will tend to fall too.

c. ADJUSTMENT AND THE CONSUMER

There is a third way in which the price mechanism will work to adjust the quantities demanded and supplied to each other. This is by inducing consumers to relent somewhat in their decision to buy less of the commodity. The decrease in prices which occurs as a result of the downward shift in the demand curve will make it cheaper to buy that good and so the quantity demanded will tend to increase somewhat as the result of a movement along the new, lower demand curve. This reduced price tends to offset to some extent, but not entirely, the original decline in the quantity demanded.

d. THE INCREASED DEMAND FOR AUTOS

By a comparable process, competition serves to increase auto output and allocate more resources to auto production in response to the increase of consumers' demands. The shift of demand means that more autos can be sold at each price and that each given amount of output can be sold at a higher price. Existing producers will expand their output, firms formerly in other lines will shift to auto production, and new firms will be formed to take advantage of the new opportunity. Their derived demand for productive resources will increase and they will bid these factors away from other industries to adjust output to consumers' choices.

e. SUMMARY

Adjustment to a fall in the consumers' demand schedule for some product will take place in several ways. (1) Reduced sales will force manufacturers to produce less. (2) Reduced prices will tend to induce manufacturers to produce less. (3) Reduced prices and manufacturers' demands for the factors of production will tend to induce owners of the factors of production to supply smaller amounts to the industry. In addition, (4) reduced prices tend to offset the original decline in the quantity demanded and to induce consumers to increase their purchases.

Thus the price system tends to effect a compromise between consumers and producers by inducing producers to change their use of resources in accord with demand shifts and inducing consumers to moderate the change in the quantity they demand. The important point for the present discussion is the first of these phenomena, the responsiveness of output composition and resource allocation to shifts in consumers' demands.

6. The Market and the Coordination of Productive Plans

We saw how the mutual interdependence of the resource allocation problems led to a need for a coordination of decisions. We showed how coal output must take into account the needs of the steel industry, and vice versa, and how the various automobile parts must be at the assembly lines in the right quantities at the time they are needed. Were there no mechanism for arranging for these things to be properly integrated and adjusted the productive system of the free-enterprise economy would indeed be anarchic and chaotic.

A. THE PRICE MECHANISM AS COORDINATOR

The price mechanism handles these problems in a manner which, at least conceptually, is rather simple. If too little cloth comes out of the textile mills to meet the derived demands of the dress manufacturers its price will rise. If too much is produced its price will fall or it will simply be unsalable and its producer will be stuck with it. In either case the maker of parts, the producer of raw materials, and the supplier of equipment will be forced to adjust his output to the needs of the maker of consumer goods, just as the latter is forced to follow the consumers' dictates.

In this way production is never permitted to get too far out of line. The supplier of productive factors who gets there with too little or too late will not long remain in business. Coal outputs must not be too small or too great to meet the demands of the steel makers and other users, or the sanction of price will soon make adjustments. In the same way, steel makers will simultaneously be kept in line.

All this may not seem like a very impressive accomplishment. Only when we examine the magnitude of the task which faces a central planner in performing these functions will we recognize the order of the achievement.

B. SUMMARY

We have shown that a free-enterprise economy can produce a number of results that are widely considered to be desirable. (1) It induces businessmen to produce their outputs efficiently—that is, at minimum cost to themselves—by choosing their scale of operations, their productive combinations, and their technology appropriately. (2) It induces businessmen to innovate, to inaugurate new methods of satisfying consumers' desires, satisfying them either better (by finding new products or more consumers for old products) or more cheaply (by new productive techniques or more economical sources of productive factors). (3) It coordinates production and tends to arrange for productive factors to be where needed when needed in the quantities needed. And (4) it tends to adjust outputs to the desires of consumers, with production increasing when the demand for a commodity rises, and vice versa.

This is a rather impressive list of achievements. However, we are not yet in a position to judge whether resources can conceivably be allocated in even closer conformity with the desires of the individuals in the economy, or whether the market mechanism does everything with society's scarce resources that society can conceivably hope for. We turn now to these questions.

7. Pure Competition and the Composition of Output

Some economists have argued that under an extreme form of competition, which they call "pure competition," production will tend to be organized in such a way as to allocate resources exactly in accord with the desires of the people in the economy and the resource cost of the various commodities. Let us look at their analysis.

A. DEFINITION OF PURE COMPETITION

To the economist, *pure competition* implies the absence of monopoly power. More specifically, it is the absence of any power on the part of any individual firm or consumer to influence prices. On the supply side, this implies a market situation in which there is a large number of sellers, each offering the same commodity, so that no seller, by holding back or dumping his goods on the market, can cause any appreciable change in the total supply or any appreciable change in the price of the commodity.

Moreover, pure competition assumes *freedom of entry* of new firms into an industry, by which we mean that any businessman who wishes may form a new firm to produce the product without being at any substantial disadvantage as compared with those already in the industry. This has two important effects. First, it permits the number of firms in the industry to become large enough so that no one of them can affect price. Second, it tends to keep profits down, for high profits will attract new firms, thereby making for increased output and reduced prices.

In practice, markets in which this is even approximately true are rather rare. Many industries, like steel, aluminum, and autos, are dominated by large firms. In many others, such as the ladies' garment industry, the firms are very small, but the products are not uniform; hence each supplier may be in danger of overstocking the market with his particular type of products, thereby forcing their price down. Very few lines outside of agriculture are characterized by many small firms producing identical products which can be, so to speak, dumped together into huge bins (the markets) from which they are sold anonymously, so that any individual seller's supply is but a drop in the bucket and can never make the difference between a glutted low-price market and one involving scarcity and high prices.

On the buyer's side, competition of the sort we are interested in is much more widespread. There we require large numbers of consumers for each product, each buying such a small proportion of the total output that no one buyer can affect price appreciably. He cannot force price up by a sudden burst of purchasing, or cause the bottom to drop out of the market by holding off for a while.

Some purchasers do have the power to influence price; they are usually large firms that buy raw materials or services. The output of a specialized product that is used only in the manufacture of some other good is sometimes bought in its entirety by a very few firms. However, the purchases of ordinary consumers present no such problem. Where is the housewife who by rearranging her purchases can break the bread or dill pickle market?

For the consumer, then, an assumption of "pure" competition appears to be roughly in accord with the facts of the market. For the firm, it is usually less justified by the facts. The significance of this will appear in Chapters 22 and 23.

B. THE FIRM UNDER PURE COMPETITION

It will be recalled that at the end of the preceding chapter we discussed the firm in an illustrative application of the principle of no wasted opportunities. We showed there that it would maximize the profit of a firm, *the price of whose product is fixed,* to produce only so much that its marginal cost (the cost of increasing the output of its product by one unit) will be (approximately) equal to the price of the product. This result is applicable to the firm under pure competition, for under this type of competition the firm has no influence over its price. The price is fixed by forces beyond its individual control. If the competitive businessman is to make maximum profits, his output must be of such a magnitude that his *marginal cost equals the price of his product.* We shall be using this result presently.

C. THE INDIVIDUAL IN THE ECONOMY

The individual members of the economy may be said to determine the composition of output and allocation of resources. In their role as consumers individuals influence output by their demands, for under private enterprise production will not long continue far above or far below the quantities demanded on the market. In their role as producers they influence output competition by deciding on the items in whose production they are willing to be occupied. But the individual decides on his demands and his occupation without considering the effect of his decision on the allocation of resources. The individual has difficulties that arise out of the scarcity of his own resources which are perfectly analogous with those of society. He has his problem of allocating his relatively scarce money resources efficiently among the different purchases (including leisure and congenial working conditions) he can make with it, and that is enough for him.

We have seen that a change in prices can lead consumers to change their occupations or to change the quantities of the different commodities they demand. Price changes can thereby cause a reallocation of resources. Under some price arrangements, individual decisions of these types may result in a rather satisfactory output composition in terms of the criterion we are using—maximum satisfaction of the public's desires. Other prices may lead consumers to misallocate resources.

D. Pure Competition and Optimal Output Composition

This suggests that there might even be a set of prices at which individuals would be led to demand and produce the product quantities which constitute optimal output composition. Those who say that pure competition achieves ideal results claim that in such a situation those are precisely the prices which will result from the operation of the market mechanism. Let us first see what sort of prices might achieve this result.

From the point of view of the individual, the price of a good represents the amounts of other commodities, including his time and effort, which he must give up to get more of the commodity in question. If prices can be set so that the amount of commodity B the individual must give up in order to buy one more unit of A is the same as the amount society gives up by shifting its resources from the production of B to provide the individual with the increased amount of A, the cost to the individual will be the same as the cost to society. For example, this would be the case if all three of the following conditions were met simultaneously: (1) The prices of shoes and other items are such that to get another pair of shoes the consumer must forego the purchase of either three hats or two leather wallets. (2) Reducing hat output by three or wallet output by two will release just enough resources to produce an additional pair of shoes. And (3) the owners of the productive factors are willing to switch their leather, labor, etc., from one of these products to another at the prevailing prices.

In this situation, the consumer who carefully husbands his own money resources will automatically be allocating the resources of society which his money commands in the same judicious manner, i.e., efficiently in accordance with his own desires. By setting the price of each commodity equal to the cost of the resources needed to produce an additional unit—that is, equal to what we have called the marginal cost of that commodity—we get the individual's money allocation problem to coincide with the community's resource allocation problem. It is as though we had given each individual a quantity of the scarce resources of society and asked him to allocate them as he saw fit. When producers offer their products for sale at prices equal to the marginal cost and the consumer spends his money, he is, in effect, hiring people —the businessmen and their employees—to carry out his decisions.

Had prices been set otherwise, people would be induced to spend their money and their efforts in such a manner as to waste resources.

Suppose that commodity A, which requires a large quantity of resources for its further production, sells much more cheaply than another item B, whose output can be increased by using very little of society's scarce resources. People would be induced to buy more of A rather than B if they considered these goods equally desirable, but by doing so they would be using a large quantity of resources where a little could do the trick.

Thus the secret lies entirely in setting prices at appropriate levels so that the marginal costs (prices) of alternative outputs to the individual are the same as the marginal costs to society. *But this is what the behavior of the firm under pure competition appears to make for,* as we have seen. The firm will produce at such a level that marginal cost is at least approximately equal to price.

This is the essence of the argument which maintains that under pure competition output composition will best conform to the desires of the individuals who make up the economy. In these circumstances the firm will tend to charge prices which reflect cost for the use of resources, and the consumer in using his money so as best to serve himself will, without knowing it, use society's scarce resources efficiently to that same end.

8. Criticisms of the Market Mechanism

Everything we have seen of the market mechanism up to this point lends support to the view that it serves to allocate resources efficiently and in accord with the desires of the individuals who constitute the economy. However, this mechanism has been severely criticized. Some critics go so far as to favor abandonment of the price system's automatic allocation in favor of a planned economy. Let us look at a few of these criticisms.

A. Pure Competition and Reality

It has been asserted that the whole discussion of pure competition refers to a never-never land which does not exist and never really did. Monopoly power is widespread and yields results that differ in important respects from those that would be produced by pure competition if it really existed. We shall consider some problems of monopoly in the next two chapters. Here we shall discuss only the criticisms of the price system that would still be valid to at least some extent even if purely competitive conditions prevailed.

B. WEIGHTING CONSUMER'S DESIRES BY THEIR WEALTH

We found earlier that to allocate society's resources in accord with the wishes of the individuals who make up society some device must be found for weighing the desires of different individuals against each other. The market weighs the desires of different consumers by the amounts of money they can produce to back up their desires. In effect, it gives the rich man many more votes than the poor man in the allocation decision.

Thus the market may not always allocate resources the way a humanitarian would. For example, if those requiring aureomycin were very poor and the demanders of yoyos were rich men's sons, the market might well supply the latter at the expense of the former. When the conflict with our ethical ideals is so flagrant, we often refuse to accept the verdict of the market. In this case we set it aside by providing aureomycin free for charity cases. But this should not conceal the fact that where the result is less dramatic, so that we are not conscience-led to interfere, the market keeps pushing large amounts of resources where the rich man wants them. Even interference in extreme cases of the sort just mentioned is by and large a fairly recent phenomenon; the lack of concern for the welfare of the very poor which characterized many of the wealthy in the eighteenth and much of the nineteenth century would shock most of us today.

Whether or not the market's decisions should be heavily weighted in favor of the rich is at least partly an ethical question, one concerning the distribution of wealth on which we offer no value judgment. This arrangement has been defended vehemently on various grounds. It has been argued that the rich are predominantly the people of sensitivity and intelligence, and so can make better use of money and resources than the rest of the public. More often used nowadays is the argument that they usually earned the money by their toil or that of their ancestors, and therefore deserve its fruits. Any redistribution to the less productive and more indolent poor would be an injustice. Arguments on the other side have been at least as vehement.

It has been suggested that even if this arrangement is not perfectly just, something less drastic than abandoning the price mechanism can be done about it. We might redistribute wealth by income taxes and other government operations, and still allow consumers to vote on resource allocation, but this time with the votes more equally distributed. To do more than this, it is argued, is to make a pointless sacrifice of a marvelous institution.

Though this method may be attractive and has been widely used, it can be employed only within limits. Too great a degree of equality of wealth, if continually enforced, must necessarily result in the break-down of the market mechanism. If wealth were redistributed only once and the public turned loose on the market again, equality could hardly be expected to remain for long. Money would again find its way into the hands of the luckiest and most astute; and though some who were formerly rich might now end up poor, and vice versa, rich and poor would almost certainly be with us again.

If, on the other hand, equality were continually enforced, the profit motive would be destroyed. There is little to be gained by seeking to be efficient in serving the desires of consumers if all earnings are to be taken away and redistributed to those who turn out to be less clever or less lucky. Though it is conceivable that other motives could to some extent take the place of the drive for profits, there is considerable danger that with the loss of the profit motive the market mechanism and its automatic allocation of resources would also be lost.

This last has been used to defend inequality of income and wealth. It is maintained that the losses of efficiency and other benefits of the market mechanism are too great a price to pay for equalizing wealth. Better to have the poor less well off than the rich but still moderately well taken care of, rather than have everyone sink to the same level of poverty. Recognition of this point was largely responsible for Soviet Russia's decision to introduce large inequalities of income and a sort of profit motive to promote productive efficiency and help allocate resources.

All this still leaves serious questions. How much inequality is necessary for the effective operation of the price system? May too much inequality actually reduce the efficiency of the system? How much efficiency should we be willing to sacrifice to secure greater equality? How much should we care about inequality, once the extremely poor have been relieved? These, together with difficult ethical problems, are involved in every decision relating to income distribution.

c. THE LAG IN ADJUSTMENT

Another criticism of the price mechanism as an allocator of resources arises from the nature of the adjustment process. It is claimed that adjustments to changes in consumers' demands often take the form of correcting mistakes already committed. A producer may proceed in blissful ignorance, continuing to use resources as before, and then be suddenly confronted with unsold goods or fallen prices. Only then, after having wasted resources on goods which are no longer wanted, does he realize that his production should be curtailed. Thus there may be a time lag in the adjustment of production to the desires of the public.

While there is some substance to this charge, there is some question about its significance in practice and there are certainly exceptions. Businessmen usually try to adjust to changes as quickly as possible, for delay adds to their losses. Moreover, producers really do attempt to forecast market trends, and to the extent that they are successful they may avoid much of the misuse of resources which results when wisdom is attained only after the event.

Planners offer little promise of adjusting resources more promptly. True, the little businessman may have neither the time nor the money to devote to a study of the market. Unassisted he may find it more profitable to operate on guesswork than to undertake the expense (which may well be tremendous) of increasing his information.[3] But this is no reason to abandon the free market. The businessman can be supplied with the information and left to adjust to it by himself. These data can be provided by private market forecasting and analysis agencies or by the government. This type of work is an important activity of the United States Department of Agriculture, whose crop forecasting and market analysis services are used by farmers, middlemen, food retailers, and speculators throughout the country. To the extent that the government gathers more relevant information than the individual businessman, it need merely pass the information along and the private businessman can then, in his speed of adjustment, have all the advantages of the planner—and perhaps more, in that he may know the details of his own firm better than a government agent could.

D. THE PAINFUL ADJUSTMENT

A complaint rather closely allied to the preceding one is that the market's adjustment process is inherently cruel and painful. It may

[3] Even for the large firm or the government, guesswork is often the most economic alternative. In some cases the costs and difficulty of obtaining information can easily outweigh the benefits. Other types of information we simply do not know how to obtain. In the former category often fall detailed computations of the cost of producing all alternative sizes of output, which can easily become prohibitively expensive. Among the latter are predictions of future demands about which even guesswork has not usually attained a highly educated level.

force resources out of an industry by driving businessmen into loss and ruin, and workers into unemployment. Unfortunately this is sometimes true, though much can be done to mitigate these effects. If the changes occur only gradually or are foreseen well in advance, much of the sting can be taken out of them. Workers can leave at their convenience as they hear of other jobs, and businessmen can save at least part of their investment by converting it to other purposes or by using up their equipment without renewing it.

There are various devices whereby the government can help soften the blow. Unemployment insurance and an information and employment service can help the workers, and loans may be useful to their employers. Loans and resettlement advice are now made available to farmers through the Department of Agriculture, apparently with some success; the agencies that administer unemployment insurance and allied measures usually act as job information centers.

Nevertheless, it must be admitted that from the point of view of the individuals involved, the transition process may be easier in the planned economy, where lost capital is the property of the state and need not be wept over by any one individual (unless someone is held to account and purged for lack of foresight), and the worker may find that the planners have a job ready and waiting for him. Whether it will be the job he prefers may be another question.

E. SOCIAL EFFECTS OF THE ACTIVITIES OF FIRMS

The market's use of resources may be questioned on yet another count, this time from the point of view of technological efficiency. We have argued that a firm is motivated to use its own resources as economically as possible—to minimize the amount of its resources used up in producing any given value of output. This will minimize social costs only if the firm itself must bear all the costs of its activities. But we discovered in an earlier chapter that a firm's activities may impose on others costs that the firm itself may not permit to influence its decisions.[4] For example, a farmer operating on a hillside may uproot trees and shrubs, thereby contributing to floods in the valley below. His own profits will not be reduced if the valley farms are flooded, so he will have no economic incentive to spend the time and effort required for flood control. Yet the interests of the economy as a whole may require just that, if a smaller investment of society's resources in flood-control

[4] See chapter 7.

measures will prevent a much greater loss in ruined property and eroded topsoil. Similar is the case of an "upstream" plant which contaminates the water used by other firms and consumers downstream.

These examples were chosen not primarily because of their importance, but because they bring the point out clearly. The behavior of every firm affects others in many ways. The proximity of the manufacturer to a supplier of raw materials will reduce transportation cost. The proximity of other firms will make it profitable to introduce railways, other means of transportation, and facilities like organized markets which improve the efficiency of the operation of the firm. The proximity of other firms that use appropriate sorts of skilled labor makes for the availability of the skills needed by the firm. On the other hand, the industrialization of the neighborhood may result in a deterioration of living conditions (e.g., air pollution) which adversely affects the inhabitants of the district and may also make it harder for all the firms to recruit and hold their labor supply.

We see, then, that when a firm makes a decision it is likely to affect the operation of other firms and the welfare of other persons; yet there is nothing in the profit motive to prompt the businessman to take these effects into consideration. The result is that even though the firm tends to use its own resources as efficiently as it can from its private viewpoint, waste and misuse of resources from the social point of view can result from failure to take into account the effects of the businessman's decisions on others. In cases like this the economist says that resources are being misused because the businessman considers only the private costs (and benefits) of his actions, whereas from the point of view of the economy it is the cost and benefit to society as a whole that must be taken into account.[5]

While the resulting social losses may be rather substantial, there is again good reason to doubt the strength of this as an argument for outright abandonment of the price system.

There is little assurance that any government is, at least at present, in a position to track down many of the wastes that result in this way. The interrelations between the decisions of different productive units, while important, are subtle and complicated. If a government planning

---

[5] This shows up an important weakness in our pure competition argument. The businessman will operate at a level where his *private* marginal costs equal price, whereas an efficient allocation of resources requires that effects on others be taken into account and price be set equal to *social* marginal cost.

board, though aware that something is wrong, cannot track down the precise sources of the trouble, it can do little by way of remedial work.

Where, as in our flood-control example, the source of the trouble is clear, much can be done to remedy it by means of only limited government intervention which will deal no mortal blow to the free market. By subsidy,[6] or special tax, or a direct employment of public works, the farmer may be induced to do something to prevent floods in the valley below him. In a similar way, other firms behaving in a manner involving a clear misuse of resources can be induced or coerced into changing their programs. The producer can be charged for any social costs caused by him and not reflected in his private costs, and he can be paid for any social benefits for which he does not collect from his customers.

F. FAILURE TO COORDINATE PLANS

A problem somewhat related to the preceding one arises from the failure of firms to coordinate their plans. The result may be bursts of optimism or pessimism, both of which are said to be rather contagious. For example, a slight fall in the price of some commodity, accompanying a minor reduction in the demand for it, should ideally result in a small reduction in the allocation of resources to that industry. Yet, if there are rumors of a complete collapse, there may be a panicky withdrawal of resources from the industry far beyond that warranted by the change in consumers' demand.

Speculative booms provide an even better example. Many gold rushes, various oil booms, and the Florida development boom of the 1920's all involved an excessive use of resources because of failure to coordinate plans. People overestimated the total profits to be made and failed to consider how many others were rushing in to take advantage of the situation.

G. COMMUNAL WANTS

Finally, but by no means least important, business firms are unlikely to supply *communal wants*—the things for which payment is not easily collected, especially the things that can be obtained only by large groups of people acting jointly. Some examples cited earlier were na-

---

[6] A *subsidy* is a government payment to the producer or seller of some commodity. Here the government would be paying the farmer's flood-control expenses. More generally a producer is subsidized by being given some amount for every unit of the good he sells. This tends to encourage him to produce more of the good and to sell it at a lower price in order to expand his market.

tional defense, lighthouses, parks and playgrounds, flood control, and educational services to the entire community. We need not discuss these communal wants in detail, having considered them at some length in Chapter 7 dealing with the functions of government.

9. Summary

In the free market economy, the organization of production and the output composition decisions are taken care of automatically. This is done in such a way as to make for a relatively efficient use of resources and a continued search for even more efficiency (innovation). Under the price system, the allocation of resources is to a considerable extent dictated by the individuals who make up the economy. Certainly the productive system cannot be dismissed as chaotic and unorganized. The accomplishments of the price system are thus astonishing and in many ways highly admirable, especially in view of the fact that the market, like Topsy, "just grew."

Nevertheless, the free market's allocation decisions have been criticized on a number of grounds. (1) The market is influenced by widespread monopoly and monopolistic elements. (2) The market gives greater weight to the desires of the rich than to those of the poor, catering to the desires that are backed up with ability to pay, and incidentally serving to produce and perpetuate inequalities of wealth and income. (3) The market adjusts to changes in demands only after mistakes have been made and registered in price changes or in increased or decreased inventories resulting from over- or under-supply. (4) The market's adjustment process is harsh and inhumane, involving unemployment and bankruptcies. (5) The price system does not make for the coordination of the decisions of firms and for consideration of the effects of a firm's decisions on others in such a way as to prevent wasteful use of society's resources. (6) The market does not supply communal wants.

These criticisms are all valid to some extent and certainly merit consideration. Despite this, most of us hesitate to take more than relatively mild meliorative action for fear of losing the benefits provided by our free market economy. As we shall see, it is quite doubtful whether the alternatives offer a more attractive prospect even if we leave out of consideration the restrictions on personal liberty and other unpalatable political attributes which often go with a centrally planned economy.

SUGGESTED READINGS
(See list at end of Chapters 6, 7, 20.)

QUESTIONS

1. a. Show how, by its effect on his income, the effect of a rise in the price of his output can sometimes induce a producer to make less of it.
    b. Why then will a rise in price not always increase supply?
    c. Why will a rise in price not always decrease demand?
    d. Why will it usually decrease demand?
2. a. Why will the price of a commodity tend to rise when the demand exceeds the supply?
    b. Explain the possible role of sellers in this process.
    c. The possible role of buyers.
    d. Explain the relevance of this to the assertion that price will tend to the level where the market is cleared.
    e. What is the relevance to clearing the market, of the effects of price changes on demand, supply, and incomes?
3. a. Which functions of price are concentrated on and which neglected by naïve advocates of price supports and ceilings?
    b. Is it true that price supports and ceilings "violate the law of supply and demand"?
    c. What does the government often do about the supply-demand difficulties which result from price ceilings?
    d. From price supports?
4. Discuss the fact that a businessman who is a pioneering innovator may reap rich rewards while the laggard may be eliminated from the market.
5. Explain why the tendency of output to rise when demand schedules rise, and vice versa, is not enough to show that the composition of output is as closely adjusted to consumers' desires as possible.
6. a. Name some commodities you think are produced under conditions approximating pure competition.
    b. Why?
    c. What sort of circumstances are necessary for the attainment of pure competition?
    d. Is this state an approximation of what the word competition has always meant to you?
    e. How might the absence of pure competition on the sellers' side affect the optimal output composition argument?
    f. How about the absence of pure competition on the buyers' side?
    g. Can you give any concrete examples?

7. a. How would the principle of no wasted opportunities require the consumer to allocate his scarce money resources?
   b. Society to allocate its scarce resources?
   c. Show that the second result automatically follows from the first when all commodities are priced at the marginal cost of producing them.
8. a. One economist has described excessively careful planning and a too painstaking search for information on which to base these calculations, whether undertaken by an individual, a firm, or a government, as "an irrational passion for dispassionate rationality." Explain.
   b. Even if a small firm is given some relevant, accurate, and detailed information by the government, it may not pay the firm to use it. Explain.
   c. Some types of information may never be obtainable. Explain.
   d. Give some reasons why not all economists are rich.
9. Consider what can be done about each of the objections to the market mechanism:
   a. By government intervention in a free-enterprise economy.
   b. In a centrally planned economy.
   c. How serious do you consider each of these criticisms?

CHAPTER 22

Monopoly and Monopoly Power

---

1. Introduction

Having discussed the allocation of resources under purely competitive conditions, we turn now to an examination of market situations involving monopolistic elements. As already noted, such situations are the rule rather than the exception in our economy. The reader is asked to defer judgment as to whether this is "good" or "bad."

"Monopoly" and "monopoly power" are subjects on which Americans usually have strong but ambivalent feelings. On the one hand, the term "monopolist" implies to them a ruthless seller who wastes no opportunity to engage in price gouging, pay unreasonably low prices to his suppliers, and crush mercilessly any would-be competitor. On the other hand, most Americans greatly admire many of the huge business firms that have at least some amount of monopoly power.

2. American Laws Relating to Monopoly

A. The Sherman Act

This ambivalence is clearly evident both in our laws and in the interpretation and administration of our laws relating to the maintenance of fair competition and the prevention of monopoly. Our first federal law dealing with monopoly and restraint of trade was the Sherman Act of 1890. The two main provisions of this law were quite simple. They declared:

Sec. 1: Every contract, combination in the form of trust or otherwise, or conspiracy, in restraint of trade or commerce among the several States, or with foreign nations, is hereby declared to be illegal. . . .

Sec. 2: Every person who shall monopolize, or attempt to monopolize, or combine or conspire with any other person or persons, to monopolize any part of the trade or commerce among the several States, or with foreign nations, shall be deemed guilty of a misdemeanor. . . .

The Sherman Act continues to be our basic law on monopoly, though it has been amended and elaborated by the Clayton Act of 1914, the Federal Trade Commission Act of 1914, and other legislation aimed at defining the proscribed acts more clearly and preventing the creation of "undesirable" monopoly power.

B. THE "RULE OF REASON"

At first the intent of the Sherman Act seemed quite clear. It was to make illegal every restraint or monopolization of any part of interstate and foreign trade and every attempt to restrain or monopolize any part of such trade. But the courts found immediately that the law could not be interpreted literally without serious disturbance to many ordinary business practices. They pointed out that every contract is to some extent a restraint of trade. If A contracts to sell and B to buy 100 tons of steel, A is restrained from selling the steel to someone else and B is restrained from buying it from other sources. Similarly, many apparently innocent acts involve some degree of monopoly. The courts therefore evolved a "rule of reason." Only "unreasonable" restraints and attempts to monopolize were to be illegal. "Reasonable" acts were not to be proscribed.

Legislators, courts, and administrators still continue their struggle to define the acts that are "unreasonable" and those that are "reasonable." It is easy to criticize the criteria they have used, to question their judgments, and even to accuse them of unreasonable prejudice in some cases. But we must appreciate their difficulties when we realize that some degree of monopoly power is inevitable in many cases, that any attempt to eradicate all monopoly power would unquestionably force us to sacrifice much efficiency in some industries, but that too much monopoly power may destroy the justification for a laissez-faire free-enterprise economy. Thus it is clear that some sort of "rule of reason" had to be evolved, though not necessarily the rule we have.

Let us now look at several aspects of the problem.

3. Monopoly Power

A. DEFINITION

In common parlance the term "monopoly" is charged with emotion. It is a label of opprobrium which usually denotes a firm that is totally unaffected by competition, that can determine its selling price and sales at will, and that does not hesitate to employ the most heinous means, including subversion of the law and even violence, to maintain its power. Though the attitude behind this is not entirely without basis in experience, the implied definition is for several reasons not usable for analytic purposes. Obviously the emotional content is not highly desirable. More important is the fact that almost no business enterprises fit the description. Taken literally, no firm has all these characteristics as we shall see, and the number of firms even vaguely matching any part of the description is very small. For these reasons the economist employs a definition which has little in common with the "man in the street's" use of the term "monopoly." It does, however, include these extreme forms of monopoly as well as many others.

When an economist uses the terms *monopoly power* and *monopolistic elements* he implies no value judgment; he does not mean that they are either "good" or "bad." He uses them in a purely descriptive sense, usually to indicate a market situation in which an individual seller or buyer, or a group of sellers or buyers acting in combination, can influence the price of a product. Each seller or buyer does not consider the market price to be completely beyond his control. Each seller knows that he can raise his selling price without losing all his sales, that he can to some extent raise his selling price by reducing his output, and that he will reduce his selling price somewhat if he increases his output. Such power on the part of a seller is usually called monopoly power. Similar power on the part of a buyer is sometimes called *monopsonistic power*. Thus a buyer may know that he can lower his buying price and still get some supply, that he can reduce the price he must pay by demanding less, and that he may raise the price he must pay if he demands more.

It should be clear that the presence of monopolistic or monopsonistic power does not imply that the seller or buyer has complete control over price in any practical sense. That sort of complete control cannot be achieved by any firm. The seller must recognize that as he raises his price he will lose some sales. In certain cases he may raise his price a lot and lose few sales, but in others he will lose lots of sales if he raises his price a little. He must always balance the advantage of higher prices against the disadvantages of lower sales. Similarly, a buyer with monopsonistic power must recognize that if he lowers his buying price he will get smaller supplies. Sometimes he can lower his buying price a lot with only a small diminution of the supplies that go to him; in other cases he will lose a large part of his supply if he lowers his buying price only a little. He must always balance the advantage of a lower buying price against the disadvantage of smaller supplies to him.

Thus, in practice, monopoly power does not mean complete control over price; it means only some control over price and it poses for its possessor the problem of balancing price against quantity.

No firm can avoid all competition. Even if one railway provided the only possible means of transportation in an area, raising fares too high would make some people give up traveling and induce them to spend their money on clothing and television sets. In this way the railway would encounter competition from the manufacturers of clothing and TV sets, competition which it could not ignore. In practice a railway monopoly also faces the competition of buses, airplanes, and passenger cars. This illustrates why there is no absolute monopoly in the sense that the term is sometimes used in everyday discourse.

We may say that monopoly or monopsonistic power is a deviation from pure competition, for we found that under pure competition each buyer or seller considers price to be completely beyond his control. This suggests that monopoly power arises out of deviations from the market conditions that characterize pure competition. To show that this is true, let us review the conditions of pure competition.

B. PURELY COMPETITIVE MARKETS

We noted earlier that a purely competitive market is one into which there is freedom of entry and in which there are many buyers and many sellers of a uniform product acting independently, so that no one seller or buyer can appreciably influence the market price. All the conditions mentioned in the statement should be noted carefully, for they suggest the ways in which pure competitive conditions can be violated—how monopoly power can arise.

1. Uniform product.
2. Many sellers.
3. Many buyers.
4. No collusion (independent action).
5. Free entry.

A *uniform product* means that, at any given price, buyers consider the output of every seller to be just as desirable as the output of every other seller. There is nothing about the product itself or the conditions under which it is sold that would lead buyers to prefer one seller's product over that of another. By *many sellers* we mean so many sellers that each supplies only a minute part of the total supply and consequently feels that he has no appreciable control over price. If any one seller tried to raise his price above the prevailing level he would lose all his sales. And no one seller believes he can raise the market price by reducing his rate of output. Similarly, by *many buyers* we mean a number of buyers so great that no one believes he can influence price; each can merely adjust his rate of purchase to the prevailing price. *No collusion* means that each seller or buyer acts independently; he does not act in any sort of concert or agreement with other sellers or buyers. *Free entry* is somewhat more difficult to define, as we shall see later. In general, however, it implies that new firms may open for business in the industry without "undue" hindrance and on much the same terms as those already there. Thus any tendency for profits in the industry to be much higher than those elsewhere can be corrected by the entry of new competing producers who drive prices down by expanding the output of the product.[1]

It is easy to see that when all these conditions are met, no one seller or buyer can influence price. No seller has a motive to restrict output in order to raise price. He cannot have a "price policy." He can have only an "output policy," which is to adjust his output to the most profitable level, considering selling price to be fixed by the market. Similarly, no buyer is motivated to reduce his purchases in order to lower price. He can only adjust his rate of purchase to the price which he takes as given.

c. Deviations from Purely Competitive Conditions

Monopolistic or monopsonistic power arises out of deviations from one or more of the conditions that are necessary for pure competition. These possible deviations may be summarized as in Table 37.

TABLE 37.   Variations in Market Situations

Conditions in Purely Competitive Markets	Possible Deviations from Pure Competition
1. Uniform product	1. Differentiated products
2. Many sellers	2. Few sellers (or one seller)
3. Many buyers	3. Few buyers (or one buyer)
4. No collusion	4. Collusion
5. Free entry	5. Difficulty or impossibility of entry

[1] For a formal discussion of these points see the Graphic Appendix, pp. 616–618.

Products may be "differentiated" in the sense that buyers do not consider the products of different sellers to be perfect substitutes for each other at the same price. Thus a seller may raise his price without losing all his sales, and he knows that he can sell more only by lowering his price or spending more on advertising or other selling devices. There may be so few sellers, each accounting for a large part of the supply, that each knows that he can affect price by varying his rate of output. Similarly, there may be so few buyers that each knows that his demand affects price. Buyers, or sellers, or both may enter into collusion instead of acting independently. Entry into the industry may be difficult, thus inhibiting the opening of new firms that would increase supply and lower prices.

We shall discuss these sources of monopoly power at some length. First, however, we should note the great variety of possible market structures.

D. TYPES OF MARKET STRUCTURES

Market structures in the United States display a wide variety, differing as to all the conditions we have described. The product may range all the way from completely uniform to highly differentiated, the number of sellers may vary from one to hundreds of thousands, the number of buyers may vary from one to millions, action by buyers and sellers may be independent or collusive, and entry of new sellers or buyers may range all the way from easy to practically impossible. Different market structures reflect almost every conceivable combination of these conditions.

These differences in market structure are often reflected in widely differing behavior of prices and output. To see why this is true we shall presently investigate each of the variables. First let us investigate a basic term we have been using.

4. Market

We often speak of the *market* for some product, of the number of buyers and sellers in this market, and of the amounts of the product bought and sold in this market. Just what does the term mean? Its general connotation is fairly clear even if it is difficult to define precisely. It implies a specific area which contains certain suppliers and demanders of a product, and in which certain supply and demand conditions work themselves out. It is sometimes difficult, if not impossible, to draw precise lines around the market area for a given product. Nevertheless, the concept of a market area for a product is highly useful.

The market for some products covers a very large area, whereas the market for other products tends to be localized. Some markets are nation-wide or even international in scope. For example, the market for wheat, Pepsodent toothpaste, Elgin watches, and many other things is at least nation-wide, for the same suppliers can operate throughout the country, and demanders throughout the country affect the price of the same supply. Other markets tend to be localized. For example, there are thousands of sellers and millions of buyers of barber services in the United States, but they are subdivided into many local markets with only tenuous connections among them. Even though they are in the same city, Joe the barber in the Bronx offers little competition to Nick the barber in Brooklyn. The same is true of electricity, of most repair, maintenance, and retailing services, and of commodities that can be moved from one area to another only at great cost.

This fact has many implications for our analysis. For one thing, it indicates that in counting the number of sellers and buyers of a product we must be wary of using the total number in the United States. There are more than 14,000 banks in the country, yet the people in any small town may have easy access to only one local bank. This bank may have at least some monopoly power because its customers find distant banks so inconvenient. There are many electric power, water, and gas companies, yet each community has access to only one. We must therefore be careful to ascertain the size of a market before trying to talk about the number of buyers and sellers in it.

The great improvements in the speed and efficiency of transportation and communication have tended to widen market areas. When both were slow and costly, a local merchant might have a considerable amount of monopoly power because his customers could get access to other sellers only at a high cost in time and money. Today they may refuse to buy much from him if his prices are considerably higher than those some miles away.

Developments during the past century or so could have increased competition and decreased monopoly power in this way even if the total number of sellers of a product decreased. In 1850 there might have been in the United States 10,000 sellers of some product, yet each buyer might have had access to only one seller. By 1950 the number of sellers might have been reduced to only 2500, yet each buyer might have achieved access to many sellers. It is always dangerous to generalize about the effects of a change in the total number of sellers without considering any accompanying changes in the size of market areas.

5. Product Differentiation

A. DEFINITION OF PRODUCT

The term *product* also presents problems of definition. Sometimes it is used in a broad sense to indicate a general category of items that have similar characteristics and are used for the same general purposes. In this sense, coal and autos are each products. But it is also used to indicate much more specific types and qualities of items. In this sense there are many "products" within the general coal category, each somewhat substitutable for others but not the same "product" because they are not perfect substitutes for each other at any given price per ton. Similarly, each model of Ford, Chevrolet, Cadillac, and Chrysler is a separate "product" within the general product category of automobiles.

This distinction between product in the broader sense and product in the narrower sense will be highly useful in our analysis.

B. UNIFORM AND DIFFERENTIATED PRODUCTS

By *uniform products* we mean those that buyers consider to be perfect substitutes for each other at the same price. There is nothing about the things themselves or the conditions under which they are sold that would lead buyers to prefer one over another at the same price. By *differentiated products* we mean any that buyers do not consider to be perfect substitutes for each other at the same price. Because of real or imagined differences in the things themselves or in the conditions under which they are sold, consumers differentiate among them. Firms that operate in a competitive market, but one in which products are differentiated, are said to be operating under conditions of *monopolistic competition.*

Products may be differentiated in many ways. Their physical, chemical, and functional properties may differ appreciably. Fords and Chevrolets are obviously not exactly the same thing, to say nothing of

Crosleys and Cadillacs. We are told that the same is true of Chesterfields and Camels, Florsheim and Walkover shoes, Coty and Houbi-
gant perfumes, and many other things. Or the differences may be
largely imaginary—illusions created by millions of dollars' worth of
advertising and selling efforts. The differences may not be in the things
themselves but in the conditions under which they are sold. A dress
sold brusquely in a basement may not be considered a perfect substitute
for the same dress sold in a swanky shop by an obsequious and attractive woman.

As soon as at least some buyers consider products to be differentiated, their sellers have some degree of monopoly power. Each seller
can raise his price without losing all his sales; at least some of his
customers will stick with the product. He can increase his sales by
lowering his price, but he must recognize that some will continue to
buy competing products even if their prices are higher. If buyers consider the differentiated products to be only distant substitutes for each
other, a seller may raise his price relative to the prices of competing
products without losing many sales, and he may lower his price relative to others without gaining many sales. But if the products are
considered to be only slightly differentiated—that is, to be very close
substitutes for each other—a seller may lose large amounts of sales by
raising his price relative to others and may gain large amounts of sales
by lowering his price relative to others.

Sellers of differentiated products face many difficult policy decisions,
of which we shall mention only a few. (1) What should be the nature
of my product? Should it be designed to hit the quality market, the
medium market, or the cheap market? Or should I offer several differentiated products in the same general category in order to cater
to all sorts of tastes? (2) What should be my advertising policy?
Should I spend a lot to increase preferences for my product? Or should
I spend little for this purpose and rely largely on the quality and price
of the product to promote my sales? What should be the nature of my
advertising? Should I try to establish a reputation for my product as
the very best in the market with no close substitutes? Or should I say
that it is practically a perfect substitute for a Cadillac that costs much
more? (3) What should be my price policy? High, relative to the prices
of other similar products? Low? The same?

Thus, to maximize his profits the seller of a differentiated product
must consider at least four variables—the specifications of his prod-

uct, the amount of his selling expenses, his price, and his rate of output.

6. Number of Sellers and Buyers

A. PURE MONOPOLY—ONE SELLER

When we count the number of sellers of a product in a market we must be sure to define both market and product. If we used product in the narrow sense there would be many pure monopolies in the American market. Every manufacturer of a branded product has a monopoly of his own brand. But we usually apply the term pure monopoly to a product in its broader sense. In this sense there is probably no pure monopoly in the United States as a whole. There are, however, pure monopolies in localized markets. Electric, gas, water, and telephone companies are outstanding examples. These monopolies are legalized and regulated.

Though a pure monopolist may have rather wide discretion in fixing his price policies he does face competition from substitute products. In the broadest sense, all products are competitors for the consumers' money. But a pure monopolist may have to compete with other products that serve much the same purpose as his own. For example, the only movie house in an isolated area may still have to compete with radios, television sets, and other forms of public and private entertainment.

B. OLIGOPOLY—A FEW SELLERS

Much more common in the United States are *oligopolistic markets* —markets in which a few sellers account for all, or at least a large part, of the output of a given product. As indicated in Table 38, there are several industries in which no more than four manufacturers account for at least 75 percent of the total national output of a product. If we looked at local market situations we would find that oligopoly is the rule rather than the exception. In some cases oligopolies sell uniform products; in others they sell differentiated products.

C. NUMBER OF BUYERS

In some markets, especially in local or regional markets, a few buyers purchase all or most of the supply of a product. Thus, A.T. & T. is the major buyer of telephone apparatus, a few auto companies are

TABLE 38. Concentration of Output in 26 Selected Manufacturing Industries, 1947[2]

	Percent of Net Capital Assets Owned by						
Industry	1 Com- pany	2 Com- panies	3 Com- panies	4 Com- panies	8 Com- panies	15 Com- panies	All Com- panies
Linoleum	57.9	80.8	92.1	93.6	....	....	100.0
Tin cans and other tinware	55.2	92.1	95.3	96.4	....	....	100.0
Aluminum	55.0	85.0	100.0	....	....	....	100.0
Copper smelting and refining	46.8	73.5	88.5	94.6	100.0	....	100.0
Biscuits, crackers and pretzels	46.3	57.0	67.7	71.4	....	....	100.0
Agricultural machinery	45.3	56.8	66.6	75.4	82.1	....	100.0
Office and store machines and devices	42.0	56.3	69.5	74.3	85.3	89.6	100.0
Motor vehicles	40.9	62.8	68.7	70.7	77.3	86.1	100.0
Cigarettes	36.6	64.4	77.6	87.8	....	....	100.0
Plumbing equipment and sup- plies	33.2	64.9	71.3	74.3	....	....	100.0
Distilled liquors[a]	29.0	53.3	72.4	84.6	94.3	....	100.0
Meat products	28.8	54.7	64.0	69.3	77.6	81.6	100.0
Primary steel	28.6	42.0	49.2	54.5	69.3	77.2	100.0
Rubber tires and tubes	27.8	49.9	70.3	88.3	94.8	....	100.0
Dairy products	27.5	48.9	55.8	59.6	71.3	....	100.0
Glass and glassware	24.9	49.1	57.4	62.2	73.9	..	100.0
Carpets and rugs	24.1	36.8	48.9	57.9	....	....	100.0
Footwear (except rubber)	23.6	39.6	43.4	46.8	53.1	57.5	100.0
Industrial chemicals	21.5	36.5	45.5	51.8	70.2	80.2	100.0
Woolen and worsted goods	16.7	23.5	28.1	30.3	36.4	....	100.0
Electrical machinery	15.8	28.8	41.7	47.5	55.2	60.7	100.0
Grain mill products	15.6	23.5	30.2	36.3	48.6	56.6	100.0
Aircraft and parts	13.6	25.4	35.2	44.0	73.7	86.2	100.0
Bread and other products (excluding biscuits and crackers)	13.0	20.0	25.4	30.6	38.2	59.2	100.0
Canning and preserving	10.7	21.4	32.0	39.4	51.0	....	100.0
Drugs and medicines	8.4	16.5	23.5	30.0	47.7	....	100.0

[a] Computed on basis of total assets.

the major buyers of automotive parts, a few cigarette companies are the major buyers of cigarette tobacco, and so on. In such cases a buyer has some monopsonistic power—some control over the price he pays. He can often lower his buying price and still get some supply, and he can to some extent lower or raise the price by decreasing or increasing his demands. In some cases this power is great; in others it is quite limited. Farmers sometimes claim that they are the victims of large industrial buyers who exercise this power.

[2] Source: Federal Trade Commission, *The Concentration of Productive Facilities,* Government Printing Office, Washington, 1949, Table 3.

7. Collusion

A. INCENTIVES TO COLLUSION

Collusion is used to denote an agreement, implicit or explicit, whereby a number of firms in a market can by common consent suppress competition and increase their monopoly power. Sellers often have a strong incentive to enter into collusion—to present a united front to buyers. In this way they may be able to raise their prices and make larger profits. Buyers, too, may find it profitable to present a united front rather than competing with each other. They may be able in this way to get more favorable prices.

In the following paragraph we shall deal only with collusion among sellers.

B. FORMS OF COLLUSION

Collusive agreements may take one or more of many forms, including the following: (1) Price agreements. All may agree on a set of prices, leaving each to get as much of the market as he can at those prices. (2) Output agreements. Each may be given an output quota which he may not exceed, but which he may sell anywhere he wishes. This may or may not be accompanied by a price agreement, but the very restriction of output will tend to keep up prices. (3) Market agreements. The market may be divided up among the sellers, either by geographic areas or by type of purchaser. Each gets his own exclusive domain. (4) Other agreements. These include many things, such as agreements among bankers as to the amount of free stationery to be given to their customers, agreements to adopt sanctions against firms who violate the collusive arrangements, and so on.

C. CHISELERS

Though there are often strong incentives toward collusion, each seller may also be strongly tempted to violate the agreement, especially if he thinks he can do so without destroying it. Suppose, for example, that a group of sellers agree collectively to raise the price of their product from $1 to $1.50. All may agree that both individually and collectively they are better off with collusion than without it. Yet each seller may reason: "Sure, I'm better off with the agreement than I would be without it. But how much better off I would be if the others refused to sell below $1.50 and I lowered my price to $1.40 and took

some of their business! I think I'll try it." Thus a chiseler is born and
the collusive agreement may be on its way out if the colluders can find
no way to police their members and new entrants. Whether the term
"chiseler" should be one of opprobrium or praise is an arguable question. Certainly chiselers have been one of the biggest headaches of
collusive groups, a frequent cause of their breakup, and a potent force
for low prices of consumer goods.

D. COLLUSION AND THE ANTITRUST LAWS

The courts are usually quite severe in dealing with cases of proved
collusion relating to prices, markets, and rates of output. However,
collusion is often difficult to prove if no member has kept incriminating
files.

8. Ease of Entry

Entry by new firms into an industry is never "free." However, it is
relatively easy to enter some industries. Only a small amount of money
is required and a new firm is at little disadvantage relative to those
already in the industry.

In other cases potential entrants may be hindered by several types
of obstacles, of which the following are illustrative. (1) The sheer
magnitude of the investment required. Not many businessmen can
raise the capital required to produce a new make of car successfully.
(2) The unavailability of raw materials. Firms already in the industry
may have established control over all the low-cost sources of raw
materials, or they may threaten to cease purchasing from any supplier
who sells to a new entrant. (3) The difficulty of getting resellers.
Wholesalers and retailers may be heavily prejudiced against the products of new producers, and they may even be under contract to handle
no products that compete with those of firms already in the industry.
(4) The difficulty of achieving consumer acceptance. Buyers may have
developed such strong preferences for existing brands that they are
reluctant to try new ones. The new firm may have to spend millions
for advertising to overcome this obstacle. (5) Patents and exclusive
licenses. New firms may be unable to produce because one firm in the
industry holds the exclusive right to use a crucial piece of equipment
or to manufacture the product or a part of the product, and refuses
to permit the newcomer to use or manufacture it even in return for
large money payments. There have even been cases when firms have
been kept out or driven out of an industry by phony patent litigation

designed to bankrupt them by the sheer expense of the legal proceedings.

Obstacles of this type can form a sort of protective wall around firms already in an industry and obstruct the inflow of additional resources. They may also serve to hold down the supply of the product, raise its price, and protect the profits of existing firms in the industry.

We have now completed our general survey of the various types of market situations and have indicated some of the ways in which differences in market structures can affect the behavior of an industry. In the course of the discussion we have seen that a very large percentage of our industry is characterized by monopolistic competition and oligopoly. Let us now look at these forms of market organization more closely.[3]

9. Monopolistic Competition

A. THE NATURE OF SUCH MARKETS

Monopolistic competition refers to a market structure containing a large number of firms, each of which offers a differentiated product or service. As we saw earlier, this differentiation may take a variety of forms. The product itself may differ from others in physical specifications and performance, packaging, brand name, and so on, or it may be differentiated solely because of the conditions under which it is sold. A seller may build up a more or less loyal clientele through convenient location, courteous service, attractive store facilities, or comely salesgirls. Thus he can get some amount of monopoly power —sometimes only a very small amount—by providing his customers with a product or service thát no one else can duplicate exactly.

Nevertheless, competition in such a market may be quite intense and take many forms. Suppose that some seller has developed a very profitable business by selecting a highly convenient location, offering a type of product that consumers like very much, or selling under attractive conditions. If entry into the market is easy, as it is likely to be if the business does not require large amounts of capital, the first seller may not be in such a favorable position very long. New sellers will come in, trying to offer close substitutes for his product. They cannot offer precisely the same product, but they can try to get a location almost as convenient, develop a product that will be con-

[3] For a formal discussion of these market forms see the Graphic Appendix, pp. 646–650, 652.

sidered about as good or better, and offer as good or better selling facilities.

We have all seen this happen as new filling stations grow up around a first one, new brands come into the market to compete with the first one, and so on. While at least some customers may continue to value the distinctive attributes of the first seller, many may turn to the products of the new entrants if they can save a few pennies, and at least some will come to prefer the products of a new seller even at the same or a higher price. Thus monopolistic competition takes many forms— competition in the specifications of products, in advertising, in location, in other selling conditions, and in price. But when the other conditions remain unchanged, each seller realizes that he can sell more only by lowering his price somewhat.

B. Profits Under Monopolistic Competition

In some cases a seller in a monopolistically competitive industry may continue to make fairly large profits. But this is unlikely if entry into the industry is relatively easy. New firms will continue to flock in, bringing additional capacity, new substitutes, and perhaps lower prices. This may even continue until all or most of the firms are having losses rather than making profits. In effect, the proprietors make less income than they could earn elsewhere. They may stay in the industry only because they are ignorant of their alternatives, or are willing to sacrifice income to be self-employed businessmen, or are hopeful that things will get better in the future.

C. Excess Capacity

The result of such an influx may be that each firm will not have enough business to secure efficient use of its resources; it will have excess capacity. The classic example is the case of filling stations which crowd together along a busy road to such an extent that most pumps and attendants are idle much of the time. Too much of society's resources is devoted to gasoline selling, not because too much gasoline is sold but because the same amount could be sold by fewer firms using a smaller total amount of labor and equipment. Professor Chamberlin and others have argued that excess capacity—an underutilization of resources—is likely to result from monopolistic competition and freedom of entry of firms.

To show how costs per unit may be reduced and resources utilized more efficiently by increasing sales, consider the following example.

Suppose a filling station's costs are 15 cents a gallon for the gasoline itself, $1 a day amortization[4] on the pump, and $9 a day for the wages of the attendant. If the station sells only 100 gallons of gasoline a day, it must sell the gasoline at 25 cents a gallon to break even. But if the same pump and attendant were to sell twice that amount—200 gallons per day—its total cost of selling each gallon would drop to 20 cents. The overhead costs of the pump and attendant, the part of cost that does not vary with the scale of output, would be spread over a greater volume of sales.

Why doesn't each seller expand his output until he has fully utilized his existing capacity and achieved the minimum cost per unit? Under pure competition each seller would do just this, for he would assume that the expansion of his output would have no effect on the price at which he could sell. But the seller of a differentiated product knows that he can expand his sales only by lowering his price. He is therefore likely to find it more profitable—or less unprofitable—to restrict his output and hold up his price, rather than to lower his price enough to achieve the volume of sales that would be necessary to utilize all his capacity. In some cases, as in our filling station example, it would be impossible for a seller to raise his sales up to capacity limits by lowering his price if his competitors also lowered their prices. If he tried it he would find that he ended up with few more sales and without enough revenue to cover his costs.

We conclude that under monopolistic competition the firm may often be expected to operate at too low a level of output to achieve all the possible economies of large-scale production. It is thus said to be characterized by excess capacity, for it has facilities for doing more business and doing it more economically.

D. Interpreting the Excess Capacity Result

The excess capacity result implies that society might be served more efficiently by fewer and larger firms—that firms might advantageously be combined, or one of the two filling stations standing side by side eliminated. This is by no means clear in every case. Under monopolistic competition, each firm produces a somewhat different good or service, or at least it appears so to buyers. A combination or elimination of firms would therefore mean a reduction in the variety of alter-

---

[4] Roughly, by the amortization of a capital good we mean the money its owner puts aside during its lifetime in order to be able to replace it when it wears out, becomes obsolete, or is finally discarded for any other reason.

natives available to consumers; it would mean a tendency toward standardization of products. This may be a higher price than consumers are willing to pay for greater "efficiency." No doubt we could get our clothing more cheaply if we were all willing to wear uniforms, but at least the ladies seem to consider this a particularly unattractive opportunity of saving money.

However, there are cases in which reasonable judgment would probably favor less differentiation and more standardization. Eliminating one of two or more neighboring gas stations might reduce the motorist's choice of road maps and perhaps the courtesy of the attendant. Yet most motorists would probably favor the change if it would save them two cents on the gallon. Sometimes the variety of differentiated items becomes so great that it serves only to confuse the consumer.

10. Oligopoly

We saw that oligopoly is another very common form of market organization. This is the case where a few sellers account for all or most of the output of some commodity.

A. THE OLIGOPOLISTS' STRATEGY PROBLEMS

The very fewness of sellers gives each oligopolist some control over price. A seller who accounts for 25 percent of the total output of his industry's product cannot assume that his own output decisions will have no effect on price. Moreover, the problem becomes quite complicated because the oligopolists are so mutually interdependent. What one does is likely to have a sharp impact on each of the few others and they may be expected to retaliate. The manufacturer of Camels cannot expect that his price cut or multimillion-dollar advertising campaign will go unheeded by the producers of Chesterfields, Old Golds, Luckies, and Philip Morrises.

An oligopolist, like a poker player, must constantly ask questions of this sort: If I lower my price, will my competitors lower theirs? If so, how soon and how much? If they do lower their prices immediately I won't take away their markets. If they don't, I can take some business away from them. If I raise my price, what will they do? If they don't raise their prices I shall lose sales to them. But if they do follow my price increase I shall not lose sales to them. What will be their response if I put on a big sales campaign? Will they retaliate or not?

Because of this mutual interdependence of oligopolists it is difficult to generalize about markets of this type. Sometimes the few firms en-

gage in price wars and cutthroat competition in a life-and-death struggle. More often, however, they come to realize that highly aggressive
behavior by one, such as price cutting, will only draw retaliation from
the others, and that it is better for all concerned to establish some sort
of *modus vivendi*. They must, of course, beware of the antitrust laws.

A common way of establishing peace is through *price leadership*.
Under this arrangement one firm, usually one of the larger firms, takes
the lead in setting prices, and the others follow suit. Each knows that
if he fails to follow a price increase by the leader or reduces his price
when the leader does not he may touch off a bitter price war or some
other sort of retaliation. Even in the absence of a formal price leadership arrangement, oligopolists are likely to decide that aggressive price
competition is almost certain to elicit retaliation and is not a wise
practice.

It has been observed that prices in oligopolistic industries tend to
be "stickier" than prices in industries with larger numbers of sellers.
Prices in the many-seller industries tend to change frequently, to decline quickly during depression, and to rise quickly during inflation.
In contrast, oligopolistic prices tend to change less frequently, to fall
more slowly during depression, and to rise less quickly during inflation.

B. REASONS FOR THE FEWNESS OF SELLERS

Why are there so many markets that have too few sellers to produce
purely competitive conditions? The answer is clear in the case of
electric, gas, and water utilities. To have a very large number of electric companies serving the same city would be preposterous. Every
one of the many electric companies would have to be so small that
its costs would be far above those of a single company serving the
entire area. In short, in this case we can get maximum efficiency in the
use of resources only by having one, or at most a few, firms supplying
the product. In any local or regional market the same is true of water
and gas utilities, railroads, buses, brick kilns, and many other things.

Though in a less obvious way, the same principle applies in some
other industries. A few large firms can produce the demanded quantity
of output more cheaply than a much larger number of small firms.
We saw earlier that under competitive conditions each firm tends to
expand toward the size that will enable it to achieve all the net economies of scale and the lowest possible cost per unit of output. In some
industries, such as agriculture, the firm reaches this least-cost size with
a rate of output that is only a very small fraction of the total demand

for its type of product. Any further expansion of the firm would bring increased, rather than decreased, cost per unit. In such industries the competitive process tends to establish a very large number of small firms.

However, in some other industries, such as automobile manufacturing, the competitive process tends to establish a small number of very large firms because each firm can achieve net economies of scale and decreasing cost per unit up to a point at which it can supply a large part of the total quantity demanded. Suppose that we start with a very large number of competitive auto manufacturing firms, each far too small to achieve minimum costs. Each will seek to expand toward its most efficient size. One way of doing this is to buy up other firms. Another way is for each to expand its own plants, thereby increasing the supply of cars and driving their prices down. If at the beginning there was just enough capacity to satisfy the demand, there will now be excess capacity. Many firms are likely to fail or be bought up by the others. Thus the competitive process itself may tend toward the establishment of oligopoly in industries in which a firm must be big enough to satisfy a large part of the demand if it is to achieve maximum efficiency and minimum costs.

This fact is quite important for public policy. Suppose that we became very much aroused about the monopoly power that goes with oligopoly and set out to break up existing firms and to form such a large number of new firms as to establish purely competitive conditions. In the process we would sacrifice the efficiency that can be achieved only with large-scale firms. It might well turn out that the oligopolists, with all their monopoly power, were selling at lower prices than the many smaller and purely competitive firms could afford to take. Moreover, oligopoly would tend to be reestablished as the small firms struggled to expand toward their least-cost size.

On the other hand, it is dangerous to assume that the emergence of oligopoly is due solely to the struggle of firms in each industry to achieve the most efficient size. In some cases the motive for mergers is to increase monopoly power rather than to lower costs. A local hauler may buy out a competitor who has been cutting prices or refusing to go along with price increases. In the same way, much larger firms may buy out troublesome competitors in order to clear the way for more favorable prices. Promoters have made large amounts of money buying up several firms that formerly competed sharply and combining them into one large firm which they expected to earn much higher profits.

In some cases the higher profits were expected to come out of lower costs; in others they were expected to come out of lessened competition.

The courts and policymakers face very difficult problems in this field, for within limits they are empowered to dissolve companies that have too much monopoly power, and to prevent the merging of companies when the result would be an undue increase of monopoly power. To arrive at rational decisions they must ponder several questions. How would the proposed dissolution or merger affect the degree of competition and monopoly in the industry? If in any case there will be only a small number of firms in the industry, what difference will it make whether there are a few more or a few less? What difference will it make in the efficiency of the industry? If a merger would raise efficiency, how much if any of the benefits will go to buyers? These problems are always difficult, but especially so when a proposed merger of firms seems likely to increase both efficiency and monopoly power, or when a proposed dissolution seems likely to decrease them both.

11. Summary

This chapter has indicated some of the many possible types of market structures and some of the relationships between the structure and functioning of an industry. It has also dealt with the sources and types of monopoly power and suggested a few of their implications.

In the next chapter we shall examine more closely some of the effects monopolistic power has had in practice. We shall try to get some idea why monopoly has become so widely used as an appellation of infamy and to see both the benefits and the disadvantages which have resulted for the community from the presence of monopolistic elements.

SUGGESTED READINGS

Lynch, David, *The Concentration of Economic Power,* Columbia University Press, New York, 1946.

Oxenfeldt, Alfred R., *Industrial Pricing and Market Practices,* Prentice-Hall, New York, 1951.

Purdy, Harry L., Lindahl, Martin L., and Carter, William A., *Corporate Concentration and Public Policy,* Prentice-Hall, New York, 1950.

Stocking, George W., and Watkins, Myron W., *Monopoly and Free Enterprise,* Twentieth Century Fund, New York, 1951.

QUESTIONS

1. a. Give some example of restraints of trade which you would consider reasonable.
    b. Unreasonable.
    c. Try your hand at formulating criteria of reasonableness.
2. a. Show how the extreme monopolist of everyday discussion is also a possessor of monopoly power in the economist's use of the term.
    b. Show that many firms that have monopolistic power in the economist's definition are not monopolists as the term is ordinarily used.
    c. In particular, why may this be true of the grocery around the corner?
    d. Of the Republic Steel Corporation?
3. Discuss to what extent a seller of second-hand cars competes with:
    a. Railroads.
    b. New Chevrolets.
    c. New Cadillacs.
    d. Clothing manufacturers.
    e. Will he ever be an absolute monopolist?
    f. Can he ever vary his sales without changing his prices, or vice versa?
4. List some ways in which products can be differentiated.
    a. In their physical characteristics.
    b. In the way in which they are sold.
    c. In the imagination of the consumer only.
    d. In other ways.
    e. Give actual examples wherever possible.
5. Show how the potential chiseler:
    a. Can gain by violating a collusive agreement.
    b. Can lose if he is the last one to start chiseling.
    c. Can lose if he and everyone else in the industry violates a collusive agreement.
    d. In what circumstances do you think a collusive agreement can last?
    e. Will rapidly break down?
    f. What can the members of a collusive group do to protect it—questions of legality aside?
6. Show how the entry of new firms can eliminate very high profits in an industry.
    a. By its effects on the selling price of the product.
    b. By its effects on the costs of producing the product.
7. Monopolistic competition is likely to be characterized by firms whose output is too small to achieve all the economies of large-scale production.
    a. Explain.
    b. Why does it not necessarily follow that society would be better off

if all the firms in such an "industry" were to expand their production; i.e., why do we say that it may call for *fewer* and larger firms? (Hint: what would be the effect on the allocation of scarce resources?)

8. Hazard some guesses as to why oligopolistic prices are often "sticky."
   a. Take into account the nature of the products manufactured by the leading oligopolistic industry, and the demand for their products.
   b. Take into account the possibility of fear of retaliation by competitors.
   c. In both respects contrast some oligopolistic industries with wheat production.

9. Suppose all suppliers of some item sell it at identical prices.
   a. Might this establish a presumption of collusion?
   b. Of pure competition?
   c. What further evidence would you want?

CHAPTER 23

Consequences of Monopoly Power

---

1. Monopoly Output and Competitive Output

A. THE ARGUMENT

One of the major arguments against monopoly is that it gouges the public by creating artificial scarcities of its products, thereby misallocating resources. In an earlier chapter we examined the argument that resources will be allocated most efficiently in line with the choices of the public under pure competition because competitive forces will adjust outputs so that the price of each commodity is equal to the marginal cost of producing it. Building on this contention, some have argued that a monopolist will misallocate resources by producing a smaller output of a commodity than would a purely competitive industry in order to sell it at a higher price.

Let us develop the argument.[1] We shall discuss pure monopoly—a one-seller situation. With some modifications the analysis can be applied to other closely related monopoly power situations. Our assumptions should be noted carefully, for they will prove to be crucial. (1) The monopolist's cost conditions are the same as those that would prevail if production were organized on a purely competitive basis. (2) The demand schedule for this product is the same as it would be if the industry were organized on a purely competitive basis. (3) The monopolist tries to maximize his profits. (4) Other products are produced and sold under pure competition.

Building on these assumptions, let us see why the monopolist will arrive at a rate of output at which his marginal cost is below the price

[1] For a formal exposition see the Graphic Appendix, pp. 650–651.

of his product. Suppose he starts off with his output at the level where his marginal cost is equal to price. Now he considers reducing his output by one unit. In doing so he will save the cost of the last unit (marginal cost), but will lose the revenue from its sale (its price). Since he starts out with price just equal to marginal cost, this gain and loss will just cancel out. However, with the fall in the amount he puts on the market, he will be able to charge a higher price on the units he continues to sell. This will be pure gain. Thus a reduction in his output will increase his total profit, and it will pay him to produce less than "the competitive" output.

An example will make the argument clearer. Suppose a manufacturer is selling 100,001 units of the product at $500 each, with his marginal cost also equal to $500. Suppose that by decreasing the amount of his product by one unit he can increase his price by one cent. If he makes this reduction in his output, the following changes affect his profit position:

1. He saves $500 in costs by not producing the last unit.
2. He loses $500 in revenue by not having that unit to sell.
3. He gains $1000 by selling each of his remaining 100,000 units of output at one cent more for each.

The reduction in output below the "competitive level" has netted him $1000, a profitable proposition. The figures used may not be particularly convincing, but the argument is not dependent on them. It is based essentially on the observation that a monopolist can increase the price of his product by reducing the amount he offers for sale. Thus under monopoly the price may be higher and both the rate of output and the amount of resources used may be lower than they would be if the industry were organized on a purely competitive basis. However, we cannot be sure that this will result in every case, or even usually.

B. CRITICISMS OF THE ARGUMENT

It should be noted that the validity of our conclusions in the preceding paragraphs depends to a considerable extent on the validity of our assumptions. Each of these assumptions is subject to question in at least some industries.

In the first place, the monopolist's cost conditions may differ from those that would prevail if the industry were organized on a purely competitive basis. The monopolist may organize production quite differently. He may use fewer and larger plants, a more efficient technology, mass buying, and so on. In this way he may achieve considerably lower costs than could a purely competitive industry. It could therefore turn out that even though the monopolist's price was set considerably above his own marginal costs, it would be below the marginal cost and price that would prevail if the industry were organized on a purely competitive basis. And simply because the monopolist's price is lower, people may buy more of the product than they would if the industry were purely competitive, had higher costs, and charged higher prices.

In the second place, the demand schedule for the product may not be the same under monopoly as it would if the industry were purely competitive. This is because a monopolist may organize advertising and selling campaigns that would not be undertaken under pure competition. Under pure competition it could never pay a firm to advertise. An individual Kansas wheat farmer never advertises his particular product, for he knows that everyone else knows that his wheat is just like everybody else's. Moreover, he is not going to pay out his own good money to raise the demand for wheat in general, because he would bear all the expense and most of the benefit would go to others. But a monopolist, getting all the benefits of his own advertising, may spend much for this purpose. The result may be an increase in the demand schedule for the product, and perhaps a greater rate of output and sales than would occur if the industry were purely competitive. Whether the price will be higher or lower than it would be under pure competition will depend on many circumstances, only one of them being the monopolist's cost conditions as compared with those that would prevail if the industry were purely competitive.

In the third place, the monopolist may not try to maximize his profits. For this there may be several reasons—fear of regulation or dissolution by the government, fear of public opinion, and so on. In such a case we cannot predict what his price and output policy will be.

Thus we find it hard to generalize about the height of prices, the rate of output, and the use of resources by a monopoly as compared with those that would hold true for a purely competitive organization of a given industry. Suppose, however, that the monopolist's cost and demand conditions actually are the same as they would be if the industry were purely competitive, and that his output is lower and his prices higher.

It does not follow inevitably that in the real world the monopolist should, from the point of view of the body of consumers, increase his output. This would follow if (1) we accepted the validity of the argument that resources will be allocated most efficiently in accord with the desires of the public when all industries are purely competitive, and (2) all other industries were actually purely competitive. In such a case the monopolization of a single industry would result in too little of society's resources being allocated to it. But suppose the other industries are also monopolistic. It could happen *by coincidence* that if all industries were monopolistic something like a purely competitive allocation of resources among them could occur. If so, it is not at all clear that one monopolist should be forced to increase his output to the point where price equals marginal cost if the monopolists in the other industries do not. With its higher rate of output and lower price the industry might then obtain too large a proportion of society's resources. The demand of the different industries for society's scarce resources may be likened to a tug of war. A monopolist sometimes does not pull for these resources as hard as a purely competitive industry would. If there is a single monopolistic industry, not enough resources may go to it and it may be desirable to make that monopolist pull harder. But in a world of monopolies, getting just one of them to pull harder may just as clearly cause resource misallocation.

Thus even if the perfection of the purely competitive allocation of resources is granted, a "competitive rate of output" in a particular industry may be undesirable if other industries are not also purely competitive.

c. CONCLUSION

We see that it is not so simple to prove that the monopolist gouges the public by unduly restricting the output of his product. There are all sorts of subtle points to be considered before valid conclusions can be drawn. No wonder the courts have found that their rule of reason yields no simple unequivocal answers.

Certainly monopoly sometimes has advantages as compared with competition. The efficiency of the large firm in many industries is well known. In some cases small competing firms are unthinkable. Visions of competing telephone companies and competing railroads between Dogpatch and Skunk Hollow are equally ludicrous. Even where pure competition is feasible it may be uneconomic. It has been argued that a great advantage of the giant monopoly lies in its great resources which enable it to conduct large-scale industrial research, and to institute innovations without difficulty. Competition can of course force firms to adopt new techniques, new products, and other innovations, for competition is a race in which each firm tries to outrun its rivals and never be left behind. The monopolist, faced with weaker pressures of this sort, can better afford to delay or even suppress new ideas. Moreover, the smaller firm can sometimes recoup some of the advantage the large firm has in research facilities. This has been made possible by the rise of specialized research firms whose inventions and discoveries are sold to businessmen who find it uneconomic to conduct their own research. Despite the added incentives for research provided by competition and the commercial and governmental research facilities available to the small firm, it is nevertheless maintained by some that the advantages of the monopolist—his great resources and facilities—make him in many cases the more effective instrument of innovation.

But we must not go to the other extreme and conclude that monopoly is always for the best. For several reasons it may be desirable to break up a monopoly or regulate its activities.

1. Even if it turns out that a monopoly is more efficient than a competitive industry and sells greater quantities at lower prices, better yet may still be hoped for. The feeling may be that regulated prices will induce the firm to sell more and still leave it adequate profits. This idea is at the heart of the logic behind our public utility regulation. We permit the so-called public utilities—gas, electricity, telephones, etc.—to be monopolized because of the efficiency that results. But we also carefully regulate the price and output policies of these firms because of the obvious possibilities of exploiting the public.

2. In some cases we may not be able or wish to break up an industry into many small units to the point where something like pure competition is achieved. Again there are obvious cases where this is out of the question. Yet we may prefer to break up a monopolistic firm which controls such an industry into several competing firms, an oligopoly. This may leave us the advantages of large-scale production and yet deprive the manufacturer of the luxury of "letting the public be damned." The presence of competitors may make him pay attention to the quality of his product and lead him to offer services to the public for which he would otherwise have no motivation. The services offered to the public by oligopolistic industries—road maps, ice water on trains, courtesy, reliability, and perhaps even sponsored radio and television programs—might be reduced or eliminated if the competing firms in the industries were to combine.

3. Monopoly has many other effects and attributes besides its

consequences for production and selling price. Much of the public's distaste for monopoly results from some of these monopolistic practices. Though they are not all obviously undesirable, some of them can lead, and have led, to serious abuses. We must therefore delve further into the consequences of monopoly.

2. Price Discrimination

A. THE NATURE OF THE PRACTICE

Price discrimination refers to the practice whereby a seller sells the same product to different buyers at different prices. More precisely, it means that the seller gets different *net* prices on his sales to different buyers. That is, the net price to him, after allowances for differences in transportation and selling costs, is greater on sales to some buyers than to others. This is clearly a device that a seller might use to charge "what the traffic will bear" in different markets.

For price discrimination to be feasible, at least these two conditions must be met. (1) The seller must have some degree of monopoly power. A purely competitive seller would not charge different prices to different buyers. He could not charge more than the market price for a uniform product, and he would be foolish to charge less than the market price. But a seller with a degree of monopoly power has at least some control over his price and may find it profitable to discriminate. (2) The seller must be able to create distinct markets for the product, so that it cannot easily be bought up in one and resold in another. If the seller cannot separate the markets, someone could make money by purchasing the good in the lower-price market and reselling it in the higher-price market, thereby tending to equalize prices in the two markets.

The seller may separate his markets and charge discriminatory prices on two different bases. In the first place, he may charge different net prices to different classes of buyers in a given geographic area. Thus he might charge higher prices to independent grocers and lower prices to chain stores. In the second place, he may separate his markets on a purely geographic basis, charging more in some than in others. This frequently occurs within the United States. It also occurs as sellers charge one price here and another price abroad. The price charged foreigners is often lower than that charged domestically. Once the goods are delivered abroad it is costly to get them back here for resale, because of both transportation costs and tariffs. This practice of selling at lower prices in foreign markets is often called "dumping," the implication being that excess outputs are dumped abroad and that this may be an unfair stealing of markets. In other cases, however, a seller may charge higher net prices abroad than at home. This may result when sellers compete somewhat in the domestic market but engage in collusive selling to foreigners.

To many the term discrimination implies unfairness and reprehensibility. Yet some cases of price discrimination meet with approval. A doctor who charges high prices to the rich and low prices to the poor is a price discriminator, though this is usually considered an act of mercy and justice. But by doing this the doctor may derive a considerable part of his revenues from the poor who would contribute very little to his income if he charged them the higher fees paid by the rich. This is not to question the doctor's motives, which may be commendably altruistic; it is only to point out that his behavior may also be consistent with profitable business practice.

We shall see that there are other cases in which price discrimination may lead to results that meet widespread approval.

B. DISCRIMINATION AND COMPETITION

We have noted that price discrimination cannot occur under pure competition. It is also difficult to maintain if there are several firms which have some monopoly power but compete for sales. This is because each rival firm can make profits by undercutting the discriminator in the higher-price markets, and the discriminator will find it advantageous to lower his prices there. The firms may, of course, enter into collusive agreements to establish and maintain discriminatory pricing. This may work if there are only a few firms. However, it becomes increasingly difficult with larger numbers of firms, for each will be tempted to direct a large part of its output toward the higher-price markets, perhaps by offering secret price concessions.

C. PROFIT, PRICE, AND OUTPUT UNDER DISCRIMINATION

If properly worked, price discrimination will usually yield higher profits than uniform pricing. Certainly the firm that can discriminate is better off than the firm that cannot, for it can always choose whichever of the two is the more profitable. If by accident it happens to be profitable to sell at the same price in all markets there is nothing to prevent the discriminator from doing so. But the seller who is in no position to discriminate must stick to his uniform pricing no matter which would be the more lucrative.

Discrimination is usually profitable because it enables the firm to skim the cream off each market—to charge low prices in the market where high prices would eliminate too much trade, without at the same time spoiling the other markets where higher prices are more in order.

Under discrimination sales will tend to be greater than with uniform pricing. Markets which would otherwise be impossible to reach are opened up to the seller. The poor who cannot afford to pay much and the foreigner who has access to the cheaper products of other countries are induced to buy, or to buy larger quantities. If it is felt that the monopolistic firm produces too small an output, the tendency of price discrimination to increase sales should perhaps be regarded with approval.

Nor is it always possible to object strongly to these pricing arrangements. If the firm is producing under conditions that involve economies of large scale, it is conceivable that even the highest-price market will obtain its goods at a lower price than it would in the absence of discrimination. The increase in production, if it occurs, will simply have lowered costs to such an extent that it pays to sell more cheaply everywhere, though more so to some buyers than to others.

An examination of the role of overhead is suggestive here. Suppose that the firm has capital equipment which it amortizes at $1 million a year. If the operations are to be lucrative and 1 million units of output are sold per year, the purchaser of each unit must contribute $1 toward replacement of the equipment. Suppose, however, that an additional million units can be produced at an additional cost of half a million dollars. If they can be sold (dumped) abroad at 75 cents each, this will yield three-quarters of a million in revenue, or a quarter of a million above the additional cost incurred in producing them. This quarter of a million can be devoted to amortization of the equipment, and the firm may then consider whether it is worth reducing the domestic selling price, which it can now do without danger of incurring a loss.

This argument is not conclusive, but it does suggest what can be shown more rigorously—that discrimination may make it profitable to lower selling prices to everyone. In such a case buyers in the dearer market can only object out of envy, which may, of course, be very real and quite unanswerable. In at least some cases, legitimate objections could be directed against the existence of the monopoly power that made price discrimination feasible, but perhaps not against price discrimination itself.

However, there are some uses of price discrimination that raise serious questions of public policy.

D. PRICE DISCRIMINATION TO ELIMINATE COMPETITORS

Price discrimination is sometimes used to drive competitors out of businesses or force them to sell out cheaply. Suppose that Firm A, a big chain store, operates in many different markets and has different competitors in each market. It would like to drive out these competitors by lowering its selling prices, but it cannot afford to lower its prices in all markets simultaneously and uniformly. However, it may accomplish its purpose through price discrimination. Holding its prices at their most profitable levels in other markets, it drops its prices to very low levels in only one or a few markets at a time. This may drive the competing sellers in these areas into bankruptcy or make them willing to sell out at low prices. In this way Firm A may enhance its monopoly power even though it is no more efficient than the competitors who are forced out. This use of price discrimination is generally outlawed as an unfair competitive practice.

Somewhat similar is the use of price discrimination by a supplier of one product to enable the seller of another product to harry competitors. Most famous was the use of railroad rate discrimination in the late nineteenth century to help the Standard Oil Company drive out its competitors. Under pressure from Standard, the biggest shipper of oil, the railroads charged Standard very low freight rates on its shipments, while charging extremely high rates to other oil companies. This obviously tended to give Standard an advantage and to increase its monopoly power regardless of its efficiency as compared with the efficiency of the other companies. It is easy to understand why this use of price discrimination has also been outlawed.

E. PRICE DISCRIMINATION IN THE FORM OF QUANTITY DISCOUNTS

A highly controversial form of price discrimination is the granting of very large discounts on purchases of large quantities, and of no discount or only a small discount on small quantities. For example, a manufacturer or other supplier may in this way charge small dealers a much higher price than it charges Macy's or a great chain of stores. This is sometimes defended on the ground that large orders can be filled more economically. On the other hand it is charged that this tends to discriminate against small dealers, to drive them out of business, and to create and increase monopoly power for the big dealers and chains. The law now provides that differences in prices may not exceed actual differences in costs. We shall not go into the difficult problems of determining actual cost differences.

Such price discrimination undoubtedly tends to put small dealers at a disadvantage. In some cases it may even harm consumers in the long run by increasing the monopoly power of the big outlets. But this need not be true in every case. In some cases consumers may actually benefit, and in others the great outlets may get no competitive advantage they could not achieve in the absence of price discrimination. We shall develop this point further.

We noted earlier that the manufacturers and other suppliers would not practice price discrimination if they did not have some monopoly power. If price discrimination were outlawed they might charge high prices to all dealers, and this would be reflected in high prices to consumers. But if the great outlets, with their monopsonistic power, can force the manufacturers to give them lower prices, they may pass along to consumers at least part of the price decrease. The small stores obviously will not like this. However, in some cases the great outlets could get the advantage of lower-cost goods by producing the goods themselves. In effect, A. & P. may say to a manufacturer: "I'll not give you more than this price, for I can produce it myself for no more than this." If this price offer is refused, A. & P. may simply go into the manufacturing business, continue to get low-cost supplies, and continue to undersell the smaller stores.

Here again we see that price policy can have an important effect on the behavior of the economy. If this type of price discrimination is permitted, it may tend to discourage small outlets, expand large outlets, and bring pressure on the smaller stores to form voluntary chains in order to get the advantage of bulk purchases. If such price discrimination is outlawed it may in some cases encourage small outlets and discourage the growth of large outlets. But in other cases it may only drive the great chains into the manufacturing business. Thus price policy can have an important effect on the structure of retail markets, the structure of the manufacturing industry, the volume of sales, and actual prices to consumers.

We offer no value judgment on policies in this field. Even if it were shown that the prevention of price discrimination in the form of excessive quantity discounts tended to lower efficiency and raise prices to consumers, the public might still be willing to pay the price in order to preserve independent small retailers.

3. Fair and Unfair Competition

As indicated earlier, it is our avowed national policy to prevent "unreasonable" monopolization and restraints on trade and to preserve competition. At the same time it is our avowed policy to promote only "fair" competition and to prohibit "unfair" competition. This seems sensible enough. But just how are we to define "fair" and "unfair" competitive practices? To whom is a competitive practice "unfair"? What type of result leads us to the conclusion that it is "unfair"? Unfortunately, the popular uses of the term are not very helpful; sometimes its users mean only that they are injured by the particular practice or are piqued because they didn't think of it first.

Some practices are considered unfair because they offend our sense of morality or sportsmanship. We just don't like to see people get along by lying about their product, spreading false stories about their competitors, bribing competitors' employees to divulge trade secrets, spoiling their competitors' merchandise, and so on. We all disapprove of the company that once hired people to pour glue into the ink tanks of its competitors' duplicating machines and the other company that hired workers to tamper with the cash registers sold by its competitors. The history of big business provides many examples of resort to violence and physical destruction in the process of eliminating competitors and keeping chiselers in line. Milk pasteurization plants have been bombed, chickens poisoned, and businessmen beaten by thugs. Business rivals have even hired gangs of hoodlums to "fight it out" for them. Corruption of government officials has also been undertaken for such purposes. Of course this is not meant to imply that such unsavory practices are standard business behavior. Especially in the twentieth century they have become increasingly unpopular until today they are more or less freak occurrences.

But there are other less obviously scandalous competitive practices that may be adjudged unfair even though they do not reflect any malicious intent. This is because they may harm consumers, make business success depend on factors other than efficiency, and create or enhance monopoly power.

We shall be able to give only a few illustrative examples of practices that are said by some to be unfair. Many of these are highly controversial.

4. Misrepresentation of Products

Misrepresentation includes every form of misinformation about a product—misbranding, the use of misleading names, and misleading advertising and other claims. Until recent decades our general public policy was embodied in *caveat emptor*—let the buyer beware. The more recent trend has been toward outlawing misrepresentation as an unfair competitive practice. No attempt is usually made to force the seller to "tell the whole truth and nothing but the truth." Ordinary commercial puffing is still legal; Johnny can still be told that a bowl of Jumbo Snappies each day, together with plenty of milk, sugar, and fruit, will undoubtedly make him a better hitter than either Ted Williams or Mickey Mantle. One of the big problems is to determine what types of misrepresentation are serious enough to warrant being outlawed.

The first laws were concerned primarily with fairness to competitors rather than to consumers. This is illustrated by the famous Raladam case, decided in 1931. The Raladam Company sold an obesity cure which it advertised as safe, effective, and easy to use. In fact, however, it contained a dangerous drug which could be used safely only under medical supervision. The Supreme Court agreed that the advertisements were dangerously misleading and that the public had an interest in prohibiting the use of such methods. Yet it ruled that under the existing law the practice could not be prohibited because the company had no competitor to be injured by it. The law has since been amended to outlaw misrepresentation which would be seriously injurious to consumers.

Many cases of concealment of the harmful effects of commercial products can be found in the annals of business. But even if misrepresentation does not injure the consumer's health it may lead to inefficiency in the use of resources. Misinformed, the consumer buys a product for what he thinks it to be rather than for what it actually is. He may thereby deny his support to firms that could produce better products for the price. Misinformed consumers are hardly equipped for their function of efficiently guiding the composition of output and the allocation of society's resources.

5. Tying Agreements and Exclusive Dealer Arrangements

A. TYING AGREEMENTS

Tying agreements are a highly controversial practice under which a seller will supply one product only if the buyer will also take one or more of the seller's other products. These usually are made when one of the seller's products is much desired, or perhaps even essential for some purpose, while his other products face greater competition. Suppose that a shoe machinery company has a machine that has no close competitor in the efficient manufacture of shoes, but that its other machines face heavy competition. The shoe machinery company may refuse to sell or lease its essential machine unless the buyer or lessee will also use all its other machines. The obvious effect is to reduce the sales of competitors' machines even though theirs may be better and cheaper.

This same practice may be employed by a manufacturer in selling to dealers. He may refuse to allow dealers to handle any one of his products unless they handle them all. This type of tying agreement is called *full-line forcing*.

B. Exclusive Dealer Arrangements

These are arrangements under which a dealer is permitted to handle a manufacturer's line of products only if he will agree to handle no competing products of other firms. Sometimes a manufacturer insists on both tying agreements, perhaps even full-line forcing, and exclusive dealer arrangements.

C. Some Implications

It should be clear that a manufacturer may have no malicious intent when he insists on full-line forcing and exclusive dealer arrangements. He may simply reason as follows: "I don't want any dealer to handle only my most popular product and refuse to handle those that don't sell themselves. Moreover, I want all my dealers to devote all their efforts to promoting the sale of my products. I don't want them to be indifferent whether customers buy my product or those of my competitors." This desire is quite understandable, and the practices may not be objectionable if other sellers can in fact find efficient sales outlets. But under other circumstances they can have important effects.

Suppose that a dominant manufacturer of popular electrical appliances has full-line forcing and exclusive dealer arrangements with the principal retail outlets in most areas. Other competitors, both those already in existence and those that would like to enter, may be put at a serious disadvantage. They may have no efficient means of bringing their products to the attention of consumers, and potential new entrants may be effectively prevented from entering. These arrangements may therefore serve to protect and preserve the dominant position of existing large firms, even if they are less efficient than their actual and potential competitors.

Laws and court decisions now indicate that exclusive dealing and tying arrangements are illegal if they "substantially lessen competition in any given line of commerce." But the definition of these terms and the gathering of the information necessary to make them meaningful pose very difficult problems.

6. Fair-Trade and Unfair-Practices Laws

Some of the laws we have mentioned were enacted despite the opposition of most sellers. But at least two types of laws now in effect in more than half the states—the laws to prohibit "unfair price practices" and to establish and preserve "fair trade"—reflect the untiring legislative efforts of sellers.

A. UNFAIR-PRACTICES ACTS

The purpose of these laws is to prohibit dealers from selling below cost. They are supposed to be aimed especially at the use of loss leaders to entice people into stores, and at "chiselers" who try to get a rapid turnover of sales by cutting their prices below those of other retailers in the area. These laws are defended by several arguments. One is that loss leaders are likely to be used to mislead consumers—to entice them into believing that everything in the store is a bargain when in fact everything except the loss leader may be overpriced. It is also argued that the chiseling price cutter prospers only by getting a rate of turnover that would be impossible if other dealers also lowered their prices, and that all would be ruined if they did charge prices as low as his.

On the other hand, the methods actually used to determine "costs" often leave much to be desired. For example, the California law prohibits sales below cost, and defines cost to include not only the price paid for the article but also every possible type of distribution cost incurred by the dealer. Moreover, it provides that cost surveys conducted by an industry group or trade association may be used as *prima-facie* evidence of cost. Thus the "costs" that are used do not necessarily reflect the costs of any one firm, and they may be computed at generously high levels.

If these laws do set unduly high minimum prices which are above the prices that would otherwise be charged, they may create excess retailing capacity, both by restricting sales and by enticing too many firms into the retail business.

B. FAIR-TRADE OR RESALE PRICE MAINTENANCE LAWS

These laws, which have been enacted by most of the states, make it illegal for any dealer within the state to sell a trade-marked article at a retail price below that suggested by its manufacturer. Most of the fair-trade laws make it illegal for all dealers to sell below a price agreed upon between the manufacturer and a single dealer in the state, whether or not the other firms have signed such an agreement, if they are informed of the manufacturer's wishes. This is often called vertical price control because it enables a manufacturer to fix not only the price he charges but also prices at the retail level.

These laws are defended on several grounds. (1) They prevent the use of popular-brand products as loss leaders to fool consumers into buying things that are not worth the price. (2) They protect dealers from ruinous price cutting. (3) They are necessary to prevent the prestige of the manufacturer's brand from being destroyed as it would be if the product came to be sold at cut-rate prices. (4) Only by protecting his product from being sold at cut-rate prices can the manufacturer hold his dealers and encourage them to promote the sale of his product.

On the other hand, these laws raise several questions. Should a manufacturer be given the power to determine retail prices and to have this power enforced by law? In effect, this amounts to giving the manufacturer power to set the gross profits for retailing services, for he sets both the retailers' acquisition cost and the selling price. Should the power of the manufacturer be limited to setting his own price, leaving the prices of wholesaling and retailing services to be fixed by other forces? Can the manufacturer be depended upon to set a "fair" retail price? Of course he must realize that if he sets the price too high he may lose sales. But he may deliberately give the retailer a very wide margin to induce him to "push" this product more than others.

Well-enforced resale price maintenance laws could have far-reaching effects on the structure and practices of both retailing and manufacturing. (1) If retailers' margins are large they may induce or increase excess capacity, both by decreasing sales and by enticing new firms into retailing. (2) Since they outlaw competition in the form of price reductions, they place a premium on other types of competition, such as advertising, showy establishments, delivery service, and so on.

(3) They may greatly stimulate the creation and sales of private brands. Chain stores and others who wish to sell on a narrower margin and are legally prohibited from cutting prices and margins on the fair-traded brands may manufacture their own private brands or have them manufactured by others. On their own brands they can determine their own prices. (4) Over a period of time such laws may transfer a larger part of the retail business from small to large firms. Firms that are too small to have their own private brands and are legally prohibited from cutting prices on the fair-traded items to maintain their sales may lose business to the larger firms that have their own private brands and are free to set lower prices. (5) All this tends to induce some manufacturers, both old and new, to supply private brands to even the smaller stores and to offer their own brands without fair-trading them. "Fair-trade" laws have also proved difficult to enforce, and their constitutionality has been challenged in several states.

Again, we offer no judgment as to the desirability or undesirability of the various types of unfair-practices and fair-trade laws. We cite them only to illustrate several points—the difficulty of defining "fair" and "unfair" competitive practices, the effect of price policies on the structure and functioning of industry, and the tendency of some sellers to seek government intervention when they expect this to be advantageous to them.

7. Public Policy Relative to Competition and Monopoly

In this and the preceding chapters we have not been able to do full justice to the great variety of market structures and competitive and monopolistic practices actually prevailing in the United States. However, our discussion should have suggested the extent of this variety of structures and practices and the implications for public policy.

Almost no one suggests that the government should regulate both business structures and practices in great detail. Few would want the government to prescribe exactly the number of business firms in each industry, the size of the firms, their pricing policies, and all their competitive practices. On the other hand, almost no one suggests that the government should follow a completely "hands-off" policy, permitting unrestricted mergers of business firms, collusion, and every conceivable type of unfair competitive and monopolistic practice. Almost all agree that the government should prescribe rules for the competitive game—rules that would leave a considerable amount of discretion to the players—and then enforce these rules.

What should these rules be? Which structures and practices should be within legal bounds and which out of bounds? We have seen that it is probably both impossible and undesirable to try to establish and maintain purely competitive conditions in every market. For technological reasons we would sacrifice much of the efficiency that can be gained only through large-scale firms if we tried to establish in every industry and every market, both national and local, the very large number of firms that would be required to meet the "many-seller" conditions of pure competition. Moreover, the differentiation of finished goods would have to be eliminated and goods standardized to meet the "uniform-product" condition of pure competition. Few consumers would want to sacrifice variety in their alternatives unless they were compensated by much lower prices, and perhaps not even then. In short, some degree of monopoly power is an inevitable consequence of (1) attempts to realize the greater efficiency and lower costs made possible by large-scale firms and (2) efforts to provide a variety of alternatives to consumers.

On the other hand, excessive amounts of monopoly power may be objectionable on both economic and moral grounds. Certainly there are few who would like to see all of our industry owned and operated by one gigantic corporation, and most of us would object to a single monopolistic corporation in autos, steel, electrical appliances, and so on. A very small firm may not be able to approach maximum efficiency, but firms can also be too large for maximum efficiency. After some point is reached, a further growth in the size of a firm may bring net diseconomies of scale, or any further net economies may not compensate for the added monopoly power. Moreover, most of us would object to unlimited collusion and the complete exclusion of new entrants into our industries.

We conclude that the objective of our public policy cannot reasonably be to establish purely competitive conditions in all markets, nor can it be to permit unlimited monopoly power. It must be somewhere in between. This objective has been described as that of maintaining "effective" or "workable" competition.

We shall not try to provide a blueprint for such a policy. However, it is probable that most Americans would want at least the following factors to be considered in formulating specific policies: (1) Effects on the efficiency of producing and selling, including effects on industrial research and technological change. (2) Effects on price behavior and on the distribution of real income. (3) Effects on the variety of alternatives available to buyers, sellers, suppliers, and workers. (4) Effects on the ability of people to go into business for themselves and to shift from one industry to another. (5) Effects of business practices on moral standards. (6) Effects on the concentration or diffusion of economic and political power. (7) Effects of government intervention on the freedom of people to determine their own behavior.

These different objectives need not always conflict with each other. But in many cases they will. Here, as in other instances, we face the problem of identifying the alternatives, of analyzing their probable results, of weighing them against one another, and deciding how much of one we are willing to sacrifice to get more of another.

SUGGESTED READINGS

Edwards, Corwin D., *Maintaining Competition,* McGraw-Hill, New York, 1949.
Galbraith, John K., *American Capitalism,* Houghton Mifflin, Boston, 1952.
Mund, Vernon A., *Government and Business,* Harper, New York, 1950.

QUESTIONS

1. a. What do you mean by "undue" restriction of output?
   b. Do you think most monopolists, if left alone by the law, would restrict output unduly?
   c. Would restrict it below competitive output?
   d. Give reasons.
   e. Do you think a firm should be broken up just because it is very big?
2. a. Give some examples of price discrimination which you consider desirable.
   b. Undesirable.
   c. Under what conditions do you approve and when do you disapprove of the tendency under discrimination toward increased profits?
   d. Increased outputs?
   e. Reduced prices to at least some buyers?
3. a. Give some actual examples of advertisements which you suspect are misleading.
   b. How effective do you think they are in selling the product?
   c. Give some examples of advertising which you do not consider misleading.
4. a. How are fair-trade laws likely to affect consumers?
   b. Small retailers?

   c. Large retailers?
   d. Do you believe that small retailers ought to be protected against the competition of large retailers if the latter are more efficient?
   e. Do you believe large retailers are usually more efficient?
   f. Do you believe small retailers are ever more efficient?
   g. Explain all your answers.
   h. What is a "discount house"?
5. How "ethical" do you believe businessmen to be:
   a. At worst?
   b. At best?
   c. Usually?
   d. How altruistic do you believe they ought to be in order best to serve the interests of society?
   e. In this connection discuss the quotation from Adam Smith's *Wealth of Nations* on pages 107–108.

CHAPTER 24

Central Planning

It is not unusual to hear eloquent and enthusiastic advocates of central planning expound on the simplicity and orderliness of the conditions that would prevail under a central planning authority, contrasting these with the chaotic and anarchic conditions they claim characterize planless capitalist economies. We have already seen how misleading is the latter part of this assertion. A closer examination will indicate that the task of the central planner is by no means simple. He is beset by difficult and serious problems. These can to some extent be overcome by skill and compromise, so as to permit the planned economy to function, but they cannot be waved aside as easy and trivial.

To bring out boldly the nature of these problems we shall consider first the extreme case of a completely centralized plan. Under this arrangement all economic decisions are made by one central planning board, and absolutely no discretion as to resource allocation or output composition is left to anyone else.

1. The Composition of Output

A. GOALS

The board must first decide on its preferences and goals. It must somehow decide which of the achievable combinations of output it considers most desirable. Its choice may be much influenced by the whims of the dictating clique, though its discretion is limited by military necessity and the need to keep the people in line.

Even if the dictator desires to further only his personal aims, the choice of goals is no simple matter. It inevitably involves a great amount of work in view of the tremendous number of output decisions that must be made. When it is realized that the number of items handled by General Motors Corporation alone runs into the hundreds of thousands and that the United States Navy handles several million distinct items, both the enormous magnitude of the information required for full planning and the laboriousness of decision-making begin to be apparent. For each of the possible items, cost information must be gathered and considered, and output goals selected accordingly.

Moreover, this must all be done quickly, for production conditions may change rapidly and decisions must not be obsolete by the time they are reached. We shall have more to say about these points presently.

B. The Interdependence of Output Decisions

Though we have already found a tremendous amount of work for the planning board, we have only just begun. We have, in effect, permitted the board to examine each industry separately and to arrive at one output goal for each product without considering its relations to the goals set for other lines other than making sure that all the targets together do not require more than the available resources.

In practice, decisions cannot be made in this way. We noted in an earlier chapter that the outputs of the different industries are mutually interdependent, and that a decision on one can be made only in relation to decisions on the others. When this is brought into the picture, the complications multiply enormously. Though this task of coordinating production decisions and production processes is handled automatically by the market, it must constitute a major problem for the central planner.

C. Raw-Material and Finished-Goods Producers

To a large extent this mutual interdependence arises because each industry is dependent on others for its raw materials. Production would soon break down if the outputs of the raw-material producers were not closely geared to the needs of the industries they supply. But the relation of raw materials to finished products is not the entire problem. If it were, decisions could be reached in successive stages, with the outputs of the industries producing finished products decided first, then the outputs of those supplying them with raw materials, and so on down the line to the initial raw-material extractors.

D. MUTUAL INTERDEPENDENCE

In reality there is no such simple chain of production from industry to industry, with one related to the other only as a supplier or buyer of some one raw material. An industry which supplies another with some things is itself quite likely to need the products of the other in its own operations. The lumber industry uses all sorts of steel in its equipment, ranging all the way from saws to railroad cars and buildings. The steel industry in turn may need lumber in its buildings and it certainly needs timber to shore up the mine shafts necessary in obtaining the coal and iron ore required for steel production. Cloth is used in automobiles, and products of the auto industry are used to transport cloth. The reader can multiply such examples indefinitely.

E. THE NEED FOR SIMULTANEOUS SOLUTION

Thus the planning board cannot set its target for the steel industry before it has laid its plans for lumber production, nor can it consider lumber output first. This is the basic problem in any situation involving mutual interdependence. As we remarked before when we met a similar problem, everything should really be taken up first. To do this we must turn to what the mathematician calls simultaneous solution. Earlier, when considering mutual interdependence in determining the level of national income, we were forced to resort to graphic analysis. Here again we shall use graphs in a fairly simple example in which only two industries are involved. However, we shall find that in dealing with larger numbers of industries graphs will not help us, and that when the number of industries becomes quite large we are in serious trouble.

2. Interdependence in Two Industries: Graphic Analysis

In this section we shall assume that there are only two industries whose outputs are interdependent. For convenience, we shall call these industries coal and steel.

A. CONSUMER TARGETS

We must distinguish between the total output of an industry and the part of the output that will be left for consumption or for whatever other final purposes, such as military preparation, the planning board may have. This is the part of the industry's output that remains after deducting the quantity of its product which is employed as ingredients elsewhere. For convenience, we call this hoped-for residue the consumer target, indicating that it is the amount expected to be available for consumption by the public or the state.

For the moment we ignore the limitations imposed on the planners by the scarcity of resources. We also assume that consumer targets have somehow been set for the two industries. Let us see what this implies for their outputs.

B. GRAPHIC REPRESENTATION

In Fig. 20 we measure the output of the coal industry along the horizontal axis, and the output of the steel industry along the vertical

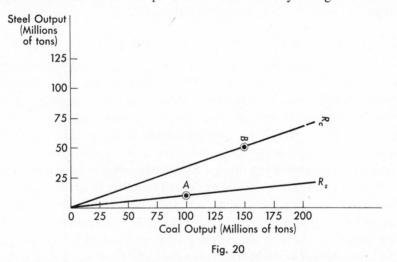

Fig. 20

axis. Point A, for example, represents an output of 100 units of coal and 10 units of steel. (Throughout this analysis each unit will represent 1 million tons.) The technological information we require is given by the two lines OR_s and OR_c. The first of these lines indicates the quantity of steel required by the coal industry. For example, it shows that with coal output at 100 million tons the coal industry will consume 10 million tons of steel. Similarly, the corresponding steel requirement for any other rate of coal output can be obtained from the graph.

To find the corresponding steel requirements by the coal industry we turn the graph on its side, this time reading along the coal requirement line, OR_c. From this we learn, for example, that 50 units of steel require for their production 150 units of coal (point B), and so on. We see that it takes some 3 tons of coal to produce 1 ton of coal; this is a rough approximation of the proportion in practice.

c. The Targets in the Graph

Suppose now that a consumer target for the steel industry is set at 33 million tons. The total steel output must then be 33 units greater than the amount required by the coal industry. For example, if coal output is to be 100 units, OR_s in Fig. 21 shows that the steel require-

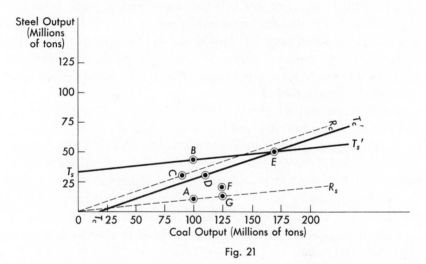

Fig. 21

ment of the coal industry will be 10 units, as given by point A. To meet the consumer target of 33 units, total steel output must then be 43 units (point B). Similarly, for every other coal output the steel output will have to be 33 units greater than the amount given by line OR_s—that is, 33 units greater than the amount needed for coal production. The total required steel output corresponding to every level of coal production will thus be given by a line T_sT_s', which everywhere lies 33 units above OR_s. T_sT_s' thus represents the total steel output required to meet both the needs of coal producers and the consumer target of 33 units. If the consumer target were greater than this, the line would lie even higher above OR_s.

Suppose also that the consumer coal target is set at 20 units. This, too, will clearly result in a shifting of the coal requirement line. However, since we have to hold the diagram on its side to show coal requirements, *in this position* the coal requirements line must be shifted 20 units upward to take care of the consumer target. The reader can check this for himself by noting that with steel output at 30 units the steel industry will require 90 coal (point C), and that to meet the consumer target of 20, total output will therefore have to be 110 (point D).

D. THE OUTPUT REQUIREMENTS OF THE PLAN

If the steel needs of the coal industry and the consumer steel target are both to be met, the steel-coal output must be given by some point along the steel target line T_sT_s'. If the output were at some point like F, which lies below that line, we would have a coal output of 125 units and a steel output of only 20. This would not be enough to meet the coal industry's 12.5 steel requirement (point G) and the consumer steel target of 33. Similarly, any point above line T_sT_s' would represent a wasteful overproduction of steel.

For the same reasons, production of exactly the amount of coal required by the steel industry and the consumer coal target together requires a coal-steel output combination that lies somewhere on the coal target line T_cT_c'. Fulfillment of both the steel and coal consumer targets therefore requires a coal-steel output combination represented by a point that lies on both of the target lines. There is only one such point, point E. This shows that to supply consumers and the state with 33 units of steel and 20 of coal, there must be produced 50 units of steel and 170 of coal.

E. COMMENTS

Observe that the required outputs are considerably greater than the amounts used by consumers. This is a common phenomenon in industry. Most of the output of many items is used "behind the scenes" and is never seen by the consumer even though its ultimate purpose is to serve him. This is clearly so for steel and coal. Corn production is another good example, some 90 percent of this crop being used as animal feed.

Note also how much greater is the required coal output, though the consumer coal target is much smaller than the steel target. This is because so much coal is needed in the manufacture of steel.

It should also be observed that an increase in the target for one of these items, taken by itself, will result in a greater increase in its output requirement of the other. For example, an increase in steel output will require more coal, which in turn will call for more steel to be used in mining equipment.

The most important thing to be observed, however, is the complexity of the process we had to go through to decide on a steel and coal output. This is because the two outputs are mutually interdependent. It is true that greater familiarity with the manipulations involved will make this two-industry case very simple, but it is still far more complicated than the two simple isolated decisions that would suffice if the industries' outputs were unconnected. Moreover, the difficulties caused by mutual interdependence increase phenomenally as the number of industries under consideration rises. We shall soon discuss this in more detail.

3. Resource Limitations and the Two-Industry Case

Up to this point our calculations have completely ignored the problem of resource limitations. These can readily be taken into account in our graphic analysis.

With output capacity limited, the planning board is no longer at liberty to pick any consumer target that suits its fancy. Every increase in the quantity of one good available to consumers must be at the expense of another. Let us see how the planning board might try to cope with the problem.

A. THE OUTPUT POSSIBILITIES

To show the sort of computations involved we use a highly simplified example. Suppose there is full employment and that labor time is the only limited resource that creates immediate difficulties. Assume that one man-hour of labor can produce four tons of coal or two tons of steel, and that during the period for which the plan is being formulated there are available 50 million man-hours for coal and steel production. The possible output combinations of these products are now easily computed. (The millions will be omitted in the following discussion.)

It is possible to allocate 25 labor-hours to steel and 25 to coal, thereby producing 50 steel and 100 coal. Alternatively, 30 labor may be allocated to steel and 20 to coal, thereby permitting the production of 60 steel and 80 coal, and so on. These figures represent the total outputs of the products. They do not indicate how much coal will be left over for consumption after deducting the amount used up in steel production, or the amount of steel that will remain for consumers. We

shall see, however, that some of the output combinations permitted by
the available supply of labor may not really be producible at all, because they do not involve enough coal production to meet the coal
needs of the steel industry, or vice versa.

In practice, of course, the calculation of the outputs permitted by
the available resources will be considerably more complicated, to say
the least. As in all highly simplified illustrations we are attempting to
indicate the nature but not the magnitude of the problems facing the
planners.

B. GRAPHIC REPRESENTATION

Once we have completed the calculations just discussed, we can
show on a graph the various outputs the planning board's resources
will permit. These are indicated in Fig. 22 by the *production possibility
line PP'*. Any point in the shaded area above and to the right of this

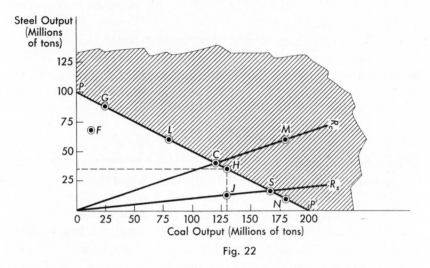

Fig. 22

line represents a steel-coal output combination beyond the economy's
ability to produce. Any point in the unshaded area below and to the
left of this line represents outputs which do not fully employ the scarce
labor resources, because they represent the production of less coal and
less steel than do points on *PP'*. (Compare point *F* and point *G* above
and to the right of *F*.) The planning board, not being able to achieve
outputs in the shaded area, and not wanting outputs in the unshaded
area, will plan to produce a steel-coal output combination represented
by a point on *PP'*.

C. THE POSSIBILITY LINE AND CONSUMER TARGETS

As before, let the steel requirements of the coal industry be given by OR_s, and the coal requirements of the steel industry by line OR_c. Let these lines cross PP' at points S and C respectively. We can now see what will be left over to meet consumption targets if the board decides to produce an output combination represented by any point, say H, on segment CS of PP'. The output combination given by H represents 130 of coal and 35 of steel. But the steel requirement line OR_s tells us that with a coal output of 130, the coal industry will use up 13 steel (point J), so that of the 35 steel produced, 22 will remain for consumption. Similarly, with the steel industry producing 35, line OR_c tells us that it will require 105 coal, leaving 25 coal for consumption. We see that point H represents an output combination that will leave 25 coal and 22 steel available for consumption.

D. THE POSSIBLE TARGETS

We can now see why we picked a point like H lying between C and S on the production possibility line PP'. Any point like L that lies above C on PP' represents an output combination which cannot really be produced. For point L represents an output of 60 units of steel and 80 of coal, and OR_c tells us that at this steel output 180 coal would be required by the steel industry alone (point M). That is, L represents an output combination for which the coal requirement of the steel industry exceeds the total coal output. Similarly, any point such as N which lies below S on PP' represents an unattainable output combination because total steel output falls short of the steel requirements of the coal industry alone.

Thus, all the output combinations of interest to the planning board will be represented by points which, like H, lie on segment CS of the production possibility line PP'. We have just seen how to compute the amounts that are left over for consumption out of each output combination. The planning board can choose among these alternative consumption targets.

Again, let us point out that this illustration is greatly oversimplified and is designed only to indicate the nature of some of the problems the planner has to solve.

4. The Three-Industry Case: An Algebraic Illustration

The interdependence of industries is much more complicated than a two-industry illustration can ever indicate. Each industry receives its raw materials and equipment from a large number of other industries; hence the mutual interdependence of output plans, which is such a great problem for the planner, must involve many more than two industries.

A. THE NEED FOR ALGEBRAIC ANALYSIS

Graphic analysis is no longer of any use when we include more than two industries. A two-dimensional graph can conveniently represent the output of only one industry on the horizontal axis and another on the vertical axis, leaving no room to record the output of any other industry. We must therefore turn to the mathematician for assistance. He provides us with the method of simultaneous solution of a system of equations. This takes us considerably further than the graphic approach, though it certainly does not provide a full solution of the planners' computational problems. To indicate as simply as possible the nature of this approach we shall use a three-industry illustration.

B. THE INPUT-OUTPUT MATRIX

Let us suppose that the economy consists of three industries—steel, coal, and agriculture. We can represent the interrelationships among our industries with the aid of Table 39, which is drawn up on the same principle as a mileage chart on a road map.

TABLE 39. Production Coefficients for Coal, Steel, and Agriculture

| | | Outputs | | |
		Steel (tons)	Coal (tons)	Agriculture (bu.)
Inputs	Steel	0.0	0.1	0.3
	Coal	3.0	0.0	0.2
	Agriculture	0.05	0.1	0.0

For example, the last column tells us that three-tenths of a ton of steel and two-tenths of a ton of coal are used in producing each bushel of agricultural produce. This table is called an *input-output matrix*.

C. THE RELEVANT RELATIONSHIPS

Suppose now that this simple economy is centrally planned. In making its plans the central planning agency has to consider the interrelationships of industries. It must somehow get hold of the data to fill in the input-output matrix. It must also set its consumption targets. Let us say that it somehow picks 41 million tons of steel, 2 million tons of coal, and 53 million bushels of agricultural products. Its planning must consider the following relationships. Let S, C, and A represent the total outputs of steel, coal, and agricultural products respectively, and let C_s, C_c, and C_a represent the amounts of each of these products available for consumption. Then we have

$$C_s = S - 0.1C - 0.3A$$

That is, the amount of steel left over for consumption must be the output of steel less the amount of steel used up in the production of other products. For example, the input-output matrix tells us that 0.1 of a ton of steel must be used in every ton of coal produced. Since C tons of coal will be produced, the coal industry will require exactly $0.1C$ tons of steel, etc. Similarly, we have the following two equations relating to the quantities of coal and agricultural products available for consumption:

$$C_c = C - 3.0S - 0.2A$$
$$C_a = A - 0.05S - 0.1C$$

Since the economy was to have for consumption purposes 41 million tons of steel, 2 million tons of coal, and 53 million bushels of agricultural products, we have $C_s = 41$, $C_c = 2$, $C_a = 53$. Our three equations therefore become

(1) $41 = S - 0.1C - 0.3A$
(2) $2 = C - 3S - 0.2A$
(3) $53 = A - 0.05S - 0.1C$

It is suggested that the reader stop at this point and make a guess as to the total quantities of steel, coal, and agricultural products that will have to be produced in order to secure the quantities desired for consumption. This may help to indicate the difficulties involved in an intuitive or guesswork approach to central planning.

D. ONE METHOD OF COMPUTATION

Multiply both the first and third equations by 10 so as to make the coefficient of C equal in all three equations. This gives us the two equations:

(4) $410 = 10S - C - 3A$
(5) $530 = 10A - 0.5S - C$

Adding the second equation to each of these in turn (to get rid of the C) gives

(6) $412 = 7S - 3.2A$

(7) $532 = 9.8A - 3.5S$

Now multiply this last equation by 2 and add it to equation (6) to get rid of the S; this gives

$$1476 = 16.4A, \text{ or } A = 90$$

To find S we substitute the value of A in equation (6), which gives

$$412 = 7S - (3.2)(90) = 7S - 288, \text{ or } S = 100$$

Finally from the second equation and these results we obtain

$$2 = C - 300 - 18, \text{ or } C = 320$$

We find that to have 41 million tons of steel, 2 million tons of coal, and 53 million bushels of agricultural produce for consumption purposes this simple economy must produce 100 million tons of steel, 320 million tons of coal, and 90 million bushels of agricultural produce. Of course the plan will work out only if these quantities are correctly divided up among the various industries using them. Table 40 shows

TABLE 40. Raw Material Requirements of Coal, Steel, and Agriculture
(In millions)

| | | Industry Using the Raw Material | | |
		Steel	Coal	Agriculture
Raw material	Steel (tons)	0	32	27
	Coal (tons)	300	0	18
	Agriculture (bushels)	5	32	0

the distribution of outputs that would make the plan effective. For example, the last column shows that agriculture would require 27 million tons of steel and 18 million tons of coal to carry out the plan.

We shall not go into the additional complications resulting from resource limitations, though the analysis can easily be extended to such a case. We have already indicated the nature of the computations, which was our primary object.

5. Problems of Computation

The general approach to the problem of planning indicated in the preceding two sections is associated with the work of Professor Leontief of Harvard. Much of this analysis was developed to meet the needs of our armed services. Professor Leontief and others have extended the analysis to take into account considerably more than three industries. However, up to the present, computations have usually been confined to systems involving less than 200 industries. Even the algebraic analysis bogs down rapidly as the number of industries under consideration increases.

A. THE NUMBER OF ITEMS OF INFORMATION REQUIRED BY THE PLANNER

Even with the most oversimplified assumptions, the number of items of information required increases as the square of the number of industries. Suppose we are dealing with ten industries. For each industry we need to know something about its relation to every other industry. Thus for every industry we require approximately 10 items of information—the steel needs of the coal industry, the steel needs of the lumber industry, the steel needs of agriculture, and so on. We need similar items of information for each of the other industries. Thus we need some 10 times 10, or 100 items of information on which to base our computations. Similarly, if we are dealing with 100 industries, we need some 10,000 items of information. A 1000-industry analysis would require about 1 million items of information, and a 100,000 industry analysis would require something in the neighborhood of 10 million items of information. When we compare this with our earlier observation that the U.S. Navy stocks several million distinct items, it is clear that the problem of collecting information for a complete analysis of an entire economy would be truly staggering.

B. THE NUMBER OF COMPUTATIONS

This is not yet the worst of the trouble. Once the planner obtains his information he must begin to calculate with it. In our algebraic example we saw that even in a three-industry case a fairly large number of distinct operations of addition, subtraction, multiplication, and division had to be carried out. It happens that the total number of these operations increases, even with the most efficient mathematical methods, much more rapidly than the number of items of information. In fact, the mathematician tells us that the number of distinct arithmetic operations increases something like the cube of the number of industries. This means that if a 10-industry model would require about 1000 arithmetic operations, a 100-industry analysis would necessitate something like 1 million steps and a 1000-industry computation would require about 1 billion steps.

c. Computing Machines

Of course it would be ridiculous to attempt this sort of thing by conventional arithmetic methods. An army of 10,000 clerks, doing one operation a minute, would take about 10 months of 40-hour weeks to complete 1 billion arithmetical operations. The expense would be tremendous and the results would probably become obsolete before they were available.

Much of this sort of computation is being done with electronic calculators, the giant "electronic brains" which have recently been and are continuing to be developed. They reduce greatly the time and cost of the operations. Yet even with their aid, only limited progress has been made so far. Of course it is difficult to say what computational possibilities the future holds in store.

d. Obtaining the Information

The detailed information required for the planners' calculations is by no means easily obtained. At present the main source in the United States is the Census of Manufactures. Other statistical sources are for the most part not sufficiently detailed, or not comprehensive enough because they deal with only small parts of the economy.

The cost of the census—including both the gathering of the information and the tabulation of the results without which it would represent a hopeless, unusable hotchpotch of figures—is tremendous. It takes two to five years after the material is collected to organize and tabulate the data and make all of them available for detailed use.

e. The Use of Broad Industrial Categories

Even the limited progress we have made in our analysis has been achieved at the expense of great oversimplification. We shall mention only two of the most important oversimplifications.

Our major one has been to use only a small number of products. The analysis deals with only broad categories, such as agriculture, iron and steel, aviation, textiles, and so on. Such broad categories can be of only limited use to a central planning board. It cannot decide merely that it wants so many airplanes or so many other motor vehicles. It must specify the precise type, and the number of each type desired. The auto industry produces trucks of various weights, passenger cars, and other items. Without guidance as to how to divide output among these specific items, plans will miscarry. A target for agriculture as a whole, or even for meat products as a whole, is equally meaningless. What is required is a goal for each variety of grain, each grade and variety of beef, and so on. Still more urgent is similar detailed planning for the production of each type of part for other products. Even if completely attained, an overall target for ball bearings may be of no use if the bearings are not of the sizes that happen to be needed. This is why a staggering number of items and decisions must face the central planner under a completely centralized system.

F. LINEARITY

Another of our important oversimplifications is the assumptions that the demand by one industry for the product of another can be represented by a straight line, like the ones in our figures. Let us see just what this means, and why it is assumed. We assumed that 3 tons of coal are used in the manufacture of 1 ton of steel. Thus, it takes 150 coal for 50 steel, 300 coal for 100 steel, and so on. This is precisely why OR_c in Figs. 20–22 is a straight line. What is assumed is that there is a fixed ratio between an industry's output and its need for any specified raw material. At least as an approximation, this is plausible for the steel industry's use of coal and of pig iron, and for the auto industry's use of steel. It takes about 10 times as much pig iron to produce 10 tons of steel as to produce 1 ton, and it takes 100 times as much to produce 100 tons. This is because pig iron is used directly as an ingredient of the steel.

In the coal industry's demand for steel we may expect a very different sort of relationship. Steel is used in mining machinery. As coal output increases, so does the wear and tear on this equipment, and this increases the demand for steel. But a doubling of coal output will not necessarily double the coal industry's demand for steel. The wear and tear on machines may more than double or less than double. Within certain ranges the wear and tear may be of no interest to the mining industry if obsolescence or simple aging is making the machines useless faster than operating them wears them out. If increased use will wear out a machine in ten years rather than twenty, but the machine would in any case become obsolete and be replaced by a more up-to-date model within five years, the increased wear may have no effect on the demand for steel.

Moreover, when mining is on a larger rather than a smaller scale, an entirely different type of machinery may be employed. The demand for steel may have no simple relation to the two levels of output. With 100 million tons of coal being produced, 10 million of steel may be required—one-tenth of a ton of steel per ton of coal. With coal output at 500 million the demand for steel may rise only to 25 million—only one-twentieth of a ton of steel per ton of coal. It is therefore quite possible that there will be economies, or diseconomies, of larger-scale production in one industry's demand for the product of another. We see then that we should not have drawn OR_s, the steel requirements line of the coal industry, as a straight line as we did in Figs. 20–22. Rather, it should have been curved, like the line OR_s in Fig. 23. There

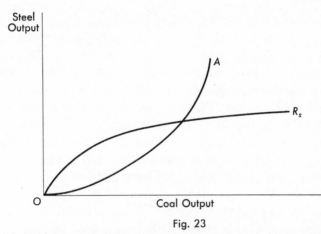

Fig. 23

we see that a doubling of the coal industry's output increases its demand for steel but does not quite double it. At the other extreme, it is also possible that in some cases the need for an input will grow faster than the industry's output, as is illustrated by line OA in Fig. 23. While the assumption of a fixed ratio between the output of an industry and its demand for raw materials is sometimes justified, it is sometimes quite false. Any planning which does not take account of this fact can be seriously misleading.

Why, then, is this somewhat unrealistic and oversimplified assumption adopted in the analysis? The answer is that it greatly decreases both the amount of information needed and the difficulty of the computational problem. The point is illustrated by going back to our example involving the steel industry's demand for coal. All the information we needed to collect and use in the subsequent arithmetic was one number—3—which summarized the information that the steel industry's demand for coal will always be three times its own output. If the coal industry always used 1 ton of steel in producing every 10 tons of coal, the information could again be summed up in a single figure, 1/10. Moreover, this figure could be found rather easily. If we knew that in a given period the coal industry used 100 million tons of steel to produce 1 billion tons of coal, we would have all the information required. Simple division then would yield the figure of 1/10 ton of steel for every ton of coal.

However, if the amount of steel used per ton of coal differs at different rates of coal output, no single figure will suffice for the planner. He will have to have a figure for the steel needs of the coal industry for every rate of coal output. From the observation that when the coal industry produces 100 million tons per period it needs 10 million tons of steel, there is no way of inferring how much steel the coal industry will require when its output is 500. This sort of information can be determined (or rather estimated) only by engineers after exceedingly expensive and elaborate calculations. Moreover, even if this information were available to the planner, his difficulties of calculation would be greatly increased because of having to deal with an array of figures where one sufficed before.

Note that the immense quantity of information needed and the huge number of computational steps are features of the planning operation even when the oversimplified assumption of strict proportionality between an industry's output and its use of raw materials is adhered to. We cannot describe here just how much more difficult the job would become if this simplifying assumption were dropped. We need only say that at present economists would be able to cope with only the simplest illustrative examples.

The large number of items in the economy and the nonproportionality between inputs and outputs are only two of the problems that our analysis has evaded by oversimplification. These techniques are not yet of much use to the planner. We have described them primarily to illustrate the complexity of the interrelationships within the economy and the nature of the problems faced by the planner under a completely centralized system of planning and control.

6. Supervision of the Individual Producing Units

A. THE ORGANIZATION AND DIRECTION OF PRODUCTION

Up to this point we have dealt only with the central planner's problems of setting output goals—his problems of determining what combinations of final output are feasible, of choosing among the many possible combinations of output and of fixing consumer targets, and of determining the types and proportions of output in the form of raw materials and equipment that must be produced in order to attain the selected consumer targets.

After having selected his goals, the planner still faces the problem of organizing and directing production to attain these goals. He must organize plants or other productive units and determine their location, size, technology, and the combination of productive factors they will use. In short, he must allocate resources not only to industries but also to individual plants and then direct their functioning. If the individual plants do not function properly the overall plans may not be fulfilled, scarce resources may be wasted, and the entire economy may get into serious difficulties.

B. CRITERIA OF EFFICIENCY

One of the great problems of the central planner in the absence of a suitable price system is the difficulty of determining whether each plant is operating efficiently. This difficulty is essentially an accounting problem. Under a price system, efficiency can be gauged in terms of costs and profits. At least as a first approximation, the firm that produces a given output at a lower money cost than another firm's is judged the more efficient of the two, and that's all there is to it.

But where there are no prices there can be no money figure for costs. Social costs are incurred just as in a money economy, for society's scarce resources are used up in the process of production. That is precisely why it is desirable to have some check on the firms' operating efficiency. This is a far more difficult task without prices and money cost calculations. It is true that records of the amounts of the different resources may be kept and examined, but the work is much more complicated and judgments much more difficult. There is always the old apple-banana problem—is it more efficient to use so much more labor and so much less steel, or vice versa? The price system solves the problem by saying that a more expensive item should be used more sparingly. For example, the price system indicates that it is better to save $50 worth of steel (whatever amount of steel that may happen to represent at current prices) than $45 worth of labor. Thus the price system implicitly solves the problem and makes unnecessary a new decision every time the efficiency of a plant is being examined.

The Soviet Union has tried to cope with this difficulty by using a pseudo price system—a system of prices which are determined arbitrarily rather than in a free market but which permit calculations of costs and profits.

c. THE MOTIVATION FOR EFFICIENCY

Checking on the efficiency of operations becomes all the more important in a planned economy because the abandonment of the price system may also destroy the profit motive. As we have seen, the profit motive is a powerful force making for industrial efficiency.

We shall not enter into the painful controversy relating to the statement "You can't change human nature." It is conceivable that over a long period other motives may replace the desire for profits and promote hard work and efficiency. National pride, pride in craftsmanship, hope of honorary recognition, and social conscience have all been urged as possibilities and they all play some role now. But for the calculable future these seem unlikely to suffice. As evidence we need merely cite the salary rewards for efficiency and special skills, and the resulting inequalities of income that have appeared in Russia. To a large extent these rewards are designed to keep up productivity. It is alleged that income inequality in Russia is now greater than in largely capitalist Britain.

7. The Allocation of Resources Among Individual Units

The central planner has another important problem relating to the individual productive units. In the process of deciding the output of some particular item he must parcel out the work among the various plants that can produce the item. This is essentially an allocation problem. For example, if the planner has at his disposal a given number of mining machines, he must allocate them among the different mines in the way that he believes will do the most good—that is to say, where they can be used most effectively. This is again a problem that is handled automatically by the market, by the competitive bidding of firms for the productive resources, and by the owners of the factors of production in their search for higher incomes and better working conditions. Workers, machines, and raw materials will tend to go to the plant which can afford to pay the most, and in general it will be the plant which needs them most, can use them most effectively, and can afford to offer them the greatest reward.

a. A SIMPLE-MINDED APPROACH

In our mining example, one approach to the problem might be for the planner to pick out the mine which by some criterion is considered most efficient and to use all the machinery there. It does not take much thought to see that this is not a satisfactory solution. The mine selected might have a limited capacity, so that if more than one-tenth the machines were sent there they might stand idle.

Moreover, efficiency in a given plant or mine will vary greatly with circumstances. In particular, it will vary with output. There may be one mine whose coal is near the surface and so can be worked with little effort. However, it may occupy a very small area and permit efficient operation on only a very small scale. Another mine may be much larger and quite efficient when operated on a scale large enough to permit the use of conveyors and other instruments of mass production. But when used for the production of only a little coal it may be quite inefficient because coal will have to be carried over long distances, miners will take a long time to cover the great distance to the pit face, and so on. The very spaciousness that permits the introduction of machinery and makes the mine efficient when output is great can be a significant disadvantage for small-scale operations. Any simple criterion of relative efficiency will not give the planner enough information for allocating the machines among the different mines. This is generally true also of the allocation of resources among the different plants in an industry.

B. THE PRINCIPLE OF NO WASTED OPPORTUNITIES AGAIN

Here we can employ the principle of no wasted opportunities which we used in earlier chapters.[1] The basic idea is simple. An optimal use of mining machinery will leave unused no possibility of increasing output by shifting machinery from one mine to another.

We may now see how the machines should be allocated between the two mines. Suppose there are 10 machines altogether, and we know in every circumstance just how much the addition of a single machine will increase the production in each mine. It is convenient to introduce a bit of terminology. We call the increase in output in mine A which results from the introduction of another machine *the marginal product of machines in mine A*.

Suppose we know the marginal product of machines in mine A and in mine B under every relevant circumstance. Let us assume to begin with that there are 2 machines in mine A. There must then be 8 machines in B, since there are 10 machines to be divided between the two mines. Assume that the marginal product of a machine in A is 5000, and of a machine in B 3000. Such an allocation would violate our

---

[1] See above, pp. 383–386.

principle of no wasted opportunities, for there would be the opportunity to add 2000 units to the total production of the two mines simply by transferring one machine from mine B to mine A.

c. Digression: Diminishing Returns

As more and more machines go to A, the acquisition of still more machines will eventually begin to add less to production. There will be less available coal face (working surface) for each of them to work on, the conveyors may become overloaded, and so on. Eventually the limits of capacity may be reached, and any further introduction of machines would be a pure waste, or even a positive nuisance. Thus, the first machine added may indeed increase A's output by 5000, and so may the second. But we may expect that soon, say with the third additional machine, output will go up only another 4500. With a fourth machine output will still be driven up, but it will rise only 3700, and so on.

This is the law of diminishing physical returns, relatively old in economic literature, which can be stated as follows: If we keep importing more and more of a resource into a plant some of whose other resources are fixed in size, after a while further additions of this resource will begin to add successively less and less to the output of the plant. That is, the marginal product of the resource will begin to fall. What we mean here by the plant's resources being fixed in size is illustrated by the availability of coal in a given seam. However much effort and equipment we put into a mine, we cannot increase the quantity of coal that happens to be there. This is a particularly strong example. More ordinarily what will be fixed, at least for a time, is the size of the building, or the quantity of land available to a farmer, or the amount of time and effort the manager or owner can devote to supervision.

The law of diminishing returns is really quite plausible, and well in accord with observation. It asserts essentially that if two or more ingredients are required in the manufacture of some item, and only one of these is doubled without the other being increased, we cannot really expect the output to double. It is because of the operation of this law that it does not pay to send all the machines to "the most efficient" mine.

d. The Optimum Allocation of Machines Among Mines

To return to our problem, we saw that with the marginal product of machines at 5000 in mine A and at 3000 in B, it pays to move machines from B to A. But as we shift more machines in this way they will become more plentiful in A and scarcer in B. By the law of diminishing returns the marginal product in A will start to fall, say from 5000 to 4500 to 3700, and so on. Meanwhile their marginal product in mine B (the loss in output resulting from the loss of still another machine) will rise for the same reason. Thus the marginal product of machines in the two mines will be closer and closer. Suppose that when there are 7 machines in mine A and 3 machines left in B their marginal products are approximately equal. No further shift of machines from mine to mine will increase output.

Thus the principle of no wasted opportunities has provided the planning board with a criterion for the allocation of its resources among plants. The principle is simply enunciated; it states that resources should be allocated in such a way as to make their marginal products in different plants as nearly equal as possible. So long as the marginal product of resources is materially greater in one plant than another it will pay to shift resources to the former from the latter. It would appear that to put this dictum into practice the planning board would merely have to obtain technical data on marginal products and make its decisions accordingly.

E. Problems in the Practical Application of the Rule

This is easier said than done. Marginal productivity data are difficult and costly to obtain. It is not even easy to define precisely what we mean by a marginal product.

Suppose an additional machine in mine A can increase next month's output by 5000 tons. But in mine B the machine can increase output by 5700 tons, but it needs a foundation because the ground is soft; hence more resources must be used to install the machine there. Moreover, because of the time needed to set it up, the machine cannot begin to increase output until the month after next. This involves a double problem: (1) How much of the output added in B can be attributed to the machine, and how much to the foundation? What is the marginal product of each? We need to know this to compare the value added by a machine in B with the marginal gain in mine A which can be attributed entirely to the machine. (2) How can we compare the value of 5000 tons of coal next month with that of 5700 tons of coal two months from now? There is no simple answer. There may be a bird-in-hand preference for coal next month, but how much weight shall we give it? Our judgment may even depend on the season. If next month is July, it may be better to wait another month to get the coal and save the extra cost of storing it till winter. But if next month is February, a ton of coal that month may be worth much more than coal the month after. It is therefore no simple matter to decide which mine should receive the machine, and our rule concerning equality between marginal products becomes a somewhat vague and equivocal guide.

This sort of problem is likely to arise in many if not most practical situations because no type of equipment can be added to production without suitable adjustments in the use of other productive factors. Another machine needs another operator and more raw materials before it can add to production, and we cannot be sure how much of the product to attribute to the machine. A machine will last longer in some places than in others and the problem of comparing outputs at different dates arises again. Very often, then, the marginal product rule will not be as helpful as might be hoped.

8. Practical Planning

From the foregoing it is easy to see that rigorous detailed planning calculations are, for the present at least, quite impractical.

A. THE IMPORTANCE OF THE COSTS

The costs of information and the tremendous job of computation mean that rigorous planning can involve an inefficient allocation of resources, precisely because too many resources are used up in the process of trying to figure out the most efficient allocation. The problem is a serious one. Guess work and groping are often the most intelligent course for the planner (or the businessman) because the high costs of information and calculation outweigh the gains.

B. THE UNDEVELOPED STATE OF THE ANALYSIS

The costs of planning are only part of the problem. As we have seen, much of the planning analysis is only partly developed, and at the present stage cannot be relied on for unequivocal and satisfactory decisions. Oversimplifications and vague concepts may be useful for pure analysis, but in practice they may mean that the planning board is offered little guidance, or perhaps is even misled.

C. POSSIBLE MAGNIFICATION OF SMALL ERRORS

The complicated processes of computation may greatly magnify small errors in the data, mild oversimplifications, and errors of computation. The way this can happen is suggested by our coal-steel example.

Any error in our steel output figure will result in an error in the coal requirements figure. This mistake would then be transmitted in our estimated steel demand by the coal industry, and in the process might make our steel figure even more erroneous. We noted above that an increase in the steel consumption target would increase the required steel output even more. In the same way an error can be magnified so much that it seriously undermines planning calculations. We know, moreover, that at the present stage of development at least minor errors must creep in.

D. THE PENALTIES FOR MISCALCULATION

Any mistakes that the planning board does make will result in a failure to meet targets. Some things will not be produced in the quantities that had been planned. In other things there will be accidental gluts. One reads of such things in the Soviet Union, when the Russian press complains of shortages of some particular item, or of a toy market flooded with a single type of rather uninspired doll. Some manager is usually called to account for it. This sort of mistake, though undesirable, is not necessarily serious.

However, the results of such mistakes can be very serious. Suppose that the production of some small but very important item falls far short of the production goal. This can bring large sectors of the economy to a standstill. The case of ball bearings comes to mind. One can easily visualize vast quantities of automobile bodies, tank parts, and unassembled machines of all sorts piling up and rusting for lack of storage space, all because ball-bearing production has fallen seriously behind the requirements of the plan, or because they happen to have been produced in the wrong sizes. Such an error can quite conceivably result in major production breakdowns, great technological depressions. There are tales to the effect that these have occurred in Russia, though verification is not easy. If so, it may be that the planned economy, having abolished unemployment of the kind that plagues the capitalist world, is afflicted with a disease whose ravages are similar, though differently produced.

This kind of breakdown, which does appear likely at least on a small and localized scale, can have serious secondary effects on the allocation of resources. Managers, fearing the consequences of failing to meet targets because their raw materials are not delivered in adequate quantity and on time, may make it their primary aim to keep their own plants running, with no thought of the consequences for the economy as a whole. If so, they will be tempted to build up large stock piles of critical raw materials as buffers, hoping this will prevent them from being caught short. The production of these stock piles may take up a significant portion of the nation's resources. A country under the pressure of extreme poverty or military necessity can ill-afford this. It is reported that this sort of stock piling is something else that plagues the rulers of the Soviet Union.

E. Planning as a Practical Proposition

Despite all these doubts about the possibility of rigorous and detailed planning, despite its pitfalls and reports of troubles, the Soviet Union appears to have been able to operate a planned economy with considerable success. The discomfort its growing military prowess has produced in the rest of the world leaves little doubt of this. The foregoing discussion suggests that things have probably not gone as smoothly or been as easy as some of the Bolsheviks envisioned before the Revolution of 1917. Yet the communists have managed to operate a planned economy and keep it going. Let us see how the feasibility of a planned economy fits in with the analysis in this chapter.

F. The Use of Trial and Error

We have shown that rigorous and detailed calculations are quite impractical. This means that practical planning must not attempt great precision. Plans must be treated as approximations, and the planners must always be prepared to look for mistakes and revise their calculations in the light of experience. In fact, trial and error becomes an essential part of the planning process, and with it the search for precise calculation is abandoned. The essence of the method is to take action on the basis of what appear to be reasonable guesses, and to make adjustments as their effects appear. Of course this can never be fully satisfactory, yet it is to some extent similar to what happens in the free market. We pointed out earlier that firms on the free market often adjust to changes in consumers' demand only after mistakenly going on as before, until they are induced by the resulting price changes to modify their ways. Moreover, in the process of trial-and-error operation, planners can hope to learn by experience and to improve the accuracy of their initial guesses.

G. Decentralized Decision

Even when operating by trial and error, the sheer work of making all the relevant decisions would certainly become too burdensome for a centralized planning board. There are simply too many items about which decisions have to be made. The practical planner must therefore delegate a certain amount of responsibility to subordinates and leave minor decisions to men who are closer to the operations. Targets become general statements of overall aims rather than detailed directives, or else they represent detailed plans that have been formulated outside the central planning board and submitted to it for its quick perusal and approval. This serves to reduce the work of the board to manageable proportions, but at the same time takes much power and control out of its hands.

H. Use of Some Sort of Price System

To aid in calculations, accounting, and supervision, the planner may find it convenient, or perhaps imperative, to operate with some sort of price system, with prices being determined at least partly by decree rather than by the market. Some market elements may be restored, perhaps in the process of distributing consumer goods where low prices may be used to get rid of excess stocks and high prices to end shortages. Wage rates may also be adjusted to promote productivity, increase the total supply of scarce skills, and induce movement from one industry or plant to another.

9. Quasi-Competitive Socialism

An alternative theoretical scheme for the operation of a socialist economy has been proposed in recent years. Some socialist writers have been highly impressed with the pure competition argument presented in an earlier chapter. When faced with the great difficulties of detailed central planning, they turned to the competitive solution as an alternative, suggesting that the proper organization of a socialist economy is an artificial, purely competitive state. As we saw when we discussed pure competition, it has been maintained that this form of organization of the economy will tend to allocate resources most effectively in accord with the desires of the individuals who make up the economy.

A. The Method

The basic idea is to grant a high degree of autonomy to the managers of the nationalized plants. While quasi-competitive socialism would not establish such a large number of small firms as to meet the formal requirements of purely competitive markets, each manager would be instructed to act as though he were in a purely competitive situation and could not influence price.

The way this is to be done is for the manager to produce and sell as much as the market will take at a price equal to the marginal cost of producing the output. For example, suppose the firm offers 1000 pairs of shoes for sale each week at their marginal cost of production, $10. If it finds that this many cannot be sold, it must reduce its output, and if in the process the marginal cost of a pair of shoes goes up to $11 because of diseconomies of smaller-scale production, the price must be raised accordingly. This adjustment process must continue until an output is found that is demanded in its entirety at a price equal to the marginal cost.

B. THE OBJECT

The object of all this is to eliminate the wastes and disadvantages of monopoly and the monopolistic elements of a capitalist economy while at the same time avoiding the great problems of calculation and bureaucratization which must beset the completely centralized economy. The automatic allocation of resources is attained by giving autonomy on output decisions to plant managers, the role of the state being confined largely to general supervision and inspection of the plants' books to see that the managers have acted in accord with the rules of the game.

The benefits of competition are achieved by prohibiting managers from manipulating prices in a monopolistic manner and by forcing prices to be set at marginal costs. This means that a consumer's cost of purchasing another unit of any good would be made to conform with the social cost of producing it. Thus, in allocating their own money resources in accord with their desires, consumers would automatically be doing the same with the resources of society.

C. REPLIES TO THE CRITICISMS OF COMPETITION

The criticisms of the operation of the market mechanism which were presented earlier have been discussed by the advocates of quasi-competitive socialism, and they have maintained that at least in some ways their system would do better.[2]

To the assertion that their market mechanism, like any other, will benefit the wealthy disproportionately, they answer that they can do as well as anyone in this respect by using stiff progressive income and

[2] See above, pp. 404–411.

inheritance taxes which will help keep wealth evenly distributed. They admit that the problem of keeping incentives alive limits the use of these devices, but they argue that in this respect their economy is no worse than any other.

To the criticism that change in the free market is painful and achieved only by hindsight, they reply that under their system the bankruptcy of a firm will harm no one directly since the firm belongs to the state, that the unemployed will be well taken care of, that plenty of jobs will be provided by vigorous full-employment policies, and that any information the state acquires through its superior foresight will be made available to managers to permit them to adjust to changes in advance.

To the criticisms that the firm will adjust price to private and not social costs and that the market neglects the interdependence of consumers, the advocates of quasi-competitive socialism reply that while these cases exist and are important, they are often difficult to discover and analyze. Unless they are located, no economic system can do much about them. Where their results are obvious, they can be handled by direct government intervention. The government can, just as it does under capitalism, produce the items clearly needed to satisfy communal wants. An industry whose private marginal costs are clearly below social costs can have its private costs raised by the appropriate amount through the levy of a special tax. Other industries may be subsidized for similar reasons. Conservation of natural resources and investment for the future generally can be stimulated by keeping interest rates low, and articles whose consumption harms others can be taxed.

d. The System as a Practical Proposition

All sorts of difficulties may be expected to beset the operation of such a system in practice. Not the least of these is the trouble and expense of determining the marginal cost of a product. Even if the concept were clearly defined, which it is not, the effort that would have to be devoted to estimating the marginal cost for every possible output would be tremendous. Our remarks on the estimation of marginal products largely apply here as well.[3]

Another difficulty in the practical operation of such a system would be in the financing of the plant. With its price equal to *marginal* cost, the plant could have either large profits or large losses. In particular, if there are economies of large-scale operation, every additional unit

[3] See Section 7E above.

will cost less to produce than the last one added before it. If in such an industry the price is equal to marginal cost (the cost of the last unit added), the price will then fully cover only the cost of the last unit produced, and the plant will lose money on every other and necessarily more expensive unit. Such a plant must end up in the red.

Many suggestions have been made for coping with this problem, including state subsidies to plants with losses. In this case the state loses an important criterion of the efficiency with which the managers are operating. There is also the danger that a plant will be kept from bankruptcy, at least until the situation becomes flagrant, even after a severe fall in the demand for its product has made it useless. Certainly the state will then have the difficult problem of deciding whether the continuance of an existing plant or the introduction of a new one is or is not justified.

Another important problem would be that of incentives to managers, for they will not be led by the urge for profits to work hard and operate efficiently.

There are other difficulties that could be cited, but we shall only remark that these problems have led many who are inclined to favor a quasi-competitive socialist system to seek even further compromises. While some of the compromises which have been suggested have less theoretical justification than a marginal cost-pricing arrangement, they would perhaps be more workable.

10. Mixed Systems

In practice, central planning usually has not involved a complete abandonment of private enterprise. Indeed in most cases it has operated in *mixed systems,* in which businessmen are permitted to operate for profit in at least some industries but are subject to varying degrees of regulation or control by the planning authority and perhaps to competition from nationalized enterprises. Economies differing as greatly as those of nazi Germany, fascist Italy, and postwar socialist Britain are all examples of mixed systems. Because of their great variety, it is difficult to generalize about the structure and functioning of mixed systems. Toward the one extreme, most of a nation's enterprises may be nationalized or subject to comprehensive central planning and control even though they are privately owned, leaving only a minimum scope for control by the market. Toward the other extreme, central planning and control may apply to only a few selected industries where there is considered to be special reason for centralization of control, leaving a very wide scope for private enterprise and for the automatic forces of the market to control the composition of output and the allocation of resources.

11. Summary

In this chapter we have examined some of the problems that the central planner must face in allocating the resources available to him. The mutual interdependence of output goals, the difficulty and cost of obtaining accurate data, the supervision of the efficiency of the economy's operations, and the allocation of resources among plants producing the same item have all been shown to involve serious difficulties, especially in view of the time-consuming nature of the operations and the danger of rapid obsolescence of data and plans. Planning was seen to involve much greater difficulties than a simple-minded view might suggest. Completely detailed and accurate plans appear to be quite out of the question. The naïve picture of the simply operated, well-ordered, centrally directed economy must go out the window.

We also saw what sort of compromises the practical planner must make, operating by trial and error, delegating authority outside the planning board, and using some sort of price system. We must recognize that by such means, and despite serious dangers of miscalculation and waste, central planning has become a practical possibility, whatever we may think of its efficiency and desirability as compared with free-enterprise systems.

SUGGESTED READINGS

Hayek, F. A., *Individualism and Economic Order,* Routledge and Kegan Paul, London, 1949, Essays VII–IX inclusive.

Lange, Oskar, and Taylor, Fred M., *On the Economic Theory of Socialism* (Benjamin E. Lippincott, ed.), University of Minnesota Press, Minneapolis, 1938.

Lewis, Ben W., *British Planning and Nationalization,* Twentieth Century Fund, New York, 1952.

Lewis, W. Arthur, *The Principles of Economic Planning,* Public Affairs Press, Washington, 1951.

Schwartz, Harry, *Russia's Soviet Economy,* Prentice-Hall, New York, 1950.

QUESTIONS

1. a. Name some industries whose outputs are mutually interdependent.
   b. Can you guess at the magnitudes of the input-output coefficients for these products?

c. Record your guess in an input-output table.

d. Explain how the outputs of these commodities are coordinated in the United States.

2. a. List some industry's demands for products of others which can reasonably be represented by a straight line like OR_c in Fig. 20.

b. Some which cannot, like OR_s in Fig. 23.

c. Explain.

d. Would curvature of these lines have made much difference to our two-industry graphic analysis?

e. Discuss the effect of this curvature on the three-industry algebraic analysis.

3. Verify our graphic numerical result in Section 2 by going through the algebraic computations for that simple two-industry case.

4. a. Discuss how the use of excessively broad categories like agriculture or aircraft can affect the usability of the calculations of the central planner.

b. Similarly, discuss the effect of the assumption of linear input-output relationships.

5. Discuss the apple-banana adding problem involved in computations of cost and efficiency.

a. Indicate why it is necessary to determine relative values for the different scarce resources of society.

b. Discuss what you consider a reasonable solution of this problem.

c. Describe the nature of the solution offered by the market, indicating the role of relative scarcity, consumers' wealth, and the distribution of income and wealth.

6. a. Criticize the idea that factories can be listed in order of efficiency without reference to the size of their outputs.

b. How does the law of diminishing returns enter here?

c. Apply the principle of no wasted opportunities to the allocation of the businessman's funds among his various factories.

d. Discuss the extent to which the businessman's decisions are likely to result in an efficient allocation of society's resources among his plants.

e. In your answer take into account and give examples of differences between private and social benefits and costs.

7. On economic grounds alone, discuss possible advantages and disadvantages of:

a. Central planning as compared with laissez faire.

b. Central planning as compared with quasi-competitive socialism.

c. Laissez faire as compared with quasi-competitive socialism.

PART VI

International Trade and Finance

CHAPTER 25

International Specialization and Trade

Fair commerce is, where equal values are exchanged for equal, the expense of transport included. Thus, if it costs A in England as much labor and charge to raise a bushel of wheat, as it costs B in France to produce four gallons of wine, then are four gallons of wine the fair exchange for a bushel of wheat, A and B meeting at half distance with their commodities to make the exchange. The advantage of this fair commerce is, that each party increases the number of his enjoyments, having, instead of wheat alone, or wine alone, the use of both wheat and wine. . . . A nation [can] acquire wealth . . . by *commerce,* which is generally *cheating.* (Benjamin Franklin, *Positions to be examined, concerning national wealth,* April 4, 1769.)

1. The Problem

We now turn our attention to an important subject which, though not completely ignored, has been given inadequate attention in the preceding pages—international economic relationships and international economic policies. We have already studied most of the economic processes and principles that will be encountered here. The economic processes are the same as those in domestic trade: specializing in various types of production, buying and selling, arriving at prices, and borrowing and lending. The mere drawing of a national boundary line between the two parties to a transaction does not change the basic nature of the transaction. Nor do basic economic principles change their nature when trade crosses national boundaries whose location may be a matter of historical accident.

Nevertheless, there are several reasons for dealing with international economic relationships and policies in a separate category. (1) Whether rightly or wrongly, large numbers of people do believe that there are great differences between domestic and international specialization and trade. For example, many who believe in the utmost freedom in domestic trade reverse their position if one of the parties to the trade resides in a foreign country. International economic policy is an area that has been peculiarly subject to widespread misunderstanding and prejudice, and this reason alone calls for careful consideration of the topic.

(2) The mobility of goods, capital, and labor among nations may be less than their mobility within a nation. Even within a country labor and capital may not readily respond to changed economic conditions that make it appropriate for them to find new jobs or geographic locales. But because of such things as feelings of patriotism, language and cultural differences, costs of migration, and unfamiliarity with or distrust of foreign conditions, their international mobility may be still lower, even in the absence of restrictions by governments. The movements of goods between nations is often also restricted by transportation costs, tariffs, and many other difficulties.

(3) Differences in the policies of different governments are an important fact with which we have to reckon. These involve many policies that we usually consider to be "domestic" rather than "international." Among them are laws and court decisions defining and protecting property rights, monetary policies, fiscal policies, wage legislation, agricultural price-support policies, and many others. Even if they are directed primarily at "domestic" objectives they may exert powerful influences on the economies of other countries. Also clearly relevant are many government policies aimed more directly at international economic relationships. Among these are policies relating to the import and export of goods and services, imports and exports of capital, exchange rates between the nation's money and foreign moneys, international migrations of people, and so on. The very fact that people in different countries live under different laws and use different moneys makes for important special problems in international trade analysis.

2. Why Trade?

Almost everyone agrees that free trade among the regions included within our national boundaries can raise our total national output and benefit all trading parties by enabling each region to specialize in producing those things for which its resources are relatively best fitted or least unfitted. In fact, a proposal that Kansas, Rhode Island, or any other state attempt to set up highly restrictive trade barriers would be considered absurd by most people. But attitudes toward interregional trade often change abruptly when the specializing and trading regions are separated by national boundary lines. Many who fight to protect and promote the freedom of domestic trade and specialization fight even more passionately to obstruct purchases from abroad.

The purpose of this chapter is to analyze specialization and trade among regions separated by national boundaries. We shall consider questions such as these: Can international specialization and trade, as compared with a system in which trade is obstructed by tariffs and other trade barriers, increase total world output and income? Can freedom of trade among nations benefit all participants? What are some of the consequences of erecting barriers to international specialization and trade?

A. THE GAINS FROM SPECIALIZATION AND TRADE

In an earlier chapter we found that specialization and trade can enhance total output and benefit all who specialize in production and trade with each other, and that, at least up to a point, the greater the degree of specialization and the broader the trading area, the greater can be productivity.[1] Enlargement of the trading area enhances productivity in 3 principal ways.

1. It permits the realization of economies of scale in production. If trading is restricted to a small area, the total demand for each type of product will be correspondingly small, and each industry may be too small to achieve or even approach its maximum efficiency. If the size of the market is enlarged, each industry will be enabled to expand toward the size that permits it to achieve the greatest possible output per unit of input of productive factors.

2. It permits differences in wants to be catered to and offers consumers a variety of products.

3. It permits a better utilization of the diverse productive factors spread over the world. As the range of trade is expanded from small localities toward a world-wide area, it becomes possible for the productive factors located in each region to specialize in the particular lines in which they are relatively most efficient or least inefficient.

[1] See especially pp. 50–54 above.

Stated in very general terms, these are the ways that international specialization and trade can enhance total world output. Let us now look at them more closely.

3. Economies of Scale and Catering to Tastes

A. ECONOMIES OF SCALE IN PRODUCTION

International specialization and trade could enhance world output even if every nation were endowed with exactly the same types and proportions of natural resources, climate, capital, labor, and technology. This is because they would enable each industry to take advantage of the potential economies of scale and to approach its most efficient size. Many industries must operate on a rather large scale in order to achieve maximum technical efficiency.

To illustrate, let us assume that there are two small countries endowed with the same types and proportions of productive factors. If each tried to produce its own steel and aircraft, neither might be able to build and use factories on a scale that would give them the most for their resources. The people of both countries may benefit by having one produce all the steel and the other all the airplanes required for both.

In many nations there seem to be industries that can reach their most efficient sizes only if they can sell in foreign as well as domestic markets. But there are fewer cases in which specialization and trade are based solely on the economies of scale. In most cases they are also based on differences in the types and proportions of productive factors available in the different nations.

B. CATERING TO CONSUMER TASTES

The items that a country produces may not be the things the inhabitants want most for themselves. If the Belgian Congo were to produce only uranium and Cuba were to grow nothing but sugar, trade would have to take place. People cannot subsist on sugar or radioactive minerals.

Trade to adapt available commodities to consumers' tastes may be useful for two reasons. (1) Specialization of production. Brazil grows more coffee than she needs and we produce more autos than we want for ourselves. If we want coffee and Brazilians want autos a trade can be mutually advantageous. (2) Differences in tastes. Even if China and India each grow both wheat and rice, trading may pay because Indians like wheat whereas the Chinese eat no cereal but rice.

4. Comparative Advantage

A. INTERNATIONAL DIFFERENCES IN PRODUCTIVE FACTOR ENDOWMENT

Nations vary greatly as to both the types and the relative supplies of natural resources, labor, capital, and technology within their boundaries. In fact, the differences are so numerous that we cannot list them, but can only illustrate them by examples. Supplies of agricultural land differ in both type and amount relative to labor and capital. Some nations have large amounts of land relative to their populations; others have but little. Some have much land well suited for wheat, corn, and hardwood production, but little or none well-adapted to the production of tropical fruits. Mineral deposits are distributed very unequally. Some nations have large amounts of easily worked coal and petroleum deposits, but little or no cheap iron or copper ore. Climate varies from country to country. And so on. The variations in natural endowments are almost endless.

Labor supplies also differ greatly. Some nations have huge amounts of labor relative to their natural resources and capital; in others labor is relatively scarce. Some have great supplies of unskilled labor, but little skilled and professional labor. Others are well provided with highly educated and skilled workers. There are also great differences in the supplies of capital relative to labor and natural resources. Some countries, such as the United States, have very large amounts of capital per worker. The state of technology varies enormously. In the United States and certain other countries technology has reached a high level of development. At the other extreme are many countries in which technology is still at a primitive stage and the supply of capable technicians is very small.

It is largely because of such wide differences in their endowments of productive factors, both in qualities and quantities, that the comparative efficiencies of nations in the production of each type of product differ so greatly. As compared with other countries, nation A may be most efficient or least inefficient in producing agricultural produce because it is relatively well endowed with land, while nation B is perhaps the most efficient or least inefficient in steel production because of its capital equipment, mineral deposits, and technical skills. Only if each nation specializes in producing the things for which its combination of productive resources makes it comparatively most efficient can the world's resources be utilized most effectively and the world output maximized.

B. COMPARATIVE VERSUS ABSOLUTE ADVANTAGE

The United States would clearly not be allocating its resources efficiently if it attempted to produce its own coffee or bananas or tin. There are some products for whose growth the country's climate is clearly unsuited, and for which our mineral deposits are so sparse or of such poor quality that it does not pay to mine them here. In products of this type we are at an *absolute disadvantage*.

But in many lines of industry our skills and abundant supplies of natural resources, our capital goods, and other productive advantages make us the most efficient producer. In these areas the foreign manufacturer cannot equal us in output per man-hour or per unit of other scarce resources. In the production of these items we are said to enjoy an *absolute advantage*.

Does it follow that in these products we can best fend entirely for ourselves and have no truck with foreign producers? We shall see that it does not. In such circumstances, even in an extreme case where we had an absolute advantage in the production of every item, it would usually pay us to import some of these products. The point is difficult, but it is essential to an understanding of international trade analysis.

Country A is more efficient than B in both food production and clothing manufacture, but A has a much greater advantage in the production of clothing. We say that A has an absolute advantage in both food and clothing but a *comparative advantage* in clothing, and that B, who is at an absolute disadvantage in both, has a comparative advantage in food. We might say that a country has a comparative advantage in lines of production in which it is "most better" or "least worse." In such circumstances we shall argue that it pays A to move in the direction both of specializing in clothing production and of leaving food production to B.

C. THE COMPARATIVE ADVANTAGE ARGUMENT: ILLUSTRATIONS

Consider the successful authoress who hires a maid to do her housekeeping. The writer herself may be by far the more efficient housekeeper, able to do the work more thoroughly and in half the time. Yet it does not pay her to give up writing time to do her own housework, for her advantage as a writer is much greater still. She has an absolute advantage in both writing and housekeeping and yet is at a comparative *dis*advantage in the latter. This example bears some thought, for it contains the essence of the logic of the comparative advantage argument. It often pays a country that is more efficient in producing cars and watches to specialize in producing only one of these items, leaving the other to its less efficient neighbor, for the same reason that it pays the writer to hire her maid.

A more direct numerical illustration may help to clarify the principle. Suppose labor is the only scarce resource in countries A and B, and the hourly labor productivity in each country is that indicated in Table 41.

TABLE 41. Productivity of Labor in Countries A and B

	A	B
Yards of cloth per day	10	2
Bushels of wheat per day	2	1

That is to say, in country A a day's labor is necessary to produce 10 yards of cloth; in country B it takes one day to produce one bushel of wheat, etc. Clearly A has an absolute advantage in each product. However, since A is five times as efficient in the production of cloth as B, but only twice as efficient as B in growing wheat, A has a comparative advantage only in cloth production.

It is now easy to show that if each country is producing both products, an increase in specialization along lines of comparative advantage will increase the total product to be shared between them. Suppose that A shifts one day of labor from wheat into cloth production. This will reduce wheat output 2 bushels and increase cloth production 10 yards. By prearrangement, let B shift enough labor in the other direction to make up for the decreased output of wheat. This will take two days of B's labor from cloth production, thereby reducing that output by 4 yards. The total wheat output will then be unchanged, but the cloth output will be increased by 6 yards—the 10 yard increased output of A minus the 4-yard reduction in B's output.

Here is something for nothing, indeed! No more work is done in either country, yet this increase in specialization has netted them together 6 yards of cloth to be divided between them. The trick consists in A's hiring B to do the work in which A itself makes the smallest net hourly gain, and concentrating on the production of the item in which its net hourly gain is greatest.

Here we see clearly that it is comparative rather than absolute advantage that determines the lines of production in which it pays to specialize, and that trade could benefit a country which was the world's most efficient producer of every item. Perhaps even more important, we see that one country's gain from trade is not necessarily at the expense of others. All countries can share the increase in output made possible by the specialization that trading permits.

d. RESOURCE LIMITATIONS

In order to simplify our examples, we have assumed that a nation has either a comparative advantage or a comparative disadvantage on all parts of its output of a given commodity. This is unrealistic in some cases. For example, we may have a limited amount of resources that are extremely well adapted to cloth production—perhaps enough to produce 1 billion yards a year. But to raise production above that rate we would have to use resources that could be better employed elsewhere. We might have to begin growing cotton on land that is so wet as to be much better suited to rice growing. Thus our comparative advantage may cease before we reach a very high rate of cloth production. The same may be true of wheat production in Britain, iron ore production in France, and so on.

Essentially the point is that a country is at a comparative advantage in the production of items that primarily use resources which are relatively abundant and of relatively good quality. But as the production of those items increases, those resources may be tied up, and hence become relatively scarce. This fact explains why it may be advantageous for a nation to produce part of its requirements for a product at home, and to import the rest.

5. Free Trade and Comparative Advantage

a. THE ROLE OF THE PROFIT MOTIVE

We have just seen that world output can be maximized only if the productive resources of each nation are used in the particular lines in which they have a comparative advantage. Now we come to a question that is crucial for public policy. Will a system of free international trade, with both production and trade carried on for profit, actually tend to allocate resources in line with their comparative advantage?

After all, producers and traders are not guided directly by some abstract theory; they are guided by prospective profits, which depend on costs and prices. We can therefore rephrase our question in this way: Will producers and traders find it profitable to use resources in the lines in which they have a comparative advantage, and unprofitable to use them in lines in which they are at a comparative disadvantage? If this is not so, unrestricted trade might lead to specialization in lines in which countries are relatively inefficient, and it could even reduce world production.

We shall argue that there is in fact a strong tendency in the direction of specialization along lines of comparative advantage, though we must recognize that it is inhibited by imperfections in the competitive process.

B. INTERNATIONAL DIFFERENCES IN COSTS OF PRODUCTION

The costs of producing different commodities in different places play an important part in determining which items businessmen will decide to produce in each place. But these costs are themselves closely related to the prices of the means of production—the labor, raw materials, and machinery used in their manufacture.

For obvious reasons natural resources cannot themselves be moved from one nation to another; as a result, supplies of these factors will differ greatly in quantity and quality and so rents on comparable types of land in the various nations may differ greatly. The international mobility of labor and capital is limited not only by government restrictions but also by feelings of patriotism, inertia, lack of knowledge, and many other factors. Because of this, there may be large and persistent international differences in the levels of wages and interest rates, and also in the productivity of labor and capital. Moreover, there are large international differences in the heights of wages, interest, and rents relative to each other.

In general, a factor or type or grade of factor that is relatively scarce in a nation tends to be relatively expensive, while those that are relatively plentiful tend to be relatively cheap.[2] For example, in the United States, where capital is in abundant supply relative to labor, interest rates (the cost of borrowing the funds with which to buy capital goods) tend to be low relative to wage rates. Where capital is scarce relative to labor, interest rates tend to be higher relative to wage rates. Where land is scarce relative to labor, rents tend to be higher relative

[2] For a formal discussion of this point see the Graphic Appendix, pp. 655–656.

to wage rates. The same principle applies to different types of labor and natural resources. Where common labor is plentiful relative to skilled and professional workers, it is likely to be cheap as compared with labor of the scarcer types. And the types of natural resources that are most plentiful will have low rents as compared with those of the scarcer resources.

c. Costs and Comparative Advantage

A nation tends to have comparatively low money costs on the things whose production requires relatively large amounts of its plentiful, efficient, and cheap productive factors, and only relatively small amounts of its scarcer, less efficient, and more expensive factors. These are the very lines in which it has a comparative advantage, for we have seen that a country tends to be at a comparative advantage in producing those items whose production makes relatively small demands on the supplies of its scarcest resources.

This suggests at once that if the producers in country A can undersell their foreign competitors in any commodities, they will be able to do so in those items in whose production the country is at a comparative advantage.

On the other hand a nation will tend to have high costs, and hence tend to be most vulnerable to foreign competition, on those things whose production requires only small amounts of its plentiful, efficient, and cheap factors and large amounts of its scarce, less efficient, and expensive factors. These are the lines in which it tends to have a comparative disadvantage.

d. Private and Governmental Price Manipulation

The foregoing argument is dependent on prices being determined by an unhampered market mechanism—by market supply and demand. Where this is the situation the prices of abundant resources will indeed tend to be low, and scarce resources will tend to be expensive, as we have said.

However, prices are not always permitted to be determined in this way. For example, some relatively scarce factor of production may be controlled by a monopolist who will force its price above what it would otherwise be. However, it is not very easy to evaluate the influence of monopoly on the channeling of international trade in relation to comparative advantage.

Perhaps more important in recent times has been government interference with the price mechanism. Governments have judged some prices undesirably low and attempted to support them (as in the case of agricultural produce in the U.S.), and in times of inflationary pressure they have put ceilings on prices to keep them from rising.

As a result, some commodities whose export would have been made profitable by comparative advantage operating through an unhampered price mechanism cannot compete on the world market without government subsidy to offset the effect of price support. American wheat may well be an example of this, for here is a commodity for whose production we are peculiarly well adapted by virtue of our abundant land and extensive agricultural mechanization. Yet the high prices produced by our farm price-support system have made it expensive for foreigners to buy our grain at U.S. market prices, and we have been able to sell wheat abroad only because the government sells it below the domestic price.

Similarly, price ceilings may make it cheap for foreigners to buy goods that we produce at a comparative disadvantage.

We see, then, that government and private interference with the operation of the price mechanism may influence foreign trade away from industries with a comparative advantage even if trade is otherwise unhampered. In such a case free trade may not always produce the full fruits of efficient international specialization. Nevertheless, productive efficiency in today's world would probably be enhanced by a reduction in restrictions on trade.

E. THE TERMS OF TRADE AND A NATION'S GAINS FROM TRADE

We have seen that international specialization can increase world production. How these gains will be shared among the nations obviously depends on the pricing of each nation's exports. It is even conceivable, though unlikely, that prices will be so unfavorable to one country as to deprive it entirely of the gains from specialization and trade, all the gains going to other countries. Prices of exports and imports will depend on a complex of supply-demand conditions and can be influenced by governmental or monopolistic interference.

The relation between the prices of a nation's exports and the prices of its imports (the exports of the rest of the world to it) are referred to as the nation's *terms of trade*. This can be of great importance to its welfare. If it can sell its exports dearly and buy its imports cheaply, this may be very advantageous. Its terms of trade are then said to be in its favor. If a nation's terms of trade turn against it, the real cost of its imports can go up substantially. It has been said that the deterioration in Britain's terms of trade resulting from the Korean war (when prices of raw materials and foodstuffs which she imports rose so much more than the prices of her exports) cost her more than the amount of aid she received from the United States under the European Recovery Program (the Marshall Plan).

Though the terms of trade are very important in determining a nation's gains from international trade, they can be somewhat overemphasized. For a nation as for an individual businessman, high selling prices may not be desirable if they reduce sales too much. Nations have sometimes quite clearly benefited when an increase in their productivity has increased their supplies of exports, lowered the selling prices of these exports, and turned the terms of trade against themselves, for the disadvantages of lower prices for their exports were more than offset by the advantages of increased sales. This is likely to happen to many economically underdeveloped countries as their development programs increase their real output and enable them to sell more of their products abroad.

6. Comparative Advantage in the United States

The principles we have been discussing can be illustrated by the experience of the United States.

A. Prices of American Factors of Production

As compared to other countries, labor is one of our scarce resources. Our population is not very dense. We have an average of 20 people per square kilometer, as against some 77 in France, 117 in India, 207 in the United Kingdom, and 317 in the Netherlands.[3] Thus we have a large amount of land per person. Our nation is abundant in natural resources and we have accumulated large quantities of capital. Hence wages in this country tend to be high, whereas rents of land and some other types of natural resources as well as interest rates tend to be relatively low as compared with some other countries. Low interest rates mean, as we have seen, that businessmen find it cheap to borrow the funds with which to obtain capital goods.[4] Thus American business

---

[3] These figures are as of 1951. Source: *United Nations Yearbook,* 1952, Table 1, pp. 89 ff. There are some countries, like Egypt, whose average population density is very much like ours, and Australia, which is much more sparsely settled at 1 person per square kilometer. However, both these countries have much relatively uninhabitable land. In fact, Egypt is generally considered an overpopulated country.

[4] See above, pp. 192–193.

finds it profitable to concentrate on the· production of goods whose manufacture employs much land or capital and relatively little labor.

B. Do High Wages Mean High Costs?

We frequently hear the suggestion that foreigners can undersell us on most products and in most markets, including our own, because their wage rates are so much lower than ours.

Yet at the same time numerous producers and government officials in low-wage countries complain that they cannot compete with low-cost American products. The inability of the rest of the world to sell us enough to pay for the goods they want to buy from us suggests there is something to what they say. Let us see why high wages need not mean high costs.

Even if labor cost per unit of output is higher here, it may be compensated for by lower costs of other types. Our relatively low interest rates and low rents on some types of natural resources offset higher labor costs in some industries, especially those that employ large amounts of capital and land relative to labor, and in which interest and rent are important components of total costs.

For reasons of these types we have lower costs than other countries in many lines of production. But in others, those where we are at a comparative disadvantage, our costs are higher. These are the industries for which our natural resources are not best adapted, where the productivity of our labor is less superior to that of other countries, where large amounts of expensive labor and small amounts of cheap capital are used, and so on.

But high wages do not mean that *labor* cost per unit of output must be high. A high wage rate is consistent with low labor cost if productivity is high enough. Thus an American producer may pay his workers $2 an hour and have lower labor costs than a foreign producer paying only $1 an hour, if output per man hour is 20 units in the United States and only 5 units abroad. It is common knowledge that output per man-hour in the United States is generally higher than that abroad, owing to our advanced technology, large capital supplies, favorable natural resources, the better health and education of our labor force, and so on. This is another way of saying that in general each unit of our output contains less labor than do foreign products. Basically, our real wage rates are high because our labor is so productive when devoted to the lines in which it is most efficient.

c. SOME LINES OF COMPARATIVE ADVANTAGE IN THE U.S.

One broad area in which the United States excels is the production of heavy machinery, automobiles, trucks, buses, and other similar products. This is due to a favorable combination of conditions. (1) Favorable natural resources. We have large quantities of low-cost coal, limestone, and iron ore to supply our iron and steel industry. However, the depletion of our richest and lowest-cost iron ore deposits would threaten our advantage in this field if we could not import high-quality and low-cost iron ores from the newly discovered deposits in Labrador, Venezuela, and Liberia. (2) Large supplies of capital. The foregoing are industries in which the use of very large amounts of our abundant capital relative to our scarce labor is most advantageous. (3) Advanced technology and a large supply of skilled technicians and workers. We have not only the necessary knowledge, but also many scientists, engineers, designers, and skilled workers to apply it in production. In these industries the large quantities of complex capital equipment and the technical complexity of the products give us an advantage in their production.

In manufacturing industries with these general characteristics we are likely to have a comparative advantage. We also have a comparative advantage in several lines of agricultural production. Among these are wheat and some types of tobacco. In general, our comparative advantage is in the lines of agriculture for which our natural resources are especially favorable, and in which mechanization and extensive agriculture are most advantageous. We have very large areas in which the climate, rainfall, soil conditions, and topography are especially suited to these products. We have enough of this land to permit a low ratio of labor to land, and we have a large supply of capital to permit mechanization.

Table 42, which shows our principal exports in 1952, indicates that these have indeed tended to follow the lines of comparative advantage. In the production of machinery, automobiles, cotton, iron and steel mill products, tobacco, and some types of chemicals and petroleum products our advantage is quite clear. We have already mentioned the peculiar case of wheat, where domestic price support might wipe out our comparative advantage were it not for the government's export subsidies.

But trade restrictions, as well as American subsidies and postwar gifts, have somewhat disturbed our export patterns. With completely

TABLE 42. Principal U.S. Commodity Exports, 1952[5]

Type of Product	Value of Exports (millions of dollars)	Percent of Total Exports	Some of the Largest Foreign Customers
Machinery, total................	$ 2,707.6	18.0	Canada, Mexico, Brazil, France
Selected military equipment......	2,320.5	15.4	(Secret)
Grains and preparations.........	1,481.8	9.9	Italy, West Germany, India, Japan, United Kingdom
Automobiles, parts, accessories, and service equipment.........	988.4	6.3	Mexico, Colombia, Brazil
Cotton, raw, excluding linters....	862.2	5.8	Canada, United Kingdom, West Germany
Chemicals and related products...	802.0	5.3	Canada, Mexico, Brazil, India
Petroleum and products..........	799.9	5.3	Canada, United Kingdom, France, Brazil, Japan
Iron and steel mill products......	721.7	4.8	Canada
Textiles and textile manufactures..	659.2	4.4	Canada, Cuba, Venezuela, Philippines
Coal...........................	493.9	3.3	Mexico, Canada, West Germany, France
Tobacco, unmanufactured........	245.5	1.6	United Kingdom, West Germany, Australia
Ferro-alloys and nonferrous metals	220.8	1.5	United Kingdom, France, Canada
Rubber manufactures, including synthetic rubber..............	156.5	1.1	Canada
Paper, related products and manufactures......................	154.5	1.0	United Kingdom, Netherlands
Meat products and edible fats....	143.0	1.0	Cuba, Canada, United Kingdom
Fruits and preparations..........	140.0	0.9	Canada, Netherlands, Belgium
Other.........................	2,128.2	14.2	
Total....................	$15,025.7	100.0	

free trade we might have exported more household electric appliances (refrigerators, washing machines), more automobiles, more movies, more ready-made clothing, especially those made of nylon and other synthetic fabrics, etc. Many of these things are considered luxuries by dollar-poor foreign governments, who therefore prohibit or severely

[5] Source: *Foreign Commerce Weekly,* March 23, 1953, pp. 25–26.

restrict their importation from the United States. In addition, foreign countries curtail our exports by means of tariffs and other devices designed to protect their industries from American competition.

D. SOME LINES OF COMPARATIVE DISADVANTAGE

In general, our comparative disadvantage is in the lines for which our natural resources are not best suited, where a large ratio of capital to land and labor is not so advantageous, where relatively large amounts of unskilled and semiskilled labor are used, and where great attention to detail is required, as in lace and watchmaking. In some industries we are at a comparative disadvantage on all parts of the output; in others we have a comparative advantage only so long as our output is small and by itself remains inadequate to satisfy our demands.

Among these products are many metals and minerals—tin, copper, bauxite, manganese, chromium, nickel, zinc, iron ore, and many others. In some cases, such as tin and nickel, it would be practically impossible to produce enough domestically to meet our demands. And in all cases it would be more expensive to mine these ores domestically than to produce other things and trade them for these imports. Moreover, to attempt self-sufficiency in these fields will hasten the day when our best resources will be depleted.

We are also at a comparative disadvantage in several types of agriculture and forestry. We could produce bananas, coconuts, coffee, tea, and other tropical and subtropical products in artificially heated greenhouses, but it is far cheaper to import them, paying for them with products like automotive equipment in whose production we have a comparative advantage. We produce some lumber cheaply and could become self-sufficient by reforesting large areas now being used productively for other purposes. But it is cheaper to buy part of our lumber product requirements from Canada, Sweden, and other countries whose resources are comparatively better adapted to forestry than to other uses, and to pay for them with items like heavy road-construction equipment.

In general, we are at a comparative disadvantage in the lines of agriculture, such as sugar production, that use large amounts of unskilled labor relative to capital and land. Our advantage is in lines in which larger amounts of capital and land relative to labor are most advantageous. At the other extreme, however, it is advantageous for us to import part of our requirements of beef, mutton, hides, and wool from Australia, Canada, Argentina, and other countries that have a comparative advantage in grazing, both because of their climate, rainfall, and soil conditions, and because they have even larger amounts of land per capita. Illinois, Ohio, Iowa, and Indiana would provide excellent grazing, but they are more productive in corn.

TABLE 43. Principal U.S. Commodity Imports, 1952[6]

Product	Value of Imports (millions of dollars)	Percent of Total Imports	Some of the Largest Suppliers
Coffee	$ 1,375.9	12.8	Brazil, Colombia
Paper and paper materials	925.3	8.6	Canada, Sweden, Finland
Petroleum and products	691.0	6.4	Venezuela, Near East
Crude rubber	618.7	5.8	British Malaya, Indonesia, Thailand
Textiles and textile manufactures	512.8	4.8	India, United Kingdom, Japan
Cane sugar	414.8	3.9	Cuba, Philippines
Copper	411.7	3.8	Chile, Canada, Mexico
Wool, unmanufactured	382.0	3.6	Australia, Argentina, Uruguay
Machinery and vehicles	353.6	3.3	Canada
Tin	280.7	2.6	Malaya, Indonesia, Bolivia
Chemical and related products	244.0	2.3	Canada, Chile, West Germany, United Kingdom
Sawmill products	221.5	2.1	Canada, Mexico, Sweden
Iron and steel mill products	212.8	2.0	Belgium, West Germany, Japan, France
Lead	208.1	1.9	Mexico, Canada, Australia
Cocoa and cacao beans	178.4	1.7	Gold Coast, Nigeria
Diamonds	155.8	1.4	Belgium, South Africa
Zinc	149.7	1.4	Canada, Mexico
Nickel	113.0	1.0	Canada, Cuba, Norway
Hides and skins	60.1	0.5	Argentina, Canada
Other	3,234.8	30.1	
Total	$10,744.7	100.0	

Again speaking generally, we tend to be at a comparative disadvantage in lines of manufacturing in which very large supplies of capital relative to labor are not so advantageous. Among the industries in which a relatively high level of efficiency can be achieved with smaller amounts of capital per worker are those producing handmade lace,

[6] Source: *Ibid.*, March 23, 1953, pp. 26–27.

hand-woven rugs, china and pottery, fine cloth, watches, clay and briar pipes, wooden toys, and many other things. In such industries, foreign producers are likely to have lower costs because of their relatively large supplies of labor. American producers in these lines cannot achieve sufficiently higher rates of output per man-hour to offset the higher wage rates they must pay. But we should remember that American producers are forced to pay these high wage rates because our labor is so productive in other lines where it receives maximum assistance from our large supplies of capital and natural resources and our advanced technology.

Our import statistics (Table 43) again show a remarkable correspondence between the items we import and our lines of comparative disadvantage. But more careful scrutiny suggests that the correspondence is not quite as close as at first appears. We do import the items in whose production we are at an *absolute* as well as a comparative disadvantage. Coffee, paper, natural rubber, copper, tin, sawmill products, lead, cocoa, diamonds, zinc, and nickel we cannot produce for ourselves in sufficient quantities on any sort of reasonable terms. On such lines there are usually only low tariffs or no tariffs at all.

But many other items in whose production we are at a considerable comparative disadvantage might be imported in much greater quantities in the absence of duties. Among these items are shoes and other leather goods, textiles, ceramics and chinaware, coal-tar products and certain other chemicals, watches and jewelry, briar pipes, specialty cheeses, meat, and wool.

We conclude that our export and import patterns have been markedly distorted by tariffs and other interferences with free trade and the price mechanism. Yet it is noteworthy how closely they nevertheless follow the lines of comparative advantage.

7. International Trade and the Structure of National Economies

A. ADAPTING THE ECONOMY TO INTERNATIONAL MARKETS

We often hear statements to the effect that nations export only their "surplus commodities." The implication is that the structure of each nation's economy is just about the same as it would be if the nation engaged in no international trade and were wholly self-sufficient—that each industry in a nation is of just about the size that would normally be required to meet domestic demands, so that only unplanned "surpluses" are exported.

This belief is clearly wrong. Under international trade the structure of each nation's economy may be far different from what it would be if the nation were self-sufficient. Some industries, expanded to meet both foreign and domestic demands, are much larger than they would be if the nation did not export. Other industries, which might be large if the nation did not import, may not exist at all, or may be quite small. In short, the entire structure of national economies and the allocation of resources adjust themselves to international trade. In this way the advantages of specialization and large-scale production can be obtained.

B. EXAMPLES

A large part of Cuba's land and about 20 percent of her labor are devoted to the production of sugar, most of which is exported to the United States and other nations. We can be sure that if Cuba were wholly self-sufficient, far less of her resources would be allocated to sugar and far more to other foods, fibers, and manufacturing. Canada's production of wheat and rye is three times as great as her consumption of these products. In the absence of trade she would certainly allocate less of her resources to these products and more to others. The watch and precision-instrument industries of Switzerland would be far smaller in the absence of export markets. The same is true of meat production in New Zealand, coffee in Brazil and Colombia, shoe and textile production in Great Britain, heavy machinery in the United States, and a host of other cases.

C. MORE PROFOUND CHANGES

We can go further. International specialization and trade can alter the entire structure of a nation's society, changing the size of its population, the distribution of its population between rural and urban areas, its occupational distribution, and so on. Consider the case of Great Britain. In 1800 she had a population of about 10.5 million which was fed and clothed largely from domestic production. Since that time her population has increased nearly fivefold, rising to some 49 million in 1951. In the process of growth she has become increasingly less self-sufficient and increasingly dependent on imports of food, and now it is just about out of the question for her to try to become self-sufficient in agricultural products. As indicated in Table 44, she now imports about 60 percent of her cereals, more than 60 percent of her sugar, 50 percent of her meat, and 90 percent of her fats and oils. It seems almost certain that her population would be far smaller and less urbanized and industrialized if from the beginning she had followed a policy of self-sufficiency.

Such a large population, and perhaps her world power, have been made possible by international specialization and trade, under which she has become a great producer and exporter of manufactures and of financial and transportation services to pay for the great imports of food and industrial raw materials without which many of her industries

TABLE 44. Imports of Some Principal Types of Food, Stated as
Percentages of the Total National Supply, 1950–1951[7]
(* indicates net exports stated as a percentage of production)

	Wheat and Rye	Sugar	Meat	Fats and Oils
United Kingdom	61	63	51	91
Japan	55	94	0	62
Austria	43	39	5	60
Belgium-Luxembourg	50	60*	2	61
Western Germany	34	33	10	58
Netherlands	54	2*	20*	49
Switzerland	58	87	14	57

could not operate. Thus both the size and the structure of British society have been profoundly molded by international trade. The same is true in varying degrees of Japan, Belgium, the Netherlands, Austria, Malaya, and most other countries.

D. INTERNATIONAL ECONOMIC INTERDEPENDENCE

To the extent that nations adjust their social and economic structures to a system of international specialization and trade they inevitably become dependent on each other. Each depends on others for goods and services to meet some part of its consumption needs and to provide raw materials and equipment for its industries. And each depends on foreign markets for its exports, both to earn money to pay for its imports and to provide income and employment in its export industries. Anything that upsets this orderly international exchange of goods and services can have serious effects on all the trading nations.

The flow of international trade may be interrupted in many ways. A nation's imports may be disturbed by wars which interrupt transportation, by tariffs, by export embargoes or heavy export taxes imposed

[7] Source: United Nations, *Statistical Yearbook,* 1952, pp. 258–263.

by producing countries, by an interruption of output in other nations, or by heavy competing demands from others. And the demand for its exports may be disturbed by an interruption of international transport, by an embargo or heavy taxation of imports imposed by other countries, or by a business depression abroad. A serious depression in the United States is likely to decrease markedly our demand for imports, to decrease income and employment in the export industries of many countries, and even to induce a cumulative depression in the rest of the world.

The fact of international economic interdependence often conflicts with the theory of unlimited national sovereignty. Each nation tends to insist on its "sovereign right" to determine its own economic policies in order to solve its "domestic" problems. But few of a nation's important economic policies have "purely domestic" effects; most of them influence the behavior of foreign economies. One of the great problems of our time is to find a workable compromise between the principle of national sovereignty on the one hand and the facts of international economic interdependence on the other. Some would solve the problem by maintaining and even increasing international specialization and trade, and modifying the principle of national sovereignty. They would delegate to some international body the power to make economic policies with international implications. Others would preserve the principle of national sovereignty and have each nation move toward self-sufficiency so that its economy would not be influenced by economic events and policies abroad.

Since these issues will be discussed later, we shall suggest no solutions here. However, two points are worth emphasis. The first is that both the size and the structure of national societies are now so adjusted to large amounts of international specialization and trade that any movement toward self-sufficiency by even a few large nations would necessitate long and painful readjustments throughout the world. The second is that even in the long run nations could purchase self-sufficiency only at a high cost in terms of world output.

8. Conclusion

International trade enables every nation to make the most of the productive factors it does have, and to enjoy some of the benefits of productive factors which it does not itself possess. For example, nations with highly inadequate amounts of farm land, forests, or petroleum and other mineral deposits can through trade enjoy the products of these resources located in other countries. Nations with very little capital can consume products that can be turned out efficiently only by the large capital supplies of other nations. And countries whose technology is in an undeveloped stage can enjoy the products of the advanced know-how of other countries. Trade enables populations to expand and to attain standards of living which their native soil could never support unaided. The world would certainly be poorer if each nation were self-sufficient, enjoying no goods or services other than those turned out by its own productive factors.

SUGGESTED READINGS

Hansen, Alvin H., *America's Role in the World Economy,* Norton, New York, 1945.

League of Nations, *The Network of World Trade,* Geneva, 1942.

U.S. Department of Commerce, *The United States in the World Economy,* Economic Series No. 23, Washington, 1943.

QUESTIONS

1. a. Do you think it is to the advantage of a New Yorker if trade between New York and Alabama is unhampered by tariffs?
    b. Do you think it would be advantageous to him if the South had successfully seceded from the Union?
    c. Do you think it would be to our advantage to abolish all tariffs against Great Britain if she were to become a "49th state"?
    d. How else might trade between the U.S. and Britain and mobility of resources be simplified in such an event?
2. We saw earlier that in some industries large-scale production is inefficient.
    a. Will free trade produce disadvantageous effects by its effect on these industries?
    b. Explain the asymmetry between the effects of free trade on industries with economies of large-scale production and on industries with diseconomies of scale.
3. a. Using the figures in Table 41, show what will be gained if A shifts 2 hours of labor from wheat to cloth production, with B making up the loss of wheat output.
    b. If A shifts 5 million hours of labor in this way.
    c. Compare these results and the result given in the text.
    d. What is the relevance of Section 4d?
    e. Draw up a table similar to Table 41 and make similar computations for the case of the authoress and the maid.

4. a. Show what would happen to international trading between two free-enterprise economies if abundant resources were expensive and scarce resources cheap.

   b. Why might there be some tendency in this direction when prices are rigged by a democratic government?

5. Why do you think the U.S. is likely to have a comparative disadvantage in producing:

   a. Radios and television sets?

   b. Corn?

   c. Cotton?

   d. Petroleum products?

   Give some other examples.

6. Why do you think the U.S. is likely to be in a comparative disadvantage in the production of:

   a. Lace?

   b. Briar pipes?

   c. Newsprint (paper)?

   d. Watches?

   Give some other examples.

7. a. Try to picture what sorts of interference with free trade might be capable of leading us to export goods in whose production we are at a comparative disadvantage and to import goods in whose production we are at a comparative advantage?

   b. Why then do Tables 42 and 43 not really indicate that current trade restrictions are relatively innocuous?

8. Try to describe what Great Britain would be like today if she had never permitted much freedom of international trade to her inhabitants. Discuss what might be:

   a. The composition of her output.

   b. The size of her population.

   c. Her standard of living.

   d. The commodities she might be unable to produce for lack of raw materials or other reasons.

9. Discuss and evaluate the Benjamin Franklin quotation at the head of this chapter.

CHAPTER 26

International Payments

In the final analysis trade across national boundaries, like domestic trade, is essentially barter of goods and services. But because direct barter is at least as inconvenient internationally as it is domestically, money is used as a means of payment. The monetary payment process is thus an integral part of the mechanism of international exchange.

1. The Mechanism of International Payments

The principal type of money used in international payments is the same as that used in domestic payments—bank deposits. We pay foreigners by giving them claims on deposits at banks, and they pay us in the same way.

A. METHODS OF TRANSFER

The three principal ways of transferring these deposit claims are illustrated by the following example. Suppose that you are to pay the equivalent of $100 to a London exporter. In some cases you may simply send him a $100 check drawn by you on your own bank. But if for any reason, say because he has not heard of you or your local bank, he will be unwilling to accept this, you may have a bank send him a check drawn on some other American or foreign bank. For example, you may give your own check to an American bank to buy a check which it will draw on another, perhaps larger, American or foreign bank. If payment must be made in a hurry, the deposit claim may be transferred by a cable or telegraph order rather than a slower-moving check. And the deposit claim transferred to the London exporter may be against an American bank, a British bank, or a bank in a third country.

B. INTERNATIONAL BANKING RELATIONSHIPS

This rapid and efficient mechanism for international payments is made possible by a network of international banking relationships. Every nation has its own domestic banking network, including its central bank and its commercial banks. These various national networks are interconnected in two principal ways: (1) through their central banks, which buy and sell gold, hold deposits with each other, and sometimes lend to each other; (2) through their commercial banking systems.

These commercial banks, in turn, are connected in two main ways. (1) Through their foreign branches. A number of our large banks, especially those in New York, operate branches in several foreign countries, as do also large banks in Great Britain, France, the Netherlands, and several other financially powerful countries. (2) Through international "correspondent" relationships. Under these arrangements, banks located in different countries and separately owned and operated hold deposits with each other, draw checks on each other, lend to each other, collect claims for each other, and so on.

C. THE ROLE OF NEW YORK AND LONDON

In these processes, the world's two greatest international financial centers—New York and London—play highly important roles. Large banks in many countries hold deposits in New York banks, borrow there, lend there, and stand ready to buy and sell claims against dollars. In fact, a considerable part of all international payments, including many between pairs of foreign countries, are made by the transfer of deposit claims against New York banks. For example, payments among Chile, Brazil, Argentina, and Mexico may be made by the transfer of dollar deposit claims in New York.

London occupies a similar position in international finance. Banks located throughout the British Commonwealth of Nations and in many other countries hold deposits in London banks, borrow there, lend there, and buy and sell claims on sterling deposits. Another considerable part of all international payments is made by the transfer of claims against deposits in London banks.

Thus the banking relationships between New York and London link together two great international financial centers, and through them the great areas in which the United States dollar and the British pound sterling are generally acceptable in international payments.

D. FREE MULTILATERAL PAYMENTS

In the absence of government restrictions, this mechanism provides a system of free multilateral international payments. This means that a nation receiving payment from a certain other nation is not forced to spend the money in the nation from which it was received, but can spend the money for the things it wants most wherever it can get the most favorable terms.

Suppose that a Brazilian coffee exporter receives a $100,000 check from the United States, but that neither he nor any other Brazilian wishes to buy in the United States. He may sell the dollars to a Brazilian bank in exchange for Brazilian money which he may use as he wishes. The Brazilian bank may then sell the dollars to an importer who uses them to buy nitrate from Chile. The latter may use the dollars to buy shoes from England, which then uses the dollars to buy cotton from the United States. Thus, under a system of free multilateral payments no nation has to buy from another simply because that nation bought from it, but each country can use the money it receives to buy wherever it can "get the most for its money." This tends to promote both the quantity and advantages of international trade. We shall find later that governments frequently restrict this process.

E. PAYMENT IN DIFFERENT CURRENCIES

One significant difference between domestic and international payments is that the latter usually require the exchange of one national money for another. Suppose that you are to pay the equivalent of $100 to a Swedish exporter. You might do this in several ways. (1) You might send him a check stated in dollars. It this case he would probably exchange the dollars for Swedish kronor at his local bank. (2) You might send him a check stated in Swedish kronor which you buy at your bank in the United States and which is drawn against a bank in Sweden. (3) You might pay him with a check stated in French francs. In this case you would probably use dollars to buy claims on francs, and on receiving the claims on francs the Swedish exporter would probably sell them for kronor.

Exchange transactions of these types occur on a very large scale and are facilitated by highly efficient *exchange* or *foreign exchange* markets. These include not only the ultimate buyers and sellers of moneys but also many types of exchange dealers and brokers who act as middlemen. The things that are exchanged are claims on the various national moneys, largely claims on bank deposits. When you buy foreign exchange you usually get a check stated in a foreign currency. When a foreigner buys dollars he usually gets a check stated in dollars.

F. RATES OF EXCHANGE

Every exchange of one money for another must, of course, involve a *rate of exchange* or *exchange rate,* which is merely the price of one money in terms of another. Table 45 indicates the approximate exchange rates between the United States dollar and a few of the principal foreign moneys in early 1953. Accustomed to expressing all

TABLE 45. Approximate Exchange Rates Between the U.S. Dollar and Selected Foreign Moneys, February 17, 1953

	Col. 1	Col. 2
Monetary Unit	Price of the Foreign Moneys Stated in U.S. Dollars	Price of the Dollar Stated in Foreign Moneys
British pound sterling	$2.80	0.357 pounds
French franc	0.00286	350.0 francs
Dutch guilder	0.2629	3.8 guilders
Argentine peso	0.0725	13.78 pesos
Swedish krona	0.1937	5.16 kronor
Australian pound sterling	2.26	0.442 pounds

prices in terms of our own dollar, we usually state exchange rates as the dollar price of foreign moneys (see Column 1). But for similar reasons, foreigners usually express these exchange rates as the price of a dollar in their own moneys (see Column 2). Both amount to the same thing.

2. Exchange Rates and the Prices of Imports and Exports

A. THE NATURE OF THE PROBLEM

In later sections we shall analyze in some detail the determination of exchange rates. Here we want to make only one important point—that the behavior of exchange rates can have a great influence on the prices of internationally traded goods, on the quantity of goods bought and sold, and on the behavior of national income, employment, and prices.

To make this point, we shall consider the exchange rate between the U.S. dollar and the British pound, letting the latter represent all foreign moneys. To indicate the influences of exchange rates on the dollar and pound prices of imports and exports, we shall compare two exchange rates: £1 = $2 and £1 = $3.

B. EXCHANGE RATES AND THE DOLLAR COST OF IMPORTS

The dollar cost of importing any commodity from Britain depends on both the price of the commodity in pounds and the price of each pound in terms of dollars. This may be stated more precisely as follows:

$$\left\{\begin{array}{l}\text{The dollar}\\ \text{cost of im-}\\ \text{porting a}\\ \text{good from}\\ \text{Britain}\end{array}\right\} \text{equals} \left\{\begin{array}{l}\text{The price of}\\ \text{the good in}\\ \text{pounds}\end{array}\right\} \text{multiplied by} \left\{\begin{array}{l}\text{The dollar}\\ \text{price of each}\\ \text{pound}\end{array}\right.$$

Suppose that the price of some commodity in Britain is £2. If the exchange rate is £1 = $2, the article will cost the American importer $4, but if the exchange rate is £1 = $3 the article will cost him $6. Thus a rise of the exchange rate on foreign moneys, which is the same as a decline of the exchange rate on the dollar, will make foreign goods more expensive to us if it is not offset by a decline in their prices in terms of foreign moneys. A decline of the exchange rate on foreign moneys—a rise of the dollar in exchange markets—will have the reverse effect, tending to make our imports cheaper in terms of dollars.

C. EXCHANGE RATES AND THE COST OF OUR EXPORTS TO FOREIGNERS

Similarly, the cost of our exports to foreigners, stated in foreign money, may be expressed as follows:

$$\left\{\begin{array}{l}\text{The cost of}\\ \text{an American}\\ \text{export in for-}\\ \text{eign money}\end{array}\right\} \text{equals} \left\{\begin{array}{l}\text{The price of}\\ \text{the good in}\\ \text{dollars}\end{array}\right\} \text{multiplied by} \left\{\begin{array}{l}\text{The price of}\\ \text{each dollar in}\\ \text{terms of for-}\\ \text{eign money}\end{array}\right.$$

Suppose that the price of some good in the United States is $3. If the exchange rate is £1 = $3, the article will cost a British importer £1. But if the pound falls in terms of dollars—that is, if the dollar rises in terms of pounds—to a point where the exchange rate is £1 = $2, the American good will cost the British importer £1.5. This indicates that a rise of the exchange rate on the dollar will tend to make our exports more expensive to foreigners unless offset by a decline in the dollar prices of our exports. On the other hand, a decline of the exchange rate on the dollar will tend to lower the cost of our exports to foreigners in terms of their own moneys.

D. SOME IMPLICATIONS

These simple aritmetic examples illustrate principles that are very important in international economic relationships.

1. Considered by itself, a rise in the dollar prices of foreign moneys —a decline of the dollar in the exchange markets—tends to increase the dollar prices of our imports and to lower the prices of our exports in terms of foreign moneys. This will make American goods cheaper relative to foreign goods, unless offset by a rise of prices in the United States in terms of dollars relative to prices abroad in terms of foreign moneys.

2. Considered by itself, a decline in the dollar prices of foreign moneys—a rise of the dollar in the exchange markets—tends to decrease the dollar prices of our imports and to raise the prices of our exports as measured in foreign moneys. This will make American goods more expensive relative to foreign goods, unless offset by a decline of prices in the United States in terms of dollars relative to prices abroad in terms of foreign moneys.

For these and other reasons, nations have a great interest in the behavior of exchange rates. For example, they sometimes cheapen their money in the exchange markets in order to promote their exports and discourage their imports.

E. COMMENTS ON THE DETERMINATION OF EXCHANGE RATES

We shall now proceed to analyze the determination of exchange rates. Fortunately, we shall find that we can use an ordinary supply and demand analysis, for an exchange rate is only the price of one national money in terms of another. We supply dollars to demand foreign money in order to make payments to foreigners. They supply foreign money to demand dollars with which to make payments to us.

Let us now look at a balance of international payments to discover the various types of receipts and payments.

3. A Nation's Balance of International Payments

A. DEFINITION

A clear understanding of balances of international payments is indispensable to an understanding of international economic relationships. This concept has been well defined by the United States Department of Commerce: "The balance of payments of a country consists of the payments made, within a stated period of time, between the residents of that country and the residents of foreign countries. It may be defined in a statistical sense as an itemized account of transactions involving receipts from foreigners on the one hand and payments to foreigners on the other."[1]

Several basic points in this definition should be noted.

1. A nation's balance of payments includes all payments between the residents of that country, including its government, and all of the rest of the world during a stated period of time. The length of the period during which the flows occur should always be noted carefully.

2. All the transactions in a nation's balance of payments are divided into two broad classes: receipts and payments. *Receipts* include all the transactions that involve receipts from the residents of foreign countries during the stated period. Foreigners may pay us by giving us claims on foreign moneys, by using their moneys to buy dollars to remit to us, or by paying us in dollars which they had previously accumulated. We may therefore look upon receipts in our balance of payments as the supply of foreign money for dollars or as the demand for our dollars. On the other hand, the *payments* of a nation include all transactions that involve payments from the residents of that nation to the residents of other nations during the stated period. Thus, our payments include all the transactions that involve payments by us to foreigners during the stated period. These payments may be made in either dollars or foreign moneys. In either case, they require us to offer dollars for foreign currencies, either in our own exchange markets or in exchange markets abroad. We may therefore look upon payments in our balance of payments as the supply of dollars to foreigners, and receipts as the demand for American money by foreigners.

3. The receipts of one nation are, of course, the payments of others.
Let us now look at the various types of receipts and payments.

B. TYPES OF RECEIPTS

The sources of a nation's receipts may be classified as follows:

A. Exports of goods and services.
    1. Exports of merchandise (goods).
    2. Exports of services.
        a. Sales to foreigners of such services as transportation, finan-

---

[1] U.S. Department of Commerce, *The Balance of Payments of the United States,* Washington, 1937, p. 1.

cial services, services to foreign travelers in this country, and
so on.
b. Income from investments in foreign countries—interest, dividends, rents, royalties, etc.
B. Exports of capital claims.
1. Exports of long-term claims, such as stocks, bonds, and mortgages.
2. Exports of short-term claims, such as short-term promissory
notes.
C. Unilateral transfers received—gifts and grants from foreigners.
D. Exports of gold.

It is easy to see why a nation's exports of goods and services result
in receipts from foreigners. Some of the other items require more discussion. Our exports of capital claims produce receipts because foreigners must pay us for them. These include our sales to foreigners of
ownership and debt claims against the United States, and our resale to
them of claims that we had previously held against foreigners. Unilateral transfers, more commonly called gifts and grants, received by
us are receipts because they require foreign payments to us. And our
gold exports result in receipts because foreigners must pay for them,
either by offering us dollars or by supplying foreign currencies to us.

C. TYPES OF PAYMENTS

The transactions involving payments are, of course, just the reverse
of those which produce receipts. They include:

A. Imports of goods and services.
B. Imports of capital claims.
C. Unilateral payments to foreigners—both government grants and
private gifts.
D. Imports of gold.

We make payments to foreigners, thereby supplying dollars, to buy
goods and services from them, to buy capital claims from them—that
is, to lend to them, to buy ownership claims against them, or to re-
purchase from them their claims against the United States—to make
gifts to them, and to buy gold from them.

D. SUMMARY

The sources of a nation's receipts and payments may be summarized
as follows:

Transactions Producing Receipts	Transactions Requiring Payments
1. Exports of goods and services.	1. Imports of goods and services.
2. Exports of capital claims.	2. Imports of capital claims.
3. Unilateral transfers (gifts and grants) received.	3. Unilateral transfers (gifts and grants) to foreigners.
4. Exports of gold.	4. Imports of gold.

In tables showing a nation's balance of international payments, its receipts are often designated by (+) and its payments by (−). For some purposes it is convenient to deal not with total receipts and total payments in each category, but only with net receipts (+) or net payments (−) in each category.

Tables 46 and 47 show the balance of international payments of the United States in 1952. In that year we had large net receipts in the

TABLE 46. Balance of International Payments of the United States, 1952[2]
(In millions of dollars)

Item	Receipts (+)	Payments (−)	Net Receipts (+) or Net Payments (−)
Goods and services, total	$20,701	$15,728	$+4973
Goods	15,859	11,519	+4340
Transportation, travel, and other services	2,931	3,788	− 857
Income on investments	1,911	421	+1490
Loans			−1350
Gifts and grants			−5043
Gold purchases (−) or sales (+)			− 394
Foreign dollar accumulation			+1576
Statistical errors and omissions			+ 238

TABLE 47. Balance of International Payments of the United States, 1952[3]
(In millions of dollars)

What Foreigners Pay Us For		Methods Used by Foreigners to Finance Payments to the U.S.	
Purchases of U.S. exports	$20,701	U.S. imports	$15,728
Net purchases of gold and dollar balances from U.S.	1,182	U.S. government grants	4,628
	$21,883	U.S. government loans	454
Statistical errors and omissions	238	Private gifts from U.S.	415
Total	$22,121	Private loans from U.S.	896
		Total	$22,121

[2] Source: *Survey of Current Business,* March, 1953, p. 8.
[3] Source: *Ibid.*

categories of net exports of goods and net income on foreign investments, balanced by net payments for imported services, net imports
of capital claims, net unilateral payments to foreigners, and net imports of gold.

Table 47 gives essentially the same information as does Table 46,
which is in more standard form. However, Table 47 is designed to
show more clearly how the balance of payments table derives its name.
In effect it balances the payments made by foreigners against the funds
used to make these payments, the funds being classified by the sources
from which they are obtained.

4. The Determination of Exchange Rates: General Principles

A. THE NATURE OF THE ANALYSIS

Having noted the various types of international payments for which
moneys are demanded and supplied, we can now proceed to analyze
the determination of exchange rates.

The following analysis will rest on two simplified assumptions: (1)
that governments do not restrict the freedom of international payments, (2) that the British pound sterling represents all foreign
moneys. Actually, of course, there are exchange rates between the
dollar and all other national monetary units, but it will be convenient
to assume that the exchange rate between the dollar and the British
pound represents exchange rates between the dollar and all foreign
moneys. In each case we shall state the exchange rate as the price of
the foreign monetary unit in terms of dollars, such as £1 = $2.80.
A rise in the price of the pound, say to $2.83, is the same as a fall in
the exchange rate on the dollar in terms of pounds; less English money
is required to buy a dollar. And a decline in the price of the pound,
say to $2.78, is the same as a rise of the dollar in terms of pounds;
more English money is required to buy a dollar.

Our analysis will be stated in terms of supply and demand—the
supply of dollars to buy foreign money, and the demand for dollars by
those who offer foreign moneys.

B. THE COMPONENTS OF SUPPLY AND DEMAND

As already noted, the quantity of dollars supplied to buy foreign
money in exchange markets may be looked upon as all our payments
to foreigners—as our payments to them for goods, securities, and gold
to make gifts and grants to them. Thus an analysis of the supply of
dollars or of our demand for foreign moneys requires an investigation

into all the factors that determine the amount of foreign money we would demand at each exchange rate in order to make these various types of payments.

On the other hand, we found that the number of dollars demanded, or the amount of foreign moneys supplied to buy dollars, arise out of all our receipts from foreigners. These include foreign payments to us for goods, securities, and gold and any gifts and grants that foreigners make to us. Thus to analyze the supply of foreign money offered for dollars we must look at all the factors that determine the amounts of dollars that would be demanded at each exchange rate to make payments to us.

c. The Quantity of Dollars Supplied for Foreign Money

Among the principal factors that determine the dollar demand for foreign money are the following: (1) The level of national income in the United States. When our national income is high, we are likely to import larger physical amounts of finished goods and raw materials than when our national income is lower. (2) The prices of domestic goods and services relative to the costs of imported goods. When most goods can be purchased more cheaply abroad than at home, our imports are likely to be larger than when most domestic goods are cheaper than imports. (3) The preferences of our people for foreign goods as against domestic products. (4) Appraisals of the relative safety of securities at home and abroad, and the relative interest rates. If foreign investments are considered relatively safe, and interest rates abroad are high relative to those here, we may offer large amounts of dollars to buy capital claims from foreigners. But in the reverse situation we may offer no dollars for this purpose, and we may even sell some of our foreign holdings. (5) The availability of gold abroad and its relative prices at home and abroad. We may offer large amounts of dollars to buy gold abroad if it is available there at prices that are favorable relative to the price in the United States. But we may offer no dollars for this purpose if gold is unavailable abroad or is priced too high. (6) Our desires to make gifts and grants to foreigners.

Because of changes in these and other factors, the supply of dollars to demand foreign moneys can shift markedly.

d. The Quantity of Foreign Moneys Supplied for Dollars

The quantity of foreign moneys supplied for dollars—our receipts from foreigners—depends on factors similar to those discussed above:

(1) the level of national incomes abroad; (2) the costs of our exports relative to the prices of foreign goods and services; (3) foreigners' preferences for our exports as against their own products; (4) the safety of securities here relative to the safety of funds abroad, and interest rates here relative to those in other countries; (5) the availability of gold here, and its relative prices here and abroad; (6) the desires of foreigners to make unilateral payments to us.

E. SUMMARY

As in other cases of price determination, exchange rates at any time will tend toward the level at which the quantities supplied and demanded are equal. Moreover, the level of exchange rates can be shifted by anything that changes demand-supply relationships. For example, it can be shifted by changes in the relative income levels of different countries, relative price levels, relative interest rates, and so on. We shall return later to these points. In the meantime we shall study pegged exchange rates and flexible exchange rates.

5. Pegged Exchange Rates and an International Gold Standard

A. THE MEANING OF PEGGED EXCHANGE RATES

A common practice has been for governments to *peg* exchange rates —to hold them stable or within very narrow limits for long periods of time. We shall deal here with government pegging, private buyers and sellers being free to make international payments without government interference.

Essentially, a government pegs exchange rates the same way it can stabilize the price of wheat or any other commodity. It does so by purchasing and selling moneys at a fixed or nearly fixed price. Suppose the United States government, acting alone or with the British government, decided to peg the dollar-pound exchange rate at £1 = $2.80. It could prevent the pound from falling below $2.80 by supplying dollars to buy all the pounds that are offered and that other buyers are not willing to take at that price. And it could prevent the pound from rising above this price by supplying all the pounds that are demanded at this price.

It should be noted that our government should be able to keep the price of pounds from falling below $2.80, for all it has to do is offer a sufficient number of dollars to buy pounds. But it can keep the price of pounds from rising only if it has or can get enough pounds to satisfy all the demands at the $2.80 price. Attempts to peg exchange rates on foreign moneys have often failed because a government did not have and could not get enough foreign money to meet all the demands at the fixed price.

Governments have often pegged exchange rates through this device of directly exchanging one national money for another. More often, however, they have achieved the same result by buying and selling gold at a fixed price and permitting the free import and export of gold. Let us now see how exchange rates are pegged under an international gold standard.

B. THE PEGGING OF EXCHANGE RATES UNDER AN INTERNATIONAL
   GOLD STANDARD

We have already noted the essential characteristics of a gold standard.[4] A nation keeps its monetary unit at a constant value in terms of gold by standing ready to buy at a fixed price all the gold that is offered to it and to sell at approximately the same fixed price all the gold that is demanded from it. This requires that the nation do the following: (1) Fix the price of gold. The official price of gold in the United States is $35 an ounce; the dollar is worth $\frac{1}{35}$ of an ounce of gold. (2) Buy at the fixed price all gold offered to it. This prevents the price of gold from falling. (3) Sell at the same fixed price all the gold that is demanded from it. This prevents the price of gold from rising. In these ways a nation stabilizes the price of gold; in other words, it stabilizes the gold value of its monetary unit.

When the monetary units of two countries are both fixed in terms of gold in this way, the exchange rate between them must remain approximately stable at a rate reflecting the relative gold content of the monetary units. To illustrate this point, let us assume that the price of gold in the United States is $35 an ounce, and that the price of gold in England is £12.5 an ounce—that the value of a pound is 1/12.5 of an ounce of gold. So long as the dollar is kept equal to 1/35 of an ounce of gold and the pound is kept equal to 1/12.5 of an ounce of gold, the gold value of the pound will be 2.8 times that of the dollar $\left(\frac{1/12.5}{1/35} = \frac{35}{12.5} = 2.8\right)$. In terms of gold, £1 = $2.80. This is called the *par of exchange* between the two moneys.

So long as the United States stands ready to sell gold at $35 an

4 See pp. 266–268, 297–298 above.

ounce and the British to buy it at £12.5 an ounce, the actual exchange rate on the pound cannot rise above the par of exchange by more than the cost of transferring title to the gold from persons in the United States to those in Britain, the cost including the necessary profit to those handling the transactions. This is because banks and other competing exchange dealers can obtain pounds by purchasing gold here with dollars and selling the gold to Britain for pounds. For example, any exchange dealer can get 12.5 million pounds by exporting a million ounces of gold which cost him $35 million and incurring transfer costs of $100,000, making a total cost of $35.1 million, or $2.808 per pound. So long as this method of acquiring pounds is open to all exchange dealers, the actual exchange rate on the pound cannot rise much above this level, for competing exchange dealers will supply at this price all the pounds that are demanded.

Similarly, the actual exchange rate on the pound could not fall below the par of exchange by more than the cost of transferring gold from Britain to the United States. This is because dealers can buy claims on pounds, use the pounds to buy gold in Britain, and sell the gold for dollars in the United States.

In summary, the maintenance of an international gold standard is one way of keeping exchange rates relatively stable. In fact, stability of exchange rates is often cited as one of the great advantages of an international gold standard. We shall examine this issue later. However, two important points should be made here.

1. To prevent its money from depreciating in exchange markets, a nation must be both willing and able to export gold at a fixed price, and to whatever extent is necessary to balance its international payments. On some occasions it may have to permit large gold exports to balance its net payments to foreigners on account of its net imports of goods, services, and capital claims. This contractive influence on its domestic economy may at times be unwelcome.[5]

2. To prevent its money from appreciating in exchange markets, a nation must be willing to purchase gold at a fixed price. That is, it must increase the supply of its money issued in exchange for gold and do this to whatever extent proves to be necessary to balance its international payments. It may therefore have large gold imports if it has large net receipts in its other international accounts. This expansive influence on its domestic economy may be unwelcome in times of actual or threatened inflation.

[5] See below, pp. 543–546.

6. Flexible Exchange Rates

A. EXCHANGE RATES IN THE ABSENCE OF PEGGING

It should be clear that exchange rates, like other prices, are likely to fluctuate in the absence of pegging. For example, the dollar price of pounds may rise if the United States will not sell gold for export at a fixed price or if Britain will not supply pounds for gold at a fixed price. The number of pounds demanded may become so large relative to the number supplied as to raise the exchange rate considerably. On the other hand, the dollar price of pounds may fall if the British will not sell gold for export at a fixed price or if the United States will not issue dollars for gold at a fixed price. The quantity of pounds supplied could become so large relative to the quantity demanded as to lower the exchange rate on the pound.

This leads to a number of important questions. How are exchange rates determined in the absence of pegging? They depend, of course, on supply and demand, being at the level that equalizes the supply of dollars for pounds and the supply of pounds for dollars. But can we go further and find any "normal" rate toward which actual market exchange rates will tend at any time?

B. PURCHASING-POWER PARITY

The purchasing-power parity theory attempts to provide such a norm. In its simplest form this theory states, "Moneys will tend to exchange for each other at a rate reflecting their relative purchasing power over goods and services in their respective countries." Suppose, for example, that price levels in the United States and Britain are such that £1 will buy in Britain as much as $2.50 will buy in the United States. Only at an exchange rate of £1 = $2.50 would the cost of buying in Britain and the United States be equal. At a higher exchange rate for the pound, say £1 = $3.00, British goods would be more expensive than American, so that both Americans and Englishmen would tend to buy in the U.S., and the quantity of sterling demanded in order to buy in Britain would probably be less than the amount of sterling supplied to buy in the United States. At a lower exchange rate on the pound, say £1 = $2.00, British goods would be cheaper than American, so that the amount of sterling demanded would probably exceed the amount supplied.

It should be evident that every change in the relative levels of prices in the countries involved will change purchasing-power parity. Suppose that while prices in Britain remain constant the level of prices in the United States doubles; that is, the dollar loses half its purchasing power. In this case purchasing-power parity would change from £1 = $2.50 to £1 = $5.00. Only if the exchange rate on the dollar fell to this level would American goods be as cheap as those in Britain.

Unfortunately, we shall have to conclude that the purchasing-power parity theory has serious shortcomings. Nevertheless, it contains important elements of truth and is quite useful for some purposes.

C. APPLICATIONS OF THE THEORY

In the first place, it helps to explain why a nation's money tends to depreciate in exchange markets when the nation undergoes serious internal inflation not matched in other countries. In such cases people often espouse a devil theory of exchange depreciation, placing the entire blame on nasty speculators or some sort of international conspiracy among financiers. Speculative sales of a nation's money may, of course, accentuate its depreciation in exchange markets, but the purchasing-power parity theory makes it clear that a great rise in a nation's internal price levels should be expected to lower the exchange rate on its money if its inflation is not matched in other countries. In fact, failure of its exchange rate to fall sufficiently would make its goods and services more expensive than those of other countries.

In the second place, the purchasing-power parity theory provides a very rough guide for the fixing of exchange rates. Suppose that the world has gone through a world war with varying degrees of inflation in different countries, and that it now has the problem of setting a new network of exchange rates. The relative purchasing powers of the various monetary units in their respective countries are certainly relevant to the setting of exchange rates that will balance international payments at appropriate levels. If the exchange rate on a nation's currency is fixed far above this level, the nation's goods will tend to be more expensive than those in other markets, and its imports will tend to exceed its exports. On the other hand, if its exchange rate is set far below this level its goods will tend to be cheaper than those of other countries, and its exports will tend to exceed its imports.

D. SHORTCOMINGS OF THE THEORY

Despite its attractiveness, the purchasing-power parity theory of exchange rates has several shortcomings.

1. The logical difficulty of selecting appropriate price levels for measurement and comparison. Which prices should be compared— only those of internationally traded goods? All prices within the country? The prices of immovable things, such as gravel pits? The wages of domestic servants? How should the various prices be weighted?

2. The effects of exchange rates on domestic price levels. Those who hold to this theory often assume that domestic price levels are determined independently of exchange rates, and that the latter merely reflect the relative heights of domestic price levels. But exchange rates themselves can exert a great influence on domestic prices. Consider the case of Britain, whose imports and exports are very large relative to her national output. A decline of the exchange rate on the pound might well tend to raise British price levels. Her imports of both finished goods and raw materials would then tend to cost more in terms of pounds unless foreign prices declined sufficiently. The prices and the quantities demanded of her exports would also tend to rise in terms of pounds, for each unit of foreign money received for her exports could be exchanged for more pounds.

3. The influence of other factors on actual exchange rates. Factors other than changes in relative price levels can influence actual exchange rates. For example, the pound might depreciate because many pounds are supplied to buy capital claims abroad, because of a decrease in foreign preferences for British exports, and so on.

E. SUMMARY

In short, we can offer no simple and logically neat theory of exchange rates in the absence of pegging. Actual rates are determined by the supply of and demand for the various national moneys, and these demand and supply conditions are influenced by all the factors we mentioned earlier. Among these are the levels of national income in the various countries, relative price levels, relative preferences for the products of the various countries, the relative safety of claims, relative interest rates, unilateral payments, the prices and availability of gold, and so on. The purchasing-power parity theory is not broad enough to encompass all these factors.

7. A "Favorable" Balance of Trade

A. DEFINITION

One of the oldest goals of international commercial policy is to achieve what is often called a "favorable" balance of trade, meaning a net excess of exports over imports of goods and services. In fact, some insist that exports should be increased as much as possible and imports depressed to a minimum in order to achieve as large a "favorable" balance as possible. This raises at least two questions: How could such an export surplus be achieved and maintained? Even if attainable, would an export surplus be "favorable" to a nation?

B. The Mechanics of a "Favorable" Balance

An export surplus means that we are shipping away more of our goods and services (measured in money) to foreigners than we are getting from them. If we are unwilling to let foreigners pay for their purchases from us out of their production, they can offer to pay us gold, or try to buy the goods on credit or to get them free. We can send to foreigners more goods and services than we receive from them only by taking gold, by granting them loans, or by giving the goods away. A favorable balance of trade therefore means that we must be receiving gold from abroad or making loans or gifts to foreigners. Moreover, any decrease in a nation's imports must be accompanied by a decrease in its exports unless the nation increases its payments to the rest of the world in the form of net gifts, loans, or purchases of gold.

The ability of a nation to achieve and maintain an export surplus is limited by many factors. Neither its people nor its government may be willing to continue making large gifts to foreigners, and in some cases the foreigners may refuse them. Its net purchases of securities from foreigners are limited by its willingness to lend and by the willingness of foreigners to borrow. And its ability to import gold is limited not only by the available gold supply abroad, but also by the willingness of foreigners to part with it. For all these reasons, and for others that will be mentioned later, a nation's attempt to expand its exports while decreasing its imports may be unsuccessful. For all nations to have export surpluses is obviously impossible.

C. Is a "Favorable" Balance Favorable?

The second question—whether an export surplus has "favorable" economic effects on a nation—can be put this way: Is it favorable to a nation to use part of its receipts from exports to make gifts to foreigners, to lend to them, or to buy gold from them, rather than to import goods and services?

The most naïve answer that has been given to this question is that a continuing "favorable" trade balance is good because it will make a nation rich. The nation's accumulation of gold and debt claims against foreigners is taken to measure its wealth and prosperity, and an unfavorable balance to indicate an improvident spendthrift country.

D. A "Favorable" Balance as a Gift to Foreigners

It is not difficult to see what is wrong with this argument. If a country consistently has a favorable balance, it is constantly depriving itself of goods and services, giving them to foreigners and refusing a *quid pro quo* (aside from I.O.U.'s). A nation that does this must be keeping down the standard of living of its people by giving things to foreigners without real reimbursement. True, it is receiving gold and I.O.U.'s in return, but these are valuable only if they will someday be used to buy goods and services from abroad—to finance imports in years when its balance is "unfavorable." The gold itself, especially when buried in a Fort Knox, is neither edible nor wearable. It does not make houses more comfortable or otherwise contribute directly to the material well-being of the citizens as will an automobile, a hat, or a bunch of bananas. Large gold receipts can seriously disturb the nation's economy by leading to an expansion of money supplies and inflationary pressure. I.O.U.'s have even less value in themselves than has gold, for they cannot be used for jewelry or filling teeth. In seeking to achieve a perpetually "favorable" balance of trade a country is therefore attempting to give away the useful for the useless—real wealth for symbols of wealth.

Of course it is not wise for a nation to go to the other extreme and deliberately seek to achieve a chronic deficit in its balance of payments. Other nations will not stand for it, and will refuse to keep making gifts and credit extensions after the deficit country's gold stock has been spent. The country with the payments deficit will then not be able to get the imports that it wants or needs. That is the problem which has faced many nations since the end of World War II. Moreover, while a huge gold stock may be of little use to a nation, it is possible for a country's gold supplies to fall to undesirably low levels. Because of their use in meeting temporary deficits and because of the effects of gold supplies on the quantity of money in a country, it can be most inconvenient for a nation if its gold stocks fall too low.

Despite the weakness in the argument we have just examined, a "favorable" trade balance can sometimes produce desirable results for short and sometimes even for protracted periods.

E. CAPITAL LENDING AND A "FAVORABLE" BALANCE

One case in which a favorable trade balance can produce favorable results is that of orderly international lending by countries with abundant capital and low capital yields to countries where capital is scarce and yields high. This leads to a favorable balance of trade, for it permits foreigners to buy from the nation goods which are not currently balanced by their exports of goods and services to the nation. Suppose that in the United States capital is so abundant that many of the best investment opportunities are used up at least for the moment and therefore the domestic use of additional capital goods will increase national output by an amount equal to only 4 percent of the new investment. Let us assume that in Brazil, on the other hand, capital is so scarce that additional capital applied where it is most sorely needed will increase annual national output by an amount equal to 10 percent of the new investment. An international loan at an intermediate rate of interest, say 7 percent, may benefit not only Brazil but also the United States.

Because of the dollar loan, Brazil can increase her capital supply, either by importing capital goods or by importing consumer goods and diverting some of her workers and other productive factors away from the production of consumer goods toward the construction of machinery, factories, roads, etc. If this increases annual national output by an amount equal to 10 percent of the new capital, while interest payments are only 7 percent, the net national income remaining at the disposal of Brazilians may be increased by an amount equal to 3 percent of the increase in the capital supply.

The United States may also benefit if in fact she receives the promised interest payments and the principal remains safe. The annual interest receipts from Brazil can be used to import goods and services worth more than the additional goods and services that might have been produced at home by adding to the domestic supply of capital goods. We shall find presently that whether or not the U.S. actually collects the promised interest payments and repayments of principal will depend not only on the willingness of foreigners to pay us, but also on our willingness to accept payments.

F. A "FAVORABLE" BALANCE AND EMPLOYMENT

An export surplus financed by net gifts, loans, and gold purchases may also benefit a country in two other ways. In the first place, it may be a way of aiding other countries and of earning their diplomatic, military, and economic cooperation. But the results may be just the reverse if the country gets its export surplus by restricting imports, or if it clumsily uses its economic aid as an excuse for trying to dominate the policies of other countries.

In the second place, an export surplus may aid a country in averting or remedying deflation and unemployment. By making gifts to other countries, by lending to them, or by purchasing gold from them, it may expand its export sales, thereby raising output, employment, and incomes in its export industries. This initial increase may stimulate further increases in national income by inducing increases in domestic consumption and investment. Any net gold imports may also tend to be stimulating by creating additional money and bank reserves.

However, this argument for striving to achieve an export surplus must be used with care. (1) It is relevant only if unemployment and deflation are really a threat. In a period of inflationary pressure a "favorable" balance will strengthen the upward pressures on prices. (2) A nation may not succeed in achieving and maintaining an export surplus if it tries to do so by reducing its imports. Other nations may respond by decreasing their purchases from it. A "favorable" balance in the one nation must mean an "unfavorable balance" elsewhere and must result in deflationary pressure elsewhere. These other countries may not appreciate the deflationary effect on their own countries and will therefore retaliate. We shall come across this process of "exporting unemployment" again.

(3) Even if an export surplus would be an effective means of preventing or remedying unemployment, it may be less desirable than an expansion of domestic demand. After all, we can always increase our own demand for our own output through such measures as reducing taxes, increasing government expenditures, and increasing the money supply and lowering interest rates. Increasing employment through a "favorable" trade balance often turns out to be merely getting rid of unsalable commodities by giving them away to foreigners. While this may be more useful than killing pigs and plowing under cotton, it must be realized that the goods going abroad could be used to enhance our own living standard.

G. UNFAVORABLE EFFECTS OF A "FAVORABLE" BALANCE

In many cases an export surplus may have highly unfavorable effects on a nation. Large gifts to foreigners may fail to purchase their good will and instead actually create ill will. Large export surpluses and gold imports in times of actual or threatened inflation may create or accentuate inflationary pressures by expanding a nation's money supply.[6] And loans to foreigners to finance the export surplus may prove to be uncollectable, especially if the nation perists in trying to maintain an export surplus. This point is worth elaboration.

A nation can make net collections of interest and debts from foreigners only to the extent that these net receipts in its balance of payments are balanced by net payments to foreigners as net gifts, net imports of gold, and net imports of goods and services. These are the only ways foreigners can get the money to pay interest and repay debts to the nation. To the extent that a nation is willing to have net imports of goods and services, it provides foreigners with money that they can use to repay debts and pay interest to it. But it is not at all uncommon for a nation to insist on having net exports of goods and services at the same time that it is trying to collect interest and debt from foreigners. This is possible only to the extent that the country makes net gifts to foreigners or gets gold from them. Making gifts to foreigners is indeed a strange way of collecting debts. And continuous gold flows in one direction are well calculated to disturb the economies of both the gold-importing and gold-exporting nations.

We often hear the complaint that foreigners have defaulted on their promises to pay interest or to repay debt to us. Before placing all the blame on them, we should ask ourselves whether our own trade policies have not been such as to make these payments extremely difficult or even impossible. We might also ask ourselves whether we have not refused to accept payment in the one form that provides the wherewithal to enhance our living standard—the real goods and services that make up our wealth and income.

SUGGESTED READINGS
(See list at end of Chapter 25.)

QUESTIONS

1. Show, using numerical examples, how when Britain devalued the pound from £1 = $4.03 to £1 = $2.80 in 1949:
   a. She made British cars cheaper to Americans.

[6] See below, pp. 542–544.

b. She made American cars dearer to Englishmen.

c. She made it more expensive for British manufacturers to produce cars because they have to buy raw materials from abroad.

d. Show how the rise in the cost of producing cars might have results which partially offset their increased cheapness to Americans after the devaluation.

e. What is likely to be the initial effect of such a devaluation on British living standards?

2. Suppose exchange rates are £1 = $5, £1 = 20 Swiss francs, $1 = 10 Swiss francs.

a. Show how you can make some money.

b. Show how in the process of making this money (the process is called *arbitrage*) these exchange rates will be driven back into line by the effects of supply and demand.

c. Give some numerical examples of exchange rates which are in line and some which are not.

3. By means of the accountant's magic a nation's balance of payments always balances.

a. In terms of Table 47, show how this is accomplished.

b. How is this possible for a nation with a "favorable" or an "unfavorable" balance of payments?

4. a. Explain why America's exports constitute an American demand for foreign money.

b. Why foreigners' exports constitute part of the supply of foreign money.

c. Why America's imports partly constitute our supply of dollars to foreigners.

d. What else constitutes an American supply of dollars to foreigners?

e. What makes up the foreign demand for dollars?

f. Compare these results with those in Table 47.

5. If all countries were on a gold standard:

a. Why would a large gold discovery not affect the dollar price of gold?

b. Why would it not affect the dollar price of pounds?

c. How might it affect the money supply in the United States, and American commercial bank reserves?

d. How might it affect the dollar price of wheat?

6. Explain exactly how a depression in the United States would affect the exchange rate of the dollar under flexible exchange rates. In your answer describe in detail the effects on supplies of and demands for dollars.

7. Suppose some European nation had been permitted to pay her debts to the United States in produce.

a. What might be the effect on the U.S. in the absence of an effective high-employment policy?
b. If effective monetary and fiscal policies maintain a high level of employment in the U.S.?
c. What can this country do to repay us if we refuse to import from it?

8. Show the ways in which receipts of gold from abroad can be:
a. Desirable to the U.S.
b. Undesirable.
c. Useless but innocuous.

CHAPTER 27

Balance of Payments Problems

Since World War II we have been hearing that Europe is suffering from a serious dollar shortage and a chronic balance of payment deficit. This situation has affected price levels and national income in this country and elsewhere. In turn, the balance of payments has been affected by the behavior of prices and incomes. In this chapter we shall examine this type of problem and the fundamental relationships between international payments and national income, employment, and prices in the trading countries.

1. Equilibrium and Disequilibrium in Balances of Payments

A. AN UNFAVORABLE BALANCE OF PAYMENTS

The statement that a nation is having "balance of payment difficulties" suggests that in some sense the country is finding it difficult to meet its payments to foreigners. We shall use this term balance of payments difficulties to mean a tendency toward an "unfavorable balance of payments." This means that the country can bring its total receipts from foreigners up to the level of its payments to foreigners only by exporting part of its gold reserves, by drawing down its holdings of foreign moneys, or receiving gifts or loans from abroad.

As popularly used, the term also implies one or both of the following: (1) The nation is temporarily balancing its international accounts in ways that cannot be sustained over a long period. For example, it is exhausting its reserves of gold and foreign moneys, or at least is reducing them to undesirably low levels. (2) It can continue to balance its

536

international accounts in these ways only at the expense of adverse effects on its economy.

As we saw earlier, a decrease in its holdings of gold and foreign moneys is not always harmful to a nation. In fact, it may be advantageous for a country with large holdings of gold and foreign moneys to trade part of them to other nations for goods, services, or earning assets. Indeed, this is precisely the function of these reserves—to cover temporary payments deficits. Moreover, the export of gold and foreign moneys may at times be useful in curbing internal inflation. Nevertheless, large and persistent losses of gold and foreign moneys can force a nation to curtail its supply of money and credit, raise its interest rates, discourage investment, and suffer serious deflation and unemployment.[1] This has happened many times.

B. CHRONIC DISEQUILIBRIUM

This brings us to a highly important problem in international economic relationships. Suppose that balances of international payments are out of equilibrium, some countries tending to have large and persistent "favorable" balances and others large and persistent "unfavorable" balances. How can balances of payments be adjusted so that some countries will no longer tend to increase their holdings of gold and foreign moneys at the expense of the others?

This requires, of course, that international payments and receipts for goods, services, and other capital claims balance out over a reasonable period of time so that no *net* payments of gold and moneys need occur. The nations that tended to have favorable balances must increase their payments relative to their receipts on these other accounts, and those that tended to have unfavorable balances must increase their receipts relative to their payments on these other accounts. But we have yet to answer the question that is basic to economic policy: By what methods can these adjustments in international payments be made?

2. Methods of Adjusting Balances of Payments

Balances of international payments may be brought into equilibrium by one or more of the following six types of adjustments: (1) of relative levels of national income, (2) of relative national price levels, (3) of relative levels of interest rates, (4) of exchange rates, (5) of the rate of unilateral transfers, and (6) of direct government controls

[1] See above, pp. 297–298.

over trade and payments. While these are listed separately, they are frequently interrelated, as we shall see.

A. ADJUSTMENTS IN THE RELATIVE LEVELS OF NATIONAL INCOME

The level of a country's national income is a major determinant of its international payments. Because it increases the purchasing power of its citizens, each increase in a country's national income tends to raise its demand for imports from foreigners and perhaps to reduce the amount of its produce available for export by increasing its domestic demand for its own products. A rise in its national income thus tends to reduce a nation's favorable balance. On the other hand, each decrease of its national income tends to reduce its demand for imports and perhaps also to raise its exports by lowering the domestic demand for its own output and in this way working to reduce any balance of payments deficit.

Thus a rise of national income in countries with favorable balances relative to the levels of national income in countries with unfavorable balances tends to equilibrate international payments. In response to their relatively higher levels of national income the countries that previously had favorable balances tend to increase their payments relative to their receipts. And in response to their relatively lower levels of national income, the countries that previously had unfavorable balances tend to decrease their purchases relative to their sales.

B. ADJUSTMENTS OF RELATIVE NATIONAL PRICE LEVELS

International payments may also be adjusted, at least in part, by a decline of prices in countries with unfavorable balances relative to prices in countries with favorable balances. This makes the countries which previously had unfavorable balances more attractive markets in which to buy and less attractive markets in which to sell; their exports tend to increase relative to their imports. The reverse occurs in the countries which previously had favorable balances.[2]

C. ADJUSTMENTS IN RELATIVE LEVELS OF INTEREST RATES

A rise of interest rates in countries with unfavorable balances relative to rates in countries with favorable balances may also be helpful, at least in curtailing a temporary imbalance. This tends to induce a flow of loans from the now relatively lower-interest countries with favorable balances to those with unfavorable balances, or at least to

[2] But see the reservation below, pp. 547–548, especially footnote 6.

curtail any flow in the opposite direction. If international lending is considered quite safe, even a small difference in interest rates may induce a sufficient flow of credit to balance international payments, at least temporarily. But this method is likely to be ineffective when international lending is considered risky.

d. Adjustment of Exchange Rates

Another method of adjusting international payments is by reducing exchange rates on the moneys of countries with unfavorable balances and raising exchange rates on the moneys of countries with favorable balances. The immediate effect is the same as that of a relative lowering of prices in the country with the deficit. The countries whose moneys have been cheapened find it easier to export and more expensive to import, for in terms of foreign moneys their goods have become cheaper, and in terms of their moneys foreign goods have become more expensive.[3] Those whose moneys have become more expensive in exchange markets find it harder to export and cheaper to import. Some of the limitations on this method of balancing international payments will be considered later.

e. Adjustments of the Rate of Unilateral Transfers

Payments may also be adjusted by unilateral transfers, the government or people of the countries with favorable balances making gifts or grants to countries with unfavorable balances. This of course requires a willingness to give and to receive such aid.

f. Direct Government Controls

Governments can utilize many types of direct controls to adjust international payments. Governments of countries tending to have unfavorable balances may restrict payments to foreigners by such devices as higher tariffs on imports, direct limitations of the quantities of imports, complete prohibition of some types of imports, and limitations on purchases of claims from foreigners. They may also seek to expand exports by subsidizing them, by forcing producers to sell in foreign rather than in domestic markets, and by other similar methods. They may also impose strict controls on sales and purchases of foreign money. Governments of countries with favorable balances may attempt to increase their international payments relative to their receipts by comparable measures to promote imports and discourage exports.

[3] See above, pp. 515–517.

G. SUMMARY

In summary, the six general methods of adjusting international payments are direct government controls affecting receipts and payments, changes of exchange rates and of the magnitude of unilateral transfers, and adjustments in the relative levels of national income, prices, and interest rates of the countries dealing with each other. One of the great problems in international economic relationships is to determine which method or combination of methods should be employed to establish and maintain equilibrium in balances of payments.

An international gold standard, it has often been claimed, will achieve this result automatically, without government control and supervision. Let us see how it would operate.

3. Adjustments Under an International Gold Standard

A. EXCHANGE RATE STABILITY

As we found earlier, exchange rates among national moneys that are fixed in terms of gold must remain almost stable. They cannot vary beyond the rather narrow limits determined by the cost of transferring gold.[4] This stability of exchange rates is one of the great advantages claimed for the international gold standard. It enables people to hold or owe foreign moneys and to agree to buy or sell them in the future without assuming the risk of the large losses or gains that might result from wide fluctuations in exchange rates. But the proponents of this type of standard also claim that it provides an effective method of adjusting international balances, and that it does so with no more than small changes in exchange rates, without necessitating unilateral transfers and without requiring any direct government controls over international receipts and payments.

B. THE MEANS OF ADJUSTMENT

Of the six methods of eliminating balance of payments disequilibrium, three play no part in the ordinary gold-standard adjustment mechanism as ordinarily described. These are changes in exchange rates, direct government controls, and unilateral transfers. This is what is meant by the mechanism's being "automatic," for any of these three methods requires direct government intervention. The mechanism must therefore work via its effects on national income, price levels, and interest rates.

[4] See pp. 523–525 above.

The proponents of the gold standard recognize that balances of payments can get out of adjustment temporarily, with gold flowing from country to country. But they argue that the initial payments disequilibrium and the accompanying gold flow will, without planning or interference, readjust national incomes, prices, and interest rates in such a way as to restore equilibrium in balances of payments and terminate gold flows.

The country or countries with favorable balances and gold inflows would tend to have higher national incomes, higher prices, and lower interest rates, thereby increasing their international payments relative to their receipts. At the same time, the country or countries with un-favorable balances and gold outflows would tend to have lower national incomes, lower prices, and higher interest rates, thereby in-creasing their receipts relative to their payments. This process would continue until equilibrium in balances of payments had been restored and the gold flow ended.

To illustrate the adjustment process in more detail, let us assume the following situation. There are only two countries—the United States and Great Britain, the latter representing the rest of the world. Owing to the emergence of a large export surplus for the United States, bal-ances of payments get out of equilibrium and gold flows from Britain to the United States. This initial disequilibrium will tend to bring about readjustments of two types—those resulting from the multiplier effects of the trade balance, and those resulting from the monetary effects of the gold flows.

c. The Direct Effect on National Incomes

By the multiplier effects we mean the sum of the direct and indirect effects of the trade balance on the levels of national income. Suppose that the export surplus of the United States has resulted from an actual increase of our exports. This means higher incomes for enterprisers and workers in our export industries. With higher incomes, they are likely to increase their rate of consumption, which will increase in-comes in the consumption goods industries. In turn these recipients of increased incomes will increase their expenditures, and so increase the incomes of the people from whom they buy, and so on.

Thus an increase in our export balance, like an increase in our rate of domestic investment, can lead to a larger rise in our national income by inducing an increase in consumption. Moreover, both the increase of our exports and the rise of our consumption may induce an increase in our rate of domestic investment. These increases in our national income tend to raise our international payments relative to our receipts. With higher incomes, and perhaps a tendency toward higher domestic prices, we are likely to import more finished goods and raw materials for consumption and investment purposes. We may also export less because of our larger domestic demands for our own products.

In the meantime, the initial import balance of Great Britain may have set off a downward multiplier movement there. The net drain of income to pay for imports tends to decrease the British demand for her domestic consumption goods and perhaps also her expenditures for domestic investment. To the extent that her national income falls, Britain will tend to import less and perhaps also to export more because of the lower home demands for her own products.

D. THE GOLD FLOW AND INTEREST RATES

We come now to the monetary effects of the international gold flow. As we found in an earlier chapter, an inflow of gold to the United States initially increases by an equal amount all of the following: (1) the public's money supply, (2) the supply of commercial bank reserves, and (3) the gold certificate reserves of the Federal Reserve banks.[5] The direct increases in the public's money supply and commercial bank reserves tend to increase the supply of money and credit, and so to lower interest rates and stimulate investment even if the Federal Reserve takes no action. But the liberalization of money and credit will be even greater if the increase of its gold certificate reserves leads the Federal Reserve to lower its discount rates (the interest rate on its loans to commercial banks) and to purchase government securities, thereby raising the price of securities (lowering interest rates).

In Britain the loss of gold tends to have the reverse effects—to lower the public's money supply, the reserves of commercial banks, and the gold reserves of the central bank. The direct decreases in the public's money supply and commercial bank reserves tend to curtail money and credit and to raise interest rates, even if the Bank of England takes no action. But the tightening of credit will be even greater if its loss of gold reserves leads the Bank of England to raise its discount rates and sell securities.

E. THE GOLD FLOW, INTEREST RATES, INCOMES, AND PRICE LEVELS

The tendency toward easier credit in the United States and tighter credit in Britain serves to readjust balances of payments in two princi-

[5] See pp. 266–268 above.

pal ways. In the first place, the tendency for interest rates in London to be higher relative to those in New York may induce a flow of loans to London, or at least to curtail any flow to New York.

In the second place—and possibly of more importance—the changes in credit conditions affect the levels of national income and perhaps also price levels. The more liberal supply of money and credit and the lower interest rates in the United States tend to encourage investment and expenditures generally and so to raise the level of our national income. Our prices also are given an upward push as money supplies and expenditures increase. This serves to increase our exports relative to our imports. On the other hand, the tightening of credit in Britain tends to lower British investment and national income, and her price levels. This tends to decrease British imports relative to her exports.

F. SUMMARY OF THE ADJUSTMENT PROCESS

Under an international gold standard, with its relatively fixed exchange rates, adjustments are made through the multiplier effects of trade balances and the monetary effects of gold flows.

In our example we assumed that the adjustment was achieved through both an expansion in the United States and a contraction in Britain. It should be evident that if either country fails to adjust, a greater burden of adjustment will be thrown on the other. For example, failure of income and prices to rise in the United States would force a greater contraction on Britain, and failure of the British to contract would force a larger expansion on the United States. If both refuse to adjust adequately, as has sometimes been the case, the disequilibrium may continue until one has lost all its gold or has resorted to other measures, such as depreciating its currency or initiating direct controls on international payments.

G. THE GOLD STANDARD AND INTERNATIONAL INTERDEPENDENCE

This adjustment process indicates the international interdependence of monetary policies and of the levels of national money incomes, prices, and interest rates under an international gold standard with stable exchange rates. Any change in monetary policy, national income, prices, or interest rates in one country affects international payments and the distribution of gold, thereby spreading its influence throughout the world.

At the same time, the adjustment process tends to limit the freedom of each country to determine its own monetary and fiscal policies. If a country combating inflationary pressure tries to hold its national money income and prices "too low" relative to those in the rest of the world, it is likely to have a "favorable" balance of payments and persistent gold inflows, both of which will tend to raise its national money income and price levels. On the other hand, if a country fighting depression tries to hold its national income "too high" relative to that in the rest of the world, it is likely to have an "unfavorable" balance of payments and a gold outflow, both of which tend to lower its levels of money income and prices. As its gold reserves decline, the country may have to choose between departing from the gold standard and substituting a contractionary monetary policy whether it likes it or not.

Many have viewed with approval this limitation on the freedom of each nation to determine its own monetary and fiscal policies. They claim that it is desirable because it produces not only stable exchange rates but also favorable relationships among the various national income, price, and interest rate structures. But criticisms of this adjustment mechanism have mounted during recent decades. Many nations have complained that it subjects them to unwanted inflationary and deflationary pressures originating in other countries, and that it imposes an intolerable restriction on their freedom to adapt their monetary and fiscal policies to the attainment of domestic objectives, such as full employment or stable prices, or both. The gold standard can prevent protracted balance of payments disequilibria if nations allow their monetary policies to be heavily influenced by gold flows. But the cure by inflation and depression has sometimes been judged worse than the disease.

H. THE GOLD STANDARD, INFLATION, AND DEPRESSION

Nations have sometimes refused to allow a favorable balance of payments and gold inflows to exert their full expansionary influences on their domestic economies, especially when the favorable balance resulted from inflationary pressures in the rest of the world. To counteract such expansionary influences they have had their central banks sell securities in the open market, raise discount rates, or adopt other restrictive policies. In a few cases they have refused to buy any more gold, or have taken direct action to restrict exports and other receipts.

Much more common, however, is national opposition to the contractionary influence of an unfavorable balance of payments and gold outflows. The common complaint is that a downward adjustment of national money income and prices produces widespread unemployment, or at least militates against the maintenance of full employment, because cost structures cannot be lowered fast enough.

National opposition to downward adjustments of money incomes and prices is especially strong when an unfavorable balance of payments results from business depressions in other countries. Suppose, for example, that the United States slides into a serious depression, with a falling national income, declining prices, and decreasing employment. We are likely to decrease our imports sharply, to offer our products on the world market in larger amounts and at lower prices, to have a favorable balance of payments, and to drain gold from the rest of the world. In short, our depression imposes unwelcome deflationary pressures on the entire world. In this way the gold standard tends to increase the contagiousness of depression (or of inflation).

Other countries may resist these contractionary influences in various ways. They may refuse to allow the gold outflows to restrict their supply of money and credit, calling on their central banks to do such things as buy securities and lower their discount rates. They may also initiate expansionary fiscal policies to compensate for the reduction of their export trade. However, it should be evident that if they are unwilling or find it politically impossible to lower their levels of national income and prices along with those in the United States, their losses of gold are likely to be prolonged. In the end, they may have to choose between lowering their incomes and prices, or going off the gold standard and ceasing to peg exchange rates.

I. DISSATISFACTION WITH THE GOLD STANDARD AND PEGGED EXCHANGE RATES

This mounting dissatisfaction with the adjustment mechanism under an international gold standard and other methods of pegging exchange rates has several very important implications. (1) It helps to explain why the international gold-standard system with fixed exchange rates has broken down. If nations refuse to permit adjustments in their money incomes, prices, and interest rates, there is no reason why a disequilibrium in balances of payments should not continue, and why gold should not be concentrated in a few countries. (2) It helps to explain why some countries now consider the maintenance of a gold standard or any other system of fixed exchange rates to be of no more than secondary importance. They want greater freedom to protect their economies against foreign fluctuations and to regulate their do-

mestic levels of money incomes, prices, and interest rates. To achieve
this greater freedom, they prefer to adjust their international payments
by varying their exchange rates or by employing direct government
controls over payments and receipts.

4. Alterations of Exchange Rates

A. A Device for Equilibrating Payments

The basic theory of adjusting international payments by appropriate
alterations of exchange rates is quite simple. Nations which tend to
have "unfavorable" balances of payments should reduce the value of
their moneys in the exchange markets relative to the moneys of nations
which tend to have "favorable" balances. The countries whose exchange rates are lowered tend to have larger exports and smaller imports. The reverse is true of countries whose exchange rates have been
increased.

To illustrate this principle, let us consider the British devaluation
of the pound in 1949. For some years prior to that time, the dollar-
pound exchange rate had been $£1 = \$4.03$, or what is the same
thing, $\$1 = £\dfrac{1}{4.03}$. At this exchange rate and with the prevailing
levels of national incomes, prices, and interest rates, there tended to be
a large "dollar shortage" or "sterling surplus" in the exchange markets.
The British wanted to pay out far more than they were receiving, and
their payments were being balanced only by large dollar grants from
the United States, by a drain on their holdings of gold and foreign
moneys, and by strict government limitations on payments to foreigners.

It was under these conditions that the British lowered the exchange
rate on the pound from $£1 = \$4.03$ to $£1 = \$2.80$. To put the same
thing another way, the exchange rate on the dollar was raised from
$\$1 = £\dfrac{1}{4.03}$ to $\$1 = £\dfrac{1}{2.8}$. This was a 30 percent depreciation of
the pound in terms of dollars, or a 40 percent rise of the dollar in terms
of pounds. This cheapening of the pound tended to promote British
exports by making them less expensive relative to exports from the
United States. Even though the British exporter charged the same price
in terms of pounds, or (as is almost inevitable) a slightly higher price,
British goods were made cheaper in terms of the foreign currencies
that would now buy more pounds. At the same time, the rise of the ex-

change rate on the dollar discouraged British imports by making them more expensive in terms of pounds.

B. THE EFFECT ON EXPENDITURES OF FOREIGN MONEY

At first glance, it would appear that devaluation of the pound would surely tend to end the dollar shortage, both by promoting British exports and by discouraging British imports. But such success cannot be assured in every case. The depreciation of the pound in the exchange market may not tend to increase Britain's dollar receipts relative to her dollar payments. It will almost certainly tend to decrease British dollar payments for imports from us. As our exports become more expensive in terms of pounds, the British will almost certainly buy smaller physical quantities of our goods and expend a smaller number of dollars in paying for them. The dollar price of our exports to Britain being unchanged, it will certainly save her dollars to buy fewer goods from us.

C. THE EFFECT ON RECEIPTS OF FOREIGN MONEY

The effect of the pound devaluation on the total dollar value of British exports is much more difficult to predict. As they become cheaper in terms of dollars, British exports are almost certain to increase somewhat in physical volume. But if the price in sterling remains constant or fails to rise enough to offset the lower exchange rate on the pound, each physical unit of British exports will earn fewer dollars. Suppose, for example, that both before and after the devaluation of the pound the British price of a pair of shoes is £1. Before devaluation a British export of one pair of shoes would earn $4.03; after devaluation it would earn only $2.80. Thus, a devaluation of the pound will actually decrease the total dollar earnings of Britain if the physical volume of her exports fails to rise enough to offset the decreased dollar value of each unit of her exports. But the total dollar value of her exports will rise if the physical volume of her exports rises more than enough to compensate for the decline in the dollar price of each unit. If, for example, the exchange value of the pound is cut 50 percent, British exports must at least double if the British are not to lose dollar revenue as a result.[6]

Even a small devaluation of the British pound may be quite effective

---

[6] This same difficulty applies to a fall in a deficit country's price level as a means of balancing its payments. A fall in British prices will encourage Americans to buy in England; but only if American purchases increased substantially would this increase Britain's dollar receipts, for each item sold would earn fewer dollars than before the price fall. Cf. Graphic Appendix, pp. 614–615.

in equilibrating the British balance of payments under the following conditions: (1) If British imports are reduced sharply in response to each increase of their prices in terms of sterling. (2) If the foreign demand for British exports is quite responsive to each decrease in their prices in terms of dollars and other non-British moneys. Each decrease in the dollar price of British goods leads foreign customers of Britain to buy much larger quantities. (3) If the British supply of exports is quite responsive to each increase in their price in terms of sterling. Such a high responsiveness of exports could reflect a large increase in the British production of exportable types of products in response to each rise in their sterling prices, a large decrease in the British consumption of their exportable products as their sterling prices rise, or some combination of the two. Under these conditions, relatively small decreases in the exchange rate on the pound will be quite effective in reducing British dollar payments for imports and decreasing British dollar receipts for exports.

Under other conditions, however, devaluation of the pound may be quite ineffective in equilibrating the British balance of payments, and may even make things worse. British imports may decline very little as their prices rise in terms of sterling. One case in which this may occur is in a nation whose imports have already been reduced severely by government restrictions, as in Britain after World War II. The foreign demand for British exports may be quite unresponsive to the decline in their dollar prices. The likelihood of this is increased to the extent that other countries impose inflexible quotas or high tariffs on their imports of British goods. Or the British supply of exports may increase very little, because the British production of exportable goods does not rise much, or because British consumption of these goods does not decline very much, or because of some combination of the two.

A noteworthy example of nonresponsiveness of supply to devaluation was provided by Scotch whiskey, whose production in 1949 could not be increased for various reasons. When she devalued her money, England therefore saw fit to raise the pound price of export Scotch at once by an amount sufficient to prevent any reduction in its dollar price. Otherwise the devaluation would have cost England dollars by forcing the same quantity of whiskey to be sold at a lower dollar price.

In short, it is difficult to generalize about the effectiveness of alteration of exchange rates as a device for equilibrating balances of payments. This depends on conditions that may vary from one case to another.

D. EXCHANGE RATES AND DOMESTIC PRICE LEVELS

The relationship between the value of a nation's money in foreign-exchange markets and the level of its domestic prices is complex. We have already seen that the level of prices in a country is a major determinant of the exchange rate on its money. For example, a steep rise of prices in Britain relative to prices in the rest of the world would make British exports more expensive, tend to decrease the demand for pounds in the exchange markets, and lower the exchange rate on the pound. But the level of domestic prices can itself be affected by changes in exchange rates, and this influence may be great if a nation's imports and exports are very large relative to its total production and consumption.

Suppose, for example, that the British lower the exchange rate on the pound by 30 percent. Their lower price to foreigners will increase British exports. Therefore, because the supplies of these goods remaining for domestic consumption is decreased, their (sterling) prices will tend to rise. So will the prices of British imports. The British will face higher sterling prices on food, cotton, wool, petroleum, and other imports of raw materials and finished goods. This may touch off a general rise of domestic prices, especially if prices are not held down by direct government controls, if workers demand wage increases to offset every increase in the cost of living and if the central bank allows the money supply to increase enough to support higher prices.

This inflationary effect will tend to offset the effect of the devaluation on the balance of payments. A given fall in the value of the pound may reduce export prices by a considerably smaller percentage if in the meantime British domestic prices have risen. Such a price rise can usually be expected to occur if many of a country's exports require imports for their manufacture. British textiles use American cottons whose dollar prices will not have been reduced by the English devaluation. A 50 percent fall in the exchange rate on the pound will then reduce the dollar price of British textiles much less than this amount because it will automatically have doubled the pound price of the cotton from which the textiles are made.

Under some circumstances, especially during depressions, nations may welcome the buoyant influence of devaluation. Suppose that the world is sliding into a depression, with declining demands for imports and declining prices. The British might devalue the pound so as to make British goods cheaper in terms of foreign moneys and at the same time prevent domestic prices in terms of sterling from falling.

At other times, however, the buoyant effects on domestic prices may be quite unwelcome. This has been true in many countries during the period since World War II. These countries were already under strong inflationary pressures as a result of their large domestic expenditures for consumption, investment, and government purposes. These pressures not only tended to push up domestic price levels, but were also largely responsible for the tendency of these countries to have "unfavorable" balances of payments at existing exchange rates. Under these conditions the countries were highly reluctant to reduce their exchange rates and add still further to their inflationary pressures. In view of their inability, or at least their unwillingness, to reduce their domestic levels of money incomes and prices, and their unwillingness to reduce their exchange rates, it is no wonder that they had to maintain rigid direct controls over international transactions in order to balance their international payments.

In a few cases countries have deliberately increased exchange rates on their moneys in order to discourage their exports relative to their imports and to prevent inflationary pressures in other countries from invading their domestic economies.

E. COMPETITIVE DEVALUATIONS

In the preceding discussion we assumed that a nation alters its exchange rate only for "defensive" purposes—to remedy a disequilibrium in its balance of payments or to prevent inflationary or deflationary pressures originating in other countries from invading its own economy. But it should be clear that a nation may be quite aggressive in its use of this device. It may reduce its exchange rate in order to make an already favorable balance of payments still more favorable or to expand its exports and reduce its imports to offset a decline in the domestic demand for its products.

Suppose that country A already has a favorable balance of payments, but that its national income and employment are declining because of a decline of its domestic consumption and investment. The country may decide to reduce its exchange rate in order to cheapen its exports to foreigners and enhance its share of the world market and to make imports more expensive and thereby retain a larger share of its home market for its home producers.

It is obvious that this can have highly deleterious effects on the exports and national incomes of other countries. Any rise of national income and employment in country A may be largely at the expense of decreased income and employment in the rest of the world. Attempts by nations to improve their position by actions of these types are often called "beggar-my-neighbor policies."

This is, of course, a game at which all can play, though it is most unlikely that all can win. There may ensue a round of competitive devaluations, every country trying to lower the exchange rate of its own money in terms of all foreign moneys. Obviously, all cannot succeed. The result may well be confusion, ill will, and little or no contribution to world recovery. One of the purposes of the International Monetary Fund, an international organization set up in Washington after World War II, is to provide for international consultation and agreement on exchange rates in order to avoid such conflicts.

5. Direct Government Controls over Trade and Payments

The preceding discussion assumed that governments do not impose direct controls on international transactions but rely on adjustments in the levels of national income, prices, interest rates, and exchange rates to adjust international payments. However, one of the outstanding events in international economic relationships during recent decades has been the growth of direct government controls as a device for regulating trade and payments. These controls are of many types, and relate to both receipts and payments, but more especially to payments.

A. DIRECT CONTROLS OVER EXPORTS AND OTHER RECEIPTS

The principal direct controls over exports are export taxes, subsidies, and quantitative controls. Although these are frequently employed to promote or discourage particular types of exports, we shall consider only their use to influence balances of payments, national incomes, and prices.

A nation can discourage its exports by reducing subsidies on them, by taxing them more heavily, or by imposing direct quantitative limitations. This is sometimes done to make a nation's balance of payments less favorable, to maintain a larger amount of home production for home use, and to inhibit inflation at home. Suppose, for example, that inflationary pressures in world markets are very strong. Country A may use direct controls over its exports to decrease foreign spendings in its own economy and to inhibit domestic inflation. This may serve to increase inflationary pressures in other countries by increasing the bidding for goods which are in short supply in these countries.

A nation can encourage its exports by reducing or removing taxes

on them, by subsidizing them, by relaxing or removing quantitative restrictions on them, or even by forcing its export industries to sell larger
amounts in foreign markets. In this way a country can tend to increase
its receipts and raise its level of national money income. In some cases
these devices are used largely for "defensive" purposes—e.g., to remedy an unfavorable balance of payments or to prevent a decrease in
foreign demand from lowering a nation's export sales. In other cases
they are employed more aggressively. For example, a country whose
balance of payments is already favorable may try to make it still more
favorable by promoting its exports. This, too, may be part of a "beggar-my-neighbor policy."

B. DIRECT CONTROLS OVER IMPORTS AND OTHER PAYMENTS

Much more pervasive are direct government controls over payments.
These are of several principal types: (1) alteration of tariffs on imports, (2) quantitative controls of imports, and (3) exchange controls.

In earlier periods, nations tended to rely largely on tariffs to regulate
imports, reducing them to increase imports and raising them to discourage imports. In recent decades direct quantitative controls have
become increasingly important. Many nations go so far as to require
licenses for all imports and use their licensing powers to regulate the
total amounts of imports, their particular types, and their sources.

Exchange controls include direct government regulation of international payments. A full-fledged exchange control system is likely to
include the following provisions: (1) The government sets exchange
rates and declares that transactions at other rates are illegal. (2) All
receipts of foreign exchange must be sold to the exchange control authorities at the officially determined rates. And (3) no payment may
be made to foreigners unless permitted by the government regulations.
Thus the government can ration foreign exchange and determine the
total amounts of payments to foreigners, the purposes for which payments may be made, and the countries to which payments may be
made.

These direct controls over imports and other payments may be used
for many purposes. They may be used to limit exports of capital funds.
They may be used to protect selected industries from foreign competition. And they may be used either defensively or aggressively to affect
balances of payments and the behavior of national income and prices.
Suppose that at the existing exchange rate a country tends to have an
unfavorable balance of payments. It may use direct controls over its

payments to hold them down to the level of its receipts. But these powers may also be used aggressively to make favorable balances of payments still more favorable and to maintain or raise the level of its national income by retaining a larger part of its home market for home producers.

The power of these controls to diminish world trade, interfere with international specialization, and affect the behavior of national incomes and prices should not require elaboration. One of the great problems in restoring freer international trade and capital flows is to secure a relaxing or removal of these controls. If these controls are to be relaxed, their function of equilibrating international payments must be served by a greater use of adjustments in the levels of national incomes, prices, interest rates, and exchange rates.

6. Conclusions

The central theme of this chapter has been the interdependence of national money incomes, employment, prices, and interest rates among countries that trade with each other. Changes originating in one country tend to spread to all the others through the various types of international payments.

One of the great problems in international relations is to get each national government to recognize the international effects of its economic policies. To the extent that this problem remains unsolved, each country is likely to try to solve its own economic problems without considering the possible deleterious effects on others. And so long as each takes this position, all may fail to achieve their objectives. It would be some gain if each would try to solve its problems in ways that would not be injurious to others. But the gain could be even greater if each would employ methods that would actually help others.

The greatest single contribution each country could make would be to maintain continuously high employment and relatively stable price levels by using methods that would not tend to cause fluctuations of real output, employment, and prices in other countries. Economic instability has been one of the greatest enemies of free international trade and payments. Fluctuations of national money incomes, fluctuations in employment, and fluctuations in national price levels have been the principal sources of balance of payment difficulties.

"Beggar-my-neighbor policies," under which each nation tries to enrich itself in ways which happen to impoverish others, may occasionally succeed in raising the level of income and employment for one country, but it cannot succeed in all. A much more fruitful approach would be for every country to use its monetary and fiscal policies to prevent extreme fluctuations in its levels of real output, employment, and prices, thereby tending to stabilize its demand for foreign products and to stabilize the prices at which it would supply exports to the rest of the world.

Even if this were done, there would still remain a problem of equilibrating international payments. Receipts and payments would still not coincide in each period for each country, because of such things as changes in buyers' preferences for the products of different countries, changes in relative productivity, and differing rates of national growth. But if every country maintained continuously high levels of employment and relatively stable price levels, the flow of international payments would be much more stable, so that only much smaller and more gradual adjustments of the relative levels of national money incomes, prices, interest rates, and exchange rates would be required.

In showing how disturbances arising in one country affect international payments and influence the economies of other countries, we may have created or reinforced the impression that economic fluctuations will be more frequent and perhaps wider under a system of international specialization and trade than they would be if each country were largely self-sufficient. This need not be true. Even if the United States were wholly self-sufficient—if she had no dealings with the outside world—all our people, business firms, and regions would still be highly specialized and dependent on markets. Our real output, employment, and price levels would still fluctuate for the reasons discussed in earlier chapters. Whether these fluctuations would be more or less frequent, or wider or narrower than under a system of free trade, we do not know.

SUGGESTED READINGS

Harris, Seymour, *The European Recovery Program,* Harvard University Press, Cambridge, 1948.

Lutz, Friedrich A., and Buchanan, Norman S., *Rebuilding the World Economy,* Twentieth Century Fund, New York, 1947.

QUESTIONS

1. a. How is it possible that a fall in a nation's income (production) can increase its exports?

    b. If prices do not fall but national income goes down, show why the nation's imports will tend to fall. Specifically, show who will buy fewer foreign goods and why.

2. a. Show how a fall in a nation's price level can conceivably worsen its balance of payments deficit.

    b. Show how this is analogous to the difficulty that may arise in trying to use devaluation for that purpose.

3. Why are improvements in a nation's balance of payments deficit that result from a relative rise in its interest rates likely to be temporary?

4. a. In terms of our balance of payments position, show in detail how the gold imports and exports required by a gold standard can conflict with the income stabilization goals of the Federal Reserve's monetary policy.

    b. Show when each of the gold standard's balance of payments equilibrating effects may be considered desirable and when undesirable.

    c. Explain how the gold standard may make depressions and inflations more contagious.

5. a. State a variety of reasons why a 50 percent devaluation in the pound will probably reduce the American price of English cars by much less than 50 percent.

    b. Show that it will then pay Britain to raise the pound price of some of her exports.

    c. Which exports?

6. a. What is a "beggar-my-neighbor policy"?

    b. What are some of the instruments a country can use in pursuing such a policy?

    c. Show the unfavorable effects of each on the rest of the world.

    d. Show the unfavorable effects on everyone if such a policy becomes competitive, i.e., if all countries go in for it.

    e. Show why any one nation may believe it to be irrational not to pursue such policies.

CHAPTER 28

Economics of Protectionism

We deliberately bring about unemployment through importing the product of low-wage living standard and slave labor. . . . (Senator George W. Malone, *Congressional Record*, 1950, p. 3597.)

While we talk of a scientific tariff to balance the difference in cost of production at home and abroad, conditions change so fast that rates can be only approximate. We do not wish to exclude foreign goods but to give our people only a fair chance in their own markets under our scale of wages and standards of living. (Calvin Coolidge, *New York Herald Tribune,* date line September 10, 1930.)

. . . [By tariff reduction] we deliberately set out to destroy the American workingmen and American investors through free and unlimited imports of the products of foreign industries in which labor is paid at sweatshop wages, as compared to American industries in which our labor is paid $10 to $12 to $15 a day. In contrast, much of the foreign labor is paid at the rate of 5 cents to $2.50 per day. The purpose of those who advocate such a program is to permit the goods manufactured in the United States to be displaced by the goods manufactured by the sweatshop labor of European and Asiatic countries. Such a situation would virtually be free trade. (Senator George W. Malone, *Congressional Record,* 1952, p. 7103.)

The American rubber footwear industry can stand no further [tariff] cuts. . . . The manufacture of rubber footwear is an essential part of our national economy. It is vital to our national defense. (T. R. Behrman, Industrial Relations Manager, Naugatuck Footwear Plant, and George T. Froehlich, President, Local

45, United Rubber, Cork, Linoleum, Plastic Workers of America, CIO, letter, *Congressional Record,* 1951, p. A1530.)

We have been told that we are buying strategic materials from those countries—things to help us stockpile for our defense. But what are we getting? . . . Rubber footwear. . . . Will rubber overshoes from Czechoslovakia be used for guided missile purposes? (Representative J. Glenn Beall, *Congressional Record,* 1950, p. A4218.)

We have already considered the one great argument for unrestricted international trade—it permits greater specialization and a greater world output to be shared among the specializing and trading nations. Yet trade restrictions are widespread. National restrictions on exports are far from absent, but restrictions on imports are much more important as barriers to international trade. The purpose of this chapter is to survey and analyze some of the arguments most frequently advanced to justify import restrictions. We shall give most of our attention to tariffs, but with modifications our comments will also apply to other methods of restricting imports, such as quotas, other direct quantitative limitations, and the use of exchange controls to prevent or limit payments for imports.

Tariffs have been advocated on many grounds. Protectionists have claimed that tariffs can help increase world output, increase the proportion of the world output going to our country, protect us from unfair foreign wage and price competition, and help the nation's military security. Some of the arguments are partly or even largely valid. But in tariff debates, notoriously shoddy, superficial, and often fallacious reasoning has been used to support weak or untenable positions. Our aim is to explore the grounds on which policy measures can rationally be weighed, not to advocate or oppose any particular proposal. The fact that some arguments which have been advanced for protection are totally untenable does not imply that a tariff will never benefit the nation imposing it.

1. Tariffs and the Efficiency of World Production

The main argument for free trade is, as we saw, based on the comparative advantage analysis, which shows that unhampered specialization and exchange can usually increase total world output. But we must qualify the conclusion that restrictions on free trade can only reduce living standards. There are several cases in which tariffs might even increase the efficiency of world production. Let us see how this can come about.

A. THE INFANT-INDUSTRY ARGUMENT

Tariff advocates often say we ought to tax imports to protect some of our newest industries. They argue that such industries, being small and lacking experience, specially trained workers, and a well-developed technology, may find it difficult if not impossible to survive competition with older and more experienced foreign producers. Many an infant industry that might become highly efficient after a period of development is killed in its early years by foreign competition. So runs the argument.

Properly formulated and administered, such a policy could indeed be economically beneficial in the long run even though it lowered real national income in the short run. However, this would be true only under the following conditions: (1) Protection would be granted only to the industries that appeared to be well suited to the economic resources of the country so that they could reasonably be expected to have a comparative advantage after a period of development and in the long run increase real national income *more than enough to compensate for the decrease of real income during the development period.* (2) Protection would be removed after a reasonable period, forcing the industry to prove its right to survive.

In practice, however, it is wise to consider very carefully before supporting a tariff to protect some infant industry. This is particularly important in the United States in her present state of development. For this there are several reasons. (1) It would be difficult to demonstrate that protection is necessary for the establishment and survival of industries that really have a good chance of developing a comparative advantage in the long run. We are bountifully supplied with alert, imaginative, and venturesome enterprisers who have at their disposal huge amounts of capital and large numbers of workers whose general education enables them to learn quickly and adapt to new occupations. If our enterprisers will not establish a specific industry here without protection, this is strong presumptive evidence that in their judgment the long-run prospects of the industry are not favorable. The judgment of political bodies on this subject may not be superior to that of businessmen.

(2) It is difficult to confine protection to the infant industries that have a reasonable chance of developing a comparative advantage. The

political process being what it is, protection is likely to be granted indiscriminately. (3) It is politically difficult to remove protection from an industry, no matter how inefficient it may prove to be. Investors, managers, and workers in the protected industry develop a vested interest in continued protection and use all their power to perpetuate the tariff. In fact, the political power of the "infant" is likely to increase as time goes by. Moreover, even when the industry reaches "maturity," inefficient "marginal" firms that may be able to survive only under protection will fight tariff elimination with every possible means.

Therefore, though the infant-industry argument is formally valid, it must be applied with extreme caution.

B. "ARTIFICIAL" PRICE DISTORTIONS

There is another way in which tariffs might actually increase the efficiency of world production. Businessmen can be depended on to produce along lines of comparative advantage under free trade only if they are led to do so by the profit motive. In a completely unhampered competitive market we have said that it will ordinarily pay them to do so, for under those conditions a nation's abundant resources tend to be relatively cheap, and its scarcer resources expensive.[1] Businessmen can then best compete with foreign producers in the lines of comparative advantage in which relatively small amounts of scarce expensive resources are needed in the production process.

But prices are often influenced by monopolists or the government. This can draw production away from lines of comparative advantage. We cited the case of wheat, in whose production we have a considerable comparative advantage that arises from our abundant land and agricultural equipment. Because the government is supporting wheat prices at "artificially" high levels we are frequently unable to compete with foreign wheat growers without further government intervention. Perhaps in these circumstances a tariff on wheat imports or a subsidy on exports can promote efficiency in American and world production. The tariff can prevent the foreign wheat producer, whose prices are not supported, from taking the domestic market away from the comparatively more efficient American grower.

Wherever there is this sort of interference with the price mechanism some form of protection may conceivably prove desirable. But where we have interfered with the price mechanism by imposing price ceilings it is the foreigner who, in line with this argument, is able to

[1] See above, pp. 496–499.

increase world productive efficiency by taking protective measures against our exports. Artificially low prices may let us export products in whose production we are really at a comparative disadvantage.

From the free-trade view it is better to try to eliminate artificial price disturbances than to use protective measures to offset them. But this is sometimes easier said than done, especially when it is the foreigner who is doing the price controlling in his own country. Anyhow, price-control and price-support legislation involves complex political, social, and economic issues on which such simple final judgments cannot always be passed.

c. Conclusion

Protective tariffs need not always decrease world production and productive efficiency. Nevertheless, we must proceed with extreme caution before advocating tariffs for these purposes. We rarely know just where they will help and where they will do serious damage. A mistake in enacting a tariff is politically most difficult to undo. There is also the danger that foreigners will interpret the tariff as an aggressive act. If it leads to retaliation and a tariff war, everyone can lose.

2. Increasing the Nation's Share of World Output

Even if a tariff serves to reduce the world's output it may benefit the nation that imposes it by giving that country a larger slice of the smaller pie. The country then necessarily benefits at the expense of others.

A. "Exporting Unemployment"

By reducing our imports, say tariff advocates, we may in times of unemployment secure a larger part of the American market for American producers and increase the number of jobs for Americans. Thus, it is suggested, by taxing imports we can create more jobs in our industries that compete with imports; and as the workers and other producers in these industries earn higher incomes they will spend more for the products of our other industries, thereby creating greater prosperity and more employment for the entire nation. Moreover, by restricting our imports we can get a favorable balance of trade, an inflow of gold, easier credit conditions, a higher rate of investment, and still more employment.

As we have already seen, such a "beggar-my-neighbor policy" may indeed enable a country to increase its level of employment at the expense of employment elsewhere if it can decrease its imports without a comparable decrease of its exports. This is most likely to occur if the protectionist country is so small that its decreased spending for imports has very little effect on the incomes of other nations and does not lead others to erect barriers against its exports.

However, the argument is inapplicable or invalid in many cases. In the first place, it is applicable only if unemployment actually threatens. It is clearly inapplicable when the outlook is for practically full employment and even for inflation, when upward pressures on prices would only be aggravated. In the second place, such a policy may fail to increase employment even in the country that employs it, for it assumes that the country can decrease its purchases from others without a comparable decrease of its exports. A decrease of our spending for foreign products decreases the dollar earnings of other nations, tends to decrease their national incomes (and incidentally employment), and is likely to reduce their demands for our exports even if they do not retaliate by raising their tariffs or other barriers against our products.

In the third place, such a policy of "exporting unemployment" may be less desirable than alternative types of recovery policies even if it succeeds in restoring a high level of domestic employment. It has the great disadvantage of tending to waste productive resources by shifting them from export industries where they are more productive to industries competing with imports where they are less productive. This need not be true of well-conceived expansionary types of monetary and fiscal policies. Moreover, any export surplus achieved by restricting imports may itself represent a wasteful use of resources from our own point of view. The gold or other claims on foreigners that we get for our surplus of exports may be less useful to us than the goods and services we could otherwise have produced for domestic use with the same resources. New schools, hospitals, highways, housing, and other goods may be more beneficial to us than an addition to our gold stock, especially in view of the fact that we already hold about two-thirds of the world's monetary gold. There have been few occasions during recent decades when we needed more gold to support a larger money supply. An expansion of Federal Reserve loans would have been just as effective in increasing the supply of money and lowering interest rates.

There is a considerably more sophisticated argument that advocates trade barriers as an instrument for protecting a country against unemployment. We saw earlier how contagious are depressions and unemployment under a gold standard.[2] A large country suffering from strong deflationary forces will drag other countries down too. Its low incomes and prices will cause its trade balance to become more favorable and foreign gold will flow in. Other countries must consequently be driven toward a payment deficit and a gold loss. Inflation can equally well be transmitted to a country from the outside.

A country may then feel that in the absence of explicit assurances from other nations that they will pursue vigorous contracyclical policies, it will pay it to give up the benefits of free trade to protect itself from the outside forces of expansion and contraction. The idea is not for the country to export its unemployment elsewhere. Rather, protection becomes part of a program designed, so far as possible, to seal the country off from the rest of the world so that it can be left to pursue its own income stabilization policies. This decision, though it may be rational, is certainly grave. In any country it may mean a serious economic loss and a blow to living standards. Such isolation is out of the question for many highly specialized economies like Cuba (sugar) and Malaya (rubber), and for others like Great Britain and the smaller countries of the Continent, whose crowded populations cannot possibly be supplied out of native resources alone.

B. TARIFFS FOR REVENUE

Another proposal claims that the nation can benefit at the expense of the foreigner through the so-called revenue tariff. A tax on our imports, it is maintained, must be paid by foreigners, who are thereby forced to bear part of our tax burdens. If kept low enough, its proponents argue, such a tariff loses its protective character and will therefore cause no serious misallocation of resources. It is true that import tariffs, which are a special type of sales tax, can be made to yield large amounts of revenue. But the argument has its pitfalls.

1. There is no clear-cut distinction between a tax for revenue and a tax for protective purposes. Any tax on imports is a penalty on the transaction. If it is borne by the buyer in the form of a higher price, it discourages purchases from abroad. If it is borne by the foreign seller in the form of lower net receipts for his product, it discourages sales to us. Any tariff, however low, can cause an inefficient reallocation of the world's resources away from the lines of comparative advantage. Only by matching any tax on imported goods by an equally heavy tax on domestically produced items can the protective character of the

[2] See pp. 544–546.

revenue tariff be eliminated. But an offsetting domestic tax is rarely advocated.

2. We cannot even be sure that the foreigner will pay most or even any of the tax. As we saw when we discussed taxes, the person who actually hands the money over to the government may not be the one who bears its burden.[3] He can often shift that burden on to someone else. If the foreign exporter of the good on which the tariff is levied can raise the price of his product without too much loss in sales here, a considerable portion of the tax will be borne not by him but by consumers in this country.

There are probably some cases in which we can make foreigners bear part of the tax burden. Some of the tax payment must come out of the exporter's pocket if he believes a significant rise in his selling price will lose him a substantial proportion of his market here and if he is determined not to lose our business. Even then we may bear part of the cost ourselves if the tariff significantly diminishes the foreigner's ability to buy from us. But if foreigners can easily sell their goods elsewhere or if they refuse to produce our import commodities rather than pay the tariff, we will have to submit to the higher prices or else go without the goods. This means that consumers in this country are really paying the tax.

3. If our consumers bear some or all of the tax, the cost to them may be far greater than the amount of revenue collected by the government. The government collects taxes only on imports, but consumers may have to pay higher prices for both imported and domestically produced goods.

This can be illustrated by an example. Suppose that without any tariff the price of woolen cloth, both imported and domestic, is $2 a yard. Now suppose that a tariff of $1 a yard is imposed and that the price rises by the full amount of the tariff. Suppose further that at this price of $3 a total of 100 million yards of woolen cloth is purchased, of which half is imported and half is produced domestically. The government collects only $50 million of import duties—$1 on each of the 50 million yards imported. The rise in the cost to consumers—the "tax" on consumers—totals $100 million. What becomes of the other $50 million? It goes directly to domestic producers in the form of higher prices for their product; it is a kind of tax paid by consumers to subsidize domestic producers. But this part of the tax paid by consumers never appears in government revenues, and the subsidies provided

[3] See above, pp. 326–327. See also the Graphic Appendix, pp. 625–627.

to domestic producers never appear in government expenditures. One of the insidious aspects of import tariffs is that there is no easy way of knowing how much they cost consumers or how much they subsidize domestic producers. This much is certain, however—the amount of revenue collected by the government is no accurate indicator of the "tax" on consumers.

In our example we assumed that the price to consumers rose by the full amount of the tariff. It should be clear, however, that the total of the increased costs to consumers may exceed the tariff revenues to the government even if the price rises by somewhat less than the full amount of the tariff.

In summary, the revenue tariff is a tricky instrument for collecting money from foreigners, and one that can very easily backfire.

C. TARIFFS AND THE TERMS OF TRADE

Tariffs may benefit a country at the expense of foreigners in a third way, by manipulating prices to the disadvantage of other countries. By appropriate tariffs a country can act like a monopolistic buyer and manipulate prices so as to get the most for its money. Like a large firm who is a major purchaser of some raw material, the nation can force prices down by keeping its purchases low. Finding that the demand for their product is low, sellers will be forced to sell on favorable terms.

By an appropriate tariff against imports we can reduce American purchase of those commodities. This can force the foreigner to export on more liberal price terms. Our exports will then pay for more foreign goods—every American automobile exported will buy 20 percent more foreign tin than it did before. In technical jargon, the terms on which the exchanges are made—the terms of trade—will have been turned in our favor.

This advantage can be achieved by skillful tariff manipulation. But, again, it is no easy matter to decide where the tariff should be levied and what its magnitude ought to be. To maximize the advantages of terms of trade we must know how foreigners will respond price-wise to our reduced purchases. For we must always balance against the reduced foreign prices the fact that we are buying and consuming less of a good than we want. The cut in consumption which results from too high a tariff will outweigh the price gain.

D. RETALIATION

There is a more important fly in the ointment. The foreigner can retaliate against any of these devices designed to benefit a country at his expense. If he sees tariffs and other barriers being erected against his exports he will not—indeed he cannot afford to—sit passively and do nothing. So long as they are levied by only one nation, tariffs may be able to increase its wealth at the expense of others, thereby increasing that nation's share of the world's wealth. Simultaneously, they are likely to cause the world's production to decline. Another nation who does nothing about it will probably receive a smaller slice of a smaller pie. That country must retaliate if it is to preserve its share of even the reduced world output.

If a tariff race begins, everyone is likely to lose. Each runner cannot come in ahead of the others in the race. It is impossible for everyone to increase the proportion of world output going to him. And world output will be seriously affected by a widespread and indiscriminate imposition of tariffs.

3. Protection Against Foreign Competition

We come now to two particularly weak protectionist arguments in whose defense many a *non sequitur* has been mustered.

A. TARIFFS TO EQUALIZE COSTS OF PRODUCTION

According to the protectionists, foreign sellers who have lower costs of production than our domestic producers have an unfair competitive advantage in our markets. Competition, it is said, can never be fair until the production costs of foreign and domestic suppliers are equalized. According to this view we should impose on every imported commodity a tariff high enough to equalize its cost of production at home and abroad. This is, moreover, claimed to be an unambiguous formula for tariff making and on these grounds is called "scientific."

Appealing to our respect for science and our sense of fair play and sportsmanship, this argument has been effective in enlisting support for protective tariffs. The principle of "equalizing costs of production at home and abroad" has been professed in several tariff acts. On closer scrutiny, however, it fares rather badly. In the first place, the tariff-making bodies could not arrive at any one figure for the difference between costs at home and abroad. In part this is because of their lack of reliable data. They have usually had far less than complete information about the costs of domestic producers, and their information about foreign costs has been even more fragmentary and probably less reliable. Knowing the purposes for which it is to be used, foreign producers are understandably uncooperative in supplying information.

Even if they had complete information, the tariff makers would probably find that for any commodity there is not just one cost of production at home and just one cost of production abroad. Both here and in the rest of the world there are wide ranges of costs. Tariff makers would therefore be able, within a wide area of discretion, to adjust the height of tariffs to suit their prejudices. If they wanted a high tariff they could set it equal to the difference between the lowest cost they could find in the rest of the world and the highest cost they could find in the United States. If they wanted a low tariff or no tariff at all they could compare the highest cost in the rest of the world with the lowest cost in this country. The claim that this formula removes discretionary power from tariff makers and indicates one definite height for a tariff cannot be supported.

Even if the tariff makers possessed full information and there were just one cost of production in the rest of the world and one in the United States, this tariff formula would be subject to a second and more fundamental objection—it would tend to decrease world output by inducing a less efficient use of the world's resources. An import tax cannot in any meaningful sense "equalize costs of production at home and abroad." By the cost of production of a commodity we mean the value of resources used up in producing it. When we levy a tax on an import, we do not raise its cost of production; we merely penalize its entry by the amount of the tax. And if we tax the product because foreigners use up a smaller value of resources in producing it, we are penalizing them because of their greater efficiency. This is hardly the way to maximize world output.

Would a policy of penalizing the more efficient so as to put them on a competitive level with the less efficient promote "fair competition" and "sportsmanship"? On this ethical question we offer no judgment. But if the answer is "yes," it would appear that the principle might be applied in domestic as well as in international affairs. We might tax all our low-cost firms so heavily that even the highest-cost firms could compete successfully. In athletics this principle of "fair competition" suggests that the fastest sprinters should be forced to carry so many lead weights that they could do no better than run a dead heat with the slowest plodder who cared to enter the race.

B. TARIFFS AGAINST CHEAP FOREIGN LABOR

Protectionists have argued with seeming plausibility that we must tax imports to protect and raise the standard of living of the American workingman. They tell us that so long as we persist in our policy of

free trade, American producers can compete in our markets with foreigners only if American wage rates fall to the lowest level prevailing
anywhere in the world. By taxing imports we can permit American
employers to raise wage rates and still compete.

Stated in such broad terms, this argument is really very weak. As
we have already seen, high wage rates do not necessarily mean high
costs per unit of output if accompanied by high output per man-hour
—and generally speaking, the productivity of American labor is the
highest in the world. In fact, many of our industries that pay the highest
wages to be found in our economy are able to undersell producers in
the lowest-wage countries. These are the industries in which we have a
comparative advantage. Only in the industries in which we are at a
comparative disadvantage are American employers unable to pay at
the American level of wages and still compete with foreign producers
who have lower wage rates. The basic problem of these employers is
that they cannot make their workers produce a value of output as great
as those workers could produce in other industries.

By taxing imports a country can of course reduce the volume of its
imports, raise the prices of its domestic goods that compete with imports, and expand employment and perhaps raise wage rates in these
particular domestic industries. But by reducing its imports it discourages its exports and reduces employment opportunities in its export
industries. Thus it tends to shift workers from its export industries,
where they are relatively more productive, to its import-competing industries, where they are relatively less productive. The result is very
likely to be a decrease in the country's real income and in average
standards of living.

There is no doubt that some workers may have their real wages increased by a tariff on imports that compete with the products they produce, even though the tariff lowers the real income of the country as a
whole. Suppose, for example, that we impose a tariff on imports of
certain types of woolen cloth on which we are at a comparative disadvantage. The domestic price of woolens will rise, as may also wage
rates in the industry, though the latter is not inevitable. The workers in
the industry must now pay higher prices for the woolen cloth they buy,
but since they spend only part of their incomes for this product they
may enjoy higher real wages. In effect they are subsidized by all the
consumers who pay higher prices for their woolens—including the
workers in other industries.

Can we properly say that if this works for one industry alone it will work equally well for all industries? The answer is clearly "no." If the woolen industry is the only one receiving protection, its workers may have to pay higher prices only for woolens. But if the tariff on woolens can be enacted only if accompanied by tariffs on imported foods, shoes, and all other consumer goods, their wage increases may be completely offset, or more than offset, by the increase in the cost of living. The same may be true of workers in the other protected industries.

Employing an analysis far more subtle than that with which we started, economists have demonstrated that under certain circumstances it might be possible for a country like the United States to raise her level of real wages by taxing or otherwise restricting imports. They admit, and even emphasize, that obstructing imports is likely to lower the total real income of the country. However, they point out that the percentage share of the decreased national income going to labor might be increased enough to raise the absolute level of real wages.

Their argument runs as follows: Under free trade we tend to import commodities whose production requires relatively large amounts of labor and relatively small amounts of capital and natural resources. We tend to export commodities whose production requires relatively small amounts of labor and relatively large amounts of capital and natural resources. Through tariffs or other restrictions on imports we could increase the size of our industries that compete with imports and decrease the size of our export industries. This would tend to expand the industries that use high amounts of labor and so would increase the demand for labor relative to the demand for capital and natural resources, thereby tending to raise wage rates relative to the rewards of capital and land. The proportion of income going to labor might be increased so much that the absolute level of real wages would rise despite the decline of total real income. The reduction of nonlabor real incomes would be greater than the rise of real wages.

That these results are theoretically possible cannot be denied. Yet for at least two reasons this argument for protective tariffs is of questionable validity. In the first place, it is doubtful that actual conditions correspond with those that would be necessary to produce the claimed results. With labor already receiving considerably more than half of the national income, it is doubtful whether tariffs could raise labor's percentage share enough to offset the resulting decline of total real income.

In the second place, if it is a national objective to raise labor incomes at the expense of others, there are alternative ways of accomplishing this that would probably have less deleterious effects on total real income. For example, we could maintain free trade to maximize total real income and then tax nonlabor incomes and subsidize workers. Most of the receivers of nonlabor income would undoubtedly oppose such a policy, and we suspect that among them would be some of the most ardent advocates of protection against cheap foreign labor.

4. Tariffs for National Defense

We come, finally, to a much more urgent protectionist argument. It admits that unrestricted international trade, the distribution of industries over the world's surface in accordance with the principles of comparative advantage, and international economic interdependence might be fine if we lived in a world of assured, continuous peace. But this is not the kind of world we live in. In this real world, it is suggested, the first concern of every nation should be its own security, and no nation can be secure if it is dependent on other countries for the materials of war and essentials for civilians. Every nation should therefore strive for self-sufficiency in all these essential things. Using tariffs, subsidies, and any other appropriate methods, it should build up within its own boundaries during peacetime all the industries whose products are needed to support its people and assure success for its military effort in case of war.

An economist cannot quarrel with the value judgment that national security should take precedence over greater real incomes. He must also admit that in at least some cases a protectionist policy may promote national security even though it lowers real incomes. Nothing that follows is meant to deny these facts. Yet it is clearly true that the national defense argument for tariffs and other measures to promote national self-sufficiency is frequently abused.

In the first place, it is used to justify tariffs on commodities that are not "essentials." And in the second place, there are some cases in which national self-sufficiency is not the most effective way of promoting national security, and others in which it would actually weaken a nation's defenses. To illustrate these points, let us consider briefly the types of international commercial policies that might contribute most to a nation's security.

A. PROTECTION AND "NONESSENTIAL" INDUSTRIES

To promote its security, a nation probably would not provide any protection to domestic industries that produce "nonessentials" and

whose productive facilities could not be converted to the efficient production of "essentials" in time of war. In fact, it would probably encourage the import of nonessentials in peacetime so that its own productive factors could be heavily concentrated in the industries that
would be most useful in wartime. For example, the United States might
actively encourage the import of such things as lace, rugs, toys, liquor,
and other nonessentials so as to build up such export industries as iron
and steel, automobiles, machinery, and chemicals—industries that are
most useful for military purposes. As it happens, the United States is at
a comparative advantage in producing most of the goods whose export
is desirable for national defense, and at a comparative disadvantage in
producing the goods which we just said should be imported. This suggests that in our case military expediency may justify much less tariff
interference in international trade than in the case of some other countries.

B. STOCK PILING

The nation would also recognize that producing certain goods at
home may be less advantageous, even for security purposes, than purchasing them from other countries. This is especially true if it can
count on the continuing cooperation of those countries and keep transportation lines open in case of war. For example, it might be wise for
us to import freely during peacetime from Canada and Central and
South America in order to develop large sources of supply in those
areas. Similarly, it may in some cases be wise to buy large amounts of
strategic materials from other countries in peacetime if the cost of producing them at home would be much higher or if we are in danger of
depleting our domestic supplies. Instead of trying to develop domestic
supplies of tin, nickel, and other alloys, we should perhaps build up
large stock piles through imports. And in peacetime we should perhaps
encourage large imports of such things as oil, iron ore, copper, uranium, and mercury in order to conserve our best domestic reserves for
use in wartime.

C. SELECTIVE PROTECTION

But there are some industries important for national defense which
must be protected by tariff, subsidy, or other devices if they are to
continue to exist. Artificial rubber manufacture in the United States
and watch production in Great Britain are industries that have been

developed at least partly for military purposes. Even if our rubber cannot compete with the natural product and American or English watches cannot meet Swiss competition, we may find it necessary to keep them going, by tariff protection if no more efficient way can be found.

We cannot discuss here the many strategic and tactical factors that should be considered in developing the economic side of a national security program. It should be clear, however, that although selective tariffs may be warranted, an *indiscriminate* protectionist policy is not necessarily most appropriate for this purpose and may actually decrease national security as well as real incomes.

5. Reducing Tariffs

Once they have been enacted, the removal of undesirable tariffs may involve some difficult problems. Their reduction or elimination is almost certain to injure some people in the protected industries, just as their continuance is almost certain to lower the general level of real incomes. Thus in deciding whether or not to reduce protective tariffs, a nation may face the difficult problem of balancing a general rise of real incomes against the probable harm to at least some of the people who work or have invested in the protected industries. Though tariff reduction will probably raise total national income in real terms—benefiting others more than it harms those who lose protection—it may impose severe hardships, at least temporarily, on some workers and investors. Often almost all of these hardships fall on a few towns or localities in which production of the protected item was centered. This may add considerably to the problems of the people affected who may not be able to find alternative local business or employment opportunities.

Facing such a problem, a nation has three principal policy alternatives. (1) It may refuse to reduce tariffs, thereby avoiding hardships for those in the protected industries but forgoing the general rise of real incomes that tariff reductions would permit. (2) It may reduce tariffs to raise real national income, forcing those in the industries losing protection to bear the burdens of adjustment. This might be justified on the basis that these people can have no legitimate vested interests in continued protection at the expense of the nation as a whole. (3) It may reduce tariffs to raise real national income and spread the burdens of adjustment by compensating those in the industries losing protection. Such compensation might take the form of liberal unemployment benefits, assistance to workers in finding other jobs and in training for them, and grants to cover losses of capital value. Whether or not these people have a "right" to compensation, such a policy may increase the possibility of lowering tariffs and leave the country as a whole better off than it would be if tariffs were not reduced.

On this policy issue we offer no judgment. However, we may note that at least two other points are relevant. The first is that tariff increases as well as tariff reductions may impose adjustment problems on specific industries. Tariff increases that lower imports are likely to reduce exports and injure those engaged in export industries. If consideration for those who may be injured is to lead us to compensate those who are injured by tariff reductions or to refuse to reduce tariffs, we might consider showing the same concern for our export industries when tariffs are increased. In the second place, adjustment problems for workers and investors are created not only by tariff changes but also by shifts in consumer demands and changes in technology. We might perhaps (and sometimes do) consider doing something for those who are injured by a shift of domestic demands and changes in technology as well as for those who may be injured by tariff reductions.

6. Conclusions

It is not easy to present a balanced and unprejudiced view on protectionism. Several points do emerge clearly from the foregoing discussion.

First and perhaps most important, indiscriminate protection is very likely to result in misallocation of world resources, and so reduce world production, living standards, and real incomes. It may benefit some nations and some sections of a nation's economy at the expense of others. But tariffs also harm a nation's export industries even if other countries do not retaliate. Tariffs can have this effect by reducing the foreigner's purchasing power.

Second, many of the arguments that have been advanced by protectionists are weak, some are fallacious, and others appeal to specious ethics.

Third, there may be valid reasons for seeking to protect particular industries in particular circumstances. Perhaps most persuasive is the national defense argument, though even this can at most support only a severely limited number of carefully selected tariffs. An honest advocacy of protection on military grounds must not gloss over the re-

duction in real national income that may result. It can only argue that
this is part of the price we must pay for national security.

SUGGESTED READINGS

Ellis, Howard S., *The Economics of Freedom,* Harper, New York, 1950.
Gordon, Margaret S., *Barriers to World Trade,* Macmillan, New York,
   1941.
International Monetary Fund, Washington, *Annual Reports;* also many
   special studies.
U.S. Public Advisory Board for Mutual Security, *A Trade and Tariff Policy
   in the National Interest,* Washington, 1953.

QUESTIONS

1. a. Discuss the circumstances under which the infant-industry argument
      might be valid.
   b. Can you think of any industries today or in the past to which it might
      validly apply?
   c. Why do you believe that enterprising businessmen would not have
      invested in these industries even without a tariff? Would they not
      have taken temporary losses in the hope of future profits?
   d. If the expected future profits were not great enough to justify their
      doing this, why might one suspect that the infant-industry argument
      is not valid in these cases?
2. a. If artificial price distortions move production out of lines of com-
      parative advantage, what devices other than tariffs might be used to
      correct for this?
   b. When might some of these other devices have advantages as against
      tariffs?
3. a. Do you think that the rise in tariff restrictions in the United States
      at the beginning of the great depression was judicious?
   b. Why or why not?
   c. Did other countries retaliate?
   d. Were we sealing ourselves off from the contagion of depression else-
      where?
4. List the various groups that will be affected by the imposition of a
   revenue tariff and show how each will be affected.
5. "Our efforts are not only to protect our own people from cheap goods,
   which President McKinley said meant cheap men, but we propose to set
   up a standard that will discourage other nations from exploiting their

people by producing cheap goods. Our policy requires fair wages for both domestic and foreign production. We have no market for blood and tears." (Calvin Coolidge, *New York Herald Tribune,* date line November 26, 1930.) Discuss.

6. a. Discuss the quotations on rubber footwear at the beginning of the chapter.
   b. What elements of validity are there in both points of view?
   c. Are either or both misleading to any extent? Explain.

PART VII

Distribution of Income

CHAPTER 29

Income Inequality

1. Introduction

Up to this point we have not said much about the division or distribution of income among the members of the community; instead we have concentrated largely on the determinants of the size and composition of national output or income. In other words, we have centered our attention on the size and content of the pie rather than on the way it is divided up. However, we have not completely neglected this important problem.

In the first chapter we noted that determining the distribution of income is almost certain to be a highly controversial issue, if for no other reason than because there cannot be enough to satisfy everybody. In our discussion of economic instability, including both depression and inflation, we found that fluctuations in national money income, employment, and price levels are almost certain to shift the distribution of both income and wealth as well as changing the total amount of real income available for sharing.

Moreover, we saw that under a free-enterprise system the same competitive processes that determine the composition of output and the allocation of resources also determine simultaneously the prices paid for the use of productive factors. The competitive processes determine wage rates for each of the many types of labor, interest rates on the various types of loans, rental rates on the many types of natural resources and other durable assets, and profits of enterprisers. These prices, of course, are determinants of the money incomes of the owners of productive factors.

577

In fact, the amount of money income that any person receives for his participation in productive processes depends on the quantity of productive factors he supplies for use and on the price he receives for the use of each unit. For example, your money income as a producer during any period depends on the quantity of labor services you sell and on the wage rate you receive for your type of labor, on the quantity of savings you have out on loan and on the interest rate you receive, on the quantity of natural resources and other durable assets you rent out and on the rental rates you receive, and on the amount of profits you receive as owner or part-owner of one or more business firms.

Thus the inequalities of income arising out of the competitive process reflect both inequalities in the quantities of productive factors that the different families are able to supply for use, and also differences in the prices they receive for the use of each unit. As an example, Mr. A may receive twice as much labor income as Mr. B either because he sells twice as many labor-hours of work or because he receives twice as much wages per hour. The same is true of all types of income-yielding wealth.

We also found that the distribution of income as determined by market competition is modified considerably by taxation, government transfer payments, and government supplies of goods and services.

In this chapter we shall discuss three broad aspects of income distribution. We shall first examine the facts, getting some idea as to how income is actually distributed and comparing the current situation with that prevailing earlier. We shall then examine the grounds on which the distribution of income has been criticized and defended. Finally, we shall consider some of the things that can and have been done to modify it.

Because value judgments are involved, the economist can say little about how income ought to be distributed. Any change in the distribution of income will necessarily be disadvantageous to some and advantageous to others. This inevitably raises such questions as these: Which person is the more deserving? Will this do A more good than it will B?

2. The Distribution of Income in the United States

A. THE CURRENT SITUATION

Some indication of the current distribution of income is given in Table 48. The income data are based on "spending units." We may think of these as households; more precisely, a spending unit is defined as "all persons living in the same dwelling unit and related by blood, marriage, or adoption, who pooled their incomes for their major items of expense." Income per spending unit is higher than income per person, because some spending units include two or more earners.

TABLE 48.   Income Groupings of Spending Units, and of Total
Money Income Before Taxes, 1952[1]

Money Income Before Taxes	Percent of Spending Units	Percent of Total Money Income
Under $1,000	11	1
$1,000–1,999	14	5
2,000–2,999	16	10
3,000–3,999	18	15
4,000–4,999	15	16
5,000–7,499	17	25
7,500–9,999	5	10
10,000–and over	4	18
All cases	100	100

Addenda:	
Median income	$3,420
Mean (or average) income	$4,070

The reader who is not already familiar with the data is likely to be struck by the high percentage of spending units earning very low incomes. The median figure means—if the survey is accurate—that 50 percent of all spending units receive less than $3420 a year. Some 11 percent receive less even than $1000 a year. Collectively, the latter have only 1 percent of the nation's total money income. One-quarter of all spending units have annual incomes below $2000 and receive only 6 percent of the nation's total money income. At the other end of the scale, 9 percent of the spending units have annual incomes above $7500 and receive 28 percent of the nation's money income. To the college student, whose family's earnings are likely to be above the average, these data are often startling.

For a number of reasons the figures may exaggerate the gravity of the situation. (1) For a variety of reasons people may understate their incomes when reporting to an official or semiofficial agency. (2) Many

[1] Source: "1953 Survey of Consumer Finances," *Federal Reserve Bulletin,* June, 1953, p. 589. Median income is that of the middle spending unit in a ranking of all units by size of money income before taxes. Fifty percent of American spending units earn more than this amount and 50 percent earn less. Mean income is the average, obtained by dividing aggregate money income before taxes by the number of spending units.

of those who earned less than $1000 in 1952 were farmers or business-
men who happened to have a bad year; some even took a loss. At least
some of them may have been well to do. Some may have suffered
temporary financial troubles because of illness. (3) Many low earners
were farmers who were able to raise food for themselves, and thus were
better off than their money incomes indicate. In general, the poorer
people tend to live in areas where living costs are lower. (4) Higher incomes often come from skilled professional work which involves long
and costly training. Averaged over his lifetime, such a person's earnings may be much less extraordinary. (5) Some of those with low incomes were elderly people who had ceased work and were living on
their accumulated wealth. (6) Statistics show that up to a point larger
families tend to have larger incomes. This means that the income per
person is likely to be less unequal than income per family or per spending unit. However, for quite large families (six and over), income
tends to decrease with family size.

But these figures should not be discounted too much, even if they
do somewhat exaggerate the degree of inequality. The very low-income
groups include old people, sharecroppers, the permanently disabled,
and others for whom the figures represent stark and chronic poverty.
This must be contrasted with the estimate that some 200 persons were
reporting annual incomes in excess of a million dollars in 1950.
Despite all the exaggeration that may be attributed to the figures, income inequality and poverty are significant and undeniable.

B. TRENDS IN THE DISTRIBUTION OF INCOME

Though we may feel that this is a rather surprisingly lopsided distribution of income, there are some indications that at least during recent
decades the trend has been in the direction of greater equality.

This trend seems to have begun during the great depression. One
writer says that at the end of the 20's "relative income inequality was
about as great as at any earlier time for which we have adequate records. During the first few years of the Great Depression, a complex set
of changes apparently diminished income inequality sharply at the upper end of the scale of incomes but increased it at the lower end. But
it is clear that since then income inequality has diminished to previously unrecorded levels."[2] This is shown in Table 49.

Even before taxes, the share of the highest 1 percent of income earn-

[2] Geoffrey H. Moore, "Secular Changes in the Distribution of Income," *American
Economic Review,* May 1952, p. 528.

ers has fallen from some 17 percent in 1929 to an estimated 9 percent in 1948, and the share of the next highest-income group—those earning less than the preceding group but still in the top 5 percent—fell from some 15 percent to about 10 percent in the same interval. Obviously the share of the rest of the community has risen correspondingly.

TABLE 49. Changes in the Distribution of Income Before Taxes, 1913–1948[3]
(Percentage Shares in Countrywide Income)

Year	Top 1 Percent	2nd to 5th Percentage Band	Lower 95 Percent	Lower 99 Percent	Total
1913	16.2	n.a.[a]	n.a.[a]	83.8	100.0
1920	13.6	12.1	74.2	86.4	100.0
1929	17.2	14.7	68.1	82.8	100.0
1939	13.3	14.8	71.9	86.7	100.0
1948	9.0	10.5	80.4	91.0	100.0

[a] n.a.: not available.

Moreover, more recent figures indicate that this trend has continued. As to the details, we may again profitably quote Moore:

Taking the period as a whole, the average per capita income for the upper group rose from $5,700 in 1913 to $12,500 in 1948, a gain of $6,800; the average for the lower 99 per cent rose from about $300 to $1,300, a gain of only $1,000. Nevertheless, relatively the gain was much larger for the lower group; that is, the mass of the population. Their per capita income in 1948 was more than four times what it was in 1913, whereas the income of the upper group had little more than doubled. Moreover, a doubling of dollar income in this period does not appear to have been enough even to maintain real income; the BLS consumers' price index in 1948 was two and a half times its 1913 level. In real terms, if this price index is representative, the "poor" grew richer and the "rich" poorer. Certainly there was a shift towards a smaller relative difference: the individuals in the upper 1 percent had an average per capita income nearly twenty times as large as the average in the lower 99 percent group in 1913 and only ten times as large in 1948.[4]

Perhaps even more significant is the fact that poverty has been significantly reduced. Though they certainly do not suggest that nothing more ought to be done in this direction, the figures give grounds for

[3] Source: *Ibid.*, p. 530. Moore discusses at length the sources of his data and his methods of analysis.
[4] *Ibid.*, pp. 529–531.

some satisfaction. More indicative than stark income statistics are data like those in Table 50.

TABLE 50.   Some Changes in Housing Conditions, 1940–1950[5]

	1940	1950
Persons per dwelling unit	3.78	3.54
Rooms per person in occupied dwelling houses	1.28	1.33
Percent of houses having:		
Electric lights	78.7	94.0
Radio receivers	82.8	95.6
No refrigeration	27.4	8.7

It is noteworthy that despite the cessation of housebuilding during the war and the increase in population, the number of homes per person has increased. Nevertheless, there remain rather startling reminders that poverty is by no means entirely gone. For example, the table suggests that nearly 9 percent of American homes do not have even iceboxes, let alone refrigerators. Moreover, in 1950 approximately a quarter of all American dwellings had no flush toilet, not even one shared by several families. This lack was by no means confined to rural areas.

3. The Desire for More Equality

Though it has diminished in recent times, the contrast between extreme wealth and poverty remains a characteristic of our economy. To many this is reprehensible, and it has given rise to a body of literature as well as to political pressures designed to promote increased equality.

This widespread egalitarian bias is not, of course, universal. It is to a considerable extent opposed by many of those who stand to lose in the process, as well as by others, perhaps less acutely involved, who see practical difficulties. But we must not conclude that division on this question runs entirely along lines of self-interest. Some of the leading exponents of egalitarianism have come from the wealthy or upper-middle classes. These people have sometimes worked with extraordinary zeal to undermine their own vested interests.

The desire to reduce inequality has not always been so popular. For example, in the England of the eighteenth century concern with the lot of the poor, even when voiced, was often little more than an affecta-

[5] Source: *Statistical Abstract of the United States,* 1952, pp. 738–743.

tion. The modern attitude can be said to have developed in the Victorian period and may be ascribed at least partly to the incredible lot of the poor under the industrial revolution. Their misery was compounded of extreme poverty and the intolerable working conditions in so many of the earlier factories and workshops. The movement for greater equality was manifested in a variety of ways, including the rise of a romantic literature typified by the works of Dickens, Elizabeth Barrett Browning, and Thomas Hood, and in a variety of revolutionary movements.

The supporters of increased equality have argued their case on a number of grounds, not all of which we shall consider here.

A. ARGUMENTS BASED ON ETHICAL GROUNDS

These are the most widely used and undoubtedly the most effective. Essentially, they assert that poverty is inherently wrong and offensive to all our concepts of justice. In particular it is maintained that it is wrong for luxury and riotous living to be permitted in the face of acute need. In such terms runs the argument that wealth be taken away from the affluent and distributed among the impecunious. There is little or nothing the economist in his professional capacity can say about these views, for they involve judgment as to what is right and what is wrong —a decision which, as we have said more than once, is beyond his field of professional competence.

A different but related viewpoint is worthy of mention. This involves advocacy of equality of opportunity rather than actual equality of income or wealth. It is held that perfect equality is quite undesirable because it would permit no reward for ability and hard work. On the other hand, it is maintained that unequal incomes should be permitted to arise only from superior effort or peculiar talent, and that the head start the rich man's son has is unfair and in conflict with our democratic ideals. The rich man's son may or may not turn out to be wealthy, but whether or not he does should depend on his own efforts. The practical proposals that stem from this particular ideal are clearly somewhat different from those that are called for by pure egalitarianism.

B. THE DIMINISHING MARGINAL UTILITY OF INCOME ARGUMENT

This is in part an argument employed by some economists and demolished by other economists. In general terms it maintains that a wealthy man has so many dollars (and so much of the things they represent) that the gain or loss of a few dollars will mean very little to him. To a poor man, however, that same number of dollars may mean a great deal. This, it is maintained, follows from the introspective observation that the more of any item one possesses, the less an additional unit of that item will be worth. That is, the so-called marginal utility of the item will diminish.

It is therefore maintained that a transfer of $5 from a wealthy person to someone less affluent will generally result in a net gain; the rich man will hardly miss his loss, while the gain to the poor man will be of considerable importance. Thus income redistribution and equalization would appear to be appropriate for the practical reason that without it we would not be deriving the maximum amount of utility from our resources. That is, inequality prevents us from achieving the maximum total happiness for the community.

This particular argument is generally rejected today on two grounds. First, as we shall see, it is not valid to assume that equality would necessarily leave unchanged the size of the pie to be divided. If it results in decreased productive efficiency and so decreases the total amount of income to be divided, any gains in welfare attained through equalization may be wiped out, and more.

In addition, it is usually agreed that this argument involves comparisons among individuals that we are not entitled to make. How are we to compare the feelings of one man with those of another, especially when one is the abstract entity entitled "the typical rich man" and the other "the representative pauper"? Is it really legitimate to argue that most rich men will miss $5 less than a poor man will? What if the first is a miser and the latter a spendthrift? True, we might then be even more tempted to take from that rich man and give to the poor, but this would be because our sense of merit is offended, not because we believe the change will, on balance, increase happiness. It is not legitimate to argue from a single individual to the group, maintaining that if a dollar becomes less valuable to B as he becomes richer, it must be worth more to A than to B because A is the poorer of the two.

c. The Social Cost of Poverty

There is another more practical line of argument for income equalization. This is the view that the upper- and middle-income groups can harm themselves by living in a community which includes very poor people. If poverty results in poor health and education it may well result in a severe loss in national productivity.[6] It may thus prevent the rich man from adding even further to his welfare. This becomes particularly plausible when we realize how much better off in terms of material comfort the modern rich man is, compared with his counterpart of several centuries ago, mainly because of inventions and discoveries then undreamed of. Many of these were produced by men of poor family who in the absence of educational assistance (which is one form of real income redistribution) might not have had the technical background necessary to produce them.

There are other ways in which widespread poverty can harm everyone. It may increase the prevalence of disease. It may weaken a country militarily and increase the military duties falling on the wealthy and middle classes. In a democracy it may make for political incompetence and corruption, which affect the lives of everyone. Thus it appears that too great a degree of inequality may not be a paying proposition even to those who come off best under such an arrangement.

d. Practical Problems of Equality

However, as we stated earlier, there are practical objections to egalitarianism, or at least to its being carried too far.[7] For one thing, there is the crucial problem of incentives. In a market economy, direction and control are achieved through an automatic system of pecuniary rewards and punishments. This requires that the man who produces what consumers want and produces it efficiently obtains a higher income than someone who does not. Complete equality must eliminate such incentives and leave us with no alternative but strict central control over the economy and complete reliance on nonpecuniary rewards and penalties. Even in the Soviet Union it has been found that the economy does not operate well in the absence of income incentives. The result has been a system of rewards making for a high degree of income inequality. It is to be noted, however, that the Soviets say they still look forward to a time when people's awareness of their social responsibility will have grown and their motivations will have become less venal, so that their economy can proceed to that ultimate communist state so often described by the phrase "from each according to his ability, to each according to his needs."

But in a market economy, equality may be a self-defeating ideal, for

[6] See pp. 41–43, 124.
[7] See pp. 330, 406.

if carried too far it may reduce productivity so much that we all become equal by becoming equally poor. This is not to deny that some degree of further equalization may be possible or even desirable. We saw in the preceding section that too much inequality may also reduce productive efficiency. Moreover, some of us, for reasons of equity, may be willing to pay the price of some loss in productivity. Where to stop, and where the productive inefficiency which can result from equalization begins, is impossible to say. We can only be certain that there are voices that cry we have already gone too far, and others that reply that we have not gone far enough.

4. Education as a Method of Reducing Inequality

One of the important steps that can be taken to reduce inequality of income is to reduce inequality of opportunity, an objective that is often considered to be an end in itself. It is obvious that those who are handicapped for the more lucrative professions by lack of education and training or by poor health resulting from inadequate medical care are thereby deprived of economic opportunities. The increased availability of subsidized education and medical care to the public at large serves to reduce inequality of opportunity.

The effect of such programs on income inequality is likely to be quite important. However, they are not "quick remedies"—it may take a long time for their effects to be widely felt. The educational process itself takes time, and it sometimes takes time to get people out of their ruts and into active competition in the more lucrative professions. The long-run effects may be to drive down the wages of highly skilled labor and of professional workers and to drive up the rate of remuneration of the relatively depleted ranks of the unskilled.

It should be clear that such a program can reduce but not eliminate inequality, though the more limited objective may be all that is desired. It will not wipe out the profits of the more astute or luckier businessman, nor will it increase the earning capacity of those whose poor abilities or ill health are beyond the meliorative abilities of existing educational or medical techniques. Thus many of the very poorest and the very richest members of the economy may not be directly affected by programs of this sort. Yet it must be recognized that the increase in public education in the United States during the past century, to the point where many now go from kindergarten through a university without paying tuition, has undoubtedly been a powerful influence toward the reduction of inequality.

5. Taxation as a Method of Reducing Inequality

A. THE TAX SYSTEM

We have already discussed at some length the tax system of the United States, its effects on the distribution of income and wealth, and some of the limits on its use as an instrument for redistributing income and wealth.[8] We found that some of our taxes are regressive, tending to accentuate inequality; others may be proportional, tending to leave income distribution unchanged; still others are progressive, tending to reduce inequality. The two most important clearly progressive taxes are the personal income tax and inheritance and estate taxes. Because of our ignorance concerning both the amount of benefits received from the government by the various income groups and the final incidence of taxes, we can generalize only broadly about the effects of taxes on the distribution of real income after taxes. This much is clear, however; the very wealthy pay a higher percentage of their income in taxes than do the very poor. This obviously tends to narrow the range between the very rich and the poor. But the effects in the wide middle-income range are more difficult to assess.

B. EFFECTS OF THE PERSONAL INCOME TAX

Table 51 may give the reader some idea of the effectiveness of the federal personal income tax in redistributing money income. This shows, for example, that the most well-to-do 10 percent of our spending units have their incomes reduced by the income tax from 31 to 28 percent of the total incomes received by all households. The percentage of our income going to all spending units below the top 20 percent is either increased or not reduced.

This table does not tell the whole story, however. Moore, whom we quoted earlier on the trend toward decreased inequality of incomes before taxes, speculates that much of this trend can be ascribed to increased taxes and increasingly progressive tax rates.[9] His reasoning is that many of the wealthy have been driven by high taxes to invest in tax-exempt bonds whose return is very low. Indeed, the demand for such bonds by the wealthy must have served to keep up their price, i.e., to keep the yield per dollar of their price very low. Thus the *pre*-tax incomes of the rich may have fallen as a result of their attempts to avoid high taxes.

[8] See chapter 17.
[9] Geoffrey H. Moore, *op. cit.*, pp. 542–543.

Similarly, Moore suggests that the very well-to-do may have taken increasingly less of their corporate earnings in dividends, more being retained in the firm to build up its capital. The purpose of this is to avoid the personal income tax altogether. The phenomenon may be particularly significant in closely held, e.g., "family," corporations.

TABLE 51. Percentage of Total Money Income Received by Each Tenth of the Nation's Spending Units, When Ranked by Size of Income, 1951[10]

	% of Income Before Federal Income Tax	% of Income After Federal Income Tax
Highest tenth	31	28
Second	15	15
Third	12	13
Fourth	10	11
Fifth	9	9
Sixth	8	8
Seventh	6	7
Eighth	5	5
Ninth	3	3
Lowest tenth	1	1
All groups	100	100

Though the net effect of this is not to reduce the income and wealth of the upper-income groups, it can tend to restrict the amount available to them for personal expenditure.

6. Government Expenditures as a Method of Reducing Inequality

A. THE POSSIBILITIES

The government affects the distribution of real income not only through its tax policies but also through its provision of goods and services and its transfer payments.

It can and does reduce inequality by providing somewhat the same amount of goods and services to the members of all income classes regardless of the amount of taxes they pay. Some examples are publicly supported parks, playgrounds, beaches, school lunch programs, and dental inspection programs in the schools.

B. PROVISION OF SERVICES TO THE POOR

The government also helps eliminate extreme poverty by providing the poor with services for which it either makes no direct charge or

[10] Source: "1952 Survey of Consumer Finances," *Federal Reserve Bulletin,* September, 1952, p. 979.

charges less than the market price. Examples are public medical and dental clinics, hospital care, and subsidized low-cost housing for which the higher-income groups are ineligible.

c. Transfer Payments

An outstanding development during the past 25 years has been the use of government transfer payments to augment the money incomes of those who would otherwise be at least temporarily in the very low-income groups. The most important of these are benefits to the aged and the unemployed.

Before the institution of these programs many of the aged were in extreme poverty. Because of low incomes during their working lives, illness, improvidence, or other reasons, they had not accumulated enough to live well after retirement. A federal old-age insurance program now provides benefits to a large proportion of the aged, and it seems likely that the coverage of the plan will be extended. This insurance program is supplemented by state-administered but federally subsidized old-age relief systems to make additional payments to those whose insurance benefits are clearly inadequate and to provide for the needy aged who are not covered by the insurance plan.

The great depression gave birth to unemployment insurance systems in practically every state and to much more liberal unemployment relief than previously prevailed. Under a typical unemployment insurance system a man who loses his job becomes eligible for weekly benefits after a short waiting period and can continue to draw benefits for 26 weeks. He receives these payments as a matter of right under the insurance program and does not have to prove need. If he is still unemployed after his unemployment insurance benefits cease, he may be eligible for unemployment relief payments, but he must prove his need for them.

7. Programs to Help Special Groups: The Example of Agriculture

At times it has proved convenient or politically expedient to try to reduce inequality through programs designed to help certain relatively impoverished groups. In some cases the issues are likely to be confused because the ostensible purpose of the program is to reduce inequality, though the actual motivations and effects may be considerably more complex. In other cases the political situation may dictate that the egalitarian effects of a program be played down. This will become clearer as we consider an example. We might mention a number of other examples—the TVA, other river valley development programs which can, at least in part, be used as a method of assisting particular regions, and tariff protection or subsidies to ailing industries. However, we shall concentrate on special assistance to agriculture. Though other sectors have received assistance, in almost no other case has the aim of reducing inequality been proclaimed so explicitly and repeatedly.

A. THE NATURE OF THE FARM PROBLEM

Taken as a whole, American farmers have indeed been in the lowest-income group for a considerable period. Among them are perhaps the most impoverished single occupational group—the sharecroppers, especially the colored sharecroppers of the South. But many other farmers have been relatively underprivileged.

Agricultural prices were quite low relative to other prices even during the prosperous 20's, and they fell precipitously with the onset of the great depression. They revived somewhat under the New Deal, but most farmers were still in the low-income category at the outbreak of World War II. During and after the war farm incomes in real terms rose to their highest levels in several decades. But Table 52 shows that

TABLE 52.   Median Incomes of Spending Units, Classified by
Occupational Groups, 1952[11]

Occupation of Head of Spending Unit	Median Income Before Taxes
All spending units	$3420
Professional and semiprofessional	5310
Managerial and self-employed	5000
Clerical and sales	3850
Skilled and semiskilled	4000
Unskilled and service	2470
Farm operator	2190

even in 1952 many farmers were in the lowest income groups. While the median income of all spending units was $3420, and the median income of those headed by unskilled and service workers was $2470, the median income of spending units headed by farm operators was only $2170. By the definition of the median, 50 percent of all farm operators received money incomes below this level. Though the figures include only money income and exclude the farmer's consumption of his own output, the fact remains that many farmers are in our lowest-income groups. On the other hand, many of the larger and more prosperous farmers have had high incomes since the early 1940's.

[11] Source: *Federal Reserve Bulletin*, June, 1953, p. 589.

B. SOURCES OF THE FARM PROBLEM

During periods of depression the farmer suffers because of his customers' lack of spending power. As people's money incomes decline, they reduce somewhat their demands for farm products. This decrease of demand in the face of the farmers' continued large supplies depresses farm prices to very low levels. Farmers would be among the principal beneficiaries of a successful program to maintain continuously high employment in urban areas. In the following section we shall say little more about depression conditions and shall concentrate on longer-term problems.

It is generally agreed that the basic source of the farmers' difficulties is the excessive allocation of resources to agriculture. This has tended to result in chronic overproduction of farm commodities, low prices, and low incomes. Three basic reasons may be suggested—the fact that agriculture is so much more highly competitive than most other sectors of the economy, the continuing technological revolution in agriculture, and the low mobility of the farmer.

Farmers must deal with the other sectors of the economy in which monopolistic elements are more prevalent and in which it may be suspected that output will tend to be restricted to relatively profitable levels. This impinges on the farmer in two principal ways. First, it tends to hold up the prices he has to pay. Second, it may impede the movement of people away from farms and into other occupations.

The tendency toward chronic overproduction has been greatly aggravated by the continuing rapid rise of agricultural productivity attributable to the greater use of capital and improvements in technology. We mentioned earlier the tremendous growth of capital on farms during the past four decades—tractors, complex farm machinery, trucks and autos, milking machines, irrigation systems, electrical equipment, and so on. At the same time there have been many technological changes relating to plant and animal selection, breeding, and feeding; insect and fungus control; and many other farm needs. All these changes have led to great and continuing increases in agricultural output per man-hour, and most have increased output per acre. This use of more resources in the form of capital and technology need not have induced or accentuated agricultural overproduction if it had been offset by a sufficient movement of labor out of agriculture and into other industries. But the movement of labor into other occupations has not been fast enough to prevent a strong tendency toward agricultural overproduction.

It is easy to underestimate the mobility of people away from farming. It is estimated that between 1929 and 1952 the number of persons employed in agriculture decreased more than 25 percent. This occurred despite high birth rates on farms, so that the total number migrating from farming to other occupations must have been many millions. Nevertheless, the rate of migration out of farming has not been high enough to offset the import of capital and technology and to prevent the tendency toward overproduction. To some extent this inadequate mobility of workers has been due to a scarcity of job opportunities elsewhere. During the great depression a poor farmer had little incentive to leap from the frying pan of low farm prices into the fire of urban unemployment. But there are also other limitations on mobility—ignorance of existing alternatives, insufficient money to finance a move, lack of education and training for other jobs, love of independence and outdoor work, and so on.

c. REMEDIES

Many types of programs have been proposed to deal with the problems of low farm prices and incomes. At the heart of current legislation is the idea that the price of each basic farm product should be prevented from falling below some stated percentage of its "parity." The basic notion is that the prices of farm products should be kept at an "equitable" level relative to the prices of nonfarm products.

For most items the period 1910–1914 was selected at the time when farm prices were "fair" in relation to nonfarm prices. In general, the parity price of any farm product at any given time is the price that has the same percentage relationship to its level in the 1910–1914 period that nonfarm prices have to their level in the same base period. For example, if in 1954 an index of nonfarm prices doubled from its 1910–1914 average, parity would require that farm prices double too. It is important to note that the direct effect of applying the parity formula is not to stabilize the real income or purchasing power of a farmer; it is to stabilize the purchasing power of a unit of farm produce over other things—for example, to stabilize the real buying power of a bushel of wheat or a pound of cotton.

To support prices at 90 percent or some other stated percentage of parity at a time when they are tending to fall below, the government usually offers to lend the farmer a stated proportion of the value of his crop at parity prices, the crop being stored as security. This will take part of the crop off the market and will tend to reduce current supplies up to a point at which the market offers terms that are as good as the government's. The farmer may then redeem his loan at some future date when market prices happen to rise above the selected percentage of parity, or he may not redeem it at all, treating his original transaction as a sale to the government.

We cannot describe all the important and complex consequences of such a price-support program or evaluate its desirability as a device for raising farm incomes. However, we may note a few of its implications. In the first place, it gives the largest benefits to the farmers whose incomes are already high. The well-to-do farmer who sells great quantities of produce on the market sometimes receives large payments from the government. At the other extreme, the poor subsistence farmer who produces primarily for his own consumption and sells very little on the market receives only small payments from the government, if any. Any system of benefits based on the amount of products marketed rather than on the income of the producer may do nothing to reduce the great inequalities in the distribution of income among the farming population, and it may even aggravate them.

In the second place, such a price-support program can have far-reaching effects on the composition of output, the allocation of resources, and the degree of efficiency in the use of resources. We can give only a few examples. It may encourage too many people to remain in agriculture and inhibit their shift to other occupations where they could produce a greater value of output. If the price-support program is not accompanied by crop restrictions, the government may have to destroy or to dump in foreign markets at very low prices a considerable part of the output of agricultural products. If crop restrictions are employed, the crops that are grown may not be produced as efficiently as possible. Some land that is no longer used to grow a certain crop might be more efficient for that crop than some of the land that remains in use.

Moreover, the parity prices of different products may be such as to induce too much output of some types of farm products and too little of others. Suppose the costs of producing commodity A have fallen greatly relative to the costs of producing commodity B. If attempts are made to keep their price relationships the same as in the 1910–1914 period, the effect will be to give much more encouragement to the production of A than to the production of B.

We do not cite these problems in any attempt to judge whether the government should or should not support farm prices at 100 percent or any other fixed percentage of parity. We do it only to indicate that attempts to redistribute income by regulating the prices of any commodity or service are likely to have many effects other than their direct effects on the incomes of the sellers and buyers of the item in question.

Some have suggested that because of these difficulties it would be wiser policy for the government to help people leave such industries by lending them money, providing assistance in training for other occupations, and supplying them with information as to job opportunities. But it should be recognized that even these policies have their limitations. They may operate too slowly to suit some people, whereas others oppose any speeding up of urbanization.

It should also be recognized that the extreme view that farmers ought to be abandoned to their own devices and "detached from the public funds" may be unsatisfactory even from the selfish viewpoint of the rest of the community. We have seen how the existence of large impoverished groups can affect the entire economy adversely. In addition, the agricultural sector can prove to be a potent source of economic instability. For these reasons no simple answers to "the farm problem" seem to be in prospect.

8. Labor Unions and the Distribution of Income

A. GOVERNMENT POLICIES RELATIVE TO LABOR UNIONS

American public policies concerning labor unions have changed greatly over the years. In earlier periods unions were highly suspect as monopolies. They were frequently prosecuted under the antimonopoly laws and were successfully sued by employers for heavy damages. Gradually, however, government policy shifted from antagonism to active support of unionization. This was clearly evident in several pieces of legislation during the 1930's—the Norris-LaGuardia Act of 1932, the National Industrial Recovery Act of 1933, and the National Labor Relations Act of 1935 (the Wagner Act). Implied in this policy change was a desire to raise workers' living standards, to alter the distribution of income in their favor.

In particular, the Wagner Act required an employer to bargain collectively with representatives of his employees that were certified by the National Labor Relations Board as representing the majority and having exclusive bargaining rights. This meant that any union that could get a majority of the workers in a firm to join it was given *exclusive* power to represent the employees in their dealings with the firm. Moreover, employers were prohibited from interfering with the unions in their efforts to organize workers.

From this high point of labor's political achievement there was some retreat in the Taft-Hartley Act of 1947, which has incurred the severe displeasure of unions. Yet in a sense even this law is indicative of the increased status of organized labor. In comparison with their pre-New Deal position, the unions still remain substantially ahead. The relative mildness of the restraints imposed by a Congress anxious to curb the power of labor, and later the promises of both the Republican and Democratic parties to change the Taft-Hartley Act point to the eminent status the unions have achieved.

Along with the enactment of more favorable legislation, but perhaps not solely because of it, union membership increased greatly, rising from less than 5 million in the 1920's to about 15 million in the early 1950's. It therefore becomes important to evaluate the role that the unions can and do play in affecting wages and employment. Unfortunately, the available information on these subjects is in general inconclusive.

B. THE OBJECTIVES OF LABOR UNIONS

Though we shall concentrate on the effects of unions on wages and employment, we should note that unions also negotiate on many other things—seniority rights of workers, working conditions, the pace of work, hiring and firing procedures, and so on. Moreover, they negotiate not only wage rates to be received currently by workers, but also the amount of vacation to be given with pay, sickness benefits, old-age pensions, and other so-called "fringe benefits." We shall use the term wages in a broad sense to include the values of all these benefits.

Our concentration on the unions' effects on wages and employment is justified by the fact that the principal function of unions is generally considered to be raising wages and the real incomes of workers. In fact, many consider unions to be effective agencies for altering the distribution of income, presumably in favor of workers.

C. DO UNIONS RAISE WAGES?

At first this may seem like a silly question. It is perfectly obvious to anyone who will look at the facts that wages have risen markedly along with the growth of union membership, and that the wage increases in unionized industries have been negotiated by union officials. But this merely tells us that in fact wages have risen; it does not indicate the effects of unions on wages. To highlight this issue we should reword our question and ask, "How much more or less would wages have risen if unions had not grown in strength but everything else had occurred as in fact it did?" Of course we cannot hope to answer this question, for it implies performing an experiment that we cannot perform. However, identification of the true question will enable us to make a few relevant comments.

Some rise of both money and real wages would almost certainly have occurred during this period even in the absence of unions. We have already noted that output per man-hour has risen markedly. This should serve to drive up real wages, either by inducing business firms to bid up wage rates or by making cost-of-living items cheaper. Moreover, the period since 1940 has been predominantly inflationary, with high levels of employment and rising prices of output. As the prices of their outputs rise and labor becomes scarcer, employers can be expected to bid up wages even if they have no unions to contend with.

We are sometimes told that it is obvious that unions drive up wages, for that is their business. But this, too, is inconclusive. The machinery for wage adjustment is sometimes slow and ponderous. It often involves waiting for a wage contract to expire, long negotiations, and sometimes lengthy strikes. It could even turn out that a large wage increase received after a long interval would be less than the total of several smaller wage increases that would have been received in the absence of collective bargaining.

Thus we come to the rather unsatisfactory conclusion that we simply do not know whether the general effects of unions on their members' wages have been to make them higher than they would otherwise have been or to make them lower than they would otherwise have been. This probably varies from one union to another.

D. EFFECTS OF UNIONS ON WAGES OF NONUNION WORKERS

It is also difficult to generalize about the effects of labor unions on the real wages of workers whose pay is not determined through collective bargaining. On the one hand, it is contended that unions tend to raise the wages of the unorganized by acting as pace setters. It is argued that employers of nonunion people raise their wages whenever unions get increases, both because this establishes a precedent and also because they fear unionization if they do not.

On the other hand, unions may in two ways tend to lower the real wages of the nonunionized. In the first place, they may so restrict the number of people employed in unionized jobs as to force large numbers into other lines, thereby lowering wages for the nonunion jobs. The union may do this either by directly restricting the number of workers allowed in union jobs, or by setting wage rates so high as to restrict the number that employers will hire. This may force more people into nonunion jobs and tend to lower wage rates there. In the second place, unions may raise the cost of living and lower the real wages of nonunion workers by forcing up the wages and labor costs of firms producing consumer goods and their components, thus pushing up their prices. Here again we cannot be sure of the net results.

E. SUMMARY

It is clear that labor unions can exert important influences on wage rates, the distribution of income, the quantities of labor employed in the various types of unionized and nonunionized jobs, and many other aspects of the economy. A more exhaustive description and analysis than we can undertake here would probably throw more light on both the nature and the extent of these effects. But we should remember that in trying to assess the effects of unions we must not simply ask, "What actually happened?" The more relevant question is, "In what ways and to what extent would things have been different in the absence of unions?" Though this is the right question, it is usually very difficult if not impossible to find conclusive answers.

9. Conclusions

We have seen that the distribution of income in our economy involves what to many people is a surprising degree of inequality and poverty. There seems to be a marked trend toward the reduction of both of these. Taxation, particularly income and inheritance taxes, can be used to hasten this process, if such a goal is desired. Aid to special groups is subject to the economic objection that it is likely to result in misallocation of resources, though in particular cases it may be desired because it is more feasible politically than an overall move for increased equality, or for other reasons.

This area is particularly likely to arouse ire and political passions. Income redistribution is essentially a process that cannot benefit everyone. It must involve some people's feeling that they are being preyed upon to benefit other groups whose moral claim they consider questionable. Yet in this region and for just this reason we are least able to make definitive judgments. We can only suggest, given whatever goal is adopted, its incidental economic consequences and the ways it can be achieved. It is to this limited task that this chapter, and indeed this volume, has been devoted.

SUGGESTED READINGS

Fisher, Allan G. B., "Alternative Techniques for Promoting Equality in a Capitalist Society," *American Economic Review,* May, 1950, pp. 356–368.

QUESTIONS

1. a. In what ways, if any, do you find the data in Table 48 surprising?
   b. Discuss the reasons given for suspecting that the data in this table exaggerate the degree of inequality, and assess the significance of each.
   c. Make a guess as to how the table might be changed as you correct for each of these points.
2. a. Try to account for the trends in income distribution.
   b. Do you think Table 49 or Table 50 is more suggestive and informative?
   c. Would you agree that in the 1930's one-third of the nation was "ill-fed, ill-housed and ill-clad"?
   d. How about now?
3. Show how inheritance taxes might help to promote:
   a. Decreased income inequality.
   b. Decreased inequality of opportunity.
   c. Under our present economic and social structure, what are some practical limits to the equality of opportunity that is achievable?
4. a. Explain in detail Moore's contention that progressive taxes can indirectly reduce the income and consumption spending power of the wealthy.
   b. Can the impulse toward more undistributed profits be considered a form of expropriation of the stockholders' earnings?
   c. Consider the possible effects of these undistributed profits on the productivity of the economy.
   d. On the level of employment.
   e. How can these effects vary with the decisions of corporations on the use of these funds?
   f. Sum up by evaluating the effects of increased undistributed profits on capitalists' living standards and on the economy as a whole.
5. a. Show how in an inflationary period sharply progressive taxes can *increase* the real incomes of the lower earning groups.

    b. How can this occur if the government does not spend the money it collects in taxes.

    c. If the government does spend it.

6. Show how the present farm price-support program:

    a. Can cause a misallocation of resources.

    b. Can cause an increase in the inequality of farm incomes.

    c. Show how willingness on the part of the government to buy at a fixed price whatever the farmer produces can increase the amplitude of the fluctuation in his income which results from a change in the weather.

    d. Can you think of any alternative programs which may be more satisfactory?

    e. Explain in detail some possible objections to doing nothing at all to assist farmers.

7. Design some investigations which might throw some light on the effect of trade unionization on wage levels. Evaluate them and point out their pitfalls.

GRAPHIC APPENDIX

This appendix is devoted to an exposition of portions of price (value) theory and of the theory of distribution. These treat, respectively, the determination of the market prices of individual commodities and of the factors of production. Wherever appropriate we shall employ the graphic techniques commonly associated with the subjects.

The reader will recognize that in a number of points the analysis in the body of the book consists of applications of this theoretical material. We have made frequent cross references to help bring this out and to make it easier to use this appendix as a supplement to the text. Nevertheless, the material we are about to present represents a departure from the direct policy orientation of this book. For this reason we have chosen to set it off by itself as an appendix where it can be used by those who find it helpful. Though it may perhaps shed light on the reasoning we have used in other parts of the book, we emphasize that an understanding of the analysis in the volume does not necessarily depend on separate study of the areas on whose discussion we now embark.

PART I

Demand, Supply, and Price

In this part of the Appendix we shall examine those oft-referred-to "laws" of supply and demand. We will see how demand and supply together can determine price in a competitive industry. In many cases the individual steps in our analysis and their applications may be of as much interest as the final summation in a supply-demand price equilibrium.

1. Demand and Utility

We saw in the body of the volume how a consumer's demand can be represented in the form of a curve that shows the quantity of a commodity he is willing to buy at each conceivable price.[1]

Let us first go behind this schedule and examine its relation to the desires and preferences of the individual consumer. From there we proceed to discuss the demand for a product by the entire body of consumers. Finally, we shall describe a much used measure of the responsiveness of demand to price, the *elasticity of demand*.

A. UTILITY AND PRICE

Economists have long been aware that there is no obvious relationship between the subjective evaluation we place on the goods we buy and the amount we pay for them. We need water to exist, whereas we can often get along without diamonds. Yet we pay little or nothing for the former and fortunes for the latter.

This apparently chaotic relationship between the utility of a good and its price was shown to display an orderly pattern, and suddenly

[1] See above pp. 381–383.

everything seemed to fall into place when late in the nineteenth century several economists independently developed the following rather
remarkable analysis.

B. Diminishing Marginal Utility

These economists maintained that the utility of a good depends on
the quantity possessed by the consumer. Although water is necessary
for our existence, we would not think highly of a birthday gift of a
bucket of water because so much of this item is available to us. Our
attitude would be different if we were on a desert and that bucket were
the only water available to us for a week. Then we might save all the
water for drinking and use none of it for frills like bathing or window
washing. Should we suddenly acquire a second bucket we could treat
it a bit more cavalierly. We might acquire a pet or even a wife and a
mother-in-law to share our supply. Thus a second bucket of water,
while giving us pleasure, does not yield as much satisfaction as the
first. The introspective evaluation of the satisfaction yielded by the
acquisition of an *additional* unit (a bucket) of water, ill defined as
the concept must be, is called its *marginal utility*.[2] We see now that
the marginal utility of the second bucket is likely to be smaller than
that of the first. A third bucket will have still less marginal utility. It
might enable us to shave, bathe, or wash the floors, all minor uses
when compared with the use of water as a life-giving beverage. There
is no need to carry this illustration further. It has suggested the introspective proposition that, as more and more units of a commodity
become available to us, we put a declining evaluation on the acquisition of yet another unit.

C. Marginal Utility, Price, and the Demand Curve

If water is available to us in unlimited quantities at 10 cents a bucket,
we can be sure that we will buy at least one bucket. For one bucket is
worth life itself to us, and there is no telling how much we would pay
for it to a black marketer of the desert who held out for all the traffic
would bear. Suppose our top price is $8 for the second bucket and $5
for the third. We will certainly buy a second and a third bucket if they

[2] It is easy to make the exposition more rigorous by translating it into money terms.
For diminishing marginal utility we can substitute the principle that the consumer
is willing to give less money for additional units of a commodity as the quantity at
his disposal grows. In this way we avoid reference to ill-defined concepts like "utility."
In the economists' jargon the additional money he is willing to pay for another unit
of a commodity is called his *marginal rate of substitution of money for the commodity*.

are available at 10 cents each. Going on in this way we might find
that our top price for a seventh bucket is 15 cents and we would still
buy it for a dime, but we would stop short at buying an eighth bucket
which is worth less than 10 cents to us. The reader will recognize that
this is an application of the principle of no wasted opportunities.[3] In
this case it tells us that the consumer will buy up to a point at which
the price of the good is equal to its marginal utility.

In this way we can derive the demand curve of the consumer. For
example, we know that at a price of 10 cents he will buy seven units,
at a price of $6 each he will buy two buckets, at $9 he will buy only

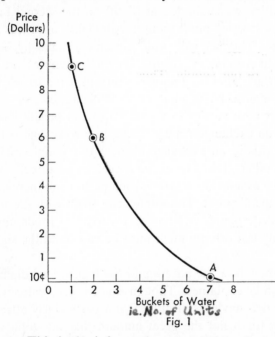

Fig. 1

one, etc. This is the information we need to draw his demand curve.
This is shown in Fig. 1, in which points *A*, *B*, and *C* represent the
price and quantity-purchased combinations just mentioned. At every
price, then, we can relate the quantity of the commodity the consumer
will buy to the marginal utility he assigns to the commodity.

D. REMARKS

An objection frequently raised by students encountering this proposition for the first time is that the purchaser is doing something wrong
here—that he should have stopped while the going was good, while

---

[3] See above, pp. 383–384.

he was getting a good return on his money. Perhaps he should have stopped at the second bucket so that he would have gotten $8 worth of goods for 10 cents. But this is surely wrong. It involves the consumer's wasting the opportunity to make more net gain for himself by buying a third unit of the good which is worth $5 to him and which still costs him only 10 cents. It would even be an opportunity wasted if he failed to buy the seventh unit, which is worth only 15 cents to him.

We can now see that the consumer usually does make a net gain in buying some good; that is, he is not really charged all the traffic will bear. This we saw clearly in the water example, in which the consumer made a net gain which we evaluated at $7.90 on the second bucket alone. Only when he stopped purchasing, on an eighth unit, was there no net gain for him. This net gain that consumers make by buying commodities is called *consumers' surplus*. It explains why we are willing to buy goods at all. That is, it shows what's in it for us when we buy some good at the grocers, or a hat, or some cigarettes.

It also shows that both parties to an exchange can benefit from it, that the gain from an exchange need not simply involve one person's cheating the other, for in an exchange each of two people makes a purchase from the other. This can be seen even more directly when we view an exchange as a means whereby each person can increase the variety of items at his disposal. The hunter can trade with the fisherman and each be made happier by having a variety of foods, instead of having to eat only fish or only meat until he can stand the sight of it no longer.

N.B.

Conclusion

We can also see now how the paradox of the high-priced diamonds and cheap water can be explained. Though water is very valuable, we have so much of it that having still more is not particularly attractive to us. We thus pay for it not the great amount that our total water consumption is worth to us, but only the smaller amount we are willing to give up for a further increase in the quantity we have. In a similar manner we can attribute the high price of diamonds to their scarcity and their consequently high marginal value.

2. The Negative Slope of the Demand Curve

A. PRICE AND DEMAND

Earlier in the volume we discussed the effect of a price change on consumption.[4] We pointed out that price is a deterrent to consumption

[4] Above, pp. 390–391.

and that a rise in price will tend to decrease purchases by consumers. This it is likely to do in two ways: (1) the substitution effect—by making substitutes relatively cheaper; thus a rise in the price of a Ford might reduce its sales to the benefit of Chevrolets or even Mercurys. And (2) the income effect—by reducing the purchasing power of the prospective buyers' income; thus a rise in the price of clothing can make the pauper retrench on all his purchases including clothing.

Where these arguments hold, the demand curve will slope downward to the right. That is, a rise in price will be associated with a reduction in consumers' purchases, a fall in price with an increase in the quantity demanded.

B. EXCEPTIONS

There are several noteworthy exceptions, cases where demand may rise with price.

1. Snob appeal. Some things are bought to impress our neighbors or our social rivals. Often we consider our purchases more worth while when they are more expensive. Therefore, within limits, more silverware and jewelry may be sold at a higher price.

2. Quality judged by price. Many of us are likely to think a commodity is better when its price is higher. There are many recorded cases of identical commodities sold under different labels, with more being sold of the more expensive batch. Commodities like milk which are bought by mothers for the health of their children may be particularly vulnerable to this sort of operation. Similarly, identical automobile tires have been sold at two different list prices, partly because some consumers judge quality by price.

3. Inferior goods. Inferior goods are defined as items of which we buy less the richer we get. Such goods are common enough. Standard examples are bread, which we no longer want to fill up on when we can afford meat, margarine which we will give up for butter, and cheap clothes which we may give up for custom-made items when we can afford them. Suppose that a housewife has a strict budget with $2 a week earmarked for margarine and a little butter for Sundays. When the price of margarine rises, her $2 will leave her less money to buy butter and so she must make up for it by increasing her margarine purchases. Here a rise in price has increased the quantity of the commodity she demands. This occurs because through the income effect, the rise in the price of the good decreases the purchasing power of her money and forces her to buy more of the inferior good.

But it is at least equally possible that the purchase of the inferior good will decrease when its price increases. The buyer may wish to make up for his decreased purchasing power elsewhere, especially since the fall in the price of the inferior good makes the "superior substitute" relatively less expensive. If the margarine price rises from a quarter to half the price of butter, the housewife may decide that the difference in taste now justifies the purchase of butter despite the difference in price, and though she has less money to spend she will use some of it to buy butter. In this case the substitution effect will have offset the income effect.

Though demand curves for inferior goods sometimes slope upward to the right, they will not usually do so because we spend only a small proportion of our incomes on most commodities. Hence a fall in the price of such an item will not increase the consumer's purchasing power very much.[5]

c. Summary

Demand curves usually have a negative slope. That is to say, consumers will buy more of a good as its price falls. This is because a fall in price makes substitutes less attractive (the substitution effect) and increases the purchasing power of the consumer's income (the income effect). We have seen three classes of exceptions. Inferior goods may (but will usually not) be an exception, because with them the income effect works in a direction opposite to the usual one. The increase in his purchasing power resulting from a fall in the price of the item leads the consumer to want less of it. The other two exceptions, snob appeal and the judging of quality by price, occur because the satisfaction which the commodity yields to the consumer increases with its price.

3. Individual and Aggregate Demand

If we know the demand curve for every consumer on the market, we can often quite easily determine the total demand facing sellers of the commodity. This may be a purely mechanical procedure.

a. Construction of the Aggregate Demand Curve

For brevity we assume there are only two consumers; however, the same method applies unchanged to any number. If at 10 cents con-

---

[5] In the body of the text we also considered another case in which a decline of price might actually reduce purchases. This was the case in which a price decline led to a downward revision of expected future prices. See pages 247–249.

sumer A will buy 3 pounds of peas and consumer B will buy 6 pounds, the quantity demanded by the market at that price will be 9 pounds. It's as simple as that.

The graphics are equally simple. In Fig. 2A and 2B let AA' and BB' be A's and B's respective demand curves for peas. Fig. 2C shows their aggregate demand. Thus we see that at price 20 cents a pound A wants 2 pounds (point E) and B wants 3 pounds (point F); hence the market will demand 5 pounds (point G). We say that the market's demand curve DD' is obtained by adding the individual demand curves horizontally. This means that at any price (say OP), the distance PH from the vertical axis of the market graph to the market demand curve

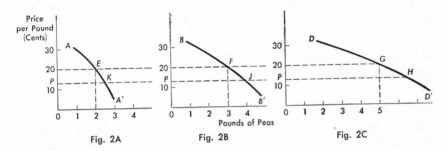

Fig. 2A   Fig. 2B   Fig. 2C

will be the sum of the vertical distance PJ, from the second consumer's vertical axis to his demand curve, plus the distance PK, from the first consumer's vertical axis to his demand curve.

B. EXCEPTIONS

This method of going from the individual to the aggregate demand curves will work so long as the demands of A and B are independent. But if A watches B eagerly to see how many he plans to buy before making his own purchases, and vice versa, things will not be so simple. We cannot even draw A's demand curve unless B's purchases are fixed, because the curve will shift with the level of B's purchases.

There is no simple technique for dealing with this sort of case, which will occur, for example, in trying to "keep up with the Joneses." For us this does not matter particularly. More important is the observation that something which is true of each of a number of things taken in isolation is not necessarily true of them taken together. When the price falls 10 cents, in the absence of any move on B's part A might buy an additional pound, and B under similar restrictions might buy an additional 2 pounds. Yet it may turn out that the fall in price induces them to buy 5 more pounds between them.

4. The Price Elasticity of Demand

It is convenient to have a measure of the responsiveness of the quantity of a commodity demanded to a change in its price. This measure, which applies equally to the demand of a single consumer and of all consumers together, is called the *price elasticity of demand*.

A. THE NATURE OF THE MEASURE

The obvious approach to measuring responsiveness of demand to price is to have price go up one unit, say $1, and compare this with the resulting decrease in the quantity demanded. It has been argued that this is most inconvenient in economics. The increase in the quantity of the commodity demanded is not easily comparable from item to item. How do you compare an increase in car purchases with an increase in pea consumption? Do we compare pounds of peas with pounds of cars or do we compare the number of cars with the number of peas? The trouble is that commodity quantities are not commensurable.

Even the price changes cannot readily be compared meaningfully. A $1 rise in the price of a pound of peas is a different beast from a $1 rise in the price of a car. The one is tremendous, the other negligible. As a result the "obvious" measure we are discussing is often not helpful. From the statement that a $1 price rise practically eliminates purchases of peas but has little effect on car sales we would not wish to conclude that pea demand is highly responsive to price changes, whereas car demand is not. The information about the two commodities is not comparable in the form in which it is given.

To avoid these difficulties economists prefer to deal in percentage changes. This method scales price changes down to size. A 1 percent change in pea and auto prices is more meaningfully comparable than a rise of $1 in both prices. It also makes it possible to compare changes in quantities of different commodities. A 50 percent rise in pea sales means the same thing whether we measure it in terms of peas, pounds of peas, or bushels. And a 100 percent rise in pea sales can be compared with a 50 percent rise in car purchases more plausibly than can the sale of 2 more pounds of peas with 1 more car. We therefore compute the price elasticity of demand as *the percentage increase in the quantity demanded when the price goes down by 1 percent*. A second way of expressing the price elasticity of demand for commodity A is:[6]

$$\frac{\% \text{ rise in sales of } A}{\% \text{ fall in price}}$$

For students acquainted with the elements of calculus we give the more unequivocal elasticity formula:

$$\frac{-\dfrac{dq}{q}}{\dfrac{dp}{p}}$$

where q is the quantity of the commodity sold and p is its price.

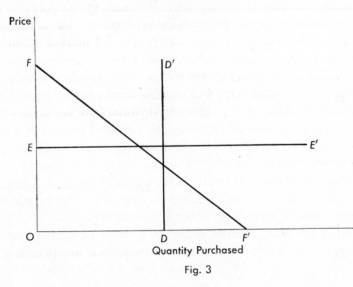

Fig. 3

B. ELASTICITY AND THE SHAPE OF THE DEMAND CURVE

We begin with the most extreme cases. Curve DD' in Fig. 3 shows that the fixed amount OD will be bought no matter what the price. Such a demand curve is said to be perfectly inelastic, or of elasticity zero (the quantity sold goes up zero percent when the price falls 1 percent). Within our ability to pay for it, our demand curve for a medi-

[6] The two ways of expressing this are roughly equivalent. For if price goes down by an amount other than 1 percent, say 5 percent, and the quantity demanded goes up 25 percent, we may say approximately that a 1 percent fall in price results in a 5 percent price rise, and 5 is clearly also the elasticity figure which is given by the formula.

cine required to save the life of someone in the family may look like this. We are prepared to pay almost anything for the quantity prescribed by the doctor, but any additional amount isn't worth a penny more to us.

In the same figure, demand curve EE' is said to be perfectly or infinitely elastic. At the slightest rise in price above OE, the consumer will have none of it. This is the most extreme sort of responsiveness to price. An example, though far-fetched, might be a buyers' strike when the price of a good goes above a level that the consumers consider "just." We shall consider a more important example later.

The question may then arise, how elastic is a straight-line curve like FF'? It happens that because of the use of percentages in the elasticity measure, the elasticity of FF' keeps changing all along the curve and runs all the way from zero near point F' to infinity at point F. How this queer result arises can be made clear as follows. When price is so high (OF) that the quantity demanded is zero, a 1 percent fall in price will increase sales by some amount, say 3 pounds of peas. But percentage-wise the rise in sales from nothing to 3 pounds is *infinite*. Another equal decrease in price will increase sales another 3 pounds, or 100 percent this time, so that elasticity is then down to about 100. A third equal fall in price still increases sales about 3 pounds, but this is now only a 50 percent increase above the 6 pounds consumers were buying before the last price fall. Thus the elasticity of curve FF' falls from infinity to about 100 to about 50, etc., with successive price decreases. This is because equal additions to ever-increasing purchases mean successively smaller percentage increases.[7]

We shall presently see the shape of a curve of unchanging unit elasticity, that is, a curve whose elasticity equals 1 everywhere in the graph.

C. ELASTICITY AND TOTAL EXPENDITURE

We come now to a very important feature of the elasticity concept. If a demand curve is unit elastic and the price of the commodity rises or falls, *the amount of money consumers spend on this commodity will not change*. Suppose the price of the item rises. The price rise will tend to increase the money consumers lay out on its purchase, but at the same time the quantity purchased will drop and this will work in the

[7] This result is strengthened by a similar phenomenon on the price side. Successive equal falls in prices mean ever-greater percentage decreases. Thus as we move toward point F', it will take ever-smaller price falls to constitute the 1 percent fall used in the elasticity measure.

opposite direction. It is plausible that the two will balance out when the price goes up by exactly the same percentage that the quantity falls. But this is what we mean by unit elastic demand—a 1 percent fall in price leads to an offsetting 1 percent rise in consumers' purchases.

When elasticity of demand is less than 1 (we call such a demand curve *inelastic*), a fall in price will reduce total consumers' expenditures and a rise in price will increase them. For while a 1 percent fall in prices reduces consumers' expenditure, the less than 1 percent rise in purchases that accompanies it will not completely offset the fall in price.

When elasticity of demand is greater than unity (the demand is *elastic*), a fall in price increases expenditures and a rise in price reduces them. The decrease in expenditures resulting from a 1 percent fall in price is more than offset by the resulting greater percentage rise in sales.[8]

Most of the applications of the elasticity measure make use of this feature of the concept.

D. A CURVE OF UNIT ELASTICITY OF DEMAND

In Fig. 4, DD' is a curve of unit elasticity of demand. A curve of this shape is called a rectangular hyperbola. If we pick any two points on the curve, say R_1 and R_2, they have the following relationships. The area of rectangle $OQ_1R_1P_1$ will be the same as that of rectangle $OQ_2R_2P_2$. This is because the first area is OQ_1, the initial quantity purchased, times OP_1, the initial price. That is, it represents the initial total expenditure. Similarly, the area of the second rectangle represents

---

[8] Rigorous proof of these propositions requires the calculus definition of elasticity or a somewhat more careful statement of the noncalculus definition. If the price rises from $5 to $10, our definition does not tell us whether to call this a 100 percent rise (a rise of $5 from the original price of $5) or a 50 percent rise (a rise of $5 is 50 percent of the final price of $10). It is customary to split the difference between the initial and final prices and call $5 a 66⅔ percent rise in terms of the average price of $7.50. With a similar convention for the percentage rise in the quantity demanded, the proof becomes a matter of simple algebra. The definition of elasticity becomes:

$$\text{The percentage rise in quantity} = \frac{q_f - q_i}{\tfrac{1}{2}(q_f + q_i)}$$

$$\text{The percentage fall is price} = \frac{P_i - P_f}{\tfrac{1}{2}(P_f + P_i)}$$

where P_i, P_f, q_i, and q_f are respectively the initial price, final price, initial quantity bought, and the final quantity bought, and $\tfrac{1}{2}(P_f + P_i)$ is therefore the average price, etc. If we set this formula equal to 1 (unit elasticity), a little manipulation yields $P_i q_i = P_f q_f$, so that final price times quantity (expenditure) is unchanged from its initial level.

final total expenditures. Thus, since total expenditures do not change along a curve of unit elasticity, these two areas must be equal.

This shows that the curve can never touch the axes anywhere, for at such a point either price or quantity, and hence total expenditure, will be zero; and this is contrary to the requirement that expenditure does not change anywhere along the curve.

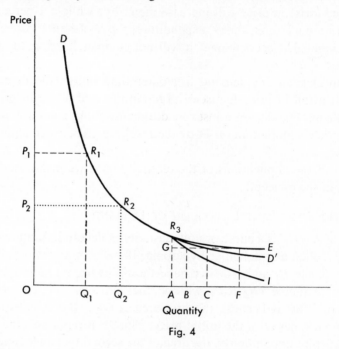

Fig. 4

R_3E is a segment of an elastic curve. Price fall R_3G increases sales by quantity AF, whereas with the unit elastic curve it increases sales only by AC. Thus R_3E shows more responsiveness of sales to price and must be elastic. For the same reason R_3I is a segment of an inelastic demand curve.

E. APPLICATION TO A NATION'S BALANCE OF PAYMENTS

In discussing balance of payments problems in the text we saw that a nation with a payments deficit might help alleviate it by lowering the prices of its exports or by devaluing its currency.[9] We noted, however, that these measures would not always help. For convenience, call the devaluing country Britain, and let the United States be the only importer of British goods. We can now see wherein lies the rub.

[9] See chapter 27, especially pp. 546–548.

If Americans' demand for British exports is elastic, it is true that a fall in British prices can increase Americans' total expenditures on imports from the United Kingdom. In other words, it will increase Britain's dollar receipts and help her balance of payments problem.

But if the United States' demand for British exports is inelastic, a fall in British prices will decrease her dollar receipts, and this part of the consequences will aggravate her balance of payments problems further. It follows that a nation in balance of payments difficulties should not rush headlong into devaluation. It may help, but sometimes it will make things worse. There is of course more to the analysis of this problem than is indicated in these two paragraphs. Some of the complications have been discussed in the text. Our object at this point is more to illustrate the elasticity concept than to analyze balance of payments problems fully. We therefore content ourselves with this warning.

F. OTHER ELASTICITY MEASURES

Elasticity is essentially a measure of the responsiveness of one variable to changes in another variable. The same measure can be used for relationships other than that between price and demand. For example, the responsiveness of quantity demanded to a change in consumers' income is measured by the *income elasticity of demand*. This is defined as the percentage rise in demand that results from a 1 percent rise in consumers' incomes. Note that this will be negative for inferior goods because a rise in consumers' incomes will decrease purchases of these items.

We may similarly use the concept of *price elasticity of supply* as a measure of the responsiveness to price changes of the quantity of a commodity that sellers are willing to offer for sale on the market. Several other such elasticity measures have also been used by economists. We mention only one other, the *cross elasticity of demand* between Ford automobiles and Chevrolet prices, which measures the responsiveness of Ford sales to changes in the prices of its competitor's product.

G. SUMMARY

We have said as much as we are going to on the role of the consumer and consumers' demands. We have discussed the relation of the demand curve to consumers' desires and preferences and shown how it is related to the consumer's evaluation of the marginal rather than the total benefits he derives from the commodity. We also examined the reasons for the usually negative slope of the demand curve and showed how we could aggregate the demand curves of the individual buyers in the market into a demand curve for the market as a whole. Finally, we examined the concept of price elasticity of demand. Designed to measure responsiveness of the quantity demanded to price changes, it also indicates the responsiveness to price changes of total consumers' expenditures (sellers' money receipts) for a commodity. The latter feature is perhaps the more important, and we showed how it can be applied to an examination of the efficacy of price cuts and devaluation as a method of eliminating a balance of payments deficit.

We turn now to the other side of competitive market price determination, a discussion of supply.

5. Supply and Cost

Like demand, supply varies with economic circumstances. We may therefore expect that it too must be represented as a schedule or curve. Sometimes the situation is too complicated for this approach. However, under the circumstances we have described as "pure competition" we can describe supply by means of a curve.

A. PURE COMPETITION DEFINED

For clarification of this point we must return once again to the meaning of the "pure competition" concept. As we indicated earlier, an industry under conditions of pure competition is usually assumed to have the following characteristics:[10]

N.B.　　1. A large number of small firms.
2. All firms producing identical products.
3. No collusion among firms.
4. Mobility and free entry of resources into or out of the industry. If the industry proves profitable, new firms can open up at will and without legal or monopolistic opposition. Firms can also cease operations and reinvest their capital in other lines if the industry becomes unprofitable.

Together these four characteristics are designed to assure us of the absence of monopolistic elements in the industry. The fourth characteristic prevents the exclusion of competitors and potential competitors. The other three together deprive the firm of power to rig and manipulate prices. They provide that the output of the firm shall have

[10] Above, pp. 417–418. The present statement is more detailed and explicit.

no identifying characteristics and be no more than a negligible proportion of the industry's total output. Hence a firm's threat to withhold some of its product in the hope of forcing prices up by making the item scarce would be totally ludicrous in these circumstances. It would remove one not particularly noteworthy grain of sand from the beach. The firm therefore cannot influence the market price of its product without the cooperation of other firms in the industry. Such cooperation is precluded by the third characteristic of pure competition—no collusion.

These two major consequences flow from the definition of pure competition:

✳1. The seller has no control over the price of his product. He cannot rig or manipulate it, and therefore takes it as a datum given him by the market to which he must adjust his plans and decisions.

✳2. Whenever profits in an industry go up very high, new firms can set up business in that line and compete with those already there.

We shall make considerable use of both these characteristics in the rest of this appendix.

B. PURE COMPETITION, COST, AND SUPPLY

We can see now why it may not be possible to construct a supply curve in the absence of pure competition. The supply curve asks how much the seller of a product is willing to supply at each possible price. When the price is subject to rigging by the seller, this question is not really meaningful. He does not accept a price and adjust to it—he picks the price. The monopolistic seller will adjust to the demand curve for his product rather than its price. Given the demand curve, he will probably pick a price which he believes will milk the greatest possible profits out of buyers.

Under conditions of pure competition, however, we can draw up supply schedules. This follows from the first consequence of pure competition listed above. We can also see something of the relations between the cost of producing the commodity and the supply curves. The second consequence of pure competition suggests that high profits may be expected to attract new competing firms into the industry. This will tend to increase the quantity of the commodity supplied, and hence to lower prices, and very likely it will raise costs as well by bidding up wages and the prices of the other factors of production. Thus profits cannot long remain very high in a competitive industry. Similarly, losses will not last very long, for firms will then pull up stakes and leave the industry, permitting a rise in prices and possibly a fall in costs.

This means that under pure competition prices will tend to approximate per unit (or average) cost of production, for otherwise either a substantial profit or a substantial loss must be realized on each unit of the product sold. Here, then, is the connection between supply and price. Whatever the price of the commodity, the amount supplied will tend to be such that the cost per unit approximates price. In order to be more specific several distinctions must be made.

C. THE INDUSTRY AND THE FIRM

As in the case of demand, there are individual and aggregate supply curves. The individual firm is the smallest unit of supply, whereas the aggregates of firms are classed as industries. We can derive aggregate industry supply curves from the individual firm's supply schedule by adding the latter horizontally as we did in the case of demand.[11] We need not repeat the details.

Now our rule about price tending to equal average costs applies in a sense to both the firm and to the industry. But the way in which it applies to the individual firm merits a little explanation.

In any industry some firms are likely to be more efficient than others. When the price of a commodity is equal to the unit cost of an inefficient firm, it would seem that it must be greater than the unit cost of the more efficient enterprises. But the difference in efficiency will arise out of something specific, such as superior location, better management, etc. However, the landlord who owns a better location will generally charge more rent for it, and the better manager will tend to earn a higher salary. If each charges what the traffic will bear, he will be able to command most of the savings that the use of his superior productive factor permits. Thus the savings which superior resources permit the more efficient firm will tend to enter the remuneration of those resources. When we take this into account, we see that money costs of production, including payment for the quality of superior resources, will tend to be the same for both efficient and inefficient firms. Hence

---

[11] See above, pp. 608–610. Again there are important exceptions when the scale of operations of one firm affects the costs and hence the scale of operations of others. (For examples, see above, pp. 408–409.) Here the simple addition of curves would again be illegitimate, for though a rise in price might induce firm A by itself to expand 2 units, and firm B by itself to expand 6 units, the two together might in fact expand only 4 units, each reacting to the expansion of the other.

if the price is close to the per unit or average money cost of one firm, it will tend to approximate the average cost of every firm in the industry.

We conclude that the quantity which the *firm* offers to supply at any price will tend to be such that the price is approximately equal to the money cost of production. But clearly if it applies to every firm, it must also apply to the industry as a whole. Hence the rule holds for both firm and industry.

Before we conclude this discussion of the relation of the firm and the industry, we should note that once we leave the area of pure competition we may run into trouble if we try to deal with industries. In the absence of pure competition each firm can produce more or less different products in which the difference may be real or fancied. When this happens, we are never sure where the industry begins and ends. From the point of view of the consumer a deodorant or a perfume may be a closer substitute for toilet soap than the powerful soaps used by commercial laundries. What, then, are the borders of the toilet soap industry?[12]

D. THE LONG RUN VERSUS THE SHORT RUN

Even if an industry is making very high profits, some time will be required before new competitive firms can open up, swing into full production, and cut the abnormal profits down to size. To deal with this lag the economist makes a distinction between the long and short run which is purposely left somewhat vague.

The long run is defined as the period of time in which most or all of the adjustments anyone desires to make to a changed situation can be completed. The time it will take new firms to set up business fully in a profitable line, the time it will take a firm to retool and reequip in response to technological changes and get back in full operation—these are examples of the long run.

The short run can be defined only residually as a time not sufficiently great for adjustments to be made to a changed situation. Consequently the distinction between the short and long run is bound to be vague. Some changes take longer than others. Partial adjustment will always create a classification dilemma. Yet for our purposes the distinction between the short and long run is sufficiently sharp.

Observe that in the short run the price of a commodity need have

[12] For further discussion, see above, pp. 419–422.

no relation to its cost of production. Both high profits and losses will be eliminated only after firms have had a chance to move into or out of the industry. In the short run either profits or losses can occur.

This we know happens in practice. The first firm to invade a new market often makes large profits for a while. A bumper crop may force farmers to accept losses at least for one year.

Short-run supply, therefore, has little relation to cost. We may go further and remark that short-run supply curves will tend to be rather inelastic (the quantity supplied is unresponsive to price changes). This is because it takes time for production to adjust substantially to

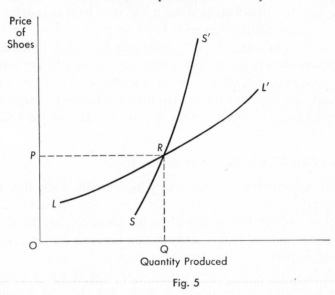

Fig. 5

price changes. In the short run an increase in demand can often be met only out of warehouse inventories because production changes cannot be made quickly enough. For a highly perishable commodity which cannot be stored in significant quantities even this much response to price changes may be impossible.

E. THE LONG-RUN SUPPLY CURVE AS AN AVERAGE COST CURVE

In the long run, however, we have seen that price tends to equal per unit cost since there will be neither substantial profits nor substantial losses.

We have defined the supply curve as the curve showing the quantities of a commodity that will be supplied at every possible price. We may define an average cost curve as one which shows per unit costs of production of that item at every possible level of output. It is now easy to show that in the long run these curves will approximately coincide. In Fig. 5 let *LL'* be the shoe industry's long-run supply. It shows, for example, that at price *OP* the industry will produce *OQ* pairs of shoes. To show that this is also (approximately) the average cost curve, let us see what would be the unit cost of producing, say, output *OQ*. Since price will tend to equal per unit cost, the answer is that per unit cost will be approximately *OP*. Thus, the long-run supply curve will tend to be a curve of average costs.

In the same figure we have drawn in a short-run supply curve (*SS'*) through point *R*. This shows how output will respond at first to a sudden shift in price from *OP*. This curve is much less elastic than the long-run curve *LL'*. The reader should be able to verify that along supply curve *SS'* a given change in price from *OP* will result in a smaller change in supply than it will along supply curve *LL'*.

F. DECREASING AND INCREASING COST: THE FIRM

It is well known that an increase in the scale of operation of a firm can sometimes reduce its unit costs. Probably the illustration most often cited is the great economy that was introduced in the production of automobiles when Ford began producing on a large scale. It should be clear, for example, that with a plant turning out 2 autos a week, there is no room for the installation of a belt system that automatically transports the unfinished vehicle from specialized worker to specialized worker. In a mass-production industry economies can be achieved in a variety of ways—no loss of time as there would be when the unspecialized worker moves from operation to operation, more skill on the part of the worker in his oft-repeated and highly limited task, and less cost in training him.

While economy of large-scale production is a familiar, well-publicized phenomenon, the possibility that costs may increase with a firm's scale of operation is less generally recognized. One source of rising costs may be found in the manager or owner losing contact with his workers and with the details of the firm's operations generally as it expands in size. He must increasingly delegate authority, with loss of the personal touch and with all the disadvantages of bureaucracy that generally result. Physical problems also arise. For example, the operations of the firm may come to be spread over too wide an area, making transportation a serious and costly problem.

It is surmised that most firms will have a technically optimal size with higher average costs if production is carried out on too small or too large a scale. In this case the firm's long-run supply curve will be characteristically U-shaped as in Fig. 6. Here output OQ yields minimum average costs. From zero up to that point, cost will decrease as output rises and beyond that point costs will increase as output rises.

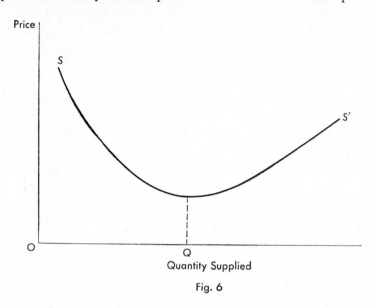

Fig. 6

G. INCREASING AND DECREASING COSTS: THE INDUSTRY

In an industry, too, costs may rise or fall as the size of output increases. Many of the reasons why costs may decrease for the firm hold true also for the industry. A tiny automotive, aviation, shipbuilding, or chemical industry does not permit firms to be big enough to reap the advantages of economical mass-production techniques.

A rise in its scale of operations can also sometimes effect economies through the reaction of agencies external to the industry. An increase in production in a district may lead to an improvement of road and rail facilities in the district, thereby lowering the producer's costs. All sorts of services that it does not pay to provide for a few small firms may be available to a Gargantuan industry.

There are also special reasons why costs to an industry may rise with increased production. The available supplies of specially suited factors of production may grow scarcer with the industry's scale of output. Skilled mechanics and engineers may be fully employed. Factories may be operating to capacity. Inefficient laborers may have to be hired. These are partly short-run difficulties. More engineers can be trained and more factories built in due time. But the stock of raw materials and specially suitable land may not be augmentable. When the industry must use lower-grade ores or costlier mines for its metal supply its costs may go up and stay up.

Under pure competition there is some reason to argue that increasing costs will be rather frequent. For in those industries in which economies of large scale are attainable by individual firms, these will

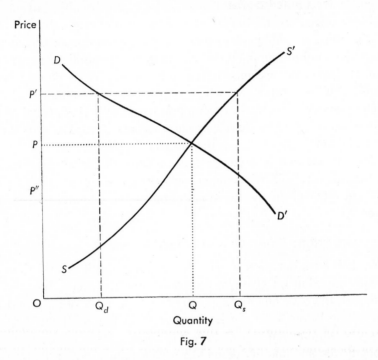

Fig. 7

tend to grow large. Steel, automobiles, electric power, telephone service, and railroad transportation are all supplied by large firms partly for that reason. But we saw that pure competition requires many small firms, each of which controls only a small proportion of the industry's production. This alone assures us that none of the industries just listed can be classed under pure competition. Thus under pure competition the industry's long-run supply curve is likely to slope upward to the right (positive slope) because its average costs rise with the scale of its operations. An example is provided by LL' in Fig. 5.

6. Industry Supply, Demand and Price

Let us now focus our attention exclusively on a competitive industry. We have derived the demand and supply curves for its product and these can now be drawn on the same diagram (Fig. 7). Here *DD'* is the demand curve and *SS'* the supply curve.

A. THE DETERMINATION OF COMPETITIVE PRICE

If the price of the product happens to be at level *OP'*, the quantity demanded, OQ_d, will fall short of the quantity supplied, OQ_s. We may then expect that prices will fall because sellers cut their prices in competing for the limited demand, and perhaps also because buyers, besieged by offers, are no longer willing to pay the original price. The reduced price should serve to increase the quantities demanded and reduce the amounts supplied. When the quantity supplied exceeds the quantity demanded, we may expect price to be driven down toward *OP*, the equilibrium price at which supply equals demand.

In the same way we may expect a price like *OP''*, which is below the equilibrium price, to be driven upward because it produces an excess of the amount demanded over the amount supplied.

We conclude that in a competitive industry the price of a product and the quantity sold will tend toward the price-output combination (*OP* and *OQ*) given by the intersection of the demand and supply curves.[13]

B. ILLUSTRATION: PRICE CEILINGS AND SUPPORTS

We shall have occasion to use the foregoing result several times in this appendix, but we give two illustrative applications at once.

Suppose the government desires to prevent the price of a commodity from falling below a certain level, say *OP'* in Fig. 7. If this price is above the equilibrium price, there will be an excess of the quantity supplied over the quantity demanded (OQ_s minus OQ_d). To prevent this from happening, the government must step in and buy up this excess. This explains why farm-support programs have resulted in agricultural commodities piling up in warehouses.

Suppose on the other hand that the government wishes to prevent the price of the commodity from rising above a certain level, say *OP''*. If it simply enacts a law making higher prices illegal, the quantity demanded will exceed the quantity supplied. Shops will run out of goods.

[13] The reader will note that our analysis of price determination is analogous to the procedure we used in discussing the determination of national income (chapters 10–12). There we said that income and interest rates would tend to equate the quantities supplied and demanded for both goods and money, and we used this to locate the level of national income and the interest rate. Here we locate the price and quantity of a commodity sold from the observation that the price will tend to equate the amounts demanded and supplied of that item.

Queuing up and shortages will result. Rationing may be the only alternative to chaos or to flagrant inequities in the distribution of goods, such as shops running out of things before working women can make their purchases. This suggests why rationing is so persistent a companion of price controls. The price controls, rightly or wrongly, have prevented the market mechanism from rectifying shortages by cutting the quantities demanded down to size and inducing bigger supplies. Something else must then replace the market in distributing the goods, and rationing often gets the job.

c. Illustration: Tax Shifting

In discussing who pays which taxes, we remarked that a man from whom the government collects the tax may bear only part of the burden, that he may be able to shift the burden on to others.[14] Our supply-

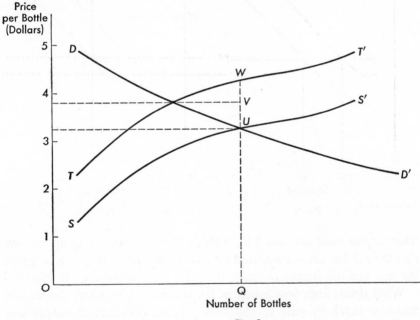

Fig. 8

demand-price result will indicate more distinctly how this can occur. In Fig. 8 let SS' and DD' be the supply and demand curves for bottles of toilet water which would prevail in the absence of taxes. Suppose that the government then imposes a $1 tax on the seller for every bottle he sells. The long-run effect must be to raise the supply curve by

[14] See above, pp. 326–327.

$1 all along the line; that is, it will make a parallel shift upward from SS' to TT'. The reason is that the seller's cost of getting a bottle to the consumer will have gone up by $1; the average cost curve will have shifted from SS' to TT', and we know that the supply curve must soon follow.

The price of toilet water will then rise from QU to QV (in our diagram from about $3.25 to $3.80 a bottle). This means that though the tax is paid by the seller, the consumer is bearing a substantial part of the burden through the price rise. In general, the burden will be divided between buyer and seller. Here the price rose only 55 cents,

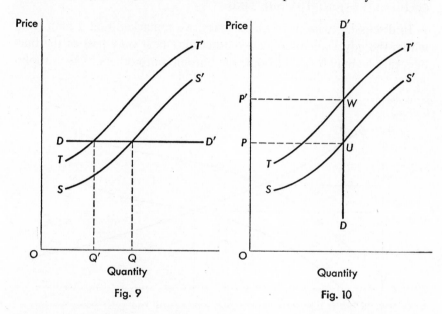

Fig. 9   Fig. 10

whereas the total tax was $1 a bottle. In more general terms we see that though the tax is measured by UW (the vertical distance between the new and old supply curves), the price will have risen only by UV.

What determines how much of the tax will be borne by consumers and how much by sellers? The answer is the elasticity of supply and demand. We illustrate this by showing what will happen in two extreme cases: zero and infinite demand elasticity. In Fig. 9 the horizontal demand curve DD' is perfectly elastic. We see there that the shift in the supply curve reduces sales substantially from OQ down to OQ'. Price, however, does not rise with the tax and the burden must then be borne by the seller.

On the other hand, the vertical demand curve DD' in Fig. 10 is of zero elasticity. Here the imposition of the tax brings no change in sales; but the price rises from OP to OP', by the full amount of the tax, UW. In this case the tax is borne by the buyer.

These results are quite in accord with common sense. A perfectly inelastic demand means that consumers are determined to buy a certain quantity and are prepared to pay any price to get it. To keep sellers from reducing their production to this level, consumers must be prepared to prevent any reduction in returns to the seller, and so consumers must absorb the tax costs in their entirety. On the other hand, an infinitely elastic demand means that consumers will buy absolutely nothing if the price rises (in effect a buyers' strike); hence unless sellers go out of business they must bear the tax.

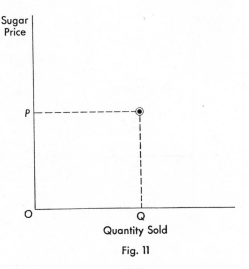

Fig. 11

The reader should be able to obtain similar results for zero and infinitely elastic supply curves, showing that the tax is borne by the seller in the first case and by the buyer in the latter case.

This discussion does not pretend to cover all aspects of the tax-shifting problem. This is a difficult, complicated, and subtle subject. The discussion does show, however, that in tax payment all may not be what it seems—he who "pays" the tax may not be the one who suffers from it.

D. EMPIRICAL DETERMINATION OF SUPPLY AND DEMAND CURVES

Before leaving the determination of price by supply and demand, let us see how much can be done about determining statistically what the shape and location of such schedules really are. This task is not easy and it is beset by pitfalls.

Suppose the demand and supply curves for sugar never changed. We would then have absolutely no way of determining their shape statistically, for both the price of sugar and the quantity sold would presumably never change. All our information could be summed up in the one dot in Fig. 11, which tells us that quantity OQ is being sold

year after year at price *OP*. This is obviously not enough information
on which to base a supply and demand diagram.

It is helpful from this point of view that supply and demand curves
do shift, and that prices and quantities sold do change. Suppose that
we have a statistical series represented by the dots in Fig. 12. The date
next to each dot indicates the year in which this particular price-quantity combination was observed. If we are looking for a demand curve
for sugar, it is tempting to draw a line like *DD'*, which roughly indicates the pattern formed by the points. But it is easy to see how wrong

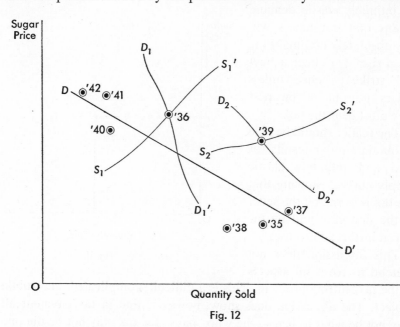

Fig. 12

we can be in making such a guess. The 1936 prices and sales could
easily have been produced by any supply and demand curves like S_1S_1'
and D_1D_1' through point '36, and the 1939 figures could be the results
of these curves shifting, say, to S_2S_2' and D_2D_2'. In a similar way any
other of our statistical dots might have been on a demand curve not
remotely related to *DD'*. The statistics have as yet refused to yield up
their secrets.

E. THE "IDENTIFICATION" APPROACH

This problem of identifying our curves from the statistics plagues us
not only in supply-demand analysis. It applies to almost all economic
analysis. It applies, for example, to the statistical determination of the

schedules used in our analysis of the determination of national income.[15] In recent years an ingenious approach to this problem has been developed under the leadership of the Cowles Commission at the University of Chicago. While it has by no means eliminated all the difficulties, it does show that the problem may be soluble.

Returning to our search for the demand curve for sugar, suppose that we have somehow obtained the following information: In 1927, 1936, and 1940 the demand curve was the same, though for each of these years the supply curve was different. In Fig. 13 dots are drawn in showing the price-quantity combinations for these three years. This tells us absolutely nothing about the shape of the supply curve in those years, but we do know that the demand curve must have looked something like *DD'*, for these dots must be on or near it.

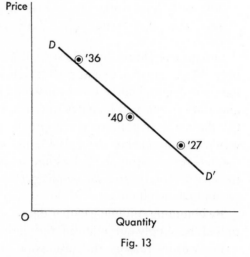

Fig. 13

We can thus *identify* the demand curve if some informer will group together the years in which the demand curve was the same. If we could somehow find out that the same demand schedule prevailed for sugar in 1928, 1929, 1941, and 1942, whereas another such schedule prevailed for 1927, 1936, and 1940, our problem would be well on the way to solution. Similar information for the supply curve would clearly be equally helpful in locating that schedule.

F. WHAT SHIFTS THE SCHEDULES?

Some information of this sort can in fact be provided. To obtain it we must ask what makes supply and demand schedules shift.

Obviously a change in consumers' income can affect demand, and changes in the weather can affect supplies, especially of agricultural commodities. There are many other things that can cause demand and supply schedules to shift, and presently we shall list some of them. But to avoid complicating our exposition, let us assume that the weather is

[15] See above, chapters 10–12.

the *only* thing that affects the supply schedule, and that the demand curve will shift only in response to national income changes.

Let us then examine the national income figures for the period for which we are seeking to construct supply and demand curves. Taking as an example the period from 1940 to 1951, we have the figures given in Table 1.

TABLE 1. Real National Income, 1940–1951[16]
(1940 = 100)

1940	1941	1942	1943	1944	1945	1946	1947	1948	1949	1950
100	116	130	146	157	153	138	139	144	144	154

On our oversimple hypothesis that national income changes are the only things causing demand shifts, this suggests that approximately the same demand curve for sugar would have prevailed in 1943, 1948, and 1949, when real incomes were respectively at 146, 144, and 144. On the same hypothesis an approximately common demand curve would have applied to 1944, 1945, and 1950. Therefore by connecting the dots representing the prices and quantities of sugar sold in each of these last three years, we would get some idea of the shape of that common demand curve.

By obtaining suitable weather data a similar approach could be used to find the supply curve at different times.

For various reasons this discussion greatly oversimplifies the problem of the statistical determination of supply and demand curves. There are hosts of other difficulties. Data are inaccurate. There is no unique 1951 price, because the price will vary from day to day and from seller to seller. The price may sometimes be temporarily out of equilibrium and hence the dot representing the supply-demand combination may not lie on the demand or supply curve. A very large number of variables can cause shifts in demand and supply curves. The following list gives but a few examples whose role should be obvious:

Some Variables Which Can Shift Demand Curves	Some Variables Which Can Shift Supply Curves
Size and distribution of national income and wealth.	Rainfall, temperature, and other weather conditions.
Population.	Prices of raw materials and other productive factors.
Prices and availability of other	

[16] Source: U.S. Department of Commerce, *National Income,* 1951.

Some Variables Which Can Shift Demand Curves (*Continued*)	Some Variables Which Can Shift Supply Curves (*Continued*)
products (a change in beef price affects pork demand).	Level of inventories.
(Changes in) consumers' tastes.	New productive techniques.
New products (the appearance of television affects radio demand).	Expectations of future business conditions.
Expectations of future prices and incomes.	

All of these difficulties suggest that we still have a long way to go before we can be at all satisfied with our ability to determine economic relationships statistically. In view of the impracticability of large-scale experimentation on many economic questions, our hopes must be tied to the prospects of advances in our statistical techniques. The analysis we have just completed should suggest the nature of some of the problems, and at least indicate that there is hope for the future.

7. Summary

In this part of the appendix we have discussed the determination of the market price for competitive products. We have seen how this is affected by demands, which are themselves related to the (marginal) desires of consumers, and by supplies, which are (in the long run) determined by costs. Our emphasis has been primarily on the theory of the industry. We shall now examine the operation of the firm more carefully. This is particularly relevant because, as we have seen, there is no well-defined industry to be analyzed in some forms of markets —e.g., monopolistic competition.

PART II

Theory of the Firm

In this part of the appendix we shall examine the determination of the output of the firm under pure competition, monopolistic competition, and monopoly. In order to do so it will be convenient to use total cost, average cost, marginal cost, and other related concepts. It will therefore be necessary to discuss these terms in somewhat greater detail before we embark on the analysis proper.

1. Total, Average, and Marginal Relations

Basically the terms total, average, and marginal have arithmetical rather than economic connotations. As such they can be (and are) applied to a variety of economic variables: cost, revenue, utility, production, etc. We have already encountered several of these uses and we shall encounter most of them again.

To begin with, we shall frame our discussion in terms of total, average, and marginal costs, in order to make it easier for the reader to conjure up specific pictures in his mind. But he should not forget that the use of costs here is purely for illustrative purposes, and that the relationships we are getting at are essentially arithmetical.

A. DEFINITIONS

We are primarily interested in keeping track of what happens to costs (or whatever other variable we are considering) as changes occur in the size of output or, more generally, in the number of relevant units produced, consumed, or sold, etc.

For our purposes the meaning of "the total cost of producing 5000 units of output" should be sufficiently clear. It means the total amount of money the firm must lay out on factors of production in order to get that much of the commodity manufactured.

The average or per unit cost of that output is defined equally in accord with common usage. It is the total cost of producing that number of units divided by the number of units produced. It is the total cost averaged over the items manufactured.

The marginal cost of producing, say, a 5000th unit of output is the only one of our three concepts that does not occur in common parlance. Yet it too is not difficult to understand. It is defined as the amount by which total cost rises when output increases from 4999 to 5000 units (or the amount by which total cost falls when output declines from 5000 to 4999 units).

B. NUMERICAL ILLUSTRATION

These relationships are perhaps best brought out by a numerical example. In Table 2 we compute hypothetical total, average, and marginal costs of producing cucumbers on a small farm for sale in a local market. The student may note that we assume the absence of

TABLE 2.   Total, Average, and Marginal Cost, and Marginal Revenue of
Producing Cucumbers

Production (Bushels per day)	Total Cost (Cents)	Average Cost (Cents)	Marginal Cost (Cents)	Marginal Revenue (Cents)
0	0	. . .	0	0
1	100	100	100	150
2	180	90	80	140
3	240	80	60	120
4	320	80	80	100
5	425	85	105	90
6	540	90	115	65
7	490	70	−50	. . .

overhead costs, so that by cutting production to zero, total costs fall to nothing.[1]

It is easy to see what we have done here. For example, for an out-

[1] An overhead cost is defined as a cost which, within limits, does not vary with the scale of output. For example, the cost of renting a theater may be the same whether no one, 50, or 200 people turn up to see the performance. It costs the same to move a bus, whether it has 10 or 20 passengers. A machine may cost the same whether it stands idle or runs 2 or 7 hours a day. In each case, after the commitment is made, it is to be noted that cutting production to zero will not avoid these overhead costs.

put of 5 bushels per day we have taken the imaginary total cost figure $4.25. Average cost is therefore $4.25 divided by 5 (bushels), or $0.85. Marginal cost is $1.05 because increasing the output from 4 to 5 bushels raises the total cost from $3.20 to $4.25, i.e. by $1.05.

Note that the marginal cost of the seventh unit is negative because total costs decrease when production goes up from 6 to 7 bushels. This obviously weird figure is thrown in to emphasize our interest in the arithmetical relationships, and to show the manner in which these relationships continue to hold in a circumstance that may be found in economic data relating to items other than costs. For example, an increase in sales can actually decrease total revenue (if demand is inelastic).

C. RELATIONSHIPS AMONG THE CONCEPTS

There are several ways in which these concepts are related aside from the ways that are stated explicitly in the definitions (e.g., average equals total divided by the number of units). We list several that will be used in the discussion that follows.

1. In the absence of overhead, average, total, and marginal costs for the first unit are equal. The reason is obvious. The average value of $5 is $5—if the total cost of one unit is $5, so is its average cost. In the absence of overhead, a reduction of output from one unit to zero cuts costs to zero, and hence the saving in total cost (the marginal cost) will be the (total) cost of producing one unit, also $5 in this illustration. In the table we see accordingly that the total, average, and marginal costs of the first unit are each equal to $1.

2. A second relationship between total and marginal costs is that total cost is equal to the sum of the preceding marginal costs. For example, the total cost of the first four bushels ($3.20) is the sum of the marginal costs of the first ($1.00) plus the second ($0.80), plus the third ($0.60), plus the fourth ($0.80). The reader can easily verify that this holds for the total cost of any other output.

This result is a direct consequence of the definition of marginal cost. Since marginal cost represents the step-by-step increases in total cost from zero to x units, the total cost of the xth unit must be the sum of these increases.

3. Our third relationship is between marginal and average costs. The average cost is the average of the preceding marginal costs. This follows from the preceding relationship—from total cost being the sum of the preceding marginals. Since average cost equals total cost

divided by the number of units, it is equal to the sum of the preceding marginals divided by their number (the number of units). But this is just how we would average them. For example, for 3 units, average cost =

$$80 = \frac{\text{total cost}}{\text{number of units}} = \frac{240}{3} = \frac{100 + 80 + 60}{3} = \text{average of } 100 +$$

$80 + 60 =$ average of the preceding marginals.

4. Our fourth relationship is also between marginal and average cost. If marginal cost is above average costs, average costs will rise. If marginal costs are below average costs, average costs will fall. If marginal costs equal average costs, average costs will neither rise nor fall.

This is again illustrated by the table. When (for the second unit) marginal cost ($0.80) is below average cost ($0.90), average cost has fallen from the previous $1 to $0.90. When (for the fifth unit) marginal cost ($1.05) is above average cost ($0.85), average cost has risen from $0.80 to $0.85. Finally, when (for the fourth bushel) marginal cost equals average cost (both $0.80), the average cost is unchanged from its preceding value.

The reason for this phenomenon is that the average cost is the average of the preceding marginal costs. If the marginal is above the average, this means recomputing the average, this time averaging in a new unit whose cost is above the old average. This must raise that average.

An example will make this clear. Suppose that we are considering the average weight of some large dogs in a kennel, and that we now interpret the table as representing total, average, and marginal weights, rather than costs. If the average weight of the first two dogs is 90 pounds and we add a third 60-pound dog (marginal weight 60 pounds), the average weight will obviously fall to 80 pounds. Similarly, the addition of an above-average dog will raise the average weight of the dogs in the kennel. But the addition of a dog of just average weight will not affect the value of the average.

Thus average costs (or the average of any other variable) will rise, fall, or remain unchanged, depending on whether the marginal lies above it, below it, or at the same level.

D. GRAPHIC INTERPRETATION

We can illustrate the first and last of these relationships by considering the U-shaped average cost curve which we said in Part I of this appendix might perhaps represent the costs of a typical firm. In Fig. 14

this is reproduced as curve CA. What will the corresponding marginal cost curve look like?

The first relationship just considered indicates that the curves must start together, for in the beginning marginal and average costs are the same. From then until output OQ, the point of minimum average costs, average costs fall with the size of output. The last relationship just considered tells us that this is possible only if for that stretch the marginal curve lies below the average curve. To the right of point OQ average

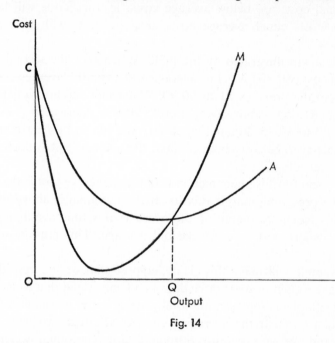

Fig. 14

costs are rising, and hence a curve representing marginal costs must lie above CA there. Finally, since at output OQ average costs are neither rising nor falling, marginal costs must there coincide with average costs.

A curve representing marginal costs must therefore have the general appearance of CM, starting with CA at the vertical axis, lying below it from there to output OQ, coinciding with CA directly above Q, and lying above it farther to the right.

2. Maximizing Profits

Let us now apply these arithmetical relationships to the operation of the firm.

A. THE DEMAND CURVE AN AVERAGE REVENUE CURVE

Suppose the firm is faced with a demand for its product that is represented by *DD'* in Fig.15. From it the firm can deduce how much revenue it can hope to earn by selling different alternative quantities of its product, for the curve tells the price at which consumers will be willing to purchase each quantity.

We shall see now that this demand curve is a curve of average revenue for the firm. We define an average revenue curve as one which

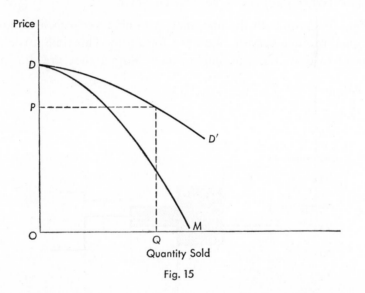

Fig. 15

shows for every possible output how much the firm will receive per unit sold. If the firm takes in $5000 (total revenue), having sold 1000 units of its product, its average revenue will be $5. Note that the term revenue refers to earnings before deduction of costs. The businessman may be expected to be primarily interested in profit rather than revenue. He may therefore prefer to earn a small revenue with very little cost outlay rather than a large revenue with a huge cost outlay, because the former will net him greater profits than the latter does.

To see that *DD'* is a curve of average revenue we need merely note that at any output *OQ* the firm will obtain price *OP* on every unit sold. Thus the owners will take in *OP* dollars per unit if they sell *OQ* units; that is, their average revenue will be *OP*. It's as simple as that.

We conclude (1) that the demand curve for a firm's product is the firm's average revenue curve, and (2) that the price at which a firm can sell some quantity of a good is its average revenue; that is, price (*OP*) equals average revenue.[2]

When the demand curve slopes downward to the right (as in our diagram), the average revenue decreases with the size of output. From the last of our average-marginal relationships this means that the marginal revenue curve must lie somewhere below it, except at their common beginning on the vertical axis. The marginal revenue curve will therefore look something like *DM*.

B. THE TOTAL PROFITS FROM ANY OUTPUT

Fig. 16 shows both the marginal cost curve (broken line) and the marginal revenue curve (solid line) for a firm. This time it is convenient not to draw these as smooth lines. Rather they are drawn with

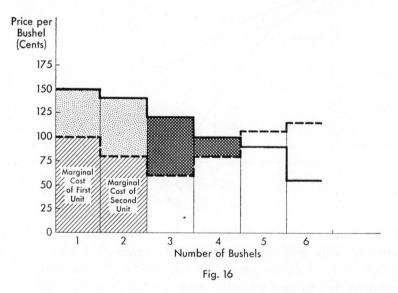

Fig. 16

steps indicating distinctly how costs and revenues change each time another unit is added to output. The marginal cost curve is taken directly from our numerical example (Table 2). The marginal cost of the first unit is 100, of the second 80, etc. The interpretation of the marginal revenue curve is similar; the figures are given in the same table. The smoothness of the curves we have been drawing all along is thus seen to be a simplification for expository convenience.

[2] This is true so long as the firm does not practice price discrimination. If it sells its goods to some consumers at one price and to other consumers at another price, its average revenue will not equal either price. Rather it will be somewhere between them.

What is the total cost of producing, say, 2 units of output? It is the marginal cost of the first, plus the marginal cost of the second (by the second of our total-marginal relationships). In the diagram it is represented by the area with the striped shading. It is the area under the cost curve to the left of the point representing 2 bushels of output, for that area is the sum of the bar representing the marginal cost of the first unit, plus the bar representing the marginal cost of the second unit.

In the same way, the total revenue from the sale of 2 bushels is represented by the area under the marginal revenue curve which lies to the left of the point representing 2 bushels. It is the striped shaded area plus the dotted area.

Since total profit equals total revenue minus total cost, total profit from the sale of 2 bushels is represented by the area between the marginal revenue and the marginal cost curves to the left of the point representing 2 bushels. In the diagram it is represented by the dotted area; it is the area representing total revenue minus the area representing total cost.

c. MAXIMIZING PROFITS

In the case represented by Fig. 16 it does not pay the firm to stop producing at 2 bushels if maximum profits are its aim. Greater profits can be earned by increasing output still further, for the next unit will still add to total revenue more than it adds to total cost. The student can see that by increasing output to 4 units, profits can be increased by the dark area in the diagram.

When does it pay the firm to stop increasing output? When the marginal cost and the marginal revenue curves cross, for beyond that point further expansion will add more to costs than to revenues.

This is again an application of the principle of no wasted opportunities.[3] Here it tells us that a firm can never maximize profits if it produces an output at which marginal cost and marginal revenue fail to coincide. If marginal revenue exceeds marginal cost the firm is wasting an opportunity to increase its earnings, for an additional unit of output will add more to revenue than to costs and hence must increase total profits. Similarly, if marginal costs exceed marginal revenue, the firm is wasting the opportunity to add to profits by *decreasing* output. A unit reduction in output must then reduce total costs more than it reduces total revenue, and hence must add to total profit.

The student may find it useful to use the marginal revenue and

[3] See above, pp. 383–386.

marginal cost columns in Table 2 to compute total profits for the various outputs, verifying that profits are indeed maximized when marginal revenue is as close as possible to marginal cost.

We therefore conclude our preliminary discussion with the basic rule that *the firm can maximize its profits only if it is producing an output at which marginal cost equals marginal revenue* (or they are as close together as they can come).

D. THE ASSUMPTION OF PROFIT MAXIMIZATION

In most of the rest of Part II we shall be concerned with what this rule tells about the operation of the firm. But to be able to apply the rule we must assume that firms maximize their profits, for profit maximization is what the rule tells us about. This premise has frequently been questioned and criticized. Some of the arguments are as follows: (1) That businessmen have other motives, such as altruism, friendship, love of power, etc. They may give up some profits to avoid hurting a friend, or take on another factory even though it brings only more power and prestige. (2) That businessmen make decisions along conventional rather than calculating patterns. For instance, they may prefer to take a markup of 10 percent above costs, which is accepted and traditional in their industry, even if this does not squeeze out the last drop of profit from consumers. (Interviewers have found that many businessmen describe their decision processes in this way.) (3) That even if businessmen want to maximize profits, they will rarely succeed because their information (especially about the future) is imperfect and because some of the calculations necessary for taking in every possible bit of profit are either too complex and hence beyond their ken or are too expensive to be worth while.

These assertions are not to be sneered at. They all contain substantial elements of truth. That economic calculations are imperfect is well known—perhaps most obviously so when economists go badly wrong (as they so often do) in their predictions. It is equally clear that businessmen are not money-making machines but complex human beings with complex conscious and subconscious desires, motivations, and passions. Like the rest of us they behave in ways that are sometimes rational, sometimes apparently irrational. Custom, tradition, and accepted practices necessarily influence them in their dealings as they affect the rest of us.

Yet the view that profits do not play an important part in business behavior is quite unacceptable. The businessman does not have the option of forgoing profits. Were he to do so he would soon be driven out of business by more calculating rivals and by the unwillingness of the money market to extend funds to him in preference to those who have been more successful earners. The business world is not a tea party; it is more in the nature of an arena where victory and even continued existence are often confined to the shrewdest and most calculating.

The upshot is that although the premise that businessmen always maximize their profits is a gross exaggeration, perhaps even a caricature, it can suggest to us the sort of behavior toward which they are driven by the forces of the market. The results we shall obtain are therefore valid only as general indicators of tendencies, as indications of the directions in which market forces lead. Yet to deny them even this vestige of validity may also be a distortion, and in the process we may be depriving ourselves of a crutch which, however imperfectly, helps us progress toward better understanding of the economy in which we live.

E. A NOTE ON TAX SHIFTING

In discussing taxes in the text we remarked that it would sometimes pay a businessman to shift part of the taxes to the consumer by raising the price of his product.[4] One may be tempted to ask why, if the firm finds it profitable to raise prices, it hadn't bothered to do so before the tax was imposed.

Our analysis of the conditions for profit maximization permit us to give an easy answer. The change in costs resulting from the tax now makes it profitable to charge a price which would not have been most profitable before.

A diagram will help make things clear. In Fig. 17 let DA and DM represent the firm's average and marginal revenue curves. Let CM be its marginal cost curve before the tax. It will then pay the firm to produce output OQ at which the marginal cost and revenue curves intersect. From the demand curve DA, we see that this will sell at price OP.

Since the tax increases the costs of the firm, it will cause an upward shift in the marginal cost curve to TM'. This indicates that OQ' is now the most profitable output. This is because beyond that point marginal cost exceeds marginal revenue, so that failure to reduce output from the old level OQ to OQ' wastes an opportunity to increase profits by reducing costs more than revenues. The output which is now most profitable, being smaller, can be sold at the higher price OP'. Thus the

[4] Above, pp. 326–327.

rise in price becomes profitable only because of the tax. For by raising costs the tax makes it unprofitable to produce as large an output as before.

We can also conclude from this discussion that a fall in costs due to such things as a fall in wages will make it profitable for the firm to produce more. This suggests that a fall in wages will induce the firm to hire more workers.[5]

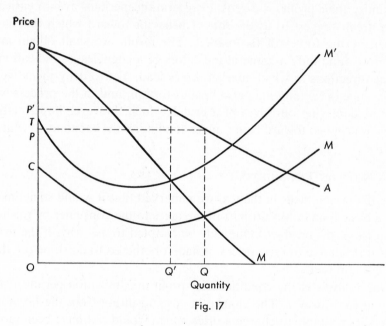

Fig. 17

3. The Competitive Firm

Let us now use our basic marginal cost = marginal revenue rule to discuss what will happen if the firm under pure competition maximizes its profits.

A. MARGINAL AND AVERAGE REVENUE UNDER COMPETITION

Each time we have discussed the concept of pure competition we have emphasized that it is characterized by inability of the firm to influence price. The firm contributes a negligible proportion of the out-

---

[5] But this tells us nothing about whether a wage cut occurring simultaneously in all firms could reduce unemployment, for this general wage cut might reduce workers' incomes. By reducing their ability to make purchases, it could cause a downward shift in the demand curve for the produce of every firm which would offset the influence of the cost reduction. For a more detailed analysis of a general wage cut, see chapter 13.

put of the industry, so no increase or decrease in its production will be sufficiently significant to affect the commodity's market price.

This tells us a great deal about the demand curve for the product of the competitive firm. It tells us that the curve must be perfectly flat (perfectly elastic) over the range which represents all outputs that it is practical for the firm to consider producing.[6] The firm will be able to sell as much as it wants to at whatever market price (such as OP in

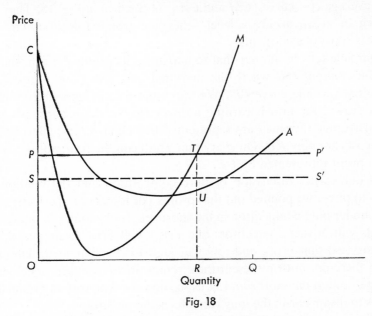

Fig. 18

Fig. 18) happens to be set by supply and demand conditions in the industry. The demand curve will then be the horizontal line PP', since the firm will be able to market *any* quantity, OQ, of its product at that price. It will not be forced to lower price in order to sell more of its product (as in the case of a negatively sloping demand curve).

Like any other demand curve, this will also be the firm's average revenue curve, since the firm's earnings per unit on any level of sales, OQ, will be the price, OP, at which each item is sold.

However, under pure competition there is also the remarkable result that this curve will also be the firm's marginal revenue curve. For the average revenue curve being perfectly horizontal, average revenue neither increases nor decreases with the scale of output. This, as we have seen, means that marginal revenue must neither exceed nor fall

[6] This is the example of a perfectly elastic demand curve which was promised when we first discussed the concept (above, p. 612).

short of average revenue; that is, the two curves must coincide everywhere.[7] Thus under pure competition the horizontal curve PP' represents demand, price, average revenue, and marginal revenue.

B. Profit Maximization, Short Run

To determine the firm's production decision, we must know its costs as well as its revenues. We therefore have indicated a marginal and average cost curve (CM and CA) for the firm in Fig. 18. They are drawn in at an arbitrary level—they are where fortuitous circumstances have placed them.

Our rule tells us at once that to maximize its profits the firm should produce output OR where the marginal cost curve CM crosses the marginal revenue curve PP'. We may note that as these curves have been drawn, the firm is earning a fat profit. For its receipts per unit sold (average revenue) are represented by height RT, whereas its per unit costs are only RU. On every unit produced the firm must be earning a profit represented by UT.

In our earlier discussion of pure competition and the relation of costs to price, we pointed out that profits (or losses) are perfectly possible under pure competition in the short run. In the long run, however, profits will attract competitors and losses will drive firms out of the industry, so that profit and loss will tend to be eliminated. The diagram therefore must represent the circumstances of a firm under pure competition *in the short run*. Let us see how the tendency of profits and losses to disappear in the long run affects the picture.

C. Profit Maximization, Long Run

The entry of new competitors in a profitable, purely competitive industry works to eliminate profits in two ways. First, by increasing supplies of the product in the market, its price will be driven down. (Exercise: Show how this operates on a supply-demand diagram for the industry.) Second, by demanding more productive factors, their prices (and hence costs) will be driven up. The first of these influences will make for a downward shift in PP', say to SS' (Fig. 18). The demand curve for the firm's product is now given by the decreased price OS. The second influence will serve to raise costs and hence will shift the cost curves upward.

When will this upward movement in the cost curve and this downward movement in the demand curve cease? To eliminate profits (or

[7] Above, p. 635.

losses) it must stop where the average cost curve and the demand curve just barely touch—that is, where they are tangent. This is illustrated in Fig. 19. To see why this is so, suppose that the movement of the curve does not continue quite that far, so that part of the average cost curve lies below the demand curve, as in Fig. 20. In that case the firm could still continue to earn a profit by producing an output like OQ, at which on each unit of product revenue QR is greater than cost QD. If on the other hand the shifting of the cost and demand curves continued until the average cost curve no longer touched the demand curve anywhere (as in Fig. 21) any output must result in a loss to the firm, for its per unit revenue QR must then fall short of its unit costs. Only if the average cost curve and the demand curve are tangent will there be neither profit nor loss.

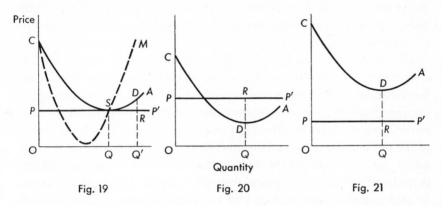

Fig. 19   Fig. 20   Fig. 21

We see, then, that the preceding analysis was for the short run because of the purely accidental relationship we gave the firm's cost and revenue curves. In the long run these will tend to be related to each other in the manner shown in Fig. 19, as we have just seen.

To complete our analysis of the output of the firm under pure competition in the long run we must find where the marginal cost curve CM cuts the marginal revenue curve PP' (Fig. 19). We may guess that it will be at output OQ, where the average cost curve touches the demand curve. At any other output, such as OQ', the firm must sustain a loss (the average revenue $Q'R$ is less than the average cost $Q'D$). Hence OQ is the only point at which the firm breaks even, and so it must be the point of maximum profit where marginal cost and marginal revenue are equal.

There is another way in which we know this must be true. Since point S is the lowest point on the average cost curve, average cost there must be neither rising nor falling with the size of output. To the left of this point marginal cost must lie below average cost, because anywhere in this part of the diagram any increase in output means a decrease in average cost. To the right of point S marginal cost must exceed average cost for the same reason. But at point S, where average cost is neither rising nor falling, average costs and marginal costs must coincide. At this point, however, average cost touches the demand curve, which is also the curve of marginal revenue. Here, therefore, marginal cost and marginal revenue must both be equal to average cost and hence to each other. Thus we conclude that the profit-maximizing output will be OQ, where the average cost curve touches the demand curve for the firm's product.

We may note in summary that profit maximization in the long run under pure competition requires that output be such that price = average revenue = marginal revenue = marginal cost = average cost = minimum average cost.

In particular, we see here that price will tend to be equal to marginal cost, a relationship we have already noted earlier in this volume. It will be remembered that this phenomenon was used there in discussing an argument which maintains that a system of pure competition could be particularly effective in allocating resources in accord with the desires of the public.[8] The price equals marginal cost result holds only because under pure competition the demand curve for the product of the firm is horizontal. This makes price everywhere equal to marginal revenue, so that equating marginal cost to marginal revenue will incidentally and automatically equate marginal cost to price.

4. Other Forms of Market Organization

As we saw earlier in the book, many economists have adopted a four-way classification of types of market organization. At the two extremes stand pure competition and pure monopoly. In between are the two categories, monopolistic competition and oligopoly.

Monopolistic competition may be defined as a situation in which there are a large number of small firms making or selling products that are similar but not identical. It differs from pure competition essentially in that each firm has a little partial monopoly of its own product. Rather than monopolizing some product as broadly defined, it monopolizes only a few distinctive product characteristics—a brand name, wrapping, or a slight difference in the texture of a soap. Other

[8] See above, pp. 402–404.

firms can and will compete effectively by selling very similar products which to most consumers are close substitutes. Under monopolistic competition, just as under pure competition, profits and losses will in the long run tend to be rendered insignificant by the competition of rival firms.

By contrast, under oligopoly the number of firms is small and the firms are relatively large. Unlike the situation in pure or monopolistic competition, the firm is a power. Its output is no longer a "drop in the bucket." The firm knows that its actions will visibly affect other firms and evoke responses from them. A distinguishing feature of oligopoly is that in making its decisions the firm must take cognizance of the responses of its competitors.

It is noteworthy that advertising may be expected to be undertaken primarily by the oligopolist and the firm operating under monopolistic competition. The pure monopolist has no rivals from whom he must steal business by using this device. He may sometimes advertise, but his purpose will be to increase the public's use of the commodity rather than to get them to switch from a rival's brand to his own.

Under pure competition there is even less reason to advertise. The firm can sell as much as it wants to at the going price, and has no need to expand its market. Basically, it does not pay that firm to advertise because everyone knows that its product is the same as that of twenty thousand other producers. Jones, a cotton grower in Texas, cannot by advertising persuade the members of the Cotton Exchange to bid a higher price for his cotton than they do for identical cotton grown hundreds of miles away.

5. The Firm Under Monopolistic Competition

A. THE DEMAND CURVE

Under monopolistic competition the demand curve for the product of the firm generally slopes down to the right, the way we usually expect demand curves to do. For if the enterprise wishes to increase its sales, it must attract customers away from products that are close substitutes. By reducing its price it can hope to win over the customers who at the old price were on the border line of indecision between its products and those of a competitor.

As the firm charges lower and lower prices, it may be able to increase its sales more and more. By lowering its price 2 cents on the gallon a gas station may be able to steal a few of the less loyal customers of nearby stations. A 5-cent price cut (if it does not start a price war) will bring customers from many blocks away and will strain the loyalty of some of its rivals' most faithful patrons.

The lower the price, then, the more the firm can sell under monopolistic competition. This is precisely what we mean when we say that the demand curve has a negative slope.

B. MONOPOLISTIC COMPETITION, SHORT RUN

To see how the firm's selling price and output are determined, the demand curve for its product, DD', and its average and marginal cost curves, CA and CM, are drawn as in Fig. 22. From the demand curve,

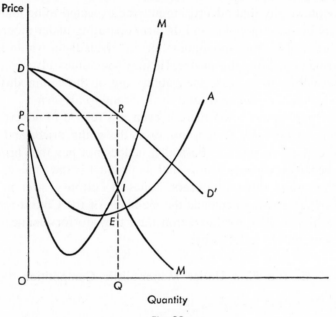

Fig. 22

which as always is an average revenue curve, we can deduce a marginal revenue curve, DM. Since the average revenue is decreasing, the marginal revenue curve must lie below it, as shown.

The firm will earn maximum profits at the output, OQ, at which the marginal cost and marginal revenue curves intersect (point I).

Unlike the competitive situation, the price at which a firm can sell is not here predetermined by outside forces. Each firm must set its own price in accordance with its profit calculations. The price is determined along with the firm's output. In deciding to produce output OQ, the firm commits itself to sell at price OP. For the demand curve DD' tells us that only at that price can the firm sell the quantity OQ it proposes to dispose of.

Again, in the short run the firm can earn substantial profits or losses. The firm whose circumstances are described by the figure will earn substantial profits because on each unit of output its costs, QE, are greatly exceeded by its revenues, QR. However, that is an accident of drawing; it would have been just as easy to have depicted a firm that is losing heavily.

c. Monopolistic Competition, Long Run

In the long run profits or losses will tend to be driven down by the entrance or exit of competitive firms that produce close substitute products. We need not repeat the discussion of the process, for it in-

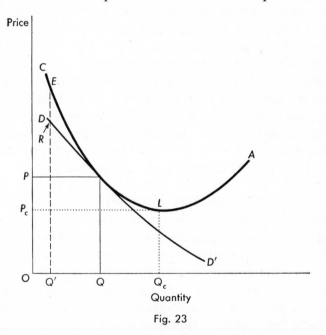

Fig. 23

volves shifts in the demand and cost curves of exactly the same nature as described for the competitive case.

Suffice it to say that again profit and loss will be eliminated when the average cost and demand curves have shifted to a position where they are tangent, as are DD' and CA in Fig. 23. However, this differs from the competitive long-run case in that the point of tangency is no longer at the lowest point L on the average cost curve. Instead the point of tangency must lie to the left of point L because of the U-shape of the cost curve.

We need not draw in the marginal curves to see that OQ, the output at which the two average curves are tangent, is the point of maximum profits. For any other output like OQ' must involve unit costs $Q'E$ that are greater than unit revenues QR, and hence must bring losses to the firm. In such circumstances, the firm will be forced to produce output OQ. The demand curve DD' tells us that it will be able to sell this output at price OP.

Had a firm with this same cost curve been operating under perfect competition, we know that in the long run it would be producing output OQ_c at which average costs are at their lowest point (compare Fig. 19). A competitive firm with this cost curve would sell its product at price OP_c.

We see, then, that long-run competitive output must be greater than the long-run output of the firm under monopolistic competition. On the other hand, the unit cost of production and the selling price of the product must be lower for the competitive firm.

This suggests at first glance that pure competition is far superior to monopolistic competition from the point of view of society. Actually this conclusion has only limited validity, and even then it is in need of careful interpretation and qualification. We have already discussed it in the text in considerable detail, and the reader is referred to that analysis for the policy implications of our conclusion.[9]

6. Pure Monopoly

We shall discuss only one point on the theory of monopoly, comparing it again with pure competition. As far as we are concerned at present, the distinguishing feature of pure monopoly is the identity of firm and industry. The firm has swallowed up the entire industry; this is what we mean by monopoly. Unlike monopolistic competition where we compared the firm with the competitive firm, we must compare the monopolistic firm with the competitive *industry*.

The mechanics of such a comparison are rather simple. We first construct another supply-demand diagram (Fig. 24), which gives us the long-run output (OQ) and price (OP) for the competitive industry. We know that under pure competition the long-run supply curve SS' is a curve of average costs.[10]

Suppose now that a monopolist comes in and "takes over" the indus-

[9] See above, pp. 427–430.
[10] See above, pp. 617–621.

try. How will he modify price and output policy? As usual, the demand curve for the firm's product (DD') is his average revenue curve, and SS' is his average cost curve. We can then construct the corresponding marginal cost and revenue curves. The marginal revenue curve, DM, lies below the average revenue curve DD', because the latter is falling. Since, as we have drawn it, average cost (SS') is rising, the marginal cost curve, SM, must lie above it. The monopolist will maximize his profits by producing output OQ' at which marginal cost and marginal

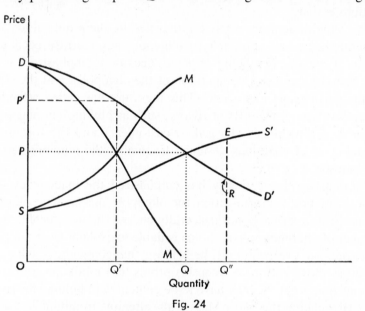

Fig. 24

revenue are equal. The demand curve DD' tells us that this output must be sold at price OP'. We note that this output will be smaller and the price higher than are the competitive price and output.[11]

At first glance this result suggests that the monopoly price-output combination leaves much to be desired from the point of view of society. But as in our conclusion relating to monopolistic competition, this needs careful interpretation and qualification, for which the reader is referred to our discussion earlier in the book.[12]

[11] This argument depends on our assumption that the average cost curve is rising. Though we suggested (see above, pp. 622–623) that this may be the more plausible cost situation for pure competition, the result can be extended to cover a significant range of cases of economies of large-scale production. For we can argue that it will not pay the monopolistic firm to produce an output like OQ'', which is greater than competitive output, because for such an output the unit costs $Q''E$ will exceed price $Q''R$ so long as the demand curve falls more rapidly with scale of output than do average costs.

[12] Above, pp. 436–439.

7. Oligopoly and Game Theory

The theory of oligopoly has until recently been confined to the analysis of a series of particular problems and situations. This piecemeal approach results from difficulties inherent in the subject. Under oligopoly almost anything is possible. Oligopolistic price wars, collusion, cartel arrangements—all have been observed frequently in past and recent history. Several special oligopolistic problems were discussed as illustrations earlier.[13]

We should mention in passing that despite these difficulties, a new general theoretical approach to oligopoly has recently been undertaken. It is called the theory of games because it emphasizes the analogy between the direct competition of the oligopolist and the struggle of the participants in a game. This literature has called attention to several aspects of this sort of rivalry, such as bluffing (in negotiations or in disguising prices charged to customers) and the forming and breaking up of coalitions designed to combat the remaining firms in the industry.

Particularly, game theory has emphasized the inadequacy of the concept of profit maximization for oligopoly theory. The oligopolist cannot simply sit back and peacefully choose the most profitable of a number of alternatives. His choice is liable to evoke a most unpleasant reaction from competitors. If he believes that competitors will counter his every move and try to keep his profits to a minimum, rather than maximizing profits he may have to be content with holding his rivals at bay. His making the best of his rivals' attempts to minimize his earnings is described by the theory as "minimax" strategy. He maximizes under the limitations imposed by the fact that his competitors are trying to force his returns to a minimum. In the game theory, then, the minimax principle has replaced the assumption of profit maximization.

The analysis is very new, is in a fluid stage, and has evoked some controversy. Its analysis is highly technical and has attracted many competent mathematical minds.[14]

8. Summary

In the second part of the appendix we have shown how the marginal analysis can shed light on the behavior of a profit-maximizing firm. The principle of no wasted opportunities showed that to earn maxi-

[13] Above, pp. 430–433.

[14] It was first developed by mathematician John Von Neumann and economist Oskar Morgenstern.

mum profits the firm must produce an output at which marginal cost and marginal revenue are equal. Using this result we discussed short- and long-run output and price determination in situations of pure competition, monopolistic competition, and pure monopoly, and made some comparisons. In this way we indicated the theoretical background for some of the policy discussions presented in the book itself.

PART III

The Pricing of Productive Factors

In this last part of the appendix we shall describe portions of the theory of pricing the factors of production. In part this is but a special case of the theory of value—the theory of pricing any commodity. Yet there are several reasons for separating the productive factors for special study. The demand for them is not a demand by ultimate consumers. They are purchased by the firm on the basis of considerations of profitability rather than the tastes of the buyer. The demand for productive factors is a derived demand—it is a demand by firms which is derived from consumers' demands for the final products in whose manufacture these items will be used.

There are also distinctive features that mark the production and sale of some of the productive factors. Some of the factors are not manufactured or manufacturable commercially. This is notably true of labor, but it also applies to a great extent to supplies of natural resources. Their extraction and processing can be accelerated or retarded by business conditions, but supplies in the mines and oil wells (known or not yet discovered) cannot always be augmented by human effort.

The pricing of some productive factors is also distinctive in that their sale is regulated by various legal devices, of which labor legislation is a well-known example.

Finally we may say that the main source of our interest in the pricing of productive factors stems from the part it plays in determining the distribution of incomes. It is in our role as owners of the factors of production that most of us obtain our income, whether we are owners of our own labor power or of vast mineral deposits. The level of wages and the prices of minerals will then be very important in determining

654

how national income is shared among workers, the owners of factories, the landholders, and lenders.

1. The Pricing of Scarce Resources

Very important for our analysis of the allocation of resources, particularly in international trade, is the pricing of a nation's scarce resources. If the pricing mechanism is to work effectively, it should encourage the use of items which are relatively plentiful and discourage

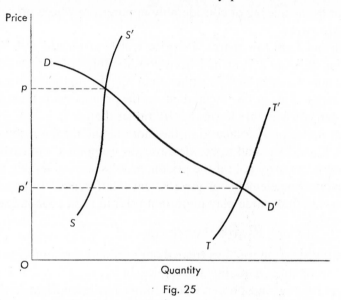

Fig. 25

the use of those that are in particularly short supply. In short, as an item gets scarce relative to the need for it, its price should rise.

In studying the comparative cost argument we saw how this applied.[1] Under a free-enterprise system prices must behave in this way if nations are to specialize in the lines of production in which they enjoy a comparative advantage. For if abundant resources are relatively cheap, businessmen will be encouraged to specialize in lines of production which use these resources liberally and the scarce resources sparingly. And these are the items in whose production the nation will tend to have a comparative advantage.

A. The Influence of Scarcity on Price Under Competition

Under pure competition we may expect that resources will be priced in the way this requires. The more abundant the item, the lower its

[1] Above, pp. 496–498.

price. A simple supply-demand diagram like that in Fig. 25 will make this clear. Let *DD'* be the (derived) demand curve for the scarce resource, and let *SS'* be its supply curve. The supply curve is almost vertical, indicating that little can be done to increase the quantity of the item. It is not perfectly vertical because a considerable increase in the price of the item can slightly increase the quantity supplied. For example, a sharp rise in the price of a scarce mineral will lead to its being mined in poorer mines where the cost of obtaining it is exceedingly high, or to the mining of considerably impurer ore whose processing is very expensive.

With our item this scarce, its price will tend toward *OP*. Suppose now that this same item had been considerably less scarce—that its supply curve had been *TT'* rather than *SS'*. In that case, because of the negative slope of the demand curve, the price of the resource would have been considerably lower, at *OP'* rather than *OP*.

Thus under pure competition the more abundant the resource, the lower will its price tend to be. However, as we pointed out earlier, this does not necessarily hold if the pricing process is considerably affected by monopolistic elements or government interference.[2] In practice, as we know, both of these play important roles in most economies today.

B. DIFFERENTIAL FACTOR PAYMENTS

In this discussion we have treated our productive resource as though all of it were alike in quality and serviceability. In reality this is not so. There are better and poorer woods, more fertile and less fertile soil, more efficient and less efficient workers. Complexity is added by the fact that the factor which is better or more efficient in one use may be less efficient in another. A may make a better machinist and a poorer farmer than B. Briar may make better pipes and poorer furniture than mahogany.

Often, therefore, different prices will be set on different specimens of the same resource. A more efficient worker may get higher wages via a bonus, more rapid promotion, or a piecework arrangement which pays him in proportion to the number of items he produces rather than a fixed amount per hour. A fertile piece of land, or one situated in the middle of a city where it is much desired by businessmen, will rent for much more than does a less serviceable piece.

How are these differentials in earnings determined? We confine our analysis largely to pure competition. In these circumstances the factors

[2] Above, pp. 496–499.

of production will "migrate" to the industries that can use them most efficiently, for those industries can afford to pay them most. Briar will go to pipe manufacturers and mahogany to furniture makers. Good mechanics will not usually become ditch diggers. Of course this is all a matter of degree and it depends on demand. With the decline in demand for buggies very skilled workers in this trade found themselves forced to go elsewhere because even their inferior ability to paint houses or do carpentry would pay them more than buggy making.

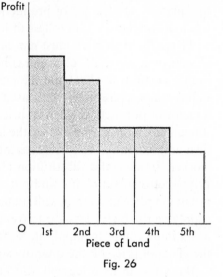

Fig. 26

What about the pricing of factors that differ in efficiency within the same industry? We have already implicitly seen the answer to this.[3] The more efficient worker will enable his firm to produce more cheaply than another. But under competition this worker can get most of these savings back in the form of a higher salary. If his present employer refuses to give him this additional pay he can (at least in the long run) hire himself out on better terms to a rival firm. The competitor will be happy to have him, because even at the higher salary the more efficient worker can still save the plant something, and the principle of no wasted opportunities says that this should not be spurned, no matter how little it amounts to.

It is easy to treat this diagrammatically. Suppose (to show that this holds for other productive factors as well) that five pieces of land are each used to produce wheat. Because of differences in fertility, costs of irrigation, etc., they return different amounts of profit (total revenue minus total costs other than land rent). In Fig. 26 these profits are indicated by the areas of the five bars corresponding to each of the pieces of land. It will be seen that the pieces of land are numbered in order of profitability, the first one being the most lucrative. The shaded area in each bar indicates how much more profit each piece of land earns than is earned by the poorest piece. This extra profit will be taken by the

[3] Above, p. 618.

landlords in extra rent. The owner of the first piece of land will therefore earn more than the owner of the fifth. The amount of his differential earnings is shown by the shaded area in the first bar.

c. NEGATIVELY SLOPING SUPPLY CURVES OF PRODUCTIVE FACTORS

We have already said a little about the shape of the supply curves of
productive factors. In this connection there is one possibility that is
worth some attention. In some cases the effect of a change in price on
the quantity of a factor of production supplied may be "perverse"—a
rise in its price may lead to less of it being supplied.

To see the reason we must remind ourselves that the effect of a price
change on a buyer or seller can conveniently be divided into two parts
—the substitution effect and the income effect.[4] The substitution effect
in this case represents the increased relative attractiveness of supplying
a factor of production when its price rises. A rise in land values makes
it relatively more expensive for the landlord to keep his property for his
own amusement. A rise in wages makes leisure more expensive for the
worker. In sum, the substitution effect represents the shift in relative
prices between supplying and not supplying a factor. In every case a
fall in the price of a factor will, in terms of the substitution effect, make
supplying the factor less attractive, whereas a rise in its price will serve
as an inducement to supply it. So far no "perversity" has appeared in
the effect of price on the quantity supplied.

But a rise in its price will also increase the real income of the supplier of the factor, just as it reduces the real income of the buyer. However, because of specialization, the effect on the producer's income is
likely to be much greater. When the price of one of our purchases rises,
it affects the cost of only one of the many things we buy, and the effect
on our total cost of living may be small. But its supplier often sells only
the one item, and for him the rise may have a substantial effect on his
income. Feeling substantially richer, he may now be able to *afford* to
cut back on sales, even though the substitution effect tells us that this
has become more expensive. The worker may feel he can afford more
of that expensive leisure; the saver who puts money away so that he
can lend it out for the interest earnings may feel that he can afford to
spend more; and the landlord may become affluent enough to turn
more of his land to flower gardening. In this way a rise in the price of
a factor of production may lead to less of it being supplied, and vice
versa.

[4] See above, pp. 606–607.

We list several applications, but remind the reader again that this sort of negatively sloping supply curve of productive factors is likely to be an exception.

1. The incentive effects of taxation. We pointed out earlier[5] that a rise in taxes can reduce the efforts of workers and businessmen and so act as a deterrent to production. We noted, however, that a rise in taxes sometimes makes people work harder. We see now how this can come about—through the income effect. People may feel that with the new taxes they cannot keep up their accustomed standard of living unless they work harder to make up for the taxes. It is said that this device has been used to increase the willingness of primitive peoples to work. To get them to work, colonial administrations first had to impose a tax on them.

2. The effects of higher national income. As our own productivity and that of other nations has risen and hourly real wages have gone up, workers have obtained shorter and shorter work weeks. The income effect has induced them to buy more leisure.

3. The fixed-purpose saver. Some people may try to save just enough for a special purpose—to send a son through college or to buy a house or a car (or to pay for houses and cars already bought on credit). A rise in interest rates can induce these people to save less. For if they have been earning interest on the money they saved (in an interest-earning savings account or by buying government bonds, for example) a rise in their interest earnings will speed the day when they have enough to buy what they have been saving for. Though the price of providing loans has risen, it will pay them to supply less, because their income from lending has risen.

D. CONCLUSIONS

We see, then, that under pure competition the price of a factor of production will depend on its scarcity and its productive efficiency. The scarcer (relative to demand) and more efficient the factor, the higher will tend to be its price. Monopolistic elements can distort these relationships. A monopoly of the supply of the product can force its price up by keeping the quality of it artificially scarce.

Some factors of production may also face a buyers' monopoly—one large firm or a cartel may do all the purchasing of some specialized item. For example, until a few years ago the purchase of bauxite for use in making aluminum in the United States was confined to one firm.

[5] Above, p. 330.

By artificially restricting its purchases a buyers' monopoly can depress the price of its purchases, just as a sales monopoly can force up the price of its product.

Government interference by means of minimum wage laws or price ceilings also can and does influence the prices of the factors of production in practice.

2. Marginal Productivity Theory

The price of a factor of production having been determined on the market, how much of that item will be bought or hired by the firm? How will the revenues of the firm be divided up among the various productive factors it hires? For answers to these questions economics has turned to marginal analysis.

A. THE MARGINAL PRODUCT OF A FACTOR

We defined the marginal product of a factor as the increase in total product that will result from the employment of an additional unit of the factor.[6] The marginal product of a farm hand is the increase in the production of a farm that results from hiring another worker.

In the same part of the book we discussed the law of diminishing marginal product, which states that as more and more of factor A is employed by an enterprise, without the concomitant hiring of any more of the other factors, the marginal product of A will begin to fall. Because the farm becomes overrun with farm hands, another worker will contribute very little additional output. For details the reader should go over the earlier discussion.

B. PROFIT MAXIMIZATION AGAIN

How many workers should a firm hire if it is to maximize its profits? Here again we can conveniently use a step diagram of marginal productivity like that in Fig. 27.

The height of the steps measures the *marginal revenue product* of labor in the firm. This is the additional *money returns the worker brings to the firm*.[7] Suppose that the worker's wage is *OW*. In that case

---

[6] Above, pp. 474–476.

[7] Under pure competition this is directly related to his marginal product; it is his marginal product multiplied by its price. If an additional worker can increase production by 10 bushels of wheat a day and wheat sells at $1.50 a bushel, his marginal revenue product will be $15 per day. But in the absence of pure competition the price of the product is not fixed; its magnitude varies with the sales of the firm. A factor's marginal revenue product is then equal to its marginal product times the increase in revenue each additional unit of output brings in. It is equal to the factor's marginal product multiplied by the firm's marginal revenue.

the first worker will bring in *OF* and cost the firm *OW*. His employment will therefore increase the profits of the firm by the shaded area in the first bar. Similarly, it will be profitable to the firm to hire a second worker, for he will increase the firm's profits by an amount indicated by the shaded area in the second bar. In the same way (though marginal products have now begun to diminish), the hiring of a third, fourth, and fifth worker will add to the firm's profits, but a sixth worker will cost the firm more than he earns.

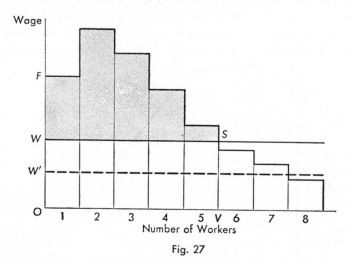

Fig. 27

Thus *it will pay the firm to hire a factor of production up to a point where its wage (price) is equal to its marginal revenue product.*

More specifically, it will never pay the firm to hire a number of workers such that the marginal revenue product of a worker is not equal to his wage. If his wage is less than his marginal revenue product, the firm is wasting an opportunity to increase its profits by hiring still another worker. If his wage is more than his marginal revenue product, it is wasting an opportunity to reduce costs more than revenues by firing a worker.

C. THE EFFECT OF A CUT IN THE PRICE OF A FACTOR

Over much of its range, the marginal revenue product curve will be falling. This is the result of diminishing marginal productivity and also of the fact that the price a firm can get for its product often falls as output increases. Thus it is easy to see that a fall in wages will induce the firm to hire more workers. In Fig. 27 a fall in wages from OW to OW' will increase the firm's employment from 5 to 7 workers. A similar result holds for the other factors of production.[8]

D. DIVIDING THE REVENUES OF THE FIRM

Also in this figure we see that the total wage payments of the firm will be five times OW, because 5 workers are hired, each at a wage of OW. Total wage payments are then represented by the area of rectangle $OVSW$—that is, by the wage OW times OV, the number of workers hired.

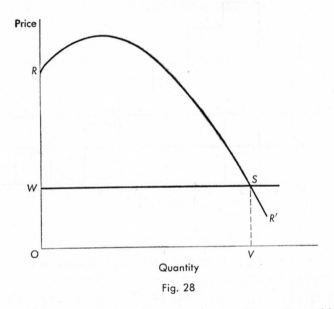

Fig. 28

Since without employees a firm can presumably earn nothing, the total revenue of the firm consists of the revenue yielded by each of the 5 workers. But the revenue yielded by the first worker is given by the area of the first bar, the additional revenue yielded by the second worker is given by the area of the second bar, and so on. The total revenue of the firm must therefore be given by the area of the first five bars taken together.

If from this total revenue we deduct wage payments, the remainder must be what is left for payment to other factors of production. This

---

[8] It does not necessarily follow that cutting wages everywhere is a sure cure for unemployment. See chapter 13 for a detailed analysis of the effect of a general wage cut.

residue of revenue after wage payment is indicated by the shaded area, for this is the area of the five bars together (total revenue) minus area $OVSW$ (total wages).

This shows the share of the revenue of a profit-maximizing firm that will go to any factor of production. It is obtained by drawing the marginal revenue product curve RR' for the factor and indicating the price of the factor, OW (Fig. 28). The firm will then hire OV units of this factor, paying out to this factor a total given by area $OVSW$. Since the firm's total revenue is area $OVSR$, the share of the factor is given by the ratio between these areas.

E. ETHICAL IMPLICATIONS

We have seen that the profit-maximizing firm will hire a factor of production in such an amount that its marginal revenue product is driven to equality with its price. There was once an economist who stated that this result had considerable ethical significance. He argued that it shows that workers and other factors will be paid exactly what they produce, and he implied that this justifies the distribution of income that results under a market economy.

We bring this up to indicate the dangers in jumping to ethical conclusions from geometric results. At first glance the idea seems attractive—everyone earns the value of his marginal product; *ergo,* justice is done. But when we examine its implications more closely we find that all is not quite what it seemed. The rule provides that all contributors to production be paid—the workers, the machines, mother nature who supplied the raw materials, etc. Without nature's contribution of soil, wheat cannot be grown. Therefore the soil must be paid its marginal revenue product. Since mother nature is unwilling or unable to collect this reward, the landholder obligingly takes it for her by proxy. This is of course a caricature, but it indicates that the rule has really given us no help toward answering the question which the theorem purported to settle—does the landlord, for instance, deserve as much as he gets or does he deserve more or less than that?

Note also that under the rule which says that the wage equals the marginal revenue product, the worker's reward does not depend only on the magnitude of his efforts. If land is plentiful and there are many acres per worker, his marginal product will tend to be high. Scarcity of land or of other factors of production will decrease his share. A monopolistic owner of a factor of production can in this way increase his share at the expense of other factors by keeping his factor artificially scarce. This is possible even though all the factors continue to be paid their marginal revenue products.

The entire argument involves a sort of linguistic chicanery. Because we named our abstract analytic concept the marginal *product* of a factor, we decide that this must be the proportion of the commodity *produced* by it in some ultimate sense. Actually a product made cooperatively by a group of factors cannot "truly" be divided among them in proportion to their contributions. Each factor's contribution is essential to the entire product. Wheat cannot be produced or brought to market without labor or without land.

Few of us would therefore be willing to go along with the ethics implied by the argument. Though the argument which purports to defend the distributive *status quo* is unsatisfactory, it does not of course follow that the current state of affairs either is or is not desirable on the basis of whatever ethical standards one chooses to adopt.

F. CONCLUSION

We have seen that marginal productivity analysis can provide us with an analysis of employment (or demand) by the firm. It describes how much of any factor the firm will hire, given the wage or price of the factor. The curve of the factor's marginal revenue product is therefore the firm's demand curve for that factor.

The analysis also enables us to examine the proportions in which the firm's product is divided among the various factors. Given the price of each factor and how much of it is bought by the firm, we can easily compute the firm's total expenditure on that item. We saw how we can go about this graphically.

3. The Four-Way Classification of Factors

The prices of the different factors are affected by their peculiar characteristics or circumstances. In order to study some of these effects, the factors of production have often been classified in four general categories. This is convenient for the discussion of the special characteristics and special circumstances (e.g., legal status) of the different factors. These categories are:

   1. Land. This term is taken to represent the factors contributed by nature which cannot be produced by human effort. Mineral deposits, for example, are included in this category.
   2. Entrepreneurship or business enterprise. This includes the or-

ganizing, risk-bearing, and innovating function of the active businessman.

3. Capital, or man-made factors of production.

4. Labor.

Each of these factors receives a remuneration which is known by a different name. The pay of the worker is his wage, the payment for land is rent, the payment on capital is interest, and payments to entrepreneurs are profits.

4. The Rent of Land

We shall not have much to say on the subject of land rent. These days there are no outstanding special circumstances concerning rent determination that have attracted widespread attention like the effects of unionization, collective bargaining, and wage legislation.

A. THE CLASSICAL RENT THEORY

In this part of the appendix we have already implicitly described the classical rent theory. Lands and other natural resources vary greatly in accessibility, fertility, and other qualities. Some swamplands and desert wastes are unemployed and earn no rent. Land in midtown New York is available only at tremendous prices.

For any type of use—whether wheat farming, house building, or copper mining—supply and demand, by determining the quantity of land to be used, incidentally determine which will be the poorest piece of property in use. As demand increases, users may be forced to resort to inferior lands they formerly would not have considered using. Inaccessible areas then come into use and arid lands are irrigated.

The poorest piece of property in use will earn very little rent; it is so undesirable that with current demands its use is just barely worth while. The rents for other better pieces of land will then tend to be determined by their productivity. Such lands will tend to earn the additional revenues which accrue to a firm from using them rather than inferior land. Their rents will then be determined in the manner described in Section 1B of this part of the appendix, where differential factor payments are discussed.

B. INELASTICITY OF LAND SUPPLY AND TAX SHIFTING

The distinguishing characteristic of land as we have defined it is its perfectly inelastic supply. Land consists of the resources that cannot be augmented by human effort. The supply curve of land must therefore be perfectly vertical. No matter what its price, the quantity of land supplied will be the same. Still the price may affect the size of the portion a man offers to rent instead of keeping for his own use.

In discussing the shifting of taxes we remarked that if supply is perfectly inelastic, the seller of the taxed item will bear the full burden of the tax.[9] This is because the seller is determined to dispose of what he has at any price. Since any rise in price will cause some fall in the amount demanded, he cannot pass any of the increased tax cost on to consumers.

It has therefore been argued that a tax on rents cannot be shifted. This, it is said, is one tax you can keep track of. It is collected from landlords, and will be paid by landlords. Actually the argument is not quite valid, for the landlord may in fact keep more of his land off the market when his rent return is cut by taxes. This means that the renter of land may have to pay more to get what he wants, thereby bearing part of the tax.

c. Land Taxes, Incentives, and Resource Allocation

A related view is that a tax on land is desirable because it will not have the incentive effects of other taxes. A tax on income can reduce overtime work or the businessman's efforts. A tax on theaters may discourage attendance and thereby reduce the number of movies produced. However, since land can neither be made nor destroyed, a tax cannot affect its supply. It is concluded that a land tax will be less harmful than other taxes in causing resources to be misallocated. Ordinary taxes will cause resources to move away from the fields where the taxes hit, even though consumers' desires would be better satisfied by their remaining where they were. Since no resources go into land production, it is argued that land taxes cannot cause such a resource misallocation.

Again the argument is weak because a tax on land can affect the supplies available on the market. A land tax of sufficient magnitude may induce landlords to let their acres grow wild or use them as hunting grounds rather than renting them out for industrial building. The less effectively he can shift the taxes on to the person to whom he rents his land, the greater may be a landlord's inducement to hold it back for his own use.[10] A land tax can also affect the profitability of resource al-

---

[9] Above, p. 627.

[10] The rise in taxes may work the other way. With smaller earnings on each acre he may be forced to rent out more acres to earn a living. The income effect (see pp. 658–659 above) of the tax will then mean that he cannot keep as much land for his own use as before. What matters for our argument is that in this case, too, the tax will affect the allocation of resources.

location to fertilization and irrigation of arid land and the use of resources for soil conservation. Thus for better or worse the land tax can affect the allocation of resources.

These, then, are important weaknesses in the arguments of those who advocate levying taxes only on land.[11] However, this is not the place to go into the complicated ethics of the question.

5. The Profits of Entrepreneurship

We shall have even less to say about profits, partly because we have already said so much on the subject in discussing the behavior of the firm. Essentially all we shall say is that three basic sources of profit are traditionally distinguished.

1. Risk-bearing. The businessman who undertakes an investment can never tell in advance how it will work out. Demand for his product may fall, the equipment bought may suddenly be made obsolete by a new invention, or he may be hit by a depression. The lucky risk-bearer, or the one with better foresight, will make a profit. Others will have losses. It is a debatable question whether on the whole more losses or more profits have accrued to businessmen from risk-bearing.

2. Innovation. We have already seen how a businessman who is the first to use a new product or a new machine or who exploits a new market or source of raw materials will earn profits in the short run before new firms can come in and cut down the profits by their competition. Since these profits of innovation were discussed earlier in the book, we shall add no more about them here.[12]

3. Monopoly profit. Monopoly is a third source of profit. Here again, enough has already been said on the subject. We should note only that it is not easy to think of a demand for and a supply of risk-bearing, innovation, and monopoly in the same way as we think of supply of and demand for other factors. It is perhaps easier to think of profit as the residual earnings of the firm after it has paid other factors, and to analyze it, as we have, as "that which is maximized by the firm," rather than by supply-demand reasoning.

A frequent source of confusion is the difference between the economist's use of the term profit and the way it is used by some laymen. A small shop owner may feel that he is earning rather satisfactory profits and would be surprised to be told by the economist that he is suffering losses. The economist, however, is considering the amount of labor the

---

[11] This was essentially the view of Henry George, founder of the single-tax movement.
[12] Above, p. 395.

owner is performing, and the funds he has invested in his enterprise. If from his earnings we deduct wages for his labor and interest payments on his money, there may indeed be no profits left for the storekeeper. In the same way the economist may consider part of the earnings of a large factory owner to be managerial salary rather than profits. By doing his own supervisory work the businessman is saving himself the cost of a hired supervisor. He has, in effect, hired himself as a manager and is paying himself a managerial salary.

6. Interest on Capital

A. INTEREST ON MONEY AND ON REAL CAPITAL

These questions may naturally arise in the student's mind: What is interest doing here again, this time as the earning of real capital, factories, machinery, inventories, etc.? Formerly we spoke of the rate of interest as the price of a money loan. Are we using the same word in two different ways, or do these two uses coincide?

Actually, it turns out that they do—that the rate of earning on capital will under competition tend to be driven to the interest rate. One way to see this is to realize that he who has funds can have equipment, and he who has equipment can sell it for money. If a $100 piece of equipment is certain to earn $10 a year, and the rate of interest is 5 percent, no one will lend any money. Everyone will prefer buying machines to lending money.

Potential borrowers will have to increase the interest they are willing to pay in order to get any funds. This will tend to drive the interest rate up toward the earnings of the machines.

Meanwhile, the increased use of the machines will tend to drive down the price of their products and to bid up the prices of the raw materials, etc., used in their manufacture. Thus the profits from the machine will tend to be driven down toward the interest rate.

The same sort of process, only in reverse, would be set in motion if the interest rate on money were much above the earnings of a machine. Thus the rate of interest and the rate of return on a machine or other piece of real capital can, under competition, differ substantially only in the short run.

This is a special case of our conclusion that under pure competition price will be driven to unit costs. For the cost of buying a machine can be considered the interest payments on the money tied up in its purchase. The per unit earnings of the machine are then in the long run driven toward equality with these interest costs.

B. THE DETERMINATION OF THE INTEREST RATE

We have already examined rather carefully the determination of the rate of interest.[13] This was done during our analysis of the determination of national income. We saw that the rate of interest was determined, along with national income, by the forces of supply and demand in the goods and money markets.

There is only one point to be added here. We see that the interest rate is determined only partly by monetary conditions. Demand and supply in the goods market cannot be said to be less important in their influence on the rate of interest. The "real" (as opposed to monetary) influences work largely through the demand for and supply of investment goods. With increases in the demand for investment goods and other purchases, there must be an increase in the demand for money with which to conduct transactions. This is the influence of the level of national income on the demand for money in the money market.[14] In this way investment demand will influence the interest rate.

In turn, the interest rate will influence the level of investment by increasing or decreasing investment costs. The upshot is the process that we just discussed, whereby the rates of return on money loans and on investment goods are driven toward equality one with the other. It is therefore impossible to say that one is determined by the other, or that either real influences or the monetary influences are "more important" in determining interest rates.

How is the determination of the rate of interest related to our supply-demand analysis of the factors of production? The answer is easily indicated. The earnings of machines will be determined by their supply and by the demand for them. But these will in turn be influenced by the availability of credit and the cost of borrowing money. For example, a lowering of interest rates will make investment more expensive, thereby lowering the demand for machinery. It will cause a downward shift in the demand curve for investment. Thus, simple supply-demand-price analysis is another correct way of looking at the determination of the rate of interest. It fails to emphasize some aspects of the problem brought out in our other analysis (particularly the role of the money supply), and leads us to emphasize others which are only

[13] Above, chapters 10–12.
[14] This is Assumption 4 of chapter 10.

implicit in our explanation of interest determination as part of the national income analysis.

C. THE PLURALITY OF INTEREST RATES

There is really no such thing as *the* rate of interest. One man or one firm has better credit than another, and the United States government or General Motors Corporation can get better terms than a speculative oil concern.

The interest rate also varies with the length of the loan. Usually (but not always) a loan for several days can be obtained on better terms than one for ten years—that is, at a lower cost per day—because the former involves less of a commitment by the lender. The upshot is that there are really many rates of interest.

Though exceptions are many and not unimportant, these rates tend to move up and down together. A lender has his choice as to where he will lend, and if the return offered by General Motors rises and the speculative oil company's does not, the latter will soon be unable to obtain funds. For without a substantial differential, lenders will not consider it worth the added risk to extend funds to that enterprise. Similarly, if the oil company's terms go up sufficiently they may attract funds away from less risky enterprises, whose interest rates will also have to rise if they want to obtain more money.

In the case of long and short loans, lenders and borrowers again have their choice. A ten-year loan can be made by borrowing (or lending) for one year at a time and renewing the loan annually. If short-term rates are too high compared to long-term rates, no one will want to lend for a ten-year period; in the reverse case, with ten-year loans relatively high, no one will want to borrow for a ten-year period.

Thus in general we may expect some similarity in the movement of the various rates of interest. This provides some justification for our speaking of a rise or a fall in "the" rate of interest as we have done throughout the book.

7. Wages

A. WAGE DETERMINATION, LEGAL RESTRICTIONS, AND COLLECTIVE BARGAINING

Our simple supply-demand analysis of the determination of the earnings of factors of production cannot nowadays be used without some modification. Minimum wage legislation prevents some wages from falling as low as they otherwise would. Other laws affect the nature of the supply by keeping out underage potential employees. Even more significant is the fact that most wages are not now determined automatically by market forces. These forces are wielded around collective-bargaining tables by union and employee representatives. By haggling and negotiation, sometimes involving the threat of or actual strikes or lockouts, wage and other employment conditions are determined. No neat diagram can sum up the outcome of such a negotiation process. It will depend on many intangibles, such as the skill of the bargainers and the morale of the union membership. Yet somehow in that bargaining process wage levels will be set.

B. The Role of Marginal Productivity

In these circumstances our marginal productivity still retains some validity. Marginal productivity can still influence in two ways the share of income going to workers.

1. It will help determine the attitude of employers. How much they are willing to concede depends on how badly they need the workers, how much they are worth to the firm. The workers' marginal revenue productivity function tells precisely that—just what having these workers can gain for the business.

2. If the agreement with the union does not specify the number of workers to be hired, the firm's employment of workers will still be determined by marginal productivity. It will still pay the firm to hire only so many workers that the marginal revenue product of one man will be equal to the negotiated wage. Then everything we have said in our marginal productivity analysis will be applicable.

This is because we have not treated marginal productivity analysis as a direct determinant of wage levels. Rather we have considered it as a theory of the demand for factors and their employment by the firm. When wages are somehow decided, marginal productivity will determine how many workers the firm will hire and it will also fix the share of the total revenue of the firm to be allotted to total wage payments.

C. The Aims of the Union

There is no unambiguous criterion for the behavior of a union like that which profit maximization provides for the firm. This may easily be illustrated by some oversimplified examples.

Suppose in Fig. 29 that DD' is the marginal revenue product curve of labor in the firm with which the union is negotiating. This is the firm's demand curve for labor. Suppose SS' is the supply curve of workers potentially willing to work in the firm.

1. The union may wish to maximize the firm's employment. In this case it will desire to have wages set at OW_1, where the quantity of labor supplied and the quantity demanded are equal at level OQ_1. The union may follow such a policy in self-interest if it wishes to become powerful by acquiring a large membership. Often, however, the union members may wish to restrict the number of employees available to the firm in order to obtain higher wages.

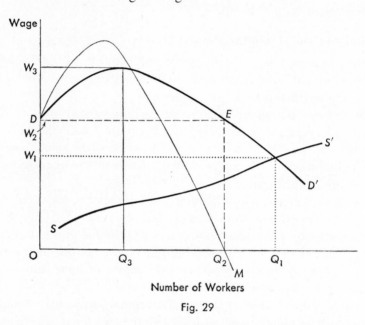

Fig. 29

2. In such a case the union might prefer to have the wage level at OW_2 and employment at OQ_2, at which the total earning of its members—the total wage bill of the firm—is a maximum. If this is shared among union members by an unemployment fund, even the unemployed members may be better off. For now the greatest possible total earnings are shared among the same number of persons, the members of the union.[15]

[15] The reader may be curious to know how we decided that OW_2 is the wage which maximizes total wage revenue. We can find this level of wages by drawing in an appropriate marginal curve. DD' being the demand for workers by the firm, it is the union's average revenue curve. From this we draw in the marginal revenue curve DM. Total revenues being the same as total profits when costs are zero, we maximize total revenue by treating all costs as though they were zero. Total revenue will then be at a

3. A small hard core of union members may prefer to keep membership severely restricted to raise their own earnings to the highest possible level. A tight little union like this may want to set wages at OW_3 and keep employment down to OQ_3.

Of course all these alternatives are exaggerations of what usually occurs in practice. Few unions openly adopt such blatant policies. Usually the aims are not even clearly defined, and they sometimes vary with circumstances and the moods of leaders and the membership.

One thing does emerge, however. As we remarked earlier in the text, it may pay unions to act in a way that makes it difficult to eliminate unemployment.[16] Only the first of the three policies listed above involves the union's permitting and encouraging employment in its industry to grow to its maximum level. If all unions try at the same time to prevent maximum employment, each in its own industry, it may not be possible to eliminate unemployment even with the most powerful fiscal and monetary techniques. A rise in the demand for labor might at once be reflected in a rise in wages rather than in employment. The inflationary implications are obvious.

D. WOULD WAGES EVER RISE WITHOUT UNIONS?

Before we leave our analysis we shall apply it to one more problem. We may ask whether wages would ever rise if all workers were unorganized or whether, on the other hand, all wage rises must be ascribed to unionization.

We can easily see that at least some wage rises might be expected in the absence of union pressure. Suppose there is an upward shift in the marginal revenue productivity curve of labor in some industry. This can occur for a variety of reasons: (1) because demand for the product is rising, (2) because price levels are rising (inflation), (3) because workers are working harder and more efficiently, (4) because more machinery and equipment increases the proportion of capital to labor and makes labor relatively scarce. (Clearly this must be "production-increasing" rather than "labor-saving" equipment.)

---

maximum when marginal revenue equals this "marginal cost" equals O. Looked at another way, this is because so long and only so long as marginal wage revenue is greater than zero, getting the firm to hire another man will add to total wage revenues.

We may also note that point E is the point at which the elasticity of DD' is exactly equal to unity. To the left of this point a reduction of wages adds to the firm's total wage payments, so that the elasticity of demand must be greater than unity. For similar reasons, the curve must be inelastic to the right of this point. (See above, pp. 612–613.)

[16] Above, p. 252.

All of these will mean that the firm's demand curve for labor has shifted upward. In that case the demand curve for labor generally will rise, and a simple supply-demand diagram will readily show that this can increase the price of labor.

Thus, wage competition will sometimes force employers to raise the wages of workers who are not organized. Whether a union could or would have raised their wages even more is a question into which we shall not enter here. Suffice it to say that some economists have argued that wage levels might have been higher without unions, but the evidence either way is inconclusive.[17]

[17] Cf. above, pp. 595–597.

INDEX

Ability to pay, 329
Absolute advantage, 494
Accounting, double-entry, 165; national income, 163–182
Ad valorem tax, 322
Advertising, 381, 422, 426, 428, 450, 647; misleading, 126, 447; monopoly, 438
Aggregate demand, 608–610
Aggregation, 20, 237–238
Agriculture, comparative advantage and disadvantage of U.S. in, 502, 504; competition in, 591; Department of, 407, 408; in 1800, 60; excessive allocation of resources to, 591; government aid to, 359, 407, 408, 592–594; impact of depression on, 145–146; mobility in, 591, 592; number of operators in, 100; overproduction in, 591; price-support program for, 149, 316, 391–392, 499, 592–593, 624; prices in, 27–28, 65, 590, 591, 592; problem of, 590–592; resources for, 39–40; revolution in, 63–65, 80, 591; unimportance of corporation in, 99
   See also Farmers; Land
Air pollution, 125
Aktiengesellschaft, 86
Algebraic analysis, interdependence of three industries, 463–466
Allen, Frederick Lewis, quoted, 67–68
Allocation of resources, 5, 6, 71, 115, 375, 384, 478–479, 667; adjusted to changing demands, 397–398; between present and future and between future and future, 376–377; and complementarity, 377–378; goals in, 379–383; role of technology in, 378–379
Alternatives and choices, 1–2, 9–10, 107, 109, 110, 111–113, 129, 375, 379–383, 384, 393–394; changing, 396–399; constant, 394–396; among uses of productive resources, 5, 6, 71
American Telephone and Telegraph Co., 93, 95, 423
Amortization, 429 n., 443
Antitrust laws, 414–415, 426, 431
Argentina, comparative advantage in, 505
Armament program, 150
Assets, 264; bank purchases of, 280, 281–282; bank sales of, 282; fear of loss in value of, 286–287; types of, 265, 280–281, 283
Australia, comparative advantage in, 505; population density in, 500 n.
Austria, 508
Automobiles, demand for, 396, 398
Average cost curve, 635–636, 644, 645, 646, 651 n.
Average revenue curve, 637–638, 643–644

Balance of payments, 517–521, 525; and alterations of exchange rates, 546–551; disequilibrium of, 537; favorable, 546; government control over, 551–553; and international gold standard, 540–546; methods of adjusting, 537–540, 554; price elasticity of demand and, 614–615; sources of difficulties in, 553; unfavorable, 536–537, 544–545, 546, 550
Balance of trade, favorable, capital lending and, 531; definition of, 528–529; and employment, 531–532; favorableness of, 529–530; as a gift to foreigners, 530, 533; mechanics of, 529; unfavorable effects of, 532–533
Bank deposits, *see* Checking deposits
Banking crises, 262
Bankruptcy, 148, 397
Banks, central, 268–270, 513; commercial, *see* Commercial banks; failures of, 148; Federal Reserve, *see* Federal Reserve System; largest U.S., 94; policies of, and economic instability, 287–288; relations among, in various countries, 513
Barter, 44, 54, 512
Beall, J. Glenn, quoted, 557
"Beggar-my-neighbor policies," 551, 552, 553, 560
Behrman, T. R., quoted, 556
Belgium, 508
Benefit principle in taxation, 328
Big Change, The (Allen), quoted, 67–68
Bluffing, 652
Bonds, 89, 225, 344; government, 272–273, 274; market price of, 273; perpetual, 363
"Boondoggling," 368–369